Strategic Marketing
Communications

Make the Grade.
Your Atomic Dog Online Edition.

The Atomic Dog Online Edition includes proven study tools that expand and enhance key concepts in your text. Reinforce and review the information you absolutely 'need to know' with features like:

- **Review Quizzes**
- Key term Assessments
- Interactive Animations and Simulations
- Notes and Information from Your Instructor
- Pop-up Glossary Terms
- A Full Text Search Engine

Ensure that you 'make the grade'. Follow your lectures, complete assignments, and take advantage of all your available study resources like the Atomic Dog Online Edition.

How to Access Your Online Edition

- **If you purchased this text directly from Atomic Dog ....**
  Visit atomicdog.com and enter your email address and password in the login box at the top-right corner of the page.

- **If you purchased this text NEW from another source....**
  Visit our Students' Page on atomicdog.com and enter the **activation key located below** to register and access your Online Edition.

- **If you purchased this text USED from another source....**
  Using the Book Activation key below you can access the Online Edition at a discounted rate. Visit our Students' Page on atomicdog.com and enter the **Book Activation Key in** the field provided to register and gain access to the Online Edition.

Be sure to download our *How to Use Your Online Edition* guide located on atomicdog.com to learn about additional features!

This key activates your online edition. Visit atomicdog.com to enter your Book Activation Key and start accessing your online resources. For more information, give us a call at (800) 310-5661 or send us an email at support@atomicdog.com

170QHFAPM

THOMSON™

*Some online Editions do not contain all features.

Strategic Marketing Communications

A SYSTEMS APPROACH TO IMC

M. Joseph Sirgy
Virginia Polytechnic Institute and State University

Don R. Rahtz
The College of William and Mary

THOMSON

Australia · Canada · Mexico · Singapore · Spain · United Kingdom · United States

THOMSON

Strategic Marketing Communications: A Systems Approach to IMC
M. Joseph Sirgy and Don R. Rahtz

Executive Editors:
Michele Baird, Maureen Staudt, and Michael Stranz

Marketing Manager:
Mikka Baker

Senior Developmental Editor:
Laureen Palmisano Ranz

Marketing Coordinators:
Lindsay Annett and Sara Mercurio

Production/Manufacturing Manager:
Donna M. Brown

Production Editorial Manager:
Dan Plofchan

Rights and Permissions Specialists:
Kalina Hintz and Bahman Naraghi

Cover Image:
© 2007 Getty

© 2007 Thomson, a part of the Thomson Corporation. Thomson, the Star logo, and Atomic Dog are trademarks used herein under license.

Printed in the
United States of America
1 2 3 4 5 6 7 8 09 08 07 06

For more information, please contact Thomson Custom Solutions, 5191 Natorp Boulevard, Mason, OH 45040. Or you can visit our Internet site at
http://www.thomsoncustom.com

ALL RIGHTS RESERVED. No part of this work covered by the copyright hereon may be reproduced or used in any form or by any means—graphic, electronic, or mechanical, including photocopying, recording, taping, Web distribution or information storage and retrieval systems—without the written permission of the publisher.

For permission to use material from this text or product, contact us by:
Tel (800) 730-2214
Fax (800) 730 2215
http://www.thomsonrights.com

The Adaptable Courseware Program consists of products and additions to existing Thomson products that are produced from camera-ready copy. Peer review, class testing, and accuracy are primarily the responsibility of the author(s).

Strategic Marketing Communications
M. Joseph Sirgy and Don R. Rahtz—First Edition

BOOK ISBN 1-592-60283-5
PACKAGE ISBN 1-592-60284-3

Library of Congress Control Number: 2006929295

International Division List

Asia (Including India):
Thomson Learning
(a division of Thomson Asia Pte Ltd)
5 Shenton Way #01-01
UIC Building
Singapore 068808
Tel: (65) 6410-1200
Fax: (65) 6410-1208

Australia/New Zealand:
Thomson Learning Australia
102 Dodds Street
Southbank, Victoria 3006
Australia

Latin America:
Thomson Learning
Seneca 53
Colonia Polano
11560 Mexico, D.F., Mexico
Tel (525) 281-2906
Fax (525) 281-2656

Canada:
Thomson Nelson
1120 Birchmount Road
Toronto, Ontario
Canada M1K 5G4
Tel (416) 752-9100
Fax (416) 752-8102

UK/Europe/Middle East/Africa:
Thomson Learning
High Holborn House
50-51 Bedford Row
London, WC1R 4L$
United Kingdom
Tel 44 (020) 7067-2500
Fax 44 (020) 7067-2600

Spain (Includes Portugal):
Thomson Paraninfo
Calle Magallanes 25
28015 Madrid
España
Tel 34 (0)91 446-3350
Fax 34 (0)91 445-621

To my wife, Pamela, and my four daughters, Melissa, Danielle, Michelle, and Emmaline

—M. Joseph Sirgy

To my family and to the people of Cambodia, who have come back from the brink of despair and shown me the value of the small things in life

—Don R. Rahtz

Brief Contents

Preface xvii
About the Authors xxi

Part One — Overview — 1

- **Chapter One** — The World of Integrated Marketing Communications 3
- **Chapter Two** — Macro and Societal Issues in Marketing Communications 30
- **Chapter Three** — Building the Foundation of Strategic Marketing Communications 57
- **Chapter Four** — A Systems Model for Integrated Marketing Communications 72

Part Two — The Marketing Communications Portfolio — 89

- **Chapter Five** — Advertising 92
- **Chapter Six** — The Buzz: Public Relations, Word of Mouth, and More 117
- **Chapter Seven** — Direct and Interactive Marketing 138
- **Chapter Eight** — Personal Selling, Trade Promotions, and Consumer Promotions 161

Part Three — Strategy Development: A Hierarchical Perspective — 193

- **Chapter Nine** — The Corporate Level: Analysis and Planning for Corporate Strategy and Tactics 196
- **Chapter Ten** — The Marketing Level: Analysis and Planning for Marketing Strategy and Tactics 219
- **Chapter Eleven** — The Marketing Communications Level: Analysis and Planning for Marketing Communications Strategy and Tactics 258

Part Four — Building, Executing, and Assessing Your Integrated Marketing Communications Plan — 289

- **Chapter Twelve** — Setting Objectives and Assessing Performance: Setting Goals and Measuring Performance of the Strategy Marketing Communications System 291
- **Chapter Thirteen** — Analysis Guiding Objective Setting: Linking Strategies and Tactics to Objectives and Performance Measures 326

Chapter Fourteen Strategic Allocation of Resources: Budgeting in the Strategic Marketing Communications System   341

Chapter Fifteen Takeaways from the Strategic Marketing Communications Process: Lessons in Monitoring, Control, and Integration   367

Case A An IMC Plan for Cable & Wireless Using the Systems Approach   393

Case B UnitedHealth Group Roanoke Call Center: IMC Plan   403

Case C Hancock Rack's IMC Plan   413

Glossary   419

Index   435

Contents

Preface xvii
About the Authors xxi

Part One   Overview   1

Chapter One
The World of Integrated Marketing Communications   3

1-1 Introduction: Operating in a World of Unity and Diversity   4
1-2 Definition of Integrated Marketing Communications   7
1-3 Characteristics of an Integrated Marketing Communications Campaign   8
1-4 A Developmental View of Integrated Marketing Communications   10
    1-4a Awareness of the Need for Integration   10
    1-4b Image Integration   11
    1-4c Functional Integration   11
    1-4d Coordinated Integration   11
    1-4e Consumer-Based Integration   11
    1-4f Stakeholder-Based Integration   12
    1-4g Relationship-Management Integration   12
    1-4h In Conclusion   12
1-5 Conditions or Trends That Paved the Way for Integrated Marketing Communications   12
    1-5a Trend 1: Decrease in Message Credibility   12
    1-5b Trend 2: Decrease of Cost of Database Marketing   13
    1-5c Trend 3: Increase of Cost and Decrease in Effectiveness of Mass-Media Communications   13
    1-5d Trend 4: Increase in Mergers and Acquisitions of Marketing Communications Agencies   15
    1-5e Trend 5: Increase in Media and Audience Fragmentation   15
    1-5f Trend 6: Increase in Parity or "Me-Too" Products   15
    1-5g Trend 7: Shift of Information Technology   15

1-6 Approaches to Planning Integrated Marketing Communications   16
    1-6a The Mandated "One-Look" Approach   16
    1-6b The Theme-Lines or "Matchbooks" Approach   16
    1-6c The Supply-Side Planning Approach   17
    1-6d Ad Hoc Approach   17
    1-6e Consumer-Based Approaches   18
    1-6f The Moore and Thorson Integrated Marketing Communications Model   18
    1-6g The Shultz, Tannenbaum, and Lauterborn Integrated Marketing Communications Model   19
    1-6h Why Evolve to the Strategic Marketing Communications Approach?   25
Summary   26
Discussion Questions   27
Practice Quiz   27
Web Exercise: What's Hot, What's Not   28
Suggested Readings   28
Notes   29

Chapter Two
Macro and Societal Issues in Marketing Communications   30

2-1 Introduction   31
2-2 Economic Issues   32
2-3 Legal and Regulatory Issues   34
    2-3a Federal Regulation of Marketing Communications   34
    2-3b State and Local Regulation of Marketing Communications   36
    2-3c Self-Regulation of Marketing Communications   37

2-4 Social and Ethical Issues 39
    2-4a Offensive Promotion 40
    2-4b Advertising to Children 41
    2-4c Cultural Beliefs and Values 44

Summary 47

Discussion Questions 47

Practice Quiz 48

Web Exercise: How to Advertise Distilled Spirits Responsibly 49

Suggested Readings 49

Notes 49

Chapter Three
Building the Foundation of Strategic Marketing Communications 57

3-1 Introduction 53
    3-1a Strategic Marketing Communications: A Framework to Aid in Strategic Decision Making 53
    3-1b Systems Concepts 54

3-2 Strategy and Tactics 55

3-3 Setting Objectives 58
    3-3a Strategy = Goal 58
    3-3b Objective = Quantitative Formulation of a Goal 59
    3-3c How Objectives Are Set 59
    3-3d Linking Strategy, Tactics, and Objectives 60

3-4 Budgeting 61

3-5 Monitoring and Control 62
    3-5a Change Strategy and Tactics 62
    3-5b Change Objective 62
    3-5c Change Budget 62

3-6 Analysis and Planning 63
    3-6a Selecting Effective Strategy and Tactics 63
    3-6b Setting Objectives 64
    3-6c Budgeting 64

3-7 System Integration 65

Summary 68

Discussion Questions 69

Practice Quiz 69

Web Exercise: Theory 70

Suggested Readings 70

Note 71

Chapter Four
A Systems Model for Integrated Marketing Communications 72

4-1 Introduction 73

4-2 The Systems Model of Integrated Marketing Communications 75

4-3 Strategy → Objectives → Tactics 75

4-4 Budgeting 78

4-5 Setting Objectives 78

4-6 Monitoring and Control 82

4-7 Analysis and Planning 83
    4-7a Strategy Selection 83
    4-7b Setting Objectives 84
    4-7c Budgeting 84

4-8 Marketing Communications Integration 85

Summary 85

Discussion Questions 86

Practice Quiz 86

Web Exercise: Yellow Pages versus Search Engines 87

Suggested Readings 87

Notes 88

Part Two   The Marketing Communications Portfolio 89

Chapter Five
Advertising 92

5-1 Introduction 93

5-2 Broadcast Media 97
    5-2a Television 98
    5-2b Radio 100

5-3 Print Media 103
    5-3a Magazines 103
    5-3b Newspapers 106

5-4 Out-of-Home Media 109
    5-4a Outdoor 109
    5-4b In-Store/Point of Purchase 111

5-5 Miscellaneous Advertising 113

Summary 114

Discussion Questions 114

Practice Quiz 115

Web Exercise: Which Advertising Does the Job for You? 115

Additional QuickLinks 116

Suggested Readings 116

Notes 116

Chapter Six

The Buzz: Public Relations, Word of Mouth, and More   117

6-1 Introduction   118
6-2 Corporate or Institutional Advertising   122
   6-2a Characteristics   123
   6-2b Audience/Target Market   123
   6-2c Measurement   123
   6-2d Best Case: Ben & Jerry's Ice Cream   123
6-3 Sponsorship and Event Marketing   124
   6-3a Characteristics   124
   6-3b Audience/Target Market   128
   6-3c Measurement   128
   6-3d Best Case: Yoplait and Breast Cancer   128
6-4 Corporate Communications   128
   6-4a Best Case: Canon USA   131
   6-4b Audience/Target Market   131
   6-4c Measurement   131
6-5 Product Placement and Alternative Buzz   132
   6-5a Audience/Target Market   133
   6-5b Measurement   133
   6-5c Best Case: MINI in *The Italian Job*   133

Summary   134
Discussion Questions   135
Practice Quiz   135
Web Exercise: Energy Companies and the Environment   136
Additional QuickLinks   136
Suggested Reading   137
Notes   137

Chapter Seven

Direct and Interactive Marketing   138

7-1 Introduction   139
7-2 Direct Marketing and Databases   142
7-3 Telemarketing   145
   7-3a Characteristics   145
   7-3b Measurement   145
   7-3c Best Case: Ferguson Enterprises—Servicing and Selling   146
7-4 Broadcast Direct Response   146
   7-4a Strategic Marketing Communications Elements   146
   7-4b Characteristics   146
   7-4c Measurement   147
   7-4d Best Case: The Food Network and Shop at Home   147
7-5 The Internet and Electronic Communications   147
   7-5a Strategic Marketing Communications Elements   148
   7-5b Characteristics   150
   7-5c Measurement   151
   7-5d Best Case: Shop Goodwill Online   152
7-6 Direct Mail, Catalogs, and Print   152
   7-6a Strategic Marketing Communications Elements   152
   7-6b Characteristics   153
   7-6c Measurement   154
   7-6d Best Case: L.L.Bean Catalog—More Than a Walk in the Woods   155
7-7 Direct Selling   155
   7-7a Strategic Marketing Communications Elements   155
   7-7b Characteristics   155
   7-7c Measurement   156
   7-7d Best Case: Avon Crosses Cultures to Bring Beauty Directly to the Home   156

Summary   156
Discussion Questions   157
Practice Quiz   157
Web Exercise: Map Your Experience on the Information Superhighway   158
Additional QuickLinks   158
Suggested Readings   159
Notes   159

Chapter Eight

Personal Selling, Trade Promotions, and Consumer Promotions   161

8-1 Introduction   162
8-2 Personal Selling   165
   8-2a Strategic Marketing Communications Elements   165
   8-2b Characteristics   165
   8-2c Measurement   170
   8-2d Best Case: Abbott Laboratories—An Educated, Motivated, and Profitable Team   170
8-3 Trade Promotions (Reseller Support)   171
   8-3a Strategic Marketing Communications Elements   172
   8-3b Characteristics   174
   8-3c Measurement   179
   8-3d Best Case: Consumer Products Manufacturer and Channel Master—Procter & Gamble   180
8-4 Consumer Promotions   180
   8-4a Strategic Marketing Communications Elements   181
   8-4b Characteristics   182
   8-4c Measurement   187
   8-4d Best Case: Driving Home a Deal—General Motors Employee Discounts   188

Summary 188

Discussion Questions 189

Practice Quiz 189

Web Exercise: Servicing Different Markets Differently—Web Contact Points 190

Additional QuickLinks 190

Suggested Readings 191

Notes 191

Part Three Strategy Development: A Hierarchical Perspective 193

Chapter Nine

The Corporate Level: Analysis and Planning for Corporate Strategy and Tactics 196

9-1 Introduction 197

9-2 Corporate Strategies and Tactics 199
- 9-2a The Growth Strategy and Corresponding Tactics 200
- 9-2b The Maintain-Position Strategy and Corresponding Tactics 201
- 9-2c The Harvest Strategy and Corresponding Tactics 202
- 9-2d The Innovation Strategy and Corresponding Tactics 203
- 9-2e The Divestment Strategy and Corresponding Tactics 203

9-3 The Use of Situation Analysis in Corporate Strategy Selection 204
- 9-3a The Boston Consulting Group (BCG) Matrix 205
- 9-3b The Multifactor Portfolio Matrix 207

Summary 215

Discussion Questions 216

Practice Quiz 216

Web Exercise: Analysis and Planning for Strategic Decision Making in the Airline Industry 217

Suggested Readings 218

Notes 218

Chapter Ten

The Marketing Level: Analysis and Planning for Marketing Strategy and Tactics 219

10-1 Introduction 220

10-2 Marketing Strategies and Tactics 221
- 10-2a Strategic Product Focus and Corresponding Strategies and Tactics 227
- 10-2b Strategic Price Focus and Corresponding Strategies and Tactics 233
- 10-2c Strategic Place Focus 236
- 10-2d Strategic Prospects Focus 240

10-3 The Use of Situation Analysis for Marketing Strategy Selection 247
- 10-3a Consumer-Related Factors 247
- 10-3b Product-Related Factors 250
- 10-3c Market-Related Factors 251

Summary 253

Discussion Questions 253

Practice Quiz 254

Web Exercise: Cruising on the Web 255

Suggested Readings 256

Notes 256

Chapter Eleven

The Marketing Communications Level: Analysis and Planning for Marketing Communications Strategy and Tactics 258

11-1 Introduction 259

11-2 An Analytic/Planning Model 260
- 11-2a High Involvement/High Thinking: Informative (Thinker) Strategy 263
- 11-2b High Involvement/High Feeling: Affective (Feeler) Strategy 274
- 11-2c Low Involvement/Low Thinking: Habit-Formation (Doer) Strategy 276
- 11-2d Low Involvement/Low Feeling: Self-Satisfaction (Reactor) Strategy 281

Summary 285

Discussion Questions 285

Practice Quiz 286

Web Exercise: Marketing Communications Strategies and Website Congruity 287

Suggested Readings 287

Notes 288

Part Four — Building, Executing, and Assessing Your Integrated Marketing Communications Plan 289

Chapter Twelve
Setting Objectives and Assessing Performance: Setting Goals and Measuring Performance of the Strategic Marketing Communications System 291

12-1 Introduction 292

12-2 Advantages of Stating and Quantifying Objectives 292

12-3 Setting Objectives 295
- 12-3a Identifying Campaign Execution Objectives 295
- 12-3b Identifying Appropriate Measures for Each Objective 296
- 12-3c Identifying Desired Levels and Appropriate Time Frames for Each Objective 297

12-4 Examples of Objectives 298
- 12-4a Corporate Objectives 298
- 12-4b Marketing Objectives 298
- 12-4c Marketing Communications Objectives 299

12-5 Measures of Corporate Objectives 300
- 12-5a Profit and Cash Flow 300
- 12-5b Brand Sales and Market Share 301

12-6 Measures of Marketing Objectives 302
- 12-6a Recognition Measures of Brand Knowledge 303
- 12-6b Aided-Recall Measures of Brand Knowledge 304
- 12-6c The Image Measure of Brand Knowledge 304
- 12-6d The Cognitive-Structure Index 304
- 12-6e The Belief-Strength Measure 305
- 12-6f Projective Measures of Brand Associations 305
- 12-6g Associative-Strength Measures of Brand Awareness 307

12-7 Measures of Marketing Communications Objectives 308
- 12-7a Brand Awareness (*Aware*) 308
- 12-7b Brand Attitude (*Feel*) 310
- 12-7c Brand Trial or Purchase (*Do*) 315
- 12-7d Repeat Purchase (*Repeat*) 317

Summary 320

Discussion Questions 320

Practice Quiz 322

Web Exercise: Let Me Count the Ways—Measurement of Communications 323

Suggested Readings 323

Notes 324

Chapter Thirteen
Analysis Guiding Objective Setting: Linking Strategies and Tactics to Objectives and Performance Measures 326

13-1 Introduction 327

13-2 Using Situation Analysis to Set Corporate Objectives 327
- 13-2a Industry Average in Relation to Sales, Market Share, Profit, and Cash Flow 330
- 13-2b Forecasted Sales, Market Share, Profit, and/or Cash Flow 330
- 13-2c Past Sales, Market Share, and Profit of Key Competitors 330
- 13-2d Anticipated Profit, Sales, and/or Market Share of Key Competitors 330
- 13-2e Anticipated Market Changes That May Affect Future Sales, Market Share, and/or Profit 330
- 13-2f Anticipated Changes within the Firm That May Affect Future Sales, Market Share, Profit, and/or Cash Flow 331

13-3 Using Situation Analysis to Set Marketing Objectives 332
- 13-3a Industry Average in Relation to the Use of This Particular Measure of Brand Association 333
- 13-3b Forecasted Changes in the Brand Association in Question 333
- 13-3c Past Brand Association of Key Competitors 333
- 13-3d Anticipated Brand Association of Key Competitors 333
- 13-3e Anticipated Market Changes That May Affect the Brand Association in Question 333
- 13-3f Anticipated Changes within the Firm That May Affect the Brand Association in Question 334

13-4 Using Situation Analysis to Set Marketing Communications Objectives 335
- 13-4a The Industry Average in Relation to the Use of the Selected Measure of the Communications Objective 335
- 13-4b Forecasted Changes in the Selected Measure of the Communications Objective 336
- 13-4c Past Performance of Key Competitors along the Selected Measure of the Communications Objective 336
- 13-4d Anticipated Performance of Key Competitors along the Selected Measure of the Communications Objective 336

13-4e Anticipated Market Changes That May Affect Communications Objectives 336
13-4f Anticipated Changes within the Firm That May Affect Communications Objectives 337

Summary 337
Discussion Questions 337
Practice Quiz 338
Web Exercise: Is Image Everything? 339
Suggested Readings 339
Notes 340

Chapter Fourteen

Strategic Allocation of Resources: Budgeting in the Strategic Marketing Communications System 341

14-1 Introduction 342
14-2 Ratio-to-Sales Methods 345
  14-2a Percentage of Anticipated Sales 345
  14-2b Percentage of Unit Anticipated Sales 345
  14-2c Percentage of Past Sales 345
  14-2d Percentage of Unit Past Sales 345
14-3 Competitive-Parity Methods 346
  14-3a Match Industry Norms 346
  14-3b Share of Voice/Market 346
  14-3c Match or Outspend Competitors 347
14-4 Quantitative Methods 347
  14-4a Experimental 347
  14-4b Historical Statistical 348
14-5 Return-on-Investment (ROI) Method 348
14-6 Objective-Task Method 350
14-7 All-You-Can-Afford Method 350
14-8 Previous-Budget Method 351
14-9 A Strategic Marketing Communications Budgeting Method 351
  14-9a Determine the Corporate Objectives 351
  14-9b Determine the Corporate Mix to Achieve the Stated Objective 351
  14-9c Determine the Marketing Strategy to Achieve the Corporate Objective 351
  14-9d Determine the Marketing Objective That Operationalizes the Marketing Strategy 351
  14-9e Determine the Marketing Communications Strategy to Achieve the Marketing Objective 351
  14-9f Determine the Marketing Communications Objective That Operationalizes the Marketing Communications Strategy 353
  14-9g Determine the Marketing Communications Mix to Achieve the Marketing Communications Objective 353
  14-9h Determine the Cost of Implementing the Selected Marketing Communications Programs 354
  14-9i Adjust the Marketing Communications Budget as a Function of Monitoring/Control and Analysis/Planning 354
14-10 Analysis for Budgeting Decisions 354
  14-10a Organizational Factors 356
  14-10b Industry Factors 358
  14-10c Product Factors 360
  14-10d Customer Factors 361

Summary 362
Discussion Questions 363
Practice Quiz 364
Web Exercise: An Exercise of Dollars and Cents 365
Suggested Readings 365
Notes 366

Chapter Fifteen

Takeaways from the Strategic Marketing Communications Process: Lessons in Monitoring, Control, and Integration 367

15-1 Introduction 368
15-2 Monitoring and Control of Marketing Communications 369
  15-2a Failing to Meet Marketing Communications Objectives 373
  15-2b Failing to Meet Marketing Objectives 374
  15-2c Failing to Meet Corporate Objectives 376
15-3 Integrating the Marketing Communications System 377
  15-3a The Link between Strategy, Objective, and Tactics 377
  15-3b The Link between Strategy-Objective-Tactics and Budget 380
  15-3c The Link between Monitoring and Control 381
  15-3d The Link between Monitoring-Control and Strategy-Objective-Tactics 381
  15-3e The Link between Monitoring-Control and Objectives 382
  15-3f The Link between Monitoring-Control and Budget 383
  15-3g The Link between Analysis and Planning 383
  15-3h The Link between Analysis-Planning and Strategy-Objective-Tactics 384
  15-3i The Link between Analysis-Planning and Objectives 387
  15-3j The Link between Analysis-Planning and Budget 387

Summary 388
Discussion Questions 389
Practice Quiz 390
Web Exercise: Brand Unity and Marketing Communications Assessment 391
Suggested Readings 392
Notes 392

Case A An IMC Plan for Cable & Wireless Using the Systems Approach 393

Case B UnitedHealth Group Roanoke Call Center: IMC Plan 403

Case C Hancock Rack's IMC Plan 413

Glossary 419

Index 435

Preface

Introduction to the Book

Marketing is about delivering value to a given consumer. Marketing communications is about transmitting that value to the given consumer. In today's world, the transmission of that value is far more complex and multifaceted than it has ever been before. There is increasing diversity in the marketplace in regard to both the consumers and the products/services. The media environments are increasingly cluttered, and new technologies are arriving daily. Taken together, these environmental factors are creating a constantly shifting and evolving world. Needless to say, effectively delivering marketing communications in such an environment has itself become a process that requires constant adaptation and evolution. Consequently, it is absolutely crucial for marketing communications practitioners to be able to effectively measure and monitor the impacts of the myriad of marketing programs they use across the entire product/service portfolio of the firm. It is only then that they can truly manage *any* of their activities. To that end, this book is written not only for marketing communications students but also for current and future marketing communications practitioners with the aim of helping them to effectively manage their marketing programs.

A Unifying Theme Throughout

The uniqueness of this book lies in its integration of marketing communications and strategic marketing. It connects these two important topics using an approach that is well grounded from both a theoretical and a practical standpoint. That approach is the systems approach. One of the real problems that we have run into over the years are books and materials that offer their examinations of advertising or public relations or, more recently, integrated marketing communications (IMC) in a "stand-alone" type of format. That is, students are provided with "all the pieces" but not "the finished product." The use of the systems approach provides that finished product for a complete evaluation. It offers the ability to see how well all those pieces fit together to deliver the "total value" of the product. At the same time, this approach delivers on another level by providing a theoretically sound framework in which outcomes can be monitored and used to strategically adjust the entire marketing program for optimal performance. This allows the marketing communications student and the marketing communications manager to better understand the complex interactions of today's market and help answer questions like: How can I *strategically* plan and manage all the varied marketing communications tasks as a system? How can I coordinate among the various elements of marketing communications to ensure consistency? How can I create a learning system that will help me make periodic adjustments in the communications elements to achieve better performance? How can I plan and manage the marketing communications tools to ensure the attainment of marketing and corporate-level goals? How can I assemble the elements of the marketing communications mix and adjust them periodically in such a way to achieve marketing and corporate-level goals?

Organization of the Book

This book is divided into four parts: (1) Overview; (2) The Marketing Communications Portfolio; (3) Strategy Development: A Hierarchical Perspective; and (4) Building, Executing, and Assessing Your Integrated Marketing Communications Plan. The book is laid out to allow you to examine the entire process from theoretical foundations to execution and adjustment. The format of the book is one based on process levels *within* the system. That is, we begin with environment, build theoretical foundations, offer an analysis and planning framework in which to lay out the strategies and tactics for all levels, and then move to the issue of assessment of the system in the later sections. If so desired, the book can also be used from a particular system level perspective. That is, after reading the entire book for process integration, you may go back and choose to focus on the chapters that deal with "corporate-level" development of strategy and tactics, resource and control, and analysis and planning, thereby examining only the one level without the entire system being at play. In this manner, you may select the particular level of management that concerns you most. As noted, though, we suggest that you first examine the entire systems approach as presented in order in the book. Even when focusing on just one management level, you should be cognizant of the entire system in which that level is operating. A brief rundown of each of the four parts is presented next.

Part 1 introduces you to the world of marketing communications. It is a world that is defined by consumers, competitors, and the legal and social environments of today. Integrated marketing communications (IMC) systems concepts are used to build the systems model of strategic marketing communications (SMC). Specifically, in *Chapter 1*, we start out with a basic definition of IMC and provide an analysis of different conceptualizations and planning approaches to IMC. We also review Professor Schultz's model of integrated marketing communications; Schultz is the foremost authority and a pioneer in IMC. In *Chapter 2*, we examine the legal and social environments that influence decision making on the part of the SMC manager. In *Chapter 3*, we introduce the systems theory and discuss a particular systems model in the generic sense. The systems model involves five major components: (1) strategy and tactics, (2) objectives and measures, (3) budget, (4) monitoring and control, and (5) analysis and planning. You are introduced to each of these systems components, and we describe their dynamics. The concept of system integration, that is, how systems can be effectively integrated by building and strengthening linkages among the systems components, is then put forth. In *Chapter 4*, we present an overview of the model at large. The model is described as involving three levels of analysis—corporate, marketing, and marketing communications. It is within this multitier approach that the true power of the systems approach lies. By using a complete picture of the planner's corporate environment, the model offers the ability to truly integrate all aspects of the IMC planner's world into his or her decision. Each level involves a subsystem, and the components of that subsystem are strategy/tactics, objectives/measures, budget, monitoring/control, and analysis/planning.

Part 2 is comprised of four chapters that examine the particular marketing communications components that could be used in an SMC campaign portfolio. The purpose here is to provide an overview of the various tools that managers could employ when building their integrated strategy. Specifically, in *Chapter 5*, we offer an examination of advertising. In *Chapter 6*, we look at the "buzz" component of SMC, including such things as public relations and word-of-mouth communications. In *Chapter 7*, we explore direct and interactive marketing. In *Chapter 8*, we evaluate sales promotions, personal selling, and other reseller support components.

Part 3 moves the systems approach into the corporate realm of planning and execution by using the core of the systems model, namely, strategy and tactics. Here we concentrate on showing the marketing communications manager how to integrate a meaningful situation analysis into a selection of the best strategies at the corporate, marketing, and marketing communications levels. We describe the kind of situation analysis that can assist the marketing communications manager in setting objectives at the three hierarchical levels. Strategy and tactics are viewed as a process hierarchy or what some systems experts call a decision tree. Marketing communications programs (advertising, sales promotion, reseller support, direct marketing, public relations, and word-of-mouth communications) are viewed as elements of the marketing communications mix selected and guided by an overall marketing communications strategy (informative, affective, habit formation, and self-satisfaction). Marketing communications strategy is viewed as an element of the marketing mix (product, price, distribution, and marketing communications), which in turn is selected and guided by an overall marketing strategy (product-focus, price-focus, place-focus, and customer-focus strategies) and focus, as well as various positioning operationalizations of these strategies—positioning by product attribute, positioning by intangible factor, positioning by customer benefit, etc.). Fifteen positioning strategies are described in this book as directly related to marketing strategy. Similarly, marketing strategy is viewed as an element of the corporate mix (marketing, manufacturing, R&D, engineering, accounting, finance, employee relations, etc.), which in turn is selected and guided by corporate strategy (grow, maintain, harvest, innovate, and divest).

Part 4 describes performance measures (*Chapter 12*) for the entire SMC system, links of strategies and tactics discussed in Part 3 to executions in the system (*Chapter 13*), budgeting and allocation of resources (*Chapter 14*), and a look back at the entire system and how it needs to be considered in an integrative and holistic manner (*Chapter 15*). In *Chapter 12*, our focus is on objectives and performance measures. Also, specific performance measures related to corporate, marketing, and marketing communications objectives are described. In *Chapter 13*, we describe how objectives are set at the corporate, marketing, and marketing communications levels. We show how the marketing communications manager can monitor communications performance and make corrective adjustments in the system at various levels to align future performance with objectives. In *Chapter 14*, we look at the resource allocation and discuss how a marketing communications budget can be effectively determined through a top-down procedure. In this last part of the book, we have included a chapter devoted to highlighting the principles of systems integration. In *Chapter 15*, we discuss those principles in some detail and advise the marketing communications manager on how to best use these principles.

Finally, we present three cases to provide you with situations applying the various concepts and models described in the book. These cases show how the systems model of IMC can be used to plan future IMC campaigns as well as evaluate the effectiveness of current and past campaigns.

Pedagogy

In addition to all of the interactive capabilities of the Online Edition of the text, both the Print and Online Editions of the book have a number of learning aids that make this text especially friendly, involving, and appealing:

- *SMC Marketplace Watch* boxed features offer more detailed looks at specific topics. These features present additional relevant and current examples and interesting sidelights and generally add to the landscape of the chapter and your understanding.
- *SMC QuickLinks* provide you with quick access to web information regarding the topic or company that is being addressed in the body of the text. You can quickly gain a wealth of contextual information regarding the discussion taking place in the text to help you gain a clearer understanding of the issue and its application to real-time decision making/strategy.
- *Key Terms* in both the Print and Online Editions of the text are highlighted and defined on first appearance. In the Print Edition, key terms are also defined in the text margins and listed in alphabetical order at the end of each chapter. A Glossary at the end of the Print Edition presents all of the definitions alphabetically. In the Online Edition of the text, "pop-up" definitions of key terms provide you with immediate clarification of a term's meaning.
- *Discussion Questions* at the end of each chapter encourage critical thinking and discussion and require you to actively apply chapter concepts.
- *The Practice Quiz* at the end of each chapter allows you to check your comprehension of the chapter's major concepts. Each chapter has ten multiple-choice review questions.
- *Web Exercises* at the end of each chapter direct you to relevant web pages and guide you through a content-related activity.
- *Suggested Readings* at the end of each chapter provide you and/or your instructor with additional readings for further review of chapter topics.
- *Notes* are provided at the end of each chapter for your convenience. These can be used to study the entire article from which an in-chapter citation came or as the basis for further study on the topic.
- *Cases* are provided at the end of the book to provide you with situations applying the various concepts and models described in the book.

Online and In Print

Strategic Marketing Communications is available online as well as in print. The online chapters demonstrate how the interactive media components of the text enhance presentation and understanding. For example:

- Animated illustrations help to clarify concepts.
- Fully customizable chapter quizzes test your knowledge of various topics and provide immediate feedback.
- Clickable glossary terms provide immediate definitions of key concepts.
- Interactive key term matching exercises at the end of each chapter randomly generate a quiz of glossary terms to reinforce your understanding.
- Highlighting capabilities allow you to emphasize main ideas. You can also add personal notes in the margin.
- The search function allows you to quickly locate discussions of specific topics throughout.

Supplemental Course Support Materials

Atomic Dog offers a competitive suite of supplemental materials for instructors using its textbooks. These ancillaries include a test bank, PowerPoint® slides, an instructor's manual, and other items as listed here. Please contact your Atomic Dog sales representative if you are interested in these products.

- A full set of over 375 *PowerPoint slides* is available for this text. This is designed to provide instructors with comprehensive visual aids for each chapter in the book. These slides include outlines of each chapter, highlighting important terms, concepts, and discussion points.

- The *test bank* for this book includes over 1,500 questions in a wide range of difficulty levels. The test bank offers not only the correct answer for each question but also a rationale or explanation for the correct answer and a reference—the location in the chapter where materials addressing the question content can be found. This test bank comes with ExamViewPro software for easily creating customized or multiple versions of a test and includes the option of editing or adding to the existing question bank.
- The *instructor's manual* for this book offers sample lesson plans, chapter outlines/important topics, key terms, teaching ideas and suggestions, suggested answers to Discussion Questions and essay questions with suggested answers.

To the Student

We hope that you will enjoy reading this book and walk away with a good sense of strategic *integration* as it relates to marketing communications. We hope you will understand and appreciate how marketing communications campaigns can be *strategically* planned and managed and integrated throughout the entire system. Ultimately, we hope that this book allows you to better appreciate the importance of planning marketing communications campaigns *guided by systematically linked corporate and marketing strategies.*

About Atomic Dog

Atomic Dog is faithfully dedicated to meeting the needs of today's faculty and students, offering a unique and clear alternative to the traditional textbook. Breaking down textbooks and study tools into their basic "atomic parts," we then recombine them and utilize rich digital media to create a "new breed" of textbook.

This blend of online content, interactive multimedia, and print creates unprecedented adaptability to meet different educational settings and individual learning styles. As part of *Thomson Custom Solutions,* we offer even greater flexibility and resources in creating a learning solution tailor-fit to your course.

Atomic Dog is loyally dedicated to our customers and our environment, adhering to three key tenets:

Focus on essential and quality content: We are proud to work with our authors to deliver a high-quality textbook at a lower cost. We focus on the essential information and resources students need and present them in an efficient but student-friendly format.

Value and choice for students: Our products are a great value and provide students with more choices in "what and how" they buy—often at a savings of 30 to 40 percent less than traditional textbooks. Students who choose the Online Edition may see even greater savings compared to a print textbook. Faculty play an important and willing roll—working with us to keep costs low for their students by evaluating texts and supplementary materials online.

Reducing our environmental "paw-print": Atomic Dog is working to reduce its impact on our environment in several ways. Our textbooks and marketing materials are all printed on recycled paper. We encourage faculty to review text materials online instead of requesting a print review copy. Students who buy the Online Edition do their part by going "paperless" and eliminating the need for additional packaging or shipping. Atomic Dog will continue to explore new ways that we can reduce our "paw-print" in the environment and hope you will join us in these efforts.

Atomic Dog is dedicated to faithfully serving the needs of faculty and students—providing a learning tool that helps make the connection. We hope that after you try our texts, Atomic Dog—like other great dogs—will become your faithful companion.

Acknowledgments

The authors would like to give special thanks to Steve Scoble, Laureen Palmisano Ranz, Victoria Putman, Sarah Blasco, Mary Monner, Jeanne Patterson, and the entire Atomic Dog Publishing team.

About the Authors

M. Joseph (Joe) Sirgy is a consumer psychologist (Ph.D., University of Massachusetts, 1979), Professor of Marketing, and Virginia Real Estate Research Fellow at Virginia Polytechnic Institute and State University (Virginia Tech). He has published extensively in the area of marketing communications, consumer behavior, and macromarketing. He is the author/editor of several marketing communications, consumer behavior, and macromarketing books. He presently serves as section editor of the *Journal of Macromarketing*. He has served the Academy of Marketing Science in many positions, dating back to the early 1980s (e.g., member of the board of governors, vice president, co-chair of several AMS conferences, conference track chairs). He is a Distinguished Fellow of the Academy.

Don R. Rahtz is a marketing/marketing communications researcher (Ph.D., Virginia Tech, 1984) and a Professor of Marketing at The College of William and Mary in Virginia. His expertise is in marketing communications programs, marketing research, survey methodology, analysis, and market assessment. He has had a particular interest in quality of life, environmental issues, economic sustainable development, business/community interface evaluation, and health systems. Dr. Rahtz has traveled and worked extensively in the South and Southeast Asian area. He has published a variety of articles in journals from the social, behavioral science, communication, and marketing areas. Professor Rahtz is a Distinguished Research Fellow of the International Society for Quality of Life Studies (ISQOLS).

Overview

Part One

1 The World of Integrated Marketing Communications
2 Macro and Societal Issues in Marketing Communications
3 Building the Foundation of Strategic Marketing Communications
4 A Systems Model for Integrated Marketing Communications

The Orlando/Orange County Convention and Visitors Bureau, Inc., is charged with directing a total marketing communications program to attract visitors to the area year-round. The bureau's specific mission is to promote the area worldwide as a premiere leisure and business destination. It caters to a diverse group of stakeholders: organizational members such as Disney World, local community leaders, visitors to the area, convention planners and delegates, and the travel industry. To communicate with these various stakeholders, the bureau has used all forms of marketing communications, including, among others, advertising, public relations, consumer promotions, trade promotions, and direct marketing.[1]

Now suppose you are hired as the marketing communications director at the bureau to plan and manage the total marketing communications program. What a challenge! Where do you start and what do you do? To do a good job planning and managing the bureau's total marketing communications program, you need to figure out strategy and tactics. What is the overall strategy of the bureau at the highest level? That is, what is the corporate strategy? Is it to increase visitors in the area? Or is it to maintain the current level? What are the specific objectives in quantitative figures? What is the current level of visitors and what level of increase is desired? What is the time frame to achieve the stated objectives? Next quarter? A year from now? How can you measure the number of visitors that come to the area? How do you monitor progress toward the stated objectives and take corrective actions when needed?

SMC QuickLink
OrlandoInfo.com
http://www.orlandoinfo.com

What should the marketing strategy be? Could it be a differentiation strategy? That is, should you focus on convincing tourists that the Orlando area is better than other tourist destinations? If so, exactly how should the Orlando area be effectively positioned? What positioning approach should you take? Should you position the Orlando region by customer benefits, highlighting all the different tourist attractions that are "fun, fun, fun" and located in one small area not requiring much traveling? Exactly what are the marketing objectives? Should you state a marketing objective in terms of brand association, for example, associating Orlando in the minds of tourists with a variety of attractions that are "fun, fun, fun"? How do you measure this to keep track of how well you are doing?

How about selecting the most effective tools of marketing communications? Should you work with advertising? Why or why not? How about sales promotion? Why or why not? Direct marketing? Public

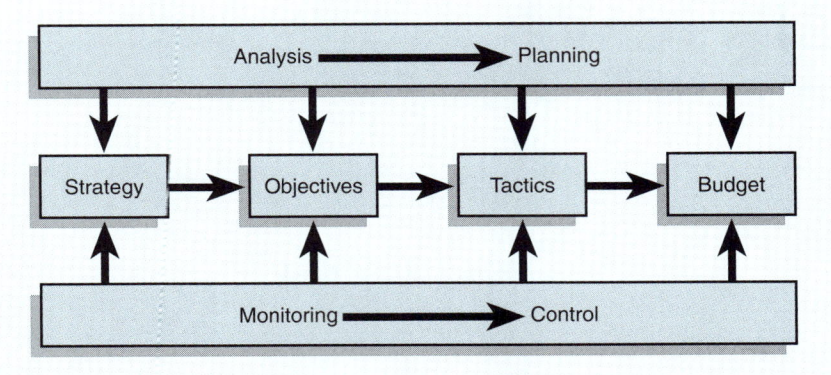

Figure 1
Major Decisions in Marketing Communications

relations? Trade promotions? Do you need some sort of strategy to help you choose the right mix of marketing communications elements? What would this strategy be? What are the objectives of the total marketing communications program? Should you state the objectives in terms of awareness, knowledge, attitude, action, and repeat action in relation to the Orlando region? How do you go about doing this? Should you come up with a total marketing communications plan that has different objectives over time? How will you measure marketing communications performance and monitor performance against the stated objectives? How do you figure out an optimal marketing communications budget? Mind boggling, isn't it?

This book is designed to help you use conceptual tools to come up with answers in an integrative framework. The book is written in a strategic manner with the focus on tying all the parts together for enhancing the decision-making abilities of managers. Part One of the book is designed to introduce the reader to the concept of integrated marketing communications (IMC), strategic marketing communications (SMC), systems concepts, and a model of IMC based on systems concepts. Specifically, Chapter One introduces you to a basic definition of IMC and provides an analysis of its various conceptualizations. It also shows how IMC is linked to the SMC idea. Chapter Two offers a look at the macro and societal issues in marketing communications. Chapter Three describes the five major components of the systems model: (1) strategy and tactics, (2) objectives and measures, (3) resource allocation, (4) monitoring and control, and (5) analysis and planning. We introduce you to each of these systems components and describe their dynamics. Then we address the concept of system integration—that is, how systems can be effectively integrated by building and strengthening linkages among the systems components. Chapter Four presents an overview of the systems model at large. The model is simply described as involving three levels of analysis: corporate, marketing, and marketing communications. Each level involves a subsystem; the components of that subsystem are strategy and tactics, objectives and measures, resource allocation, monitoring and control, and analysis and planning (see Figure 1).

Note

1. For a complete discussion of the bureau's total marketing communications activities, see Chapter 20 of the following book: William Wells, John Burnett, and Sandra Moriarty, *Advertising: Principles and Practice* (Englewood Cliffs, NJ: Prentice Hall, 1995).

The World of Integrated Marketing Communications

Chapter One

Key Terms

ad hoc approach (p. 17)
brand (p. 4)
brand equity (p. 4)
brand identity (p. 4)
brand unity (p. 6)
campaign continuity (p. 8)
consumer-based integration (p. 11)
contact management (p. 21)
coordinated integration (p. 11)
diversity (p. 4)
functional integration (p. 11)
integrated marketing communications (IMC) (p. 7)
message/media consistency (p. 11)
one-look approach (p. 16)
physical continuity (p. 8)
psychological continuity (p. 9)
relationship marketing (p. 7)
relationship-management integration (p. 12)
segmentation (p. 19)
stakeholder-based integration (p. 12)
strategic marketing communications (SMC) (p. 26)
strategic orientation (p. 9)
strategic partnering (p. 4)
supply-side planning approach (p. 17)
theme-lines or "matchbooks" approach (p. 16)
unity (p. 4)

Chapter Outline

1-1 Introduction: Operating in a World of Unity and Diversity
1-2 Definition of Integrated Marketing Communications
1-3 Characteristics of an Integrated Marketing Communications Campaign
1-4 A Developmental View of Integrated Marketing Communications
    1-4a Awareness of the Need for Integration
    1-4b Image Integration
    1-4c Functional Integration
    1-4d Coordinated Integration
    1-4e Consumer-Based Integration
    1-4f Stakeholder-Based Integration
    1-4g Relationship-Management Integration
    1-4h In Conclusion
1-5 Conditions or Trends That Paved the Way for Integrated Marketing Communications
    1-5a Trend 1: Decrease in Message Credibility
    1-5b Trend 2: Decrease of Cost of Database Marketing
    1-5c Trend 3: Increase of Cost and Decrease in Effectiveness of Mass-Media Communications
    1-5d Trend 4: Increase in Mergers and Acquisitions of Marketing Communications Agencies
    1-5e Trend 5: Increase in Media and Audience Fragmentation
    1-5f Trend 6: Increase in Parity or "Me-Too" Products
    1-5g Trend 7: Shift of Information Technology
1-6 Approaches to Planning Integrated Marketing Communications
    1-6a The Mandated "One-Look" Approach
    1-6b The Theme-Lines or "Matchbooks" Approach
    1-6c The Supply-Side Planning Approach
    1-6d Ad Hoc Approach
    1-6e Consumer-Based Approaches
    1-6f The Moore and Thorson Integrated Marketing Communications Model
    1-6g The Shultz, Tannenbaum, and Lauterborn Integrated Marketing Communications Model
    1-6h Why Evolve to the Strategic Marketing Communications Approach?
Summary
Discussion Questions
Practice Quiz
Web Exercise: What's Hot, What's Not
Suggested Readings
Notes

The multitude which does not reduce itself to unity is confusion.

—Blaise Pascal (1623–1662), French scientist, mathematician, physicist, philosopher, moralist, and writer

---

brand A name, term, design, symbol, or any other feature that identifies one seller's good or service as distinct from that of other sellers. The legal term for brand is *trademark*. A brand may identify one item, a family of items, or all items of that seller. If used for the firm as a whole, the preferred term is *trade name*.

brand identity Brand image. The perception of a brand in people's minds. The brand image is a mirror reflection (though perhaps inaccurate) of the brand personality or product being. It is what people believe about a brand—their thoughts, feelings, and expectations (AMA website: http://www.ama.org).

SMC QuickLink
NFL.com
http://www.nfl.com

strategic partnering The process by which two (or more) entities, who on their own lack the resources to create the desired market offering, will come together to gain synergies and optimize resource utilization to meet performance demands of a given marketplace.

brand equity A marketing goal. The term is used interchangeably with terms such as *brand association*, *brand image*, and *brand knowledge*. It describes a desirable situation in which target consumers associate the brand with desirable features, events, and/or people.

1-1 Introduction: Operating in a World of Unity and Diversity

The unity in today's world is the **brand.** The diversity is the marketplace. The elevation, maintenance, and protection of brands drive companies in almost everything they do today. Branding has become central to many of the world's largest corporations, local mom-and pop-operations, and entrepreneurial start-ups. Entities both large and small, private and public, and profit and nonprofit have come to realize that a good **brand identity** (brand image) can contribute greatly to both the short-term and long-term well-being of that entity. Consider the image and your feelings when someone mentions Coca-Cola. A clear set of images will flash through your mind regarding that brand. Bring up Exxon Corporation, and even though the *Exxon Valdez* disaster happened years ago, someone will undoubtedly comment that he or she refuses to buy that brand due to that disaster and the way in which Exxon handled the aftermath. The National Football League (NFL) has profited greatly in consumer attitudes toward it by **strategic partnering** with one of the best-known nonprofit organizations in the United States, the United Way. The NFL now has expanded its activities in a number of community-based projects. A new start-up can attract venture capital funding by simply having a "name" individual associated with it who is well known as being successful in such endeavors in the past or is just known as a smart investor. Tell any investor that Warren Buffet is interested in this company and that "personal brand" being transferred into bottom-line "brand value" becomes clear. Michael Eisner's departure from Disney had a direct impact on investors, and the departure of Bill Gates from Microsoft would reverberate throughout all levels of the financial and consumer markets.

The role of marketing communications in nurturing and building **brand equity** is crucial. How did the NFL arrive at the decision to partner with the United Way? What is that relationship worth to both partners in this relationship? Over time, is the partnership aiding both entities or hurting both or one of them? How much? Should the overarching message be changed? If so, to what? Think of the examples we have given in terms of strategic marketing communications. Questions like these are crucial for the plethora of global brands that now occupy the landscape.

Some people may think that diversity in the consumer population is the only diversity that marketers need to consider. In today's world, there is much more to the concept. **Diversity** is the myriad of demographic segments, cultures, lifestyles, nationalities, suppliers, companies that own that particular brand and others (in both the same company and other companies that may be owned by a higher level multinational corporate entity), and the brands themselves that occupy the landscape where brands seek to maintain **unity** of image and message. Needless to say, maintaining unity is a very daunting task.

Put yourself in the position of a brand manager for Crest toothpaste. Internal to the company, there are eighty-five different subbrands of Crest. These subbrands make up Crest, "the brand." This brand, in turn, is one of twelve brands of toothpaste that are put out by Procter & Gamble, which has hundreds of brands. This number got even larger recently when Procter & Gamble acquired Gillette. Now

Diversity in Consumers and Products

Diversity is the myriad of demographic segments, cultures, lifestyles, nationalities, suppliers, companies that own that particular brand and others (in both the same company and other companies that may be owned by a higher level multinational corporate entity), and the brands themselves that occupy the landscape where brands seek to maintain unity of image and message.

Sources: (Left) © 2006 JupiterImages Corporation. *(Middle)* and *(right)* © 2006 Stockbyte.

Figure 1-1
Today's Marketing Interface

who are the consumers being served with those brands? Obviously, Crest has eighty-five different subbrands to serve specific needs of market subsegments of toothpaste users. Are these subsegments broken out on age demographics, benefits sought, ethnic splits, lifestyle orientation, or a combination of these dimensions? Because these subsegments all have perceived different needs, they may also have different contact points in their relationship with that brand. It is an unbelievably complex task to keep track of all these contact points, keep track of what messages are best developed, and assess their impact on the greater entity of the Crest brand. Figure 1-1 gives an idea of the complexity of the marketplace environment in which today's manager must operate.

As Figure 1-1 shows, there is no single entry point for relationship building between a brand and the customer. Either the consumer or the seller can initiate

diversity (see p. 4) Variety; noticeable heterogeneity.

unity (see p. 4) The state or quality of being in accord; harmony. There is a combination or arrangement of parts into a whole. There is a singleness or constancy of purpose or action.

these relationships at any point of the contact. What becomes clear is that today's world of marketing communications is one of complexity at all levels of operation. There is, in general, no single channel by which marketers can channel all of their messages to a single target market. Monitoring and responding effectively to any of those interactions can be crucial in maintaining an effective relationship. Even a small, single-product company needs tools to track a myriad of elements that are at play in such an environment. It is to this diverse and dynamic environment that *integrated marketing communications* (*IMC*) seeks to bring a unity of message in brand communications and all its marketing activities.

Consider the following case of the ACUVUE disposable contact lens.[1] Marketing scholars agree that Johnson & Johnson (J&J) launched a successful integrated marketing communications (IMC) campaign. Johnson & Johnson started out with a direct-response advertising campaign in magazines such as *Newsweek*. The direct-response campaign introduced the lens and discussed its benefits. Each print advertisement allowed readers who became interested to receive an information packet by returning a mail-in card to J&J and identifying their optometrist. Johnson & Johnson then sent direct-mail kits to their optometrists. The optometrists, in turn, contacted their patients to set up appointments. Then optometrists notified J&J of appointments. Using this information, J&J mailed discount coupons (first-time trial offer) to patients who made an appointment to see their optometrists. These patients turned in their coupons and placed their first order with their optometrists. The optometrists, in turn, notified J&J about the first order. After some time, J&J mailed the eyecare patients another discount on second orders (see Figure 1-2).

Running a complicated marketing communications campaign such as the one for J&J's ACUVUE lens involves multiple communications tools directed to multiple audiences in multiple stages using a sophisticated coordination mechanism. This is what a complete IMC campaign is all about. A successful marketing communications program has to create unity of message and **brand unity** (brand consistency) in a marketplace that has become increasingly diversified. No longer is the relationship between a marketer and the final consumer one of a single contact point. Today's marketplace interactions exist in a world of continuous interaction between the marketing manager and the consumer and the consumer and his or her world. Constantly monitoring all events occurring within the broader environment while at the same time adjusting messages based on ever-evolving relationships with the consumer is a daunting, yet obviously crucial, endeavor.

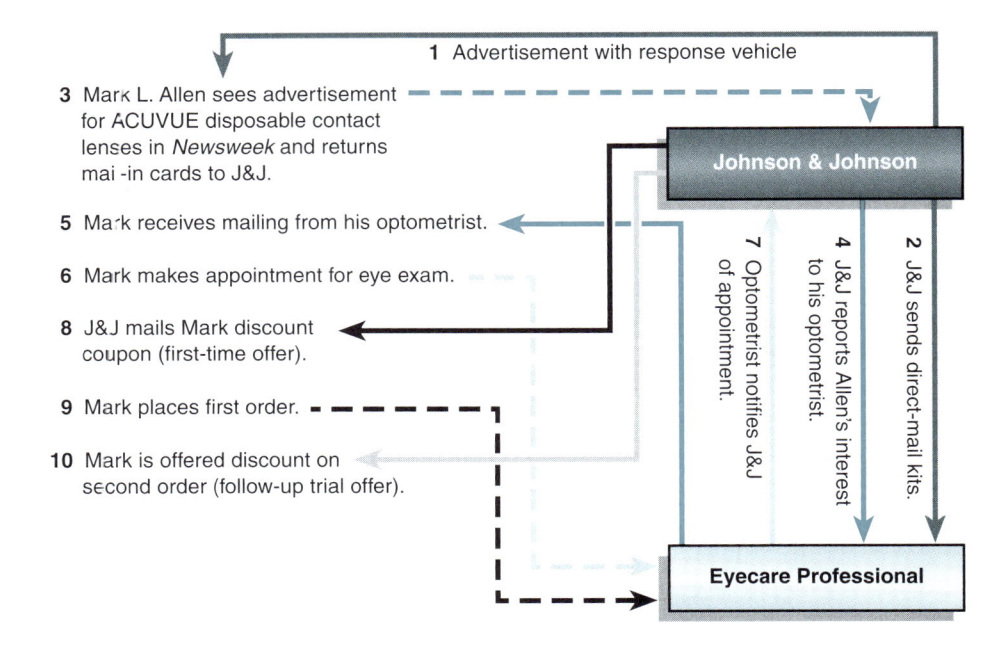

SMC QuickLink
ACUVUE® Brand Contact Lenses
http://www.acuvue.com/contact_lenses.htm

brand unity Brand consistency. How well the marketer has tied together and maintained all elements of the brand into a consistent and unified image in the mind of the consumer and target markets. This includes such things as marketing communications, promotions, product design, consumer promotions, imagery, and so on.

Figure 1-2
ACUVUE Integrated Communications Program

1 Advertisement with response vehicle

3 Mark L. Allen sees advertisement for ACUVUE disposable contact lenses in *Newsweek* and returns mail-in cards to J&J.

5 Mark receives mailing from his optometrist.

6 Mark makes appointment for eye exam.

8 J&J mails Mark discount coupon (first-time offer).

9 Mark places first order.

10 Mark is offered discount on second order (follow-up trial offer).

2 J&J sends direct-mail kits.

4 J&J reports Allen's interest to his optometrist.

7 Optometrist notifies J&J of appointment.

Johnson & Johnson

Eyecare Professional

The purpose of this chapter is to introduce you to the concept of IMC and the need for the continuing evolution of IMC to what is called *strategic marketing communications (SMC)*. We start by defining IMC. Second, we discuss the characteristics of an IMC campaign. Third, we describe the concept of IMC from a developmental perspective. Fourth, we explore the conditions that paved the way for IMC. Finally, we introduce you to several planning methods or approaches to IMC.

1-2 Definition of Integrated Marketing Communications

In today's world of **relationship marketing,** marketers must strive to optimize their exchange of information with both their suppliers and their consumers. At the same time, an exponential increase in the development of new communications technologies and methods is taking place. Marketers are compelled to use many of these technologies to reach and communicate with target consumers more effectively and in more cost-efficient ways. To do this in an optimum manner, marketers need a framework upon which they can build and complete an integrated program. They need help in knowing how to plan and implement a unified marketing communications campaign. They need conceptual tools to guide them in linking it all together. They need to create synergies among the various marketing communications programs. This is why many marketing and marketing communications scholars have come to recognize the importance of an integrated marketing communications perspective. **Integrated marketing communications (IMC)** is defined as follows:

> Integrated marketing communications is a concept that recognizes the added value in a program that integrates a variety of strategic disciplines—for example, general advertising, direct response, sales promotion, and public relations—and combines these disciplines to provide clarity, consistency, and maximum communication impact.[2]

Professor Don Schultz, considered by some to be a founding father of IMC, defined IMC as follows:

> [Integrated marketing communications is] the process of managing all sources of information about a product/service to which a customer or prospect is exposed, which behaviorally moves the consumer toward a sale and maintains customer loyalty.[3]

Integrated marketing communications embraces the idea that a firm coordinates all of its communications activities. This is very important because many firms are often content to let an advertising agency take care of their advertising. The firm farms out its public relations (PR) work to a PR agency. The firm's marketing department handles the sales promotion program. As a result, the firm's advertising goes off in one direction, public relations in another, and the sales promotion program in still another. As a result, the overall effectiveness of the firm's marketing communications suffers significantly. In today's world of unity of brand image, this can be very costly, as markets are unsure of which separate message should be considered. As a philosophical concept, IMC dictates that all parties involved in the firm's communications efforts coordinate their efforts to speak to target consumers with one voice, a unified message, and a consistent image.

Marketers have come to recognize the value of the IMC concept.[4] Four out of five marketing practitioners, when provided with a definition of IMC, indicated that the concept is very valuable and that it would increase the effect and effectiveness of their marketing communications programs. They indicated that IMC provides greater consistency in marketing communications programs, reduces media waste, and gives a company a competitive edge.[5]

---

relationship marketing
Marketing with the conscious aim to develop and manage long-term and/or trusting relationships with customers, distributors, suppliers, or other parties in the marketing environment.

integrated marketing communications (IMC)
A concept that recognizes the added value in a program that integrates a variety of strategic disciplines—such as general advertising, direct response, sales promotion, and public relations—and combines these disciplines to provide clarity, consistency, and maximum communications impact.

1-3 Characteristics of an Integrated Marketing Communications Campaign

The Body Shop has been proclaimed to be a highly successful international chain of retail stores. The company has an image of being socially and environmentally concerned. The image is consistent with the personality and values of The Body Shop founder Anita Roddick. The product ingredients are all natural and are bought from developing countries, and none of the testing is done on animals. The company does not use traditional advertising. The company uses a variety of marketing communications tools and has done well integrating the disparate components to create impact. SMC Marketplace Watch 1-1 shows how this company has adhered to this unity of message and delivery concerning its brand, thus successfully practicing IMC. What characteristics of The Body Shop's marketing communications campaign make it *integrated*?

To define IMC in terms of effectiveness, however, falls short of the true IMC perspective. Simply inferring that the marketing communications campaign must have been integrated because it achieved its marketing goals is clearly incorrect. This kind of thinking is what philosophers call "tautology" or "circular thinking." An IMC campaign needs to be defined in terms of two distinct characteristics: campaign continuity and strategic orientation.[6] **Campaign continuity** means that all messages communicated in different media through different marketing communications tools are interrelated. Campaign continuity involves making both the physical and psychological elements of a marketing communications campaign continuous. **Physical continuity** refers to the consistent use of creative elements in all marketing communications. Physical continuity in a marketing communications campaign can be achieved by using the same slogan, taglines, and trade characters across all advertisements and other forms of marketing communications. For example, for so many years, every Maytag advertisement reflected the same lonely repairman. For years, Wendy's used its CEO and founder Dave Thomas in its advertisements. Even though Dave died in 2002, Wendy's has recently returned to using him in their advertisements in an effort to recapture that continuity of brand that seemed to have faded in consumers' minds since Dave had stopped appearing as a spokesperson. He still holds a hallowed spot in the company's memory and message as can be seen at the Wendy's website. Visit Wendy's website (see Exhibit 1-1) to learn more about the personality of Wendy's founder.

campaign continuity The situation in which all messages communicated in different media through different marketing communications tools are interrelated.

physical continuity The consistent use of creative elements in all marketing communications.

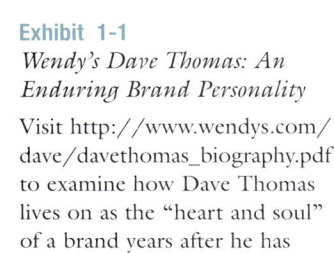

Exhibit 1-1
Wendy's Dave Thomas: An Enduring Brand Personality

Visit http://www.wendys.com/dave/davethomas_biography.pdf to examine how Dave Thomas lives on as the "heart and soul" of a brand years after he has passed away.

Source: AP/Wide World Photos.

SMC Marketplace Watch 1-1

The Body Shop—Unity of the Brand Message

Allister Jackson of The Body Shop says that the firm is totally committed to building community with its operations in Harlem. While some of the big chains may not "give back" to the community, The Body Shop believes its brand is about giving back. Five percent of sales (or 50 percent of profit, whichever is bigger) goes from the Harlem operation in support of that commitment by The Body Shop. The commitment does not stop with simply donating the money. The store's management meets with the Harlem Community Board to coordinate the dispersion of the monies in the community to various programs. This second "community store" (the first in the United States) was based on the store in Brixton, England, where the community has some of the same characteristics as the Harlem community. In Brixton, the focus is more on domestic violence and AIDS issues; but the monies and program support provided by The Body Shop in both communities are strong drivers in providing money for various entrepreneurial programs for the youth of these urban minority communities. These two stores are the only *community* stores of more than 1,800 worldwide Body Shop stores. By involving the community, The Body Shop has built a strong brand for the community and by the community as the staff and market. Eighty percent of both the staff and store customers are women from the surrounding community.

Source: Adapted from http://www.jrn.columbia.edu/newmedia/projects/masters/harlem/bodyshop.html.

In addition to physical continuity, *psychological* continuity is equally important. **Psychological continuity** refers to a consistent attitude toward the firm and its brand(s). It is consumers' perception of the company's "voice" and its "persona."[7] Psychological continuity can be achieved by using a consistent theme, image, or tone in different advertisements and other forms of marketing communications. The Virginia Slims marketing communications campaign has a consistent theme, that of "the liberated woman who chooses to smoke because she now has a mind of her own." Marlboro cigarettes are another example of the use of a consistent image across all forms of marketing communications—the cowboy image of being tough and rugged. Many cosmetic and apparel communications are good examples of consistent tone. For example, all Calvin Klein advertisements and other forms of marketing communications are sexual in tone. United Colors of Benetton seeks that continuity in "shock" and controversy. In the automobile industry, Volvo and safety are inextricably linked, whereas, as Exhibit 1-2 shows, BMW is the "Ultimate Driving Machine."

The second characteristic of an IMC campaign is **strategic orientation.** Integrated marketing communications campaigns can be effective because they are designed to achieve strategic company goals. The focus is not to develop a creative advertisement that simply attracts attention or gets an audience to laugh. Some marketing communications specialists may get carried away by the production of extraordinary creative work—advertisements that may win them communications awards (e.g., a Clio). If, however, these communications do not help achieve the firm's strategic goals—goals such as sales, market share, and profit—they are IMC failures. What really makes a marketing communications campaign integrated is its strategic focus on execution and performance assessment.

That strategic orientation is the emphasis of this book—hence, its title: *Strategic Marketing Communications.* It is crucial for the manager and the marketing student to have a well-grounded theoretical and practical framework within which they can make marketing communications decisions. Systems theory provides that. Chapter Two covers the systems approach and its value for decision making and monitoring in much

psychological continuity
A consistent attitude toward a firm and its brand(s).

SMC QuickLink
BMW International
http://www.bmw.com

strategic orientation
An orientation that attempts to provide consistency of marketing communications strategies with product/market strategies and the organization's mission, goals, and resources in the face of relevant market environmental factors.

Exhibit 1-2
BMW

The Lexus brand may be about value, but BMW has a clear message for its brand of luxury. It is "The Ultimate Driving Machine."

Source: Reprinted by permission of BMW of North America, LLC.

more depth. When used in the strategic marketing communications (SMC) framework, messages from every element in the campaign are designed to achieve specific strategic goals and media are selected with strategic goals in mind. The entire marketing and communications system of the firm is integrated toward delivering a unified strategic impact. That systems perspective is crucial when developing a "true" IMC or SMC perspective.

1-4 A Developmental View of Integrated Marketing Communications

Integrated marketing communications can occur in different forms at different levels of development. Seven levels of development have been identified (see Table 1-1).[8]

1-4a Awareness of the Need for Integration

In its most rudimentary form, IMC can be simply marketers' *awareness* or recognition of the need for integration of marketing communications. Consider the following example. A media planner is involved in buying and placing advertisements for a political candidate who is running for the presidency. The media planner comes to

TABLE 1-1	Developmental Stages of Integrated Marketing Communications
1. Awareness of the need for integration	5. Consumer-based integration
2. Image integration	6. Stakeholder-based integration
3. Functional integration	7. Relationship management integration
4. Coordinated integration	

recognize that media vehicles within and across media categories should be selected to reflect a consistent image of the political candidate. This is a first step toward implementing the IMC concept.

1-4b Image Integration

The second stage involves making decisions to ensure *message/media consistency*. **Message/media consistency** refers to consistency achieved between written and visual elements of an advertisement and between one advertisement placed in one media vehicle and one placed in another. That is, the picture has to reinforce and illustrate the written message. The advertisement also has to be slightly varied as a function of the editorial or programming content of the media vehicle, yet consistent with other advertisements placed in other media vehicles.

Derrith Lambka, the strategic planning and customer data manager for computer products at Hewlett-Packard, defined IMC in a manner consistent with image integration. She views IMC as "integration of messages and visual themes across the marcom [marketing communications] mix to maximize impact of messages in the marketplace. A consistent user benefit is clearly communicated in all marcom pieces."[9]

message/media consistency
Consistency of message between written and visual elements of an advertisement.

SMC QuickLink
Hewlett-Packard
http://www.hp.com

1-4c Functional Integration

The third level of development involves *functional integration*. **Functional integration** is the process in which the various marketing communications programs are formulated as a direct function of marketing goals, such as sales and market share. That is, the strengths and weaknesses of each element of the marketing communication mix are analyzed and the mix is assembled to achieve specified marketing objectives. To reiterate, marketing goals are employed to guide the selection and implementation of the marketing communications programs.

functional integration
A goal of marketing communications in which decisions are made as a direct function of marketing goals, such as sales and market share.

1-4d Coordinated Integration

In **coordinated integration,** a still higher level of development, the personal selling function is directly integrated with other elements of marketing communications (advertising, public relations, sales promotion, and direct marketing). That is, measures are taken to ensure consistency between interpersonal and impersonal forms of marketing communications. What one salesperson says has to be consistent with what the advertisement says.

coordinated integration
A goal of marketing communications in which the personal selling function is directly integrated with other elements of marketing communications (advertising, public relations, sales promotion, and direct marketing).

1-4e Consumer-Based Integration

In **consumer-based integration,** the fifth level of IMC development, marketing strategy is planned by understanding the consumers' needs and wants, targeting certain consumers, and effectively positioning the product to target consumers. In other words, marketing strategy is integrated. Messages are created to reflect strategic positioning in the minds of the consumers in a selected market segment.

consumer-based integration
A goal of marketing communications in which marketing communications decisions are guided by marketing strategy.

stakeholder-based integration The goal of marketing communications in which messages directed to target consumers, employees, suppliers, distributors, stockholders, the community, and certain government agencies are coordinated.

relationship-management integration A marketing communications goal in which messages are guided not only by marketing strategy but also by corporate strategy.

1-4f Stakeholder-Based Integration

The sixth level of IMC development is **stakeholder-based integration.** At this level, marketers recognize that target consumers are not the only group with which the firm should be communicating. Other stakeholders that should be included in the overall IMC campaign include the firm's employees, suppliers, distributors, stockholders, the community, certain government agencies, and others.

1-4g Relationship-Management Integration

Finally, **relationship-management integration** is considered to be the highest level of IMC development. To effectively communicate with the various stakeholders, the firm needs to develop effective strategies. These strategies are not only marketing strategies; they are manufacturing strategies, engineering strategies, finance strategies, human resource strategies, accounting strategies, and others. That is, in order to enhance relationships with organizational stakeholders, the firm has to develop management strategies within each functional unit (manufacturing, engineering and R&D, marketing, finance, accounting, human resources, etc.) that reflect coordination among the various functional units. Once this integration is achieved, the marketer attempts to communicate to the various stakeholders in a manner reflecting total integration.[10]

1-4h In Conclusion

We believe that the IMC model described in this book reflects an IMC perspective consistent with the highest three levels of IMC development—consumer-based integration, stakeholder-based integration, and relationship-management integration. We hope that you will agree with this assessment upon completion of the book.

1-5 Conditions or Trends That Paved the Way for Integrated Marketing Communications

At least seven conditions or trends have been identified that paved the way for IMC.[11, 12] These are shown in Table 1-2.

1-5a Trend 1: Decrease in Message Credibility

Consumers are continuously bombarded with marketing communications on all fronts. The enormity of this message bombardment has caused "clutter" in the landscape of marketing communications. This clutter is responsible for the fact that a single advertisement in a single medium cannot create significant impact. This clutter is responsible for a decreasing trend in message impact, which in turn has paved the way

TABLE 1-2	Conditions or Trends That Paved the Way for Integrated Marketing Communications

1. Decrease in message credibility
2. Decrease of cost of database marketing
3. Increase of cost and decrease in effectiveness of mass-media communications
4. Increase in mergers and acquisitions of marketing communications agencies
5. Increase in media and audience fragmentation
6. Increase in parity or "me-too" products
7. Shift of information technology

to the recognition that message effectiveness is dependent on multiple messages, multiple media, and multiple forms of marketing communications tools. Therefore, marketers are beginning to feel the need for understanding the science and art of IMC. They are beginning to realize that they need to understand and implement IMC to be effective in today's cluttered marketing communications environment.

1-5b Trend 2: Decrease of Cost of Database Marketing

The advent of computer technology has created a large industry of mailing-list organizations. Now, more than ever, marketers are capable of gathering specific information about targeted consumers. For example, if marketers want to target, let us say, physical therapists, they can buy a database that provides an extensive profile of these people. Part of this profile is the various sources of information they use in making purchases related to their professional practice and their media habits. Armed with this information, a marketer targeting this population can create multiple messages using different forms of marketing communications tools. Because of the sophisticated computer technologies used in database management and the fierce competition in this industry, the cost of using databases has dramatically decreased over the years. The increased viability of database marketing has made IMC increasingly attractive to many marketers.

1-5c Trend 3: Increase of Cost and Decrease in Effectiveness of Mass-Media Communications

The cost of television advertising, as well as that of other mass-media advertising, has continuously spiraled over the years. Consumers are no longer watching television as they used to. SMC Marketplace Watch 1-2 examines what is happening to the traditional television viewer environment. In other areas, consumers are not reading newspapers as they used to.

Radio listenership is also down. Consumers are turning to other entertainment media and leisure activities such as playing Nintendo games and surfing the Internet. Those who watch television are now zipping through and zapping the commercials. Many are watching pay cable television to avoid commercials. Marketers are becoming more cost conscious than ever. They are increasingly recognizing that they can launch

Consumers in the New Millennium

Consumers are turning to other entertainment media and leisure activities, such as playing Nintendo games and surfing the Internet.

Source: © 2006 JupiterImages Corporation.

SMC Marketplace Watch 1-2

Consumers Are Watching Fewer Network Television Shows—The Changing Landscape of America's Media Habits

American society today is far more diverse and commercially self-indulgent than a decade or two ago. The country has atomized into countless market segments defined in terms of demographics and psychographics. Prime-time network ratings and newspaper circulation numbers have been sliding since the 1970s. Digital and wireless communications channels are proliferating into hundreds of narrowcast cable television and radio channels; thousands of specialized magazines; and millions of computer terminals, video-game consoles, personal digital assistants, and cell-phone screens.

In the 1960s, a marketer could reach 80 percent of U.S. women with a spot aired simultaneously on CBS, NBC, and ABC. Today, an advertisement would have to run on one hundred television channels to come close to reaching 80 percent of that market. According to Nielsen Media Research, the average U.S. household receives one hundred television channels compared with twenty-seven in 1994. Cable now rules prime time, with a 52 percent share compared to broadcast's 44 percent.

In 2004, McDonald's devoted a third of its U.S. marketing communications budget to television, compared with two-thirds 5 years earlier. Network television does not reach a mass audience as it used to. Money that used to go for 30-second network spots now pays for closed-circuit sports programming shown in Hispanic bars and advertisements in *Upscale*, a custom-published magazine distributed to barber shops with a customer base of black people. McDonald's is segmenting its mass market into many segments and reaching its segments using targeted media.

Consumers are spending more time in front of the computer than in front of the television set. American Express launched an advertising campaign starring longtime spokesman Jerry Seinfeld on the company's website. The two, 4-minute "Webisodes" costarring an animated Superman have attracted more than two million visitors in through American Express's Internet portal. American Express is now running the first website in conjunction with TBS reruns of *Sex and the City*. The combined campaign of television and Internet is said to be highly effective in reaching young urban professionals, the same type of consumers that used to watch *Seinfeld*.

The media habits of active young mothers—the prime target of Pfizer's new product, RELPAX, a prescription medicine for migraine headache relief—are changing. These mothers are listening to the radio in the car, going on the Internet late at night, or reading a magazine in a quiet moment. They are not watching television that much. Consequently, Pfizer is no longer using television to reach this market.

Procter & Gamble (P&G) is becoming choosier in its use of television advertising in its marketing communications programs. From 1999 to 2003, P&G cut its spending on television commercials for Tide by nearly 16 percent to $69.4 million. Spending on network television plummeted 75 percent to $25.3 million. Procter & Gamble has now doubled its budget for Hispanic television to $12.4 million

Table 1 summarizes how changes in media viewing habits in the last two decades have affected advertising.

Source: Adapted from Anthony Bianco, "The Vanishing Mass Market: New Technology. Product Proliferation. Fragmented Media. Get Ready: It's a Whole New World," *Business Week*, July 12, 2004, 60–68.

TABLE 1 Effects of Changing Media Viewing Habits on Advertising

	Old	New
Consumers	Couch potatoes passively receive whatever the networks broadcast.	Empowered media users control and shape the content, thanks to TiVo, iPod, and the Internet.
Aspirations	To keep up with the crowd	To stand out from the crowd
Television Choice	Three networks plus PBS station, maybe	Hundreds of channels plus video on demand
Magazines	Age of the big glossies: *Time, Life, Look,* and *Newsweek*	Age of special interests: A magazine for every hobby and affinity group
Advertisements	Everyone hums the Alka-Seltzer jingle.	Talking to a group of one, ads go ever narrower.
Brands	Rise of the big, ubiquitous brands, from Coca-Cola to Tide	Niche brand, product extensions, and mass customization mean lots of new variations.

an aggressive and effective marketing communications campaign using marketing communications tools that are less costly than mass-media advertising. As they rely on other forms of marketing communications tools and combine these programs to achieve sales, market share, and profitability goals, marketers are beginning to realize that they need to better understand the science of integrated communications—thus, IMC.

1-5d Trend 4: Increase in Mergers and Acquisitions of Marketing Communications Agencies

In the last decade or so, we have witnessed an unprecedented level of mergers and acquisitions in the marketing communications agency business. These mergers and acquisitions may have been the result of agency executives realizing the need to offer clients comprehensive marketing communications services. A large marketing communications agency that can assemble teams from various marketing communications departments to meet the needs of its clients is likely to be in a better competitive position than agencies that cannot offer this type of service. Those agencies that are now in a position to offer comprehensive marketing communications services are increasingly appreciative of the science and art of IMC.

1-5e Trend 5: Increase in Media and Audience Fragmentation

The fierce competition in mass media has forced the industry to become highly fragmented. Radio stations are springing up all over with specific programming formats. Television channels are specializing by content area, for example, history, classic movies, learning, science fiction, family, news, politics, and so on. There are hundreds or thousands of magazines and trade publications that are specialized. Consumers are no longer watching a television station that caters to everyone. They do not have to. They tune in to those media that have programming or editorial content that matches their interest. This trend of media and audience fragmentation has been a challenge for marketers. Marketers can no longer place, say, a 30-second television commercial in, say, *CBS Evening News* or *60 Minutes* and expect to get large exposure. That used to be the case—but no more. Marketers have to identify the media habits of their target consumers and develop and place multiple messages in specialized and possibly nontraditional media. To do this effectively, they realize now more than ever that they need to fully understand IMC.

1-5f Trend 6: Increase in Parity or "Me-Too" Products

Competition is becoming fierce. Many businesses are developing and marketing products that cannot be significantly differentiated from competitor brands. Marketing communications has become essential in an age of "me-too" products. The name of the game is now *share of voice*. Share of voice becomes an effective means to achieve desired returns and market share—that is, the more messages in more media, the better the chance for higher returns and greater market share. The increased emphasis on marketing communications has brought with it increased marketing communications clutter, decreased message credibility, database marketing, increased cost and decreased effectiveness of mass-media communications, mergers and acquisitions of marketing communications agencies, and increased media and audience fragmentation. These, in turn, have made marketers very cognizant of the need for and power of IMC.

1-5g Trend 7: Shift of Information Technology

Professor Schultz has argued that changes in information technology are likely to provide consumers with the ability and capability to communicate and even purchase through a variety of means. That is, consumers can communicate interactively and purchase products directly from the manufacturer. Traditionally, the manufacturer announces the availability of its product to consumers and attempts to transmit messages to consumers in the hope of making them purchase. The trend points to the scenario in which the buyer announces his or her readiness to purchase using the latest interactive information technology. The sellers attempt to respond to the buyer's readiness. The buyer becomes the advertiser; and the traditional use of advertising, sales promotion, public relations, and direct marketing changes dramatically. This shift in information technology dictates a redefinition of the traditional use of the various elements of marketing communications.[13]

1-6 Approaches to Planning Integrated Marketing Communications

Several approaches to planning IMC have been identified and discussed.[14] These are listed in Table 1-3.

1-6a The Mandated "One-Look" Approach

one-look approach
An approach that attempts to create unity in all forms of marketing communications through maintaining a "single look and feel" in all executed messages including colors, fonts, visuals, logos, and so on.

Some marketers understand and implement the concept of IMC in terms of *common look*. This **one-look approach** usually translates into having unity through common colors, graphics, and logo treatments in all forms of marketing communications. For example, a company hires an advertising agency to develop an advertising campaign for one of its products but makes the decision to develop other communications materials in-house. In this case, the company makes an attempt to develop those in-house materials in a manner consistent with the advertising campaign. In other words, the company tries to maintain a "look" of the in-house communications materials that is consistent with the colors, visuals, and logo treatments shown in the advertisements developed by the advertising agency.

The major shortcoming of this approach is the fact that a common look to all forms of marketing communications is not likely to suffice. A strategic focus is lacking; hence, IMC decisions cannot be made effectively.

1-6b The Theme-Lines or "Matchbooks" Approach

theme-lines or "matchbooks" approach
Used by marketers who attempt to coordinate all supporting forms of marketing communications around an advertising theme. The goal is to use nonadvertising forms of marketing communications to trigger consumers to remember the advertising message.

Marketers who attempt to coordinate all supporting forms of marketing communications around an advertising theme are using the **theme-lines or "matchbooks" approach.** The goal is to use nonadvertising forms of marketing communications to trigger consumers to remember the advertising message. For example, the television commercial of Coppertone suntan lotion uses a theme line of "Tan, don't burn." The same theme line is then used in skywriting over the beaches during the summer while the target market is engaged in the tanning process itself.

Some research has been conducted in this area.[15] Examples of findings and their managerial usefulness are outlined here:

- Advertising retrieval cues such as key visuals or distinctive slogans can be placed on point-of-purchase displays and packaging. These cues can help consumers remember the advertising message.
- Consumers can be made to remember a television commercial through a radio commercial by using the same audio script.

TABLE 1-3 Planning Approaches to Integrative Marketing Communications

1. The mandated "one-look" approach	4. Ad hoc approaches
2. The theme-lines or "matchbooks" approach	5. The consumer-based approach
3. The supply-side planning approach	

- Before running a television commercial, marketers can run radio and print advertisements that are directly linked to the television commercial. The print and radio advertisements in this case serve as teasers and increase consumer motivation to fully process the television commercial when it is finally run.
- Television commercials can be viewed as consisting of different elements that marketers can choose to combine in different ways over time. Examples of these interchangeable elements include visual scenes, characters, symbols, verbal phrases, and slogans.

As with the one-look approach, the theme-line approach is necessary but not sufficient. Marketers need to be guided by both continuity and a strategic focus.

1-6c The Supply-Side Planning Approach

Many companies offer a **supply-side planning approach,** which is a system of marketing communications services that has the appearance of integration. For example, an advertising agency may have a package deal with the local cable company, several radio stations, and a local newspaper. The package deal allows a local business to advertise its offerings through a combination of cable channels, the two radio stations, and the local newspaper. The price of the package deal is highly attractive. The benefit that the advertising agency highlights in selling this package deal to prospective businesses is integrated communications. That is, the advertising agency will create advertisements with a common look and theme and place them across varied media vehicles.

The major shortcoming of the supply-side planning approach is the fact that the package deal may not fit the exact needs of the business client. Businesses may be inclined to move in this manner because they may think that they are being efficient and getting a good bargain, but in reality the bargain may not provide "true" integrated value.

1-6d Ad Hoc Approach

Some marketers may use an **ad hoc approach,** which is an attempt to integrate the disparate elements of their marketing communications programs by arranging meetings with all the interested parties. For example, a variety of people representing different interests attend a meeting and attempt to achieve consensus. Included among

supply-side planning approach Using a system of marketing communications services that has the appearance of integration. A combination of marketing communications outlets that are put together to increase value to the buyer. Communications with a common look and theme are placed across varied media vehicles.

ad hoc approach An attempt to integrate the disparate elements of marketing communications programs by arranging meetings with all the interested parties.

Ad Hoc Approaches
Some marketers may attempt to integrate the disparate elements of their marketing communications by arranging meetings with all interested parties. Different people representing the different suppliers/contributors present their ideas of marketing communications and discuss ways to establish common threads.

Source: © 2006 JupiterImages Corporation.

these people may be the account executive from the advertising agency, the public relations representative, the salesperson from the sales promotion firm, and the marketing research people, among others. The meeting is organized and led by the marketing director. Different people representing the different suppliers/contributors present their ideas of marketing communications and discuss ways to establish common threads.

The major shortcoming of this approach is that the process is not likely to be efficient. There is no underlying model or plan to guide the integration efforts. Second, the outcome may be highly influenced by group dynamics. Certain parties with strong opinions may take over and lead the integration effort with inappropriate and ineffective results.

1-6e Consumer-Based Approaches

There are two consumer-based approaches to IMC—one developed by Moore and Thorson[16] and the other developed by Schultz, Tannenbaum, and Lauterborn.[17] The IMC model developed by Schultz and colleagues is considered to be the standard model. This model is fully discussed and critiqued in order to help set the stage for a presentation of this book's IMC systems model. While truly not the standard that is the Schultz, Tannenbaum, and Lauterborn model, the Moore and Thorson model is briefly described here to, again, set the stage for a systems model perspective.

1-6f The Moore and Thorson Integrated Marketing Communications Model

The Moore and Thorson IMC model involves five basic steps, which are shown in Table 1-4.

Step 1, *identifying the market,* is the process by which the marketer identifies those consumers who are most likely to buy the company product. For example, consider the scenario of two possible segments for Evian, a brand of bottled water—the health-conscious adult and the new mother. New mothers would be inclined to buy pure water to feed their babies. Step 2 involves *segmenting the market based on the stage of the purchase cycle.* The typical stages in the purchase cycle include awareness, acceptance, preference, search, purchase, usage, and satisfaction. The stage of the purchase cycle is then identified for each market segment. For example, one can identify the two market segments as having tried the bottled water so that most of the consumers are at the satisfaction stage. Step 3 involves *the identification of messages and communications vehicles for each target segment.* Knowing in which stage most of the consumers are allows the marketer to identify the kind of message needed. In this case, the message has to reinforce the consumers' satisfaction. The message directed to the health-conscious consumers has to be created in a way that allows the health-conscious audience members to identify with the characters in the advertisement, perhaps by using a health-conscious celebrity as a referent. Similarly, the message directed to the new mothers has to appeal to this audience. Advertisement executions could be created using a new mother as a spokesperson. Furthermore, Evian would attempt to identify those media vehicles that can reach both segments in the most cost-efficient way. For example, certain magazines can be identified for each of these

TABLE 1-4 The Moore and Thorson Customer-Based Approach to Integrated Marketing Communications

1. Identifying the market
2. Segmenting the market based on the stage of the purchase cycle
3. Identifying messages and communications vehicles for each target segment
4. Allocating resources
5. Evaluating program effectiveness

two segments. Once both the message and media are identified for the given market segment, attempts to ascertain the costs of creating and placing a certain number of messages in certain media are undertaken. This is Step 4, the *resource-allocation* step. Finally, Step 5 involves *evaluating program effectiveness*. For example, tracking studies can be employed to monitor brand awareness, consumer attitude, and so on for each of the segments targeted.

This approach to IMC is highly consistent with the systems approach discussed in this book. However, the systems model is more comprehensive and rigorous than the Moore and Thorson model in a number of ways. The model we present shows explicitly how decisions made at the corporate level are tied to decisions made at the marketing level, which in turn are linked to decisions made at the marketing communications level. You are now in a position to better understand and appreciate the systems model of IMC that is proposed in this book.

1-6g The Schultz, Tannenbaum, and Lauterborn Integrated Marketing Communications Model

The most authoritative work in IMC is that of Schultz, Tannenbaum, and Lauterborn (1994) in their book *Integrated Marketing Communications: Pulling It Together and Making It Work*.[18] Schultz and colleagues describe IMC as a way of conceptualizing the whole process instead of focusing on parts such as advertising, public relations, sales promotion, direct marketing, and so forth. Their IMC model involves a sequence of marketing communications planning activities (see Figure 1-3).

Database Development

The first step in planning, according to the Schultz, Tannenbaum, and Lauterborn model, is developing a database. Database development involves gathering and assembling information (demographics, psychographics, purchase history, and category networks) about the product users (consumers). For example, an airline sends information to members of its frequent-flier program through direct mail and emails and solicits replies from them. The members may be asked if they want information on air travel to some exotic island in the Caribbean to spend the Christmas holidays. The reply can be in the form of a return direct-mail piece, an email response, or merely a telephone call. Part of the reply asks for additional information about the members, their likes and dislikes involving travel, the way they would like to spend their Christmas vacation, and so on. The reply information is used to create the database about potential customers who may be interested in flying to the Caribbean for a Christmas vacation and the kind of travel/tourist services that the airline company may be able to provide to meet the needs of the members of its frequent-flier program.

Gathering data about consumers is important, and marketing scholars have always advocated exactly the same thing. That is, knowing customers better allows firms to serve customers better. The problem here is knowing exactly what elements are needed to better know the consumer. That analysis has to be strongly linked with planning. Every piece of information gathered needs to be useful in bettering delivery to the consumer. One needs to figure out exactly what kind of decisions need to be made first and then try to gather *relevant* information that can help decision makers execute these decisions more effectively. In the systems model, analysis and planning are essential and directly tied to strategy selection, objective setting, the formulation of tactics, and resource allocation at the corporate, marketing, and marketing communications levels.

Segmentation

Segmentation is a basic and long-lived marketing process in which consumers are divided into subsegments that group around certain homogeneous similarities. Schultz and colleagues advance the notion of segmentation as one of breaking the

SMC QuickLink
AirTran Airways
http://www.airtran.com

segmentation The process of breaking up a larger, heterogeneous market into smaller subsegments that group around homogeneous similarities.

Figure 1-3

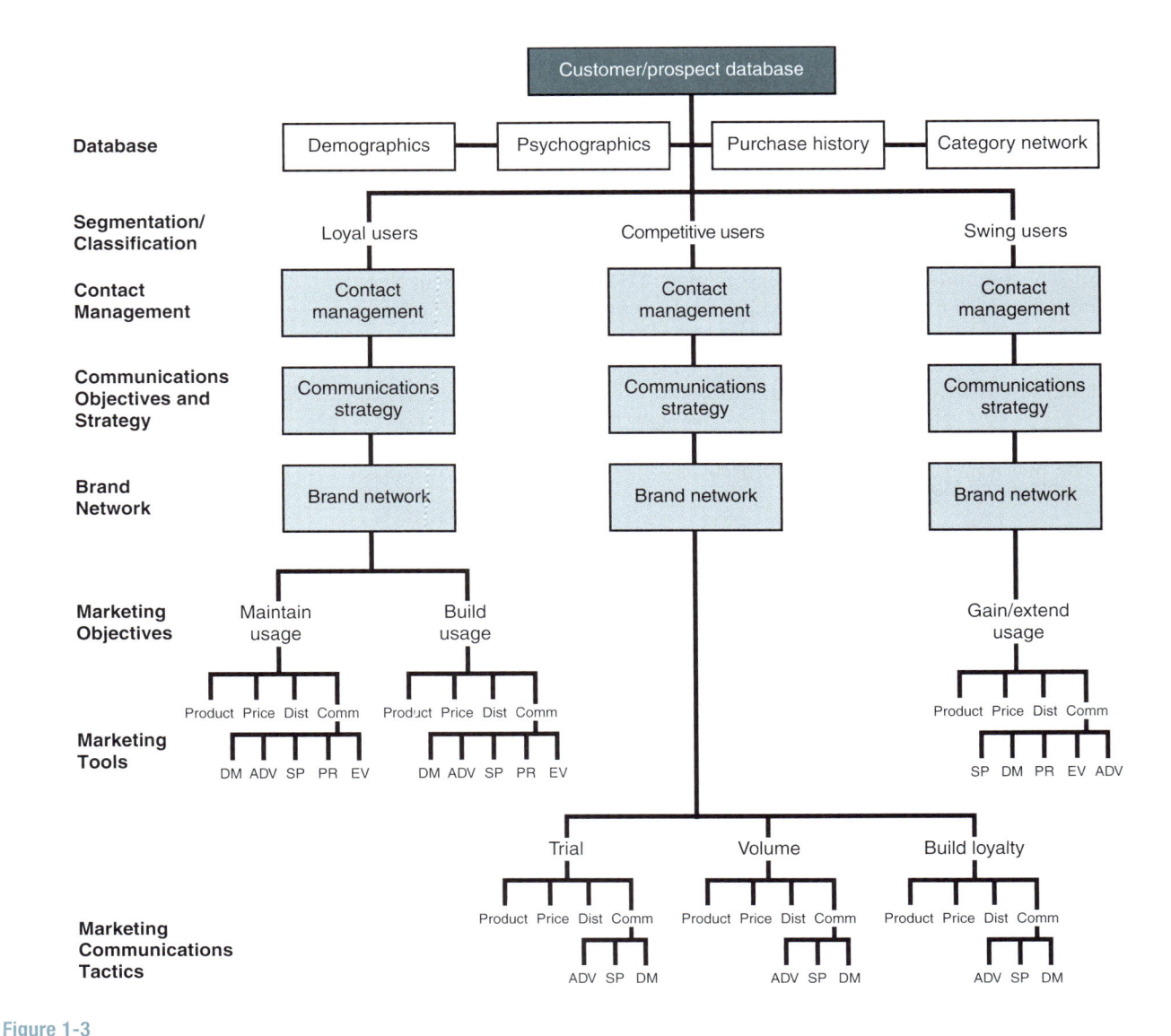

The Schultz, Tannenbaum, and Lauterborn Integrated Marketing Communications model (DM = Direct marketing; ADV = Advertising; SP = Sales promotion; PR = Public relations; EV = Event marketing)

market into the segments of loyal users, competitive users, and swing users. Consumer profiles of these various segments are developed. *Loyal users* are consumers who have a history of repeat use of the product brand. *Competitive users* are those who use the brand in question together with other competitive brands. *Swing users* are not loyal to any one brand or combination of brands. They are opportunistic. They buy a brand because of its price and accessibility.

Take the Olive Garden (an Italian restaurant national chain) as an example. The marketing director would be interested in developing consumer profiles of those who are loyal to the Olive Garden—people that eat at the Olive Garden whenever they feel the need to eat Italian food in a sit-down restaurant. The marketing director wants information about these loyal customers to serve them better and retain their business for the long term. What is the relevant kind of information that the marketing director needs concerning the loyal customers? Relevant information would concern their likes or dislikes regarding the different items on the menu, information about their likes or dislikes concerning the possibility of introducing new dishes, information about their media habits, and so on.

What about competitive users? The marketing director of the Olive Garden would desire information concerning this segment, too. The goal here may be to get these people to increase their patronage of the Olive Garden. Again, information about their likes and dislikes concerning the menu items and about their media habits can be very helpful in developing appeals to move this segment toward a stronger relationship with the Olive Garden in the future.

How would the marketing director of the Olive Garden use information regarding the swing customers? Perhaps the marketing director could find a way to appeal to the swing customers to fill gaps in the dining periods when business is slow—off-peak periods, perhaps during lunch and dinner in the middle of the week. This group may respond to discounts, perhaps through coupons distributed in the local newspaper. Thus, the marketing director needs to gather information concerning which local newspapers these group members read. If the consumers do not read newspapers, what other media vehicles can reach them in the most effective and cost-efficient way? Information about media habits is important.

Schultz, Tannenbaum, and Lauterborn advanced brand use as the method of segmentation. As noted earlier, they suggest that consumers should be segmented into loyal users, competitive users, and swing users. While this segmentation is well known in the marketing literature, a multitude of other segmentation bases exists. Marketing scholars have long described a plethora of ways of segmenting the market using all kinds of different segmentation criteria (e.g., demographic segmentation, psychographic segmentation, segmentation based on product criteria, geographic segmentation, sociocultural segmentation, and so on). Schultz and his colleagues' concept of segmentation limits the process to one very specific method of segmentation based on a product criterion—brand use. In essence, Schultz and his colleagues advocate that we abandon all other uses of segmentation and adopt the brand-use segmentation as the best and only method. Their prescription of segmentation is extremely constrictive. There are hundreds of scenarios in which segmentation by brand use is not likely to be the most effective or even appropriate. The systems model does not limit managers to a single, specific segmentation criterion. The systems model incorporates Porter's model,[19] which posits that segmentation can and should only be attempted when the best marketing strategy is one of focus. Other marketing strategies such as differentiation and cost leadership do not require any market segmentation at all. Only in the context of the focus strategy should the manager implement segmentation; and, in the context of focus, the systems model recommended the use of any of the following three positioning strategies: customer benefits (commonly known as *benefit segmentation* in marketing), use or applications, and user or customer. Thus, the brand-use segmentation restriction of Schultz, Tannenbaum, and Lauterborn is really only one variation of the user or customer strategy.

Contact Management

Contact management is the process by the which the marketer determines the time, place, or situation in which to communicate to the customer or prospect. For example, the Olive Garden's marketing director would consider the situation in which most customers (potential and actual) are most likely to be most favorably disposed to actively processing an advertising message about the Olive Garden. Should the advertisement appear on the local television news program before dinnertime? Those who may be planning to eat out may consider the Olive Garden if they were to see an advertisement about the Olive Garden just before they were getting ready to go out to dinner. Effective contact management in this scenario would be buying advertising space on the local television news program between 5 P.M. and 7 P.M.

Why talk about contact management as a strategic decision? Contact management, although it is important, is a tactical decision. In the systems model, contact management is a tactical decision made in the context of each element of the marketing communications mix. For example, when advertising is selected as an effective element of the marketing communications mix, the marketing communications manager makes media placement decisions and only in this context should the time,

SMC QuickLink
Olive Garden Italian Restaurant
http://www.olivegarden.com

contact management The process by which the marketer determines the time, place, or situation in which to communicate to the customer or prospect.

place, or situation be considered. The systems model treats marketing and corporate decisions as more strategic than tactical. Contact management is strictly a tactical decision but nevertheless important.

Communications Strategy

The marketer at this point determines what main points the consumer should take away from the communications and what action the consumer should take as a result of the communications. That is, the marketer tries to identify the most effective message possible. What can be said? The goal is to create a change in the customer or prospect's category and brand network, the kind of change that is likely to induce the desired behavior given the right situation.

For example, Dell Computers tries to identify the most effective message to those who have bought an older version of a Dell computer. The goal is to get them to upgrade and buy new hardware from Dell. The Dell marketer has to find a compelling reason that can be effectively communicated to these people to get them to upgrade. Should the message focus on the proliferation of the use of multimedia software and on the premise that older-hardware Dell users are missing out on this wonderful new technology? Or should it be focused on the speed of computer processing or Internet and wireless communications systems? Which message is likely to be most effective? For the marketer to be able to identify effective messages, he or she needs to know something about the value systems of these customers or prospects. What are the salient attributes regarding the way in which they use computers? This information should be part of the consumer profile that the marketer gathers about target customers or prospects.

According to Schultz, Tannenbaum, and Lauterborn, the marketer at this point determines what main points the consumer should take away from the communications and what action the consumer should take as a result of the communications. That is, the marketer tries to identify the most effective message possible. The problem is not that what Schultz and his colleagues say is wrong or unimportant but that the term *communications strategy* is not used clearly and perhaps improperly. What is described is in essence what marketing scholars refer to as *positioning*, which is the way to communicate important things about the product and cause target consumers to adopt the product. The systems model describes at least three marketing strategies and how the "selling points" that reflect the essence of these strategies are communicated through positioning. Well-established concepts of positioning, such as positioning by product attribute, positioning by intangible factor, positioning by product class, positioning by competitors, and so on, are all applicable within the systems model. This positioning decision is highly strategic and governs what, in the context of the systems model, are "marketing communications strategy, objectives, and tactics."

Marketing Objectives

According to Schultz, Tannenbaum, and Lauterborn, the message has to induce some overt behavior and this behavior is captured and measured in relation to marketing objectives. Some examples of marketing objectives follow.

- Maintain or increase usage for brand loyal customers.
- Generate product trial, build volume, or build loyalty for competitive users.
- Gain or extend usage for swing users.

Note that marketing objectives are stated in relation to selected target markets (loyal customers, competitive users, and swing users). Note also that these marketing objectives are directly deduced from the communications strategy, that is, the message. For example, suppose the Dell marketer who is targeting the loyal customers (previous users of Dell) settles on the following message: "You should update your Dell because the new Dell has much more power for just a few dollars more." This message should be tied to a marketing objective such as increasing usage by previous Dell customers through an increase of 20 percent in sales of the new Dell series in the next 6 months.

SMC QuickLink
Dell USA
http://www.dell.com

Of course, marketers and the systems model presented here call it *marketing strategy,* and Schultz, Tannenbaum, and Lauterborn call it *communications strategy.* They are correct in talking about the message as a strategic decision, which we place at the marketing level, and about how the message (i.e., positioning strategy) dictates marketing objectives. As you read more in this book, you will note that their *marketing* objectives are partly accounted for in our *communications* objectives. Our conception of communications objectives involves the well-accepted hierarchy of effects that starts with brand awareness, goes to brand learning, moves into brand attitude/liking, then into brand trial/purchase, and finishes off with repeat purchase. Our conception of marketing objectives is directly tied to the marketing strategies of differentiation, cost leadership, and focus, which in turn are further operationalized in terms of positioning. Depending on which positioning strategy is invoked, the corresponding marketing objective is also invoked. For example, if a differentiation strategy is selected, the marketer may choose to operationalize this strategy in terms of positioning by product attribute. In this context, the corresponding marketing objective may be stated in terms increasing or maximizing brand association with an important product attribute. On the other hand, if a focus strategy is operationalized in terms of positioning by customer application, then the corresponding marketing objective can be stated as maximizing brand association with a certain customer application.

Marketing Tools

At this point, the marketer uses the elements of the marketing mix (product, price, place, and promotion) as marketing communications tools to implement the communications strategy and achieve the stated marketing objective. The message is not solely communicated through marketing communications elements such as advertising, sales promotion, public relations, and so on. The product itself with the package, its price, and the way it is distributed can communicate different messages. The challenge lies in ensuring message consistency across all marketing mix elements.

For example, suppose the marketer of an upscale market apparel manufacturer such as Polo Clothing decides that the message is, "Polo clothes are for classy people." However, the price of Polo clothes is "cheap." Polo clothes are distributed through discount clothing stores. This example shows inconsistency between the message itself and the price and method of distribution. Consumers are getting conflicting messages. The advertising campaign is informing them that Polo clothes are for classy people, yet they are sold cheaply and through discount stores. Consumers would expect Polo clothes to be sold at premium prices and sold through clothing boutiques and upscale apparel stores. Thus, the message must be consistently reflected in all elements of the marketing mix, not just the communications mix.

Schultz and his colleagues' idea of marketing tools is "on target." That is, according to Schultz, Tannenbaum, and Lauterborn, the marketer then uses the elements of the marketing mix (product, price, place, and promotion) as marketing communications tools to implement the communications strategy and achieve the stated marketing objective. If what is meant by "communications strategy" à la Schultz and his colleagues is what marketing scholars talk about as positioning, then our systems model appears to be highly compatible with the Schultz, Tannenbaum, and Lauterborn model. This is because the systems model asserts that the marketing strategy is translated in terms of marketing objectives, which in turn are achieved through marketing tactics (i.e., the elements of the marketing mix—product, price, place, and promotion).

Marketing Communications Tactics

At this point, the marketer chooses tactics such as advertising, direct marketing, sales promotion, public relations, and event marketing to implement the communications strategy and achieve the marketing objective. In the Polo clothes example, the Polo marketer attempts to choose an effective mix of communications elements to

Exhibit 1-3

Striving for Effectiveness and Efficiency in Choosing Advertising Placement

The marketer has to choose what form of advertising would be most effective in implementing the communications strategy. *(a)* If magazine advertising is selected, the marketer must select a magazine that offers the best environment for message effectiveness but also one that delivers cost efficiencies. *(b)* To help with cost efficiencies, brands will sometimes cooperate and feature more than one product in the advertisement if the creative brand connection makes sense to consumers. For social advocacy messages that rely on contributions for funding of paid advertisements or free space if the magazine offers, these things can be much more difficult to accomplish.

Sources: (a) Used with permission of CDC-Division of Cancer Prevention and Control. *(b)* Reprinted by permission of MasterCard and Brooks Brothers via McCann Erickson NY.

communicate the message of *class*. Which communications elements are *most* effective in implementing the communications strategy of "classy clothes"? Would advertising be effective? What form of advertising? Television advertising? Radio advertising? Magazine advertising? If magazine advertising is selected, which magazines should be selected as the most effective and cost-efficient vehicles? *The New Yorker Magazine*? *Forbes Magazine*? Exhibit 1-3 gives an example of how some marketers may try to optimize cost efficiency for the magazine they have selected.

As we have already noted, according to Schultz, Tannenbaum, and Lauterborn, the marketer chooses tactics such as advertising, direct marketing, sales promotion, public relations, and event marketing to implement the communications strategy and achieve the marketing objective. This is fine, of course, except for the fact that the approach misses an entire layer of decision making. Before the marketing managers get to make decisions about marketing communications tools, they need to have marketing communications strategies in place. The systems model, upon which this book is based, uses the traditional Foote, Cone, & Belding (FCB) model to identify four communications strategies: informative (thinker), affective (feeler), habit formation (doer), and self-satisfaction (reactor). Choosing a strategy is an important decision because the strategy allows the marketing communications manager to figure the communications performance dimensions (marketing communications objectives). According to the FCB model, an informative (thinker) strategy leads to developing a marketing communications campaign that focuses on brand awareness and learning. The affective (feeler) strategy prompts the marketing communications manager to single out brand attitude or liking as the goal for the marketing communications campaign. The habit-formation (doer) strategy motivates the manager to set the campaign objectives in terms of brand trial/purchase and brand learning. Finally, the self-satisfaction (reactor) strategy nudges the manager to set the campaign goals in terms of brand trial/purchase and brand attitude/liking. According to the systems model, all marketing communications objectives have to be spelled out in terms of the various dimensions of the hierarchy-of-effects model. The FCB planning model allows the marketing manager to select a communications strategy and then to figure out the appropriate performance dimensions of the communications campaign.

1-6h Why Evolve to the Strategic Marketing Communications Approach?

Besides the problems with the conceptualization of the various stages or components of the Schultz, Tannenbaum, and Lauterborn model, the model is also lacking in three areas: (1) not dealing with budgeting issues—an important decision in marketing communications; (2) not dealing with issues of monitoring and control; and (3) working with a model that involves a narrow and highly select use of concepts not yet fully grounded in the marketing communications, marketing, and business strategy literature.

Budgeting Issues

Developing a marketing *budget* that allows marketing communications managers to accomplish the stated campaign objectives is crucial. Schultz and his colleagues do not deal with budgeting at all. They briefly talk about compensation, which is entirely different from budgeting for marketing communications. Even in relation to compensation (e.g., how to compensate the advertising agency based on performance), we do not know much about how this decision fits in the overall scheme of the model. Budgeting is not a decision in the model at all, and the entire topic of budgeting is conspicuously absent. This is a major shortcoming of the Schultz, Tannenbaum, and Lauterborn model.

Monitoring and Control Issues

Also conspicuously absent from Schultz and his colleagues' model are the issues of monitoring and control. Monitoring and control are crucial in every aspect of business. Most marketing and marketing communications books do at least some justice to this very important concept.[20] Any marketing communications campaign cannot be effectively managed without assessing performance and taking corrective action. How can we have *integrated* marketing communications without monitoring and control functions? The Schultz, Tannenbaum, and Lauterborn model does not address the topics at all, let alone show how they can be used to enhance marketing communications integration.

Narrowness of Concepts and Lack of Theoretical Grounding Issues

Most important is the fact that Schultz and his colleagues' IMC model does not clearly show students and practitioners of IMC how to put all the *pieces* together. The problem is that this model does not recognize all of the pieces equally. Many decisions, concepts, and models that are well accepted in marketing communications, marketing, and overall business strategy are not acknowledged in the Schultz, Tannenbaum, and Lauterborn model. Students and practitioners of IMC have to put aside most of the concepts and models they have learned (and possibly felt very comfortable using throughout the years) to adopt this model. The systems model described throughout this book, on the other hand, builds on well-accepted concepts and models in marketing communications, marketing, and business strategy. The systems model uses concepts such as the FCB planning model, which is highly popular in advertising and marketing communications, Porter's model of marketing strategies (differentiation, cost leadership, and focus), and much of the rich literature on positioning and positioning methods, as well as the Boston Consulting Group matrix and the multifactor portfolio model that are very popular in business strategy. The point is that the systems model focuses on the process rather than the content. If IMC students or practitioners are highly satisfied with a particular strategic model at the corporate, marketing, or marketing communications level, they can change the content but follow the same process. The marketing communications manager has to select a marketing communications strategy that is designed to achieve marketing objectives. The marketing objectives have to reflect the selected marketing strategy. The marketing strategy has to be selected in such a way to achieve corporate objectives. Corporate objectives have to reflect the goal of corporate strategy. *The process is the same. The content may differ.* The process dictates that the marketing communications budget be determined by taking into account the marketing communications tactics (or tasks). The process dictates that each objective has to be quantified and measured using reliable and valid measures—measures with established norms. The process dictates that objectives should be set to capture the essence of a superordinate strategy. The process dictates that objectives set at one hierarchical level should guide the selection of programs or tactics at the subordinate level—and so on. This systems model emphasizes the process and has the versatility of changing content whenever the state of the science reveals better strategy models (the kind of models that help us select effective marketing communications, marketing, and corporate strategies).

Strategic marketing communications is, in essence, the logical extension of IMC into the entire organization. It offers the manager a theoretically grounded and applied framework in which to work. Using the classic "forest from the trees" saying, this hybrid gives the manager the ability to see contours of the forest while looking at the trees themselves. Therefore, we arrive at the definition of **strategic marketing communications (SMC)**:

> [Strategic marketing communications is] a systematic approach that guides the marketing communications manager to fully integrate strategies and objectives at the corporate and marketing organizational levels with all elements of the marketing communications campaign at the planning, execution, and monitoring stages.

strategic marketing communications (SMC)
A systematic approach that guides the marketing communications manager to fully integrate strategies and objectives at the corporate and marketing organizational levels with all elements of the marketing communications campaign at the planning, execution, and monitoring stages.

Summary

This chapter introduces you to the concepts of IMC and SMC. Integrated marketing communications (IMC) is defined as added value in a program that integrates a number of marketing communications programs such as general advertising, direct response, sales promotion, and public relations. The goal is to provide clarity, consistency and maximum communication impact. The logical extension of IMC is that of strategic marketing communications (SMC), which is guided by a systems theory approach laid out in the next chapter.

An SMC perspective extends the notion of an IMC perspective through the application of systems theory. Strategic marketing communications still recognizes the two distinct characteristics of IMC—continuity and strategic focus—but examines these issues in the context of a much stronger and more measurable theoretical framework. In both approaches, campaign continuity involves making both the physical and psychological elements of a marketing communications campaign continuous. Physical continuity in a marketing communications campaign can be achieved using the same slogan, taglines, and trade characters across all advertisements and other forms of marketing communications. Psychological continuity can be achieved by using a consistent theme, image, or tone in different advertisements and other forms of marketing communications. With respect to strategic orientation, the focus is to make marketing communications decisions to achieve the firm's strategic goals—goals such as sales, market share, and profit.

Integrated marketing communications can occur in different forms at different levels of development. Seven levels of development have been identified: (1) awareness of the need for integration, (2) image integration, (3) functional integration, (4) coordinated integration, (5) consumer-based integration, (6) stakeholder-based integration, and (7) relationship-management integration.

At least seven trends have been identified that paved the way for IMC: (1) decrease in message credibility, (2) decrease of cost of database marketing, (3) increase of cost and decrease in effectiveness of mass-media communications, (4) increase in mergers and acquisitions of marketing communications agencies, (5) increase in media and audience fragmentation, (6) increase in parity or "me-too" products, and (7) shift of information technology.

Several approaches to planning IMC have been identified and discussed: the mandated "one-look" approach, the theme-lines or "matchbooks" approach, the supply-side planning approach, ad hoc approach, and the consumer-based approaches. These approaches are described and a critique is provided. We end the chapter with the definition of strategic marketing communications (SMC).

Discussion Questions

1. Develop your own definitions of integrated marketing communications (IMC) and strategic marketing communications (SMC). Then compare and contrast your definitions with those provided in the chapter.
2. Find two magazine advertisements of the same brand. Examine the two advertisements in terms of campaign continuity. Do the two advertisements have physical continuity—same slogans, taglines, and trade characters? How about psychological continuity? Do the two advertisements have a consistent theme, image, and tone? Describe in some detail.
3. Try to remember a recent television commercial. Think for a moment about its contents and purpose. Can you figure out the corporate goals of this commercial? In other words, what is the strategic focus of this commercial?
4. Pick one of the SMC QuickLink examples, visit the website, and do an evaluation of the advertised brand. What does it stand for? What does the brand mean to you? Did this brand's website maintain consistency with the perception you had of that brand before the visit?
5. How do marketers try to achieve image integration in their marketing communications efforts?
6. How do marketers try to achieve functional integration in their marketing communications efforts?
7. How do marketers try to achieve coordinated integration in their marketing communications efforts?
8. How do marketers try to achieve consumer-based integration in their marketing communications efforts?
9. How do marketers try to achieve stakeholder-based integration in their marketing communications efforts?
10. Pick an industry that you are somewhat familiar with—any industry such as banking, telecommunications, computer software, or computer hardware. Try to think about the industry dynamics in relation to marketing communications. Do you think marketers in that industry recognize the importance of IMC? Is IMC practiced in that industry? What are the conditions or trends that have made marketers in that industry adopt or not adopt IMC? Describe those conditions.
11. Discuss the various approaches to IMC planning. What are their advantages and disadvantages?

Practice Quiz

Note: You can find the correct answers to these questions by taking the quiz and then submitting your answers in the Online Edition. The program will automatically score your submission. If you miss a question, the program will provide the correct answer, a rationale for the answer, and the section number in the chapter where the topic is discussed.

1. _____ is the concept that recognizes the added value in a program that integrates a variety of strategic disciplines and combines them to provide clarity, consistency, and maximum communications impact.
   a. Strategic marketing communications
   b. Integrated marketing communications
   c. Relationship marketing
   d. Strategic partnering

2. The IMC campaign includes all of the following terms as a part of its characteristics except _____.
   a. campaign continuity
   b. physical continuity
   c. strategic orientation
   d. sociological continuity

3. Which of the following refers to the process in which the various marketing communications programs are formulated as a direct function of marketing goals, such as sales and market share?
   a. coordinated integration
   b. image integration
   c. functional integration
   d. awareness of the need for integration

4. In the _____ level, the personal selling function is directly integrated with other elements of marketing communications.
   a. coordinated integration
   b. consumer-based integration
   c. relationship-management integration
   d. functional integration

5. Identify a trend that paved the way for IMC.
   a. increase in message credibility
   b. increase of cost of database marketing
   c. increase of cost and decrease in effectiveness of mass media
   d. decrease in media and audience fragmentation

6. Which approach uses nonadvertising forms of marketing communications to trigger consumers to remember the advertising message?
   a. theme-lines approach
   b. the mandated one-look approach
   c. supply-side planning approach
   d. ad hoc approach

7. Who described IMC as a way of conceptualizing the whole process instead of focusing on parts such as advertising, public relations, sales promotion, direct marketing, and so forth?
   a. Kotler
   b. Derrith Lambka
   c. Schultz, Tannenbaum, and Lauterborn
   d. Moore and Thorson

8. Identify the process by which the marketer determines the time, place, or situation in which to communicate to the customer or prospect.
   a. positioning
   b. relationship marketing
   c. contact management
   d. segmentation

9. According to the FCB model, a (an) _____ leads to developing a marketing communications campaign that focuses on brand awareness and learning.
   a. affective (feeler) strategy
   b. habit-formation (doer) strategy
   c. self-satisfaction (reactor) strategy
   d. informative (thinker) strategy

10. _____ is a systematic approach that guides the marketing communications manager to fully integrate strategies and objectives at the corporate and marketing organizational levels with all elements of the marketing communications campaign at the planning, execution, and monitoring stages.
    a. Strategic marketing communications
    b. Supply-side planning
    c. The one-look approach
    d. Integrated marketing communications

Web Exercise

What's Hot, What's Not

Using the search engine of your choice, visit the AdAge.com, Adweek, and Brandweek websites. Look for themes that seem to be common on the three websites. How might you characterize what those themes are? What do you think the implications are for those in the marketing communications field? Pick one of those themes and do a wider web search for information over the past 12 months using the keyword of your theme. Is this a hot topic to the greater marketing field? What does the future hold for those in this field?

AdAge.com
http://www.adage.com

Adweek
http://www.adweek.com

Brandweek
http://www.brandweek.com

Suggested Readings

Duncan, Tom, and Clarke Caywood. 1996. The concept, process, and evolution of integrated marketing communication. In *Integrated communication: Synergy of persuasive voices,* ed. Esther Thorson and Jeri Moore, 13–34. Mahwah, NJ: Erlbaum.

Duncan, T., and S. E. Everett. 1993. Client perceptions of integrated marketing communications. *Journal of Advertising Research* 33 (3): 30–39.

Hamper, Robert J., and L. Sue Baugh. 1992. *Strategic market planning.* Lincolnwood, IL: NTC Business Books.

Jackson, Rob, and Paul Wang. 1994. *Strategic database marketing.* Lincolnwood, IL: NTC Business Books.

Keller, Kevin Lane. 2000. The brand report card. *Harvard Business Review* (January–February). Repr. no. RR00104.

Medill School of Journalism. 1992. *Integrated marketing communications symposium.* Lincolnwood, IL: NTC Business Books.

Moore, Jeri, and Esther Thorson. 1996. Strategic planning for integrated marketing communications programs: An approach to moving from chaotic toward systematic. In *Integrated communication: Synergy of persuasive voices,* ed. Esther Thorson and Jeri Moore, 135–52. Mahwah, NJ: Erlbaum.

Roman, Ernan. 1995. *Integrated direct marketing.* Lincolnwood, IL: NTC Business Books.

Schultz, Don E., Stanley I. Tannenbaum, and Robert F. Lauterborn. 1994. *Integrated marketing communications: Pulling it together & making it work.* Lincolnwood, IL: NTC Business Books.

Special Issue of Integrated Marketing Communications. 1996. *Journal of Business Research* 37 (3).

Stern, Barbara. 1996. Integrated communication: The company "Voice" and the advertising persona. In *Integrated communication: Synergy of persuasive voices,* ed. Esther Thorson and Jeri Moore, 87–102. Mahwah, NJ: Erlbaum.

Thorson, Esther, and Jeri Moore, eds. 1996. *Integrated communication: Synergy of persuasive voices.* Mahwah, NJ: Erlbaum.

Notes

1. John Deighton, "Features of Good Integration: Two Cases and Some Generalizations," in *Integrated Communication: Synergy of Persuasive Voices,* ed. Esther Thorson and Jeri Moore, 243–56 (Mahwah, NJ: Erlbaum, 1996).
2. Bob Stone, *Successful Direct Marketing Methods,* 5th ed. (Lincolnwood, IL: NTC Business Books, 1994), 7.
3. Northwestern University's brochure (1991).
4. C. L. Caywood, D. E. Schultz, and P. Wang, *A Survey of Consumer Goods Manufacturers* (New York: American Association of Advertising Agencies, 1991); T. Duncan and S. E. Everett, "Client Perceptions of Integrated Marketing Communications," *Journal of Advertising Research* 33, no. 3 (1993): 30–39.
5. Reported in Tom Duncan and Clarke Caywood, "The Concept, Process, and Evolution of Integrated Marketing Communication," in *Integrated Communication* (see note 1).
6. Donald Parente, Bruce Vanden Bergh, Arnold Barban, and James Marra, *Advertising Campaign Strategy: A Guide to Marketing Communications Plans* (Fort Worth, TX: The Dryden Press, 1996).
7. Barbara Stern, "Integrated Communication: The Company 'Voice' and the Advertising Persona," in *Integrated Communication* (see note 1).
8. Duncan and Caywood, "Concept, Process, and Evolution," 13–34.
9. Cited in Don E. Schultz, "Problems That Practitioners Have with IMC," *Marketing News,* November 4, 1996, 11.
10. See note 8.
11. Ibid.
12. Don E. Schultz, "The Inevitability of Integrated Communications," *Journal of Business Research* 37, no. 3 (1996): 139–46.
13. Ibid.
14. Jeri Moore and Esther Thorson, "Strategic Planning for Integrated Marketing Communications Programs: An Approach to Moving from Chaotic toward Systematic," in *Integrated Communication* (see note 1), 135–52.
15. Kevin Lane Keller, "Brand Equity and Integrated Communication," in *Integrated Communication* (see note 1), 103–32.
16. See note 14.
17. Don E. Schultz, Stanley I. Tannenbaum, and Robert F. Lauterborn, *Integrated Marketing Communications: Pulling It Together & Making It Work* (Lincolnwood, IL: NTC Business Books, 1994).
18. Ibid.
19. Michael E. Porter, *Competitive Strategy and Techniques for Analyzing Industries* (New York: The Free Press, Division of Simon and Schuster, 1980).
20. See, for example, Phillip Kotler and Kevin Lane Keller, *Marketing Management,* 12th ed. (New York: Pearson Prentice Hall, 2006); and George E. Belch and Michael A. Belch, *Advertising & Promotion: An Integrated Marketing Communications Perspective* (New York: McGraw-Hill/Irwin, 2004).

Macro and Societal Issues in Marketing Communications

Chapter Two

Chapter Outline

2-1 Introduction
2-2 Economic Issues
2-3 Legal and Regulatory Issues
    2-3a Federal Regulation of Marketing Communications
    2-3b State and Local Regulation of Marketing Communications
    2-3c Self-Regulation of Marketing Communications
2-4 Social and Ethical Issues
    2-4a Offensive Promotion
    2-4b Advertising to Children
    2-4c Cultural Beliefs and Values
Summary
Discussion Questions
Practice Quiz
Web Exercise: How to Advertise Distilled Spirits Responsibly
Suggested Readings
Notes

Key Terms

administrative complaint (p. 35)
advertising to children (p. 41)
Better Business Bureau (BBB) (p. 37)
Bureau of Alcohol, Tobacco, Firearms and Explosives (ATF) (p. 34)
cease and desist order (p. 35)
Children Online Privacy Protection Act (COPPA) (p. 36)
Children's Advertising Review Unit (CARU) (p. 37)
consent order (p. 35)
consumer information (p. 34)
consumer sovereignty (p. 32)
corrective advertising (p. 35)
Federal Communications Commission (FCC) (p. 34)
Federal Trade Commission (FTC) (p. 34)
Food and Drug Administration (FDA) (p. 34)
Lanham Act (p. 36)
market power (p. 34)
materialism (p. 45)
National Advertising Division (NAD) (p. 37)
National Advertising Review Board (NARB) (p. 37)
National Association of Attorneys General (NAAG) (p. 37)
offensive promotion (p. 40)
puffery (p. 34)
Robinson-Patman Act (p. 36)
social stereotypes (p. 31)
substantiation of marketing claims (p. 35)
Telephone Consumer Protection Act (TCPA) (p. 36)
trade regulation ruling (p. 35)
United States Postal Service (USPS) (p. 34)
Wheeler-Lea Amendment (p. 34)

Even the most rational approach to ethics is defenseless if there isn't the will to do what is right.

—**Aleksandr Solzhenitsyn** (1918–), Russian novelist and Nobel Laureate

2-1 Introduction

Do advertising and other forms of promotion affect society? Sure they do, many social critics would say. The promotion industry as a whole affects society in many ways. Consider the case of how advertising and other forms of promotion affect our image of different groups of people, that is, our **social stereotypes.** Marketers have traditionally employed a wide variety of female stereotypes to sell their wares. Most consumer magazines carry advertisements of female stereotypes that psychologists and sociologists agree are harmful. These stereotypes have been linked to the etiology of dieting behavior and eating disorders. These harmful female stereotypes come through in the media in many forms. The typical stereotype is that of the dumb blond who is half-witted, indecisive, childlike, frivolous, a ding-a-ling, a sexual object submissive to men, overly concerned with her looks, thin yet with much cleavage, and so on. This stereotype not only is demeaning to women but also is dangerous because it promotes an image of the "thin ideal" that suggests that super-slim women are more desirable and successful in many ways. This obsession with thinness contributes to deadly eating disorders in the form of anorexia and bulimia.

According to *Ladies Home Journal,* the ideal figure back in 1905 was 38-27-45. Today, the standard is much different. The standard reflects the Barbie doll image: 38-18-28. Female role models have evolved from being wholesome to being very thin. This stereotype affects women's self-esteem because they compare their own body image with that of the "ideal" and finding themselves to be far from the ideal. Thus, they feel dissatisfied with their body image, which in turn leads to eating disorders. This problem is particularly accentuated among college women. They are obsessed with thinness. The "slim ideal" is the accepted social norm among college women.

Marketing scholars Robert Gustafson, Mark Popovich, and Steven Thomsen conducted a fascinating study to demonstrate this point. The study involved female college students who rated forty current magazine advertisements featuring harmful female stereotypes. The subjects rated them on a 9-point scale varying from "least harmful" to "most harmful." The advertisements included a variety of stereotypes: sexual objects, women submissive to men, women obsessed with men, frivolous women, dumb blondes, and the ultra-thin model. The majority of the subjects reacted strongly and negatively to most of the images—except the ultra-thin model image. In fact, the "thin model" image was consistently rated as "least harmful" compared to the other images. The findings of this study show that college women are socialized to accept the ultra-thin look as the standard of female beauty.[1]

In this chapter, we explore a variety of issues dealing with the effects of advertising and other forms of promotion on society and how society attempts to deal with the harmful effects through regulation and consumer education. We first address economic issues by exploring the various arguments making the case for both the positive and negative effects of the promotion industry on economic well-being. Then we shift focus and explore regulatory issues, that is, how society deals with promotion problems using our legal system. Finally, we address some of the social and ethical issues such as the effects of promotion on the evolution of consumer culture; our sense of materialism and the extent to which materialism leads to good or bad quality of life; and, most important, the way promotion reinforces social norms as in the case of the harmful image of the ultra-thin model.

social stereotypes A form of media representation by which instantly recognized characteristics are used to label members of social or cultural groups. While often negative, stereotypes can contain an element of truth and are used by the media to establish an instant rapport with the audience.

SMC QuickLinks

Barbie Collector
http://www.barbiecollector.com

Barbie.com
http://barbie.everythinggirl.com

2-2 Economic Issues

Marketing communications plays an important role in free economies. It does so by providing consumers with information about available goods and services. Society benefits when consumers use information intelligently and make purchase decisions based on quality and price. Competitor brands that have high-quality goods and services for low prices are likely to be selected by consumers who know—that is, consumers who have information about quality and price. Companies that fail to provide brands high in quality and/or low in price are not likely to gain consumers' economic votes (i.e., money), which in turn may cause the demise of those firms. Thus, firms that serve consumers' best interest by marketing high-quality/low-price goods and services are likely to prosper, and firms that fail to serve consumers in that manner are likely to fold and fade into oblivion. The concept of how consumers' economic votes weed out bad businesses and reward good businesses is referred to as **consumer sovereignty.** Thus, economists and marketing scholars argue that marketing communications does indeed play an important role in society. Marketing communications provides consumers with information about a variety of aspects of brands, including quality and price. It is the effective use of this information by consumers in the marketplace that makes the market function to serve the best interests of consumers and society. Let us try to analyze this argument in greater detail.

Economists and marketing scholars have long argued that marketing communications is used to help businesses differentiate their brands from competitor brands by persuading consumers that their brands are better than competitor brands based on quality, price, or some other distinguishing features. Thus, marketing communications encourages businesses to innovate and develop better goods and services, because if they develop better goods and services they can be more competitive by informing consumers of the availability of their "better" brands. Thus, marketing communications plays an important role of encouraging competition and innovation, which in turn translate into consumer choice. That is, consumers end up with many brand choices because marketing communications allows firms to communicate the availability of their innovations to target consumers. Without marketing communications, firms may not have the incentive to innovate and market goods and services that serve to meet consumers' needs because they cannot effectively communicate the availability of their innovations.[2]

In contrast, other economists and social critics of marketing argue the opposite. That is, they argue that marketing communications discourages (rather than encourages) innovation, which in turn limits (rather than enhances) consumer choice. Marketing communications tends to diminish competition because only the large companies benefit significantly from marketing communications. Large companies with large marketing communications budgets tend to promote their goods and services heavily, and the result of their marketing communications campaigns is customer loyalty. Consumers stick with brands with which they are familiar, and they are familiar with those brands because of heavy promotion. Thus, large companies with large marketing communications budgets tend to be effective in selling their brands—not because their brands are better in quality and/or low in price but because they promote heavily. Smaller firms that do indeed have better-quality goods and services at lower prices cannot effectively compete with the large companies because they do not have the financial muscle to spend on marketing communications the way the large companies do. Social critics maintain that the reality of how marketing communications is used in the marketplace stifles competition and reduces consumer choice, not the other way around. The power of large firms with huge promotion budgets effectively erects barriers to entry, and those barriers prevent smaller companies with better goods and services from reaping the fruits of their hard work and innovation. The evidence for this argument is strong. Social critics point to the fact that heavily advertised brands dominate the market in certain product categories such as soft drinks, beer, and cereals.[3] Let us focus on the U.S. beer market. The number of national brewers has declined significantly. Industry giants such as Anheuser-Busch and Miller managed to increase their marketing communications budgets and reaped huge market shares. Procter & Gamble and PepsiCo spend

---

consumer sovereignty
The concept of how consumers' economic votes weed out bad businesses and reward good businesses.

over $2 billion a year each on marketing communications.[4] However, the evidence is not that clear-cut. There is also evidence to the contrary.[5]

Marketing scholars rebut the social critics by saying that it is somewhat naïve to believe that marketing communications is the only factor that leads to customer loyalty. Other factors such as price, product quality, distribution effectiveness, promotion efficiencies, and competitive strategies play an interactive role with marketing communications. Defenders of marketing communications point to the example of Hershey's chocolate. Hershey's did not advertise at all until 1970. For 66 years, the company established its reputation based on the quality of its product and its extensive channels of distribution. Therefore, the argument goes that industry leaders dominate not because they have large promotion budgets but because they have good products, good prices, and good distribution. Marketing communications does not help much with the other elements of the marketing mix being effective. In other words, there is an interactive effect among the four Ps (product, price, place, promotion) that significantly influences brand sales and market share.[6]

Another criticism of marketing communications is that the large budgets allocated for promotion contribute to the high prices of goods and services, and there is some evidence to suggest the positive relationship between prices and advertising expenditures.[7] For example, many consumers buy private-label brands to save money. Critics of marketing communications attribute the high price of the national brands to the high cost of promotion.[8] Proponents of marketing communications counter by pointing to the fact that promotion helps achieve economies of scale in production and distribution by providing information to and stimulating demand in the mass market. These economies of scale serve to reduce prices, not increase them. Marketing communications also helps reduce prices by allowing competitors to compete on price. Price competition usually leads to price reductions.[9]

Table 2-1 summarizes the arguments pointing to the positive and negative economic effects of marketing communications. The table captures the pro and con

TABLE 2-1 Does Marketing Communications Equate with Market Power or Consumer Information?

	Marketing Communications = Market Power	Marketing Communications = Consumer Information
Brand Preference	Marketing communications affects consumer preferences by changing consumer values of certain brand costs and/or benefits. For example, a consumer exposed to a Reebok advertisement may form a preference for Reebok shoes because: "Reebok advertises its shoes as stylish; style must be important because it is advertised as such; I like Reebok because it is stylish."	Marketing communications affects consumer preferences by informing consumers about availability of certain brands with certain costs and benefits. For example, a consumer exposed to a Reebok advertisement may form a preference for Reebok shoes because: "Reebok advertises its shoes as stylish; style is important to me; I like Reebok because it is stylish."
Brand Purchase and Repeat Purchase	Marketing communications makes consumers more loyal to brands that are heavily promoted; consumers become less price sensitive and perceive fewer substitutes for promoted brands.	Marketing communications makes consumers more aware of brand differences in terms of quality and price; they shop around and purchase brands with best value, that is, brands of high quality and low price.
Barriers to Entry	Small firms cannot afford to spend the kind of money to compete against large firms with large budgets having entrenched and loyal customers. Therefore, barrier to entry is high for small firms despite the fact they may have higher-quality (and/or lower-price) goods or services.	Marketing communications allows firms with a new product of higher quality and/or lower price to compete and gain market share by reaching it to target consumers.
Industry Structure and Competition	Marketing communications rewards the large firms with huge promotion budgets and punishes small firms with small budgets. Doing so leads to market concentration in the form of monopolies or monopolistic competition.	Marketing communications encourages consumers to shop around for best value. Doing so rewards firms that serve consumers with better-value goods and services and weeds out firms that are inefficient in terms of marketing goods and services with high value. Therefore, marketing communications increases the likelihood of a competitive industry structure.
Market Conduct	Large-promotion expenditures by large firms allow them to dominate the market and establish brand loyalty. Market dominance and entrenched customer loyalty take away the incentive to innovate and develop higher-quality goods and services for lower prices.	Marketing communications allows consumers to be more informed. Thus, marketing communications through consumer information is an incentive for firms to innovate and develop higher-quality goods and services for lower prices.

market power The ability of a market participant, as a result of its control of sufficient or essential facilities, to profitably set prices above or reduce supply below that which would occur in a fully competitive market.

consumer information Resources that help a consumer make decisions about a purchase.

Wheeler-Lea Amendment An amendment to the Federal Trade Commission Act that added the phrase "unfair or deceptive acts or practices in commerce are hereby declared unlawful" to the Section 5 prohibition of unfair methods of competition in order to provide protection for consumers as well as competition.

puffery An exaggerated claim made by a firm in relation to one of its products or services, without making an overt attempt to deceive or mislead.

Food and Drug Administration (FDA) Government agency whose mission is to promote and protect the public health by helping safe and effective products reach the market in a timely way and monitoring products for continued safety after they are in use.

Federal Communications Commission (FCC) An independent U.S. government agency, directly responsible to Congress. The FCC was established by the Communications Act of 1934 and is charged with regulating interstate and international communications by radio, television, wire, satellite, and cable. The FCC's jurisdiction covers the fifty states, the District of Columbia, and U.S. possessions.

arguments in terms of two schools of thought: (1) marketing communications = **market power,** and (2) marketing communications = **consumer information.**[10]

2-3 Legal and Regulatory Issues

In the United States, there are federal and state laws designed to protect consumers from unfair and deceptive marketing communications practices. Furthermore, there are self-regulation measures. We discuss all of these in some detail.

2-3a Federal Regulation of Marketing Communications

At the federal level, there is the **Wheeler-Lea Amendment** (1938) to Section 5 of the Federal Trade Commission (FTC) Act. The FTC Act's original intent was to create an agency to enforce antitrust laws and fair trade. The Wheeler-Lea Amendment expanded the FTC's authority into all forms of marketing communications.

The Wheeler-Lea Amendment prohibits deceptive or misleading promotion. An advertisement or any form of promotional material is deemed deceptive or misleading when a substantial number of "average people" form the impression about the product's benefits and costs that are not real and the promotional material induces "average people" to make a purchase. This law allows individuals or businesses to sue the offending firm in court.[11]

It is important to note the difference between deception and puffery. Puffery is allowed by law; deception is not. **Puffery** is defined as an exaggerated claim made by a firm in relation to one of its products or services, without making an overt attempt to deceive or mislead. Examples of words used in puffery include *best, greatest,* and *finest.* When a fast-food restaurant claims that it has the best burgers in town, the restaurant can get away with it because the claim is considered puffery. In contrast, if the same restaurant claims that its burgers are from Angus beef when in actuality they are not, this is deception.

The Wheeler-Lea Amendment is enforced by a variety of government agencies such as the **Food and Drug Administration (FDA;** http://www.fda.gov); the **Federal Communications Commission (FCC;** http://www.fcc.gov); the **United States Postal Service** (**USPS;** http://www.usps.com); the **Bureau of Alcohol, Tobacco, Firearms and Explosives** (**ATF;** http://www.atf.treas.gov); and the **Federal Trade Commission (FTC;** http://www.ftc.gov). The FDA regulates and oversees the packaging and labeling of "food and drug-related products." This agency is primarily concerned with food quality and drug safety; however, it also monitors advertising on food packages and advertisements for drugs. The FCC regulates television, radio, and the telecommunications industry. Although its primary responsibility is to grant (and revoke) operating licenses for radio and television stations, it has responsibility to monitor advertising directed toward children. Federal Communications Commission rules dictate that television stations are limited to 12 minutes per hour of children's advertisements during weekdays and 10 minutes per hour on weekends.[12] The USPS watches over all mail-type promotional materials. The agency investigates mail-fraud schemes and brings those perpetrators to justice. The ATF gets involved in cracking down on firms engaging in deceptive and misleading promotion when the product or service is related to alcohol, tobacco, or firearms and explosives. The FTC is the agency that has greatest jurisdiction over marketing communications. The FTC is authorized to stop unfair or deceptive marketing communications practices by levying fines and suing violators in federal court.

Specifically, the FTC enforces the law by conducting investigations, taking court actions, ordering corrective advertising, and issuing trade-regulation rulings. Complaints from consumer advocacy groups, businesses, Congress, or the media typically induce the FTC to investigate a specific violation. Once an investigation is conducted and the FTC determines that the law was indeed violated, the FTC may issue a **consent order.** This means that the agency orders the firm to stop the illegal promotion immediately. The firm can sign the consent order and stop further promotion without admitting guilt. Most FTC investigations end with the signing of a consent order.

If the firm refuses to sign the consent order, the FTC issues an **administrative complaint,** which entails a formal hearing held before an administrative law judge; the judge makes a ruling after he or she hears testimony from the firms and the FTC. If the judge determines that the firm indeed violated the law, the judge issues a **cease and desist order**—an order that requires the firm to halt the disputed practice immediately and refrain from similar practices in the future. The firm can appeal to the full FTC commission if they are not satisfied with the ruling. If the firm appeals, the *full commission* holds hearings and makes its own ruling. If the firm is still not satisfied with the full commission's ruling, then it can appeal to the Court of Appeals and then to the Supreme Court. When the company decides to pursue the case at higher levels, it risks paying high civil penalties if found guilty.

Here is an example of FTC court action. The offender was Screen Test USA. The FTC investigated this company and found that it is a bogus front used to sell expensive modeling services. The company created the impression that it screens prospective models for modeling and acting jobs and, in doing so, persuades customers to purchase an assortment of products and services (e.g., a photo shoot). In actuality, the company was not a real agent to other companies that look for models. The modeling agency was bogus, and the company made money on the products and services they sold to customers. Customers hoping for a modeling job were deceived.[13]

The FTC can order a firm to engage in **corrective advertising.** This can occur when the FTC realizes that the damage is done through deception and the only way to undo the damage is to not only stop the damage but also make an attempt to undo it. That is, corrective advertising is designed to force the offending firm to launch a marketing communications campaign to change the false beliefs—to restore consumers' beliefs about the product to match their beliefs prior to the offending campaign. For example, Ocean Spray Cranberries, Inc., was found guilty of deceptive advertising about its cranberry juice because it claimed that the juice had more "food energy" than orange or tomato juice but failed to note that "food energy" means "calories." The FTC ordered the company to spend 25 percent of the company's annual media budget to run corrective advertising. The corrective advertisement stated: "If you've wondered what some of our earlier advertising meant when we said Ocean Spray Cranberry Juice Cocktail has more food energy than orange or tomato juice, let us make it clear: we didn't mean vitamins and minerals. Food energy means calories, nothing more. Food energy is important at breakfast since many of us may not get enough calories, or food energy, to get off to a good start. Ocean Spray Cranberry Juice Cocktail helps because it contains more food energy than most other breakfast drinks. And Ocean Spray Cranberry Juice Cocktail gives you and your family Vitamin C plus a great wake-up taste. It's . . . the other breakfast drink." This advertisement was run in one of every four advertisements for one year.[14]

The FTC can also issue a **trade regulation ruling,** which is designed to implicate an entire industry in case of unfair or deceptive practices. For example, in both 1984 and 1994, the FTC issued a trade regulation ruling against the funeral home industry. The ruling requires funeral homes to disclose as much information as is possible about what consumers are buying—an itemized list of funeral goods and services and a detailed description of each good and service.[15]

The FTC can move against offending firms by enforcing rules of **substantiation of marketing claims.** Specifically, the rule states that if a company uses an endorser to make claims about product benefits, the company has to substantiate these claims based on legitimate tests performed by experts. Consider the following example. The FTC issues a consent order to Fitness Quest, Inc. The company used endorsers to

---

United States Postal Service (USPS) (see p. 34) Government agency that watches over all mail-type marketing materials and investigates mail fraud schemes and other fraudulent marketing practices.

Bureau of Alcohol, Tobacco, Firearms and Explosives (ATF) (see p. 34) Government agency that rules when the sale, distribution, and advertising of alcohol and tobacco are at issue.

Federal Trade Commission (FTC) (see p. 34) A government agency established in 1915 whose purpose is to enforce a variety of federal antitrust and consumer protection laws. The FTC seeks to ensure that the nation's markets function competitively, vigorously, efficiently, and free of undue restrictions. It also attempts to eliminate acts or practices that are unfair or deceptive.

consent order An FTC order to stop illegal advertising immediately.

administrative complaint In the event that a firm refuses to sign an FTC consent order, the FTC continues with an administrative complaint. This complaint entails a formal hearing held before an administrative law judge, and the judge makes a ruling after he or she hears testimony from the firms and the FTC.

cease and desist order A court order that requires a firm to immediately halt the disputed advertising practice and to refrain from similar practices in the future.

corrective advertising Advertising designed to attempt to return consumers' beliefs to those that they held before a damaging advertising campaign.

trade regulation ruling (see p. 35) An FTC ruling designed to implicate an entire industry of unfair or deceptive practices and force the industry to correct these practices.

substantiation of marketing claims (see p. 35) An FTC rule that if a company uses an endorser to make claims about product benefits, the company has to substantiate these claims based on legitimate tests performed by experts.

Lanham Act This act provides for the registration and protection of trademarks.

Robinson-Patman Act This is an amendment to the Clayton Act that prohibits price discrimination when the effect "may be substantially to lessen competition or create a monopoly"; prohibits payments of broker's commission when an independent broker is not employed; forbids sellers to provide allowances or services to buyers unless these are available to all buyers on "equally proportional terms"; and prohibits a buyer from inducing or receiving a prohibited discrimination in price.

Telephone Consumer Protection Act (TCPA) A federal law that imposes restrictions on the use of automatic telephone dialing systems (also called autodialers), artificial or prerecorded voice messages, and fax machines to send unsolicited advertisements.

Children's Online Privacy Protection Act (COPPA) A congressional act to prohibit unfair or deceptive acts or practices in connection with the collection, use, or disclosure of personally identifiable information on the Internet from and about children under 13 years old.

make claims about how their gliders and abdominal machines are effective in weight loss. The exact claims were that the glider would burn calories at the rate of 1,000 per hour, that it would burn three times more calories than walking, and that it would burn nearly twice the calories of cross-country skiing.[16]

In addition to the Wheeler-Lea Amendment and its enforcement by federal agencies, most notably the FTC, we also have another law that companies have been using to sue their competitors for deceptive advertising. This law is the **Lanham Act** of 1947. This piece of legislation was originally adopted to protect words, names, symbols, or other devices used to identify and distinguish a manufacturer's products. The law was amended to encompass deceptive advertising. Here is an example of a company suing its competitor using the Lanham Act. Energizer Holdings, Inc., filed a suit against Duracell in 2002 over an advertisement claiming the superiority of the DURACELL CopperTop brand over "heavy-duty" competitors. The advertisement failed to mention that all alkaline batteries outlast so-called heavy-duty batteries (inexpensive, old-fashioned zinc batteries).[17]

Sales promotion typically involves promotion material that reflects pricing. The FTC has broad powers to control discriminatory pricing (and, therefore, all forms of promotion involving pricing) through the **Robinson-Patman Act.** Empowered by this law, the FTC requires marketers using contests, games, and sweepstakes to make certain all of the details are given clearly and to adhere to prescribed sets of rules to ensure fairness. Marketers have to disclose the exact number of prizes to be awarded, the odds of winning, the duration and termination dates of the promotion, and the availability of lists of winners of various prizes.[18]

Congress also passed the **Telephone Consumer Protection Act (TCPA)** of 1991. This law prescribes that telemarketers have to follow a complex set of rules that the FCC developed. Telemarketers have to maintain an in-house list of residential telephone subscribers who do not want to be called. Consumers who receive unwanted calls can sue a telemarketer in state court for damages up to $500. Federal Communications Commission rules also ban telemarketing calls to homes before 8 A.M. and after 9 P.M. and automatic dialer calls. The ban also extends to recorded messages to emergency phones, health-care facilities, and numbers for which the call recipient may be charged.[19]

In 1993 the FTC issued its *900-Number Rule* for advertising directed at children. Many companies (companies involved in sleazy sex, contest scams, and other unscrupulous activities) advertise to encourage consumers to call telephone numbers with the 900 prefix, whereupon they are automatically billed for the call. The rule requires that 900-number advertisements directed at children (under 18 years old) must contain clear and conspicuous disclosure requiring the caller to have parental permission to make the call. The rule also requires advertisers to disclose the cost of the call and give the caller the opportunity to hang up without incurring any costs. In 1998 the rule added new provisions to combat telephone bill *cramming* (placing unauthorized charges on consumers' phone bills).[20]

The FTC has recently begun enforcing the **Children's Online Privacy Protection Act (COPPA)** of 1998. The law restricts companies from collecting information from children via the Internet. Furthermore, websites directed at children are required to post the privacy policy on their home page and other web pages where information is collected.[21]

2-3b State and Local Regulation of Marketing Communications

In addition to federal regulations of marketing communications, firms have to contend with state and local regulation. The vast majority of the states in the United States have their own unfair and deceptive marketing practices laws borrowed mostly from the FTC's rules and regulations. Typically, the state's attorney general enforces state laws regarding false or deceptive advertising.

The states' attorneys general have banned together to form the **National Association of Attorneys General (NAAG;** http://www.naag.org), which sometimes takes action against offending firms when the FTC fails to do so. For example, the NAAG developed enforcement guidelines on airfare advertising, car rental pricing advertising, and advertising related to nutrition and health claims in food advertisements, among others. The vast majority of the states have adopted these guidelines.[22]

2-3c Self-Regulation of Marketing Communications

Most allegations or complaints about unfair and deceptive marketing communications are handled and settled within the industry through self-regulation. The primary organization that oversees self-regulation in the United States is the **Better Business Bureau (BBB;** http://www.bbb.org). This is how it works. Any consumer (consumer advocacy group) or business (or trade association) files a complaint with the BBB against a firm engaging in unfair or deceptive promotion. Complaints are collected, summarized, and publicized by the BBB. The goal is to provide complaint information to consumers about a variety of businesses to encourage consumers to make intelligent purchasing decisions—by avoiding doing business with firms with a significant record of complaints.

Complaints about deceptive advertising (typically national-level advertising) are typically referred to the **National Advertising Division (NAD;** http://www.nadreview.org) for review. The NAD is a subsidiary of the BBB. The NAD investigates the charge and determines whether the advertiser's claims are real or false. If false, the NAD negotiates with the offending firm to modify or discontinue the advertising campaign. If the NAD does not resolve the complaint or the advertiser appeals the NAD's decision, the complaint goes to the **National Advertising Review Board (NARB;** http://www.narcpartners.org), a board composed of advertising professionals and prominent civic leaders. If the NARB determines that the firm's advertising claims are deceptive, it orders the offending firm to discontinue the advertising campaign. If the offending firm refuses to comply, then the NARB refers the case to the FTC for legal action against the firm. Consider the NARB example involving AT&T. MCI objected to AT&T's advertising claim that calling 1-800-CALL-ATT always costs less than MCI's 1-800-COLLECT. MCI filed a complaint with the NAD that was ultimately referred to the NARB. The NARB did not find the AT&T message claim to be deceptive because the pricing claim was substantiated by AT&T.[23]

The BBB has also been involved in regulating the advertising industry in relation to children. The BBB has the **Children's Advertising Review Unit (CARU;** http://www.caru.org), which has strict guidelines to help firms that advertise to children to do the right thing. The guidelines address standards related to the type of appeal, product presentation and claims, disclosure and disclaimers, the use of premiums, safety, and techniques such as special effects and animation. See these guidelines on the CARU's website at http://www.caru.org/guidelines/index.asp.

Other forms of self-regulation include specific rules and regulations about advertising and other forms of marketing communications developed by specific industry association and media groups. Consider the example of the liquor industry. The Distilled Spirits Council of the United States (DISCUS; http://www.discus.org) has maintained a ban on radio advertising since 1938 and television advertising since 1948. Seagram's, the second-largest distiller in the world, broke the industry's long-standing ban in 1996. The explanation from Seagram's was that DISCUS's voluntary ban has placed the distilled spirits industry at a competitive disadvantage with the beer and wine industry. Late in 1996, DISCUS overturned the self-imposed ban on broadcast advertisements. The broadcast industry (the four major broadcast television networks, as well as major cable networks such as ESPN and MTV) countered by refusing liquor advertisements. Nevertheless, affiliate stations (those not owned by the four major television networks), as well as local cable channels and

National Association of Attorneys General (NAAG)
A professional association whose membership is comprised of state-level attorneys general.

Better Business Bureau (BBB) The Better Business Bureau, founded in 1912, is an organization based in the United States and Canada devoted to honest business. On its website, it lists its core services as: "Business Reliability Reports," "Dispute Resolution," "Truth-in-Advertising," "Consumer and Business Education," and "Charity Review."

National Advertising Division (NAD)
A subsidiary of the Better Business Bureau (BBB) to which complaints about deceptive advertising (typically national-level advertising) are typically referred.

National Advertising Review Board (NARB)
A committee composed of advertising professionals and prominent civic leaders who decide whether a specific ad is deceptive or misleading.

Children's Advertising Review Unit (CARU)
An organization belonging to the Better Business Bureau (BBB) that focuses on regulating the advertising industry in relation to children. CARU has strict guidelines to help firms that advertise to children to do the right thing. The guidelines address standards related to the type of appeal, product presentation and claims, disclosure and disclaimers, the use of premiums, safety, and techniques such as special effects and animation.

SMC Marketplace Watch 2-1

Advertisements Rejected Because They Violate Community Norms about Sex

Plugg Jeans Co.'s shot of a woman holding a man's leg close to his privates has been rejected for a billboard in Times Square.

The mMedia advertising agency working for the suburban youth denim brand, a division of Andrew International, produced an advertisement designed to "stop traffic, literally" on a billboard at 41st Street and 7th Avenue near Times Square. The advertisement featured a picture of a sweaty, entwined couple. The hand of the woman in the picture is grasping the young man's upper thigh. The advertisement was intended to attract the suburban 15- to 22-year-olds aspiring for the city grit they do not get at home.

Boston Properties, the building's landlord and owner of the billboard at 41st Street and 7th Avenue near Times Square, prevented the placement of the advertisement because it was "too suggestive." The media company that represents Boston Properties indicated that in spite of the fact that some may think the advertisement is hip, others may see it as too suggestive and offensive. Executives at *Elle Girl* and *Teen People* reached the same conclusion; however, *Cosmo*

Too Suggestive?
This Plugg advertisement was rejected by teen magazines *Elle Girl* and *Teen People* as well as by a Times Square building owner as being too suggestive.
Source: Reprinted by permission of mMedia.

---

independent broadcast stations, began accepting liquor advertisements. Late in 2001, NBC made a decision to accept liquor advertisements. However, NBC would accept liquor advertisements only under certain conditions: liquor companies had to run 4 months of social responsibility advertisements on subjects like designated drivers before general product promotion spots could air. Furthermore, the advertisements would air in programs for which 85 percent of viewers are documented as age 21 or older. The other major networks followed NBC's footsteps and adopted similar guidelines. However, social critics, the media, and public advocacy groups lambasted the networks for accepting liquor advertisements (even with the social responsibility guidelines). In early 2002, NBC reversed its decision to accept liquor advertisements. NBC's retreat failed to slow down the avalanche of liquor advertising in the broadcast media. Industry experts have documented the fact that liquor advertisements are becoming very prevalent, reaching over two-thirds of U.S. households.[24] See SMC Marketplace Watch 2-1 for an example of how the media regulate advertising.

Some companies have specialized in collecting Internet usage data and information about consumers and sharing this information with marketers. This practice has generated quite a controversy because of possible violation of privacy laws. In

Girl accepted the advertisement in its original form with only minor touch-ups and *Jane* accepted it wholly without any touch-ups.

The decision to reject the advertisement was supported by the Times Square Business Improvement District and New York State and corporations such as Morgan Stanley and Conde Nast Publications. The sentiment is that there is quite a difference between creativity and pornography, and the advertisement by mMedia is more pornographic than creative.

mMedia is now working to appease Boston Properties and the magazines that rejected the advertisement. The creative staff at the agency have softened the muscle definition in the male model's chest, raised the waistline of the jeans on the male model a bit to cover the so-called GI Joe Muscle, and even changed the position of the couple. The new tagline for the brand is an irreverent plug for Plugg: "Get used to it."

Source: Adapted from Stephanie Thompson, "Sexy Jeans Ad Rejected by Magazines and Times Square." AdAge.com QwikFIND ID: AAQ63X, June 8, 2005.

Toned Down Enough?

This Plugg advertisement was redone in response to the criticisms. What do you think? Is it toned down enough?

Source: Reprinted by permission of mMedia.

response to this controversy, leading companies in this area have joined together under the banner of the Network Advertising Initiative (NAI) to develop a self-regulatory code. With the help and encouragement of the FTC, the NAI has launched a website to help explain how Internet advertising practices affect consumers and the Internet itself (http://www.networkadvertising.org). The website also allows consumers to "opt out" of targeted advertising delivered by NAI member companies.[25]

2-4 Social and Ethical Issues

We addressed the issue of false and deceptive promotion in Section 2-3a. Of course, false and deceptive promotion is socially and ethically unacceptable as well as illegal. There are many promotion practices that are socially and ethically unacceptable, but they are legal. Therefore, we need to address the social and ethical issues of marketing communications independently from the legal issues. Examples of promotion practices considered socially and ethically unacceptable include offensive promotions, advertising to children, materialism, and stereotyping.[26] Exhibit 2-1 is an example of a credo to which an advertising agency pledging and asserting its commitment to high ethical standards might adhere.

Exhibit 2-1
An Advertising Agency's Credo

> Our purpose is to create and implement outstanding ideas to help clients' businesses grow, benefit the user, and contribute to the well-being of society.
>
> To provide this vital service, our experience has led us to believe in the importance of certain values—the characteristics of deeply committed people working in a supportive community.
>
> **Statement of Organizational Values:**
>
> Growth
> Fairness
> Responsibility
> Respect
>
> **Statement of Personal Values:**
>
> Attitude
> Integrity
> Hard work
> Talent

2-4a Offensive Promotion

Many advertisements and other promotional materials are offensive; tasteless; irritating; boring; obnoxious; or, simply stated, "done in bad taste." Much evidence points to the fact that about half of consumers report that they have felt offended by advertising and other sources of promotion at least sometimes.[27] Consumers are offended by this **offensive promotion** in a variety of ways. For example, there are many goods and services that are promoted openly and conspicuously that should not be: contraceptives, personal hygiene products, drugs related to sexual dysfunction, beer and liquor, tobacco, pornographic films and videos, guns and assault rifles, and violent video games, among others. One can categorize these goods and services as *sin products* and *personal products;* contraceptives and personal hygiene products are examples of "personal products," whereas beer/liquor, tobacco, and pornographic film and videos are examples of "sin products." In the arena of social marketing, there are many social causes that should not be promoted openly and conspicuously, as in the use of condoms to avoid sexually transmitted disease (e.g., HIV/AIDS).[28]

Besides being offended by personal and sin products, consumers are also offended by certain types of message appeal such as fear and sex appeal. Sex appeal, in particular, has been strongly hit by social critics. Sex appeal involves the use of sexually suggestive advertising and nudity. Social critics maintain that many advertisements involving sex appeal tend to demean women by depicting them as sex objects. Advertisements that use women's sex appeal to capture attention to goods and services that have very little to do with sexuality tend to dehumanize women. Social psychologists and sociologists have long linked violence against women with actions that dehumanize women. Sex appeal advertisements using women as sex objects tend to reinforce the image of women's sexual submission to men.[29] How many times have you seen advertisements by local car dealers using sexy models or spokeswomen to attract attention? How about advertisements that equate sexy cars with sexy women? SMC Marketplace Watch 2-2 is a case in point. Advertisers try to exploit sex to draw attention—but at what expense?

What is worse is the use of women's sex appeal to promote sin products such as tobacco, beer, liquor, and guns. Firms selling sin products have used sex appeal because they know that sex sells, particularly among teenagers and the young.[30] The use of sex appeal to attract attention is known in advertising circles as "shock advertising." The rationale of the creative people who develop those advertisements is that advertising clutter is a significant problem and that one must find ways to break

offensive promotion
A message issued in behalf of some product or cause or idea or person or institution and is defined as "offensive" because it elicits unsavory or morally offensive feelings in the consumer.

SMC Marketplace Watch 2-2

Carl's Jr. Makes No Apologies for Sexy Paris Hilton Advertisement

Hamburger chain Carl's Jr. developed a television commercial that has stirred controversy. The commercial introduces Carl's Jr.'s new Spicy Burger featuring Hilton hotel heiress and reality television star Paris Hilton. Paris Hilton is shown in a skintight swimsuit soaping up a Bentley and crawling all over it before taking a big bite out of the burger. The advertising campaign was launched on May 19, 2005 and has run during sports programs, on ABC's *Desperate Housewives* finale Sunday, and on the season-ending episodes of Fox's *The OC* and NBC's *The Apprentice*.

The company also features the advertisement on its website (http://www.carlsjr.com) and also built a separate website called SpicyParis.com (http://www.SpicyParis.com) to play a 60-second version of the commercial. A company spokesperson said that SpicyParis.com was so overwhelmed with traffic at one point that the website crashed.

Television watchdogs, including the Los Angeles-based advocacy group Parents Television Council (PTC), criticized the advertisement. A PTC spokesperson said, "This commercial is basically soft-core porn. . . . The way she moves, the way she puts her finger in her mouth—it's very suggestive and very titillating." The spokesperson also said that because the advertisement is airing during sports programs and FOX's *OC,* which are heavily watched by teens, it promotes sexuality to an audience that may not be ready for it.

The PTC plans to mobilize its more than one million members to contact the restaurant chain and complain about the advertisement; however, the PTC does not plan to petition the FCC to make Carl's Jr. remove the advertisement. The PTC argues that unlike a television program, parents have no way of knowing when the advertisement is going to appear on television and, therefore, parents cannot prevent their children from seeing the advertisement.

Instead of appeasing the PTC, Carl's Jr.'s Andy Puzder, CEO of Carl's Jr., rebutted the advocacy group by saying the group needs to ". . . get a life . . . This isn't Janet Jackson—there is no nipple in this. There is no nudity, there is no sex act—it's a beautiful model in a swimsuit washing a car." Puzder says he has shown the advertisement to his three children, ages 12, 9, and 7, and they have shown no signs of being corrupted.

Source: Adapted from Caleb Silver, "No Apologies for Sexy Paris Hilton Ad: Burger Chain Carl's Jr. Tells Watchdog Group Infuriated over Scantily Clad Soap-Up to 'Get a Life.'" CNN Business News, May 25, 2005, 10:24 A.M. EDT, http://www.money.cnn.com/2005/05/24/news/newsmakers/carls_ad.

---

through the clutter. Shocking the audience with outrageous sex scenes is one way to penetrate the clutter.[31]

2-4b Advertising to Children

Social critics have long criticized marketers for targeting **advertising to children**.[32] The gist of their argument is that children are highly impressionable. Our free economy works best when consumers are well informed about goods and services, they shop around for brands with best value (high quality and low price), and they purchase those brands based on value. Doing so requires that consumers acquire information about brand options, study those options for quality and price, and make purchase decisions "intelligently." Children, by definition, do not have the cognitive capacity to make intelligent decisions. They do not shop around. Quality and price are not necessarily guiding criteria in the purchase decision making. They are highly impressionable. They make purchase decisions based on experiential factors such as style, color, feel, taste, smell, sound, and so forth. Their purchase decisions are heavily influenced by peer pressure—they buy things to gain social approval and to avoid disapproval from their significant others such as friends. In other words, they pay less attention to functional or utilitarian criteria such as quality and price.[33] If so, children, by definition, cannot make intelligent purchase decisions required in a free economy. Consider the concept of *consumer sovereignty* we discussed in Section 2-2. Consumer sovereignty is required to ensure that a free economy provides the maximal

advertising to children
A paid, mass-mediated attempt to persuade a certain audience, in this case, children.

Advertising and Children
Children are highly impressionable, and they make purchase decisions based on experiential factors such as style, color, feel, taste, smell, sound, and so on. Their purchase decisions are heavily influenced by peer pressure—they buy things to gain social approval and to avoid disapproval from their significant others such as friends.

Source: Photo by Eric Dungan.

benefits to society. In conclusion, if we cannot trust children to make intelligent decisions in the marketplace, then we have to have a mechanism to ensure that most purchase decisions are relegated to the adults in their lives such as their parents or guardians. A recent survey of young adults' attitudes toward advertising revealed that two-thirds of the respondents believed that the main goal of advertising is to make them buy things; only 11 percent felt that the goal is to provide information.[34]

So we have a system in place to prevent firms from targeting children with promotion, right? The reality is not the case. The current system does exploit children by targeting promotion to them. Firms targeting children do not provide functional or utilitarian information about their offerings. Unfortunately, most of the promotion targeting children is based on purchase criteria that are experiential and social in nature, not functional. The reality is that television is frequently and commonly used to reach children between the ages of 2 and 11. These children watch an average of 21.5 hours of television a week. They are exposed to around 25,000 commercials a year.[35] Studies show that television is an important source of information for children about goods and services. Children are highly impressed by what they see and hear on television, and they do make purchase decisions based on what they see and hear on television.[36]

In 1979 the FTC held hearings about advertising to children and recommended banning all television advertising for any product directed to children under age 8 because they are too young to understand the selling intent of advertising. Unfortunately, business and the advertising industry argued strongly against this recommendation. Their argument is that banning television advertising to children is a violation of their right of free speech protected by the First Amendment. They also argued that parents should be the primary agent to regulate children's television viewership, not the government. In the end, the FTC's initiative was defeated. Instead, Congress passed the Children's Television Act of 1990. This law requires that television stations limit the amount of commercial time in children's programming to 10.5 minutes per hour on weekends and 12 minutes on weekdays.[37] Furthermore, the major networks have strict guidelines for advertisements targeting children. For example, only 10 seconds can be devoted to animation and special effects in network television advertisements; the last 5 seconds of the commercial should display the entire product and accessories and disclose whether they are sold separately.[38]

See SMC Marketplace Watch 2-3 for an example of a company that acted responsibly in relation to advertising to children.

SMC Marketplace Watch 2-3

Product Is Targeted to Children While in Fact It May Be Dangerous to Children

Procter & Gamble will stop advertising its Secret Sparkle Body Spray to children under age 12 following a ruling by the Children's Advertising Review Unit that P&G's marketing program violates safety provisions of the group's self-regulatory guidelines.

Procter & Gamble has recently launched the first mass-market body spray (Secret Sparkle) directed at girls. Part of the promotion campaign included sampling and cobranded sweepstakes giving away iPod Shuffles at Limited Too, a fashion chain for girls ages 7 to 14. Television advertising has focused mainly on teen programming and both teen and "tween" publications. Publicis Groupe's Leo Burnett USA, Chicago, handles advertising for Secret Sparkle; and sibling Starcom Mediavest Group, New York, handles media planning and buying.

The culprit is the fact that the body spray carries a "Keep Out of Reach of Children" warning. Isn't it paradoxical? The product is unsafe for children; it has a warning label to keep out of reach of children; and, at the same time, the company is targeting children in most of its promotions. The BBB's Children's Advertising Review Unit (CARU) guidelines explicitly state that products inappropriate for use by children should not be advertised directly to children.

Procter & Gamble's position is that there is no evidence of misuse of the product by children. Furthermore, the sweepstakes required parental permission to enter. The company believes that its promotion campaign was conducted within CARU guidelines. The company has targeted girls because younger and younger girls are now using deodorant. The company's rationale is if P&G does not target the consumer as she starts using the product, the company is likely to lose a competitive advantage.

Source: Adapted from Jack Neff, "P&G Pulls Children's Body Spray Advertising." AdAge.com QwikFIND ID: AAQ64O, June 10, 2005.

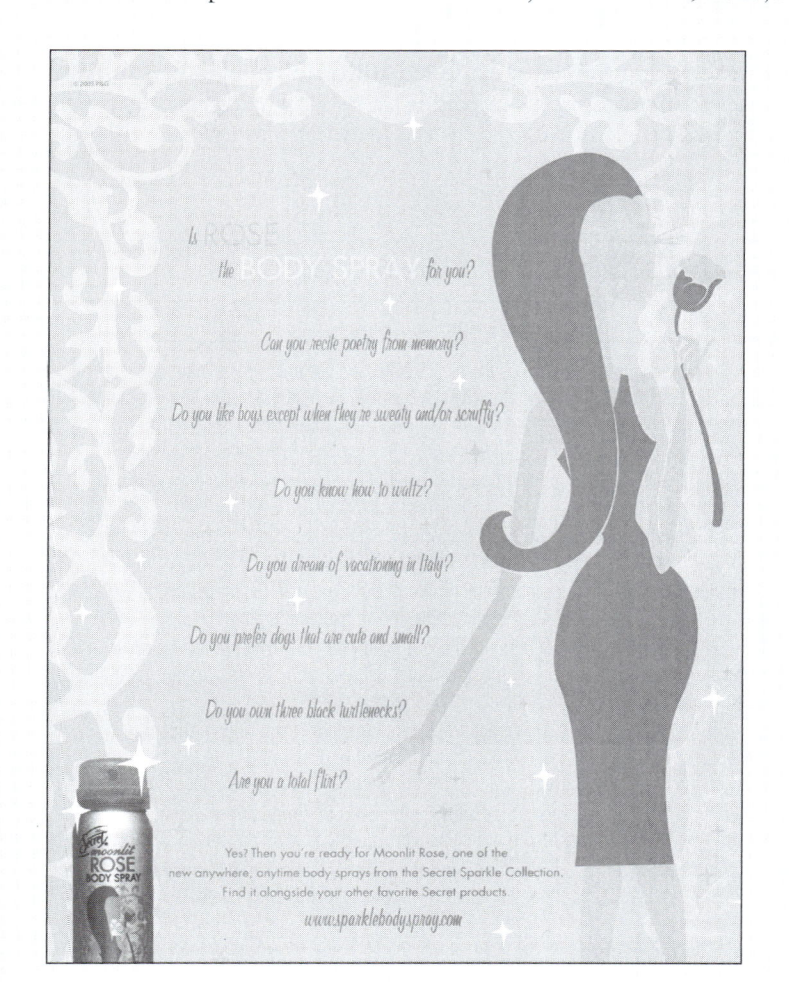

Self-Regulation Requires Companies to Be Committed to the Spirit of the Law and Not Just the Letter of It

Although Procter & Gamble had monitored and complied with what it thought were the legal requirements of product advertising for children, The Children's Advertising Review Unit thought that P&G had crossed over the safety provisions of the group's self-regulatory guidelines. In the spirit of industry self-regulation, P&G withdrew the initial advertising and promotions. This is the advertisement ultimately used for Sparkle Body Spray, aimed at young girls.

Source: Reprinted by permission of The Procter & Gamble Company.

2-4c Cultural Beliefs and Values

Advertising and other forms of promotion do play a significant role in shaping cultural beliefs and values.[39] Social scientists have noted that the institutions of family, religion, and education have weakened over the past three generations. The media and advertising seem to have replaced the traditional institutions of family, religion, and education in shaping our beliefs about the world and our sense of what is important in life. Advertising and other forms of promotion establish fashion and style. For example, when IKEA launches an aggressive campaign showing advertisements with a gay couple, the message is that being gay is acceptable, perhaps even "cool." When Gap shows advertisements with white, black, and Hispanic young adults dancing together, the message that filters through is that interracial and interethnic dating and marriage are no longer socially taboo.[40]

The Effects of Marketing Communications on the Consumer Culture

Marketing in general and marketing communications in particular are influential in speeding the development of a consumer society. Marketers not only supply products but also encourage the demand for them by making them culturally desirable. Marketers achieve this largely through the use of cultural symbolism. Table 2-2 describes the types of symbols that marketers purposely associate with their products, thus investing them with the cultural desirability of those symbols. Through the use of symbols, marketers tell us that certain characteristics—power, youth, and beauty, for example—are culturally desirable. The associations that marketers make between their products and these cultural characteristics affect not only the consumption of those products but also our perception of the culture at large.[41]

An excellent example of how symbols work is the success of the long-running campaign for Nike shoes featuring the serious-minded athlete. The marketers of Nike shoes have managed successful promotion campaigns by associating the product with characteristics admired within the culture, such as competition, hard work, athletics, and winning.

TABLE 2-2 Categories of Cultural Meaning for Material Objects

Symbol	Cultural Meaning
Ancestral Totem	This category of symbols describes the significance of objects valued as statements of ethnicity or kinship. Examples of ethnicity symbols include a sari, a prayer shawl, a set of bagpipes, and a framed portrait of Martin Luther King Jr. Examples of kinship symbols include a bronzed baby shoe, a grandmother's china cup, and old family photographs.
Social Status Communication	Material objects can signal belonging or division. Examples include a white lab coat, an expensive briefcase, a tube of lipstick, flashy earrings, or a red Corvette.
Interpersonal Medium	Material objects can signify social observances. Examples include flowers and clothes to signal shared rejoicing or mourning dress to share sorrow.
Self-Expression	Material objects may reflect the development of the ideal self. Examples include medical books, a college diploma, a tennis trophy, or an exercise machine.
Utility	Material objects can be valued strictly for the useful function they serve. Examples include an iron used to press clothes, a stapler used to bind sheets of paper together, or a telephone used to communicate with others.
Pleasure Giving	Material objects can be used in ways to provide pleasure to the user. Hence, the symbols associated with these products are related to pleasure giving. Examples include drinking brandy after dinner, smoking a pipe, and using a whirlpool tub.
Experiential Memoir	Material objects such as mementos can also be used to remember the past. Examples include a photo album, travel souvenirs, or a child's first drawings.
Transcendence	Material objects can be used to transcend the limits of one's own existence. Examples include a Greenpeace bumper sticker, a collection of crystals, or a rosary.

Source: Adapted from Marye Tharp and Linda Scott, "The Role of Marketing Processes in Creating Cultural Meaning," *Journal of Macromarketing* 10 (Fall 1990): 47–60.

SMC Marketplace Watch 2-4

Advertising and the Development of Consumer Societies

Hand in hand with a country's economic growth comes the development of a consumer society. At first, that society reflects utilitarian values—people buy only the essentials. As the economy develops, hedonistic values come to the fore. People buy not out of need but for the pleasure of ownership.

The style of advertising used reflects a country's stage of development. Within a utilitarian society, for example, an advertisement for a refrigerator is likely to focus exclusively on price and performance. Within a hedonistic society, appearance, special features, and other aspects that communicate status are likely to be the center of the advertisement.

A comparison of advertising from Hong Kong, the People's Republic of China, and Taiwan showed some marked differences. In Hong Kong, advertising stressed hedonistic values with a focus on having. In the People's Republic of China, utilitarian appeals with a focus on being were prevalent. Taiwanese advertising fell between the two extremes.

Source: David K. Tse, Russell W. Belk, and Nan Zhou, "Becoming a Consumer Society: A Longitudinal and Cross-Cultural Content Analysis of Print Ads from Hong Kong, the People's Republic of China, and Taiwan," *Journal of Consumer Research* 15 (March 1989): 457–72.

It is important for marketers to understand the effects of advertising and other forms of promotion on the development of the consumer culture because, through both the creation of products and their affiliation with cultural symbols, they contribute to the subtle changes that over time transform the culture in which we live. Those changes are not always positive. Consider, for example, advertising for a product like premium whiskey. To build sales to professional businesspeople, the marketer decides to associate the product with such images as success and aggressive competitiveness.

From a micromarketing perspective, by exulting these characteristics, the marketer simply hopes to sell more whiskey. From a macromarketing perspective, however, the potential effects on consumers and on the culture in which we live are much more complex. The advertising promotes behavior that is potentially dysfunctional and presents whiskey as culturally desirable. It encourages the development of cultural values and behaviors that are not always—as in this example—in the best interest of society at large. There are of course social ills that are indirectly related to marketing. Understanding how their actions potentially contribute to social malaise may help marketers make decisions that result in the selling of their products in a socially responsible manner. SMC Marketplace Watch 2-4 describes how advertising contributes to the development of consumer societies.

The Effects of Marketing Communications on Materialism and the Quality of Life

Materialism is a cultural value that places emphasis on the role of material possessions in achieving the good life. There is much evidence that suggests consumers in higher income brackets own more material possessions than those in lower brackets. Material possessions (e.g., a house, a car, and furnishings) do play an important role in the quality of life. Ownership of economic goods enhances subjective well-being.[42] Quality-of-life researchers typically treat subjective well-being as an indicator of quality of life. For example, in a large-scale study, satisfaction with life was found to increase with income. Life satisfaction also was found to be positively related to the possession of products such as new home entertainment equipment and financial instruments.[43] Those who have new home entertainment centers (have more financial investments) seem to be happier with their lives than those who do not have the home entertainment centers (have no financial investments). Furthermore, shopping enjoyment was positively related to life satisfaction. That is, those who are more satisfied with their lives report higher levels of shopping enjoyment than do those less satisfied with their lives.[44]

materialism A cultural value that places emphasis on the role of material possessions in achieving "the good life."

Materialism and Quality of Life

For the highly materialistic, satisfaction with material possessions plays an important role in subjective well-being.

Source: © 2007 JupiterImages Corporation.

45

SMC Marketplace Watch 2-5

How Others View Us

As the first and probably the strongest consumer culture in the world, how is the American culture perceived? Muslims who are fundamentalists all over the world see Levi's jeans, Hollywood movies, and popular music as signs of a cultural invasion of their society by the United States and are up in arms to fight it. American brands invade their landscape as fast-food chains like McDonald's, Burger King, Taco Bell, and Pizza Hut set up in major cities and in smaller towns. From cigarettes to cereals to computers, American brands are infiltrating the Muslim landscape.

Mexico, too, sees often unwelcome influences creeping into its culture, where the best-selling piñata figure is not of the traditional burro but of the American cartoon character Bart Simpson. American football—and the consumption that surrounds it—has been exported to Russia, where the Russian Association of American Football has launched its own Super Bowl. In Japan, where American brands enjoy enormous popularity, consumers rejected a specially designed Japanese Barbie doll introduced by Mattel. The doe-eyed Japanese beauty was turned down in favor of the original American Barbie.

What positive and negative impressions of the American culture do these and other examples give to consumers in other nations?

Sources: Adapted from Morley Safer, *60 Minutes,* November 6, 1994; Tim Padgett, "The Gringos Are Coming," *Newsweek,* November 30, 1992, 55; William E. Schmidt, "West Sets Up Store and the Russians Are Seduced," *The New York Times,* September 27, 1991; David Kilburn and Julie Skur Hill, "Western Barbie," *Advertising Age,* October 7, 1991, 40; John F. Sherry Jr. and Eduardo G. Camargo, "'May Your Life Be Marvelous': English Language Labeling and the Semiotics of Japanese Promotion," *Journal of Consumer Research* 14 (September 1987): 174–88.

In another study, consumer researchers have found that satisfaction with material possessions tends to contribute to overall life satisfaction, but only for materialistic people. This is because materialistic people tend to value material possessions and place much importance in the significance of material possessions and wealth in life. As such, any satisfaction in the material life domain spills over to other life domains affecting one's overall feelings about life. Thus, for the highly materialistic, satisfaction with material possessions plays an important role in subjective well-being. By the same token, dissatisfaction with material possessions makes these people feel miserable about their lives. Satisfaction with material possessions in this study was measured as a composite of satisfaction with the following material items: house/condo, consumer electronics, furniture and appliances, auto vehicles, clothing/accessories and jewelry, and savings and investment.[45]

The Effects of Marketing Communications on Stereotyping

Social critics have long accused the marketing communications industry of perpetuating social stereotypes of women, ethnic minorities, and other groups.[46] With respect to women, critics have argued that marketers often depict women as preoccupied with beauty, household tasks, and parenting. Marketers also often show women as decorative objects and sexually provocative. Specifically, studies focusing on television and print advertising have demonstrated that girls and women are associated with traits such as passivity, deference, lack of intelligence and credibility, and punishment for high levels of effort. In contrast, boys and men are associated with being constructive, powerful, autonomous, and achieving.[47]

The National Organization for Women (NOW) and the Sexual Assault Prevention and Awareness Center have argued that depicting women as sex objects in advertising contributes to a climate that propagates violence against women. Furthermore, many social ills such as women's obsession with thinness have contributed significantly to an epidemic of eating disorders, smoking (to control weight), and other health problems among women. These social ills are all connected to the depiction of women as decorative items and beauty symbols.[48] SMC Marketplace Watch 2-5 shows how people around the world perceive Americans.

Summary

In this chapter, we explore a variety of issues dealing with the effects of advertising and other forms of promotion on society. We also describe how society attempts to deal with the harmful effects of the promotion industry through regulation and consumer education. We first address economic issues by exploring the various arguments making the case for both the positive and negative effect of the promotion industry on economic well-being. In sum, scholars have argued that advertising and other forms of promotion can be viewed as consumer information or market power. Viewing advertising and other forms of promotion in terms of consumer information is considered a good thing for society. In contrast, viewing advertising and other forms of promotion as a means for large firms with large budgets to monopolize the market is considered to be bad for society.

We then shift focus and explore regulatory issues: how society deals with promotion problems using our legal and justice system. Specifically, we describe how the marketing communications industry in the United States is regulated by laws such as the Federal Trade Commission Act and its Wheeler-Lea Amendment, the Robinson-Patman Act, the Telephone Consumer Protection Act, the Lanham Act, and the Children's Online Privacy Protection Act. We also describe how these laws are enforced by many federal agencies such as the FTC, the FCC, the FDA, the ATF, and the USPS and how these agencies have their own rules and regulations. We also describe how the various states have their own consumer protection laws and how these are enforced. The promotion industry has its own self-regulatory policies that are overseen and enforced through the BBB and its various divisions.

Finally, we address some of the social and ethical issues such as the effects of promotion on the evolution of consumer culture. We describe the effect of advertising and promotion on cultivating our sense of materialism and the extent to which materialism leads to good or bad quality of life. We also discuss how advertising and other promotion reinforce social norms as in the case of the harmful image of the ultra-thin model.

Discussion Questions

1. What is the effect of advertising and other forms of promotion on economic well-being? In other words, is promotion good for society because it provides consumers with information about the availability of goods and services in the marketplace and their quality and prices? Discuss the issues in some detail.
2. Consider the same question again: "What is the effect of advertising and other forms of promotion on economic well-being?" Now focus on the notion of "market power." Is promotion bad for society because it serves only the marketing giants with large communications budgets? Discuss the issues in some detail.
3. Discuss the Federal Trade Commission Act and its effect on society.
4. Discuss the Wheeler-Lea Act and its effect on society.
5. Discuss the Robinson-Patman Act and its effect on society.
6. Discuss the Telephone Consumer Protection Act and its effect on society.
7. Discuss the Lanham Act and its effect on society.
8. Discuss the Children's Online Privacy Protection Act and its effect on society.
9. How does the FTC regulate the promotion industry? Discuss.
10. How does the FCC regulate the promotion industry? Discuss.
11. How does the FDA regulate the promotion industry? Discuss.
12. How does the ATF regulate the promotion industry? Discuss.
13. How does the USPS regulate the promotion industry? Discuss.
14. How does the BBB regulate the promotion industry? Discuss.
15. Can you think of any advertisements you have seen lately that you think are offensive? Please describe and discuss.
16. Does promotion propagate materialism? If so, how? Discuss.
17. Does advertising propagate social stereotypes? Discuss.

Practice Quiz

Note: You can find the correct answers to these questions by taking the quiz and then submitting your answers in the Online Edition. The program will automatically score your submission. If you miss a question, the program will provide the correct answer, a rationale for the answer, and the section number in the chapter where the topic is discussed.

1. Which of the following refers to the concept of how consumers' economic votes weed out bad businesses and reward good businesses?
   a. consumer capital
   b. business evolution
   c. better business approach
   d. consumer sovereignty

2. Which of the following expanded the FTC's authority into all forms of marketing communications?
   a. Lanham Act
   b. Hart-Scott-Rodino Antitrust Improvements Act
   c. Wheeler-Lea Amendment
   d. Robinson-Patman Act

3. A fast-food restaurant claims that it has the best burgers in town. Can the restaurant legally get away with this claim? Why or why not?
   a. no, because the claim is considered deceptive
   b. yes, because the claim is considered puffery
   c. no, because it is potentially misleading
   d. no, because the claim has to have research backing

4. Identify the agency that has greatest jurisdiction over marketing communications.
   a. Food and Drug Administration
   b. Federal Communications Commission
   c. Bureau of Alcohol, Tobacco, Firearms and Explosives
   d. Federal Trade Commission

5. What is the objective of a trade regulation ruling issued by the FTC?
   a. It is the only way to undo the damage done by deception and is not only to stop the damage but also to make an attempt to undo it.
   b. It is designed to implicate an entire industry in case of unfair or deceptive practices.
   c. If a company uses an endorser to make claims about product benefits, the company has to substantiate these claims based on legitimate tests performed by experts.
   d. It is designed to halt the disputed practice immediately and prevent similar practices in the future.

6. Energizer Holdings filed a suit against Duracell in 2002 over an advertisement claiming the superiority of the DURACELL CopperTop brand over "heavy-duty" competitors. The advertisement failed to mention that all alkaline batteries outlast so-called heavy-duty batteries. Which legislation did Energizer Holdings use to sue Duracell?
   a. Lanham Act
   b. Hart-Scott-Rodino Antitrust Improvements Act
   c. Wheeler-Lea Amendment
   d. Robinson-Patman Act

7. Empowered by the _____, the FTC requires marketers using contests, games, and sweepstakes to make certain all of the details are given clearly and to adhere to a prescribed set of rules to ensure fairness.
   a. Lanham Act
   b. Hart-Scott-Rodino Antitrust Improvements Act
   c. Wheeler-Lea Amendment
   d. Robinson-Patman Act

8. Identify the organization that oversees self-regulation in the United States.
   a. Federal Trade Commission
   b. Better Business Bureau
   c. National Advertising Review Board
   d. Best Practices Bureau

9. There are many goods and services that are promoted openly and conspicuously that should not be: contraceptives, personal hygiene products, drugs related to sexual dysfunction, beer and liquor, tobacco, pornographic films and videos, guns and assault rifles, and violent video games, among others. How can we categorize such goods and services?
   a. addictive products and personal products
   b. sin products and personal products
   c. social evils and taboo products
   d. taboo products and addictive products

10. Consumer researchers have found that satisfaction with material possessions tends to contribute to overall life satisfaction, but only for _____.
    a. materialistic people
    b. women
    c. adults over the age of 40
    d. adolescents

Web Exercise

How to Advertise Distilled Spirits Responsibly

Visit the website of the *Distilled Spirits Council of the United States* at http://www.discus.org. Analyze its code of responsible practices, read the DISCUS semiannual code report, its press releases, the reaction to DISCUS code revisions and the FTC report, the highlights of the revised code, and the media buying guidelines. Be prepared to discuss this information in class.

Suggested Readings

Berger, Arthur Asa. 2004. *Ads, fads, and consumer culture*. Lanham, MD: Rowman & Littlefield.

———. 2005. *Shop 'till you drop: Consumer behavior and American culture*. Lanham, MD: Rowman & Littlefield.

Berman, Ronald. 1981. *Advertising and social change*. Beverly Hills, CA: Sage.

Courtney, Alice E., and Thomas W. Whipple. 1984. *Sex stereotyping in advertising*. Lexington, MA: Lexington Books.

Featherstone, Mike. 1991. *Consumer culture and postmodernism*. Thousand Oaks, CA: Sage.

Leiss, William, Stephen Kline, and Sut Jhally. 1986. *Social communication in advertising: Persons, products, & images of well-being*. Toronto: Methuen.

———. 1990. *Social communication in advertising: Persons, products, & images of well-being*, 2nd ed. Toronto: Nelson Canada.

Rotzoll, Kim B., and James E. Haefner. 1990. *Advertising in contemporary society*. Cincinnati, OH: South-Western.

Sheehan, Kim. 2004. *Controversies in contemporary advertising*. Thousand Oaks, CA: Sage.

Wernick, Andrew. 1991. *Promotional culture: Advertising, ideology, and symbolic expression*. Thousand Oaks, CA: Sage.

Zukin, Sharon. 2003. *How shopping changed American culture*. New York: Routledge.

Notes

1. Robert Gustafson, Mark Popovich, and Steven Thomsen, "The 'Thin Ideal' Study: Students Seem Numb to Dangers of Stereotype," *Marketing News*, March 15, 1999, 22.
2. Kim B. Rotzoll and James E. Haefner, *Advertising in Contemporary Society* (Cincinnati, OH: South-Western, 1990); Kim Sheehan, *Controversies in Contemporary Advertising* (Thousand Oaks, CA: Sage, 2004).
3. Ibid.
4. Paul N. Bloom, "The Cereal Industry: Monopolies or Super Marketers?" *MSU Business Topics* (Summer 1978): 41–49.
5. Lester G. Telser, "Advertising and Competition," *Journal of Political Economy* (December 1964): 537–62.
6. Robert D. Buzzell, Bradley T. Gale, and Ralph G. M. Sultan, "Market Share—A Key to Profitability," *Harvard Business Review* (January–February 1975): 97–106.
7. See note 2.
8. Robert D. Buzzell and Paul W. Farris, *Advertising Cost in Consumer Goods Industries*, Marketing Science Institute, Report no. 76 (August 1976), 111; Paul W. Farris and David J. Reibstein, "How Prices, Ad Expenditures, and Profits Are Linked," *Harvard Business Review* (November–December 1979): 173–84; Thomas M. Burton, "Reining in Drug Advertising," *The Wall Street Journal*, March 13, 2002, B1, 4.
9. Lee Benham, "The Effect of Advertising on the Price of Eyeglasses," *Journal of Law and Economics* 15 (October 1972): 337–52; Robert L. Steiner, "Does Advertising Lower Consumer Price? *Journal of Marketing* 37, no. 4 (October 1973): 19–26.
10. Paul W. Farris and Mark S. Albion, "The Impact of Advertising on the Price of Consumer Products," *Journal of Marketing* 44, no. 3 (Summer 1980): 17–35.
11. James A. Calderwood, "False and Deceptive Advertising," *Ceramic Industry* 148, no. 9 (August 1998): 26.
12. Doug Halonen, "30% Disobey Kids' Ad Limit," *Electronic Media* 17, no. 10, March 2, 1998, 3.
13. "Bogus 'Talent Scouts' Use Smoke Screen to 'Screen Test' Consumers," Federal Trade Commission, May 27, 1999, http://www.ftc.gov/opa/1999/9905/screen.htm.
14. Dick Mercer, "Tempest in a Soup Can," *Advertising Age*, October 17, 1994, 28–29.
15. "FTC Reviews Funeral Rules," Federal Trade Commission, April 30, 1999, http://www.ftc.gov/opa/1999/9904/funeral.rev.htm.
16. Jack Redmond, "Marketers Must Be Familiar with FTC Guidelines," *Inside Tucson Business* 5, no. 51, March 18, 1996, 18–19.
17. Daniel Golden and Suzanne Vranica, "Duracell's Duck Will Carry Disclaimer," *The Wall Street Journal*, February 7, 2002, 7.
18. "Trade Regulation Rule: Games of Chance in the Food Retailing and Gasoline Industries," Federal Trade Commission, 16 C.F.R., Part 419 (1982).

19. Mary Lu Carnevale, "FTC Adopts Rules to Curb Telemarketing," *The Wall Street Journal*, September 18, 1992, B1, 10.
20. Scott Hume, "900 Numbers: The Struggle for Respect," *Advertising Age*, February 18, 1991, S1; *Federal Register*, "Rules and Regulations," August 9, 1993, 42, 364–406; "Commission to Seek Public Comment on 900-Number Rule Revisions," Federal Trade Commission Press Release, October 23, 1998; Russell N. Laczniak, Les Carlson, and Ann Walsh, "Antecedents of Mothers' Attitudes toward the FTC's Rule for 900-Number Advertising Directed at Children," *Journal of Current Issues and Research in Advertising* 21, no. 2 (Fall 1999): 49–58; "US FTC: FTC Workshop to Address Proposed Changes to Its Pay-per-Call-Rule," *M2 Presswire*, May 20, 1999.
21. James Heckman, "COPPA to Bring No Surprises, Hefty Violation Fines in April," *Marketing News*, January 31, 2000, 6.
22. Steven Colford, "ABA Panel Backs FTC over States," *Advertising Age*, April 10, 1994, 1.
23. "AT&T Wins NARB Case over Collect-Call Ads," *Advertising Age* 68, no. 8, February 24, 1997, 2.
24. Kate Fitzgerald, "Cable Wrestles with Liquor Ads," *Advertising Age*, June 10, 2002, S-16; Stuart Elliot, "Facing Outcry, NBC Ends Plan to Run Liquor Ads," *The New York Times*, March 21, 2002, C1; Joe Flint and Shelly Branch, "In Face of Widening Backlash, NBC Gives Up Plan to Run Liquor Ads." *The Wall Street Journal*, March 21, 2002, B1, 3.
25. "NAI Launches Privacy-Awareness Web Site," AdAge.com, May 28, 2001; "Online Advertisers Launch Two Privacy Tools," *Network Advertising Initiative*, May 23, 2001, http://www.networkadvertising.org/aboutnai.
26. See note 2.
27. Banwari Mittal, "Public Assessment of TV Advertising: Faint Praise and Harsh Criticism," *Journal of Advertising Research* 34, no. 1 (January–February 1994): 35–53; J. C. Andrews, "The Dimensionality of Beliefs toward Advertising in General," *Journal of Advertising* 18, no. 1 (1989): 26–35; Ron Alsop, "Advertisers Find the Climate Less Hostile Outside the U.S.," *The Wall Street Journal*, December 10, 1987, 29
28. David A. Aaker and Donald E. Bruzzone, "Causes of Irritation in Advertising," *Journal of Marketing* (Spring 1985): 47–57; Stephen A. Greyser, "Irritation in Advertising," *Journal of Advertising Research* 13 (February 1973): 3–10: Ron Alsop, "Personal Product Ads Abound As Public Gets More Tolerant," *The Wall Street Journal,* April 14, 1986, 19; Joan Voight and Wendy Melillo, "Rough Cut," *Adweek*, March 11, 2002, 27–29; Joanne Lipman, "Censored Scenes: Why You Rarely See Some Things in Television Ads," *The Wall Street Journal*, August 17, 1987, 17.
29. Leanne Potts, "Retailers, Ads Bare Flesh for Bottom Line," *Albuquerque Journal*, December 20, 2002, D1.
30. John P. Cortez and Ira Teinowitz, "More Trouble Brews for Stroh Bikini Team," *Advertising Age*, December 9, 1991, 45; Bob Garfield, "Miller Lite's Latest in a Return to the Bad Old Days of Beer Ads," *Advertising Age*, January 20, 2003, 37; Hillary Chura, "Lap Dancer, Toilet Jokes Hawk New Whiskey," July 2, 2001, http://www.adage.com.
31. Michael McCarthy, "Shockvertising Jolts Ad Viewers," *USA TODAY*, February 23, 2000, 68.
32. See note 2.
33. Scott Ward, Daniel B. Wackman, and Ellen Wartella, *How Children Learn to Buy: The Development of Consumer Processing Skills* (Beverly Hills, CA: Sage, 1979); Thomas Robertson and John R. Rossiter, "Children and Commercial Persuasion: An Attribution Theory Analysis," *Journal of Consumer Research* 1, no. 1 (June 1974): 13–20; Scott Ward and Daniel B. Wackman, "Children's Information Processing of Television Advertising," in *New Models for Communications Research*, ed. G. Kline and P. Clark, 81–119 (Beverly Hills, CA: Sage, 1974); Merrie Brucks, Gary M. Armstrong, and Marvin E. Goldberg, "Children's Use of Cognitive Defenses against Television Advertising: A Cognitive Response Approach," *Journal of Consumer Research* 14, no. 4 (March 1988): 471–82; Tamara F. Mangleburg and Terry Bristol, "Socialization and Adolescents' Skepticism toward Advertising," *Journal of Advertising* 27, no. 3 (Fall 1998): 11–21.
34. Dan Lippe, "What Children Say about Media and Advertising," February 4, 2002, http://adage.com.
35. David Lieberman, "Broadcasters Crowd the Playground," *USA TODAY*, February 7, 1996, 1, 2B.
36. Ward, Wackman, and Wartella, *How Children Learn to Buy*.
37. *FTC Staff Report on Advertising to Children* (Washington, DC: Government Printing Office, 1978); Ben M. Enis, Dale R. Spencer, and Don R. Webb, "Television Advertising and Children: Regulatory vs. Competitive Perspectives," *Journal of Advertising* 9, no. 1 (1980): 19–25; Richard Zoglin, "Ms. Kidvid Calls It Quits," *Time*, January 20, 1992, 52; Elizabeth Jensen and Albert R. Karr, "Summit on Kids' TV Yields Compromise," *The Wall Street Journal*, July 30, 1996, B12; Sally Goll Beatty, "White House Pact on TV for Kids May Prove a Marketing Bonanza," *The Wall Street Journal*, August 2, 1996, B2.
38. Ronald Alsop, "Watchdogs Zealously Censor Advertising Targeted to Kids," *The Wall Street Journal*, September 5, 1985, 35.
39. See note 2.
40. Ronald Berman, *Advertising and Social Change* (Beverly Hills, CA: Sage, 1981), 13; Joan Voight, "The Consumer Rebellion," *Adweek*, January 10, 2000, 46–50.
41. Marye Tharp and Linda Scott, "Role of Marketing Processes in Creating Cultural Meaning," *Journal of Macromarketing* 10 (Fall 1990): 47–60.
42. Ed Diener, Jeff Horwitz, and Robert A. Emmons, "Happiness of the Very Wealthy," *Social Indicators Research* 16 (1985): 263–74; Robin A. Douthitt, Maurice MacDonald, and Randolph Mullis, "The Relationship between Measures of Subjective and Economic Well-Being: A New Look," *Social Indicators Research* 26 (1992): 407–22; Richard A. Easterlin, "Does Economic Growth Improve the Human Lot? Some Empirical Evidence," in *Nations and Households in Economic Growth*, ed. Paul A. David and Melvin W. Redder, 89–121 (New York: Academic Press, 1974); Randolph Mullis, "Measures of Economic Well-Being As Predictors of Psychological Well-Being," *Social Indicators Research* 26 (1992): 119–35.
43. R. S. Oropesa, "Consumer Possessions, Consumer Passions, and Subjective Well-Being," *Sociological Forum* 10, no. 2 (1995): 215–44.
44. Ibid; for an interesting and insightful analysis of the effects of the availability of too many brand options on consumers, see David Glen Mick, Susan M. Broniarczyk, and Jonathan Haidt, "Choose, Choose, Choose, Choose, Choose, Choose, Choose: Emerging and Prospective Research on the Deleterious Effects of Living in Consumer Hyperchoice," *Journal of Business Ethics* 52 (June 2004): 207–11.
45. M. Joseph Sirgy, Dong-Jin Lee, Val Larsen, and Newell Wright, "Satisfaction with Material Possessions and General Well-Being: The Role of Materialism," *Journal of Consumer Satisfaction, Dissatisfaction and Complaining Behavior* 11 (1998): 103–18.
46. See note 2.
47. Alice E. Courtney and Thomas W. Whipple, *Sex Stereotyping in Advertising* (Lexington, MA: Lexington Books, 1984); Daniel J. Brett and Joanne Cantor, "The Portrayal of Men and Women in U.S. Television Commercials: A Recent Content Analysis and Trends of 15 Years," *Sex Roles* 18, no. 9/10 (1998): 595–608; John B. Ford and Michael La Tour, "Contemporary Perspectives of Female Role Portrayals in Advertising," *Current Issues and Research in Advertising* 28 (1996): 81–93; Beverly A. Browne,

"Gender Stereotypes in Advertising on Children's Television in the 1990s: A Cross-National Analysis," *Journal of Advertising* 27, no. 1 (Spring 1998): 83–96; Richard H. Kolbe, "Gender Roles in Children's Advertising: A Longitudinal Content Analysis," *Current Issues and Research in Advertising* 22 (1990): 197–206; Debra Merskin, "Boys Will Be Boys: A Content Analysis of Gender and Race in Children's Advertisements on the Turner Cartoon Network," *Current Issues and Research in Advertising* 24 (Spring 2002): 51–60.

48. Cate Terwilliger, "Love Your Body Say Auraria Event Takes Aim at 'Offensive' Images, Ads," *Denver Post*, September 23, 1999, E3.

Building the Foundation of Strategic Marketing Communications

Chapter Three

Chapter Outline

- 3-1 **Introduction**
  - 3-1a Strategic Marketing Communications: A Framework to Aid in Strategic Decision Making
  - 3-1b Systems Concepts
- 3-2 **Strategy and Tactics**
- 3-3 **Setting Objectives**
  - 3-3a Strategy = Goal
  - 3-3b Objective = Quantitative Formulation of a Goal
  - 3-3c How Objectives Are Set
  - 3-3d Linking Strategy, Tactics, and Objectives
- 3-4 **Budgeting**
- 3-5 **Monitoring and Control**
  - 3-5a Change Strategy and Tactics
  - 3-5b Change Objective
  - 3-5c Change Budget
- 3-6 **Analysis and Planning**
  - 3-6a Selecting Effective Strategy and Tactics
  - 3-6b Setting Objectives
  - 3-6c Budgeting
- 3-7 **System Integration**
- Summary
- Discussion Questions
- Practice Quiz
- Web Exercise: Theory
- Suggested Readings
- Note

Key Terms

- analysis (p. 54)
- control (p. 54)
- decision tree (p. 55)
- feedback (p. 62)
- feedback mechanism (p. 62)
- feedforward (p. 63)
- goal (p. 58)
- higher order (p. 57)
- linkage (p. 53)
- lower order (p. 57)
- model (p. 53)
- monitoring (p. 54)
- objectives (p. 54)
- planning (p. 54)
- process hierarchy (p. 55)
- situation analysis (p. 63)
- strategy (p. 54)
- subordinate (p. 55)
- superordinate (p. 55)
- system (p. 54)
- system integration (p. 65)
- tactics (p. 54)
- theoretical framework (p. 53)
- theory (p. 53)

Theories are nets to catch what we call "the world": to rationalize, to explain, and to master it. We endeavor to make the net finer and finer.

—**Karl Popper** (1902–1994), Austrian philosopher and scientist

3-1 Introduction

Again consider the case of Crest toothpaste. As noted in Chapter One, the brand itself comes in eighty-five varieties. When you consider the number of possible communications avenues open to a brand manager for each of those particular subbrands of Crest, it simply staggers the mind. How can a manager hope to be able to link all the communications activities for a given subbrand (1) to other Crest subbrands, (2) to the Crest brand, (3) to other Procter & Gamble oral care brands, and (4) across the entire family of Procter & Gamble brands?

SMC QuickLink
Crest
http://www.crest.com/home/index.jsp

3-1a Strategic Marketing Communications: A Framework to Aid in Strategic Decision Making

Believe it or not, a good *theory* is the only means to establishing those **linkages** or relationships at a variety of levels. Perhaps a definition of what a theory is would be helpful to begin this chapter. While there are many definitions of theory, one from the marketing area is offered here:

> A **theory** is a systematically related set of statements, including some lawlike generalizations, that are empirically testable. The purpose of a theory is to increase scientific understanding through a systematized structure capable of both explaining and predicting phenomena.[1]

The first thing that should jump out here is that theories have to be empirically testable. In other words, you have to be able to take a theory into the real world, use it, and then measure the outcomes. If you cannot actually apply it and get some data that tell you that you should keep the theory around because it works or throw it away because it does not perform, it is not a theory. The second thing is that it has to have a structure to it and needs to explain and predict things. Those things can be changes in consumer attitudes, changes in sales, and so on. If you were the manager making decisions about Crest and you did not have some sort of valid **theoretical framework** to help you evaluate how your marketing communications was impacting all the far reaches of your brand's universe, you would be completely lost. Theories and theoretical **models**, methods of turning marketing objectives into practical strategies, make the complex less confusing. They do this by acting as frames of reference, aiding in integration of massive amounts of data from the consumer market and internal sources, and providing a road map to managers on how to take their brands from one place to another effectively and efficiently. The bottom line is that they are tools to help managers make better decisions. The systems theory discussed in this chapter is all about how to think about using a theoretical tool to help communications managers think and act strategically at every level of their activities.

linkage The ability to establish a relationship between two or more constructs, events, or behaviors.

theory A hypothesis that has withstood extensive testing by a variety of methods and in which a higher degree of certainty may be placed. A theory is *never* a fact but, instead, is an attempt to explain one or more facts. A strict definition refers to a theory as a systematically related set of statements, including some lawlike generalizations, that are empirically testable.

theoretical framework A framework within which various suppositions and questions can be examined using the scientific method of empirical testing (see *theory*).

models A set of hypotheses or theoretical propositions tied together to convey a logical point, message, or story.

3-1b Systems Concepts

As already noted, to strategically connect one piece of the SMC plan to all others in the system and make decisions that can be tracked from the execution stage to corporate and marketing strategies, managers need to have a framework within which they can make decisions. Systems concepts and models are designed to help all people, particularly decision makers and managers, make better decisions. Decisions are not independent of environmental influences and therefore should not be made as if they were in a vacuum. The best decisions are ones that are grounded in well-articulated and measurable goals that are reached after considering all the relevant environmental variables. For marketers and managers, these decisions are made in the context of programs, projects, and campaigns. The goal is to make effective decisions that ensure the integrity of the system (i.e., the integrity of the program, project, or campaign). A given person's career is an example that almost everyone can relate to. Let us take that given career and call the entire career of the individual a **system.** Most everyone will agree that such a system has to be effectively planned and managed if a successful career is to be achieved. Systems concepts can help do exactly that. You can apply concepts such as strategy and tactics, objectives, budget, monitoring and control, and analysis and planning. Let us consider your career (current state or expected) for a minute. Think about the **strategy** you have or will set for yourself to further develop your own career. What is it? You have a variety of strategic options available to you within that career. If you think about your current or future position (job), you can follow a single approach or a mix of various approaches to the furthering of that career. You may decide to be professional in everything that you do. You may decide to follow everything your boss tells you to do. You may also focus on being able to demonstrate creativity or being able to demonstrate leadership. To take the example of a system strategy to an even simpler level, ask yourself what strategy you have for "getting rich." Everyone has seen the late-night infomercials in which any number of "how to get rich strategies" are touted by "experts" who are willing to share their "secret of success" with you for only $99.95. Why would such a strategy work for you? Or why would it not work? Think about a strategy of your own and focus on this strategy. What are the things that you have been doing lately to carry out this strategy? For example, could it be that you try to keep up with the professional trade journals and popular business press articles to be able to use the newest concepts and models at work or in the classroom? This may be a tactical thing you do to help achieve the goal of "being professional." Think about two or three **tactics,** or courses of action that you have selected, and list them.

Now focus on one or two of these career-related tactics. Can you articulate the exact **objective** pertaining to each tactic? For example, if you are starting your career at a marketing consulting firm and you subscribe to *Advertising Age* and *The Wall Street Journal,* your objective may be to read them completely and discuss the things you find interesting with your officemates and your immediate supervisor. Now think about the objective pertaining to your career strategy. Can you articulate it? For example, if you said that acting professionally is your strategy, how will you know that you are progressing to becoming an ideal professional? What are those *measures* or indicators that will tell you whether you are progressing in that direction or failing in this endeavor? Now step back for a second and think about how you budget your *resources* (and energy) to the various tasks that help you achieve your career goal. Can you think of the resources? These may be money, time, and effort. Now consider how you would assess your performance and focus on **monitoring** and **control.** How have you progressed? Are you a good learner? Are you learning from trial and error? What have you learned in the past that allowed you to enhance your career? Again, let us shift gears. Let us focus on **analysis** and **planning.** What kind of analysis do you do to help you in your career planning? For example, some people gather information about new job opportunities. Other

---

system A set of procedures and methods for the regular, planned collection, analysis, and presentation of information for use in making marketing decisions.

strategy A course of action that emphasizes certain elements of the strategic mix.

tactics Selected courses of action guided by objectives of the superordinate level of the organization's hierarchy.

objectives Formal statements of a strategy that serve as goals. These formal statements are precise and quantifiable and guide the formulation of tactics or action.

monitoring The process by which performance outcomes are measured.

control The process by which a warning signal is generated to trigger corrective action. The strength of the signal is determined by the degree of the negative deviation between an objective and a performance outcome—the greater the negative deviation, the greater the warning signal.

analysis The process of identifying factors that may assist the decision maker in selecting an effective strategy, setting objectives, determining tactics, and/or allocating resources. Once these factors are identified and specific information about the case in question is gathered (guided by the identified factors), then the decision maker is ready for planning. In other words, analysis assists the decision maker in planning.

planning Making decisions related to strategy, objectives, tactics, and resource allocation that are based on information obtained through analysis.

people gather information about opportunities to help out within the firm, and so on. Of course, analysis and planning are very much related to your career strategy. You may gather information and thoroughly analyze it to help you figure out the best career strategy for you; or you may gather information that will help you allocate your time wisely. All the tactics you use to achieve your career objectives are part of a system. Your decisions will become more effective and productive if you learn to manage the system as a whole. Take a look at the career advice at Monster.com and think about it in terms of how those suggested strategies would fit within the systems approach.

The purpose of this chapter is to sensitize you to certain systems concepts used to build the SMC model. The goal is to familiarize you with the language of the SMC systems model as a prelude to Chapter Four, in which many of these concepts will be used. It is very likely that, after reading this chapter, you will better understand and appreciate the systems concepts addressed here; hopefully, you will fully appreciate them when you have completed this book. While some may find this chapter "too theoretical," the theory part of the model has to be flushed out, articulated, and understood before it can be applied to IMC. Theory provides the foundation of the entire structure and process. Read this chapter with patience, and try to learn the language of systems theory. You not only will find it useful in better understanding the IMC systems model but also will appreciate how its "theoretical" foundations aid in its practical significance.

SMC QuickLink
Monster
http://www.monster.com

3-2 Strategy and Tactics

All decisions can be viewed as involving a **decision tree** or a **process hierarchy**, which is, in essence, a sequential set of processes that are hierarchically organized. Thus, any organizational task can be viewed as involving a set of processes organized hierarchically. At any given level of the process hierarchy, there is a mix of process elements. Focusing on a given element of the process mix allows the system designer to identify the **subordinate** elements. For example, a decision tree that we address throughout this book involves a three-level hierarchy for a company's programs—corporate, marketing, and marketing communications. Marketing communications programs at the bottom of the decision tree are considered to be elements of the marketing communications mix, and the elements of the marketing communications mix are guided by a marketing communications strategy; but marketing communications strategy is considered to be an element of the next level in the hierarchy, the marketing mix. This element is guided by marketing strategy, which is considered an element of the corporate mix, which in turn is guided by a corporate strategy.

More specifically, a process at a **superordinate** level is usually referred to as a *strategy*, while the elements of that process (the subordinate processes designed to implement the superordinate process) are usually referred to as *tactics* or *strategic mix*. Once we focus on a process, it becomes a *strategy* and the elements employed to implement that process become *tactics* (elements of the *strategic mix*). However, a *tactic* becomes a *strategy* once we move down the hierarchy of processes and focus on that tactic. Hence, the distinction between a strategy and a tactic can be appreciated as a direct function of the vantage point of the decision maker in an overall hierarchy of processes. For example, at a company's highest level, a CEO commonly makes decisions at the top of the decision tree, decisions that management scholars refer to as *corporate strategy*. A decision such as "gain market share" is considered highly strategic. This decision is carried out by the various organizational departments. In other words, all corporate strategic decisions are implemented through the deployment of the various functional units of an organization (research and development [R&D], engineering, production, marketing, accounting, finance, insurance, employee relations, etc.). The tasks performed in the various functional units are tactical decisions, not strategic ones, from the vantage point of the CEO.

decision tree or process hierarchy A hierarchy of decisions reflecting a hierarchical link between strategy, objectives, and tactics. For example, the following can be described as a process hierarchy: A corporate strategy of "Gain market share" leads the decision maker to set a corporate objective of "Increase market share by 20 percent by next quarter." Certain corporate tactics are then selected to meet this objective, such as to hold the marketing department responsible to develop a marketing program that can achieve the corporate objective.

subordinate Placed in or occupying a lower class, rank, or position.

superordinate Superior in rank, class, or status.

SMC Marketplace Watch 3-1

Will Saab Maintain Its Identity or Get Lost in the General Motors Family of Brands?

Saab executed its most ambitious new-model blitz since its founding in the late 1940s. Many experts in the field, though, think that Saab may end up getting lost in the GM family. General Motors took total ownership of the Swedish car manufacturer in 2000. Before GM and until now, Saab has been a premium niche market player whose brand was centered on two models. The most recent configuration of that two-model product line was the Saab 9-5 and the Saab 9-3. General Motors is borrowing from its other brands and joint-venture partners to expand Saab's lineup. This expansion will include a variety of other models that step outside of Saab's traditional product offering. By doing so, GM hopes to build total brand strength.

In May of 2005, Saab's first sport-utility vehicle, the 9-7X, which draws heavily on GM's Chevrolet TrailBlazer and is built in Ohio to overcome Europe's high currency exchange rates, was introduced. Executives at GM argued that the brand needed an SUV since nearly 30 percent of owners who leave Saab do so for an SUV and almost 40 percent of Saab owners have a second vehicle that is an SUV.

Todd Turner, president of CarConcepts, wonders if the 9-7X "fits the bill," because he believes it takes away the Saab identity by significant use of GM transplanted parts. Mr. Turner does, however, believe that using parts from other GM brands, like in the case of the Saab 9-3, built on one of GM's European Opel platforms, "maintains the Saab-ness" of the brand.

General Motors' Mark LaNeve, VP for sales, service, and marketing for North America, begs to differ regarding the 9-7X, saying, "There's a lot of differentiation in the two vehicles." He says, "We have brand differentiation. It's a matter of really executing the products and how we advertise them."

Saab: The Early Years

Even in its early years, Saab was part of a much larger corporate system. Managing effectively within that larger system is something that many brands in today's world of diversified, multinational firms have to find ways to deal with.

Source: General Motors Corp. Used with permission, GM Media Archives.

Saab will also continue to expand the 9-3 line by bringing out a SportCombi hatchback. With the 9-3 sedan and convertible accounting for 71 percent of Saab's annual U.S. sales, a seven-passenger crossover SUV is expected in either 2006 or 2007. This particular brand will reach even farther for parts and production. The model is being codeveloped and built by GM partner Fuji Heavy Industries. Fuji's Subaru also builds Saab's 9-2X for the United States. The 9-2X, on sale since fall 2004 and Saab's first all-wheel-drive model, has been derisively nicknamed "Saab-aru" by industry insiders.

However, the vice president for marketing can make a decision that is highly superordinate guiding the performance of the entire marketing department, and this decision is referred to as *strategy* from the vantage point of the VP for marketing. For example, "we should position our product as a quality product" is a strategic decision that guides all marketing efforts. The various marketing tasks employed to implement this decision are considered *tactics*—again, only from the vantage point of the VP for marketing. Note that the same decision made by the VP for marketing is considered a *tactic* from the vantage point of the CEO. Similarly, the marketing communications manager may make strategic decisions at the marketing communications level, which in turn are carried out as concrete tasks or *tactics* using the various tools of marketing communications. For example, the use of coupons is considered a tactical decision by the marketing communications manager because this particular task is guided by a superordinate decision, such as "develop a communications campaign that induces consumers to try the product."

Across the aisle at Ford Motor Company, the Swedish Volvo brand is doing much better than Saab, having sold 139,067 vehicles in the United States. The speculation is that it may be due to Volvo reputation and established brand image. Conjecture continues as to why Saab is not doing as well as its Swedish brother in a global automotive giant. While some suggest that Volvo had more distinctive designs, others feel that it may be that Saab is just getting lost in the GM brand system despite upping spending in advertising and product development to drive the brand sales.

Even though Saab spent nearly $61 million on advertising and promotion in the United States, Saab sold just over 38,000 vehicles in the United States in 2004, down about 20 percent from 2003. The phrase "distinctively designed, independently inspired" is prevalent in the current campaign.

Saab veteran Bob Sinclair, who retired in the early 1990s after leading Saab USA for 13 years, says GM is trying to mass market the Saab brand, something he feels is counter to what the brand is. "I see no evidence that GM management understands what the Saab brand is about."

"Saab has always been quirky and caters to that crowd, and it's a small crowd," says Jim Sanfilippo, executive VP at Omnicom Group's AMCI. "Saab is getting lost in the GM blender."

SMC QuickLink
General Motors
http://www.gm.com

Source: Adapted from Jean Halliday, "GM Struggles with 'Saabness'," *Advertising Age* 76, no. 15, April 11, 2005, S8.

The Saab Dealer Support System
The Saab subsystem within General Motors (GM) communicates with and provides standardized marketing communications elements to Saab dealers to help them maintain systemwide message consistency from GM to the Saab dealer to the Saab consumer.
Source: General Motors Corp. Used with permission, GM Media Archives.

SMC Marketplace Watch 3-1 provides an example of Saab as a **lower-order** part of a system that is in danger of losing its brand identity (and profitability) within a larger system, which is General Motors. It is a good example of a real-life need to be able to link all the marketing communications (and other marketing and product dimensions) into the **higher-order** demands of the larger corporate system and visa versa. A systems approach becomes crucial in that case to be able to strategically make those connections effectively.

In a typical decision tree or process hierarchy, the selection of one or more subordinate process elements (elements of a strategic mix) is directly influenced by the selection of the corresponding superordinate process (strategy). Correspondingly, the selection of a specific strategy (main process at any given hierarchical level) is influenced by the implicit or explicit selection of the strategic mix (process elements). That is, the process hierarchy is designed using both top-down and bottom-up approaches. It does not matter which comes first—a given process (strategy) or

lower order See *higher order* below.

higher order A term used to refer to abstract ideas or constructs that are superordinate over (or comprised of) lower constructs.

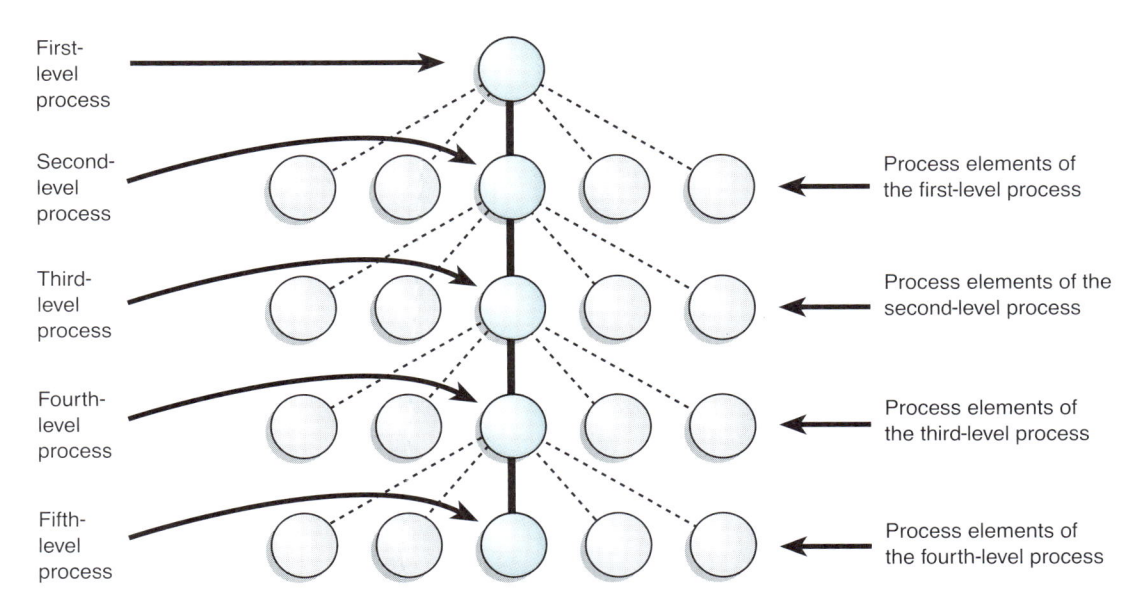

Figure 3-1
An Organizational Process Hierarchy

its elements (strategic mix). The idea is that planning entails the selection of hierarchical processes that create means-end chains, and that subordinate processes (means) are selected in such a way to achieve the goals of a superordinate process (end) at any level of the process hierarchy, and vice versa (see Figure 3-1).

3-3 Setting Objectives

The concept of objectives is very popular in the organizational and managerial sciences. Managers set goals and objectives and develop programs to meet these goals and objectives. First, let us distinguish between *strategy-tactics* and *goals-objectives* and then proceed to distinguish goals from objectives. Once we get a good feel for what objectives are, then we can discuss how objectives are set, in general.

3-3a Strategy = Goal

goal The purpose toward which an endeavor is directed; an objective.

In the context of the process hierarchy described in Section 3-2, any strategy can be described as a **goal** that can be attained through *tactics*. Managers always talk about implementing a program to accomplish or achieve a goal, and this goal is nothing more than the superordinate decision or action that we also call a *strategy*. Once a strategic decision is made and a set of tactics is conceived to carry out the strategy, progress toward achieving this strategy is considered *goal fulfillment*. In other words, we only translate a strategy into a goal after putting into action a program designed to achieve the strategy, that is, *meet the goal*. Another way of looking at this is through the distinction of planning versus management. When managers talk about *planning*, they usually talk about strategy, strategizing, strategic planning, strategic decision making, and the like. In this context, the focal point of the discourse is to make superordinate-level decisions, or decisions that are positioned more toward the top of the organizational hierarchy than toward the bottom of that hierarchy. The outcome of planning is one or more *strategies*. People who make these superordinate-level decisions are mostly upper managers.

Once the strategic plan is put into action, then the focus becomes *management*. The emphasis is now placed on implementing the strategies through programs or operationalizing the strategies into concrete action. Middle-level managers and supervisors tend to be concerned with operationalizing strategies. They are con-

Managing Achievement of Goals

Middle-level managers and supervisors are concerned with operationalizing strategies conceived by top management and are concerned about achieving goals that reflect those strategies.

Source: © 2006 JupiterImages Corporation.

cerned about *achieving goals* that reflect the strategies. In other words, goals are nothing more than middle-level management's representation of strategies to ensure that the tactics (or managerial programs) are carried out in such a way to effectively implement the strategies, that is, achieve certain goals that reflect these strategies. For example, suppose a CEO makes a strategic decision to *maintain the position* of the firm's brand in a certain market. In other words, the focus is to fend off the competition and stop customer erosion to competitor brands. This is a corporate strategy: *maintain position strategy*. This strategy can be implemented through various organizational programs—marketing, R&D, engineering, manufacturing, accounting, finance, purchasing, and so on. The marketing manager has to develop and manage product, price, place, and promotion programs in such a way to meet the goal of *maintain position*. Thus, the strategy conceived by top management becomes a goal for middle-level management.

3-3b Objective = Quantitative Formulation of a Goal

Managers usually treat objectives as quantitative operationalizations of goals. Therefore, *goals* are desired states that are articulated qualitatively, whereas *objectives* are goals' quantitative counterparts. For example, to go back to the CEO's strategy of *maintain position*, which is now treated as a *goal* by middle-level managers, this goal can be articulated quantitatively in terms of sales and market share. More specifically, the goal of *maintain position* may be quantitatively translated as, *maintain current level of market share, which is 25 percent*, or *maintain current level of unit sales of 5 million units per year*. These are objectives, and middle-level management is traditionally held accountable to achieve these *goals*.

3-3c How Objectives Are Set

Setting objectives is an organizational task involving three key processes: (1) identification of an objective (or performance) dimension, (2) identification of measures to gauge outcomes related to the objective (or performance) dimension, and (3) identification of the desired level and time frame associated with the objective dimension. We discuss each of these tasks in some detail and provide illustrations.

Identification of an Objective (or Performance) Dimension

In this process, the manager tries to select an appropriate objective. The challenge is to identify an appropriate objective that is consistent with the selected strategy and its strategic mix. Different strategies (and strategic mixes) entail different objective dimensions. For example, the objective dimension for a strategy such as *maintain position* is sales and market share. One can quantify the goal pertaining to the maintain position strategy in terms of the sales and market share dimensions. However, a strategy such as *harvest* may entail an entirely different objective dimension, namely, profit. The goal pertaining to the harvest strategy can be quantified in terms of maximizing profit, not sales and market share. The point is to select the appropriate objective dimension that closely matches the selected strategy.

Identification of Measures to Gauge Outcomes Related to the Objective (or Performance) Dimension

Once one or more objective dimensions are identified (e.g., brand awareness), the manager has to identify suitable measures of each selected objective dimension. If the selected objective is *brand awareness*, then what are those valid and reliable measures that are well established in the industry that the manager can use? Not only these measures have to be identified but also the norms pertaining to the measures. For example, suppose a *brand awareness* objective is selected. The manager should examine alternative measures of brand awareness and select a suitable measure.

Then the manager should examine the norms of that measure. Are there previous studies using this measure with a comparable product, a comparable target market, and a comparable campaign? Suppose the product is a brand of deodorant soap. The manager plans a television advertising campaign that should last 6 months. Target consumers are adult women. Suppose that the manager finds several studies that deal with comparable markets, products, and advertising campaigns. Now suppose that, based on these studies, the average increase in brand awareness after 6 months of television advertising was identified as approximately 50 percent. That is, previous "comparable" advertising campaigns have generated an increase of 50 percent in brand awareness. Now the manager is in a position to go to the next step and identify the desired level associated with the selected objective.

Identification of the Desired Level and the Time Frame Associated with the Objective (or Performance) Dimension

Knowing the norms of the measure that will be used to gauge the performance of a program (e.g., an advertising campaign), the manager is now positioned to identify the goal of that program in a very concrete and quantitative way. Should the manager set his or her objective to reflect the norm, be above the norm, or be below the norm? If 50 percent increase in brand awareness is the norm, for example, should the goal be 50 percent, greater than 50 percent, or less than 50 percent? The goal now is to determine the extent of desired deviation from the norm. This can be accomplished by considering several factors, such as past and anticipated performance of key competitors, anticipated changes in the market, and anticipated changes within the firm.

Note that implicit in this discussion is the notion that the time frame is also selected in a way to match comparability with previous studies. For example, if most of the previous studies conducted with comparable products and advertising campaigns involve a time frame of 6 months (duration of the entire advertising campaign), then the time frame of the planned advertising campaign should also be 6 months.

3-3d Linking Strategy, Tactics, and Objectives

Examine Figure 3-2. The figure shows how strategies, tactics, and objectives are linked in the context of the process hierarchy. A strategy at a 0-order level of the process hierarchy (*Strategy 0*) has a corresponding objective (*Objective 0*). To achieve Objective 0, we have to move to the first-order level of the process hierarchy. Thus, the strategy of the first order in the process hierarchy (*Strategy 1*) is essentially the

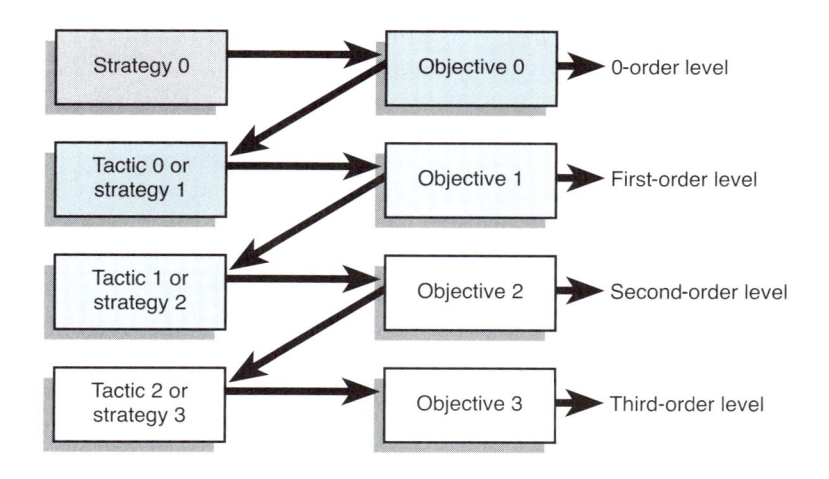

Figure 3-2
Linking Strategy, Tactics, and Objectives

tactic used to achieve the objective at the superordinate level. We can call this decision *Strategy 1* or *Tactic 0*. Similarly, at the second-order level, the strategy (*Strategy 2*) has a corresponding objective (*Objective 2*). This Strategy 2 is essentially a tactic conceived to carry out the objective of the first-order level (*Objective 1*).

Calling a decision at any given level a *strategy* or a *tactic* is very much dependent on whether this decision is seen as the starting point of many other subordinate decisions or a decision that is subordinate to others. Thus, a decision that initiates the system (considered as a starting point) is a *strategy*, whereas a *tactic* is a decision that is subordinate in nature (see Figure 3-2).

As an example to illustrate the links among strategy, objective, and tactic, let us conceive of a process hierarchy involving three process levels: corporate (0-order level), marketing (first-order level), and marketing communications (second-order level). At the 0-order level (i.e., corporate level), most organizations make decisions such as *grow, maintain position, innovate, harvest, divest*, and so forth. We can view any of these decisions as 0-order strategies. A grow strategy may be translated into a goal and quantified in terms of an objective such as *5 percent increase in sales*. This objective is then the 0-order objective. This objective becomes the goal that guides the decision maker to formulate tactics to achieve the stated objective. Now move to the marketing level (first-order level); let us say that the decision maker decides that a strategic product focus (specifically positioning by competitors to demonstrate the brand superiority against competitor brands) is best to achieve the 5 percent sales increase. This is Strategy 1 but Tactic 0. This strategy can be translated into a concrete goal such as *associate the brand with key product benefits compared to the competition so that 60 percent of consumers come to recognize the brand as superior to competitor brands*. This is Objective 1. This objective creates the impetus for the decision maker to identify a suitable marketing communications tactic that can achieve this goal. Now we are at the marketing communications level (second-order level). Perhaps an informative (thinker) communications tactic would do the job. This is Tactic 1 or Strategy 2. This decision can be translated in terms of specific goals such as *we need to increase brand awareness and learning such that at least 80 percent of consumers become aware of the brand and its key benefits compared to its competitors*.

3-4 Budgeting

Allocating resources to the elements of the strategic mix is, in essence, a budgeting decision. The manager must decide what resources are needed to implement the selected strategy and its respective strategic mix. For example, given the decision to advertise the product through television, the manager determines the amount of money needed to launch a television advertising campaign to achieve a certain level of brand awareness. This example shows the power of a particular budgeting method called the *buildup approach,* which is commonly used in advertising (sometimes this budgeting method is also referred to as the *objective-task method*). In the buildup method, a decision maker can effectively allocate resources by starting at the top of the decision hierarchy such that: strategy → objectives → tactics → strategy → objectives → tactics → and so on all the way down the process hierarchy. At the bottom of the hierarchy, the decision maker tabulates the costs of all those tasks at that level needed to achieve the stated objective at the superordinate level. The sum of these costs is viewed as the required budget to effectively achieve the stated objectives (all those objectives stated at the different levels of the process hierarchy).

3-5 Monitoring and Control

feedback The outcome or state of a system that may be utilized in the modification of the system's operation. This term is usually used in terms of compensation and, as such, relates to the system whereby information is obtained regarding performance versus compensation.

feedback mechanism A mechanism that generates a stress signal when a specific measured outcome is detected to be significantly below (or above) the stated objective.

The control function involves the use of a **feedback** mechanism. A **feedback mechanism** generates a stress signal when a specific measured outcome is detected to be significantly below (or above) the stated objective. In today's world of scanners, monitors, and databases, collection of feedback can be a continuous "real-time" process for marketers and the like. The evaluation points of performance need to be clearly articulated by the manager based on his or her particular product and planning needs. For example, a marketing communications objective may be phrased as *The marketing communications objective is a 50 percent increase in brand awareness as measured by a brand recognition method after 6 months from the launch of the advertising campaign*. After 6 months, the marketing communications manager assesses the outcome using the designated method and finds out that brand awareness only inched up 10 percent. That is, a negative deviation of forty points from the desired level of the objective dimension was detected. Significant negative deviations "raise red flags" and motivate the manager to make adjustments. These adjustments may involve one or more of the following: (1) change strategy and tactics, (3) change objective, and/or (2) change budget.

3-5a Change Strategy and Tactics

Through negative feedback, the manager realizes that the selected strategy might not have been the best strategy or that the way the strategy was implemented might have been faulty. Perhaps certain elements of the strategic mix (or tactical programs) were misconceived. Thus, based on feedback, the manager may develop a new strategy, or a new configuration of the strategic mix, for future action. This is viewed as corrective action.

3-5b Change Objective

There are many instances in which managers set their objectives too high, perhaps unrealistically high. If performance is assessed to be significantly below the objective, then perhaps the objective was too high to begin with and needs to be lowered in future planning and implementation. Conversely, some managers may underestimate their strengths and set their objectives too low. Feedback may indicate performance above and beyond the stated objective. These managers may realize that the objective was set too conservatively, and they may raise the objective in future action.

3-5c Change Budget

Corrective action can also be in the form of reallocating resources. Through negative feedback, the manager may realize that the amount of money budgeted to implement a strategy is not adequate—more money is needed. The converse is also possible—too much money has been allocated to implement a certain program, cre-

Reallocating Resources

Sometimes, the amount of money budgeted to implement a strategy must be reallocated in order to meet a stated objective.

Source: © 2006 JupiterImages Corporation.

ating misallocations to other programs, which together may have contributed to failure in meeting the stated objective.

3-6 Analysis and Planning

Analysis and planning, in systems language, is referred to as *feedforward*. **Feedforward** is analysis that examines the future situation. In many instances, managers rely on studies that have successfully predicted certain phenomena to anticipate how things are likely to unfold. These studies reflect a feedforward function, looking into the future, anticipating how things are likely to unfold by relying on our understanding of how things happened in the past. Managers usually conduct what has been referred to as **situation analysis** to help them anticipate how things are likely to unfold, thereby making decisions to take advantage of the anticipated events and attempting to counteract them. Situation analysis, as commonly used by marketing strategists, for example, involves market analysis, environmental analysis, competitive analysis, customer analysis, and self-analysis. Thus, when selecting a positioning strategy, a marketer needs to make that decision based on customer analysis, that is, how consumers perceive the ideal product and the various brands along with product attributes. This kind of analysis is used to help the marketer make a positioning decision and allows the marketer to understand how consumers perceive the marketer's brand in relation to competitor brands. Therefore, the marketer anticipates how consumers are likely to react to the brand given certain attributes in the near future. In particular, analysis and planning assist the manager in (1) selecting effective strategy and tactics, (2) setting objectives, and (3) budgeting.

feedforward Analysis that examines the future situation.

situation analysis Another term for *strategic analysis*, situation analysis refers to the process in which certain factors internal and external to the organization are analyzed to help marketers with strategic planning. Examples of internal factors include the firm's past sales, past profit, past media expenditures, past promotional messages, and so on. Examples of external factors include the competition, the market, customers, and the environment.

3-6a Selecting Effective Strategy and Tactics

Situation analysis (or feedforward) allows the manager to understand and anticipate the effects of certain actions (strategy and tactics). Specifically, the manager needs to plan a process hierarchy that is most effective and determine which elements of a strategic mix (which tactics) are likely to be most effective in achieving the goals of a superordinate strategy. For example, a CEO studies the situation pertaining to a certain product offered by her firm in a certain market. She needs to make a strategic decision, whether to attempt to further grow in that market, to maintain position, to harvest, to improve the product through innovation, or to divest. Which strategic option is likely to be most effective in enhancing the stock value of the firm? The CEO has to rely on situation analysis to make this decision. The application of models such as the Boston Consulting Group Matrix and other portfolio models may help the CEO gather appropriate information to help her select a most effective strategy. Depending on which portfolio model is used in the situation analysis, the CEO may gather information about market growth, market share, and other characteristics pertaining to both the industry as a whole and her particular business position. The models assist the decision maker in selecting the best strategy.

An example closer to the heart of marketing communications may be as follows: Suppose the marketing communications manager is working with a habit-formation (doer) strategy. That is, the manager is charged with the task of inducing consumers to try the product and experience its benefits directly. What is the best element of the marketing communications mix that can carry out this strategy? Could it be sales promotion? Advertising? Public relations? Direct marketing? Reseller support? Word-of-mouth communications? What does the marketing communications manager know about the effectiveness of each of the communications mix elements? Under what conditions are certain elements of the communications mix likely to be most effective? The manager has to apply certain marketing communications models that are designed for the specific purpose of answering these questions. Exhibit 3-1 provides an example of where the catalog communications element is used as a communications leave-behind after personal salespeople have called on retailers to explain the various product offerings. Retailers are then reinforced through this communications mix element to help select products for their final consumers. In correctly arriving at the appropriate point, the marketing communications manager applies the model, gathers the necessary information to operationalize the model, and voila!—the answer flows from the model and the process.

3-6b Setting Objectives

Situation analysis is also very important in helping managers set objectives. To set reasonable objectives, managers have to translate goals (which are reflections of strategies) into quantitative desired states. To do this effectively, the manager has to establish a conception of a desired state based on information concerning:

- *The firm's strengths and weaknesses:* What the firm can realistically achieve in the future, knowing its strengths and weaknesses
- *The competition:* How key competitors have acted in the past and how they are likely to act given certain market conditions
- *Market changes:* How these changes present opportunities or threats and how the firm can react to those opportunities or threats
- *Changes within the firm:* How these changes present opportunities or threats and how the firm should react

3-6c Budgeting

Situation analysis also can be invaluable in allocating resources. Through the analysis, managers commonly gather information about:

- *The firm's past expenditures:* How much the firm has traditionally spent on what program and how effective the various programs have been, given certain levels of expenditures
- *Key competitors:* How much the competition has spent on what program in the past and how much the competition is likely to spend in the future
- *The industry at large:* How much most firms in the industry have spent on what programs and the effectiveness of different levels of expenditures

Exhibit 3-1
Optimizing the System

This catalog execution for Saigon Cosmetics provides just one piece in the entire system that ultimately delivers the brand to the final consumer.

Source: Reprinted by permission of Saigon Cosmetics Corporation.

- *Changes in the market:* How much they are likely to increase or decrease the cost of certain programs and tools
- *Changes within the firm:* How they are likely to increase or decrease the cost of certain programs or tools

3-7 System Integration

Having laid out the different system components, it is logical to move the discussion into the concept of system integration. Exhibit 3-2 offers an example of the General Motors corporate system. The automotive system itself is a set of brand subsystems. **System integration** is achieved by ensuring strong links between the system components. In this case, that is all the brands of the General Motors Corporation. Specifically, this and any system can be effectively integrated by ensuring strong links among the following system components:

1. *Link between strategy, objective, and tactics:* Systems tend to break down and become ineffective when there is no clear logic between a given strategy, how this strategy becomes a goal-guiding tactic, and tactics formulated to achieve the objective. For a system to be effectively integrated, a strategy has to be translated into a quantifiable objective and tactics have to be developed to achieve the stated objective. Each tactic, in turn, becomes a strategy, which, in turn, is transformed

system integration
The extent to which the system components (strategy, objectives, tactics, budget, analysis, planning, monitoring, and control) are strongly or weakly linked. A system is said to lack integration if any one link between the system components is weak. In contrast, a system is said to be fully integrated when all of the system components are strongly linked.

Exhibit 3-2

The General Motors Automotive System

In the automotive family of GM, there can be interactions across the entire system from marketing communications decisions made for each of the brands and subbrands. Without a systemwide structure in which planning, monitoring, and evaluation of such interactions take place, the potential for working at cross-purposes or even chaos increases significantly.

Source: General Motors Corp. Used with permission, GM Media Archives.

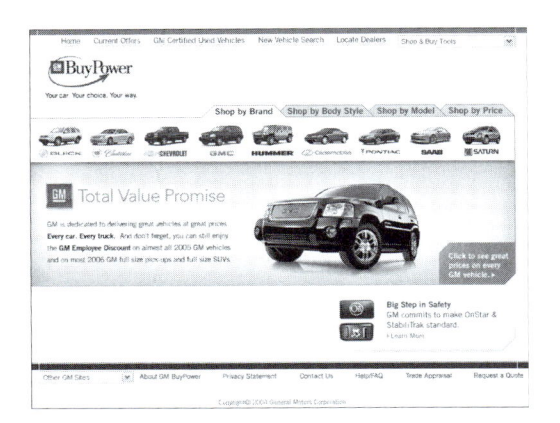

into a goal to guide subordinate-level tactics, and so on. This is a necessary but not sufficient principle of system integration. For example, suppose a marketing communications manager is charged with getting consumers to adopt the product on a trial basis. The manager has a history of using television advertising and nothing but television advertising. Consequently, he uses television advertising to accomplish this goal. The goal of getting consumers to adopt the product on a trial basis is a goal that reflects the habit-formation (doer) communications strategy. The objective of this goal is to increase consumers' product trial by a certain percentage within a given time frame. The tactics used to carry out this strategy are tools mostly related to sales promotion and direct marketing; television advertising may not be very effective in implementing the doer strategy. In this situation, there is no link between strategy, objective, and tactics. There is no logic that ties them together.

Objectives are concrete and quantitative translations of strategies. The system is jeopardized when a manager sets objectives that have little or nothing to do with the selected strategy. The supporting programs cannot be developed and effectively managed without higher-order objectives. For example, a marketing communications manager is working with a habit-formation (doer) strategy but sets an objective related to brand awareness and learning. He states that the objective is to maximize awareness and learning from the current level of 50 percent to a desired level of 80 percent. What does the awareness and learning objective have to do with the habit-formation (doer) strategy?! This strategy can only be translated in terms of product trial or purchase, *not* awareness and learning. This is another example of lack of system integration.

2. *Link between strategy-objective-tactics and budget:* The system is said to lack integration when resources are allocated in a manner that is completely oblivious to the resource requirements of the selected tactics (those programs selected to achieve specific objectives). In many instances, top management allocates resources using methods that do not take into account the resource requirements to accomplish the goals of certain strategies. Such misallocation of resources can place the system in jeopardy. For example, a marketing communications manager is working with a habit-formation (doer) strategy with the goal of trying to get target consumers to adopt the firm's product on a trial basis. The corresponding objective is to increase product trial by 30 percent in the next 6 months. She knows that such an objective will require at least two mass direct-mailing campaigns to target consumers and will cost approximately $100,000. However, top management has traditionally allocated a marketing communications budget based on 2 percent of last year's sales. Last year's sales were $4 million, and 2 percent of $4 million allocates $80,000. The marketing communications manager needs at least $100,000 to accomplish the goals of the communications strategy and its stated objective. There is a problem here! The

resources allocated do not mesh with the required strategies and the cost of the program required to achieve the goal of the strategy.

3. *Link between monitoring and control:* Lack of system integration occurs when performance monitoring is not followed by control. In other words, the manager may monitor system performance but no control is exerted. The manager fails to observe deviations from desired states and fails to respond by taking corrective action. Corrective action may have been completely dissociated from monitoring. For example, suppose the marketing communications manager observes that the direct-mail campaign that was designed to increase product trial by 30 percent in the next 6 months failed. He does nothing! There is no corrective action! There is no learning from mistakes! Failure is terminal! Effective systems learn from trial and error. Effective systems take corrective action to improve future performance. If the link between monitoring and control is weak, then the system does not learn. The system deteriorates and eventually dies.

4. *Link between monitoring-control and strategy-objective-tactics links:* We have already discussed how monitoring and control are exerted to change strategy-objective-tactics links. This is part of the monitoring and control function. If the system fails to meet certain performance objectives, corrective action can be instituted by changing the strategy, its objective, and the corresponding tactics (supporting programs). The system is said to lack integration if the monitoring-control function fails to reassess the strategy-objective-tactics link given negative feedback.

5. *Link between monitoring-control and objectives:* When a program fails, the manager must reassess the level of the objective. The manager asks whether the objective was set unrealistically high and whether it should be adjusted to reflect the system's true capabilities. The system lacks integration if the manager fails to reassess the objectives in light of poor performance outcomes.

6. *Link between monitoring-control and budget:* As previously stated, the monitoring-control function serves to motivate the manager to reassess the appropriateness of the resources allocated. If the program fails, the manager asks whether the failure may be attributed to lack of resources or the misallocation of resources. If corrections are needed, the manager should change resource allocations. Failure to reassess the method and outcomes of resource allocation given failure is a signal of system breakdown or lack of system integration.

7. *Link between analysis and planning:* Many managers engage in research; they set up elaborate intelligence apparatus and they hire consultants and gather enormous amounts of data—and they feel good about all of this. Unfortunately, much of this information is not used in planning. This is typical in the real world of planning and management. Most business strategy books and guides show managers how to conduct a *thorough* situation analysis. They assert that managers should gather information about competitors and the market. They commission consumer behavior studies to establish demographic and psychographic profiles of consumers. They urge managers to segment the market into groups and profile the various groups. They show how past sales can be analyzed and how regression equations can be developed to predict sales. Do all of these tasks result in sophisticated information gathering? Yes! The failure is in how much of this information is used. Most books provide very little guidance on using the information to plan strategies. A breakdown between analysis and planning is a strong sign of lack of system integration.

8. *Link between analysis-planning and strategy-objective-tactics links:* We have already discussed how analysis and planning are used to help managers plot strategy, articulate objectives from strategy, and formulate tactics guided by objectives. Proper analysis and planning are imperative. Strategy selection that is not

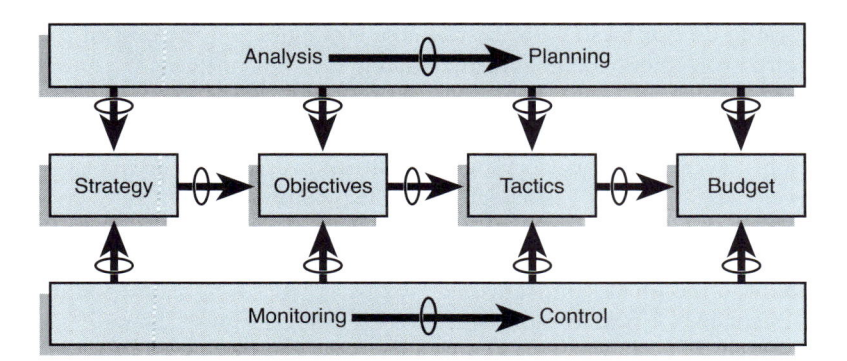

Figure 3-3
System Integration

guided by a thorough analysis of the situation can lead to a disaster. If the wrong strategy is selected, the wrong objectives are articulated and the wrong tactics are deduced. The marketing strategy and management as well as the marketing communications literatures are very rich with models that allow managers to determine what strategies are effective under what conditions. Failure to use these analytic models may lead the manager to make misguided decisions, leading to system disintegration.

9. *Link between analysis-planning and objectives:* Objective setting that is not guided by situation analysis may lead managers to set unrealistic and unreasonable objectives. This is again symptomatic of lack of system integration.
10. *Link between analysis-planning and budget:* Similarly, lack of system integration occurs when resources are allocated ineffectively with very little guidance from a thorough and suitable analysis of the situation.

See Figure 3-3 for an illustration of these links.

Summary

In this chapter, you are introduced to rudimentary systems concepts. We discuss concepts such as strategy and tactics, objective setting, budget, monitoring and control, and analysis and planning.

Strategy and tactics are described as decisions in a decision tree or a process hierarchy. Objectives are described as quantitative statements of a desired state represented as a strategy. Objectives serve as goals for lower-level decisions, that is, tactics.

Objectives are set guided by three processes: (1) identification of an objective dimension, (2) identification of measures to gauge outcomes related to the objective dimension, and (3) identification of the desired level and time frame associated with the objective dimension.

Budgeting is described as an allocation process guided by a buildup method. That is, the manager allocates resources by starting at the top of the decision hierarchy such that strategy → objectives → tactics → and so on all the way down the process hierarchy. At the bottom of the hierarchy, the manager tabulates the costs of all those tasks at that level needed to achieve the stated objectives.

Monitoring and control are described as feedback mechanisms in which a stress signal is generated when a specific measured outcome is detected to be significantly below (or above) the stated objective. Significant deviations motivate the manager to make adjustments. These adjustments may involve (1) change of strategy and tactics, (2) change of objective, and/or (3) change of budget.

Analysis and planning were described as feedforward mechanisms in which information is gathered and analyzed to predict future performance. Based on these predictions, the manager is in a better position to select effective strategy and tactics, set objectives, and budget resources.

System integration is described in terms of breakdown of links between (1) strategy, objective, and tactics; (2) strategy-objective-tactics and budget; (3) monitoring and control; (4) monitoring-control and strategy-objective-tactics; (5) monitoring-control and objectives; (6) monitoring-control and budget; (7) analysis and planning; (8) analysis-planning and strategy-objective-tactics; (9) analysis-planning and objectives; and (10) analysis-planning and budget.

Discussion Questions

Try to relate some of these systems concepts to your own personal experiences. Focus on a particular project, whatever the project is, that you have been very much involved with in the last few months. Answer the following questions.

1. Develop a process hierarchy in relation to the project. Figure out the major goals of the project, then figure out the major tasks or programs used to achieve each goal. Within each program, try to figure out the various subtasks. Lay this out in a tree form. That is, construct a decision tree.
2. Now focus on one major program or task. Try to figure out the goal of that program. Now try to quantify that goal and make it as concrete as you can. This will be the objective of the program.
3. Again focusing on that program, try to figure out the kind and amount of resources allocated to that program. Were these resources allocated effectively? Why or why not?
4. Again focus on the same program. How will you go about monitoring the performance of that program? What performance measures will you use? What will you do if the performance outcomes point to failure? That is, how will you go about controlling the program in an attempt to improve future performance?
5. Now let us focus on analysis and planning. What analysis will you need to conduct to help you make better decisions in terms of selecting the most appropriate subtasks, setting objectives, and allocating resources?
6. How can you enhance program integration? Is the program effective overall? Comment.
7. Visit the Saab.com website and see if you can link what the brand stands for in the mind of the consumer with the execution of the website. In the words of Karl Popper, Can you "make the web fine enough" to be able to uncover the reasons for the brand potentially "becoming lost" at General Motors?
8. Visit the General Motors website. How would you go about linking a strategic communications campaign for the GMC truck brand within the larger GM brand?
9. You are the marketing manager for Crest Whitestrips, the home teeth-whitening product. In putting together a direct mailing to consumers about your product, you begin to wonder how that activity will impact the sale of Crest toothpaste that has whitening added. You are also concerned about its impact on diluting the perception by the market that "Crest prevents cavities." How might you be able to think about that relationship using a systems perspective?
10. Develop your own theory on why one type of person would advance well in a given company while another type of person would be stuck in a "dead-end" career point at a certain company.

Practice Quiz

Note: You can find the correct answers to these questions by taking the quiz and then submitting your answers in the Online Edition. The program will automatically score your submission. If you miss a question, the program will provide the correct answer, a rationale for the answer, and the section number in the chapter where the topic is discussed.

1. A (an) _____ is a systematically related set of statements, including some lawlike generalizations, that are empirically testable.
   a. tactic
   b. theory
   c. integration
   d. procedure

2. A process at a superordinate level is usually referred to as _____, while the elements of that process are usually referred to as _____.
   a. systems concepts; models
   b. a decision tree; process hierarchy
   c. tactics; strategic mix
   d. a strategy; tactics

3. Any strategy can be described as a (an) _____ that can be attained through *tactics*. Which one of the following options is incorrect?
   a. goal
   b. superordinate decision
   c. program
   d. action

4. When managers talk about *planning*, they usually talk about _____.
   a. strategy
   b. strategic planning
   c. strategic decision making
   d. all of the above

5. In the _____ method of budgeting, a decision maker can effectively allocate resources by starting at the top of the decision hierarchy, all the way down the process hierarchy.
   a. strategy-tactics
   b. task-objective
   c. buildup
   d. higher-order

6. Which is the mechanism that generates a stress signal when specific measured outcome is detected to be significantly below the stated objective?
   a. feedback mechanism
   b. evaluation point-of-performance mechanism
   c. corrective action mechanism
   d. feedforward mechanism

7. Which of the following options is *not* the kind of analysis that examines the future situation?
   a. feedforward
   b. situation analysis
   c. feedback
   d. analysis and planning

8. _____ is achieved by ensuring strong links between the system components.
   a. Situational analysis
   b. Linkage
   c. System integration
   d. Theoretical framework

9. What can be described as a concrete and quantitative translation of a strategy?
   a. objectives
   b. tactics
   c. analysis
   d. budgets

10. When does lack of system integration occur?
    a. when performance monitoring is not followed by control
    b. when performance monitoring is not followed by corrective action
    c. when performance monitoring is not followed by feedback
    d. when corrective action is not followed by communication

Web Exercise

Theory

Put yourself in the position of a CEO for a company of your choice. Visit its website and select what you see as a marketing communications problem for the company that an understanding or application of theory may help solve. Explain how the theory would help your management team better understand how to approach the problem. An example may be the need to build consumer awareness of a new product that is part of the company's overall product portfolio.

Suggested Readings

Baumler, J. 1971. Defined criteria of performance in organizational control. *Administrative Science Quarterly* (September): 340.

Churchman, C. W. 1968. *The systems approach.* New York: Dell.

Cavaleri, Steven, and Krzysztof Obloj. 1993. *Management systems: A global perspective.* Belmont, CA: Wadsworth.

Flamholtz, E. 1979. Organizational control systems as a managerial tool. *California Management Review* 22 (2): 50–59.

Katz, D., and R. Kahn. 1966. *The social psychology of organizations.* New York: John Wiley.

Lerner, A. Y. 1972. *Fundamentals of cybernetics.* London: Chapman and Hall.

Miller, James G. 1978. *Living systems.* New York: McGraw-Hill.

Morell, R. W. 1969. *Management: Ends and means.* San Francisco: Chandler.

Popper, Karl. 2002. *The logic of scientific discovery.* Repr., New York: Routledge Classics.

Powers, W. T. 1973. *Behavior: The control of perception.* Chicago: Aldine.

———. 1990. Control theory: A model of organisms. *Systems Dynamics Review* 6 (1): 1–20.

Rahmation, S. 1985. The hierarchy of objectives: Toward an integrating construct in systems science. *Systems Research* 2 (3): 237–45.

Richardson, G. 1991. *Feedback thought in social science and systems theory.* Philadelphia: University of Pennsylvania Press.

Robb, F. F. 1985. Cybernetics in management thinking. *Systems Research* 1 (1): 5–23.

Simon, Herbert A. 1965. *Administrative behavior.* New York: The Free Press.

Sirgy, M. Joseph. 1989. Toward a theory of social organization: A systems approach. *Behavioral Science* 34: 272–85.

———. 1990. Self-cybernetics: Toward an integrated model of self-concept processes. *Systems Research* 7 (1): 19–32.

———. 1990. Toward a theory of social relations: The regression analog. *Behavioral Science* 35 (4): 195–206.

Note

1. Shelby Hunt, *Marketing Theory: Conceptual Foundations of Research in Marketing* (Columbus, OH: Grid Publishing, 1976), 104.

A Systems Model for Integrated Marketing Communications

Chapter Four

Chapter Outline

4-1 Introduction
4-2 The Systems Model of Integrated Marketing Communications
4-3 Strategy → Objectives → Tactics
4-4 Budgeting
4-5 Setting Objectives
4-6 Monitoring and Control
4-7 Analysis and Planning
    4-7a Strategy Selection
    4-7b Setting Objectives
    4-7c Budgeting
4-8 Marketing Communications Integration
Summary
Discussion Questions
Practice Quiz
Web Exercise: Yellow Pages versus Search Engines
Suggested Readings
Notes

Key Terms

affective (feeler) strategy (p. 77)
brand association (p. 77)
brand awareness (p. 77)
brand preference (p. 77)
brand purchase (p. 78)
brand trial (p. 78)
budget (p. 78)
buildup approach (p. 78)
conjoint analysis (p. 83)
demographics (p. 83)
divestment strategy (p. 77)
growth strategy (p. 77)
habit-formation (doer) strategy (p. 78)
harvest strategy (p. 77)
informative (thinker) strategy (p. 77)
innovation strategy (p. 77)
integration (p. 75)
means-end chains (p. 75)
multiattribute attitude models (p. 83)
psychographics (p. 83)
self-satisfaction (reactor) strategy (p. 78)

The achievement of one goal should be the starting point of another.

—**Alexander Graham Bell** (1847–1922),
Scottish-American inventor, invented telephone and phonograph

4-1 Introduction

Marketers often consider the college student market as a fairly well-defined and homogeneous type of market. While not completely true, the college market does offer a defined IMC environment to which most of us can relate. The college market is the target market for a variety of products that run the gamut from low-involvement, low-cost brands to high-involvement, high-cost brands. Marketers are constantly trying to entice this group with "free" products for trial. The college student is the recipient of shaving cream and razors, magazines, and even credit cards that offer "interest free" and no fees for a limited period of time if the student starts to use them. Food marketers such as Kellogg's and their Pop-Tarts brand have distributed free samples to incoming students at the beginning of the school year. Local and chain restaurants put two-for-one coupons in campus mailboxes; and, at sporting events, cell phone companies give away T-shirts and other paraphernalia that have their logo and contact information emblazoned on them. General Motors has worked with student groups at campuses across the country to stage brand events for their Pontiac and Chevrolet brands that include live music, vacation giveaways, and free food—all done to provide the college market with a chance to interact with the brand. College newspapers are full of advertisements from both national and local businesses. Companies also advertise their products on television programs such as *The OC* with both media buys and product placements. Reality shows, such as *Survivor*, which score high in ratings with the college demographic, are full of brand promotion executions. To further the brand relationship with students, marketers are also active in cyberspace through interactive websites, emails, and instant messaging. Specialty magazines target the college market, and many advertisers buy space in them hoping to gain exposure to the college market. Companies such as MarketSource have focused on providing full IMC solutions to attract the college-age population. SMC Marketplace Watch 4-1 gives an example of a very focused media approach to the market developed by recent college graduates.

Consider a marketing program that is centered on campus movie cross-promotion events. Marketers could place several movie trailers to run before the movies are shown. Corporate sponsors of these trailers would then promote the movies in campus newspapers and hand out literature and samples at the campus theater. However, at times, marketers have not always been as successful as they could be in the college student market due to a number of problems related to integration. In the past, for example, different promotional materials were made with different slogans and often contradictory messages. Some messages appeared to emphasize certain product benefits, while other messages emphasized other benefits. Some promotional materials had trademarks and logos, while others did not. No attempt had been made to set concrete objectives and measure performance. Tactical problems were rampant. For example, visiting high school students snapped up free samples distributed in the dorms. Posters promoting a specific event were not put up. Advertisements were run

SMC Marketplace Watch 4-1

New National Magazine Targets College Students

The college market spends over $200 billion per year. As a consequence, this market is extremely lucrative for marketers who can figure out how to tap into it. Campus Connections, a company launched by three recent college graduates—Christian Thornburg, Cristian Stenstrom, and Heather Tillett—believe they have created a great way to access that market through the development of a new marketing communications venue. Thornburg relates his experiences while a student at Notre Dame as the genesis of the idea. "Marrying the concept of a cohesive magazine with content specifically pertinent to college students inspired us to create *GenZ Magazine*." Stenstrom says, "We believe we have found the answer and, based on the outstanding response to our first issue, advertisers seem to think so too."

GenZ Magazine was launched in 2004 with an issue and a website. Initially heading out to one hundred campuses, *GenZ Magazine* positioned itself as the first magazine to be circulated exclusively through the use of pre-insertions into college bookstore bags. By doing so, they drove circulation to one million copies in the fall of 2004, and hoped to keep on growing with the strategy.

GenZ tries to blend a number of features focused on the college and university setting by delivering content specific to that setting. That content runs the gamut from a lot of "how-to" practical information kinds of things to advice on careers, travel tips, and even on such matters as politics. *GenZ* gets published twice an academic year at the start of the semester cycle. The recently graduated entrepreneurs now have an exclusive deal with the National Association of College Stores (NACS) and also have hooked up with another company that focuses on the college market, Follett Corporation (http://www.follett.com) to increase circulation in the future.

Source: Adapted from http://www.writenews.com/2004/082704_genz_magazine.htm.

in the campus paper after the target event had already taken place. Samples distributed at bookstores were not effective because the store employees were too busy to enforce the company's policy requiring students to sign a log sheet and show a school ID. Promotion materials that were supposed to go into mailboxes were not distributed. The people distributing these would stick a big pile next to the mailboxes, come back a couple of days later, and throw away whatever had not been picked up.[1] While these problems may seem to be ones that are unique to the college environment, they are not. It is not uncommon to encounter these in almost any campaign promoting all kinds of products in all kinds of markets. Often these problems can be traced directly to a lack of integration on the part of the marketer. The elements of any marketing communications program have to be managed in such a way to achieve corporate and marketing objectives. The management process requires that the elements be selected in ways to achieve the marketing objectives (which in turn should be instrumental in achieving corporate objectives). Each element of the marketing communications mix has to be driven by specific and explicit objectives that have to be monitored over time to ensure continuous progress. The objectives pertaining to each element of the marketing communications mix have to be consistent with the strategies and tactics associated with that element.

Implementing these strategies and tactics requires resources, and these resources have to be effectively budgeted. A process of control has to be in place to identify problem areas and implement immediate corrective action. These are all issues of integration, which is the focus of this book. This chapter introduces you to a systems model of marketing communications. The systems model shows how the entire process of marketing communications can be planned to ensure strategic integration. All marketing communications processes are structured hierarchically: at the top, processes are related to the corporate level; next, the marketing department level; then the marketing communications level; and, finally, each element of the marketing communications mix. In addition, specific objectives and subordinate processes can be identified as a direct function of a given process at any hierarchical level. The model shows that system integration can be effectively achieved by allocating adequate resources for the implementation of the process elements within a given hierarchical level, monitoring performance against the stated objectives, exerting continuous control, and analyzing and planning.

4-2 The Systems Model of Integrated Marketing Communications

The systems model forms the theoretical framework organizing topics in this book and shows how these topics are integrated into a "whole." The model posits that all organizational processes are structured hierarchically. Specific objectives and subordinate processes are identified as a direct function of a given process at any hierarchical level. Thus, marketing communications planning can be described in terms of a process hierarchy involving at least four levels: corporate, marketing, marketing communications, and within each element of the marketing communications mix (advertising, public relations, direct marketing, sales promotions, reseller support, and word-of-mouth communications). Within each level of this process hierarchy, the marketing communications manager selects a strategy from a pool of optional strategies. The selected strategy at a given hierarchical level guides the manager to articulate quantitative objectives consistent with that strategy. Similarly, the marketing communications manager selects a strategic mix (subordinate processes) that is designed to meet the goal of the selected strategy (i.e., its objectives). **Integration** can be achieved by building and reinforcing links among the system's components within each level of the process hierarchy (see Figure 4-1).

4-3 Strategy → Objectives → Tactics

Let us recap from the previous chapter for a moment. A systems model is developed here for the specific purpose of integrating the various elements of the marketing communications mix. The model asserts that any organizational process can be viewed as a hierarchy of processes. Thus, organizational tasks can be viewed as involving a set of processes organized hierarchically. At any given level of the process hierarchy, there is a mix of process elements. Remember, to implement a strategy, the strategy becomes a goal, which is achieved through objectives. Thus, objectives are nothing more than quantitative goal states that reflect a strategy. Objectives guide the formulation and the implementation of tactics. This perspective may be somewhat confusing to someone who has been taught in a nonintegrated manner. Those approaches tend to follow the traditional objective → strategy → tactic model for each and every level independent of the higher or lower level of a business entity. Conceptually, the only difference here is that the systems approach integrates *throughout* a system. Consequently, calling the element a strategy or objective is a function related to the particular level of the entire system from which the decision maker is viewing the process.

Also, in this systems model, the selection of one or more subordinate process elements (elements of a strategic mix) is directly influenced by the selection of the corresponding superordinate process (strategy). Correspondingly, the selection of a specific strategy (main process at any given hierarchical level) is influenced by the implicit or explicit selection of the strategic mix (process elements). That is, the process hierarchy is designed using both top-down and bottom-up approaches. It does not matter which comes first—a given process (strategy) or its elements (strategic mix). The idea is that planning entails the selection of hierarchical processes that create **means-end chains** and that subordinate processes (means) are selected in such a way to achieve the goals of a superordinate process (end) at any level of the process hierarchy, and vice versa.

integration The state of combination or the process of combining into completeness and harmony. It is one of the hallmarks of an on-demand business, and one of the four characteristics of the on-demand operating environment.

means-end chains Conceptual frameworks for advertising strategy that are used to link message elements to consumers' personal values. The standard linkages will move from the attributes presented to benefits sought by the consumer, which are then leveraged to impact personal values of the individual.

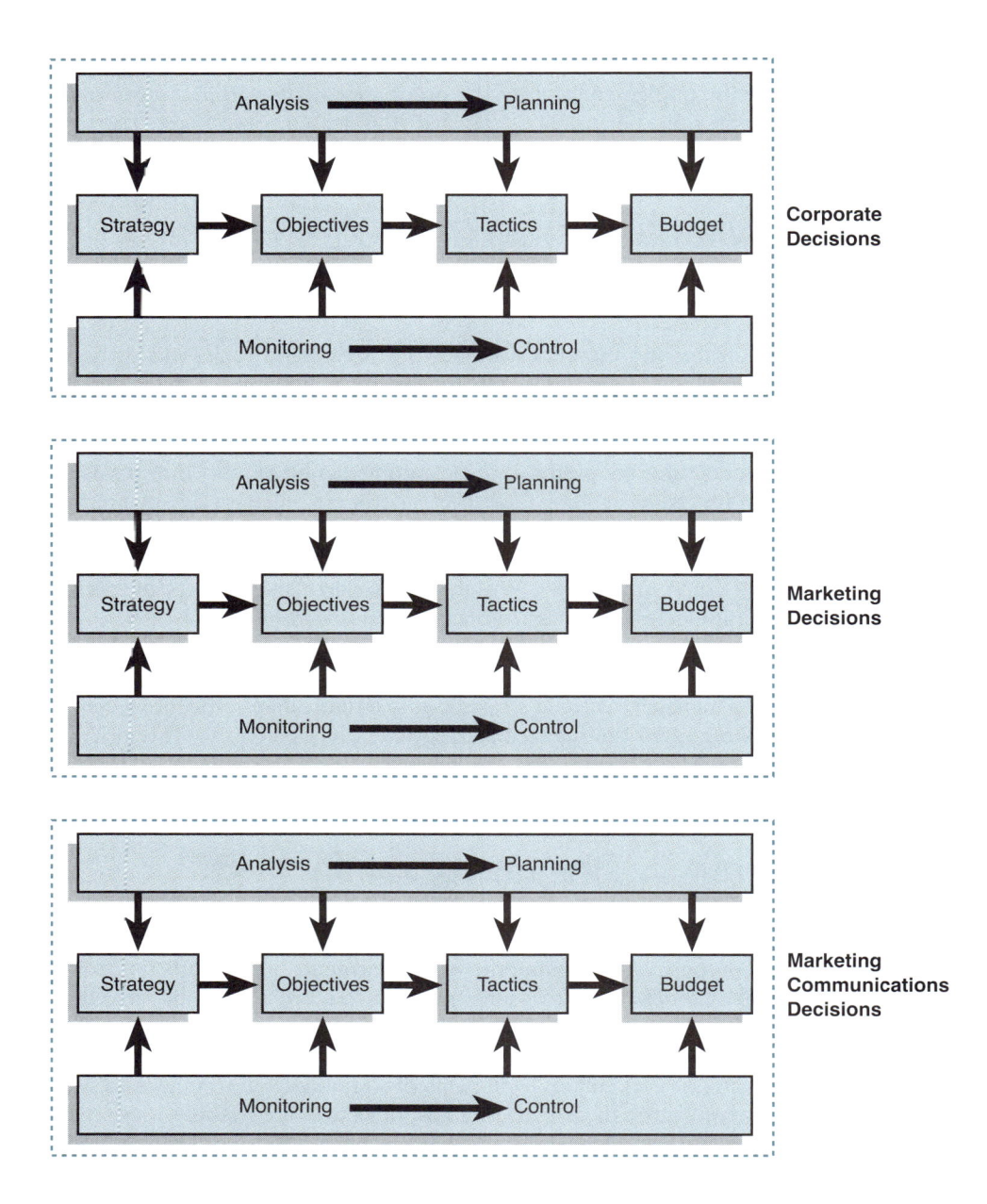

Figure 4-1
The Marketing Communications Systems at Large

Applying the process hierarchy to marketing communications, the marketing communications manager has to, first and foremost, identify all superordinate processes of marketing communications. There are two types of superordinate processes in marketing communications. These are processes related to the corporate level and, next in line, processes related to the marketing level (see Figure 4-1). Thus, at the corporate level, a given corporate strategy is implemented through a corporate mix (process elements at that level). The elements of the corporate mix may be viewed as organizational functions related to research and development (R&D), engineering, manufacturing, finance, accounting, personnel, and marketing. More specifically, the traditional corporate strategies that managers typically choose from include grow, maintain position, harvest, innovate, and divest. These corporate-level strategies are popular and commonly used. A corporate strategy is implemented through the corporate mix. The corporate mix here is viewed as involving the traditional functional units of an organization (R&D, engineering, manufacturing, marketing, accounting, finance, employee relations, insurance, legal, etc.). Thus, a corporate strategy tends to configure the corporate mix in such a way that certain elements of the corporate mix are emphasized. For example, a **growth strategy** dictates that emphasis be placed on marketing because marketing most effectively communicates the product's benefits to new consumers in new markets.[2] In contrast, an **innovation strategy** places more emphasis on the working dynamics of R&D and engineering, a **divestment strategy** places the emphasis on the finance element of the corporate mix, and so on.

The implementation of any corporate strategy necessitates the articulation of specific objectives. These objectives guide the formulation of the selected corporate strategy. For example, a growth strategy is usually articulated in terms of increases in sales and market share and is stated as corporate objectives. A maintain-position strategy is typically articulated in terms of maintenance of sales and market share. A **harvest strategy,** on the other hand, is typically expressed as maximization of profit. An innovation strategy aims for a certain level of sales. Finally, a divestment strategy typically calls for increases in cash flow.

The model acknowledges four typical marketing strategies. These are *strategic product focus, strategic price focus, strategic place focus,* and *strategic prospects focus.* Each of these strategies is described in terms of several positioning approaches. For example, the strategic product focus can be accomplished through positioning by product class, product attribute, intangible factor, competitors, and country of origin. The strategic price focus can be accomplished through positioning by relative price and positioning by low price. The strategic place focus can be accomplished by positioning through brand-distributor tie-in, distributor location, and distributor serviceability. Finally, strategic prospects focus is operationalized through positioning by celebrity/spokesperson, lifestyle/personality, customer benefits, user/customer image, and use/application. Of course the implementation of any of the aforementioned marketing strategies is predicated on the notion that the market is already segmented and a specific consumer segment is targeted.

Any of the aforementioned marketing strategies is in turn implemented through the marketing mix (product, price, distribution, and marketing communications). Also, just as each corporate strategy entails a different configuration of the corporate mix, similarly each marketing strategy entails a different configuration of the marketing mix. For example, positioning by product attribute is a marketing strategy that is effectively carried out through a host of product and marketing communications decisions, while positioning by relative price places more emphasis on the price and promotion elements of the marketing mix than other elements.

To carry out any marketing strategy through implementation of the marketing mix, the marketing communications manager has to identify the objectives that reflect the marketing strategy. For example, if a strategic product focus is selected and operationalized in terms of positioning by product attribute, then the objective is to establish a **brand association** with an important product attribute. Thus, marketing objectives are a direct function of the marketing strategy and its operationalization in terms of positioning.

With respect to marketing communications strategies and tactics, the model posits that the marketing communications manager usually has at least four strategic options. These are traditionally expressed as informative (thinker), affective (feeler), habit formation (doer), and self-satisfaction (reactor). These strategies are well known in advertising but can be easily applied to all forms of marketing communications. The **informative (thinker) strategy** is typically applied in relation to products that are highly involving and are of the thinking type. For thinking-type products, messages about the product are usually processed semantically, cognitively, or "rationally" (left-brain processing). Thus, marketing communications programs for this strategy focus on **brand awareness** and learning. That is, the objective here is to reach as many consumers as possible to create brand awareness and brand associations or knowledge. The **affective (feeler) strategy** commonly applies to high-involvement products of the "feeling" type. This strategy is typically expressed in terms of desired increases in **brand preference,** attitude, or liking. The

growth strategy A corporate strategy that guides the corporate executive to set corporate objectives in terms of increases in sales and market share. The aim here is to expand the market by going after new prospects and/or encouraging customers to purchase more.

innovation strategy A corporate strategy that guides the corporate executive to set corporate objectives in terms of increases in sales. The aim here is to develop a new product to increase sales.

divestment strategy A corporate strategy that guides the corporate executive to set corporate objectives in terms of cash flow. The focus here is to generate needed cash flow by selling off the firm's least prosperous organizational entities.

harvest strategy A corporate strategy that guides the corporate executive to set corporate objectives in terms of maximizing profit. The intent here is to stop investing and making improvements and thus reduce costs of doing business. Therefore, profit maximization can be achieved through cost reduction.

brand association A marketing goal. The term is used interchangeably with terms such as *brand equity, brand image,* and *brand knowledge.* It describes a desirable situation in which target consumers associate the brand with desirable features, events, and/or people.

informative (thinker) strategy A marketing communications strategy that guides the marketing communications manager to provide target consumers with information about the firm's brand—that is, to educate consumers about the product costs and/or benefits.

brand awareness (see p. 77) A marketing communications goal. It describes a situation in which target consumers recognize or recall the brand name as related to a product category.

affective (feeler) strategy (see p. 77) A marketing communications strategy that guides the marketing communications manager to elicit an affective response, a feeling that helps build a positive attitude toward the firm's brand. The focus here is on feelings, much more so than learning or inducing purchase.

brand preference (see p. 77) A marketing communications goal. It describes a desirable situation in which target consumers recognize the firm's brand as preferable to competitor brands.

habit-formation (doer) strategy A marketing communications strategy that guides the marketing communications manager to induce purchase or an overt behavioral response. The focus here is on inducing action.

brand trial A marketing communications goal. It describes a desirable situation in which target consumers have psychologically committed themselves to trying the firm's brand.

brand purchase A marketing communications goal. It describes a desirable situation in which target consumers have actually purchased the firm's brand.

self-satisfaction (reactor) strategy A marketing communications strategy that guides the marketing communications manager to induce purchase. That is, the focus here is on inducing action, which in turn sparks certain positive feelings for the brand.

habit-formation (doer) strategy applies to low-involvement products that are of the "thinking" type. The objectives are usually stated in terms of **brand trial** or **brand purchase** and brand learning. Finally, the **self-satisfaction (reactor) strategy** typically applies to low-involvement products that are of the "feeling" type. The objectives are articulated in terms of brand trial or purchase and attitude.

The implementation of any marketing communications strategy is done through the marketing communications mix—advertising, sales promotion, reseller support, direct marketing, public relations, and word-of-mouth communications. Also, just as corporate and marketing strategies dictate the configurations of the corporate and marketing mix, respectively, marketing communications strategy guides the marketing manager to work with certain elements of the communications mix and not others. For example, the informative (thinker) strategy can be effectively implemented through print advertising, certain forms of public relations (such as the press release), certain forms of reseller support programs (such as trade shows), and word-of-mouth communications (such as the use of referrals). A self-satisfaction (reactor) strategy can be effectively implemented through outdoor advertising, sales promotion (such as the use of premiums and contests and sweepstakes), and direct marketing (such as selling parties and teleshopping).

4-4 Budgeting

Allocating resources to the elements of the strategic mix is, in essence, a budgeting decision. Such decisions, to begin with, need to be based on solid market information regarding the target market of interest. As SMC Marketplace Watch 4-2 reveals, data on the market's behavior and use of information sources can help direct resources where they are most effective given their strategy. The manager must decide what resources are needed to implement the selected strategy and its respective strategic mix. For example, given the decision to advertise the product through Internet advertising, the marketing communications manager determines the amount of money needed to launch an Internet advertising campaign to achieve the goal of the marketing communications strategy, possibly to achieve a certain level of knowledge about the benefits of a brand. This method is referred to as the **buildup approach** commonly used in advertising (sometimes also referred to as the *objective-task method*). The buildup method can be used effectively to find out the costs of the marketing communications programs needed to achieve the marketing communications objectives. Then, the manager sums up the total costs related to the implementation of these subordinate tasks to derive the required **budget.** Of course, this method of allocating marketing communications resources is predicated upon the assumption that each task or tactic is effectively designed to meet higher-order objectives.

4-5 Setting Objectives

Setting objectives is an organizational task involving three key processes: (1) identification of one or more objective dimensions, (2) identification of the measures used to gauge outcomes related to each objective, and (3) identification of the desired level and time frame associated with each objective dimension. Since this is an introduction to the model, we will discuss how marketing communications managers go about identifying objective dimensions that reflect the selected strategies. The other remaining processes will be discussed in some detail in the following chapters.

The marketing communications manager tries to select appropriate objectives related to each strategy at the three hierarchical levels (corporate, marketing, and

SMC Marketplace Watch 4-2

Budget Allocation and Monitoring

A study by comScore Networks showed that Internet yellow pages (IYP) drew customers much more ready to buy and spend more money than search engines like Google and Yahoo! local-search services. The survey showed that consumers who used online yellow pages directories to locate retailers in their local area only did five searches before purchase, while those on Google and Yahoo! did eight. This data can be interpreted to mean that yellow page consumers were nearer to the actual transaction. Most of the major search engines like Google, Yahoo!, MSN, America Online, and AskJeeves upgraded local-search systems to target in on the local markets all across the United States. These upgrades have really heated up the competition for local-market consumers.

Head-to-head comparisons yield pros and cons to both search engines and the yellow pages. Search engines offer a lot of new technology like mapping routes to retail businesses. The consumer perceptions of Google and others lead them to think of those engines as the way to "search for anything" on the Internet. The yellow pages, though, have a long history of being the "go to" place for locating retail for consumers, and they have a sales force familiar with the local retail market to back it up. For a business that has routinely bought advertisements in the yellow pages every year, going to buy that advertisement online as well may not be a difficult readjustment in thinking and spending.

The survey data showed that online, IYP consumers spent on average between 5 percent and 17 percent more than they did on the search engines in the product category of the search. These IYP users also were more likely to visit the actual store, and they spent between 13 percent and 17 percent more there. Some suggestions gleaned from the data are that advertisements in the online yellow pages may want to focus on facilitating the transaction at the store by using such tactical things as special promotions and coupons. Since the people are closer to the sale point, they may just need a little push to get them to complete the sale.

Where the online search engines of Google and Yahoo! performed best were for those searches that are considered by consumers to have more of an online presence to them. The consumers who were using the local-search engines were more likely to visit entertainment and straight information sites, like community and gaming sites. Kids and teen sites also showed higher access possibly due to a higher interaction with the web than with traditional yellow pages by the younger user.

The data were derived from a market research firm hired by the Yellow Pages Association, but research was done independently of the association. The data were gathered in 2004 from the association's panel of 1.5 million consumers.

SMC QuickLink
YellowPages.com
http://www.yellowpages.com/Index.aspx

Source: Adapted from Kris Oser, "Online Yellow Pages Users Buy Quicker and Spend More," *Advertising Age,* April 25, 2005, http://adage.com/news.cms?newsId=44859 (accessed April 26, 2005).

---

marketing communications). The selected objective dimensions have to reflect the essence of the selected strategies. Remember that the *corporate* strategies are: grow, maintain position, harvest, innovate, and divest. The growth strategy usually entails the use of sales and market share objectives. That is, the marketing communications manager may translate the corporate vision of growth in a certain market into a marked increase in sales and market share in the specified market. Similarly, the corporate vision of maintaining position may translate into maintenance of current levels of sales and market share. In contrast, a harvest strategy may entail different objective dimensions altogether. The appropriate objective dimension for a harvest strategy is profit. Here the objective is to increase or maximize profit, not necessarily through increases in sales and market share. A harvest strategy usually signals the manager to be cost-efficient and to generate profit through cost reductions. The objective dimension for an innovation strategy is only sales. New products that are launched may not have competitors; therefore, market share is not an appropriate objective. Profit is also not an objective because new products are expected to be in the red for some time. Finally, the divestment strategy entails a cash flow objective.

buildup approach (see p. 78) A method of building up the expenditure levels of various tasks to help establish an advertising budget.

budget (see p. 78) The amount of monetary resources allocated to implement certain tactics (or a course of action).

Most firms divest strategic business units (SBUs) that are continuously losing sales, market share, and profit. The goal in divestment is to increase cash flow.

At the *marketing level*, objectives are selected in direct correspondence with the selected positioning strategy. All objectives at this level relate to brand equity (i.e., brand associations). For example, positioning by product attribute entails creating or reinforcing a brand association with an important product attribute (usually an attribute that consumers consider when making decisions); positioning by customer benefit entails creating or reinforcing a brand association with an important customer benefit (usually a benefit that is an important criterion in the consumer purchase decision); and so on.

At the *marketing communications level*, objectives are selected as a direct function of marketing communications strategies—informative (thinker), affective (feeler), habit formation (doer), and self-satisfaction (reactor). Based on these strategies, marketing communications objectives are typically articulated in terms of brand awareness, learning, attitude (or liking), trial (or purchase), and repeat purchase over an extended time frame. The *informative* (*thinker*) strategy entails a *learn* → *feel* → *do* sequence. That is, brand awareness and learning objectives are considered the most important in the initial phase of the campaign. Brand attitude is considered the most important objective in the second phase of the campaign, while brand trial or purchase is considered the most important in the last phase of the campaign. The *affective* (*feeler*) strategy entails a *feel* → *learn* → *do* sequence. That is, the initial phase of the marketing communications campaign should emphasize establishing brand liking. The second phase should emphasize brand associations, while the last phase of the campaign should emphasize brand trial and purchase. The *habit-formation* (*doer*) strategy reflects a *do* → *learn* → *feel* sequence. That is, the initial phase of the campaign should attempt to induce target consumers to buy the product on a trial basis. The second phase of the campaign tries to educate consumers about the product benefits—brand associations—while the third phase of the campaign concentrates on establishing good feelings about the product—brand liking. Finally, the *self-satisfaction* (*reactor*) strategy entails a *do* → *feel* → *learn* sequence. That is, the initial phase of the campaign should emphasize brand trial and purchase. The second phase of the campaign focuses on establishing good feelings toward the brand, while the third phase concentrates on brand learning.

For example, a communications campaign of a national pizza restaurant called Roni's has pizza places on college campuses throughout the United States. The marketing communications manager targets freshman students by directing messages that speak to the freshman students at the beginning of every school year, changing the nature of the message in the middle part of the school year and changing again during the last part of the school year. The idea is to guide freshman students through a sequence of psychological processing (any sequence such as *learn* → *feel* → *do*, *feel* → *learn* → *do*, *do* → *learn* → *feel*, or *do* → *feel* → *learn*). Doing so will ensure that these students will be able to learn about the product benefits, establish good feelings for it, and try it at least once. A freshman student having learned about the pizza, established good feelings about the pizza, and tried it at least once is likely to buy it repeatedly (*repeat*) during the next 3 years in college. The questions then are: What marketing communications strategy is most appropriate for Roni's Pizza? and How does the marketing communications manager set objectives varying in time? Table 4-1 shows examples of marketing communications objectives that reflect the four different strategies.

Note from Table 4-1 how the desired level of each communications objective changes as a direct function of the marketing communications strategy. If the manager chooses an informative (thinker) strategy, this leads the manager to initiate the campaign using educational messages. Thus, during the first 3 months of the academic year, Roni's marketing communications manager may expect that 80 percent of the freshman students should learn about the benefits of Roni's Pizza, 20 percent should be able to form a positive attitude toward Roni's Pizza, and 10 percent

TABLE 4-1 Marketing Communications Objectives as a Direct Function of Marketing Communications Strategy

Marketing Communications Strategy	Brand Learning (Learn)	Brand Liking (Feel)	Brand Purchase (Do)
Informative (Thinker) Strategy (Learn → feel → do)			
First 3 months	80%	20%	10%
Second 3 months	90%	50%	20%
Third 3 months	95%	60%	50%
Affective (Feeler) Strategy (Feel → learn → do)			
First 3 months	20%	80%	10%
Second 3 months	50%	90%	20%
Third 3 months	60%	95%	50%
Habit-Formation (Doer) Strategy (Do → learn → feel)			
First 3 months	20%	10%	80%
Second 3 months	50%	20%	90%
Third 3 months	60%	50%	95%
Self-Satisfaction (Reactor) Strategy (Do → feel → learn)			
First 3 months	10%	20%	80%
Second 3 months	20%	50%	90%
Third 3 months	50%	60%	95%

Note: The first 3, second 3, and third 3 months refer to a 9-month marketing communications campaign. The percentages in the table refer to quantitative goals. For example, if the marketing communications manager has decided to use an informative (thinker) strategy, then the first 3 months of the campaign should strive to establish awareness and learning in the minds of 80 percent of the target market, establish positive feelings toward the brand in 20 percent of the target market, and entice 10 percent of the target market to purchase the brand on a trial basis.

should have tried it. Note that the 80 percent brand learning objective is a goal that reflects the importance placed on that goal compared to brand liking and brand purchase. The next 3 months, around 10 percent *more* of the freshman students are expected to be educated about Roni's Pizza (to a total of 90 percent); but note that the emphasis is now placed on the second component of the hierarchy of effects—the *feel* component. Here the goal is established at 50 percent. The underlying assumption is that consumers are now ready to establish an attitude toward Roni's Pizza, after being educated about its benefits the first 3 months of the academic year. Thus, the nature of the message changes in tone, from that of cognitive to affective. This shift underscores the notion that brand attitude develops after brand learning (*learn → feel*). The third 3 months of the campaign focuses on brand purchase. Here the goal is established at 50 percent, that is, 50 percent of the freshman students should have tried Roni's Pizza at least once. The use of a coupon similar to that in Exhibit 4-1 may be the last piece of the plan to achieve that level of trial. Again, this reflects the notion that consumers are likely to purchase the product after feeling good about it (*feel → do*). Note how objectives pertaining to brand learning, liking, and purchase dramatically change with other marketing communications strategies—the affective (feeler) strategy, the habit-formation (doer) strategy, and the self-satisfaction (reactor) strategy. The challenge here is to identify the appropriate objectives that are consistent with the selected strategy and its strategic mix. Therefore, the point to remember is: *Select appropriate objectives that closely match the selected strategy and its strategic mix.*

Exhibit 4-1

Domino's Pizza

This is an example of an advertisement that includes coupons to facilitate purchase behavior.

Source: © Used by permission of Domino's Pizza LLC.

4-6 Monitoring and Control

The control function involves the use of a feedback mechanism. A feedback mechanism generates a stress signal when a specific measured outcome is significantly below the stated objective. Negative feedback can occur at the corporate level, the marketing level, and/or the marketing communications level. Negative deviations observed at any hierarchical level necessitate corrective action. Corrective action may take the form of changing the strategy and/or tactics, changing the budget, and/or changing the stated objectives.

For example, a communications objective may be a 50 percent increase in brand awareness as measured by a brand-recognition method 6 months from the launch of the campaign. After 6 months, the marketing communications manager assesses the outcome using the designated method and finds out that brand awareness only inched up 10 percent. That is, a negative deviation of forty points from the goal was detected. Significant negative deviations "raise red flags" and motivate the manager to make adjustments. These adjustments may involve one or more of the following:

1. *Change the strategy and corresponding tactics.* For example, through negative feedback, the marketing communications manager realizes that perhaps the informative (thinker) strategy is not the best strategy; perhaps an affective (feeler) strategy may have been more effective. Thus, based on feedback, the marketing communications manager develops a new communications campaign that is consistent with an affective (feeler) strategy.

2. *Change the budget.* For example, through negative feedback, the marketing communications manager may realize that the amount of money budgeted to implement the strategic mix of the informative (thinker) strategy is not adequate; more money is needed.

3. *Change the objective.* For example, expecting a 50 percent increase in brand awareness may not be realistic, perhaps because the marketing communications manager has failed to take into account certain conditions that are detrimental to the communications campaign. Thus, the marketing communications manager may lower the desired level to 40 percent in the planning of the next campaign.

Failure to meet objectives at either the marketing or the corporate level also requires the marketing communications manager to take similar corrective action, that is, change marketing or corporate strategy and/or tactics, change resource allocation at either the marketing or corporate level, and/or change the stated objectives to align them with actual performance.

4-7 Analysis and Planning

The marketing communications manager gathers much information, analyzes this information, and makes decisions at the corporate, marketing, and marketing communications level. These decisions involve strategy selection, setting objectives, and allocating resources. Analysis and planning facilitate decision making by providing the marketing manager with relevant information.

4-7a Strategy Selection

Remember that the marketing communications manager may be directly or indirectly involved with selecting (or changing) strategies at the corporate, marketing, and marketing communications levels. Also remember that all strategies and tactics are formulated in relation to a specific SBU. At the corporate level, optional strategies are to grow, maintain position, harvest, innovate, and divest. At the marketing level, optional strategies include differentiation, cost leadership, and focus. At the marketing communications level, optional strategies are informative (thinker), affective (feeler), habit formation (doer), and self-satisfaction (reactor). How does the marketing communications manager select the best strategy at each level? The marketing communications manager uses *situation analysis.*

At the corporate level, situation analysis is conducted through the use of a strategy-selection model such as the Boston Consulting Group (BCG) Matrix or the Multifactor Portfolio Matrix. These models direct the manager to gather specific information such as market share and market growth to assess the strengths and weaknesses of the SBU in question. For example, knowing that the SBU has a low market share but is in a high-growth market may lead the manager to select a growth strategy. This selection of corporate strategy is a direct logical deduction of the BCG Matrix.

At the marketing level, the selection of a positioning strategy is facilitated by situation analysis. The manager gathers information about a host of factors from customer **demographics** and **psychographics,** consumers' perception of the brand in relation to competitor brands, consumers' perception of the ideal product, and consumers' decision-making criteria, among others. There are many positioning models—for example, perceptual maps, means-end chains, **conjoint analysis,** and **multiattribute attitude models.** All of these models are designed to help marketing communications managers select an optimal positioning for the brand in question.

At the marketing communications level, the manager has to select one or more strategies from the following optional strategies: informative (thinker), affective (feeler), habit formation (doer), and self-satisfaction (reactor). In doing so, the manager gathers information about many factors that can facilitate strategy selection. Two factors commonly used in situation analysis are product involvement and product type (thinking versus feeling). For instance, if consumers are likely to be highly

demographics
The characteristics of people and population segments, especially when used to identify consumer markets. Popular demographics used in media planning and buying typically include gender, age, household income, education levels, household size, and ethnicity.

psychographics While demographics are objective characteristics of a population, psychographics are subjective lifestyle psychological characteristics that are based on consumers' responses to questions regarding their activities, interests, and opinions (AIO). These AIO variables are usually combined with demographics to get a more complete picture of consumer market segment types.

conjoint analysis
A multivariate statistical technique that is used by marketers to assess the consumer's relative importance and utility of levels of various attributes that a product/service possesses.

multiattribute attitude models Theoretical models used by marketers that view attitudes as being comprised of a number of attributes (dimensions) upon which consumers build up to a total attitude. The models generally include both attribute importance and a belief regarding whether or not the brand/product/service being evaluated possesses the specific attribute. The consumer's complete attitude is then a summation of the cross-products of these importance and belief components. An example would be
$A_1 = \sum B_i * E_i$
where A_1 is the attitude toward the brand, B_i is the belief regarding performance on the brand attribute being evaluated, and E_i is the importance to the consumer of the attribute being evaluated regarding the brand.

involved with a thinking-type product, they may be highly motivated to seek information and learn about the product and alternative brands. Thus, an informative (thinker) strategy may be best.

4-7b Setting Objectives

The marketing communications manager has to be involved directly or indirectly in the setting of corporate, marketing, and marketing communications objectives. Situation analysis is used to assist in this endeavor. At the corporate level, the objectives are usually stated in terms of sales, market share, profit, and cash flow. Each strategy has its own objective dimensions. Specifically, the goal of the growth strategy is usually articulated in terms of sales and market share: maintain position in terms of sales and market share, harvest to increase profits, innovate to stimulate sales, and divest to raise cash flow. The desired level of the selected objective dimension is determined by information obtained through situation analysis. The manager relies heavily on information regarding the firm's strengths and weaknesses and the competition to set a desired level of the selected objective. For example, the manager decides to increase sales by 50 percent within the next year because the product is undergoing a radical improvement (innovation strategy) and the competition is not expected to develop a comparable improvement.

At the marketing level, the manager may rely heavily on information regarding the norm of the brand association measure. Different methods used to measure brand association may have different norms. In addition to the norms of the measure, the manager may conduct a consumer survey to measure the level of brand association that has been achieved so far and to determine what can be achieved in light of the strengths and weaknesses of the firm's communications campaign and the competition. The final objective may be stated as, "Increase brand association with . . . by . . . percent in the next . . . months."

At the marketing communications level, the manager may rely heavily on the norm of the measure pertaining to the selected objective dimension (brand awareness, brand association, brand preference, brand trial or purchase, and repeat purchase). Again using a consumer survey, the manager may find out what the current level is in relation to the selected objective dimension (e.g., current level of brand awareness is 30 percent). Knowing something about the competition, the firm's skills and capabilities, and anticipated changes in the marketplace and within the firm, the manager may be in a position to set the desired level of the selected objective (e.g., "Increase brand awareness by . . . percent in the next . . . months.").

4-7c Budgeting

The marketing communications manager is likely to be directly or indirectly involved in determining the marketing communications budget. In setting the budget using the buildup method (objective-and-task method), the manager gathers much information about the cost of the various marketing communications tasks. As a matter of fact, every marketing communications manager has to have an information database about the costs of using every possible marketing communications tool, especially ones that are more frequently used than others, and the manager must update this information periodically. This is imperative if the manager uses the buildup method to determine the budget needed to accomplish various objectives.

The use of the buildup method in determining a prefinal marketing communications budget probably offers the most desirable method in the context of a systems approach. The final marketing communications budget is adjusted as a direct function of analysis and planning. That is, the manager takes into account factors such as the firm's past expenditures on marketing communications, past and anticipated expenditures by key competitors, average marketing communications expenditures by the industry at large, current and forecasted changes in the marketplace, and anticipated changes within the firm. Information about these factors should help the marketing communications manager adjust the budget. Thus, a final budget is developed.

4-8 Marketing Communications Integration

The true "integration" of marketing communications can only be achieved by ensuring strong links among the various decision processes made at the corporate, marketing, and marketing communications levels. Lack of integration may occur at any one or combination of system links. The links are between

- Strategy, objectives, and tactics
- Strategy-objectives-tactics and budget
- Monitoring and control
- Monitoring-control and strategy-objectives-tactics
- Monitoring-control and objectives
- Monitoring-control and budget
- Analysis and planning
- Analysis-planning and strategy-objectives-tactics
- Analysis-planning and objectives
- Analysis-planning and budget

An examination of one of these system links may help in seeing how integration works in terms of one of these links. Let us focus on the first link—the link between strategy, objectives, and tactics. Suppose the corporate strategy is determined to be "maintain position." This may be due to the realization that competition is becoming fierce and the best that the firm can do is to defend the current market position. However, the corporate objective is stated as "increase market share by 5 percent in the next quarter." This corporate objective is certainly not consistent with the corporate strategy of "maintain position," that is, there is no link between corporate strategy and corporate objective. To exacerbate the situation, suppose that the CEO instructed all departments to implement a drastic cost-cutting measure of 10 percent. Cost cutting is a corporate tactic that is supposed to have been guided by a "harvest" strategy, *not* a "maintain position" strategy. This is because a "harvest" strategy is most effective when the product is in the decline stages of its life cycle and the firm cannot make further improvements to the product to offset the competition. In this situation, cost cutting becomes important to maximize profitability before "the product is pronounced dead." Again, lack of consistency between strategy and tactics means *system breakdown*—or, specifically, a breakdown of an important link in the system. It is only when the system is considered as a whole that nonintegrative decisions can be identified and dealt with in a timely manner to head off such a system breakdown.

Summary

In this chapter, you are introduced to a systems model of marketing communications. An effective system, by definition, is an integrated system. System integration can be achieved through ensuring that the processes are integrated hierarchically, that the objectives of each process are consistent with the selected process elements, that resources are allocated in a manner consistent with the selected processes and their corresponding objectives, that performance is monitored against the objectives, and that control is continuously exerted throughout the process hierarchy. How the model works is described in a cursory fashion. Strategies and tactics are formulated at the corporate, marketing, and marketing communications levels. Objectives are set in direct relation to corporate, marketing, and marketing communications strategies. Determining how to allocate resources to achieve an effective marketing communications budget within the systems model is discussed. The use of an effective method—the buildup method of a budget—is introduced. Monitoring and control and how these are done at the three different levels of the system are briefly addressed. Finally, the kind of analysis and planning that marketing communications managers perform to select strategies, set objectives, and allocate resources at the three different levels are discussed.

Discussion Questions

Assume you are a marketer for a large copy and document reproduction business with a number of retail shops in a large metropolitan area and you realize that you need to launch an aggressive marketing communications campaign. You have recently bought all new digital printing equipment for your business. Digital printing is different from offset printing in that it can print directly from a computer disc and print only as many copies as needed—no more, no less. You also have a great deal of sunk cost in state-of-the-art offset printing equipment. Offset printing has the advantage of economies of scale. That is, the more copies one prints, the less cost per unit. In contrast, digital printing has the advantage of economies of scope. That is, for less cost, the consumer can print a few copies and make changes and print more copies based on the altered version. Offset printing costs too much to print a few copies and has little or no flexibility to customize orders.

1. What do you think is an effective marketing communications strategy for this copy and document reproduction business? Would you choose to work with an informative (thinker) strategy? An affective (feeler) strategy? A habit-formation (doer) strategy? Or a self-satisfaction (reactor) strategy? Why?

2. What do you think is an effective marketing strategy for this copy and document reproduction business? Select a marketing strategy and justify your selection.

3. What do you think is an effective corporate strategy for this copy and document reproduction shop? Would you select a growth strategy? A maintain position strategy? A harvest strategy? An innovation strategy? Or a divestment strategy? Why?

4. Tie the selected marketing communications strategy with the superordinate strategies at the marketing and corporate levels. Do the strategies fit together? If they do not fit, revise the strategies and make them fit.

5. Set corporate, marketing, and marketing communications objectives that are directly deduced from the strategies.

6. What kind of monitoring would you recommend for the copy and document reproduction business? What kind of corrective action would you recommend to exert control and improve marketing communications performance?

7. Think about analysis and planning. What information do you think you need to develop an effective strategy at the corporate level? At the marketing level? At the marketing communications level?

8. What information do you think you need to set effective objectives at the corporate level? At the marketing level? At the marketing communications level?

9. How would you go about determining a marketing communications budget for the copy and document reproduction business? What information do you think you need to determine an optimal budget?

Practice Quiz

Note: You can find the correct answers to these questions by taking the quiz and then submitting your answers in the Online Edition. The program will automatically score your submission. If you miss a question, the program will provide the correct answer, a rationale for the answer, and the section number in the chapter where the topic is discussed.

1. All marketing communications processes are structured hierarchically. Which of the following processes would one find at the top?
   a. processes related to the marketing department level
   b. processes related to the marketing communications level
   c. processes related to the corporate level
   d. processes related to each element of the marketing communications mix

2. Which model of IMC posits that all organizational processes are structured hierarchically?
   a. systems
   b. strategic
   c. cognitive
   d. analytical

3. In the systems model of IMC, what is a process at a superordinate level usually referred to as?
   a. action plan
   b. tactic
   c. strategy
   d. strategic mix

4. Which of the following is an incorrect observation?
   a. A tactic becomes an objective once we move down the hierarchy of processes and focus on that tactic.
   b. To implement a strategy, the strategy becomes a goal, which is achieved through objectives.
   c. Objectives are quantitative goal states that reflect a strategy.
   d. Objectives guide the formulation and the implementation of tactics.

5. Identify the corporate strategy that is typically expressed as maximization of profit.
   a. divestment
   b. harvest
   c. innovation
   d. maintain position

6. Which marketing communications strategy can be applied to low-involvement products that are of the "thinking" type?
   a. informative (thinker)
   b. self-satisfaction (reactor)
   c. affective (feeler)
   d. habit formation (doer)

7. Which of the following strategies can be effectively implemented through outdoor advertising, sales promotion (such as the use of premiums and contests and sweepstakes), and direct marketing?
   a. informative (thinker)
   b. self-satisfaction (reactor)
   c. affective (feeler)
   d. habit formation (doer)

8. Given the decision to advertise the product through Internet advertising, the marketing communications manager of a company determines the amount of money needed to launch an Internet advertising campaign to achieve the goal of the marketing communications strategy. Which approach is he or she using?
   a. plan-ahead strategy
   b. harvest strategy
   c. subjective-task method
   d. buildup approach

9. Which of the following strategies entails a *feel → learn → do* sequence?
   a. informative (thinker)
   b. self-satisfaction (reactor)
   c. affective (feeler)
   d. habit formation (doer)

10. What is conducted at the corporate level using a strategy selection model such as the Boston Consulting Group (BCG) Matrix or the Multifactor Portfolio Matrix?
    a. perceptual analysis
    b. situation analysis
    c. conjoint analysis
    d. investment analysis

Web Exercise

Yellow Pages versus Search Engines

You are the marketing communications director for a local restaurant. You would like a web presence that drives customers to visit your restaurant when they are looking for a good place to eat in your town. Using your town as a search point, go to http:www.google.com and then go to http://www.yellowpages.com/Index.aspx.

Conduct a search for the restaurant type of your choice. Which would be a better place to make sure of a good web presence? Conduct the same kind of search using the two different methods, but assume you are the marketing director for a local car dealership.

Suggested Readings

Belch, George E., and Michael A. Belch. 2001. *Advertising and promotion: An integrated marketing communications perspective.* Burr Ridge, IL: Irwin.

Kitchen, Phillip J., Don E. Schultz, IIchul Kim, Dongsub Han, and Tao Li. 2004. Will agencies ever "get" (or understand) IMC? *European Journal of Marketing* (Bradford, England) 38 (11/12): 14–17.

Kliatchko, Jerry. 2005. Towards a new definition of integrated marketing communications (IMC). *International Journal of Advertising* 24 (1): 7–34.

Kotler, Philip. 2002. *A framework for marketing management*, 2nd ed. Englewood Cliffs, NJ: Prentice Hall.

Park, C. W., and Gerald Zaltman. 1987. *Marketing management*. Hinsdale, IL: Dryden Press.

Percy, Larry, John R. Rossiter, and Richard Elliott. 2002. *Strategic advertising management*. Oxford, UK: Oxford University Press.

Schultz, Don E., and Beth Barnes. 1994. *Strategic advertising campaigns*, 4th ed. Chicago, IL: NTC/Contemporary Publishing Company.

———. 1999. *Strategic brand communication campaigns*, 5th ed. McGraw-Hill.

Schultz, Don E., Stanley I. Tannenbaum, and Robert F. Lauterborn. 1994. *Integrated marketing communications: Pulling it together and making it work*. Lincolnwood (Chicago), IL: NTC Business Books.

Thorson, Esther, and Jeri Moore, eds. 1996. *Integrated communication: Synergy of persuasive voices*. Mahwah, NJ: Erlbaum.

Wang, P., and L. Petrison. 1991. Integrated marketing communications and its potential effects on media planning. *Journal of Media Planning* (Fall): 11–17.

Weilbacher, William M. 2001. Point of view: Does advertising cause a "hierarchy of effects"? *Journal of Advertising Research* 41 (6): 19–26.

Notes

1. Cyndee Miller, "College Campaigns Get Low Scores," *Marketing News*, May 8, 1995, 1–2.
2. Note that our systems model starts out with a focus on a specific strategic business unit (SBU). Each firm can easily identify its strategic business units by developing a two-dimensional matrix in which all its products can be specified along one dimension and all markets specified along the other dimension. The starting point of the systems model is a specific SBU or a product/market unit. All decisions (corporate, marketing, and marketing communications) are then constrained to that SBU.

The Marketing Communications Portfolio

Part Two

5 Advertising

6 The Buzz: Public Relations, Word of Mouth, and More

7 Direct and Interactive Marketing

8 Personal Selling, Trade Promotions, and Consumer Promotions

Consider the relaunch of the MINI in the United States in 2002. First introduced in Europe in 1957 and imported to the United States from 1962 to 1967, the original Mini is somewhat of a legend in car circles. Known for its boxy look and small stature, the quirky little car never sold anywhere near as many units in the United States as its more successful and better known competitor, the Volkswagen Beetle. The car did, however, achieve "cult" status among some in the racing field when a high-performance version of the car, the Mini Cooper (named after John Cooper who created the racing version) came about in the early 1960s. Production continued for the non-USA market, producing millions of cars for the European (and global) marketplace. In 1994 BMW acquired the Rover Group, which included the Mini as one of its brands. In 1996 BMW announced its plans to launch a new MINI to take the place of the Mini, and in 1997 the concept car was previewed at the Frankfurt International Auto Show in Germany. The car received rave reviews. The stage was set for the MINI to reappear on the United States automotive landscape.

The management team was faced with a number of questions related to the way in which to proceed in introducing the MINI to the world. What marketing communications tools should BMW use to launch the new MINI into the marketplace, particularly in the United States? Tradition would say that you would rely heavily on the advertising component of the mix to build awareness of the new model. Automobile manufacturers had been doing that for decades, and new models from competing brands were pretty much following that time-honored practice.

BMW, however, had recently had success with the launch of their sports car, the Z3 roadster, by going against the norm and focusing on extensive use of "nontraditional" media. The Z3 roadster hooked up with James Bond in *Golden Eye* as a product placement in the film, had a launch party New York City's Central Park, had appearances on *The Tonight Show with Jay Leno,* was prominently displayed on the BMW website, and was sold in the Neiman Marcus Christmas catalog. While traditional media played a role, the Z3 launch created a great deal of demand based on its "buzz" that had been generated with the "nontraditional" elements of the marketing communications mix.[1] With the MINI launch, BMW would again "spin" the marketing communications mix in a nontraditional way and do it with even more flair.

The MINI would receive a great deal of public relations coverage in the press due to its unique heritage and stature. Automobile magazines provided a number of stories on the coming availability of this car that had been missing from the American landscape for years. Among road-racing enthusiasts, the buzz was underway. The car had also had its sights on the young adult market, which had generally shunned the traditional communications channels and viewed itself as edgy and in the possession of a whole lot of "attitude."

The introduction campaign designed by Crispin Porter & Bogusky generally shied away from the traditional and instead focused on the guerilla and buzz aspects of marketing communications. The campaign was designed to give the car its own personality and attitude.[2] In such an approach, the idea of selling cars seemed to some to be some sort of a secondary focus. MINIs were strapped on the backs of SUVs and driven around town. The MINI showed up at *The Tonight Show with Jay Leno* as well, and Jay Leno "smoked the tires" and took them for a spin in the street outside his studio. MINIs had a large web presence that allowed visitors to play MINI games, learn cool stuff, and be "on the edge." The car arrived at events, chic stores, and hotels but always the "right kind of place" to keep its 'tude intact. Outdoor oversized props, billboards, and magazines such as *Rolling Stone* also were used to reach the "right" market with the "right" feel. MINI Motoring Gear and its clothing line could be acquired at dealers (and on the web) along with a variety of promotions designed to drive dealer traffic. The video commercials of MINI could be found on the website and at dealers and in the movie theaters but, alas, not on the mass-market television.

SMC QuickLink
MiniUSA.com
http://www.miniusa.com

Where the Z3 had been a bit player in the *Golden Eye* movie, the MINI was the star in *The Italian Job* movie. The entire plot of the movie revolved around the use of the automobile in pulling off the heist. The driving scenes were tremendous displays of the performance capabilities of the MINI.

Bottom line? BMW made a conscious decision to limit imports in 2002 to 20,000 units.[3] The $25 million marketing buzz campaign could then be figured out to cost about $1,250 per unit. The long-term impact, however, is what is telling. In March of 2002, the car was available in the United States and there had been over 50,000 people who had registered on the MINI website for possible purchase. By the end of April, over 2,300 cars had been sold; in June that number was over 6,700 units; in December there was a 3-month to a year waiting list and a 20,000-unit backlog.

One could argue that this campaign, while nontraditional for the automobile industry, was quite successful. It showed that translating a good understanding of the marketplace into the appropriate mix of available marketing communications portfolio elements for the target market is crucial in the ultimate success of the product itself. Part Two of this text presents four short chapters that outline the elements that make up the marketing communications portfolio. The intent in this section is not to provide extended discussions concerning all the aspects of each of these portfolio elements; there are books written on the topics of each of these chapters that provide such in-depth examinations. Rather, our intent is to introduce (or revisit for those who have taken an introductory course in the topic) the elements and discuss their general nature and how they can be evaluated in terms of their contribution to the development and execution of an overall strategic marketing communications (SMC) campaign. To that end, the chapters are broken down into each of the types of the particular SMC element (e.g., *advertising* is broken down into eight lower-level types of advertising such as *television* and *radio*). The discussion in each chapter of each of these lower-order elements is generally laid out in a format that provides an examination of a particular medium's applications, measurement, and possible best cases. Each chapter concludes with a summary and conclusions.

Chapter Five examines all the different types of advertising that are available for use. Chapter Six presents what we like to call "the buzz elements." These are public relations, word of mouth, guerilla marketing, and a mix of supporting types of buzz generators. Chapter Seven puts the focus on direct and interactive types of elements. Finally, Chapter Eight explores the sales promotions, personal selling, and other reseller support elements. The framework for the development of the SMC campaign follows in Part Three of this book.

Notes

1. See Susan Fournier and Robert Dolan, "Launching the BMW Z3 Roadster," Harvard Business School Case 9-597-002, February 14, 1997, for a complete story of the Z3 launch.
2. Karl Greenberg, "Giving a Small Car Big 'Tude," *Brandweek* 43, 45 (2002): 31.
3. Jean Halliday, "Creating Max Buzz for the New BMW MINI," *Advertising Age* 73, 24 (2002):12.

Advertising

Chapter Five

Chapter Outline

5-1 **Introduction**
5-2 **Broadcast Media**
    5-2a Television
    5-2b Radio
5-3 **Print Media**
    5-3a Magazines
    5-3b Newspapers
5-4 **Out-of-Home Media**
    5-4a Outdoor
    5-4b In-Store/Point of Purchase
5-5 **Miscellaneous Advertising**
Summary
Discussion Questions
Practice Quiz
Web Exercise: Which Advertising Does the Job for You?
Additional QuickLinks
Suggested Readings
Notes

Key Terms

advertising (p. 93)
advocacy advertising (p. 93)
area of dominant influence (ADI) (p. 99)
average quarter-hour (AQH) audience (p. 102)
broadcasting (p. 97)
circulation (p. 105)
clutter (p. 98)
cost per rating point (CPRP) (p. 100)
cost per thousand (CPM) (p. 96)
cume or cumulative radio audience (p. 102)
daily effective circulation (DEC) (p. 110)
dayparts (p. 98)
designated market area (DMA) (p. 99)
effective net reach (p. 95)
effective reach (p. 95)
frequency (p. 95)
gross rating points (GRPs) (p. 96)
households using television (HUT) (p. 100)
narrowcasting (p. 99)
net reach (p. 95)
outdoor advertising (p. 109)
paid circulation (p. 108)
panels (p. 109)
point-of-purchase (POP) advertising (p. 111)
preferred position (p. 106)
rate base (p. 105)
rating point (p. 100)
reach (p. 94)
readership (p. 108)
recent reading (p. 105)
run of press (ROP) (p. 106)
share (p. 100)
sheets (p. 109)
showing (p. 110)
superstations (p. 99)
television households (TVHH) (p. 99)
through the book (p. 105)

Many a small thing has been made large by the right kind of advertising.

—Mark Twain (1835–1910), American writer

5-1 Introduction

Advertising is probably the best known of all the marketing communications portfolio components addressed in this section of the book, so it is appropriate to begin the discussion with advertising. It is a marketing communications tool that focuses on the mass media. That is, messages are placed in impersonal types of media such as television, radio, newspapers, and magazines, among others. Advertising is an excellent communications tool to generate the highest brand awareness possible. Advertising is by its very nature meant to influence individuals in a direction that is desirable for the advertiser. For that reason, it is often viewed with suspicion. It can also be one of the most difficult SMC elements to measure effectively. For this reason, in today's world of accountability regarding promotional spending, advertising has come under increasing scrutiny regarding its use.

This chapter provides an examination of the advertising component in the strategic marketing communications (SMC) portfolio, beginning with the nature of advertising. Each of the elements that make up the SMC advertising toolbox is then discussed in a summary manner regarding its value and appropriate uses. The chapter ends with a summary discussion that recaps the major aspects of this SMC tool. How this element can best be managed within the SMC framework is outlined in Part Three of this book in Chapter Eleven, "The Marketing Communications Level: Analysis and Planning for Marketing Communications Strategy and Tactics."

Let us start with a definition of *advertising*. **Advertising** is the placement [by an identified sponsor] of announcements and persuasive messages in time or space purchased in any of the mass media by business firms, nonprofit organizations, government agencies, and individuals who seek to inform and/or persuade members of a particular target market or audience about their products, services, organizations, or ideas.[1] Note that the definition focuses on a set of paid and mass-media communications between the marketing entity and the environment in which it operates. That marketing entity can be anything from the government to individuals like yourself, as well as anything (or group of people) in between those two anchor points. While the official AMA definition has dropped the "by an identified sponsor" line relating to the entity (reinserted in brackets in the definition), we believe it is still important to remember that dimension when using advertising. If the message is not from an identified sponsor, it becomes propaganda because the receiver cannot make a clear assessment as to the credibility of the source of that message. One may often see these types of "shadows" in advocacy types of advertising.

Advocacy advertising is a type of advertising placed by businesses and other organizations that is intended to communicate a viewpoint about a controversial topic relating to the social, political, or economic environment. Exhibit 5-1 shows an example. Such communications are also used at times when advertising sources feel that identity would be a detriment in an advocacy advertising type of campaign. For example, during the 2004 U.S. presidential election, attempts to disguise the true sponsorship of various attack advertisements and thus confuse source credibility

advertising One of the elements or tools of marketing communications for use in mass media, such as television, radio, newspaper, magazine, outdoor, transit, aerial, mobile billboards, specialty, directory, interactive, in-store, in-flight, movie theater, and videotape advertising.

advocacy advertising A type of advertising placed by businesses and other organizations that is intended to communicate a viewpoint about a controversial topic relating to the social, political, or economic environment.

Exhibit 5-1
Advocacy Advertisement for Voting

Source: Courtesy of Federal Voting Assistance Program, Department of Defense, Pentagon.

assessment of the message by the voters were made by political action committees (PACs) that were not directly connected to the given political party.

Since the domain of advertising relates to any mass media, the range of elements that need to be covered is somewhat overwhelming. It can become a laundry listing that goes on forever. The approach taken here is to examine the advertising elements under four broad categories: (1) broadcast media, (2) print media, (3) out-of-home media, and (4) miscellaneous media. In today's world, it is sometimes difficult to place an element in only one of the portfolios because everything is so integrated. For example, you will again see advocacy advertising, albeit briefly, when you read Chapter Six, "The Buzz: Public Relations, Word of Mouth, and More." What we do here is simply provide you with what is necessary for you to later consider which of the various elements has value in the SMC campaign that you put together. The portfolio of particular advertising tools available to the marketing communications manager is shown in Table 5-1. Subsequent sections provide a brief discussion on each of the subelements.

This chapter on advertising, the first of the SMC portfolio chapters, is a good place to introduce a few of the measurement concepts that are used to aid in the selection of portfolio elements that will be used in the SMC campaign. In particular, those that look at audience delivery in terms of levels and efficiency are (1) reach and frequency, (2) gross rating points, and (3) cost per thousand (CPM). A number of other specific measurement issues are tied to particular portfolio elements (that will be discussed in the context of each of them), but these particular measurement concepts are ones that are fairly universal in their application to all of mass media. The first two concepts (reach and frequency) are used extensively by marketing communications managers as a measure of the level of gross audience delivery of a given individual marketing communications element or an entire campaign. We see their use particularly when advertising is involved.

reach A percentage related to the amount of the audience who were exposed to the media vehicle.

Reach is usually defined as a percentage related to the amount of the audience who were exposed to the media vehicle. For example, a reach number of 25 percent for a single advertisement about athletic shoes placed on the Super Bowl that was directed at a target market of all male 18- to 34-year-olds would indicate that 25 per-

TABLE 5-1 The Advertising Media Universe

Broadcast Media
Television
Radio

Print Media
Magazine
Newspaper

Out-of-Home Media
Outdoor
In-store/point of purchase

Miscellaneous
Movie trailers, videotape, and DVD
Directory

---

cent of that target market was exposed to that advertisement when it was shown on the program. How effective it is an altogether different question—a question that is covered later in this book.

Frequency, on the other hand, is simply how many times an advertisement or campaign comes in contact with the target market. For example, if there were three advertisements placed in that Super Bowl broadcast, the frequency would be reported as 3. A total of three advertisements in three different magazines directed at the target market would also be a frequency of 3. Frequency is simply a gross contact count—again, regardless of actual effectiveness. As noted, these two measures are used extensively in trying to assess the impact of marketing communications programs. Determining which one is more important in decision making is a matter of which one the manager chooses. If a manager feels that the need for simple awareness to the largest number of target market members is the driving force for the campaign, then reach becomes the most important issue. If, however, the manager feels that a strongly held attitude concerning the brand needs to be changed, then it will be necessary to repeatedly expose the target market to the message. In that case, frequency becomes the driving force behind the campaign. Determining which level of reach or frequency must be achieved is dependent on the strategies by which the marketing communications planner is being guided.

You may also see the use of what is termed **effective reach,** which is tied to the level of frequency needed to achieve a given goal of exposure. This number is often set at 2 or 3, depending on the objectives of the campaign, as already discussed. That would then translate to "the percentage of the target market that was exposed to our message x times."

Net reach is one last reach measure that we touch on here concerning delivery by advertising. The application of net reach and its calculation are seen in Chapter Eleven. The net reach figure is the delivery of the number (usually expressed as a percentage) of the unduplicated target market that has been exposed to a communication as part of the campaign. While you may buy overlapping media that have good reach for the target market (i.e., you may buy a television advertisement that has a reach number of 50 percent for the target market *and* a magazine that has a reach of 60 percent for the same target market), you can never go over a net reach of 100 percent; so net reach is the percentage of the target market that sees the message at least once (people in this group may have seen the advertisement multiple times but are only counted once).

The logical extension is to **effective net reach,** which is that percentage of the target market that sees the message at least x times (where x is the effective frequency).

While both reach and frequency measurements can be used independently, they can also be used to estimate a gross measure of audience exposure to a campaign.

---

frequency How many times an advertisement or campaign comes in contact with the target market.

effective reach A level of reach that is tied to the level of frequencies needed to achieve a given goal of exposure.

net reach A measure commonly used by media planners to assess the effectiveness of a media schedule in terms of its maximum reach of a target market. It is computed by adding the percentages of reach of all media vehicles minus duplication among the vehicles. For example, a 90 percent net reach is the ability of a combination of media vehicles to reach 90 percent of the target market.

effective net reach A level of reach that is tied to the level of frequencies needed to achieve a given goal of exposure that is then assessed regarding nonduplication of audience. That is computed by adding the percentages of effective reach of all media vehicles minus duplication among the vehicles.

gross rating points (GRPs)
A gross measure can be estimated based on either a percentage of target market delivery or the number of individuals. The measure based on the percentage is called gross rating points. When multiplied together, reach (not effective or net reach) and frequency will yield the measure of gross rating points.

That gross measure can be estimated based on either a percentage of target market delivery or on the number of individuals. The measure based on the percentage is called **gross rating points (GRPs).** When multiplied together, standard reach (not effective or net reach) and frequency will yield the measure of gross rating points (GRPs). That formula is shown here.

Reach (expressed as a percentage of the target market) × Frequency (number of insertions) = Gross rating points (GRPs)

If you have two of the measures from the formula, you can always find the missing element by using this formula appropriately. For example, if you have a reach of 25 percent for your target market and a frequency of 2, then your GRP will be 50. If you change that to knowing the GRP is 100 and you have a reach of 50, then the frequency is found by dividing the GRP (100) by the reach (50), which yields a frequency number of 2.

Managers are always asking: Which is more important—reach or frequency? The classic answer here is: It depends! The importance of one over the other is a strategic issue. If there is a new product introduction with no awareness of the product and a strong latent demand for that product, then the answer is clearly, reach. If, however, there is a need to change a belief related to a product, say, from a negative feeling about an attribute (e.g., the product is dangerous), then frequency becomes much more important than reach. A few generalities about reach and frequency can be applied to help a manager to determine which is more important:

1. Other than the case with an evident strong latent demand, one exposure will probably not "do it" for the media choice.
2. A general "rule of thumb" for effective frequency is usually 3 for a brand purchase cycle of about 3 to 4 weeks.
3. Beyond an effective frequency level of about 3 or 4, continuing to increase frequency quickly creates a situation of diminishing returns on media expenditures.
4. The frequency effectiveness levels are pretty stable across a variety of media.
5. There is an interaction effect between creativity and effectiveness of media.

cost per thousand (CPM)
The cost of a given media, or media mix, in delivering one thousand individual impressions within the target market.

These measures relate to the level and magnitude of delivery by the media. The most commonly used efficiency measure related to advertising is the **cost per thousand (CPM)** measure (the *M* is from the Roman numeral for "one thousand"). The CPM measurement provides the manager with a quick and easy measure of the cost of a given media or media mix in delivering one thousand individual impressions within the target market. In other words, what does it cost me to "reach" one thousand members of my target market using this media? The calculation is most often used for print schedules but can be applied across mixed media environments. The calculation is fairly straightforward.

Cost per thousand (CPM) = (Cost of the media unit/audience delivery) × 1,000

For example, if a manager decided to buy a one-page advertisement for $100,000 in *Magazine X* that had an audience delivery (readership) of 1,000,000 people, the CPM for that buy would be $100; that is, for efficiency, the media buy cost the manager $100 to reach 1,000 people. The value of this measure becomes even more apparent when you use it in media comparisons. For example, if that same manager decided to buy a second advertisement in *Magazine Y* for $50,000 and the magazine had an audience delivery of 300,000 people, a quick calculation shows that the CPM for the media buy in *Magazine Y* is $166.67. From a straight efficiency comparison, *Magazine X* delivers more "bang for the buck." As with reach and frequency, however, it depends. The choice must also be considered within the context of the creative execution and other SMC elements. SMC Marketplace Watch 5-1 provides a look at using a myriad of different means to "reach the beach bunch."

SMC Marketplace Watch 5-1

Cool Connects with the Hot Beach Crowd

With the advent of summer, the media vehicles used to get to certain target markets can change significantly. All along the coastlines of the United States, alternative media choices are cranked up to connect with the sun and sea lovers. The good-natured assault on the markets' senses is being carried out through a variety of marketing communications that are themselves delivered by a diverse set of land-, sea-, and air-based vehicles.

From the air, we see banner-towing planes along beaches from coast to coast. One of the owners of an aerial advertising firm calls this air assault effective because "you have a 100 percent captive audience, often packed shoulder-to-shoulder in a prone position with not much else to do but notice low-flying airplanes dragging color billboards behind them." A single plane heading up and down the Jersey shore on a top summer holiday can get 550,000 impressions; in the Midwest, that may be 765,000 impressions of people visiting Lake Michigan; or there could be 1,275,000 people relaxing in southern California near Los Angeles.

From the sea, advertisements spread across sailboat sails pitch a variety of relevant products. As the vivid advertisements are displayed against the brilliant summer sky, the advertiser's message makes a visit to places where regular, more traditional billboards are often banned by local ordinances. Photosails Inc., working out of Fort Lauderdale, Florida, has had such clients as Tequiza, Bacardi, Cadillac, Volvo, and other large marketers. The company owns the boats and produces the sails, which are then paraded up and down the beaches by Photosails crews.

From the ground, promotion and event-marketing companies like Encompass Media and Grand Central Marketing lead the assault with beach campaigns. In the sand and on certain beaches' boardwalks, there are logo-laden beach umbrellas, beach chairs, towels, flip-flops, and other giveaways that promote marketers' brands. Marketers can manufacture flip-flops to have a product's logo imprinted on the soles so beachgoers can "spread the word as they wander across the sand."

Taking the spreading of the word to the next level, Beach 'n Billboard of New Jersey has a machine that can cross the beach every morning and imprint advertising messages on the sand. Such brands as Volvo, Snapple, and Skippy peanut butter have used the unique advertising approach. The imprints are part of Beach 'n Billboard's "Support-a-Beach" program and will generally last until about 1:00 P.M. on a typical beach day. To add a social responsibility dimension to each message, the company includes a message asking beach goers to not litter. Since being used, littering has gone down by 20 percent according to the president of the company.

Some beach premiums last longer than one day on the beach. Ellen Stone, director of marketing for Lifetime, said umbrellas promoting last year's new Lifetime shows *Missing* and *Wild Card* were still showing up at beaches one year later.

Segmentation is also used as these types of companies know where the teens will be, where the older consumers will be, and where any other potential subsegment of the sand and sea crowd will be. As one company spokesperson said, referring to their services, "We know whether to go to Jones Beach versus the Hamptons."

In support of these campaigns, marketers still will use the traditional media of radio and some local nighttime event marketing at nightspots around the beaches.

Source: Adapted from Anna Heinemann, "Unleashing the Ads of Summer: How Big Marketers Chase the Sunbathing Demographic," *Advertising Age,* June 20, 2005, Adage.com QwikFIND ID: AAQ65Z.

5-2 Broadcast Media

Broadcasting is a method of distributing television or radio signals by means of stations that broadcast (make public) signals over channels assigned to specific geographic areas. Broadcasting was the traditional (and only) way to deliver television and radio messages for many years. It was not until the advent of cable that the "airwaves" spilled over into a more "grounded" format of buried and overhead cables.

broadcasting A method of distributing television or radio signals by means of stations that broadcast (make public) signals over channels assigned to specific geographic areas.

5-2a Television

Television is available as broadcast (network and local), satellite, and cable. According to Nielsen Media Research, average household members in 2004 used their television a little over 8 hours per day. Television is very well suited to do certain things.

Characteristics

Television can provide very broad reach into the mass market (see "Strategic Marketing Communications Elements" on page 99). Due to the high reach, even though the actual cost of producing a television commercial and buying time may be high, overall it has a fairly low cost per exposure compared to other media. It does have some downsides to it as well. In general, television is not an overly focused medium. That is, an advertiser using television may have "wasted" exposure outside of a desired target market. **Clutter** is a severe problem for television commercials. In 2004 it is estimated that there were over 67 billion advertisements that hit the airwaves as network, spot, syndication, or cable commercials.[2] Television commercials also tend to have a short message life. Standard units for the medium are *15-second*, *30-second*, and *60-second* spots. About 38 percent and 56 percent of the commercials on television are 15- and 30-second spots, respectively.

The medium has the ability to provide the impact of sight, action, motion, and sound. For certain types of products, this can be highly advantageous in message presentation. It can also provide a certain amount of prestige ("As seen on TV"). Production costs can make the use of television commercials prohibitively expensive. If a focused message to a limited target market is necessary, television may not be the best selection. As with anything in marketing communications, though, the interactions between creative, the target market, and the message components will decide if television is appropriate.

Television is generally broken up into time-scheduling segments for a given day. These time ranges for the day are referred to as **dayparts.** Obviously, a manager would expect that there would most likely be different audiences associated with each of the dayparts. As a consequence, programming varies across these dayparts. Cost of commercial placement also varies. Table 5-2 provides a breakdown of the daypart time breaks.

---

clutter A condition that exists when many advertisements and/or commercials are placed too closely together in space or time. In today's media-rich environment, this is a constant problem for advertisers.

dayparts Time-scheduling segments for a given day, used for television and other broadcast media.

Television

Television is a very effective advertising medium for many types of products because it has the ability to provide the impact of sight, action, motion, and sound and it can provide a very broad reach into the mass market.

Source: © 2006 JupiterImages Corporation.

TABLE 5-2 Television Dayparts Breakdown

Television Daypart	Time Breakdowns
Morning	7:00 A.M.–9:00 A.M., Monday–Friday
Daytime	9:00 A.M.–4:30 P.M., Monday–Friday
Early fringe	4:30 P.M.–8:00 P.M., Monday–Friday
Prime time	8:00 P.M.–11:00 P.M., Monday–Friday
Prime-time Sunday	7:00 P.M.–11:00 P.M., Sunday
Late news	11:00 P.M.–11:30 P.M., Monday–Friday
Late fringe	11:30 P.M.–1:00 A.M., Monday–Friday

Mediaweek's cost estimates for the average 30-second spot in the fourth quarter of 2004 in the daytime slot were $29,400. In comparison to that, a prime-time 30-second spot in the same quarter averaged $230,000.

Audience/Target Market

Broadcast television tends to be mass market. Local broadcast spot buys can focus on a limited geographical region. There are certain **superstations** (e.g., WGN from Chicago) that are powerful broadcasting stations and have relationships with other local broadcasters and cable companies to provide their programming across a broad geographic region. Cable television is more limited, but the merger of cable systems has provided widespread reach in certain geographic regions and the urban/suburban setting. Cable networks are also useful in what is referred to as **narrowcasting** (a focused television buy versus the wider broadcast from traditional television outlets). Satellite has a more limited reach due to the penetration into households at this point. The demographic and psychographic segments will also vary based on the programming type and time of day for viewership (see Table 5-2).

Measurement

A great deal of discussion recently has been about how to measure television commercials.[3] Nielsen has long been the major player in setting the standard for measuring exposure and, ultimately, the cost for commercial time. Generally, what is available is based on a number of assumptions concerning the exposure of individuals to advertisements.

Strategic Marketing Communications Elements

In this section, we describe various SMC elements of television, including area of dominant influence and designated market area, television households, households using television, rating point, cost per rating point, and share.

Area of dominant influence (**ADI**) and **designated market area** (**DMA**) relate to the geographic area over which a local television station holds domination. For example, a station from Chicago would have a dominant influence in northern Illinois until it came close to where station signals from another nearby city (e.g., Milwaukee) dominated the area. Arbitron uses the ADI term, and Nielsen uses the DMA designation.

The term **television households** (**TVHH**) refers to the number of households in the market (usually reported as the entire U.S. market) that have at least one television set. As of 2005 the number of TVHH in the United States was estimated to be 109,600,000. That number translates to approximately 98 percent of all households in the United States. As a percentage of households, the percentage has remained fairly constant over the past 20 years.

---

superstations Powerful broadcasting stations that often have relationships with other local broadcasters and cable companies to provide their programming across a broad geographic region.

narrowcasting A focused television buy versus the wider broadcast from traditional television outlets. Cable buys are often used for this purpose.

SMC QuickLink
Nielsen Media Research
http://www.nielsenmedia.com

area of dominant influence (ADI) or designated market area (DMA) The geographic area over which a local television station holds domination. For example, a station from Chicago would have a dominant influence in northern Illinois until it came close to where station signals from another nearby city (e.g., Milwaukee) dominated the area. Arbitron uses the ADI term, and Nielsen uses the DMA designation.

television households (TVHH) The number of households in the market (usually reported as the entire U.S. market) that have at least one television set.

households using television (HUT) The number of television households (TVHH) that have a television "in use."

rating point This figure is equal to 1 percent of the TVHH (or broadcast media target market) and is reported as a percentage. Consequently, if a program receives a 10 rating, that rating translates as 10 percent of the TVHH in the United States were tuned into the particular program when the measurement was taken.

cost per rating point (CPRP) Cost of a commercial ÷ rating.

share Number of households tuned in to a program ÷ HUT.

SMC QuickLink
Taco Bell
http://www.tacobell.com

Households using television (HUT) refers to the number of TVHH that have a television "in use." The number does not mean that people are paying attention; it is simply a measurement regarding the number of households that have at least one television turned on.

The **rating point** is a figure equal to one percent of the TVHH and is reported as a percentage. Consequently, if a program receives a 10 rating, that rating translates as 10 percent of the TVHH in the United States were tuned in to the particular program when the measurement was taken. The formula is shown here. Following the rating point formula is the formula for calculating the **cost per rating point (CPRP),** a useful calculation in assessing the efficiency of a media buy by itself or in comparison against another buy, as is the CPM discussed previously.

Rating point = Number of households tuned in to a program ÷ total number of television households (TVHH)

Cost per rating point (CPRP) = Cost of a commercial on a given program ÷ rating of a given program

While rating relates to an absolute percentage in regard to TVHH, the **share** figure is estimated based on the HUT figure defined previously. It is used to compare programs by determining what percentage of the actual viewing public saw a particular program or commercial at a given time. The formula for calculating share is shown here.

Share = Number of households tuned in to a program ÷ HUT

Best Case: Taco Bell

There are few better product classes for television than fast food. The Taco Bell "Think Outside the Bun" campaign is an excellent example of bringing the brand essence alive creatively.[4] Using television as the major media choice to reach the broad fast-food target market, Taco Bell was able to get a clear positioning message across in an effective and efficient manner. The Foote Cone and Belding (FCB) campaign is credited with providing a strong boost to the brand. Recently, FCB's campaign focus on the portability capability of the quesadilla hybrid called the "Crunchwrap Supreme" uses a simple tagline of "Good to Go" that is effectively executed on the medium as well, through demonstration and visual elements of the product and its usage.

5-2b Radio

Radio is available as broadcast (network and local), satellite, and cable. Network radio offers the widest availability of syndicated programming. According to the FCC, there are over 13,500 radio stations in the United States. About 6,200 of those are FM band, while about 4,700 are AM band.

Characteristics

Arbitron notes that the average time spent listening to radio by the 18+ age group is almost 3 hours a day, males slightly higher than females. Those 3 hours tend to group around what could be considered as "drive-time" dayparts. The highest level of listening occurs while in the market's automobile. While television has its "prime-time" hours in the evening, radio usage drops by nearly half to 53 percent of the 18+ population in the evening (7 P.M. to 12 A.M.). During drive times of 6 A.M. to 10 A.M. and 3 P.M. to 7 P.M., usage is about 82 percent and 91 percent, respectively. Radio is very well suited to do certain things. As with television, it can provide very broad reach into the mass market. Due to the high reach, overall it has a fairly low cost per exposure compared to other media. Radio production costs are significantly lower than those of television. Radio also allows a more tightly focused targeting of a given market due to the radio station formatting approach. For example, buying a spot on an "All Sports" format radio station generally delivers a fairly homogeneous audience

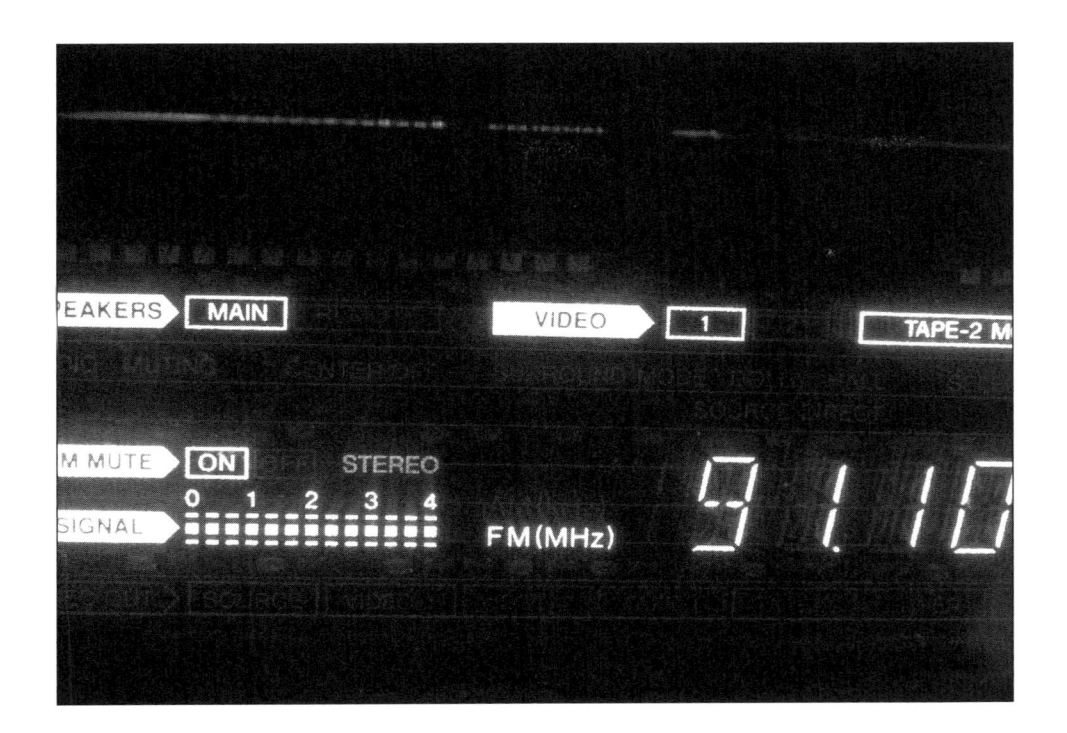

Radio

As with television, radio can provide a very broad reach into the mass market. It also allows a more tightly focused targeting of a given market due to the radio station formatting approach.

Source: © 2006 JupiterImages Corporation.

who is interested in sports, is college educated, has a fairly high income, and is male. Ethnic/race radio stations can deliver a niche market segments based on ethnic heritage as well. Stations that cater to the Hispanic language market (and even subsegments within the Hispanic demographic) continue to grow. Radio is also extremely flexible in terms of front-end time requirements and ease of changing the content of the message. It does have some down sides to it as well. In general, clutter is a severe problem for radio commercials. Commercial flights may be zapped by people changing stations. Radio is also at times used as "background noise" by commuters who may not really be listening.

The medium has the ability to provide the impact of sound but not the other senses. However, radio promoters will argue that, because of that, imagination can be brought into play with the right kind of message. "There are no bounds for imagination" goes the argument. If a message can generate high levels of cognitive and affective functioning and create the image in the mind's eye, along with the appropriate feeling, then the message can have a powerful impact. For certain types of products, this can be highly advantageous in message presentation. Production costs make radio commercials appealing. Local stations can quickly put together professional level advertisements. If a focused message to a limited target market is your need, radio may be a good selection. As with anything in marketing communications, though, the interactions between creative, the target market, and the message components will decide if radio is appropriate.

As noted previously, radio is generally broken up into time-scheduling segments for a given day. These time ranges for the day are referred to as dayparts. The drive-time dayparts are the most listened to. Top disc jockeys and programming occupy those slots. Cost of commercial placement also varies accordingly. Table 5-3 provides a breakdown of the radio daypart time breaks.

The cost-per-rating-point estimate for the average 30-second spot on network radio that reaches the 18+ adult market for weekday drive time was $2621.00 in 2004. In comparison to that, a 30-second spot in only the New York market for the same target market during drive time was $716.05. Men (18+) listen to radio for about 3 hours a day during the week while women (18+) are slightly lower in their listening habits at 2.75 hours each day during the week.

TABLE 5-3	Radio Dayparts Breakdown
Radio Daypart	Time Breakdowns
Morning drive time	6:00 A.M.–10:00 A.M.
Daytime	10:00 A.M.–3:00 P.M.
Afternoon drive time	3:00 P.M.–7:00 P.M.
Nighttime	7:00 P.M.–12:00 midnight
Late night	12:00 midnight—6:00 A.M.

Audience/Target Market

Broadcast radio generally has allowed access to the local market. Local broadcast spot buys can focus on a limited geographical region. There are certain superstations (e.g., WLS-AM from Chicago) that are powerful broadcasting stations that can be heard across a broad geographic region. Cable radio is more limited, but the merger of cable systems has provided widespread reach in certain geographic regions and the urban/suburban setting. Satellite radio (e.g., Sirius and others) is now available, but much of its appeal is based on the lack of commercial interruption from advertisers. The demographic and psychographic segments will also vary based on the programming type and time of day for viewership (see Table 5-3).

Measurement

Arbitron has long been the major player in setting the standard for measuring exposure and ultimately the cost for commercial time. Generally, what is available is based on a number of assumptions concerning the exposure of individuals to advertisements.

Strategic Marketing Communications Elements

Two SMC elements of radio include average quarter-hour audience and cumulate radio audience.

Average quarter-hour (AQH) audience refers to the number of people who are listening (tuned in) to a given program at a certain time. The measure is based on 15-minute segments (hence, the quarter hour). When this number is reported as a percentage of a given population, it becomes a *rating*. Cost per rating point (CPRP) can then be figured using the formula from the "Television" section.

Cume or **cumulative radio audience** is an estimated number that is the total number of different people who listened to radio station programming for at least 5 minutes during a given daypart.

Best Case: Bud Light

Radio can be used in support of television and other media. It can be used to provide a reinforcement of a given message that has been delivered in a more complete manner by the main media choice for the campaign. There are, however, exceptions to that rule. This is one of those cases—Anheiser-Busch, Inc.'s Bud Light "Real Men of Genius." Bud Light was able to get a clear message across in a humorous message that was fairly effective in the highly competitive beer market. Aimed at the 21- to 34-year-old male target market, the DDB Chicago campaign is credited with providing a memorable boost to the brand within the target market. The campaign pays homage to a variety of strange jobs and terms the men who have those jobs as "Real Men of Genius." An example is "Mr. Tiny Dog Clothing Manufacturer" (see Exhibit 5-2). The spots have won a number of Golden Lion Awards at Cannes and have become something of a cult, generating a huge fan base. At the same time, they are a crucial piece in staving off a concerted effort by Miller Lite to take market share from the brand in the continuing "Beer Wars."

SMC QuickLink
Arbitron
http://arbitron.com/home/content.stm

average quarter-hour (AQH) audience The number of people who are listening (tuned in) to a given program at a certain time. The measure is based on 15-minute segments (hence, the quarter hour). When this number is reported as a percentage of a given population, it becomes a *rating*.

cume or **cumulative radio audience** An estimated number that is the total number of different people who listened to radio station programming for at least 5 minutes during a given daypart.

SMC QuickLink
Bud Light
http://www.budlight.com

Announcer:	Bud Light presents . . . Real Men of Genius.
Singer:	*Real Men of Genius.*
Announcer:	Today we salute you . . . Mr. Tiny Dog Clothing Manufacturer.
Singer:	*Mr. Tiny Dog Clothing Manufacturer.*
Announcer:	Great men ask the tough questions. Where did we come from? What is gravity? How do you help a schnauzer through a fashion crisis?
Singer:	*Smashin' fashion.*
Announcer:	You see no irony in designing a thick fur coat, for an animal born with a thick fur coat.
Singer:	*It's warm in here.*
Announcer:	A dog licking himself, disgusting. A dog licking himself in an argyle sweater, adorable!
Singer:	*Smoochable pooch.*
Announcer:	So crack open an ice cold Bud Light, oh, Purveyor of the Pooch. They may be just dumb animals. But thanks to you, they'll always be smartly dressed.
Singer:	*Mr. Tiny Dog Clothing Manufacturer.*
Announcer:	Bud Light Beer. Anheuser Busch, St. Louis, Missouri.

Exhibit 5-2

Bud Light Mr. Tiny Dog Clothing Manufacturer

Radio sometimes creates striking images in the mind of the listener.

Source: Copyright © 2005 by Anheuser-Busch, Incorporated. Used with permission of Anheuser-Busch, Incorporated. All rights reserved. Audio available at www.budlight.com.

5-3 Print Media

While newer media have often grabbed the news spotlight, print continues to offer an excellent vehicle of choice to perform certain tasks and reach certain target markets effectively. Print media can be further broken down into the two subheadings of "Magazines" and "Newspapers."

5-3a Magazines

Magazines provide what is considered to be one of the most targeted and high-involvement types of mass media. Often referred to in the trade as *books,* this medium can have extremely high reproduction quality if desired. It can also be reproduced resembling newspaper quality. Magazines also offer a creative flexibility in being able to offer an integrated message using text, image, texture, and even smell (perfume vendors will often use scratch-and-sniff inserts).

Characteristics

The ability of magazines to focus on a particular audience is excellent (see "Audience/Target Market" on page 105). Advertisers can also select certain issues that provide editorial and story content that is directly related to a given product. For example, a drug manufacturer can have an advertisement for an arthritis medication placed on the same page of an article that discusses the value of new drugs in maintaining better quality of life for seniors. In such situations, the relevance and impact of the advertisement are increased significantly. Compared to broadcast media, the magazine has much greater permanence. It can be kept around (e.g., *National Geographic* has a very long retention by readers). It also will get a certain level of "pass around." Think of dentists' and doctors' offices and the ability to gain exposure to multiple people over a long magazine life. Certain magazines offer prestige as well. *Condé Nast Traveler* is viewed as one of the bibles for more upscale travel. In fact, the Condé Nast group is generally regarded as one of the most reputable publishers. Magazine publishers generally provide a high level of service for advertisers. Downside elements are also there. There is generally a long required lead time before publication dates. These lead times can be as long as 2 months in some

Magazines

As compared to the passive television and radio, magazines are an active and highly involved medium. Magazines offer a creative flexibility in being able to provide an integrated message using text, image, texture, and even smell (perfumes will often use scratch-and-sniff inserts). If an advertiser has a message that requires the audience to process a great deal of information, or information that is complex, the magazine also allows readers to process that information at their own pace.

Source: © 2006 JupiterImages Corporation.

cases. The other most discussed shortcoming is tied to magazines' strength. They are limited in reach to a wide market due to their focused delivery of a limited audience. Electronic magazines or *ezines* (either unique or online versions of print publications) are increasingly making their presence felt in publishing.

Magazines have the ability to provide very focused messages to a focused target market. If an advertiser has a message that requires the audience to process a great deal of information, or information that is complex, the magazine also allows readers to process that information at their own pace. The medium is generally considered an active and high-involvement type of medium, as compared to the passive television and radio. Visual elements can be used in conjunction with text to create a unity of image and message to a more highly involved audience than that of the broadcast media. As already noted, selection of a highly credible magazine for the target market can enhance the value of the message and, for certain magazines, drive behavior for certain readers (e.g., *Vogue* or *InStyle* may set fashion trends). If the advertiser requires the impact of vision, touch, and smell or any combination of them, magazines are generally an effective medium. As with anything in marketing communications, though, the interactions between creative, the target market, and the message components will determine whether magazines are appropriate.

Standard advertising units are full-page, half-page, and quarter-page units. Advertisements are sold as black and white, two color, four color. Black and white is available for the lowest cost, two color (black and white plus one color) is the next most expensive, and full-color advertisements (referred to as *four color*) are the most expensive. Free-standing inserts (FSIs), those little cards that drive us all crazy, are also available. Publishers generally work with advertisers to provide any special display needs as well (for a price). Standard Rate and Data Service (SRDS) provides a full breakdown of circulation and cost figures for all magazines in the U.S. market.

Mediaweek reports that there were 17,254 magazines (6,234 consumer only, which exclude trade publications) in the United States as of 2004. In 2003, they generated over $19 billion in advertising revenue from over 225,000 pages of advertising. In 2003, combined circulation figures for single copies and subscriptions were over 352 million.[5]

SMC QuickLink
SRDS Media Solutions
http://www.srds.com

Audience/Target Market

As noted, the audience can be very small and focused or fairly broad in scope. Examples of the narrowness and broadness of the medium can be seen in titles that focus on such things as quilting *(Quilting Arts)*, babies *(American Baby)*, and brides *(Brides)* to fairly broad general news (*Newsweek* and *Time*). By using regional edition buys, advertisers can focus on a certain local market down to a ZIP code level. They may also buy national and regional editions of the magazine. The demographic and psychographic segments vary based on the magazine.

Measurement

Simmons Market Research Bureau; Mediamark Research, Inc.; and Standard Rate and Data Service (SDRS) provide various measurements and data regarding magazines. Cost per thousand, cost per rating point, reach, and gross rating points (as discussed earlier in relation to broadcast media) are used in measurement of magazines.

Strategic Marketing Communications Elements

Other measurement elements from *Mediaweek*[6] and other sources include circulation, rate base, recent reading, and through the book:

- **Circulation** is the total number of issue copies sold through all channels of distribution (subscription, newsstand, bulk).
- **Rate base** is the guaranteed average issue circulation upon which a book's advertising rates are based.
- **Recent reading** is a technique used by Mediamark Research, Inc., for determining magazine readership. Respondents to the survey are shown magazine logos and asked if they have recently read or looked into any of the publications. Readership is then identified by asking if any issue has been read or looked at within the last publication cycle.
- **Through the book** is a technique used by the Simmons Market Research Bureau to estimate total readership of publications. Respondents are asked to examine a stripped-down issue of any magazine that they have read or looked into recently. Initially, they are asked whether they have read or looked into the specific issue previously. Those who answer "yes" are counted as readers of the magazine.

Best Case: Absolut

Magazines can deliver a strong message both visually and through text content in a highly involved environment. The selection of Absolut as a "best case" is based on its use of the image of its uniquely shaped bottle of vodka. It was an imagery that became one of the most successful print campaigns in history. Using a strong visual imagery tied to events and situations, Absolut built the brand into a product class powerhouse. Market share went from about 0.1 percent in 1980 (at the start of the campaign) to over 12 percent in 2000. This happened while the imported vodka market was rising from less than three quarters of a million cases in 1980 in the United States to almost forty million cases in 2001.[7] A variety of analysts attribute a major driver of that rise to Absolut and its advertising campaign—a campaign that was successful in driving awareness and product class image enhancement over that time period. Absolut has been under constant assault on its market share from other premium vodkas, and its market share has slid some recently; but the campaign remains as a great example of how a campaign largely based on print (magazines as the major element) can be successful in impacting a focused target market.

The spots won a number of awards and have become something of a legend. They have generated website tributes, spoofs, and blog boards dedicated to them. How long the simple imagery will continue to be used by Absolut has become a source of constant speculation.

---

circulation Total number of issue copies sold through all channels of distribution (subscription, newsstand, bulk). Used for magazines and newspapers.

rate base The guaranteed average issue circulation upon which a book's (magazine's) advertising rates are based.

recent reading A technique used by Mediamark Research, Inc., for determining magazine readership. Respondents to the survey are shown magazine logos and asked if they have recently read or looked into any of the publications.

through the book A technique used by the Simmons Market Research Bureau (SMRB) to estimate total readership of publications. Respondents are asked to examine a stripped-down issue of any magazine that they have read or looked into recently. Initially, they are asked whether they have read or looked into the specific issue previously. Those who answer "yes" are counted as readers of the magazine.

SMC QuickLink
Absolut
http://www.absolut.com

5-3b Newspapers

Except for a few national newspapers like *USA Today* and *The Wall Street Journal* and special group newspapers (e.g., ethnic, lifestyle, business), newspapers are usually considered to be local media. *The New York Times* and *The Washington Post* have a national presence as well, but that presence often involves the United States Postal Service or an online copy. *The New York Times* is known for additional readership of its Sunday edition, which can be purchased at newsstands in most urban and large suburban areas. In general, newspapers are an excellent choice of media for local advertisers.

Characteristics

According to *Mediaweek*, there are over 1,400 daily newspapers in the United States that are read by 53 percent of U.S. adults. On Sunday, 61 percent read a newspaper. Daily newspapers provide a five-issue net reach of around 72 percent of the adult population.[8]

Data related to the online versions of these local papers were not available; but, as with hard copies, the online copies tend to focus on local news. The national and international news is covered as well, but daily newspapers in both the hard and electronic versions remain the main source for news in the local environment. As a consequence, the newspaper is often the best advertising option for local businesses and retail establishments in reaching their target market. In general, newspapers offer a number of positive elements for the local advertiser. They provide very short lead times and flexibility for insertion and production. Thus, they offer a very timely media choice. Local newspapers often provide all the layout and production services for free. The advertisements can be in a variety of space sizes and can include inserts. Advertisers can also select the section (e.g., sports, local, world, national, life, classified, real estate, food, travel, etc.) that fits a particular product. This is called **preferred position** and is in contrast to **run of press (ROP),** which is simply buying an advertisement that can be placed anywhere in the newspaper. Executions can be in color or in black and white. The cost in comparison to other media is often much less. Coupons offer an ability to drive local traffic for retail. Readers are in an active versus passive (as in broadcast) mode and are therefore more involved in processing the message. Newspapers also entail some downsides. A great deal of clutter (many advertisements in each issue) is often present, and newspapers have selective reader exposure. The nature of the daily is such that the advertisement has a very short life. Reproduction quality is somewhat poor compared to magazines. The newspaper medium is one that has seen continuing evolution in recent years, as SMC Marketplace Watch 5-2 illustrates.

Newspapers have the ability to cover a local market very well. For gaining attention of the local market and initiating behavior through information concerning product availability and other terms of sale, the newspaper is well suited. If an advertiser has a message that requires the audience to process a great deal of—or complex—information, the medium is well suited to that task in a local environment. As with magazines, newspapers allow readers to process that information at their own pace. The medium is generally considered an active and high-involvement type of medium as compared to the passive television and radio. If timeliness is critical, newspapers allow almost immediate turnaround for advertisement placement. If the advertiser requires the impact of vision, touch, and smell or any combination of them, newspapers can offer this—albeit at a lower production quality than that of magazines. As with anything in marketing communications, though, the interactions between creative, the target market, and the message components will determine whether newspapers are appropriate.

Newspapers basically come in two different sizes—standard and tabloid. Some daily newspapers (e.g., *Chicago Sun-Times*) use the tabloid size as a competitive advantage. The tabloid size makes it much easier to read on a commuter train or bus, for example. Standard advertising units used to be offered only in agate lines (1/4" deep by one standard column wide (usually 2" wide) or column inch (1 inch deep by one column wide, with fourteen agate lines per column inch). More recently,

---

preferred position Advertisers can select the section (e.g., sports, local, world, national, life, classified, real estate, food, travel, etc.) or particular page placement that fits a particular product.

run of press (ROP) Buying an advertisement that can be placed anywhere in the newspaper or other print vehicle by the editorial staff of the publication; that is, the advertiser is not able to select certain a placement for his or her advertisement. (See *preferred position*.)

SMC Marketplace Watch 5-2

The Continuing Evolution of the American Newspaper

Printed newspapers are continuing to lose readers to online editions, according to research by Nielsen//NetRatings. Of the web users who do read newspapers, almost a quarter of them read the daily paper online.

Online newspaper readership is led by NYTimes.com, which had 11.3 million unique readers in May of 2005. The number two and number three positions were held by USAToday.com (9.2 million) and WashingtonPost.com (7.4 million), respectively. While these are thought of often as more national newspapers (*USA Today* especially), the remaining two dailies are traditional big-city papers from California. These were LATimes.com (3.8 million) and SFGate.com, website of the *San Francisco Chronicle* (3.4 million).

This research suggests that a steady shift away from paper to computer screens is taking place in the country. In support of such a contention, a Newspaper Association of America analysis of the figures from the Audit Bureau of Circulations over the first months of 2005 sees a significant slide in the print circulation numbers. The data reveal that daily newspapers' total average daily circulation dropped 1.9 percent to 47.4 million. The drop was even bigger on Sundays, falling 2.5 percent to 51 million. While men make up the majority of online readers, the difference is not that great. They are 53 percent of online readers, while women comprise 47 percent. Comparatively, women make up 57 percent of those who read newspapers primarily in print.

The appeal of the online editions may rest in their immediacy and interactivity capabilities. These online editions have also incorporated original, Internet-specific content that seeks to keep readers on the site. That content includes online message boards, editorial blogs, and up-to-the-minute news postings.

The Nielsen//NetRatings survey routinely polls 36,000 online users by telephone. For this study, they were asked, "Do you primarily read the newspaper online or offline?"

Source: Adapted from Kris Oser, "Newspaper Readers Continue Migration to Internet. Largest Online Readership Is NYTimes.com with 11.3 Million Uniques," *Advertising Age,* June 28, 2005, QwikFIND ID: AAQ70K.

---

though, most newspapers have embraced a standard advertising unit (SAU) based on the full-page, half-page, and quarter-page units. However, over fifty SAUs are available, so the system is still not as simple as some other media choices when it comes to sizing. As with magazine advertisements, they can be sold as black and white, two color, and four color (although some smaller publications do not offer the color options). Black and white is available for the lowest cost, two color (black and white plus one color) is the next most expensive, and full-color advertisements (referred to as *four color*) are the most expensive. Free-standing inserts (FSIs) are also available. Newspaper publishers and their distributors will generally work with advertisers to provide any special display needs, inserts, or outer sleeves for additional charges. Free samples can also be distributed through local newspapers in sleeves or other special inserts. Standard Rate and Data Service (SRDS) provides a full breakdown of circulation and cost figures for most major and local newspapers in the U.S. market.

Audience/Target Market

As already noted, the newspaper audience is generally a very broad but local market. The audience is generally not able to be segmented in any sort of demographic and psychographic manner. However, the audience generally is much more engaged (involved) when reading due to the local relevance of many of the stories. For specialty newspapers such as *The Wall Street Journal,* the involvement with the newspaper can be extremely high because the relevance of the information is significant to the readership in job performance. *USA Today* is often referred to as "the traveler's newspaper" because people who are traveling commonly read it. It is available in airports, motels, train stations, resorts, and so on. For this reason, you will often find advertisements that fit that particular demographic and lifestyle segment.

Newspapers

Daily newspapers in both the hard and electronic versions continue to be the main source for news in the local environment. As a consequence, the newspaper is still often the best advertising option for local businesses and retail establishments in reaching their target market.

Source: © Stockbyte.

paid circulation Number of copies from subscription or newsstand sales.

readership The circulation of a newspaper multiplied by the estimated readers per copy.

Measurement

Standard Rate and Data Service (SDRS) provides various measurements and data regarding newspapers. Cost per thousand, reach, and like measures (all discussed earlier in this chapter) can be used in measurement of newspapers. Newspapers are one of the most "passed around" of media. *The New York Times,* for example, according to a Scarborough Media report from 2004, is estimated to have 4.4 readers for a single copy of the newspaper. Cost of advertising is sometimes based on straight circulation numbers; but, in the case of newspapers like *The New York Times,* a large pass-around rate is figured into advertising cost.

Strategic Marketing Communications Elements

Other measurement elements from *Mediaweek*[9] and other sources for newspapers include circulation, paid circulation, and readership:

- *Circulation* is the total number of copies sold through all channels of distribution (subscription, newsstand, bulk).
- **Paid circulation** is the number of copies from subscription or newsstand sales.
- **Readership** is the circulation of a newspaper multiplied by the estimated readers per copy. In the case of *The New York Times,* readership would equal circulation × 4.4.

Best Case: Your Local Car Dealer

Newspapers can deliver a message to a broad local market. They can also be used to drive local retail traffic through sales, inserts, contests, and coupons. Instead of selecting one particular campaign as a "best case" example for newspapers, we have selected a group of retailers who have used the local newspaper as a major component in their media mix for years: local car dealers. Over the years, local car dealers have been able to use the local newspaper to drive local traffic into their dealerships where the deals are closed by their salesforce. By using newspapers in a number of ways (regular section space, inserts, and the classifieds) to provide awareness of availability of a certain product (make or model) and basic information on price and quantity, local car dealers have effectively used the newspaper for what it can do best in the local marketplace. In today's world, car dealers are using the Internet and websites much more than before, but the newspaper still acts as the most effective mass-media tool for driving traffic into the retail environment.

5-4 Out-of-Home Media

Out-of-home media may not be entirely a truism. It is advertising that you are exposed to while you are "out and about." While you can read your magazines and newspapers, watch television, or listen to radio while you are "not at home," this category is meant to capture media that you *cannot* bring into your home. It includes outdoor and in-store/point-of-purchase types of advertising.

5-4a Outdoor

Outdoor advertising is made up of a number of different types of presentation formats, including such things as traditional billboards, transit boards (at stops and on equipment), aerial advertising (billboards, banners, etc.), mobile billboards (painted trucks, cars, or other derivations), and inflatables (you may have seen the giant gorilla tethered near a main thoroughfare). Some positive dimensions of outdoor advertising are that the medium can be very location-specific in its application; it can provide geographic flexibility in placement; and high visual impact is possible and can be a real attention grabber.

Characteristics

With technological breakthroughs, the medium can be very innovative and creative in design. It has the ability to provide high frequency in a tightly focused market area through saturation of the area. A downside is that using the medium generally requires a very short and concise message because of the short time exposure for the passerby. While high frequency is possible, another downside is the possibility of the advertisement "wearing out" from that constant exposure. Some localities place significant restrictions on the use of outdoor advertising.

Outdoor advertising has great capabilities for building brand awareness in a defined geographic region. The strategic use of a series of outdoor panels can blanket an area and deliver a high number of impressions for a given message. The medium is also an excellent choice for delivering a high-frequency message into a geographic area. As noted in its characteristics, though, the message must be short (seven words is often posited for a good cutoff). Visual imagery that is concise and does not require a great deal of processing is best for the medium. If the advertiser has a complex or lengthy message to get across to the target market, this is not the medium to choose. It can be used effectively to supplement the main point of a more complex message that is expanded in other elements of the campaign, but the outdoor element must be clean and concise in delivery of its message. Through the use of transit media, commuters in major urban areas can be effectively targeted.

Standard billboard units are referred to as **panels** or **sheets.** In the past only a few choices were available for the size of billboards, but now many different options are available. The most common size for an outdoor panel is 30 sheets (9′ 6″ high by 21′ 7″ wide) or 8 sheets (5′ high by 11′ wide). The outdoor advertising industry reported increased revenues of 6.0 percent in 2004 compared to 2003. That translates to a total U.S. outdoor revenue of $5.8 billion in 2004, up from $5.5 billion in 2003. Figure 5-1 provides a breakdown of the four major product categories and the percentage of total revenue contributed by each.

outdoor advertising Made up of a number of different types of presentation formats, including such things as traditional billboards, transit boards (at stops and on equipment), aerial advertising (billboards, banners, etc.), mobile billboards (painted trucks, cars, or other derivations), and inflatables (you may have seen the giant gorilla tethered near a main thoroughfare).

panels or **sheets** In outdoor advertising, standard billboard units. In the past, only a few choices were available for the size of billboards, but now many different options are available. The most common size for an outdoor panel is 30 sheets (9′6″ high × 21′7″ wide) or 8 sheets (5′ high × 11′ wide).

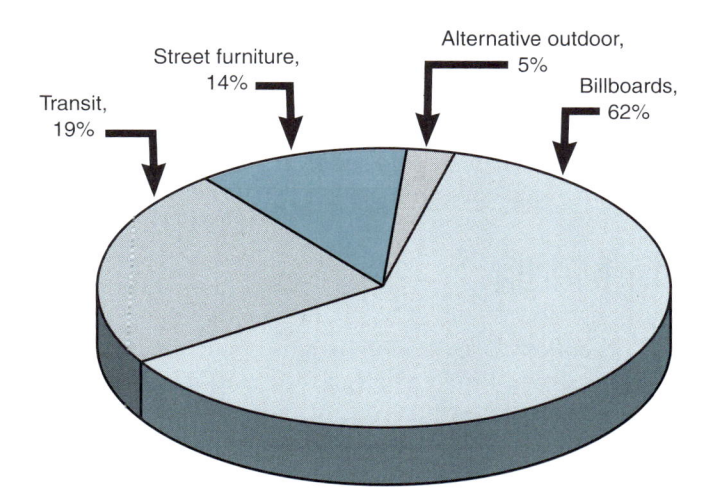

Transit, 19%
Street furniture, 14%
Alternative outdoor, 5%
Billboards, 62%

Figure 5-1
Four Major Product Categories
Source: Available from http://www.oaaa.org/outdoor.

Audience/Target Market
As already noted, the audience is generally a local market. The audience is generally not able to be segmented in any sort of demographic and psychographic manner, although placement in certain neighborhoods and commute routes can provide some targeting on a few dimensions. A wide variety of business types used outdoor as part of their media mix to reach their particular target markets. McDonald's is the top spender in outdoor media expenditures. It has an extensive outdoor presence not only in the U.S. market but also in the international market. In the developing world, outdoor advertising is the choice to reach the mass market because traditional electronic media may not be available to the mass market. See, for example, Exhibit 5-3, which shows billboards in Bangladesh.

Measurement
A number of organizations now provide measurement for outdoor advertising. Cost per thousand, reach, and like measures (all discussed earlier in this chapter) can be used in measurement of out-of-home media. Standard Rate and Data Service (SDRS) provides various measurements and data. Simmons Market Research Bureau and Mediamark Research, Inc., provide demographic and exposure types of data.

Strategic Marketing Communications Elements
Some of the measures that are unique to outdoor advertising, according to *Mediaweek*[10] and other sources, include daily effective circulation, gross rating points, and showing:

- **Daily effective circulation (DEC)** is the average number of persons age 18 or over potentially exposed to an advertising display for either 12 hours unilluminated (6:00 A.M. to 6:00 P.M.) or 18 hours illuminated (6:00 A.M. to midnight); daily effective circulation is also called *daily impressions*.
- The *gross rating points (GRPs)* measure is related to duplicated circulation over a period of time. For outdoor (and out-of-home) advertising, GRPs relate to daily circulation expressed over a weeklong time span. One rating point is equal to one percent of the target population. In outdoor and out-of-home advertising, this measure is replacing the more traditional measure of showing.
- **Showing** is the number of panels in a given market required to reach a fixed percentage of the population on a daily basis. Generally expressed as 25, 30, 74, or 100, it does not include a number of panels as it varies in each market. For example, a 100 showing means that you have provided a gross number of impressions equal to 100 percent of the local desired population. It varies for each locality. The

---

daily effective circulation (DEC) Average number of persons age 18 or over potentially exposed to an advertising display for either 12 hours unilluminated (6:00 A.M. to 6:00 P.M.) or 18 hours illuminated (6:00 A.M. to midnight); also called *daily impressions*.

showing The number of panels in a given market required to reach a fixed percentage of the population on a daily basis. For example, a 100 showing means that you have provided a gross number of impressions equal to 100 percent of the local desired population. It varies for each local. The term is only used in outdoor advertising and is generally being discarded in favor of the more common media measure of GRP.

Exhibit 5-3
Outdoor Advertising

This set of billboards in Dhaka, Bangladesh, advertises business and consumer products.
Source: Photo by Don Rahtz.

term is only used in outdoor advertising and, as noted, is generally being discarded in favor of the more common media measure of GRP.

Best Case: Chick-fil-A

Fast food again makes its appearance in the outdoor category. As a best case, we offer Chick-fil-A. The use of the cow images on the billboard created a simple yet unmistakable impression to build awareness of the Chick-fil-A brand. The "Eat Mor Chikin" misspelled by the 3D cows delivered a message that passersby could quickly process and act on.

SMC QuickLink
Chick-fil-A
http://www.chickfila.com/cfa.asp

5-4b In-Store/Point of Purchase

Point-of-purchase (POP) advertising is any facilitating advertising element that is present at the point of purchase or decision to consume by the consumer. Some people will argue that any advertisement that is in a directory (e.g., advertisements for lawyers in the yellow pages) that then generates a sale is POP advertising. In the case of online purchasing, that line is also one of discussion. Here, we generally discuss it in the context of the in-store environment. In-store and point-of-purchase advertising used to be fairly basic.

Characteristics

Times have changed, though, with the introduction of a wide variety of formats and elements intent on influencing the final decision at the point of purchase. Now we have video screens, intelligent shopping carts, electronic coupon dispensers, Plexiglas floor units, LED panels, music programmed for certain shopping times and crowd environments, scent dispensers, and motion-activated audio and video messages that inform customers about a variety of specials and product characteristics and terms of sales. In other words, the in-store environment has been optimized to create an environment in which the customer will feel more inclined to follow through on a planned

point-of-purchase (POP) advertising Advertising usually in the form of window and/or interior displays in establishments where a product is sold to the ultimate consumer. POP can also be promotional materials placed at the contact sales point designed to attract consumer interest or call attention to a special offer. Finally, there can be both on- and off-shelf display materials or product stocking that is generally at the retail level that is used to call special attention to the featured product. This latter element of POP is sometimes referred to as *point-of-sale display.*

Exhibit 5-4

In-Store/Point of Purchase

Ronald McDonald greets diners as they arrive at a McDonald's in Bangkok.

Source: Used with permission from McDonald's Corporation.

purchase, be influenced to impulse purchase, or simply have a better experience in the retail environment. Note how Ronald McDonald greets customers in Exhibit 5-4.

Such a wide variety of in-store advertising is possible that it may always be possible to use at least one element. While high-end retail environments may rely less on the obvious in-store and point-of-purchase elements, they will still need to focus on the atmospherics of the retail environment to send a message regarding the store and the brands they are carrying.

Target Audience

The target audience is any shopper in a retail environment and/or its accompanying parties. In that target market, there may be an individual shopper who is trying to make his or her way to a particular store to purchase a particular item. Men often shop in this manner. At the same time, you may have a group of teenage girls who are "out browsing" and in more of a social mode. As a consequence, marketing communications managers need to develop a mix of appropriate tactics to reach and influence the particular target market as they traverse the retail landscape.

Measurement

Since the in-store advertising is at the point of purchase, the effectiveness of its impact on a purchase is something that can often be measured in a field experiment environment. That is, over a period of time, sales can be measured for a particular product; then a particular in-store advertisement or point-of-purchase element can be inserted and the sales of a given product measured while the advertisement is in place. The advertisement can then be removed and measurements taken again in a scientific manner. These pre- and post-measurements can then evaluate any increase or decrease in store sales or other dimensions of interest to the marketer.

Best Case: Milk Processor Education Program

Chances are that when you think of milk advertising, "Got milk?" comes to mind. A point-of-purchase program by the Milk Processing Board was a huge hit in restaurants. Using restaurants like Denny's, an experiment was carried out to see if POP programs could influence people's beverage decision in the out-of-home market. The program used different visual and verbal cues. Point-of-purchase materials and servers or cashiers used verbal (suggesting ordering milk) or visual (such as "Got milk?" apparel) cues. The results for the Milk Processor Education Program (MilkPEP) across all restaurant treatments were significant. They registered increases in purchasing of at least 19 percent and several around 50 percent. In one upscale restaurant, they reported a 776 percent increase. On average, the tests increased milk sales by 42 percent. The bottom line for the industry is a potential increase of between $300 million and $500 million in yearly incremental milk sales across four food-service channels nationwide.[11]

SMC QuickLink
MilkPEP.org
http://www.milkpep.org

5-5 Miscellaneous Advertising

As the title for this section indicates, this is a catchall category. Because this is the catchall category of the remaining elements that we wish to treat as advertising, the characteristics are quite varied. You can, however, think of these as inserts in specialized media. These are executions that are focused to impact a particular segment of the population.

Characteristics

As noted, directories in some cases can be considered POP advertising because they can "close the deal" in some sense. Directories are compiled listings of entities based on some given characteristic. The directory (e.g., the Yellow Pages, specialty directories, and organizational directories) is a source of a great deal of traffic for an individual who is in search of a particular individual or firm that is a member of a given directory listing grouping. Service providers are often found in directories. Lawyers, doctors, and dentists are listed in directories that are available from professional organizations as well as in the Yellow Pages. Carpet cleaners and florists are commonly found in directories. Cost of production is fairly low. The placement of advertisements in these directories is not viewed as being intrusive because the user has initiated the search for relevant information. On the downside for directories, fairly long lead times are involved and directories can go out of date fairly quickly if not updated constantly (many now offer electronic versions to offset the currency and perishability of the medium).

Advertising in DVDs, video games, and movie theaters generally entails placing a video commercial for a given product in a nontelevision environment. You may at times see exactly the same advertisement that you saw on television or in the movie theater. The practice of embedding advertisements for other movies (either currently in release or coming) in DVDs is the old "Coming Attractions" ploy that has been used for years in movie theaters. Moving other types of products in these environments is simply shifting media placement. On the positive side of movie and home video advertising is that, first off, it reaches a fairly large audience. In 2003 there were 1.54 billion admissions to the movies.[12] Movie theaters usually have less clutter to contend with as compared to television. Local buys are fairly cheap, although national buys can be pricey on a CPM level. You may also have viewers that are "out shopping" when they are in the theater and have stopped in to "catch a movie," so immediacy may be useful in facilitating purchase behavior. The downsides are limited, but the one everyone talks about is "being sold to while out for entertainment." Older consumers seem more bothered by that than younger consumers are, who seem to take advertising's presence as an expected situation. At-home DVD insertions have many of the same characteristics without the out-of-home dimension. Fast forwarding, if possible, often renders the insertions useless. Video game advertisements are also becoming more common in an effort to reach the "gaming" target market.

Target Audience

In DVDs and in movie theaters, advertising for the target audience can be matched to the movie's projected demographic. In directories, the audiences for yellow pages types of directories are fairly broad. A directory of "advertising professionals" will attract a much narrower audience.

Measurement

National Yellow Pages Monitor (NYPM) now provides measurement for directory ratings and usage for directory advertising. Cost per thousand, reach, and like measures (all discussed earlier in this chapter) can be used in measurement of out-of-home media. Simmons Market Research Bureau and Mediamark Research, Inc., provide demographics and exposure. Many firms (e.g., Movie Ad Media at http://www.movieadmedia.com) provide services and research summaries about movie theater advertising.

Best Case: Your Local Restaurant and the Yellow Pages Directory

Local restaurants were by far the most searched for product or service in the yellow pages. A study from 2004 conducted by the Yellow Pages Publishers Association reported that there were 1,322,500,000 usages by the population to find information out about local restaurants.

SMC QuickLink
Yellow Pages Publishers Association
http://www.yellowpageblues.com/YPPA.html

Summary

Advertising is a wide and varied set of media that are used to communicate with the mass market or segments within that market. It is crucial to select the particular medium that possesses the characteristics that best suit your target audience in communicating the given message. Technology is changing the way in which advertising is delivered, but the medium can be quite effective if used properly. (Part Three covers the application of advertising in the SMC mix in much more detail.)

As noted at the beginning of Part Two, the chapters in this part are brief and not intended to provide in-depth coverage of each of the presented advertising elements. For that reason, we suggest that you spend some time on the sites that are listed in the "Additional QuickLinks" section. These sites represent associations from all the different advertising media covered in this chapter. Most of these sites offer extensive amounts of information about the media, their performance, and their customers. You will be able to learn many more details about the various advertising elements than was possible in this chapter, given our space restraints and the strategic nature of this book.

Discussion Questions

Using a brand of your choice, assume that you are the brand manager for that particular brand. There is a budget of $1 million for advertising this coming quarter (you may choose your quarter). Your boss has requested that you provide her with a comprehensive evaluation of possible choices for spending the million dollars on advertising for your brand. She asks that you conduct an evaluation of the types of advertising that would best suit your particular brand. How do each of the different media covered in the chapter figure into your plans for the brand? Television? Radio? Newspapers? Magazines? Outdoor? In-store?

1. Which would be your primary choice of advertising media? Why?
2. Which would you select (if any) as your supporting advertising? Why?
3. What characteristics of your particular media choices contribute to creating the image you want for your brand?
4. How did the characteristics of your target market influence your choices on media?
5. How did the characteristics of your product influence your choices on media?
6. What media are your major competitors relying on when they advertise? Should you mimic them or try something different? Why?
7. If you were to speculate, which is more important for your brand—reach or frequency? In your advertising buy?
8. How might recent technology changes influence your decision?
9. Does the time of year (the quarter that you chose) influence your choice of media?

Practice Quiz

Note: You can find the correct answers to these questions by taking the quiz and then submitting your answers in the Online Edition. The program will automatically score your submission. If you miss a question, the program will provide the correct answer, a rationale for the answer, and the section number in the chapter where the topic is discussed.

1. Which of the following refers to a type of advertising placed by businesses and other organizations that is intended to communicate a viewpoint about a controversial topic relating to the social, political, or economic environment?
   a. advocacy advertising
   b. opinion advertising
   c. reference advertising
   d. evaluative advertising

2. Which figure is the delivery of the number (usually expressed as a percentage) of the unduplicated target market that has been exposed to a communication as part of the campaign?
   a. reach
   b. effective reach
   c. net reach
   d. frequency

3. Which of the following when multiplied with frequency will yield the measure of gross rating points?
   a. share
   b. standard reach
   c. effective reach
   d. net reach

4. A manager decided to buy a one-page advertisement for $200,000 in *Magazine X* that had an audience delivery of one million people. What would be the cost per thousand (CPM) for that buy?
   a. $100
   b. $50
   c. $200
   d. $400

5. Television is generally broken up into time-scheduling segments for a given day. These time ranges for the day are known as _____.
   a. timeframes
   b. dayparts
   c. schedules
   d. slots

6. What is the share figure in television broadcasting based on?
   a. TVHH
   b. ADI
   c. HUT
   d. target markets

7. Which of the following is a severe problem for radio commercials?
   a. cost of production
   b. low reach
   c. loosely focused targeting of a given market
   d. clutter

8. Identify a downside of magazine advertising.
   a. long lead time
   b. passive nature
   c. low involvement
   d. low permanence

9. Which of the following is a disadvantage of newspaper advertising?
   a. clutter
   b. passive mode
   c. low involvement
   d. long lead time

10. What are standard billboard units referred to as?
    a. clubs
    b. display units
    c. panels
    d. covers

Web Exercise

Which Advertising Does the Job for You?

Using the links provided in "Additional QuickLinks," visit the website of one of the associations from each of three different types of advertising media. Make a list of the most beneficial aspects of that type of advertising (according to the association). Select a brand from a product class of your choice (e.g., soft drinks) and evaluate the use of the three selected types of advertising and how they may work to help your brand in the marketplace.

Additional QuickLinks

Eight Sheet Outdoor Advertising Association (ESOAA)
http://66.179.121.117/default.asp

Federal Communications Commission (FCC)
http://www.fcc.gov

Magazine Publishers of America (MPA)
http://www.magazine.org/home

National Association of Broadcasters
http://www.nab.org

National Association of Theatre Owners
http://www.natoonline.org

Newspaper Association of America
http://www.naa.org

The Newspaper Industry
http://www.newspaper-industry.org

Outdoor Advertising Association of America
http://www.oaaa.org

Point-of-Purchase Advertising Institute
http://www.popai.com//AM/Template.cfm?Section=Home

Summary Media Source: I Want Media Inc.
http://www.iwantmedia.com

Television Associations
http://www.tvweek.com/tvLink.cms?tvLinkId=114

TNS Media Intelligence
http://www.tns-mi.com

Yellow Pages Association
http://www.yppa.org

Yellow Pages Media
http://www.ypm.com

Suggested Readings

Aaker, David A., and James M. Carman. 1982. Are you overadvertising? *Journal of Advertising Research* 22 (4): 57–70.

Herremans, Irene, John K. Ryans Jr., and Raj Aggarwal. 2000. Linking advertising and brand value. *Business Horizons* 43 (3): 19–26.

Jones, John P. 1990. Ad spending: Maintaining market share. *Harvard Business Review* (January–February): 314–42.

Lane, W. Ronald, Karen W. King, and J. Thomas Russell. 2005. *Kleppner's advertising procedure*, 16th ed. Upper Saddle River, NJ: Prentice Hall.

Little, John D. C. 1966. A model of adaptive control of promotional spending. *Operations Research* 14 (November–December): 175–97.

Ogilvy, David. 1985. *Ogilvy on advertising*. Singapore: First Vintage Books. (Orig. pub. 1983, Multimedia Books.)

Rossiter, John R., and Peter J. Danaher. 1998. *Advanced media planning*. Norwell, MA: Kluwer Academic Publishers.

Schroer, James C. 1990. Ad spending: Growing market share. *Harvard Business Review* (January–February): 44–48.

Sissors, Jack Z., and Roger B. Baron. 2002. *Advertising media planning*, 6th ed. New York: McGraw-Hill.

Wells, William D., Sandra Moriarity, and John Burnett. 2006. *Advertising principles and practice*, 7th ed. Upper Saddle River, NJ: Prentice Hall.

Notes

1. This definition and the subsequent definitions in this chapter (unless otherwise noted) are taken from the American Marketing Association (AMA) list of definitions (http://www.marketingpower.com/mg-dictionary.php) and are used with AMA's permission.
2. *Mediaweek: Marketer's Guide to Media 2005* (New York: VNU Business Publications, 2005), vol. 28.
3. Eric Schmitt, "The :30 Is on Its Last Legs: Now's the Time to Rewire TV Ad Industry," *Advertising Age*, April 11, 2005, 46.
4. Kate MacArthur, "O'Keefe Looks to Work FCB Taco Bell Magic on KFC," *Advertising Age* 74, no.44 (2003): 52.
5. See note 2.
6. *Mediaweek: Marketer's Guide*, 148–49.
7. Christopher Lawton, "Old Premium Brands Falter as Saavy Competitors Emerge—At Absolut Super-Premium Vodka Begins to Drain Market Share: Are Those Bottle Ads Getting Old?" *Wall Street Journal* (Eastern edition), October 24, 2002, B.1. Retrieved July 18, 2005, from ABI/INFORM Global database. (Document ID: 219924651).
8. See note 2.
9. See note 6.
10. *Mediaweek: Marketer's Guide*, 82–87.
11. David Phillips, "Milk Promotions Key to Foodservice Success," *Dairy Foods* 104, no. 4 (2003): 15.
12. "Movie Revenues Up, Tickets Down," CBSNews.com (2004), http://www.cbsnews.com/stories/2004/12/22/2004/printable662569.shtml.

The Buzz:
Public Relations, Word of Mouth, and More

Chapter Six

Key Terms

blog (p. 133)
buzz marketing (p. 119)
consideration set (p. 119)
corporate advertising (p. 122)
corporate communications (p. 128)
event marketing (p. 124)
guerilla marketing (p. 133)
product placement (p. 132)
public relations (p. 118)
publicity (p. 119)
sponsorship (p. 124)
strategic partnership (p. 124)
viral marketing (p. 132)

Chapter Outline

6-1 Introduction

6-2 Corporate or Institutional Advertising
- 6-2a Characteristics
- 6-2b Audience/Target Market
- 6-2c Measurement
- 6-2d Best Case: Ben & Jerry's Ice Cream

6-3 Sponsorship and Event Marketing
- 6-3a Characteristics
- 6-3b Audience/Target Market
- 6-3c Measurement
- 6-3d Best Case: Yoplait and Breast Cancer

6-4 Corporate Communications
- 6-4a Best Case: Canon USA
- 6-4b Audience/Target Market
- 6-4c Measurement

6-5 Product Placement and Alternative Buzz
- 6-5a Audience/Target Market
- 6-5b Measurement
- 6-5c Best Case: MINI in *The Italian Job*

Summary
Discussion Questions
Practice Quiz
Web Exercise: Energy Companies and the Environment
Additional QuickLinks
Suggested Reading
Notes

Everything secret degenerates; nothing is safe that does not bear discussion and publicity.

—**Lord Acton Dalberg** (1834–1902), British historian

6-1 Introduction

The opening quote seems to speak to the very nature of public relations and publicity. If your campaign cannot manage to initiate and maintain the appropriate "buzz" for your product or service, then you can expect the degeneration process to begin regarding the market's perception of your brand. Publicity and public relations are by their very nature about creating maximum impact for your firm and/or brand or product with minimal resources. This means that you seek to leverage the aspects of your brand or product that the market and the press (media) find interesting to gain media coverage and market "buzz." This "buzz" is about getting relevant audiences talking about and spreading the word regarding the firm or product. In that sense, it is akin to word of mouth (WOM). In the buzz sense, firms can manage and facilitate positive messages about their firms to these relevant audiences through the public relations mechanisms. As everyone will tell you, word of mouth is the most persuasive type of message. Unfortunately, it is often used to pass along a negative message regarding a firm—for example, that poor service experience you had at the local restaurant. It is up to the manager to make sure that the WOM and the buzz is positive. A well-managed public relations program can hope to maximize the positive messages concerning the firm while at the same time minimizing the negatives.

This chapter provides an examination of the public relations component in the strategic marketing communications (SMC) portfolio. That examination begins with the nature of public relations. Each of the elements that make up the SMC public relations toolbox (shown in Table 6-1) is then discussed in regard to its value and appropriate uses. The chapter ends with a summary discussion of how these elements can best be managed within the SMC framework outlined in Part Three of this book.

Let us start with definitions of *public relations, publicity*,[1] and *buzz marketing*.[2] As you will see, there is overlap. In either case, the "buzz" about your organization must be well managed if you are to capture its value. Note that the definitions focus on a set of nonpaid communications between the marketing entity and the environment in which it operates. These communications can be done through the use of a variety of tools available to the marketing communications manager. These tools are the ones shown in Table 6-1.

- **Public relations** is that form of communications management that seeks to make use of publicity and other nonpaid forms of promotion and information to influence the feelings, opinions, or beliefs about the company, about its products or

public relations That form of communications management that seeks to make use of publicity and other nonpaid forms of promotion and information to influence the feelings, opinions, or beliefs about the company, about its products or services, or about the value of the products or services or the activities of the organization to buyers, prospects, or other stakeholders.

TABLE 6-1	The Public Relations Toolbox
• Corporate/institutional advertising	
• Sponsorship and event marketing	
• Corporate communications	
• Product placement and alternative buzz	

services, or about the value of the products or services or the activities of the organization to buyers, prospects, or other stakeholders.

- **Publicity** is the non-paid-for communication of information about the company or product, generally in some media form.
- **Buzz marketing** involves capturing the attention of consumers and the media to the point at which talking about your brand becomes entertaining, fascinating, and newsworthy.

Having identified what public relations and publicity are, let us briefly discuss what they can do for a firm and/or its brands or products. Public relations can deliver on a variety of promises if it is used effectively. A summary of these promises is in Table 6-2.

A firm will generally want to keep its name in the public eye. From a consumer perspective, this means that a given brand from the firm will more likely come to mind in a current or future decision-related or purchase situation. A brand has a much better chance of being in a consumer's **consideration set,** the particular brands that would be considered by a given consumer at the time of evaluation, recommendation, and purchase. Consumer (and even supplier) relationships are critical in today's environment. SMC Marketplace Watch 6-1 gives an example of the importance of "buzz" in a supplier and distributor relationship that we all can relate to: the movies. It is generally much cheaper to keep existing customers than to go out and find new ones. If consumers continue to see positive things about the firm or brand in the marketplace, they are much less likely to leave that relationship. At the same time, consumers who have strong relationships with a given firm or brand are much more likely to feel that there is a greater value in that relationship and be willing to pay for that added value in acquiring that brand.

Public relations can also be used to influence the public opinion arena outside of the consumer relationship. The public opinion arena includes the general public as well as the public policy decision makers (see Chapter Two). Well-conceived public relations executions can also act as a strong primer to the marketplace by creating buzz on the street before the arrival of a new product. In this sense, it "sets the table" for the launch. Think of all the "buzz" generated by the major Hollywood studios for a particular film long before that film's release into the movie theaters. The intent is to facilitate the formation of long lines at the box office for when "the doors open." If done well, public relations can supplement or even supplant more traditional types of advertising in the SMC mix, depending on the situation. A good manager should never overlook the critical role that public relations plays in the life of the firm through defense of the firm and its brand and products. A good manager will have a proactive public relations plan laid out for defense of the firm in times of crisis. This plan should be updated periodically and assessed using "crisis simulations." Proactive public relations planning for crisis management may end up saving the firm from major losses or even total collapse.

publicity The non-paid-for communication of information about the company or product, generally in some media form.

buzz marketing Creation of an atmosphere in which both the consumer and the media find the discussion and promotion of a particular brand to be entertaining, exciting, and newsworthy.

consideration set The group of alternatives that a consumer evaluates in making a decision (can also be referred to as the *evoked set* in a consumer behavior sense).

TABLE 6-2 Public Relations Potential Deliverables

- Keep the firm or brand in the public and consumer eye.
- Build firm or brand and consumer relationships.
- Provide extra value to the brand.
- Increase positive public opinion.
- Positively influence public policy decisions.
- Create pre-advertising and/or product launch buzz in the marketplace.
- Introduce and support a brand or product with minimal advertising expenditures.
- Defend the firm and its brands or products.

SMC Marketplace Watch 6-1

DreamWorks Built Up the Buzz for Its Zoo Movie Madagascar

In 2004 DreamWorks' Chief Executive Jeffrey Katzenberg played host to an event promoted as a seminar on animation. Several hundred Wall Street types, press, and entertainment honchos—with kids in tow—were treated to a marketing extravaganza by DreamWorks aimed at building the buzz for its new movie *Madagascar* and the company itself. As a public relations add-on, Mike Myers, the voice of the green ogre in the blockbusters *Shrek* and *Shrek 2,* and Chris Rock, the voice of the zebra in the film *Madagascar,* along with Jerry Seinfeld, the producer, writer, and lead voice for the 2007 release *Bee Movie,* all contributed to the buzz event. The event finale was a 20-minute sneak peak of *Madagascar.*

The big public relations event not only was meant to launch a movie but also was used to show off the company. Because the firm was now public, the stakes were higher and quarterly earnings and shareholder expectations were part of the package. Since the firm had gone public, competitor Pixar had a string of hits and DreamWorks had mixed success. *Madagascar,* a $90 million flick about New York zoo animals stranded on a desert island, was a hoped-for hit. Investors had to believe and feel good about the future. With the stock up 34 percent since its initial offering, this first movie had to be able to deliver on expectations.

Right around the corner to keep the buzz alive for the movie were a hippo, a giraffe, a lion, and a zebra on boxes of Honey Nut Cheerios and packages of Totino's pizzas. They also were showing up on 1,600 Denny's restaurant menus. The plan was to spend $50 million on marketing. Stars were enlisted and companies targeted to use animated cast members in their own advertising. Ben Stiller, the voice of the lion, hosted Nickelodeon's *Kids' Choice Awards* show; and Hewlett-Packard used the four psychotic penguins from the film in advertisements for its digital cameras and printers. DreamWorks is convinced of the success of the film and is preparing a direct-to-video spin-off starring the penguins. The buzz was out and about through public relations and word of mouth.

The bottom line on keeping the hoped-for franchise film alive is that DreamWorks knows such a movie can keep contributing to the value of a firm for a very long time. Films like *Shrek* can become virtual cash cows through revenue generation from products and DVD sales and sequels. Merrill Lynch & Co. analyst Jessica Reif Cohen figures that *Shrek 2,* the top-grossing animated film at the box office, eventually provided DreamWorks with $623 million in operating profits. With *Shrek 2* and *Shark Tale,* DreamWorks in 2004 earned $333 million on revenues of $1.1 billion. *Shrek 3* and *Shrek 4* are already in the works. A year earlier, without a hit film, DreamWorks lost $187 million.

Source: Adapted from Ronald Grover in Los Angeles, "A Bad Case of Pixar Envy," *Business Week* (New York), no. 3933, May 16, 2005, 97.

In a crisis, one can argue that the public relations element is the most important component for any brand. Consider the lasting impact that the *Exxon Valdez* oil spill disaster in 1989 has had on Exxon (now ExxonMobil) over the years in every corner of the global environment, from your living room to international movements. Fifteen years later, the mention of the Exxon brand will elicit negative comments from a certain number of people in almost any room. (See SMC Marketplace Watch 6-2 for the *Exxon Valdez* public relations story.) Some people still refuse to buy the brand, even if they have to drive an additional number of miles out of their way to do it. Oil company executives from other companies use the case as a training example of how not to handle a public relations disaster.

The situation that Exxon faced—and continues to face—is not the usual level of conflict in its operating environment that most firms face. It is, however, a reminder of how important all the elements of an SMC mix are. All the elements must be considered as crucial in delivering the overall message that a marketing communications manager wants to deliver. That message is one that is relevant to a number of stakeholders, not just the company's direct customers.[3] The basic definition of a *stakeholder* is one who holds a share or an interest in some endeavor. More specifically, these stakeholders can best be thought of as any group that is either directly or indirectly influenced by or influences the environment in which the brand or marketing

SMC Marketplace Watch 6-2

A Lesson from a Public Relations Failure

On March 24, 1989, the Exxon tanker *Exxon Valdez* hit Bligh Reef in Prince William Sound off Alaska. What followed was an environmental disaster of epic proportions. At the same time, the response from the company to the episode created an epic public relations disaster for the firm. Even though the company spent over $2 billion on cleanup alone, the company's image and reputation were left in tatters. The media, the general public, and public policy officials blasted the company for its response. Of particular focus was the perception of Exxon Chairman Lawrence Rawls being uninvolved or even unconcerned. This perception grew from his failure to appear in public for over a week after the spill. As one public relations writer, William Small, pointed out, " Exxon has lost the battle of a favorable public image and is still trying to regain its reputation. If public relations was an objective, it was a failed one." Companies need to take the lessons from this disaster to heart. Small summarized two of those lessons: First, the only sensible policy should be a clear demonstration of candor and repentance. Second, the chief executive officer embodies the company and should step up to the forefront and act as the spokesperson for the company. Money and good intentions are not enough when a crisis strikes.

SMC QuickLink
Exxon
http://www.exxon.com

Source: Adapted from William J. Small, "*Exxon Valdez:* How to Spend Billions and Still Get a Black Eye," Public Relations Review 17, no. 1 (April 1991): 9. Retrieved from ABI/INFORM Global database (Document ID: 9051622).

---

entity operates. These stakeholders can be your customers; your employees; the public at large; stockholders; members of an organization's channel (either suppliers or buyers); public policy makers at the local, state, national, or global level; the media; advocacy groups; lobbyists; and so on. In other words, in today's world there is a need to recognize that organizations do not exist in what we often call a vacuum. These various stakeholders are summarized in Table 6-3.

Any marketing communications manager must have a clear recognition of the breadth and the nature of the various stakeholders that are relevant to the firm. Any one of the relevant stakeholders is a valuable ally in the continued healthy existence of the firm. Failure to recognize all relevant stakeholders of a firm—and plan accordingly—in the public relations domain can spell trouble for the firm. In the broad sense, any of the groups listed in Table 6-3 have a clear share in what a given firm does and how that firm communicates with the world.

The Exxon example can again be used illustrate how all stakeholders can be affected. Starting at the top of the table, some customers stopped buying product. The news media quickly picked up the story and conveyed it to the world. The general public was by and large outraged at the damage done to the environment and demanded that something be done. The public policy officials demanded actions,

TABLE 6-3 Relevant Stakeholders in the Strategic Marketing Communications Public Relations Domain

- Customers
- News organizations and general media
- General public
- Public policy officials
- Stockholders and the investment community
- Employees
- Suppliers and other channel members
- Members of the industry

SMC Marketplace Watch 6-3

Racing for Fans and Sponsors

June 19, 2005, was the day of the Formula One U.S. Grand Prix race in Indianapolis, and Michelin Tire Company had just discovered a design flaw in its tires that made them unsafe. After a last-minute special request that would allow teams to change their tires after qualifying failed to gain approval from the Grand Prix governing body, Michelin advised all teams using their tires to withdraw from the race. With only two tire manufacturers making tires for the teams, the net result was that fourteen of the twenty drivers did not compete. With only six cars left in the race, the more than 100,000 racing fans were less than pleased.

Formula One, which has been a strong global performer outside of North America, had been working for over 5 years to build audience in the U.S. market and attract lucrative sponsorships like the kind that NASCAR has received; but June 19 loomed large as a public relations disaster that could torpedo even the best-laid plans. Sponsors were clearly not pleased with the events of that day. "We've already been re-thinking our commitment," said a marketing chief for one U.S.-based sponsor, who asked not be identified. "Even before [June 19], we talked about taking a long look at a sponsorship where, of the nineteen races, only two were in North America [Indianapolis and Montreal] and the popularity of the sport didn't seem to be growing that much. Now, I would say, yeah, what happened has kind of hastened those discussions."

Michelin quickly issued a statement concerning its decision: "Michelin deeply regrets that the public was deprived of an exciting race and therefore wishes to be the first, among the different groups involved in the Indianapolis race, to make a strong gesture towards the spectators." The company then followed up with an unprecedented offer to the fans who had come to see the U.S. Grand Prix. It would refund the entire price of the ticket. At an average price of $100.00, that worked out to about $12 million to which Michelin added another $5 million that Michelin will buy for the 2006 race.

Whether or not the public relations move will help save the Formula One series in the United States is still open to debate. Formula One President Bernie Ecclestone was not too optimistic following June 19: "The future for Formula One in the United States is not good."

Source: Adapted from Rich Thomaselli, "Michelin Responds to PR Disaster: Offers $12 Million in Formula One Race Ticket Refunds," *Advertising Age,* June 29, 2005. AdAge.com QwikFIND ID: AAQ70V.

---

brought actions against Exxon, and passed new legislation. Stockholders were upset, and shares fell in value with worries of future earnings. Employees were embarrassed and questioned by friends as to what kind of company Exxon was to let such a thing happen. Members of the channel in some cases changed brands, and retail outlets felt the consumer boycott impacts. Meanwhile, members of the entire oil industry expressed their disappointment and anger as they watched the prestige and consumer perceptions for the entire oil industry plummet. This last stakeholder realm could also be extended out to all of business, because one could expect spillover to continue out to the entire business community.

On the positive side of a reaction to a potential public relations disaster is the case of Michelin Tires shown in SMC Marketplace Watch 6-3. Michelin recognized the likely long-term impact on the entire system of a lesser response than full restitution to what it viewed as "injured parties" (the race attendees). While the short-term cost was extreme, one can speculate that the long-term cost would have been much greater. Subsequent sections of this chapter address each of the public relations elements from Table 6-1.

corporate advertising
An advertising message or campaign that has the primary purpose of promoting the name, image, personnel, or reputation of a company, organization, or industry.

6-2 Corporate or Institutional Advertising

Corporate advertising is an advertising message or advertising campaign that has the primary purpose of promoting the name, image, personnel, or reputation of a company.

6-2a Characteristics

It becomes clear from the definition of corporate advertising that this type of advertising is an element of public relations. There is no mention of "selling" a particular product or feature. In the place of selling, though, there is an unmistakable positioning characteristic regarding branding and corporate identity. Corporate advertising is about supporting or creating brand essence and the corporate identity This type of advertising is all about the brand and how the entity wants itself to be viewed in the marketplace.

We all have images of major companies and the characteristics that define those companies. Think of a few major firms. What images come to mind? When you think of Nike, what does Nike conjure up in image and words? What about Apple? What about U2 (the band)? *Nike* may generate a picture of Michael Jordan and link to words of "athletic performance." *Apple* may generate the image of its logo or an iPod and mean "technological leader." *U2* may generate a stadium concert scene and link with words such as "activists" and "Irish."

Corporate image advertising is about effectively managing those linkages to elements surrounding the entity. This type of advertising is extremely important when the consumer basically "purchases the brand or company." That is, the consumer purchases the product based on his or her relationship with the brand essence. For example, in global markets, Coca-Cola may be purchased because it represents the "American lifestyle" and its values that may be aspired to by the youth market. Trust can also be a crucial element in relationships with any of the stakeholders in Table 6-3. Therefore, the harmony in these relationships with the brand and what it stands for is crucial. How can the brand be linked in a positive manner to things that matter to the marketplace? Positive linkages can be developed in a variety of ways. They generally relate to a positioning issue. These advertisements may simply focus on the values of the target audience and show how the firm and the target audience are in harmony regarding these values. They can, for example, show how a company contributes to society through helping raise funds or public awareness for a social cause (e.g., partnerships with the American Cancer Society or similar organizations) or showing how a particular product or service that the company produces serves the well-being of the greater society in some manner. An example of this may be producing high-resolution imaging equipment that allows physicians to better diagnose and treat illnesses like cancer and heart disease.

6-2b Audience/Target Market

The audience or target market encompasses any or all of the stakeholders in Table 6-3. For an example of how Swatch targets a younger audience, see Exhibit 6-1.

6-2c Measurement

Corporate advertising uses the same measurements as outlined in Chapter Five regarding traditional broadcast and print media when it comes to exposure, reach, frequency, and GRPs. Strategic measurements of performance are covered in Part Three.

6-2d Best Case: Ben & Jerry's Ice Cream

Ben & Jerry's has become one of the most recognized brands in the high-end ice cream business. Beyond the quality of its products, its social stand has made it a favorite in the eyes of the segment of the population who feels that business should play a socially responsible role in society. Public policy people will often hold Ben & Jerry's up as an example of successful businesses that are committed to social causes. After the acquisition by Unilever, fears of a sharp departure from the socially responsible path have proved unjustified.[4]

SMC QuickLink
Ben & Jerry's
http://www.benjerry.com

124 Part Two The Marketing Communications Portfolio

Exhibit 6-1
Swatch Billboard from Swiss Mall Promoting Safe Sex

This advertisement for Swatch clearly relates to Swatch's market, which tends to be young and hip. The humor and imagery are in keeping with the brand. At the same time, it addresses the very serious problem of the need for safe sex without preaching to the target market.

Source: Courtesy of Swatch.

sponsorship A relationship executed between two or more entities that seeks to establish an association between the entities for mutual benefits. This sponsorship can exist long term or as a single event for the common promotion of a product, service, idea, or cause. The common practice is for one of the entities to provide financial and/or other types of support in exchange for brand promotion.

event marketing
The development, promotion, support, and execution related to a particular event that is designed to promote a particular brand, product, service, idea, or cause. As with sponsorship, if the event involves multiple entities, the common practice is for one or more of the entities to provide financial and/or other types of support in exchange for brand promotion.

6-3 Sponsorship and Event Marketing

Sponsorship is a relationship executed between two or more entities that seek to establish an association between the entities for mutual benefits. This sponsorship can exist long term or as a single event for the common promotion of a product, service, idea, or cause. The common practice is for one of the entities to provide financial and/or other types of support in exchange for brand promotion.

Event marketing is the development, promotion, support, and execution related to a particular event that is designed to promote a particular brand, product, service, idea, or cause. As with sponsorship, if the event involves multiple entities, the common practice is for one or more of the entities to provide financial and/or other types of support in exchange for brand promotion.

6-3a Characteristics

Clear objectives of the sponsorship should be laid out before the relationships are undertaken, and performance should be monitored throughout these relationships. Many of these relationships are well thought out and managed very closely due to their importance to all the parties involved. In this case, they are referred to as **strategic partnerships.** The discussion here centers on the characteristics of various types of sponsorships. The actual relationship is generally (1) between two or more for-profit entities or (2) between a for-profit entity and a not-for-profit entity (which often involves a social cause). These sponsorships can be long-term relationships or single events. In all cases, though, the intent is to enhance value for all the entities involved.

The first of these is increasingly seen in the high-powered field of professional sports. All major bowls at the end of the regular college football season now have "named sponsors" for the game (e.g., Nokia Sugar Bowl). In auto racing, the $750

NASCAR Sponsorship Reaches a Rabid Sports Segment

Committed sports fans from soccer to car racing can be rabid in their support "for the team" and anything they see as representing that team. Sponsorships of sporting events and the sport itself offer companies a chance to connect their brand to that highly involved consumer. It is hoped that this connection will translate into committed, brand-loyal customers for the firm's product/service.

Source: Photo by Bob Townsend.

million sponsorship deal between Nextel and NASCAR is an example of the first type that has proved highly successful in its brief history.[5] After years of NASCAR's Winston Cup Series racing, the deal has produced the Nextel Cup Series. There are also much less expensive means for entering the sports sponsorship arena. One of those inroads is through "presenting sponsorships."[6] These minor sponsorships allow logos and other messages from companies to be present at sporting events on such things as seat cushions or ticket stubs for a certain fee.

Since the 1960s, the Montreux Jazz Festival event in Switzerland has created a perfect place for the interaction of musicians, music lovers, and a variety of brands (see Exhibit 6-2). The event itself brings world-class musical acts from a variety of music genres to the shores of Lake Geneva. Swatch acted as one of the major sponsors in 2005, and Montreux Jazz Festival 2005 versions of its watch were specifically created for the event. The watches were sold in the festival's official stores, and the brand was prominently displayed throughout the venues, promotional materials, and so on. Coca-Cola was also on hand with a disc jockey and open-air booth providing music and product for the crowds. Also present were a wide variety of music-related firms such as Gibson (musical instruments) and Shure (microphones and sound equipment). The event and the brands involved in it "spill over" onto each other to create product differentiation based on a combination and a resulting synergy of what each brand stands for in the mind of the target audience. Montreux made a great deal of sense for these types of firms given the demographic and lifestyle groups in attendance. It is critical for a firm to make sure that the event provides a good match in providing access to the firm's current or potential target market.

Corporations can also use manufactured events to further the buzz about their brands. While it is crucial to have a good match and execution in a partnership situation, when the event is nothing more than a clear brand promotion, the firm must make certain that the event is one that creates the right kind of feel for the brand. It must also ensure that the presence of the brand at the event and the nature of the event itself will be enough to draw the appropriate audiences in the numbers that meet defined objectives.

While any type of event marketing is a tool that is often used to cut through clutter in the marketplace, managers working with the organizers must create a plan that anticipates every possible contingency. It must be recognized that everything involved in the event must meet the requirements to enhance brand essence. Problems that arise also "spill over" onto the brand. Years ago, the Rolling Stones

strategic partnership (see p. 124) Cooperation strategy between companies to jointly pursue a common goal. Strategic partnerships are also referred to as *collaborative agreements* or *strategic alliances*.

SMC QuickLink
NASCAR Nextel Cup Series™
http://nextelonline.nextel.com/en/promotions/nascar.shtml

SMC QuickLink
Montreaux Jazz Festival
http://www.montreuxjazz.com/index_fr.aspx

Exhibit 6-2

Montreaux Jazz Festival

Event sponsorship by *(a)* Swatch and *(b)* Coca-Cola at the world-famous Swiss music festival reaches a global target market of music lovers.

Source: (a) Courtesy of Swatch. *(b)* Coca-Cola, the Dynamic Ribbon Device, the Contour Bottle design and mycokemusic are registered trademarks of The Coca-Cola Company. Reprinted by permission.

concert at Altamont, California, and the Who concert in Cincinnati, Ohio, were each sites of fan deaths because of events at the concert. The prior was because of a stabbing by Hells Angels acting as security guards in the crowd, and the latter was because of fans rushing the door to get good seats in a festival seating concert. Both bands are linked with those events many years after the events. The deaths in Cincinnati led legislators to pass legislation banning festival seating at all future con-

SMC Marketplace Watch 6-4

Even the Best-Laid Plans....

Snapple's idea was to stage an event in which it would create the world's largest ice pop in New York's Union Square. It recruited world-renowned ice expert Max Bollkman Zuleta to oversee the construction of the 3,950 gallons of kiwi strawberry mixture into an ice pop. Prior to construction, the ice pop was kept in pieces at −15° Fahrenheit in Edison, New Jersey, and then transported to Union Square in a freezer truck. While very well planned, it turns out that Snapple forgot that outdoor events in cities can be affected by a variety of uncontrollable elements. In this case, it was the weather.

Starting at 10:00 A.M., the event went fine until the early afternoon sun and heat had wreaked havoc on the build attempt. Parts of the hoped-for 20-ton structure turned into an avalanche of slush in the day's 80° temperatures. Snapple did get a lot of buzz, though, with the kiwi strawberry slush sliding around one of New York's busy neighborhoods.

A spokesperson for Deutsch, the Interpublic Group of COS Inc.'s advertising agency that staged the event, called it a success because they did generate buzz that reached a lot of people and they provided product samples of ice pops and Snapple to 45,000 of the event's visitors from the time the ice pop began taking shape at 10:00 A.M. until mid-afternoon.

Source: Adapted from Anna Heinemann, "The Snapple Ice Pop That Ate Union Square. Story of a Promotional Stunt Gone Awry," *Advertising Age,* June 22, 2005. QwikFIND ID: AAQ67M.

---

certs in Ohio. Both bands are still touring and have had their concerts sponsored by large corporations. Other mishaps at events, while not as onerous, can have a clear effect on the event and the brand both in the near and far term. SMC Marketplace Watch 6-4 reveals one event that got a bit "sticky" for the brand.

When the sponsorship involves a relationship between a for-profit and a not-for-profit, the sponsorship and event become more related to "cause marketing." Cause marketing involves the support of an idea, charity, or program generally for the betterment of the society. Cause marketing here is considered to be a bit different from advocacy advertising in the sense that we assume a more socially noble intention. That is not to say that firms do not gain value from that nobility. These causes are often related to the support of a nonprofit organization such as the United Way or Habitat for Humanity. In today's world of seeking to build brand value, the ability to tie a particular brand to a socially desirable cause allows the firm to differentiate itself from the competition "with the company it keeps." A cause or a not-for-profit can gain access to much needed financial resources that a corporate entity may possess while the corporate entity gains value through building the desired brand essence. The fight against cancer has brought a number of firms into these types of relationships.[7] This type of cause-related marketing can be thought more of as a corporate partnership between the two entities. It is important for both entities look for a match that is consistent with the values of both entities. A mismatch can have the potential to be costly for one or both of the entities. Consider if you would the negative impact that may arise from a relationship between a liquor manufacturer and Mothers Against Drunk Driving (MADD). On the other hand, a relationship between MADD and a company that provides automobile insurance would make sense. In fact, such a relationship does exist between MADD and State Farm Insurance.

Event marketing for profits and not-for-profits can be part of cause marketing or a stand-alone relationship. Yoplait, in its commitment to fighting breast cancer among women, also supports the Race for Life, which is a series of 5K race/fitness walk events. These events attract thousands of participants yearly and offer opportunities for the Yoplait brand to build stronger relationships with its consumers, the larger marketplace, and others.

SMC QuickLink
MADD
http://www.madd.org/home

6-3b Audience/Target Market

The target audience is any or all of the stakeholders in the SMC public relations domain. Thus, it can include customers, news organizations and general media, the general public, public policy officials, stockholders and the investment community, employees, suppliers and other channel members, and members of the industry (as shown in Table 6-3).

6-3c Measurement

Performance can be measured in terms of attendance figures, tickets or coupons, booth attendance, web accesses, standard monitoring of appropriate measures of awareness, perceptions, attitudes, and purchase intention. It can also be measured through surveys (pre and post for events and tracking data for sponsorship).

6-3d Best Case: Yoplait and Breast Cancer

Yoplait Yogurt for years has provided consumers with the chance to fight breast cancer through collecting caps from their yogurt and mailing them in. The relationship has been very successful. For the not-for-profit, the relationship has provided increased awareness of the issue and funds to carry on the fight against breast cancer. For Yoplait, the relationship has contributed greatly to the marketplace's perception of Yoplait being a socially responsible and caring company.

SMC QuickLink
Yoplait
http://www.yoplait.com

6-4 Corporate Communications

Within the public relations portfolio is a group of tools that allow the corporation to directly communicate with the various stakeholders and convey specific information about what, when, why, and where the entity or corporation is doing. These **corporate communications** elements are: (1) the press release, (2) the press conference, (3) interviews, (4) annual reports and corporate websites. Each of these is briefly discussed here.

The press release is a direct written communication to the greater public about some aspect of the company that certain audiences are likely to find of interest. A well-crafted press release should draw the attention of the media and provide information that is easily transferred by the media into a newsworthy story produced by the particular media outlet (see Exhibit 6-3). When you visit any corporation's website, you should find a link that connects you to all the recent press releases from that particular corporation. A quick reading of a variety of these press releases should allow you to gain valuable information about how a company does business, what its future holds, and what its values are.

Related to the press release but having an event spin to it is the press conference. Bob Geldolf (Live Aid organizer), Bono (from the band U2), and other well-known celebrities used the press conference to announce their plans for a Live-Aid-like series of concerts to raise awareness about third world debt relief. The press conference was attended by a wide variety of media from around the world. At the press conference, media were informed as to the purpose of the event, the timing, the format, the participants, and so on. The press conference allowed the Live 8 organizers to generate a great deal of publicity for the series of concerts that were scheduled to coincide with the meetings in Scotland of the leaders of the G8 nations. The event itself was a success, attracting thousands of attendees and millions more through the Internet and television media. While most corporations may not generate as much excitement with a press conference, a press conference that is well planned and executed can deliver a very focused and positive transmission of information for the corporation or business entity.

corporate communications
Communications used to build favorable attitudes toward a particular company with competitors, consumers, the financial community, stockholders, and other publics. Can also refer to internal marketing communications that are sent throughout the organization for information dissemination or the same purpose as above.

Press Information

Summer Travel Tips from US Airways

Arlington, Virginia, June 6, 2005—To make your travel as smooth as possible in what is shaping up to be the busiest summer travel season in years, US Airways would like to remind our passengers that being informed is being prepared, and usairways.com is the ideal source for travel information. Online, customers can make flight reservations, check in for flights, find forms and procedures for children traveling alone, and check up on required documentation for international travel.

By using the "Travel Planning" feature on usairways.com, customers can see the recommended check-in arrival times at airports across the US Airways system and view up-to-the-minute weather advisories.

Here are some tips from US Airways to help smooth travel this summer:

- Check in online and leave early for the airport. Flight Check-In at usairways.com allows customers to check in for flights departing within 24 hours, and no later than 90 minutes, before departure. Customers also can select seats and print boarding passes from a home or office computer. For checked baggage, see a curbside attendant or visit one of our 565 Self-Service Check-In Kiosks located at ticket counters in 88 airports.
- US Airways is committed to our youngest travelers, and our Kids Class program for unaccompanied minors is designed to ensure that they are safe, supervised and comfortable at every step of their journey. Parents and guardians can review a thorough pre-departure checklist at usairways.com, as well as complete and print out the required forms. Even so, we advise customers to arrive extra early at the airport when seeing off their children.
- Planning on visiting Europe, the Caribbean, or another international destination? To ensure you have the proper travel documentation, which may include a passport, visa, state-issued birth certificate, or government-issued photo ID, visit the "Travel Planning" link on usairways.com for destination-specific information. The proper documentation must be presented at check-in on the day of departure.
- Limit the amount of metal carried before leaving home, like pocket change, belt buckles and large jewelry, which commonly set off metal detectors. Some shoes have reinforced metal toes or metal supports in the heels that could also trigger metal detectors. As a reminder, the Transportation Security Administration (TSA) banned all lighters onboard aircraft in April 2005. For more information, visit the TSA website at http://www.tsa.gov/public.
- Carry undeveloped film in carry-on luggage. The scanners that checked baggage goes through could affect film, making pictures look hazy or blurry. Pack medication and other essential personal belongings in carry-on baggage as well.
- Be aware of excess, oversize, and overweight baggage rules when packing for a long vacation this summer. US Airways customers can check up to two pieces of luggage without charge. With the exception of sporting equipment and special assistance devices, baggage checked on US Airways must have total dimensions less than 62 inches (157 cm) within the free baggage allowance.
- Blankets are available on our European and Caribbean flights, as well as on West Coast flights departing after 9 P.M. Cabin temperatures may vary, so for added comfort, consider personal preferences and dress accordingly, even if headed for the tropics.
- Be sure that US Airways has all customer contact information for the duration of the trip, so that we can make contact with travelers if there is a flight irregularity. Take the time to replace outdated luggage tags, and include contact information—and ideally, the itinerary—inside bags as well, in case the outside tag is separated from the suitcase.
- Customers requiring special assistance can visit our "Ask a Question" feature at usairways.com for information to make your trip go more smoothly.

US Airways is the nation's seventh-largest airline, serving 181 communities in the United States, Canada, Europe, the Caribbean, and Latin America. US Airways, US Airways Shuttle and the US Airways Express partner carriers operate approximately 3,400 flights per day. For more information on US Airways flight schedules and fares, visit US Airways online at usairways.com, or call US Airways Reservations at 1 (800) 428-4322.

Reporters needing additional information should contact US Airways Corporate Affairs at (703) 872-5100.

Exhibit 6-3
Press Release
Source: Reprinted by permission of US Airways.

Interviews and company tours give inside access to the news media and other interested parties. A well-conceived, open-access, interview policy that is appropriate for the type of firm can give all stakeholders the feeling of transparency. In today's world, such transparency can be a very positive benefit for the firm in a variety of ways. It may be as simple as the perception of being a good neighbor willing to talk to community leaders and students. It may also give public policy officials the feeling that the firm has "nothing to hide" and therefore is not in need of greater government scrutiny or legislation. An interview (and company tours as well) allows corporations or entities a chance to "tell their story" in an interactive "one-on-one"

Global Call to Action against Poverty Campaign Press Conference

At the World Economic Forum in Davos, Microsoft founder Bill Gates, British Prime Minister Tony Blair, U2 lead singer Bono, and others offered their support for the GCAP campaign at a press conference.

Source: AP/Wide World Photos.

SMC QuickLink

Nike
http://www.nike.com

manner. Nike was the recipient of a great deal of negative publicity regarding its production facilities in developing countries. To attack that view, Nike has a policy of providing factory tours of its production facilities in Vietnam and other countries. It uses the tours to "set the story straight" about negative perceptions of its labor practices. It strongly encourages people to visit and tour the facilities. One of the authors of this text frequently takes groups of students to visit Vietnam and various businesses, with Nike production facilities being one of the manufacturing stops on the visit. After one recent visit to a factory that produced Nike product in Vietnam, one student, who had started the tour with a particularly negative feeling toward Nike, was heard to say "I am going back home and buying a pair Nikes! This place was great. I had a totally wrong idea of the working conditions here."

In general, an interview or tour gives the visiting parties much greater detail and insight into the way in which the corporation or entity goes about its business. It is crucial to have those people being interviewed or leading a tour to be skilled at communication and prepared to discuss whatever topic may be covered. A well-prepared interviewee or tour leader allows the exploration of relevant issues (even negative ones) so that information that is relevant to the issue can all be placed in the open and addressed by the corporation's representatives. A poorly prepared interviewee or tour leader, though, can lead to potential disaster.

Consider one last comment on interviews and tours when they are placed in the context of exclusivity. Exclusive access granted to the media or other influential parties will often generate stories from writers who feel "privileged" to have that exclusive access to information regarding the firm. This feeling of being special can translate into a positive relationship between the interviewer and the corporation or entity. Under those conditions, it is much more likely that there will be a more positive spin to any subsequent stories or coverage.

The annual report and the corporate website are the places where a company offers a great deal of information about itself for public consumption. Prior to websites, the annual report was *the* place to go for information on the company. An annual report in a very brief format will let any interested party know what the company is about. Most companies now offer electronic versions of their annual reports that can be accessed online through various services or on the corporate website. Vision statements, corporate philosophy, products and product lines, how to acquire goods, terms of sale, and tax information are all there. In both the annual report and the website, everything counts to the interested party. The website and the annual report should present a unified message of who the corporation is and what its brand essence is. Graphic designs; colors; layouts; font; the amount of space given to vari-

Interviews and Tours

An interview or tour gives the visiting parties much greater detail and insight into the way in which the corporation or entity goes about its business. Exclusive access granted to the media or other influential parties also will often generate stories from writers who feel "privileged" to have that exclusive access to information regarding the firm. As such, it is much more likely that there will be a more positive spin to any subsequent stories or coverage.
Source: © 2006 JupiterImages Corporation.

ous topics, both business and social; and so on all need to be discussed and evaluated by the firm before they are executed. Go visit a corporate website and then read their annual report and you should get a fairly good idea about what the firm believes in and how it does business. You should also get a clear sense of unity of message about the firm. If you do not, then something needs to be fixed. The thing to remember about all corporate communications is to play to your correct audience with the right kind of message. Simply creating "boilerplate" kinds of messages may potentially even create difficulties instead of contributing to a positive feeling within and outside of the firm.[8]

6-4a Best Case: Canon USA

Canon USA produces a line of office imaging equipment for consumption in the United States and overseas. When you visit the Canon USA website and read its annual report, the sense of unity of message exists. This is a company that cares about quality in everything it does, but it also cares about community and the environment. It communicates that in press releases and access to interviewing and by sponsoring various things that support a commitment to its vision and company philosophy.

SMC QuickLink
Canon Inc.
http://www.canon.com

6-4b Audience/Target Market

The target audience is any or all of the stakeholders in the SMC public relations domain. Thus, it can include customers, news organizations and general media, the general public, public policy officials, stockholders and the investment community, employees, suppliers and other channel members, and members of the industry (as shown in Table 6-3).

6-4c Measurement

Performance can be measured in terms of the numbers of interviews given, positive stories produced following interviews, tours, web accesses, standard monitoring of appropriate measures of awareness, perceptions, attitudes, and purchase intention. It can also be measured through surveys (pre and post for events and tracking data for sponsorship).

6-5 Product Placement and Alternative Buzz

Product placement is the placing (inserting) of brands into regular entertainment, news, or other media. The intent is to create an association between the brand being placed and the audience that is interacting with the given medium. The common practice is for the placed brand to provide financial and/or other types of support in exchange for brand insertion in the regular content of the medium.

Without a doubt, the current level of product placement in today's marketplace is the result of too much clutter in the traditional channels of marketing communications. Technology has also played a major role in providing impetus for product placement by allowing consumers to zap and zip commercials or not be exposed to them at all. In the movie arena, the leader in product placement for years was (and in many ways still is) the James Bond movie series. The producers learned early on that they could "sell" space in a movie and generate additional revenues to cover the costs of producing the Bond sagas. If you rent a James Bond movie (beginning with the Roger Moore movies), you will find a plethora of branded products that make their way into the movies. Given the target market these companies were trying to reach, it was a fairly cheap exposure medium for a number of years. Placements these days can be quite expensive and are used much more strategically now than before.

Sports is another area in which product placement is used heavily to promote certain brands. The outdoor signage in the stadium can also reach millions who watch a sports event. NBC would digitally insert billboards for downhill racing that would show up on the millions of televisions tuned in for viewers to intently watch the racing slashing past the advertising message.[9] If you ever wondered why skiers always held their skis with the brand name toward the camera during interviews, that is product placement as well. Golfers are paid to wear certain brands during golf matches and in many cases are paid based on the amount of time the brand logos are shown on the program. A match leader on the last day can ring up significant earnings based on such a deal. At the same time, the brand achieves exposure and brand affiliation with sports celebrities during situations when watching fans are in a heightened emotional state.

One of the real problems for product placement has been trying to develop effective measurements to gauge its impact. Questions as to enhanced performance or diminished performance due to integration need to be examined to help set prices for inclusion in various media. However, a growing number of firms and organizations tout product placement as much more effective than traditional advertising for products. The definitive answer to that argument is yet to be arrived at. Some of the QuickLinks following the summary in this chapter are to product-placement firms who specialize in integrating brands into the movie, television program, or even magazine story content.

While placement gets the product in front of people in an unsuspecting way, so do some of the approaches to alternative buzz. Two terms that are often used in discussions of this type are *viral marketing* and *guerrilla marketing*. **Viral marketing** is about trying to get people to spread the word about your brand or product like a virus (hence the name). Bob tells Ann, Ann tells Debbie who tells Dave, and so on. Often this is done via emails or electronic media, but it can also be a word-of-mouth-driven type of marketing so we mention it here. The bottom line for viral marketing is to make the content interesting and valuable enough in the eyes of the consumer

---

product placement The placing (inserting) of brands into regular entertainment, news, or other media. The intent is to create an association between the brand being placed and the audience that is interacting with the given medium. The common practice is for the placed brand to provide financial and/or other types of support in exchange for brand insertion in the regular content of the medium.

viral marketing A marketing phenomenon that facilitates and encourages people to pass along a marketing message; nicknamed *viral* because exposing people to a message mimics the process of passing a virus or disease from one person to another.

to pass along. Doctors are always in search of diagnostic support tools but are a very tough group to get to adopt en masse. Epocrates, a software that provides basic drug data for no charge and disease profiles and lab diagnostics for a fee (starts at $60 per year), is now subscribed to by one in every four doctors in the United States. The marketing started with three hundred emails a few years ago, and the rest was by word of mouth and forwarded emails.[10]

As noted at the beginning of this chapter, buzz is about getting people to talk about your brand and products. **Guerilla marketing,** as its name implies, is sneaking up on people and delivering them your message before they know it. The unique aspect of guerrilla marketing is "thinking outside the box" in regard to traditional ways of doing things. While guerrilla marketing is often thought of as being an "in your face" kind of marketing, it does not have to be. It can be much more subtle and be used as part of a larger strategy that gets mixed in with a more traditional set of marketing communications. For example, Heineken placed "the right kind of people" in bars in major markets to be seen consuming Heineken beer.[11] It also continued to run its regular advertising for the brand. The very nature of the way in which you deliver your message can generate additional buzz and media interest, which will aid in building your brand's or product's position in the market.

Finally, buzz can be built with **blogs.** An increasing number of people use blogs to talk about topics that interest them. By definition, blogs are basically online diaries. They are a chronological online publication of personal thoughts and musings, and often include a collection of links to various websites. While blogs initially tended to be a mixture of what was going on in someone's life, they have also become a means by which marketers can "create buzz" and provide information to consumers and clients (and get them talking to each other as well) in a fairly low-cost manner.

guerilla marketing Unconventional marketing intended to get maximum results from minimal resources. The technique relies on quick-hitting, irregular, and often unexpected means by which to elevate the brand in the consumer's eyes and mind. It often requires marketing personnel to "think outside the box."

blog A hybrid form of Internet communication that combines a column, diary, and directory. The term *blog* is short for "weblog" and refers to a frequently updated collection of short articles on various subjects with links to further resources.

6-5a Audience/Target Market

For product placement, the audience generally is the same as the audience of a given movie or television show. For buzz campaigns and viral marketing, the audiences are again consistent with the product target market. Whereas buzz used to be more of a youth idea for targeting, now it is used widely in other audiences.

6-5b Measurement

For product placement, the performance can be measured traditionally based on exposures and ratings and such, but increasingly there is a move to bring new measures to bear (see, for example, SMC Marketplace Watch 6-5). For buzz and others, there are again traditional measures such as web accesses and standard monitoring of appropriate measures of awareness, perceptions, attitudes, and purchase intention. They can also be measured through surveys (pre and post for campaigns and tracking data for sponsorship).

6-5c Best Case: MINI in *The Italian Job*

As noted in the Part Two introduction, the entire movie plot of *The Italian Job* offers the chance to show what a spectacular performance car the MINI is. While there were numerous contenders for this Oscar, the MINI zipped away from the crowd by its total integration in the plot and seamless performance. This movie will continue to offer brand impact as long as the DVD plays on in households around the world.

SMC QuickLinks

Paramount Pictures: The Italian Job
http://www.italianjobmovie.com/flash/index.html

The Italian Job Children's Charity Fundraising
http://www.italianjob.com

SMC Marketplace Watch 6-5

Different Ways to Measure: Product Placement's Impact Still Not Clear to Advertisers

TNS Media Intelligence joined others in trying to provide valid measurement for product placement by launching Branded Entertainment Reporting Service. The service tries to provide that measurement by integrating branded-entertainment data into a system capable of comparing the data to advertising in eighteen other types of media.

Nielsen Media Research, a rival of TNS, monitors product placements with the Nielsen Product Placement Service. The service also uses a database. The Nielsen database is called PlaceViews. This particular database catalogs and counts all visual and audio references to products during prime-time entertainment programming on the six major television networks. Payment for placement does not matter. Data collected in this service include whether a product was used in the foreground, background, as a prop, or in the storyline; which characters were involved; and duration of time the brand was on air.

Intermedia Advertising Group (IAG) Research takes yet another approach. Their service, In-Program Performance, registers the effectiveness of advertising based on viewer responses to the content of the shows, advertisements, placements, and sponsorships, in addition to cataloging and counting occurrences of product placements.

The lack of a solid, industrywide standard and method for accurately measuring this impact has been a real concern for product placement as a business. An Association of National Advertisers survey of 118 major marketers found that 63 percent had tried a mix of product placement and branded entertainment initiatives in their marketing campaigns, but 40 percent of the group felt there was no credible measurement system that could be linked to a return on investment (ROI) assessment by the firm using it. Eighty-five percent of those surveyed reported that their primary concern was having a measurement system that quickly reported who had been reached by the product placement.

Source: Adapted from Anna Heinemann, "TNS Launches Product-Placement Measuring Service," *Advertising Age*, June 21, 2005. Adage.com QwikFIND ID: AAQ66H.

Summary

In the SMC portfolio, public relations is a key component in maintaining the image and essence of a firm and/or brand. It can also offer for-profit and not-for-profit firms with limited budgets a way to get the message out concerning who and what they are and the products and services that they offer at a much reduced cost (as compared to using the more traditional advertising and other portfolio elements covered in Chapter Seven and Chapter Eight). If done well, public relations can offer a way to add credibility to the message regarding the firm or brand. It can offer a means to cut free from the clutter that may be present if a more traditional advertising approach is used. The event- and cause-related part of public relations helps a firm define itself in the eyes of the market "by the company it keeps." As with any SMC element, in using public relations it is crucial to select the particular public relations tool that best suits your target audience in communicating the given message.

As noted in the Part Two opener, the chapters here are brief and not intended to provide in-depth coverage of each of the presented advertising elements. For that reason, we suggest that you spend some time on the sites that are listed in "Additional QuickLinks." These sites represent public relations associations, firms that work in the field whose pages offer some insights into public relations and the "buzz." This section is not to endorse any particular company or organization but, rather, to allow you to visit a few of the many sites that are out there. A few of these sites also provide some good summary listings of related public relations links. Most of these sites offer additional amounts of information about public relations, product placements, and so on and the roles that these SMC portfolio elements can play for a firm. Again, as noted in the Chapter Five, by visiting these sites, you will be able to learn many more details about the various elements than was possible in this chapter, given our space constraints and the strategic nature of this book.

Discussion Questions

Using a corporate brand of your choice, assume that you are the brand manager for that particular brand. Your boss has requested that you put together a comprehensive public relations plan for enhancing the value of the brand while still maintaining the essence and character of the brand. To help you in your evaluation and public relations plan:

1. Ask three of your friends to write down five words that best describe your brand. Ask these same people which word best describes your brand.
2. What do those words tell you about the public's perception of your brand?
3. What characteristics of your brand are strongest in the mind of the people you interviewed?
4. Which would be your primary public relations tool? Why?
5. Of all the tools available to you, which would be most useful in creating positive "buzz" for your brand? Why?
6. How did the characteristics of your target market influence your choices of tools?
7. Find a corporate image advertisement for your brand and evaluate its message about your brand. Is it successful in conveying the essence that you would like your brand to convey to the marketplace? Why or why not?
8. Find two corporate image advertisements from your competitors and compare them with your own product's corporate advertisement from Question 5. Of the three advertisements, which is the most successful in conveying the brand essence? Why?

Practice Quiz

Note: You can find the correct answers to these questions by taking the quiz and then submitting your answers in the Online Edition. The program will automatically score your submission. If you miss a question, the program will provide the correct answer, a rationale for the answer, and the section number in the chapter where the topic is discussed.

1. Identify the most persuasive form of publicity.
   a. positive news
   b. advertising
   c. word of mouth
   d. viral marketing

2. Which of the following is defined as the non-paid-for communication of information about the company or product, generally in some media form?
   a. word of mouth
   b. public relations
   c. publicity
   d. buzz marketing

3. _____ involves capturing attention of consumers and the media to the point where talking about your brand becomes entertaining, fascinating, and newsworthy.
   a. Word of mouth
   b. Public relations
   c. Publicity
   d. Buzz marketing

4. With what would one associate an advertising message that has the primary purpose of promoting the name, image, personnel, or reputation of a company?
   a. strategic partnership
   b. sales promotion
   c. brand consciousness
   d. corporate advertising

5. Which of the following observations regarding corporate advertising is incorrect?
   a. It is an element of public relations.
   b. Selling a particular product finds a place in this type of advertising.
   c. There is a positioning characteristic regarding branding and corporate identity.
   d. It is about supporting or creating brand essence and the corporate identity.

6. With what would you associate the relationship between Mothers Against Drunk Driving and a company that provides automobile insurance?
   a. relationship advertising
   b. cause marketing
   c. corporate image advertising
   d. nonprofit marketing

7. Before the advent of websites, where would one look for information on a particular company?
   a. press release
   b. interviews
   c. advertisements
   d. annual reports

8. Which of the following involves inserting of brands into regular entertainment, news, or other media?
   a. word of mouth
   b. corporate image advertising
   c. product placement
   d. press release

9. Identify the type of marketing that tries to get people to spread the word about particular brands or products by providing content that is interesting and valuable enough to pass along.
   a. awareness marketing
   b. sponsorships
   c. guerilla marketing
   d. viral marketing

10. What is the unique aspect of guerilla marketing?
    a. awareness generation
    b. creating the buzz
    c. thinking outside the box
    d. interesting and valuable content

Web Exercise

Energy Companies and the Environment

As noted in this chapter, the *Exxon Valdez* oil spill has had a major impact on the entire oil industry and how it views the public relations function. Visit the websites of ExxonMobil (http://www.exxonmobil.com) and some of the other oil companies (e.g., Chevron, Texaco, BP, to name a few). How do they portray their relationships with the environment? With society? With the consumer? Why are these relationships so crucial to firms, especially firms in industries like energy?

Additional QuickLinks

The Ad Council
http://www.adcouncil.org

Business Ranks Directory
http://www.businessranks.com/public-relations.htm

Buzz Business Summary Links
http://www.buzzbusiness.com/directory/advertising_and_marketing/corporate_branding_and_identity/positioning/product_placement

Canadian Public Relations Society
http://www.cprs.ca

Creative Product Placement Firm
http://www.acreativegroup.com/ces

Hollywood Product Placement Firm
http://www.hollywoodproductplacement.com

The Museum of Public Relations
http://www.prmuseum.com

New Age Media Concepts
http://www.namct.com/main.html

Online Public Relations Summary Links
http://www.online-pr.com

PR Firms by Infobeagle
http://www.infobeagle.com/business/pr-agencies.htm

PR Newswire Organization
http://www.prnewswire.com

Public Relations Resource Page
http://www.aboutpublicrelations.net/index.htm

Public Relations Society of America (PRSA)
http://www.prsa.org

Viral + Buzz Marketing Association
http://www.vbma.net/about.html

Women Executives in Public Relations
http://www.wepr.org

Suggested Reading

Evan, W. M., and R. W. Freeman. 1976. A stakeholder theory for the modern corporation: Katian capitalism. In *Ethical theory and business*, 3rd ed., ed. T. Beauchamp and N. Bowie, 97–106. Englewood Cliffs, NJ: Prentice Hall.

Notes

1. These definitions, and a few of the subsequent definitions in this chapter are taken from the American Marketing Association (AMA) list of definitions (http://www.marketingpower.com/mg-dictionary.php) and are used with AMA's permission.
2. The *buzz marketing* definition is taken from one of the buzz marketing firms (http://www.buzzmarketing.com).
3. W. M. Evan and R. W. Freeman, "A Stakeholder Theory for the Modern Corporation: Katian Capitalism," in *Ethical Theory and Business*, 3rd ed., ed. T. Beauchamp and N. Bowie, 97–106 (Englewood Cliffs, NJ: Prentice Hall, 1976).
4. Sarah Mahoney, "It Only Looks Easy," *Advertising Age*, March 7, 2005, 12.
5. Barry Janoff, "NASCAR-Nextel Year One: Score Points for Fans, Sponsors," *Brandweek*, November 22, 2004, 12.
6. Rich Thomaselli, "Now, Many Words from Our Sponsor," *Advertising Age*, January 3, 2005, 6.
7. Mercedes M. Cardona, "Marketers Think Pink for Breast Cancer Awareness," *Advertising Age*, October 23, 2000, 18.
8. Bob Tippee, "All That Boilerplate," *Oil and Gas Journal*, May 23, 2005, 17.
9. Vanessa O'Connell, "NBC Olympic Sports Plugs Inside Plugs—Networks Ads Show Athletes Zooming Past Movie Posters That Were Put in Digitally," *Wall Street Journal*, January 15, 2002, B-1.
10. Erick Schonfeld, "Helping Doctors Go Digital Epocrates Used Viral Marketing to Connect with Physicians—and a Shrewd Business Model to Profit from Advertisers Who Want to Reach Them," *Business 2.0* 6, no. 6 (July 2005), 54.
11. Heather Todd, "Future of . . . Guerilla Marketing," *Beverage World* (August 2004), 14.

Direct and Interactive Marketing

Chapter Seven

Chapter Outline

7-1 Introduction
7-2 Direct Marketing and Databases
7-3 Telemarketing
    7-3a Characteristics
    7-3b Measurement
    7-3c Best Case: Ferguson Enterprises—Servicing and Selling
7-4 Broadcast Direct Response
    7-4a Strategic Marketing Communications Elements
    7-4b Characteristics
    7-4c Measurement
    7-4d Best Case: The Food Network and Shop at Home
7-5 The Internet and Electronic Communications
    7-5a Strategic Marketing Communications Elements
    7-5b Characteristics
    7-5c Measurement
    7-5d Best Case: Shop Goodwill Online
7-6 Direct Mail, Catalogs, and Print
    7-6a Strategic Marketing Communications Elements
    7-6b Characteristics
    7-6c Measurement
    7-6d Best Case: L.L.Bean Catalog—More Than a Walk in the Woods
7-7 Direct Selling
    7-7a Strategic Marketing Communications Elements
    7-7b Characteristics
    7-7c Measurement
    7-7d Best Case: Avon Crosses Cultures to Bring Beauty Directly to the Home
Summary
Discussion Questions
Practice Quiz
Web Exercise: Map Your Experience on the Information Superhighway
Additional QuickLinks
Suggested Readings
Notes

Key Terms

card pack (p. 152)
catalog (p. 152)
cross-selling (p. 145)
data mining (p. 142)
database (p. 139)
database marketing (p. 140)
direct mail (p. 152)
direct marketing (p. 140)
direct selling (p. 155)
direct-broadcast commercial (p. 146)
direct-response advertising (p. 152)
electronic catalogs (e-catalogs) (p. 149)
electronic mail (email) (p. 148)
electronic newsletters (e-newsletters) (p. 149)
house list (p. 154)
infomercial (p. 146)
inserts (p. 153)
instant messages (IMs) (p. 149)
interactive marketing (p. 140)
Internet direct advertising (p. 149)
lifetime value (p. 155)
multilevel marketing (p. 155)
outside list (p. 154)
permission marketing (p. 143)
spam (p. 150)
telemarketing (p. 145)
television shopping network (p. 146)
websites (p. 149)

Think like a wise man but communicate in the language of the people.

—**William Butler Yeats** (1865–1939), Irish dramatist and poet

7-1 Introduction

The world of today showers both business people and final consumers with massive amounts of data regarding brands and products and services. Information comes at us from around every corner at every moment of every day. From a marketing communications manager's perspective, this situation is not an enviable one. In this environment of constant clutter, a major problem is getting the intended target to pay attention to information without dismissing it—not to mention getting the target to process the information at any level to move toward purchase. To paraphrase John Eden in *Images*,[1] there is indeed a great deal of roadkill on the information superhighway that has not contributed to the consumer's (both business and final) knowledge concerning brands and products and services. Two elements are critical to building relevant knowledge and generating a subsequent desired action: (1) getting through to the "right" consumers with the right communication and (2) having them respond in a timely manner so that they do not get lost again in the clutter before the communication's proposition has been accepted and hopefully acted on. The first is a necessary condition for the second to occur, but it is not sufficient by itself. The first relates to being able to identify the appropriate target audience ("think like a wise man") for a message and purchase proposition ("communicate in the language of the people"). The second relates to providing an action alternative while the recipient is still engaged with the brand and/or product or service.

Direct marketing tries to address both issues. It goes directly to business customers and consumers that the marketing communications manager has identified as prospects and offers the chance to interact with the brand and/or product or service. In this regard, it is critical that direct-marketing managers possess a good **database.** The development and maintenance of the database are essential. A good database allows the manager to "think like a wise man" by understanding and targeting and the proper audience. Without a well-developed (and well-maintained) database, the information communicated will be dismissed outright by those who are not the appropriate audience. To address the second of the critical elements, direct marketing offers the consumer the chance for immediate action regarding a marketing communication and/or purchase offer to mitigate the problem of "not closing the sale" before the consumer moves on and is again lost in the cluttered environment of competing brands and messages. In direct marketing, the offer is made when the prospect is engaged. In such a setting, the prospect has the opportunity to act to continue the process and/or purchase a brand immediately. The Direct Marketing Association (DMA) reports that such an interactive and dynamic environment led direct-marketing-related sales and nonprofit contributions to reach a level of $2.3 trillion in 2004. In 2004 direct marketers spent around $217 billion, with about $115 billion of that on the business-to-business sector.[2]

This chapter provides an examination of the direct-marketing component in the strategic marketing communications (SMC) portfolio. This chapter does not, however, get into the execution and development of direct-marketing campaigns. "Additional QuickLinks" at the end of the chapter offer the reader a number of sites

database A compendium of information on current and prospective customers that generally includes demographic and psychographic data, as well as purchase history and a record of brand contacts. This information can be from internal or external sources and includes such items as sales reports and research studies.

TABLE 7-1	The Direct-Marketing Toolbox
	• Telemarketing
	• Broadcast direct response
	• Internet
	• Direct mail, catalogs, and print
	• Direct selling

that provide a much more in-depth exploration of each of the toolbox elements. This examination is to highlight what these components may have to offer from an SMC manager's perspective when building an SMC plan. We begin with a discussion of the nature of direct and interactive marketing. Many of the direct marketers now use a combination of some or all of the direct-marketing toolbox elements displayed in Table 7-1 to conduct their business. They have found that such combinations allow greater synergy and contribute to a better overall performance for their operations. Each of these elements that make up the SMC direct- and interactive-marketing toolbox is discussed in regard to its potential value and appropriate uses following the section on databases. The chapter ends with a summary discussion of how these elements can best be managed within the SMC framework outlined in Part Three of this book.

Let us start with definitions of *direct marketing* and *interactive marketing*.[3] Because of the critical importance of the database, the AMA definition of *database marketing* is included as well. As already noted, a good database that includes updated and appropriate information can be the difference between the success or failure of direct marketing.

direct marketing
An element or tool of marketing communications. It involves various forms of marketing communications couched in direct channels of distribution, such as direct mail, catalogs, telemarketing, direct-response advertising, the new electronic media (e.g., teleshopping and videotext), and direct selling.

interactive marketing
A special case of direct marketing that occurs in the virtual world of cellular, Internet, or any other type of electronic-technology-enhanced environment.

database marketing
Marketing communications that are directly facilitated by a large database containing relevant information about customers and prospects.

Direct marketing is a form of nonstore retailing in which customers are exposed to merchandise through an impersonal medium and then purchase the merchandise by telephone or mail (retailing definition); it is the total of activities by which the seller, in effecting the exchange of goods and services with the buyer, directs efforts to a target audience using one or more media (direct selling, direct mail, telemarketing, direct-action advertising, catalog selling, cable selling, etc.) for the purpose of soliciting a response by phone, mail, or personal visit from a prospect or customer (channels of distribution definition).

The term **interactive marketing** is often used in reference to direct marketing that occurs in the virtual world of cellular, Internet, or any other type of electronic-technology-enhanced environment. In such a case, interactive marketing is a special case of direct marketing as defined in the preceding AMA definition.

Database marketing is an approach by which computer database technologies are harnessed to design, create, and manage customer data lists containing information about each customer's characteristics and history of interactions with the company. The lists are used as needed for locating, selecting, targeting, servicing, and establishing relationships with customers in order to enhance the long-term value of these customers to the company. The techniques used for managing lists include (1) database manipulation methods such as select and join, (2) statistical methods for predicting each customer's likelihood of future purchases of specific items based on his or her history of past purchases, and (3) measures for computing the lifetime value of a customer on an ongoing basis.

Having defined direct marketing, we continue our quick overview concerning the nature of direct marketing. Direct marketing for a lot of years would conjure up visions of Vegi-matics and things to store your food leftovers in. Things have changed; but then again, as Exhibit 7-1 shows, some of the classics have changed very little over the years.

Exhibit 7-1
As Seen on Television
Although direct marketing on television has evolved to include more complex programming and products, it still has some enduring pitches from its earlier years that continue to do well on the medium.
Source: Courtesy of Ronco Corporation.

It can be argued that technology and the consumer demand for convenience and efficiency in shopping have played a major role in that change and in building direct marketing to the level it now enjoys. As the hardware and software technology developed, databases showed that, if used wisely, the technology could offer much closer targeting and evaluation of consumer and business segments.[4] Consumers and businesses also seemed to find that direct marketing offered them a much more efficient way to acquire what they needed. They no longer needed to visit a "bricks and mortar" establishment. Purchases from catalogs, online, or television shopping (networks or infomercials, etc.) would be deposited at their doorstep or in their mailbox. A visit to any direct marketer's website shows the convenience with which products may be acquired and delivered to you.

At the same time, on the final consumer side, direct marketing can conjure up some pretty negative feelings. These tend to relate to the "invasion of privacy" and very real concerns about people's security of personal information. We have all been the recipient of unwanted calls at dinnertime and mailboxes (both postal service and email) full of unwanted materials. There is also a pool of individuals who are the victims of such things as identity theft. Some of the public feel the direct-marketing industry may be at least partially to blame for the situation, and the industry is taking note.[5] The industry has some apprehension about recent legislation such as the National Do Not Call Registry and potential future legislation and what it may mean to the industry.[6] You may wish to revisit Chapter Two for more legislative and macroenvironmental issues.

While direct marketing is being used more by the mainstream, for-profit sector, the not-for-profit sector has used direct marketing as a centerpiece for its appeals for funds for a very long time. *The Jerry Lewis MDA Labor Day Telethon* for the Muscular Dystrophy Association is a very good example of the use of the direct-marketing appeal by charities and not-for-profits. This television-based special is, in essence, an infomercial to engage donors. Over the years, this star-studded entertainment program has raised millions for "Jerry's Kids."

All in all, the use of direct-marketing methods by not-for-profits has been quite successful over the years. In 1998 over $60 billion was raised by not-for-profits through direct mail and telephone solicitations alone.[7] Although new restrictions on the use of databases and telemarketing could put a dent in that number,[8] the use of direct marketing will continue as a way to raise needed funds from the public.

SMC QuickLink
Home Shopping Network
http://www.hsn.com

SMC QuickLink
Muscular Dystrophy Association
http://www.mdausa.org

The Jerry Lewis MDA Labor Day Telethon for the Muscular Dystrophy Association

The Jerry Lewis MDA Labor Day Telethon for the Muscular Dystrophy Association is a very good example of the use of the direct-marketing appeal by charities and nonprofits. This television-based special is, in essence, an infomercial to engage donors. Over the years, this star-studded entertainment program has raised millions for "Jerry's Kids." Shown here are Ed McMahon and Jerry Lewis.
Source: AP/Wide World Photos.

SMC QuickLinks

U.S. Census Bureau
http://www.census.gov

The Indonesian Bureau of Statistics
http://www.bps.go.id/index.shtml

data mining The analytical process of finding new and potentially useful knowledge from data. The process includes the use of mathematical tools to find difficult patterns of intelligence. Helps to identify unforeseen patterns and behaviors.

7-2 Direct Marketing and Databases

We turn now to the interface of direct marketing and one of its most important assets, the database. As noted, synergies provided to the marketers' side of the exchange equation by linking databases and direct marketing have allowed the evolution of direct marketing over the past decade. These benefits are shown in Table 7-2. If monitored and used wisely, the direct-marketing process and a good database can deliver along a variety of dimensions.

In building a database, identifying what pieces of information need to be included is crucial. The particular database needs will vary with each type of business and/or industry. Whether it is a business-to-business or a business-to-consumer operation is one obvious distinction that would influence design and requirements. Table 7-3 provides a summary of some of the types of data that generally would go into a marketing-communications-focused database.

The sources for such data can be found both internally (at the firm) and externally. Internally, sales records and such data related to existing customers can be a starting point to build additional elements seen in Table 7-3. Externally, a variety of data sources exists, beginning with the government census data for consumers and industries. The government has a true wealth of data on a variety of dimensions that are readily available. Around the globe, Bureau of Statistics sites offer much the same for almost every country. A number of private database service providers such as Simmons and Donnelly Marketing also have large existing databases. Consumer surveys can be conducted either by the company or by consulting firms. Finally, for a firm that operates in a multitiered channel (e.g., manufacturer, wholesaler, retailer), the members of the channel will often be willing to provide or exchange data to facilitate better performance throughout their value chain.

It is up to management to spend the time to identify what elements need to be included in the database. Taking the time to plan before collecting data can save a great deal of wasted time later in **data mining,** which is sorting or analyzing information from a database to isolate patterns or trends. A cluttered database filled with irrelevant data is more of a hindrance than a help in trying to identify, track, communicate, and evaluate subsequent performance. The strategic use of information in a good database can open up all sorts of new markets and ways in which to communicate and service them.[9] Good data in a well-designed database, one that is based on a clear set of objectives, can be used to link the entire SMC process to the consumer as the information can help guide the types, placement, timing, and even cre-

TABLE 7-2 Direct-Marketing and Database Deliverables

- Better control of channel communications
- Control firm or brand and consumer relationships
- Enhanced ability to gather additional consumer data
- Reduce distribution cost
- Better ability to measure performance
- Reduction in response time to action
- Enhanced ability for cross-selling

TABLE 7-3 Potential Elements for the Database

- Names, addresses, and contact information
- Type of customer (business or consumer)
- Point of contact (first and subsequent such as "saw advertisement and called in")
- Demographics (if available psychographics)
- Types of products or services purchased
- Purchase amounts/levels
- Purchase cycles (dates of purchase and time between purchases)
- Purchase method (store, catalog, online, telephone)
- Purchase and customer financials (credit, cash, account, etc.)

ative execution of message content for communicating and building stronger relationships with the target audience.

The value of strengthening these customer relationships can be seen in the growth of such things as (1) **permission marketing,** (2) loyalty/frequency programs, and (3) corporate-sponsored online "lifestyle" communities. In the first of these programs, consumers give their permission to be contacted and sent various communications and "special" incentives for being a valued partner with the company. This approach shies away from the guerilla types of tactics that some consumers may be becoming wary of and, instead, asks them to enter the relationship.[10] (See SMC Marketplace Watch 7-1 for a discussion of permission marketing.)

The second gives an incentive to the consumer to continue in the relationship by offering incentives related to purchasing behavior. These programs involve a wide variety of products—and not just in the United States.[11] The most notable of these is the airline industry's frequent-flier program. This behavior-reinforcement program has spread from airlines to hotels, department stores, restaurants, credit cards, shopping malls, supermarkets, and just about anywhere there is a repeat purchase opportunity on a fairly regular basis. From a database perspective, both the permission marketing and the loyalty programs offer a great chance to collect purchase-related data on a regular basis. In the case of the loyalty programs, for example, every time a purchase is made and a loyalty card is scanned at the purchase point, it can be linked and integrated into the database to match up with the full data profile of the loyalty card user.

The members of online "lifestyle" communities that are sponsored by corporations and interest groups yield large amounts of personal data that can be compiled in a database for the sponsors to use. These communities can offer a wide variety of services and experiential elements for individuals interested in things from babies to hot rods.[12] The limits regarding the use of these data are generally spelled out on the website when the consumer "signs up" with the community.

Data from these "involved" and readily monitored consumers offer a wealth of information for continuing to better focus the communications and offers that can be directed to involved consumers and others like them. The corporation or the

permission marketing
Marketing centered around getting customer's consent to receive information from a company.

SMC QuickLink
Air Canada
http://www.aircanada.com

SMC QuickLink
Alloy.com (Commerce and the Youth Community)
http://www.alloy.com

SMC Marketplace Watch 7-1

Permission Marketing

The future of marketing communications is likely to take the form of *permission marketing*—marketing communications so relevant that it is actually welcomed rather than abhorred by consumers. Permission marketing is inextricably linked with database marketing. For example, academic researchers interested in research publications in their area of expertise visit the publisher's site; they register by providing information about their area of expertise and the kind of publications in which they are most interested. They provide permission to the publisher to send out announcements of new publications in their matched interest areas. When a book matching a researcher's interest comes on the market, the publisher emails that researcher an announcement about the publication (with much information about its content, such as an abstract of the article or table of contents of a book) and information about ordering that publication.

Source: Adapted from Anthony Bianco, "The Vanishing Mass Market: New Technology. Product Proliferation. Fragmented Media. Get Ready: It's a Whole New World." *Business Week,* July 12, 2004, 68.

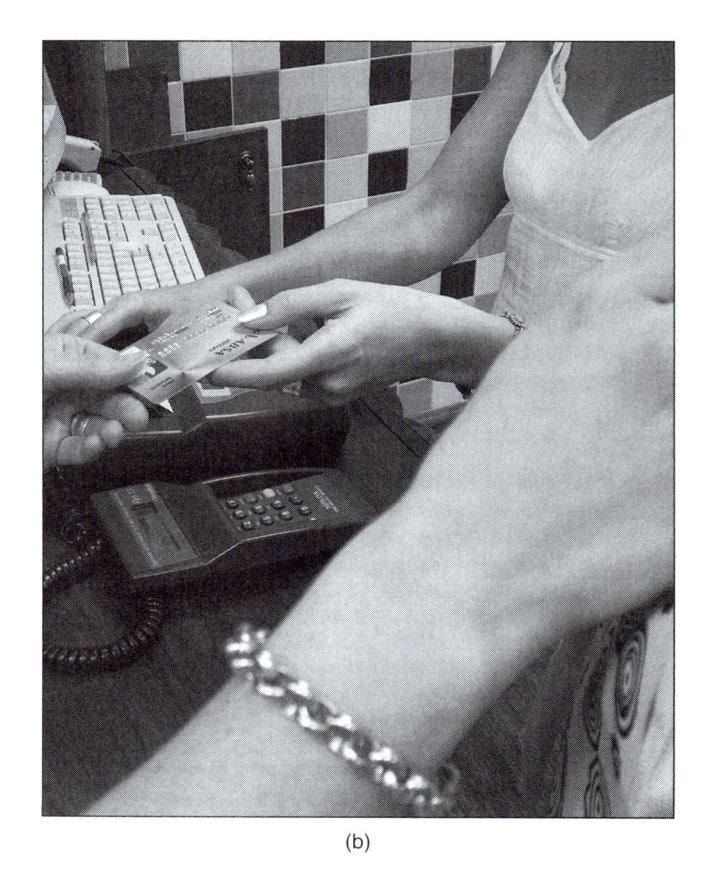

(a)

(b)

Strengthening Customer Relations

The value of strengthening customer relations can be seen in the growth of *(a)* corporate-sponsored online "lifestyle" communities and *(b)* loyalty/frequency programs. From a database perspective, the members of the online "lifestyle" communities yield large amounts of personal data that can be compiled for the sponsors to use, and the loyalty/frequency programs offer a great chance to collect purchase-related data.

Sources: (a) © 2006 JupiterImages Corporation. *(b)* Photo by Lotus Head.

not-for-profit cause can build a fairly complete lifestyle and behavior profile of the members of such programs. From a data-mining perspective, this provides some great opportunities for such things as **cross-selling** related products where the consumer can be offered a variety of related goods and services that are related to a product/service that the consumer already uses (or complementary products/services that the marketer has available) and, in the case of charities, appeals for donations to the consumer.

Hopefully, you can see that the database offers a great deal for the creation and targeting of communications within the marketplace. We now move on to the components that can deliver those communications and products to the target audience. Subsequent sections provide a look at the SMC portfolio elements that are available to the SMC manager from the direct-marketing toolbox summarized in Table 7-1.

7-3 Telemarketing

Telemarketing is the marketing of goods/services or soliciting of funds through the use of telephone services by contacting potential or existing buyers/consumers or donors. Telemarketing comes in a couple of forms. It can be used as either "in" or "out." *In* or *inbound calling* occurs when prospects or buyers call into the firm or entity to begin the exchange. *Out* or *outbound telemarketing* is the one we as consumers seem to complain about the most. The "do-not-call" lists relate to the outbound type of telemarketing. Some books may treat telemarketing in the larger category of personal selling, but we include it here with the direct-marketing group due to its use of technology to achieve contact.

7-3a Characteristics

Telemarketing allows you to have personal voice contact with your prospect or consumer. Even though *telemarketing* in the mind of the general public means annoying calls at dinner, telemarketing is used extensively in business-to-business marketing to conduct business and as a way to support the personal salesforce. Although often rigidly scripted, telemarketing allows the elements of your communications to be adjusted and adapted almost to the degree that personal selling does. Telemarketing operators, though, have much broader access and geographic reach than does a more traditional personal salesforce. With today's communications technologies, a telemarketing operator can reach anyone, anywhere, *from* anywhere. This geographic freedom has allowed the move of call centers to the far corners of the world to help reduce cost for the operation. Pay scales are much cheaper in the developing world, but use of global call centers far away from the markets being serviced must be considered as to their value in the greater strategic mix of the firm. Service, complexity of message and/or appeal, language, technical expertise, and geographic proximity may play a role in your consumers' assessments of your firm.[13] Remember that those individuals who are calling for a firm or cause are representing the firm. Training to provide the communication or service level required by the audience and consumer is a must, as is maintaining appropriate working conditions that will enhance personnel performance and, as a consequence, call effectiveness.[14] It is this call effectiveness that a user of telemarketing should strive for, not simple efficiencies or cost containment.[15]

7-3b Measurement

A number of measures are used related to telemarketing. Some relate to speed and quantity, but the bottom line relates to effectiveness. Cost per call is used as a flat measure for delivery. Measures such as revenue per call and return on investment (ROI) for selling and satisfaction of customer and effectiveness in solving the problem of the customer are useful in this regard.

---

cross-selling In retailing, the process of selling between and among departments to facilitate larger transactions and to make it more convenient for the customer to do related item shopping. In sales promotion, a consumer sales promotion technique in which the manufacturer attempts to sell the consumer products related to a product the consumer already uses or that the marketer has available.

telemarketing Marketing products or services by using the telephone to contact potential buyers.

SMC QuickLink
Ferguson
http://www.ferguson.com

7-3c Best Case: Ferguson Enterprises—Servicing and Selling

Ferguson Enterprises, a wholesaler who services the building and plumbing industry has used telemarketing on the in and out basis over the years. In-house sales are considered to be an important part of the entire Ferguson sales effort. Information is effectively transmitted to its current (or potential) consumers through well-trained personnel who understand the needs of the client base. A well-maintained database contributes to that industry understanding.

7-4 Broadcast Direct Response

Broadcast direct response covers a great number of options for the marketing communications manager regarding the broadcast media category. This particular category, while referred to as broadcast, also covers the cable environment where many of these communications elements now find their home. In a typical cable television market these days, a certain percentage of channels are almost always delivering direct programming 24 hours a day. There is a choice of the 30-second or one-minute commercial, extended-time infomercials, and/or involvement with entire shopping networks. Each of these options provides the communications manager with a variety of strategic benefits and shortcomings that need to be considered when choosing whether or not to use it in the communications mix.

7-4a Strategic Marketing Communications Elements

- The **direct-broadcast commercial** fits in the standard time formats used by traditional broadcast advertisements. It differs from traditional broadcast commercials in that it provides an access point and means for product/service purchase or continuation of the pre-purchase process.
- An **infomercial** is a program-length time period on audiovisual broadcast/cable media used to market ideas, causes, products, and services.
- A **television shopping network** is an audiovideo network whose primary programming content is direct-to-consumer marketing.

direct-broadcast commercial A commercial that usually fits in a standard time format (e.g., 30 seconds) and that gives the listener or viewer the ability to directly respond to the commercial, via a telephone number or Internet access point, to continue the purchase process by either gaining more information or actually buying the product or service.

infomercial The use of a program-length time period to advertise products and services. Usually seen on broadcast or cable television. This approach often includes a direct-response offer to sell the advertised items directly to the public.

television shopping network A network that is built around the process of showing, discussing, and selling products and services directly to viewers. Viewers often call in to be part of the shows, while hosts of certain shows can obtain celebrity-like status to buyers.

7-4b Characteristics

The growth of the direct-response broadcast media was the largest in the late 1980s and 1990s with the spread of cable networks and the increased presence of infomercials to sell a variety of products to consumers. The direct-appeal commercial was also used extensively by not-for-profit groups such as Save the Children to provide a look at the value that consumers could provide through their immediate donations. In 1997 the Arthritis Foundation took its appeal to a full infomercial.[16] Infomercials can also have a much longer life for a company and its appeals. Companies will invest upwards of $1 million in an infomercial but can recoup their costs since the infomercial has a much longer life than a traditional type of advertisement, with some running over a year or more after they are made.[17] While the direct-broadcast medium often conjures up visions of lower-cost goods, evolution in the industry has continued. In 2003 a high-end shopping network, The Ultimate Shopping Network was launched.[18] Partnerships and acquisitions in the media arena have also bred some very good strategic partnerships between "lifestyle" networks and the shopping networks. The Food Network and the Shop at Home Network (the fourth largest shopping network) have created some real synergy for communicating lifestyle and how to acquire product to support that lifestyle.[19]

Direct-broadcast commercials have standard time lengths that are generally 30 seconds, 60 seconds, or 90 seconds. The access point provided by the direct-broadcast commercial is usually a toll-free telephone number. However, interactive television technology in some cases now offers direct-purchase capability on the screen.

SMC QuickLink
The Ultimate Shopping Network
http://www.impostors.com

Infomercials can be "live" or pre-recorded. They provide an extended format (usually 20 minutes or longer) that allows the company or charity to talk about complex product dimensions and "tell their story" with much more detail and affect. As with direct-broadcast commercials, infomercials provide an access point and a means for product/service purchase or continuation of the pre-purchase process. Also the same as direct-broadcast commercials, the access point for infomercials is usually a toll-free telephone number and interactive television technology offers direct-purchase capability on the screen.

The shopping networks usually operate "live" through cable systems and provide their programming content on a 24-hour basis. Each network provides hosts and sales personnel for a variety of products shown over varying time slots, which can range from a few minutes to hour-long segments with guests and celebrities appropriate for the products being offered. These networks offer the same access points and direct-purchase capabilities already described. All major shopping networks also have a web presence to allow off-show Internet shopping by their viewers and nonviewers.

7-4c Measurement

A number of measures are used related to direct-response broadcasting. These include measures such as calls generated per commercial or program, inquiries regarding messages covered in the presentations, revenue per commercial (or part of) and/or per program, number of new orders (donors), repeat orders (donations), and size of average order (or donation).

7-4d Best Case: The Food Network and Shop at Home

The Food Network started cooking in 1993, making viewers salivate and the chefs stars. With the purchase of Shop at Home TV for $285 million in 2002 by E. W. Scripps (The Food Network's parent), the company is leveraging lifestyle with retailing to create an appetizing recipe for increased sales and revenues.[20] In doing so, The Food Network has reaped its just desserts for offerings a tasty mix of offerings to that hungry group of highly involved people.

SMC QuickLinks
Food Network
http://www.foodtv.com

Shop at Home TV
http://www.shopathometv.com

7-5 The Internet and Electronic Communications

The World Wide Web has opened up a vast communications network for use in marketing communications. The wireless revolution (see SMC Marketplace Watch 7-2) has prompted an even faster expansion and use of this communications and cellular network. This ever-expanding world is one that is interactive and direct by nature. Such an environment can allow marketing communications managers not only to send out messages but also to respond to the audience with messages or changes to the brand based on feedback, either immediately or in a delayed manner.[21] The virtual world can be used to provide communication links to customers, employees, interest groups, the public, public policy decision makers, brand franchisees, and all the interested parties mentioned in the Chapter Six discussion on audiences of public relations activities 24 hours a day, 7 days a week. There have been suggestions that this area of marketing communications may well take away from the more traditional areas of media.[22] It has been predicted that spending for online marketing and advertising will climb from around $12 billion in 2004 up to greater than $26 billion in 2010. While email is expected to be fairly flat at around $1.7 billion, expected up only $300 million, search engines are expected to leap from $4.3 billion in 2004 up to $11.6 billion.[23] The marketing communications manager has a wide variety of virtual-world tools to draw from the Internet and electronic toolbox. The choices are (1) electronic mail, (2) electronic newsletters, (3) electronic catalogs, (4) websites, and (5) instant messages. As with any

SMC Marketplace Watch 7-2

Consumer Behavior Related to Wireless Communication

Communicating by wireless communication devices came to life when the first commercial cell phone hit the market in 1984. Two decades later, around half of all Americans—about 150 million people—have cell phones. The industry made $94 billion in 2002 and is growing by 15 percent each year. By the middle of 2002, Americans were spending an average of $53 a month to talk 442 minutes on their cell phones—about 100 minutes more per month than they did in 2001. Americans have logged more than 53 billion minutes chatting.

Wireless communication is beginning to have a notable impact on our social behavior. People are changing their lifestyles because they are using mobile phones. Wireless communication is making people's lifestyle more mobile. At least four ethnographic studies in the United States and Europe released in 2001 and 2002 noted the changing habits of consumers as a direct function of wireless communication. These studies have shown that wireless communication allows people to become independent and spontaneous. Cell phone users are prone to planning at the last minute and arriving at meetings late. Because much of the use of cell phones occurs in public, users are sharing more of their personal lives in public. Basic etiquette is changing because of the use of cell phones in public places. Cell phones allow users to manage multiple roles simultaneously. Cell phones not only enhance social life but also allow work to impinge on family life. People using cell phones become more accessible to social networks. Cell phone use supports relationships; the use of mobile phones helps sustain social ties for emotional gain. By regulating who has the cell phone number, most cell phone users know that incoming calls are most likely from relatives or good friends.

Although cell phone users are split fifty-fifty between men and women, men tend to make more calls than women. Men tend to use cell phones for business more than women do. Women tend to call friends more than men.

Just a few years ago, the average cell phone user was wealthy and white. In 1999, 37 percent of African Americans and 32 percent of Hispanics had cell phones, compared to 42 percent of whites. In 2002, 65 percent of African Americans reported use of cell phones, compared with 62 percent of whites, and 54 percent Hispanics.

Source: Adapted from Hassan Fattah, "America Untethered: Wireless Communication Is Beginning to Have a Notable Impact on Our Social Behavior. A Look at What Ethnographers Have Observed about Our Changing Social Habits, Thanks to the Rise in Cell Phone Use," *American Demographics* (March 2003): 35–39.

---

electronic mail (email)
A communication format that involves sending computer-based messages over telecommunication technology. Email can include a letter-style text message or more elaborate web-style HTML messages. Users can also attach other files to the email and transmit all elements simultaneously.

electronic newsletters (e-newsletters) (see p. 149) Electronic publications (usually small in relative size to a full publication) containing news of interest chiefly to a special group or community.

audience contact, though, marketing communications managers need to monitor and keep control over the information they provide in this virtual world.[24] Nonattention can lead to miscommunications, legal difficulties, and consumer backlash.

Until around 2002 or 2003, when marketing communications managers spoke about the virtual and electronic world, they were referring to the World Wide Web of the Internet. Focus was on an audience that was "surfing the web" from business networks, home computers, or laptops hooked up to the web via dial-up or cable access. In today's world, that is not the case. The world is "wired"—or should we say "wireless"?—and so is the audience. Audience members are mobile and take their "wireless world" with them. The merging of cellular telephones, personal digital assistants (PDAs), and the web has continued to drive evolution in the electronic communications field. Marketing communications managers now contact the audience on a regular basis through a host of tools, for example, instant messages concerning today's lunch special that is beamed to audience members on their cell phones as they pass by a "wired" retailer.

7-5a Strategic Marketing Communications Elements

Some SMC elements of Internet and electronic communications include electronic mail, electronic newsletters, electronic catalogs, instant messages, Internet direct advertising, and websites:

- **Electronic mail** (**email**) is mail, which can include text and graphics, that is sent electronically to anywhere in the world over the Internet.

A Wireless Audience
Today's world is "wired"—or should we say "wireless"?— and so is the audience. Audience members are mobile and take their "wireless world" with them.

Source: © 2006 JupiterImages Corporation.

- **Electronic newsletters** (**e-newsletters**) are electronic publications (usually small in relative size to a full publication) containing news of interest chiefly to a special group or community.
- **Electronic catalogs** (**e-catalogs**) are electronic publications that offer a complete enumeration of items offered by a firm or cause and are arranged systematically with descriptive details regarding these items. In addition to the descriptive details concerning the items, e-catalogs generally include all relevant information regarding the purchase and acquisition of those items including shipping and delivery.
- **Instant messages** (**IMs**) are different than regular email because of the immediacy of the message exchange and allowing the exchange to continue as long as users are online. Most exchanges are text only, but voice messaging and file sharing are possible with some providers. Due to the immediacy of the messaging, real-time conversations are possible. The cellular telephone environment now offers this capability, though the instant messaging is usually referred to as *text messaging*.
- **Internet direct advertising** is a particular type of advertising that is limited to the Internet environment. These advertisements ask Internet users to interact with them by clicking on various offers that arrive on their screens in varied manners. These include banner, button, floating, pop-up, pop-under, and transitional advertisements. The types of advertisements on websites and various search engines are also referred to in classifications laid out by the Interactive Advertising Bureau in their Interactive Marketing Units (IMUs) specifications.
- **Websites** are a conglomeration of virtual pages on the World Wide Web containing hyperlinks to each other and made available online that were built through using various software and maintained by an individual, company, educational institution, government, or organization.

electronic catalogs (e-catalogs) Like the regular hard-copy catalogs, these electronic publications offer a complete enumeration of items offered for sale by a firm or cause. Beyond simply listing all the products and their attributes, these publications generally provide instructions on how to order and acquire the products or services directly.

instant messages (IMs) While very similar to email communication, these messages allow an immediate message exchange between parties as long as the parties stay online. Most exchanges are text only, but use of file sharing, video, and voice is growing. Cell phones are especially well-suited in today's environment for IMs, although on cell phones, such activity generally is referred to as text messaging.

SMC Marketplace Watch 7-3

The Diffusion of Email in Health Care

Email is actually a recent phenomenon. Ten years ago, people did not use email. Now email has been diffused quite rapidly in society. Nowadays, business people communicate regularly by email; students email their teachers; consumers gather information about products and services by contacting companies directly by email. But what about email communication between patients and physicians? The diffusion of email communication between patients and physicians has not been as rapid as in other sectors of society. Physicians remain reluctant to some extent.

American Demographics (http://www.demographics.com) reported the results of a survey released in April by Harris Interactive in Rochester, New York, which shows that about 90 percent of the patients that have Internet access would like to interact with their doctors online. The survey was based on a sample of 2,014 adults. The majority of the patients surveyed indicated that they would be interested in using email to ask their doctors questions when an office visit is not necessary (77 percent), to make appointments (71 percent), to refill prescriptions (71 percent), and to retrieve test results (70 percent). Patients are even willing to pay to communicate with their physicians by email. Specifically, 37 percent are willing to pay an average of $10.60 a month out of pocket or $6.90 per email for the opportunity to communicate with their doctors by email.

With respect to the physicians, they seem to be cool to that idea. A separate survey of 1,200 U.S. physicians found that most physicians expect to be reimbursed an average of $57 for a 15-minute e-consultation.* Around 23 percent of the physicians indicated that they interact with their patients by email. Of those who are not currently emailing, 54 percent said that they may be willing to do so if insurance companies would reimburse them for it; 43 percent indicated that they would do it if they reallocated staff; 42 percent said they would do it if they are presented with proof that email would save time; 37 percent indicated interest if email would help them see more patients; and 37 percent would try it if it can be demonstrated that email can help cut expenses.

Source: Adapted from John Fetto, "Virtual Docs," *American Demographics* (July–August 2002): 16.

*Though the report is no longer available, the information is from a survey conducted by Deloitte Research and Fulcrum Analytics and was cited by Fetto in the *American Demographics* article, from which SMC Marketplace 7-3 was adapted.

<u>Internet direct advertising</u> (see p. 149) Direct marketing that is limited to the Internet environment. In this setting, users are interacting with various offers that appear as banners, buttons, floaters, pop-ups, pop-unders, and transitional items on websites and search engines. The Interactive Marketing Bureau identifies them based on their Interactive Marketing Unit (IMU) specifications.

<u>websites</u> (see p. 149) A collection of interconnected electronic "pages" on the Internet and used to provide information about a company, organization, cause, or individual. The website is often a crucial IMC component in building and maintaining a consistent brand image in the eyes of the consumer.

<u>spam</u> Bulk, unsolicited email.

7-5b Characteristics

As noted previously, the Internet has greatly expanded the way in which businesses, causes, and individuals can interact with consumers at the business and final consumer level. As SMC Marketplace Watch 7-3 shows, that use has raised a number of new challenges and opportunities in markets that have traditionally shied away from new communications innovations. The use of email by marketers has, no doubt, contributed to some concerns about the future of some of the more traditional direct-marketing approaches such as direct mail.[25] Email offers a number of benefits in being able to target a specific group or a fairly broad piece of the mass market with a message and offers crafted specifically for that group. In terms of cost, this can be done much cheaper than direct mail because the cost of postage, printing, and paper is eliminated. Geographic boundaries are also virtually eliminated from the cost consideration. Email as an effective marketing communications tool is, however, under assault from one of its own hybrids: "spam." **Spam** is bulk, unsolicited email. We all have been its targets.

From as early as the mid-1990s, there has been concern from those who use email that the misuse of the tool will create severe backlash from consumers regarding brands that use it.[26] The increase over the past several years in the use of untargeted spam has kindled these types of feelings within various consumer markets. The government and the industry are taking steps to try to aid consumers who receive this spam by providing addresses to forward unwanted spam.[27] Most Internet service providers (ISPs) offer spam filters on all of their software now. The problem of spam offers a real threat to the effective use of legitimate users of email in their campaigns. Government prosecution of offenders and lawsuits from such corporations as Microsoft targeting spammers should help dissipate some of that threat, but only time will tell.[28]

E-newsletters and e-catalogs offer many of the same production cost benefits of email over regular mail. There is no need to print off thousands of the expensive-to-make and mail catalogs that may contain hundreds of pages regarding various products/services that a company has to offer. The reproductive capability of digital imaging and high-speed Internet connections have allowed both businesses and final consumers to interact quickly and effectively using the scanning and ordering capabilities of the e-catalog. When used in combination with other web-based elements in a total selling system, the e-catalogs can offer an effective combination for marketing products locally or around the globe.[29] Many small companies who would have never been able to afford to do regular mailings of catalogs can now update their e-catalogs on a regular basis quickly and inexpensively. The use of e-newsletters allows companies and not-for-profits to continue to keep a strong relationship with customers (donors, members, etc.). For both the corporations and the not-for-profits, an e-newsletter can inform interested parties of topics that may be of interest to them with increased frequency, in a very timely manner, and at a fairly low production and distribution cost. These newsletters can be used in conjunction with the organization's website to bring its constituencies into a more extensive and personal brand experience. For example, Quaker Oats provides a free newsletter on women's health from a health page on its brand site.

SMC QuickLink
Quaker Oats (Health Professionals page)
http://www.quakeroatmeal.com/healthpros/index.cfm

Instant messaging and its cellular cousin, text messaging, offer a chance to deliver marketing communications in a timely and relevant mode. When one of the authors steps off an airplane in a new city in a different country and turns on his cell phone, he immediately gets messages from a number of communications companies offering services for such things as reduced fees on overseas calling, hotels in the area, transportation options in the city, and so on. Consumers walking past department stores and restaurants can receive text messages on their cell phones regarding the sales and menu specials for lunch or dinner (depending on the time of day). The promise of the utilization of the instant message using cellular technology at a point of purchase for a product or service is just starting to be realized.[30] Expect a lot more.

The website for the profit or not-for-profit entity has become a crucial element in communicating what the entity is all about. We discuss the website and its development in regard to the corporate and marketing communications strategies. Website construction is crucial in conveying a sense of brand to the relevant constituencies. As noted in Chapter Six, the website carries a lot of public relations elements with it. The website has become a tool for communication of the brand as much as a place where product/service purchasing occurs. That is not to say that the purchase process and the ease by which a purchase or donation can be executed are not critical elements for the entity. When the website is also used in conjunction with direct-marketing pieces that direct the audience to the website for further information or purchase, the directing pieces and the website itself should be in concert regarding their ability to deliver what was promised.[31] Finally, it must be remembered by the firm or entity that the website offers a variety of services to incoming visitors. These visitors may be looking for, among other things, information, customer service problem solving, sales support, or product purchase. A good marketing communications manager ensures that the message delivered in any one of those situations is appropriate, consistent, meets visitor expectations, and provides a positive message for the firm.

7-5c Measurement

A number of measures are used related to Internet and electronic direct marketing. They include response rates and measures such as calls generated per email, inquiries regarding messages covered in the presentations, revenue per execution, number of new orders (donors), repeat orders (donations), and size of average order (or donation). In regard to e-catalogs, many of the same type of measures

SMC QuickLink
ShopGoodWill.com
http://www.shopgoodwill.com

direct mail The use of the mail delivered by the U.S. Postal Service or other delivery services as an advertising media vehicle. Direct mail can include letters, brochures, postcards, etc.

card pack A type of cooperative mailing that is usually a number of "cards" from a variety of marketers that are included in a mailing package sent to consumers. These cards are often from companies that view the other cards included in the pack as complementary products that may increase the chance for a response or sale. Mailing costs are shared by those including cards in the pack.

catalog A publication containing the descriptions or details of a number or range of products used to increase mail-order sales, phone sales, and/or in-store traffic of the sender. Generally, all the information needed for purchase and acquisition is included. See also e-catalogs.

direct-response advertising An approach to the advertising message that includes a method of response, such as an address or telephone number, whereby audience members can respond directly to purchase the advertised product or service. Direct-response advertising can be conveyed to members of a target market by a wide variety of advertising media, including television, radio, magazines, mail delivery, etc.

are used, albeit a bit more extended and complex. Data can also be measured based on any set of demographic or other types of information collected via the contact point.

7-5d Best Case: Shop Goodwill Online

When we think of Goodwill Industries and their marketing communications, most of us would think of something like a direct-mail piece that asks for your donations to be brought to a drop-off point in a nearby strip mall. The world of e-commerce has beckoned the Orange County, California, chapter of Goodwill and business is booming. Four years ago, the information technology staff set up Goodwill's first web e-commerce site. The website, which is set up as sort of an eBay clone, services over one-hundred separate Goodwill organizations from around the country. Just about everything from cars to jewelry is sold on the site. About 6,000 items a day are listed. Sales have passed the $20 million mark, and revenues are running at close to $600,000 per month.[32]

7-6 Direct Mail, Catalogs, and Print

The public commonly refer to direct mail as "junk mail." Marketers, though, do not seem to share that feeling. In 2004, total mail volume rose nearly 4 billion pieces to 206 billion, mostly in Standard Mail, which includes a significant amount of marketing materials. That level of mail gave the United States Postal Service (USPS) revenues of $69 billion, a reported increase of $265 million over 2003.[33] The numbers of print advertisements that include direct-response capability have increased, again driven by the desire for measurement performance capability. In a 2003 survey of advertising executives, 42 percent of them cited direct mail as the most-effective-return-on-investment medium. This was a clear two to one margin over the next closest choice.[34]

7-6a Strategic Marketing Communications Elements

- **Direct mail** (brochure, advertising, catalog, etc.) is a marketing communication that is sent to its intended recipient through the use of the official postal service of the given country. Direct mailings are done usually under bulk rates, which are much cheaper per unit than first-class postage. The official postal service of the given country will usually have special services that they offer to aid in the mailing and distribution of direct mail. In the United States, direct mail would entail any marketing communications that were sent via the United States Postal Service (USPS). A few SMC elements of direct mail include card packs, catalogs, and direct-response advertising.

- A **card pack** is a cooperative mailing of postage-paid, business-reply cards returned to advertisers who share the costs of mailing the card pack to potential buyers.

- A **catalog** is a publication that offers a complete enumeration of items offered by a firm or cause; the items and their descriptive details are arranged systematically (see Exhibit 7-2). Catalogs generally include all relevant information regarding the purchase and acquisition of those items, including shipping and delivery.

- **Direct-response advertising** is the use of an advertisement that offers the recipient the chance to respond directly to the offer made in the advertisement without having to go to a store for purchase (see Exhibit 7-3). This traditionally is done with a toll-free number or mail-back address. Today, the advertisement may ask the responders to visit a website to complete the sale.

Exhibit 7-2
Crate & Barrel *Catalog*

Catalogs such as ***Crate & Barrel*** offer a complete enumeration of items offered by a firm/cause. The items and their descriptive details are arranged systematically.

Source: Cover image provided by *Crate & Barrel*, reprinted by permission of Gintas Zaranka, photographer.

7-6b Characteristics

Direct mail offers the marketing communications manager some very positive things, many of them driven by the strategic use of a well-maintained database. The medium allows a very specific targeting of individuals based on the situation. Note also the frequency required to achieve a desired result. There is no one number here, but research on the topic can usually be found through the various industry associations, such as the Direct Marketing Association (DMA) (see "Additional QuickLinks" at the end of this chapter). The medium also gives the user complete control over the creative context in which the advertising is seen; that is, the marketer controls all content and packaging. Geographic segmentation down to individual housing units is possible. **Inserts** of a variety of special offers, coupons, and personalized materials are possible on an individualized basis. Potential customers can be identified by database characteristics, or existing customers can be targeted based on their personalized shopping behaviors. For example, in one case from England, a major upscale retailer sends personalized, printed and mailed-on-demand welcome packs to new customers based on the database and has created significant opportunities for cross- and up-selling.[35]

Catalogs as well have a great deal of targeting capability based on the database-supplied information. According to the DMA, 58 percent of Americans shop from catalogs with apparel being the most purchased type of item (57 percent of catalog shoppers), but home decor or furniture is a strong 31 percent; 27 percent of catalog shoppers buy electronics from catalogs.[36] In January of 2005, the mix of the different types of catalogs sent out (dropped) to consumers was: apparel, 30.3 percent; home decor and housewares, 20.5 percent; general merchandise, 15 percent; gifts and collectibles, 7.0 percent; children's products, 6.5 percent; food, 5.5 percent; crafts, hobbies, and sports, 4.8 percent; other, 10.5 percent.[37] These percentages are seasonally impacted, but the numbers from the January drop give an insight into the general distribution of catalog types.

inserts Advertisements or promotional materials that are inserted into newspapers, magazines, or other publications as either "free inserts" (not attached) or "bound inserts" (attached).

Exhibit 7-3

The Economist *Card Insert*

Direct-response advertisements, such as this *The Economist* card insert, offer the recipient the chance to respond directly to the offer made in the advertisement without having to go to a store for purchase.

Source: Used with permission from *The Economist.*

In the past, catalogs were not sent with the frequency that we now see. However, research by the industry has shown that increased frequency, in general, leads to higher yields from the market. It is also important to remember that the overuse of frequency can result in a number of these catalogs being thrown away before even being opened because the customer has a feeling that "they will just send another one next week anyway."[38] This truly does point to a feeling of "junk." This attitude can dilute the value of the catalog and end up costing the firm a great deal, not only in mailing and production costs but also in the "value" of the brand. Keeping the customers satisfied in all aspects regarding the catalog's brand is crucial. Using supplemental communications tools in concert with the catalogs themselves can help keep the relationships with valued customers strong. An industry benchmarking study from February 2005 showed that catalogers regularly contacted their best consumer market customers an average of 10.4 times a year using email, newsletters, solo product offers, and regular and special targeted catalogs. They contacted their business-to-business customers an average of 9.1 times a year using the same communications vehicles. For the business-to-business market, the use of newsletters was stronger; email was more strongly used in the consumer market.[39]

Catalogers often use lists derived from databases to identify who gets a catalog sent to them. Customers who are part of the active company list internally are called members of the **house list.** Those names that come from external sources (such as mailing list companies) are referred to as being from **outside lists.** Data from the previously mentioned industry benchmarking study showed that in the consumer market 49 percent of the mean sales came from the house list while only 12.2 percent came from these outside lists. In the business-to-business group, 60 percent came from the house list with only 11 percent from the outside list. The implication is obvious for revenue generation. The house list is almost always a more productive source of orders and revenue. This is because the cataloger maintains control over its maintenance and the member on the house list has interacted with the company before. Websites are also starting to drive higher sales, contributing almost 26 percent on the consumer side and 11.5 percent from the business side.[40] One of the consultants in the mail order industry published what amounted to his "top ten list" of catalog mistakes for the fourth quarter (a critical time for catalogs with the holidays and such). Among them are such critical things as not clearly positioning the uniqueness of the catalog brand, not staying fresh in format and look, not integrating the catalog with other marketing efforts (in particular, the website), and making it difficult to order from.[41] These seem like pretty simple things, but the simple things are often the ones that cause the problems if not given regular attention.

house list A list of customers developed and maintained "in house" by the company that is marketing the products or services. A house list is often used by catalog companies that can segment the list into a variety of categories, generally based on levels of and types of purchases.

outside list A list of customers developed and maintained outside of the company that is marketing the products or services. These lists are then sold to interested parties (e.g., catalog companies).

7-6c Measurement

A number of measures are used for measuring performance, some of which are response rates and measures such as calls generated per mail, inquiries regarding messages covered in the presentations, revenue per execution, number of new orders (donors), repeat orders (donations), and size of average order (or donation). In regard to catalogs, many of the same types of measures are used, albeit a bit more extended and complex. Catalog drops are evaluated in regard to customer responses and orders for both single drops and quarterly; yearlong and customer **lifetime values** are calculated as well. Data can also be measured based on any set of demographic or other types of information collected via the contact point.

7-6d Best Case: L.L.Bean Catalog—More Than a Walk in the Woods

L.L.Bean is the epitome of the catalog brand. Its catalogs have provided a unified core product for years while at the same time finding specialty niches that are complementary for maintaining the essence of the brand. L.L.Bean launched a new specialty catalog in 2005 called *Everyday Adventures*. The catalog sells women's apparel and gear suitable for activities such as yoga, cycling, walking, and hiking. A variety of products use specialty fabrics to "deliver the goods." Prices for the products go from $8.00 for a water bottle on up. Bean is betting that a significant portion of its female customers lead active lives that fit the catalog offerings of apparel, outdoor gear, and home decor. When the eighty-eight-page catalog was dropped to mailboxes, it went only to house file names.[42]

7-7 Direct Selling

Direct selling is the personal selling element of direct marketing. It differs slightly from the personal selling that is covered in Chapter Eight. Revenues in 2003 from direct selling were estimated at $29.55 billion. About 70 percent of those sales occurred in an individual one-on-one setting. The other 30 percent were largely in the party or group selling setting.[43] *Direct selling* and *multilevel marketing* are defined in the "Strategic Marketing Communications Elements" section.[44]

7-7a Strategic Marketing Communications Elements

- **Direct selling** is the sale of a consumer product or service, in a face-to-face manner, away from a fixed retail location.
- **Multilevel marketing** is a form of compensation in a direct-sales company in which the salesperson can earn money not only on his or her own personal retail sales but also on the sales of people he or she personally recruited into the business and on the sales of people recruited by their recruits.

7-7b Characteristics

In direct selling, the focus is on using personal relationships to create a sort of "dealer network" that operates within the consumer society. Personal selling, on the other hand, is differentiated in that it operates in the business-to-business environment and entails a variety of corporate restrictions and levels. That is not to say that direct selling does not have management levels. Many of these types of programs have district managers, senior salespeople, regional managers, and so on. Many of these direct-selling operations run as multilevel marketing companies with each level receiving compensation for the sales performance of salespeople recruited by the person at the higher level. Again, the nuance here regarding direct selling is to separate out the business-to-business salespeople from this form of direct marketing.

Some of the best known of these types of sales organizations are for home and beauty products like Avon, Mary Kay, Tupperware, and Amway. However, these types of selling operations have expanded into a variety of housewares, candles, quilting, lingerie, gourmet items, and so on. The nations of the transitional world have

---

lifetime value A method of calculating the contribution (value) of a customer over the long term. The calculation is usually based on the yearly number of visits by a customer multiplied by the average amount of money spent per visit multiplied by the customer's average life span.

SMC QuickLink
L.L. Bean
http://www.llbean.com

direct selling 1. (sales definition) A marketing approach that involves direct sales of goods and services to consumers through personal explanation and demonstrations, frequently in the home or workplace. 2. (retailing definition) The process whereby the firm responsible for production sells directly to the user, ultimate consumer, or retailer.

multilevel marketing A strategy used by direct-selling companies to have independent agents serve as distributors and resell merchandise to other agents, who eventually make sales to consumers. This is a compensation system in which salespeople earn money from the sales of other people they recruited into the business and also from the sales of the people their recruits recruited. Sometimes negatively referred to as pyramid marketing.

been the target of a number of these companies, showing great promise for expansion of the selling method. Tupperware in 2005 paid Sara Lee $557 million for its direct-sales operation, which is mostly cosmetics and other consumer goods that are concentrated in developing markets. Tupperware hopes this will expand the product mix (and hence its revenue stream) that it can offer in the social setting of direct sales, which seem to work fairly well in transitional environments.[45] Those who are acting as the salespeople are often friends of those buying; as a consequence, the direct-selling environment relies on what can be fairly heavy social pressure to buy. The group party that is hosted by a friend contributes to the social pressure as the "everyone else has bought" message may not be explicit but implicitly is present. As a result of the social aspects of direct selling, direct selling by salespeople in the single or group setting for things like personal care items or "handicrafts" can be quite successfully used. The setting can create a very positive social and interactive environment for communications about aspects of the product—such things as how to use it effectively and how to fix problems. This all allows the salesperson to build relationships that facilitate immediate purchases or set the stage for future sales. These sales presentations tend to be fairly scripted from a sales formula provided by the parent company, but there is room to adapt to each situation.

7-7c Measurement

A number of measures are used related to direct selling. These are measures such as revenue per sales call, units per call, repeat purchase, salesperson turnover, number of new orders per group meeting, repeat orders, and size of average order.

7-7d Best Case: Avon Crosses Cultures to Bring Beauty Directly to the Home

SMC QuickLink
Avon
http://www.avon.com

Avon has pioneered the use of direct selling of beauty products to women around the world. It has done so in a variety of cultures by adapting to local culture and product desires. Avon was given the ability to bring its direct-selling operation into mainland China in 2005.[46]

Summary

In the SMC portfolio, direct and interactive marketing provides the closest connection with the target audience, short of personal selling. This chapter examines the importance of a good database in all direct-marketing communications efforts. These communications include using telemarketing; broadcast direct response; Internet and electronic communications; direct mail, catalogs, and print; and direct selling. Not-for-profit and for-profit firms use direct and interactive marketing methods extensively to present extended amounts of information about a product. For example, in certain product classes, the infomercial allows up to an hour of product demonstration and audience involvement. The Internet and electronic communications have greatly expanded the way in which direct approaches have been used. Electronic and interactive media also have allowed significant cost savings in both production and distribution versus the traditional direct-mail bulk mailing. The geographical reach of the direct approach has been greatly expanded with the World Wide Web offering global access for anyone with a computer and correct software. The evolution and merging of technologies will continue to offer direct-marketing communications new and exciting opportunities in the future.

As noted in the other chapters in this section of the book, the chapters here are brief and not intended to provide in-depth coverage of each of the presented advertising elements. For that reason, we suggest that you spend some time on the sites that are listed in the "Additional QuickLinks" section. These sites allow you to access a number of the direct-marketing and interactive associations from around the world. As with the sites offered in the other chapters in this section, a certain number of these sites provide good summary listings of other direct and interactive links. You will find some overlap by using all the links, and you may find some new sites as you surf the sites. Again, as noted in the previous chapters, you will be able to learn many more details about the various elements by looking at additional sites than was possible in this chapter, given our space restraints and the strategic nature of this book.

Discussion Questions

Once again, pick a brand of your choice. Your boss has asked you to develop a direct-to-consumer campaign. Put together a strategic plan for instituting a direct-to-consumer marketing program. You will need to answer a number of questions that relate to that plan.

1. How might a database help you develop your plan?
2. What information do you want in your database related to product information?
3. What information related to the consumer would you want or need? Usage information? Demographic information? Others?
4. How would you integrate these pieces of information into your plan?
5. What options for direct marketing do you have? Which are best suited for your product?
6. Which would be your first choice for use? Why?
7. Can any of these be used in combination for better performance? Why or why not?
8. Can your direct-marketing elements be integrated with other traditional advertising approaches from Chapter Five?
9. Can your direct-marketing elements be integrated with other public relations approaches from Chapter Six?

Practice Quiz

Note: You can find the correct answers to these questions by taking the quiz and then submitting your answers in the Online Edition. The program will automatically score your submission. If you miss a question, the program will provide the correct answer, a rationale for the answer, and the section number in the chapter where the topic is discussed.

1. What are the two critical elements that direct marketing tries to addresses?
   a. establishing the right marketing mix and setting up a pricing strategy that goes with it
   b. getting through to the right customers and having them respond in a timely manner
   c. getting through to the mass in a particular market and selling maximum products
   d. targeting the right audience members and then working toward retaining them by prompt services

2. _____ is a form of nonstore retailing in which customers are exposed to merchandise through an impersonal medium and then purchase the merchandise by telephone or mail.
   a. Interactive marketing
   b. Database marketing
   c. Indirect marketing
   d. Direct marketing

3. What is the process wherein a customer database is sorted to help identify, track, communicate, and evaluate subsequent performance?
   a. data collation
   b. database management
   c. data mining
   d. data gathering

4. All of these options are measures used related to telemarketing except for _____.
   a. cost per call
   b. revenue per call
   c. return on investment
   d. revenue per program

5. _____ is a program-length time period on audiovisual broadcast/cable media used to market ideas, causes, products, and services.
   a. A television shopping network
   b. A direct-broadcast commercial
   c. An infomercial
   d. A traditional broadcast advertisement

6. _____ are electronic publications that offer a complete enumeration of items offered by a firm or cause and are arranged systematically with descriptive details regarding these items.
   a. Electronic catalogs (e-catalogs)
   b. Electronic newsletters (e-newsletters)
   c. Instant messages (IMs)
   d. Electronic mail (email) messages

7. _____ is a marketing communication that is sent to its intended recipient through the use of the official postal service of a given country.
   a. A card pack
   b. A catalog
   c. Direct mail
   d. An insert

8. In the direct-mail database list, customers who are part of the active company list internally are called members of the _____.
   a. outside list
   b. company list
   c. house list
   d. All of the preceding answers are correct.

9. In 2003, of the estimated $29.55 billion revenue, direct selling in an individual one-on-one setting was at _____ percent.
   a. 70
   b. 50
   c. 90
   d. 30

10. _____ is a form of compensation in a direct-sales company in which the salesperson can earn money not only from his or her personal retail sales but also on the sales of people he or she personally recruited into the business and on the sales of people recruited by their recruits.
    a. Multilevel marketing
    b. Multi-earning schemes
    c. Indirect compensation marketing
    d. None of the above

Web Exercise

Map Your Experience on the Information Superhighway

Take one of the legitimate direct-mail or email messages that you have received in the past week—not the email offer from the spouse of a recently deceased government official who offers to share $200 million if you send your bank information! Everyone has gotten at least one! Included somewhere on the message should be a website address to go to purchase or learn more about the good or service being offered. Before you connect to the site, write down what you expect to find on the site, including what you expect the site should look like and how you think your experience will be handled by the site. After writing those things down, visit the site and compare. Were you surprised? Was it better or worse than you expected? Was there true integration between the marketing communications appeal from the initial contact piece and the "landing" spot (the website)? Evaluate the consistency offered in both places. What would you suggest for a better integration?

Additional QuickLinks

Australian Direct Marketing Association
http://www.adma.com.au

Australian Interactive Media Industry Association
http://www.aimia.com.au

The Canadian Marketing Association
http://www.the-cma.org

The Cellular Telecommunications Industry Association (CTIA)
http://www.ctia.org

Direct Mail Information Service (United Kingdom)
http://www.dmis.co.uk

The Direct Marketing Association of Singapore
http://www.dmas.org

The Direct Marketing Association (United Kingdom)
http://www.dma.org.uk/content/home.asp

Electronic Media Marketing Association
http://www.emmadirect.com

Electronic Retailing Association
http://www.retailing.org

Federation of European Direct Marketing
http://www.fedma.org

Inside Direct Mail Association
http://www.insidedirectmail.com

The Institute of Direct Marketing (Europe)
http://www.theidm.com

The Interactive Advertising Bureau
http://www.iab.net

ListShopper.com (example of mail-list organization)
http://www.listshopper.com

The New Zealand Marketing Association
http://www.marketing.org.nz

Response Magazine (one of the direct-response magazines)
http://www.responsemagazine.com/responsemag

United States Postal Service Direct Mail
http://www.usps.com/directmail/welcome.htm?from=home&page=directmail

Suggested Readings

Bergman, Thomas P., and Stephen Garrison. 2002. *The essential guide to web strategy for entrepreneurs.* Upper Saddle River, NJ: Prentice Hall PTR.

Bly, Robert W., Michelle Feit, and Steve Roberts. 2000. *Internet direct mail: The complete guide to successful e-mail marketing campaigns.* Chicago, IL: NTC Business Books.

Jelassi, Tawfik, and Albrecht Enders. 2005. *Strategies for e-business: Creating value through electronic and mobile commerce.* Upper Saddle River, NJ: Pearson Prentice Hall.

Lautman, Kay. 2003. *Direct marketing for nonprofits: Essential techniques for the new era* (Aspen's Fundraising Series for the 21st Century). Gaithersburg, MD: Aspen Publishers.

Roberts, Mary Lou. 2003. *Internet marketing: Integrating online and offline strategies.* New York: McGraw-Hill/Irwin.

Roberts, Mary Lou, and Paul D. Berger. 1999. *Direct marketing management,* 2nd ed. Upper Saddle River, NJ: Pearson Prentice Hall.

Spiller, Lisa S., and Martin Baier. 2005. *Contemporary direct marketing.* Upper Saddle River, NJ: Pearson Prentice Hall.

Stone, Bob, and Ron Jacobs. 2001. *Successful direct marketing methods,* 7th ed. New York: McGraw-Hill/Irwin.

Notes

1. Quotation available at http://www.zaadz.com/quotes/John_Eden.
2. "US Direct Industry Boosts Revenues to $2.3 Trillion," *Precision Marketing,* April 1, 2005, 9.
3. As with earlier chapters, these definitions and a few of the subsequent definitions in this chapter are taken from the American Marketing Association (AMA) list of definitions (http://www.marketingpower.com/mg-dictionary.php) and are used with AMA's permission.
4. Joan Throckmorton, "Discovering DM," *American Demographics* (November–December 1996): 50–57.
5. Mark Roy, "Industry Cannot Afford to Take Rap for ID Fraud," *Precision Marketing,* July 22, 2005, 14.
6. Lisa Yorgey Lester, "What Can List Professionals Do Now to Prevent Future Legislation of the List Industry?" *Target Marketing* 28, no. 5 (2005): 79.
7. "Legislation Restricting Use of Marketing Data Could Cost Non-Profits $9 Billion," *Fund Raising Management* 32, no. 8 (2001): 18–19.
8. Elizabeth Schwinn, "End of the Line? New Law Forces Charities to Rethink Fund Raising by Phone," *The Chronicle of Philanthropy,* September 18, 2003. Available from http://philanthropy.com/temp/email.php?id=vuqp3xwnic7khcbk0mxgce95ugvbyz0z.
9. Steve Cocheo, "More Banks Direct-Market Small-Biz Credit," *ABA Banking Journal* 89, no. 6 (1997): 7 (3 pages).
10. Josh Linkner, "Please Remove Your Sneakers," *Brandweek* 46, no. 16 (2005): 28.
11. Jeff Shaw and Walter Gardisch, "A Question of Loyalty," *CMA Management* 79, no. 3 (2005): 44–45.
12. Ben Bold, "Babyworld," *Marketing,* June 29, 2005, 27.
13. Coreen Bailor, "5 Elements to Consider After You've Outsourced," *Customer Relationship Management* 9, no. 7, (2005): 24 (6 pages).
14. Brendan Read, "Home Sweet Call Center," *Call Center Magazine* 18, no. 8 (2005): 34 (6 pages).
15. "Address Call Effectiveness, Not Efficiency," *Precision Marketing,* October 17, 2003, 18.
16. Kim Cleland, "Arthritis Foundation Turns to Infomercial," *Advertising Age* 68, no. 23, June 9, 1997, 14.
17. Sean Mehegan, "Enviro Vac," *Mediaweek* 8, no. 3, January 19, 1998, 52.
18. Duff McDonald, "Secrets for Selling to the Idle Rich Ultimate Shopping Network Is Taking Televised Sales Upscale By Persuading Wealthy Viewers to Open Up Their Wallets for High-End Products," *Business 2.0* 6, no. 3 (2005): 44.
19. Allison Romano, "The Food Network Wants a Bigger Slice," *Broadcasting and Cable* 36, September 6, 2004, 10.
20. Ibid.
21. William M. Bulkeley, "Marketers Scan Blogs for Brand Insights," *Wall Street Journal,* June 23, 2005, B-1.
22. Patrick Barwise and John U. Farley, "The State of Interactive Marketing in Seven Countries: Interactive Marketing Comes of Age," *Journal of Interactive Marketing* 19, no. 3 (2005): 67–81.
23. Tony Kontzer, "Finding the Customer," *InformationWeek,* no. 1050, August 1, 2005, 34–39.
24. John L. Rogers and Christopher L. Bennett, "Effective Use of the Internet: A Guide for Franchise Systems," *Franchising World* 37, no. 7 (2005): 56–57.
25. "Special Report—Mailing Issues: Sizable Issue," *Precision Marketing,* July 15, 2005, 19–21.

26. Roberta Fusaro, "E-Mail Marketing: Tread Lightly," *Computerworld* 32, no. 27, July 6, 1998, 8.
27. Mylene Mangalindan, "Spotting an Internet Scam," *Wall Street Journal*, August 2, 2005, D-1.
28. Robert A. Guth, "Large Sender of Spam Email Settles Case with Microsoft," *Wall Street Journal*, August 10, 2005, D-5.
29. Susan Avery, "Intel Goes Global with Indirect Buying Strategy," *Purchasing* 134, no. 6, April 7, 2005, 16, (3 pages).
30. Ken Mandel, "New Apps Will Make Mobiles Key Drivers of Sales at POS Level," *Media,* July 1, 2005, 15.
31. Ken Burke, "The Other Half of the Equation," *Target Marketing* 28, no. 8 (2005): 27–28.
32. Ellen Messmer, "One Man's Trash Is Another's Cheap PC," *Network World* 21, no. 47, November 22, 2004, 1, (2 pages).
33. "USPS Reports Strong '04; Issues Cautionary Note," press release no. 04-088, http://www.usps.com/communications/news/press/2004/pr04_088.htm.
34. Judann Pollack, "Marketers Slap Network TV in Survey on ROI," *Advertising Age* 74, no. 41, October 13, 2003, 1.
35. See note 25.
36. Data taken from Direct Marketing Association website, http://www.the-dma.org/press/funfacts.shtml.
37. Sherry Chiger, "Out of the Gate and Into the Mail," *Catalog Age* 22, no. 4 (2005): 10.
38. Steve Johnson, "Don't Dilute the Value of Print," *American Printer*, no. 4 (2005): 84.
39. Sherry Chiger, "Benchmark 2005: Marketing," *Catalog Age* 22, no. 2 (2005), 23–25 (ABI/INFORM Global).
40. Ibid.
41. Jack Schmid, "Top 10 Catalog Blunders," *Target Marketing* 28, no. 7 (2005): 23–24.
42. Mark Del Franco, "Bean Hopes for Great Adventures," *Catalog Age* 22, no. 2 (2005): 7.
43. Direct Selling Association website: http://www.dsa.org/research/numbers.htm#SALES.
44. The definitions are taken from the website of the World Federation of Direct Selling Associations (WFDSA) at http://www.wfdsa.org/legal_reg/pyramidselling.asp.
45. Dennis Berman and Janet Adamy, "Tupperware Will Pay Sara Lee $557 Million for Direct-Sales Unit," *Wall Street Journal,* August 11, 2005, B-2.
46. Yan Yang, "Avon Given Direct-Selling Nod in China," *China Daily,* April 9, 2005. Retrieved August 10, 2005, from http://www2.chinadaily.com.cn/english/doc/2005-04/09/content_432686.htm#.

Personal Selling, Trade Promotions, and Consumer Promotions

Chapter Eight

Key Terms

- accelerated purchase (p. 182)
- advance dating (p. 173)
- advertising/display allowance (p. 174)
- agent (p. 165)
- bonus pack (p. 181)
- broker (p. 165)
- buy one, get one free (p. 182)
- buy-back allowance (p. 174)
- buying allowance (p. 174)
- channel of distribution (p. 163)
- consumer promotions (p. 163)
- contest (p. 181)
- continuity plan (p. 182)
- cooperative advertising (p. 173)
- count and recount promotion (p. 174)
- coupon (p. 181)
- coupon redemption (p. 181)
- creative selling (p. 167)
- cross-ruff (p. 181)
- cross-selling (p. 182)
- dating (p. 173)
- dealer tie-in (p. 173)
- display (p. 173)
- end-aisle display (p. 173)
- free merchandise (p. 173)
- horizontal cooperative advertising (p. 173)
- ingredient-sponsored cooperative advertising (p. 173)
- manufacturer's agent (p. 165)
- missionary sales work (p. 167)
- off-invoice allowance (p. 174)
- order taking (p. 167)
- personal selling (p. 163)
- point-of-purchase materials/displays (p. 173)
- premium (p. 181)
- price-off deal (p. 181)
- promotional allowance (p. 174)
- rebate (p. 181)
- referral reward (p. 181)
- refund (p. 181)
- sales contest (p. 173)
- salesperson (p. 165)
- sampling (p. 181)
- selling agent (p. 165)
- slotting allowance (p. 174)
- sweepstakes (p. 181)
- trade allowances (p. 174)
- trade promotions (p. 163)
- trade show (p. 173)
- vertical cooperative advertising (p. 173)

Chapter Outline

8-1 Introduction

8-2 Personal Selling
- 8-2a Strategic Marketing Communications Elements
- 8-2b Characteristics
- 8-2c Measurement
- 8-2d Best Case: Abbott Laboratories—An Educated, Motivated, and Profitable Team

8-3 Trade Promotions (Reseller Support)
- 8-3a Strategic Marketing Communications Elements
- 8-3b Characteristics
- 8-3c Measurement
- 8-3d Best Case: Consumer Products Manufacturer and Channel Master—Procter & Gamble

8-4 Consumer Promotions
- 8-4a Strategic Marketing Communications Elements
- 8-4b Characteristics
- 8-4c Measurement
- 8-4d Best Case: Driving Home a Deal—General Motors Employee Discounts

Summary
Discussion Questions
Practice Quiz
Web Exercise: Servicing Different Markets Differently—Web Contact Points
Additional QuickLinks
Suggested Readings
Notes

Character is the salesperson's stock in trade. The product itself is secondary. Truthfulness, enthusiasm, and patience are great assets to every salesperson. Without them, they couldn't go far. Courage and courtesy are essential equipment.

—George M. Adams (1878–1962), American author

8-1 Introduction

Chapter Seven, "Direct and Interactive Marketing," deals with the provider of the product or service trying to communicate with and market directly to the final consumer. Chapter Eight possesses some of those same direct-to-consumer aspects; however, it also covers some different means of contacts and communications with that final consumer. Additionally, it examines contacts and communications with the intermediaries that may be necessary for the efficient marketing of goods and services to that final consumer. If intermediaries are needed, then a number of communications and facilitation tools are available to the marketers. These personal contacts and facilitation tools are the tools that must be sharpened if the system is to be perfected.

This chapter provides an examination of three of the components in the strategic marketing communications (SMC) portfolio that are often crucial in facilitating the movement of product through the entire marketing channel between the manufacturer or service provider and the final consumer: (1) personal selling, (2) trade promotions, and (3) consumer promotions. We refer to *trade promotions* later in the text as *reseller support* because the role of the trade promotion is to support the reseller of a given product through a variety of activities and incentives provided by the manufacturer or service provider who is operating in the channel. As with the previous three chapters in this section, this chapter does not get into the execution and development of these activities and incentives. The "Additional QuickLinks" at the end of the chapter offer you a number of sites that provide a much more in-depth exploration of each of the toolbox elements. This examination is to highlight what these components may have to offer from an SMC manager's perspective when building an SMC plan. In Part Three of this book, we provide examples of how these components can be integrated strategically into an SMC execution.

The examination of personal selling, trade promotions, and consumer promotions includes the nature of these tools. As earlier chapters in this section point out, many marketers use combinations of these and other tools (shown in Chapters Five to Seven) in the executions of an SMC plan. The entire purpose of an SMC approach is to find combinations of these various tools to allow greater synergy and contribute to a better overall performance. Table 8-1 summarizes the elements of personal selling, trade promotions, and consumer promotions. Subsequent sections examine each of these three elements in greater detail. The chapter ends with a summary discussion of these elements.

Let us start with definitions of *personal selling, trade promotions,* and *consumer promotions* as they relate to SMC and "life in the channel."[1] Because these activities are taking place within the channel of distribution, the American Marketing Association definition of *channel of distribution* is included as well.

TABLE 8-1 The Personal Selling, Trade Promotions, and Consumer Promotions Toolbox

Personal Selling

Types of personal salespeople	Types of sales presentations

Trade Promotions (Reseller Support)

Contests and incentives	In-store displays and point-of-purchase materials
Cooperative advertising	Training programs
Trade allowances	Trade shows

Consumer Promotions

Coupons	Refunds and rebates
Sampling	Bonus packs
Premiums	Price-off deals
Contests and sweepstakes	

- **Personal selling** is selling that involves a face-to-face interaction with the customer.
- **Trade promotions** (also called *seller support*) are marketers' activities directed to channel members to encourage them to provide special support or activities for the product or service.
- **Consumer promotions** are externally directed incentives offered to the ultimate consumer. These usually consist of offers such as coupons, premiums, rebates, and so on that are designed to gain one or more of the following: product trial; repeat usage of product; more frequent or multiple product purchases; introduction of a new or improved product; introduction of new packaging or different size packages; neutralization of competitive advertising or sales promotions; capitalization on seasonal, geographic, or special events; encouragement of consumers to trade up to a larger size, more profitable line, or another product in the line.
- A **channel of distribution** is an organized network (system) of agencies and institutions that, in combination, perform all the functions required to link producers with end customers to accomplish the marketing task.

Having defined the main categories for our discussions in this chapter, let us, for a moment, examine the channel of distribution because this is where these SMC tools will be used. (Part Three expands the strategic aspects; the intent here is to highlight where these elements operate.) This book is about the need to consider your communications decisions in the context of the greater system of which they are a part. The channel of distribution, as the definition points out, is the system that links the end customer with the producer of the good (product or service) involved in the exchange. As can be seen from Figure 8-1, this channel can either be a very short channel or a very long channel with lots of intermediaries involved. What SMC elements play major roles in the promotion of the goods is influenced by the length and complexity of the channel.

An example of a short channel can be seen in the commercial aircraft industry. In years past, the channel was direct from the manufacturer to the airline. All of the marketing communications that went on regarding the selling of product were generally done with personal selling supported by technical information. Even though the channel now has added leasing companies to the mix (companies who buy the aircraft from the manufacturers and then lease them to airlines for use), the channel is fairly short.[2] As the number of intermediaries grows, so does the need for more and more different types of communications and facilitating offers regarding the transactions occurring within the system. Consider the number of intermediaries and transactions

---

personal selling Selling that involves a face-to-face interaction with the customer.

trade promotions Marketers' activities directed to channel members to encourage them to provide special support or activities for the product or service. Also called *seller support*.

consumer promotions Externally directed incentives offered to the ultimate consumer. These usually consist of offers such as coupons, premiums, rebates, and so on that are designed to gain one or more of the following: product trial; repeat usage of product; more frequent or multiple product purchases; introduction of a new or improved product; introduction of new packaging or different size packages; neutralization of competitive advertising or sales promotions; capitalization on seasonal, geographic, or special events; encouragement of consumers to trade up to a larger size, more profitable line, or another product in the line.

channel of distribution An organized network (system) of agencies and institutions that, in combination, perform all the functions required to link producers with end customers to accomplish the marketing task.

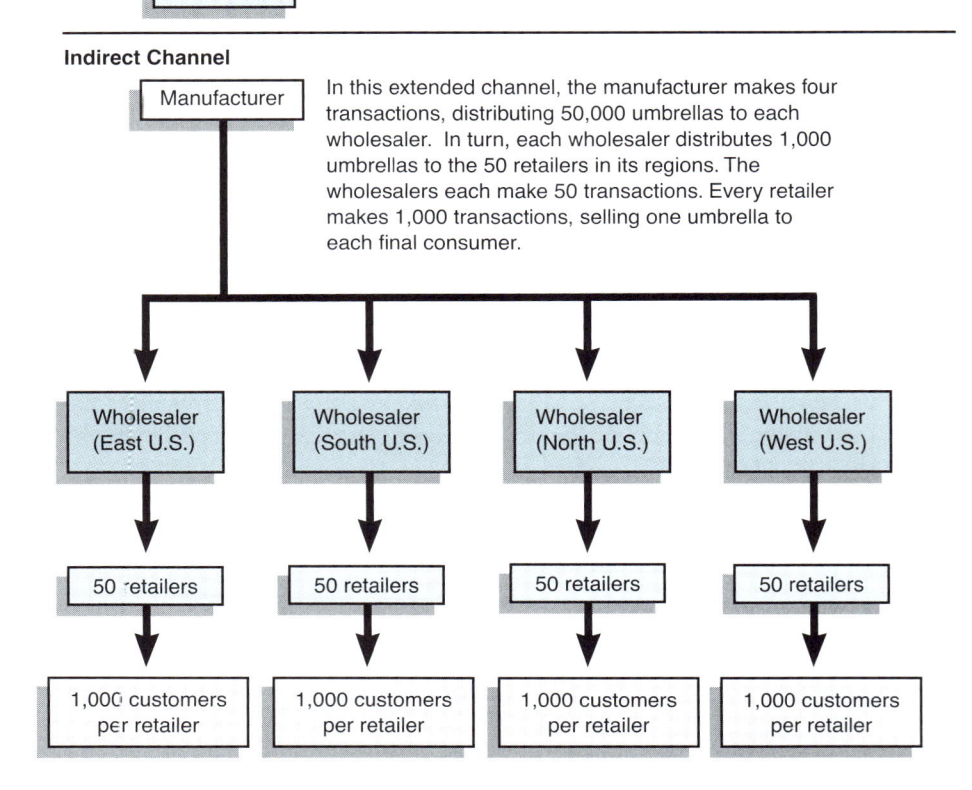

Direct Channel

Manufacturer → 200,000 customers

In this direct channel, an umbrella manufacturer sells directly to final customers. It makes 200,000 separate transactions, one for each customer.

Indirect Channel

Manufacturer

In this extended channel, the manufacturer makes four transactions, distributing 50,000 umbrellas to each wholesaler. In turn, each wholesaler distributes 1,000 umbrellas to the 50 retailers in its regions. The wholesalers each make 50 transactions. Every retailer makes 1,000 transactions, selling one umbrella to each final consumer.

- Wholesaler (East U.S.) → 50 retailers → 1,000 customers per retailer
- Wholesaler (South U.S.) → 50 retailers → 1,000 customers per retailer
- Wholesaler (North U.S.) → 50 retailers → 1,000 customers per retailer
- Wholesaler (West U.S.) → 50 retailers → 1,000 customers per retailer

Figure 8-1
The Channel of Distribution

The Channel Is Short for Aircraft Sales (left)

Aircraft manufacturers like Airbus will sell direct to the airlines or lease companies.
Source: © 2006 JupiterImages Corporation.

The End of a Long Channel (right)

Mom-and-pop outlets will generally buy a mix of products from wholesalers or other channel providers.
Source: © 2006 JupiterImages Corporation.

involved in getting a pack of Wrigley's Doublemint Gum into the "mom-and-pop" souvenir or convenience store in Tomahawk, Wisconsin. There are probably quite a few more levels of transactions and intermediaries involved than in the case of Airbus selling an A340-500 aircraft to Thai Airways for use on its route between New York and Bangkok.

While these examples are somewhat extreme, our intent is to sensitize you to the need to consider the aspects of the channel system when examining the potential SMC elements to be used. The discussion now moves on to this chapter's SMC elements that operate in that dynamic channel environment. Subsequent sections provide a look at the SMC portfolio elements that are available to the SMC manager from the personal selling and sales promotions toolbox summarized in Table 8-1.

8-2 Personal Selling

As already noted, personal selling involves face-to-face selling. The types of personal salespeople involved can vary depending on whether they are from the company or outside operators. As a consequence, some personal selling definitions are offered in Section 8-2a concerning some of the different types of sales personnel that may be used.[3]

8-2a Strategic Marketing Communications Elements

Some of the SMC elements unique to personal selling include agents, manufacturers' agents, selling agents, brokers, and salespersons.

- The sales definition of **agent** is a person who acts as a representative of a firm or individual. The retailing definitions are (1) a business unit that negotiates purchases, sales, or both but does not take title to the goods in which it deals; and (2) a person agent; one who represents the principal (who, in the case of retailing, is the store or merchant) and who acts under authority, whether in buying or in bringing the principal into business relations with third parties. The global marketing definition of agent is a company or individual that represents a company in a particular market. Normally an agent does not take title to goods.
- A **manufacturer's agent** is an independent businessperson who is paid a commission to sell a manufacturer's products or services but does not take title to the products.
- A **selling agent** is an agent who operates on an extended contractual basis. The agent sells all of a specified line of merchandise or the entire output of the principal and usually has full authority with regard to prices, terms, and other conditions of sales. The agent occasionally renders financial aid to the principal.
- A **broker** is a middleperson who serves as a go-between for the buyer or seller. The broker assumes no title risks, does not usually have physical custody of products, and is not looked upon as a permanent representative of either the buyer or seller.
- A **salesperson** is a person who is primarily involved in the personal process of assisting and/or persuading a potential customer to buy a product or service to the mutual benefit of both buyer and seller. A salesperson is also referred to as a *sales representative*.

8-2b Characteristics

As can be seen in its definition, personal selling can involve individuals who are members of your organization or individuals who exist outside your organization but still represent your organization as a member of the channel system. This leads to an issue of control of content and the manner in which the marketing communications regarding the organization are handled. The marketing communications manager

---

SMC QuickLinks

Wrigley
http://www.wrigley.com

Airbus
http://www.airbus.com

agent In sales, a person who acts as a representative of a firm or individual. In retailing, a business unit that negotiates purchases, sales, or both but does not take title to the goods in which it deals; and a person agent—one who represents the principal (who, in the case of retailing, is the store or merchant) and who acts under authority, whether in buying or in bringing the principal into business relations with third parties. In global marketing, a company or individual that represents a company in a particular market. Normally an agent does not take title to goods.

manufacturer's agent An independent businessperson who is paid a commission to sell a manufacturer's products or services but does not take title to the products.

selling agent An agent who operates on an extended contractual basis. The agent sells all of a specified line of merchandise or the entire output of the principal and usually has full authority with regard to prices, terms, and other conditions of sales. The agent occasionally renders financial aid to the principal.

broker A middleperson who serves as a go-between for the buyer or seller. The broker assumes no title risks, does not usually have physical custody of products, and is not looked upon as a permanent representative of either the buyer or seller.

salesperson A person who is primarily involved in the personal process of assisting and/or persuading a potential customer to buy a product or service to the mutual benefit of both buyer and seller. Also referred to as a *sales representative*.

needs to take this into consideration when developing the SMC campaign and choosing from among its SMC portfolio elements. With the use of internal salespeople, the control and speed to adapt are much faster. When using outside representatives, there may be a greater need to establish clearly defined criteria for the manner in which information concerning your organization and its goods is presented. A schedule for updating information provided to these representatives should also be developed that is consistent with the information needs of the market environment. That being said, the discussion now turns to the various aspects of the personal selling component.

Personal selling offers a number of positives that other types of communications do not. Of paramount importance is the potential for interactive and adaptive communications between the buying and selling parties. This dyadic relationship (as graphically displayed in Figure 8-2) offers a free and open "real-time" exchange of information regarding all aspects of the exchange. Well-trained salespeople can quickly assess all aspects of the exchange and offer valuable insights regarding the ways in which they can "help the buyers" in their decisions. A good salesperson is often viewed as almost an employee or member of the buyer's side in an exchange. The key is to get the buyers to open up and discuss the relevant issues and then adapt and respond appropriately. The salesperson is there to offer solutions to a problem, not to "sell product." One consultant put it in terms of a win-win type of environment. She also correctly pointed out that the best sales call starts with the salesperson being acutely aware of and concerned about what makes specific customers successful in what they do.[4]

The type of selling already described can be classified under a need-satisfaction approach to personal selling. This approach requires a salesperson who can see the big picture; it also requires the firm to be committed to spending a great deal of time in the process and in finding and training the right kind of salesperson.[5] Others have called this approach *consultative selling*.[6] In other words, the salesperson works with the buyer to identify needs and then provides goods that can service that need. This is the whole basis of the marketing concept. Long-term satisfaction of consumer needs leads to optimal profits. In some cases, though, this approach may not be optimal given salesperson expertise, time, cost, or other situational aspects.

The adage of sales being 90 percent preparation and 10 percent presentation is probably true, and the selection of the appropriate level of presentation delivery is part of that. The manager will need to match the requirements of the situation to the delivery used in the personal communications format and level of complexity. The personal sales presentations are generally thought of as having three levels of complexity. The highest and most complex is the *need-satisfaction or consultative selling approach* explained previously. The lowest level is the *canned or prepared sales presentation*. In this type of sales presentation, a memorized script is involved that does not change from customer to customer. Although often criticized as too inflexible, these types of sales presentations allow the use of inexperienced sales personnel in situations in which there is not felt to be a great deal of difference between the various customers' needs regarding the products or services in question.

In between the canned presentation and the need-satisfaction approach is the *selling-formula approach*.[7] In this approach, pieces from the two other approaches are borrowed for use. The approach has a basic scripted element, but the salesper-

Figure 8-2
The Buyer-Seller Dyad

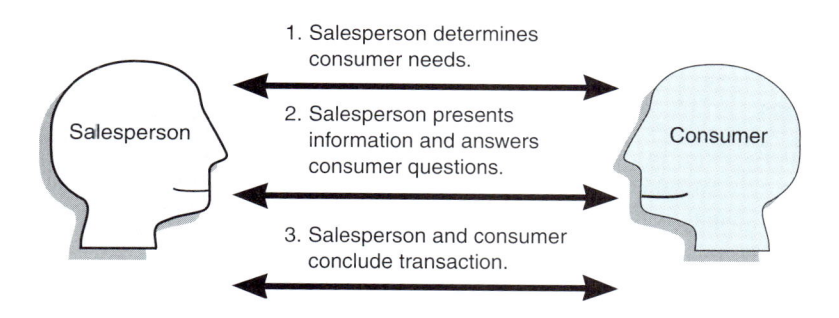

son can adapt the presentation to the particular needs of the situation. The approach allows the buyer to do most of the talking up front, giving the salesperson the chance to identify needs. Once the buyer type and needs have been clearly identified, then the salesperson can proceed with a presentation based on those elements. A vice president of a sales-force-improvement firm says that the more talking the buyer does, the better, and offers a simple three-step guide to get the buyer talking: (1) identify the relevant issues, (2) lead the buyer on, and (3) customize your presentation.[8] Table 8-2 offers a summary of the three types of sales presentations and their characteristics.

Each of the sales presentation types we have discussed acts within a communications context of moving the customer from paying attention to the salesperson and his or her pitch to the closing of the sale. The AIDA model—attention to interest to desire to action—can be applied here to provide a planning mechanism for the sales presentation. The amount of time spent on each level will vary from customer to customer; but, as with all communications, the process starts with getting the buyer to pay attention to the communications and concludes with getting some sort of action regarding the sale at the end. Training for salespeople on the way in which they can facilitate that movement is crucial. An expert in the field gives her take on the art of selling in SMC Marketplace Watch 8-1.

Linking with the types of sales presentations are what others consider to be the three types of salespeople functions or personal selling jobs to be done by salespeople: (1) creative selling, (2) order taking, and (3) missionary sales work.[9]

- **Creative selling** involves several personal selling tasks: prospecting, assessing needs, recommending a means of satisfying needs, demonstrating the capabilities of the firm, and closing the sale. Here, the salesperson is the "point person" who establishes the initial contact and has the major responsibility for completing the transaction.
- **Order taking** is very different from creative selling. The order taker services an account. This situation is commonly referred to as a "straight rebuy." That is, the order does not change much. For example, a food manufacturer's salesperson may call on a wholesale food company and present it with a list of food products to sell.
- **Missionary sales work** involves a combination of creative selling and order taking. The position calls for introducing new products and programs to both current and potential customers.

For all of the positives about personal selling, the downside is the cost. The U.S. Department of Labor reports that the median annual earnings of sales representatives, wholesale and manufacturing, technical and scientific products, including commissions, in 2002 were $55,740. For those in categories other than the technical and scientific product area, that number was $42,730.[10]

The cost of a sales call for a business-to-business salesperson can be staggering. One report from the business-to-business sector from 2003 refers to a chemical company's revealing that its average cost per sales call was $3,000 per call.[11] That same report also pegged the average cost per sales call in the industrial market at over $500 per call. This number is up significantly from just a few years ago. An industry survey

creative selling Involves several personal selling tasks: prospecting, assessing needs, recommending a means of satisfying needs, demonstrating the capabilities of the firm, and closing the sale. Here, the salesperson is the "point person" who establishes the initial contact and has the major responsibility for completing the transaction.

order taking The order taker services an account. This situation is commonly referred to as a "straight rebuy." That is, the order does not change much. For example, a food manufacturer's salesperson may call on a wholesale food company and present it with a list of food products to sell.

missionary sales work Involves a combination of creative selling and order taking. The position calls for introducing new products and programs to both current and potential customers.

TABLE 8-2 Three Types of Sales Presentations

Type	Salesperson Training Requirements	Target Group Characteristics
Canned or prepared	Minimal	Homogeneous
Selling formula	Moderate	Mixed
Need-satisfaction or consultative	Extensive	Varied or unique

SMC Marketplace Watch 8-1

Preparation and Caring Make for a Win-Win Sales Call

Mary Donato, the associate director of the Institute for the Study of Business Markets, has a chance to see a number of top salespeople in her position. She knows what can make a sales call work or not work. It seems that the adage of "a good sales call is 90 percent preparation" really does get to the heart of things. She likened watching one top-level salesperson preparing for a sales call to "a well-orchestrated play" because all the questions, client concerns, and various ways to solve the client's problems had been anticipated and plans had been laid out for the various options. She noted that he had worked out even the possible objections from the client and how he would respond to them in finding the right solution. It was, by all measures, a well-rehearsed series of conversations that would ensure that the salesman could find a solution that would meet the customer's specific needs. When Ms. Donato asked the salesman about what he would do if none of the suggested solutions would work for the client, he replied that he would "advise the prospect, stop the sales cycle, and move on to the next opportunity."

Ms. Donato feels that "[f]ar too many salespeople don't attempt—or don't know how—to truly understand client needs and what would be an effective solution for them. In the end, time, energy, and money are wasted, both on the seller's and buyer's part." She feels that the salesperson must also start with a philosophy of "caring deeply for what it takes to make the customer successful."

Using the FranklinCovey Sales Performance Group (SPG) training and coaching curriculum called *Helping Clients Succeed*, Ms. Donato provides a simple "win-win list" of those things that can make a great sales call; many relate to the attitude and caring about the needs of the client and being prepared with the right kind of information and solutions:

1. *Sales are not about selling*. They are about helping clients succeed.
2. *Intent counts more than technique*. Be very clear about your intent before the meeting. Focus on meeting the needs who you call on and not so much on your own needs.
3. *Solutions have no inherent value*. Solutions derive value only from the problems they solve and the results they produce. Know what the problem is and everything that is relevant is solving the problem. Then help the client find ways to solve it.
4. *No guessing*. Know the relevant information and what questions need to be asked. Don't spend your time trying to "guess" what the problem is.

Source: Adapted from Mary Donato, "The Win-Win Sales Call," *Sales and Marketing Management* (New York) 157, no. 6 (2005): 21.

---

in 2000 pegged the cost of a sales call at just under $170.[12] While sales call cost has gone up, so have some of the inefficiencies with the numbers of sales calls per day dropping with part of the blame on the buyers' desire to not talk with salespeople.[13] As an example of this, think of the number of pharmaceutical salespeople who pass through the doctor's office while you are waiting for an appointment who are told, "The doctor is busy and cannot see you today." Additionally, increased traffic in major urban areas in both the United States and the global market can greatly reduce the number of calls possible. For example, when making sales calls in Bangkok, Thailand, salespeople may only try for two or three meetings at the most per day due to traffic congestion in the city.

To try and counter some of the cost and travel issues involved in on-site personal selling, some business-to-business firms have supplemented their traditional personal selling with the use of new technologies that can provide some of the aspects of personal selling but at a reduced cost. It was reported that in 2002, web conferencing increased by 89 million users, a jump of 40 percent from the previous year. If used wisely, these new technologies can act to enhance the ability of a firm to provide "personal service" to clients. One firm uses teleconferencing as a chance to pair additional technical expertise with a salesperson; as a consequence, the firm has been able to prequalify its sales prospects more quickly, which helped reduce travel expenditures.[14] In general, firms in the business-to-business field are using the full range

Exhibit 8-1

The Saigon South (Vietnam) Brochure Sent to Interested Investors

In support of personal selling, the Saigon South Industrial Development Zone (Vietnam) will use a variety of appropriate tools to allow potential investors to evaluate a great deal of information before making the long trip to visit the site for meetings with the sales staff.

Source: Reprinted by permission of Phu My Hung Corporation.

of other marketing communications tools to supplement their personal selling operations to try to make the use of their highly skilled but high-cost salespeople more efficient. One such example, a brochure given to interested parties, is seen in Exhibit 8-1.

The use of personal selling in the consumer market is less expensive than in the business-to-business market, but it is still, in general, a much more costly approach than using other marketing tools. In today's retail environment, there has been continued evolution in the way in which the salesperson is used. At Nordstrom's, the salespeople are highly trained and valued by the chain. In 2001 Nordstrom's used some of the $44 million it saved by cutting national advertising to fund higher salaries for its salespeople.[15] The salespeople generally are quite well informed about the needs of their customers and will often keep databases of regular customers' product likes and dislikes. This helps them to develop a long-term relationship with their clients. Turnover in the sales force is generally lower than in the rest of the retail industry.

In other retail outlets, though, salespeople turnover, skill, and training can be highly variable—as can be pay. The U.S. Department of Labor reports that in 2002 the median hourly pay of retail salespeople including commission was $8.51. As noted, though, there is high variability. Those in the bottom 10 percent earned under $6.18 per hour, and those in the top 10 percent earned over $16.96 per hour.[16] One well-known consumer electronics firm concluded that the combination of high turnover and new product introduction meant that it had to change the way it educated its

SMC QuickLink

U.S. Department of Labor
http://www.dol.gov

In-Store Personal Help

Clerks at the retail level are often more than simple order takers. They often provide insights and information regarding the products to help the shopper make the "right" choice.

Source: © 2006 JupiterImages Corporation.

in-store sales force. It changed from spending time training sales personnel to know information about the products they carried to training them to use online-like search skills to find the answers to customer inquiries. As a consequence of this change, the company is eliminating the need for training sessions for current salespeople to update product knowledge, as well as the need for educating new personnel on the entire retail inventory.[17] On the other side of the coin, a retail bakery extended training of its in-store personnel to include how to interact more effectively and professionally with customers. They went from being simple order takers to being salespeople. Because of this enhanced communication, the store's profitability increased and maintained a strong level by overdelivering on the expectations of the clientele.[18]

8-2c Measurement

Personal selling performance can be measured through a variety of quantitative and qualitative measures. *Quantitative measures* include measures related to orders, sales volume, accounts/customers, sales calls, selling expenses, and product margins. These can be further broken down into subcategories, as shown in Table 8-3.

Qualitative measures include measures related to communication skills, knowledge of customer needs, customer satisfaction and feedback, customer relationships, marketing intelligence gathering, contribution to corporate mission, and performance.

8-2d Best Case: Abbott Laboratories—An Educated, Motivated, and Profitable Team

SMC QuickLink
Abbott Laboratories
http://www.abbott.com

Abbott Laboratories is known as one of the premier pharmaceutical companies in terms of its wide variety of consumer and industry health and education programs. It also dedicates a great deal of time and effort to training and maintaining its sales force. That sales force has made a significant contribution in maintaining good company performance. In 2005, for its second quarter, the company reported a net earn-

TABLE 8-3 Quantitative Measures and Their Subcategories

Orders

Total number achieved
Average size of order in dollars
Average size of order in units

Sales Volume

Total units
Total dollars
Market share in salesperson district
Sales quota achievement

Accounts/Customers

Accounts serviced
Number of new accounts
Number of lost accounts

Sales Calls

Calls made
Number of new account calls
Average time per call
Calls required for sale
Types of calls (selling versus service, etc.)
Road time versus call time

Selling Expenses

Average per sales call
Percentage per sales (dollar)
Percentage as sales (units)

Product Margins

Gross margins
Net margins
Product mix (different types of product categories)

ings increase of 38 percent to $877 million from $634.3 million in 2004. Total sales in the drug, devices, and nutritional product categories went up 17 percent to $5.52 billion, up from $4.7 billion in 2004.[19] The company provides a complete portfolio sales force training program and related support to make its sales force one that is comprised of well-trained, motivated, and professional people.

8-3 Trade Promotions (Reseller Support)

Trade promotions are best thought of within the context of being reseller support functions. These programs, activities, specials, and/or products are the tools that are used to facilitate the movement of goods or services through the channel system. Table 8-4 provides a listing of those tools. If the goods or services are being sold to an organization or firm for resale to the final consumer (whether that final consumer is an individual or a business entity), then it is a trade promotion. Otherwise, the activity is classified as a consumer promotion (which is covered in Section 8-4). A variety of these reseller support activities are often tied to inventory control and management issues as well. Manufacturers may at times coordinate with consumer promotions targeting the same inventory, thus creating both push and pull activities in the channel at the same time.

TABLE 8-4	Trade Promotions Toolbox
Trade Promotions (Reseller Support)	
Contests and incentives	
Cooperative advertising	
Trade allowances	
In-store displays and point-of-purchase materials	
Training programs	
Trade shows	

cooperative advertising (see p. 173) An approach to paying for local advertising or retail advertising whereby the advertising space or time is placed by a local retail store but is partly or fully paid for by a national manufacturer whose product is featured in the advertising.

horizontal cooperative advertising (see p. 173) An advertising partnership in which several retailers share the cost of a promotion.

ingredient-sponsored cooperative advertising (see p. 173) An advertising partnership in which producers of a particular ingredient or component used in a product share the cost of a promotion.

vertical cooperative advertising (see p. 173) Advertising in which the retailer and other previous marketing channel members (e.g., manufacturers or wholesalers) share the cost.

dating (see p. 173) In sales promotion, a type of trade promotion in which the retailer is allowed to buy a certain amount of product from the manufacturer and then pay for that product over a prolonged period of time. In retailing, the dates in which discounts can be taken or the full invoice amount is due.

At times, the objectives of channel members may be different. Manufacturers are usually trying to accomplish such things as obtaining either initial or expanded distribution, increasing order sizes, reducing their own inventories, supporting their brands' development, enhancing marketing communications with the final consumer, optimizing logistical performance, or simply making the system run more smoothly. Basically, manufacturers generally want channel members to carry the inventory, promote the product, and pay for as much of the expense as possible. They are concerned about market share as it relates to their brands in regard to the other competitive brands in the category. Problems can arise because, meanwhile, the channel members want the manufacturer to carry the inventory, promote the product, and pay for as much of the expense as possible. Retailers in the channel are concerned about market share for their stores (not necessarily specific brands they carry) against competing retailers.

The careful and effective use of reseller support functions can help bring peace to this situation by helping both sides to achieve their objectives in an environment that is as harmonious as possible. For example, a manufacturer may want to move excess inventory out into the channel and capture higher market share through a consumer promotion. Retailers in the channel are hesitant to take on the extra inventory required because of extra carrying costs but feel that the brand promotion may bring in additional store traffic. The manufacturer will offer a special discount to the retailers to compensate them for the additional carrying costs involved in the increased inventory that must be carried for the promotion. However, trade promotions have some dangers. One such danger is "forward buying," in which channel members "stock up" at the lower price and then have no need for product when the manufacturer is offering the product back at the normal price. In the meantime, the retailers can go "off deal" and sell the discounted product at full price to the consumers when the official promotion is over. The margins for retailers are then much higher, although they still have the higher carrying costs from taking on the extra inventory.

The power structure in the channel has shifted in recent years with the rise of powerful retailers like Wal-Mart, Target, and Costco. These giants are creating their own strong brands that are challenging those of the older brand manufacturers.[20] What type of trade promotion environment will evolve out of these new power relationships is still not clear, but changes have already been seen on a variety of fronts. Ultimately, whatever the new model becomes must operate efficiently as a delivery system to the final consumer if it is to thrive in today's highly competitive market.

8-3a Strategic Marketing Communications Elements

As already noted, trade promotions are activities directed to channel members to encourage them to provide special support or activities for the product or service. Some of the elements that are unique to trade promotions are defined here.

- **Cooperative advertising** is an approach to paying for local advertising or retail advertising whereby the advertising space or time is placed by a local retail store but is partly or fully paid for by a national manufacturer whose product is featured in the advertising.
- **Horizontal cooperative advertising** is an advertising partnership in which several retailers share the cost of a promotion.
- **Ingredient-sponsored cooperative advertising** is an advertising partnership in which producers of a particular ingredient or component used in a product share the cost of a promotion.
- **Vertical cooperative advertising** is advertising in which the retailer and other previous marketing channel members (e.g., manufacturers or wholesalers) share the cost.
- **Dating** (sales promotion definition) is a type of trade promotion in which the retailer is allowed to buy a certain amount of product from the manufacturer and then pay for that product over a prolonged period of time or (retailing definition) the dates in which discounts can be taken or the full invoice amount is due.
- **Advance dating** is an arrangement by which the seller sets a specific future date when the terms of sale become applicable. For example, the order may be placed on January 5 and the goods shipped on January 10 but under the terms "2/10, net 30 as of May 1." In this case, the discount and net periods are calculated from May 1. *Season dating* is another name for terms of this kind.
- **Dealer tie-in** is the local support by a retailer for an advertiser's promotional program through use of in-store display materials, cooperative advertising, local contests, identification in media advertisements, and so on.
- A **display** is a special exhibit of a product at the point of sale, generally over and above standard shelf stocking.
- An **end-aisle display** is an exhibit of a product set up at the end of the aisle in a retail store to call attention to a special offering or price.
- **Point-of-purchase materials/displays** are promotional materials placed at the contact sales point and on- and off-shelf display material or product stocking generally at the retail level that is used to call special attention to the featured product. It is sometimes referred to as *point-of-sale display*.
- A **trade show** (sales definition) is an exhibition in which a number of manufacturers display their products or (sales promotion definition) a periodic gathering at which manufacturers, suppliers, and distributors in a particular industry or related industries display their products and provide information for potential buyers (retail, wholesale, or industrial).
- A **sales contest** (sales definition) is a short-term incentive program designed to motivate sales personnel to accomplish specific sales objectives. In general, a sales contest is used by firms to stimulate extra effort for obtaining new customers, promoting the sales of specific items, generating larger orders per sales call, and so on. Although a contest should not be considered part of the firm's ongoing compensation plan, it does offer salespeople the opportunity to gain financial as well as nonfinancial rewards. Contest winners often receive prizes in cash or merchandise or travel that have monetary value. Winners also receive nonfinancial rewards in the form of recognition and a sense of accomplishment.
- **Free merchandise** is a trade promotion technique in which an additional amount of the product is offered without additional cost as an incentive to purchase a minimum quantity. The incentive is typically offered for a limited period of time.

advance dating An arrangement by which the seller sets a specific future date when the terms of sale become applicable.

dealer tie-in The local support by a retailer for an advertiser's promotional program through use of in-store display materials, cooperative advertising, local contests, identification in media advertisements, and so on.

display A special exhibit of a product at the point of sale, generally over and above standard shelf stocking.

end-aisle display An exhibit of a product set up at the end of the aisle in a retail store to call attention to a special offering or price.

point-of-purchase materials/displays Promotional materials placed at the contact sales point and on- and off-shelf display material or product stocking generally at the retail level that is used to call special attention to the featured product.

trade show In sales, an exhibition in which a number of manufacturers display their products. In sales promotion, a periodic gathering at which manufacturers, suppliers, and distributors in a particular industry or related industries display their products and provide information for potential buyers (retail, wholesale, or industrial).

sales contest In sales, a short-term incentive program designed to motivate sales personnel to accomplish specific sales objectives.

free merchandise A trade promotion technique in which an additional amount of the product is offered without additional cost as an incentive to purchase a minimum quantity.

trade allowances Short-term special offers made by marketers to channel members as incentives to stock, feature, or in some way participate in the cooperative promotion of a product.

buying allowance A form of trade promotion in which the retailer is offered a discount on the purchase of the product at a particular point in time.

promotional allowance In retailing, an allowance given by vendors to retailers to compensate the latter for money spent in advertising a particular item in local media or for preferred window and interior display space used for the vendor's product. In sales promotion, the payments, price reductions, or other inducements used to reward channel members for participation in advertising and/or sales promotion programs.

count and recount promotion A trade promotion technique in which inventory is counted at the beginning of the promotion and recounted at the end of the promotion period. Discounts are then allowed based on the total quantity of product moved during the promotion period.

slotting allowance In retailing, a fee paid by a vendor for space in a retail store. In sales promotion, the fee a manufacturer pays to a retailer in order to get distribution for a new product.

advertising/display allowance A form of trade promotion in which retailers are given a discount in exchange for either promoting the product in their own advertising or setting up a product display or both.

SMC QuickLink
Star Alliance
http://www.staralliance.com

- **Trade allowances** are short-term special offers made by marketers to channel members as incentives to stock, feature, or in some way participate in the cooperative promotion of a product.
- A **buying allowance** is a form of trade promotion in which the retailer is offered a discount on the purchase of the product at a particular point in time. The discount is often tied to the purchase of a particular number of units.
- A **promotional allowance** (retailing definition) is an allowance given by vendors to retailers to compensate the latter for money spent in advertising a particular item in local media or for preferred window and interior display space used for the vendor's product or (sales promotion definition) the payments, price reductions, or other inducements used to reward channel members for participation in advertising and/or sales promotion programs.
- A **count and recount promotion** is a trade promotion technique in which inventory is counted at the beginning of the promotion and recounted at the end of the promotion period. Discounts are then allowed based on the total quantity of product moved during the promotion period.
- A **slotting allowance** (retailing definition) is a fee paid by a vendor for space in a retail store or (sales promotion definition) the fee a manufacturer pays to a retailer in order to get distribution for a new product. It covers the costs of making room for the product in the warehouse and on the store shelf, reprogramming the computer system to recognize the product's UPC code, and including the product in the retailer's inventory system.
- An **advertising/display allowance** is a form of trade promotion in which retailers are given a discount in exchange for either promoting the product in their own advertising or setting up a product display or both.
- A **buy-back allowance** is a form of trade promotion in which channel members are offered an incentive to restock their store or warehouse with the product to the level in place prior to a count and recount promotion offer.
- An **off-invoice allowance** is a type of trade promotion in which the manufacturer offers the retailer a price reduction on the product price at the time of billing, generally for a limited period of time.

8-3b Characteristics

The channel for a consumer products company plays a vital role in maintaining a quality relationship between the brand and the final consumer. Members of this channel execute a variety of services and activities that can either enhance or adversely affect the consumer's brand experience. As a consequence, good channel relations must be maintained from manufacturing to consumption to expedite the movement of goods/services through the system to achieve optimal value delivery to the consumer. A constant monitoring and update of appropriate trade promotion (reseller support) can act as a crucial set of elements in making sure that happens. SMC Marketplace Watch 8-2 highlights one of the environmental changes that is occurring in the channel.

As noted previously, there are three forms of cooperative advertising programs: horizontal, ingredient-sponsored, and vertical. In *horizontal cooperative advertising*, the retailer (or same level of the channel) will share the advertising cost of a number of other retailers. Airline marketing alliances are a good example of this type of cooperative agreement. Eight airlines that were members of the Star Alliance consolidated all of their advertising into WPP in 2004. These alliance airlines were looking for significant savings in media procurement costs by the cooperative move.[21] One

SMC Marketplace Watch 8-2

The Winds of Change in the Channel Stalk the Trade Promotion

The world of trade promotions in the channel had been changing as the result of the power of retailers such as Wal-Mart. The big manufacturers are now adding to that change with some muscle flexing of their own. The big companies at the top of the food channel are trying to squeeze the most that they can out of the almost $80 billion that they spend each year on channel trade promotions. Food product company giants like Nestlé, Kraft Foods, and Hershey Foods are demanding that retailers meet new minimum-performance requirements in order to receive funds for such things as price and display promotions. In the past, these dollars were offered with very few requirements or "strings attached." The manufacturers, who now possess better tracking data, are finally demanding an accounting regarding their return on these investments. Failure to measure up can result in a retailer being dropped.

Instead of spending these "push" kinds of channel trade promotions, the companies had tried to focus on brand building. That has not had much success. The spending numbers support that supposition. According to research by Cannondale Associates, package-goods companies' trade spending rose 0.5 percent to 17.4 percent of gross sales in 2003, accounting for 54 percent of companies' marketing budgets—up from 44 percent of total budgets in 2002. For the $470 billion food industry, that translates to as much as $80 billion. The companies who are spending that money in the channel are allocating resources to the most profitable brands and accounts, leaving some retailers out in the cold.

"Over the years, trade monies have become a taken-for-granted expectation rather than a promotional vehicle," said a Nestlé executive. "Now we're re-emphasizing in our contracts that there has to be a base promotion executed upon for these funds to be paid." Each of the brands within Nestlé's food and beverage divisions now possesses a unique set of minimum-performance requirements for promotions. Cannondale Associates partner Ken Harris says that the wealth of good data from a variety of tracking systems, including such things as improved syndicated data, frequent-shopper cards, and handheld inventory devices, has allowed the drive toward pay-for-performance spending.

On the other side, retailers see "the handwriting on the wall" and have begun to reevaluate their promotions for products they carry. Some of the retail executives believe that they can pay more attention to moving product as a result of promotional supports and become more efficient, thus giving the bigger manufacturers more sales and higher profits. Some are concerned, though, that the regional and third-tier brands may now find themselves out in the cold as a result.

Source: Adapted from Stephanie Thomson, "Nestlé Warns Stores: Prove It or Lose Out," *Advertising Age* 75, no. 37, September 13, 2004, 1 (2 pages).

---

marketing consultant finds the resistance by an assortment of chain retailers to cooperate in a variety of local promotional events puzzling. He argues that it is this type of cooperative advertising that can allow funding for a number of programs at a level that can have significant local traffic impacts at places like malls and shopping centers.[22]

Ingredient-sponsored cooperative advertising is a form of advertising in which the manufacturer of a product's ingredient collaborates with other manufacturers or resellers to promote the ingredient jointly. In Exhibit 8-2 the product brand is Subaru, and the ingredient used in the product is the L.L. Bean brand. Taken separately, both these brands offer something of value to certain consumers. If the consumer perceives positive congruency between the advertised ingredient and the product brand using that ingredient, then the overall consumer evaluation of the brand to be purchased is enhanced. Creating synergy is the name of the game here.

Intel is another company with classic ingredient messages. Intel has centered a great deal of its advertising funds around the cooperative pitch that is found in personal computer advertisements from various manufacturers.[23]

buy-back allowance (see p. 174) A form of trade promotion in which channel members are offered an incentive to restock their store or warehouse with the product to the level in place prior to a count and recount promotion offer.

off-invoice allowance (see p. 174) A type of trade promotion in which the manufacturer offers the retailer a price reduction on the product price at the time of billing, generally for a limited period of time.

Exhibit 8-2

Subaru and L.L. Bean

Subaru and L.L. Bean cooperate in this advertisement for the Subaru Outback. The product brand is Subaru, and the ingredient used in the product is the L.L. Bean brand. Perceived positive congruence between these two brands enhances overall consumer evaluation of the brand to be purchased.

Source: Used by permission of Subaru of America, Inc.

Finally, *vertical cooperative advertising* is the most common form of cooperative advertising (see Exhibit 8-3). This form of advertising is seen every Sunday in the newspaper sections featuring sales and specials at a variety of retail outlets. In the business-to-business environment, this type of advertising has had increased use, especially in the technology fields in which a number of independent software vendors (ISVs) could not afford the cost of promotion on their own.[24]

When considering a partnership with current or potential channel members or other brands, the marketing communications manager should examine the fit of the brands involved in the overall message and presentation. When multiple brands are involved, some interaction effects may not be desirable for the situation.[25]

Trade allowances are the most commonly used allowances for trade promotion. They usually involve some form of a discount or deal to encourage the reseller to carry, promote, and display the product. The three types of trade allowances are *buying allowances, promotional allowances,* and *slotting allowances*. Buying allowances and promotional allowances, as seen in the definitions already given, are basically price reductions passed along to channel members for purchasing product from the manufacturer. Readjustment of these allowances from time to time can, in essence, have the same impact as that of price increases or decreases. Phillip Morris, for example, reduced the "off-invoice" discount it gave to wholesalers by $1.00 to $5.50 a carton for a number of its brands, including its iconic brand, Marlboro. The reduction effectively raised cigarette prices by about 10 cents a pack to the channel members.[26]

Retail power, as noted, has grown quite substantially in the past several years. There has also been a significant increase in the use by retailers of house brands. With more new products hitting the retail market every year and those new house brands, there is a significant squeeze being put on available retail shelf space. For manufac-

Exhibit 8-3

Sprint and BMW Cooperative Advertisement

Sprint and BMW cooperate to advertise Sprint cell phone service, thus helping both carmaker and service provider benefit from the alliance.

Source: Reprinted by permission of BMW of North America, LLC and by permission of Sprint and David Reinbold, illustrator.

turers trying to get new product into the retail arena, this has led to some major concerns. If a marketer is trying to get a new product into retail outlets, there is now often the requirement to provide an incentive for retail stores to stock the product on their shelves. The most commonly used incentive is the slotting allowance.[27] Some recent research has suggested that the slotting allowance is a good way for retailers in a highly competitive market to help balance the risk of new-product failure between manufacturers and retailers, as well as serving to widen retail distribution for manufacturers through the mitigation of retail competition.[28] Another study likened the slotting allowance to real option pricing, in which retailers hold call options on their shelf space and the manufacturers/suppliers must buy these options to introduce their new product.[29]

In-store advertising and *point-of-purchase displays* were discussed in the context of out-of-home advertising in Chapter Five. We revisit them for a brief moment here to recognize that they can be an integral part of a channel reseller support function. A manufacturer can set up point-of-purchase displays and promote its products within the store, which can be a very attractive perk to the reseller. These point-of-purchase (POP) executions, which are also referred to as *point-of-sale* (POS) executions, can run the gamut from whole racks of products to inflatable balloon types of merchandise that grab attention and generate sales. Labatt's Brewery in Canada had retailer response and success with an inflatable blue snowmobile that was the centerpiece of its winter sales promotion.[30] As noted later in the chapter, these types of displays can

SMC QuickLink

Displays2Go (POP display site)
http://www.displays2go.com

Trade Shows

Trade shows offer the ability to have personal contact with buyers from an entire industry in just a few days.
Source: AP/Wide World Photos.

SMC QuickLink
McCormick Place
http://www.mccormickplace.com

increase sales for the manufacturer's products, which increase the retail outlet's sales numbers at no cost to the retailer.

The trade show offers the chance for companies in various industries to come together and see what is going on throughout the industry. In 2004 the average show spread out across 243,847 net square feet of space, had 760 exhibiting companies, and drew 17,793 attendees.[31] For certain industries, the trade show has been a staple in the marketing communications toolbox. While trade shows used to be the second expenditure behind advertising for the business-to-business marketing communications budget,[32] they have slipped in importance in some industries as the Internet has allowed companies to provide more information and product demonstrations in the cyberworld.[33] The trade show still has a strong role to play in a variety of industries that require face time for product explanation and demonstration. For example, trade shows in the medical field have continued to grow in attendance. In 2004 the medical industry average show had 358 exhibiting companies and was attended by 8,098 professionals.[34] Tourism, hardware, and consumer and home products shows are some of the biggest. Only a limited number of cities have the facilities with the capacity to host some of these groups. Chicago's McCormick Place has long been the venue for many of the larger shows and continues to expand its facilities for future shows. An estimated 70,000 individuals from the print and graphics field were at McCormick Place from September 9 to September 15, 2005, for the PRINT 05 & CONVERTING 05. At the event, attendees were awash in technology, equipment, and supplies related to producing trade show graphics, posters, point-of-purchase displays, vehicle wraps, package prototypes, large banners, fine art reproductions, photo enlargements, and a multitude of other products.[35]

The last of the trade promotions examined here involves personal selling either directly or indirectly. These are sales contests and incentives and sales training. Sales contests and incentives are drivers to increase the volume of product "out the door." Such short-term incentives have been used for years to motivate salespeople to perform. The effectiveness of such contests both from an internal sales force application and dealers can be quite varied. Some research on the subject has been done on sales contest effectiveness,[36] but its application in any channel can be a complex endeavor. When using the promotion, marketing communications managers need to do a thorough analysis of the method as it may apply to their particular circumstances. In using incentives and contests, some ethical concerns are involved as well. The use of contests by a well-known Wall Street firm to sell certain of proprietary mutual funds also ran into legal trouble.[37]

Training Programs for Channel Members Can Be an Important Part of the Sale.

Firms have long known the value of training for those who handle their products because training helps the sellers to understand all the aspects of the product features, ingredients, applications, and other use-related issues.

Source: © 2006 JupiterImages Corporation.

Training is a form of manufacturer-sponsored educational program. Business-to-business firms have long known the value of hands-on training being provided by the manufacturer when a new product or adopter is involved.[38] For example, in the medical equipment industry, manufacturers usually offer to both train physicians and health-care personnel (the buyers) how to best use the equipment and also educate them about the product's benefits. In the aviation arena, when a new aircraft is sold to an airline, training, both initial and refresher courses, for the airlines pilots is often a crucial and expensive element in the terms of sale.[39] You may also see extensive training for retail sales personnel in the beauty products categories. As the beauty boutique retail arrangement (in which each brand has its own retail space) has spread across most department stores and the brands have opened their own boutiques, the brand has trained the retailers' sales personnel regarding all the aspects of the product ingredients, application, and other use-related issues.[40] Table 8-5 provides a summary of the sales promotions that can be directed at channel members to facilitate the movement of product through the channel. In most cases, a mix of the elements is used to optimize channel performance.

8-3c Measurement

Trade promotions offer a discrete time in which to evaluate the performance of a given tool. You can take a measure, run the promotion, and then follow up with another measurement. That is a very appealing aspect for managers. Taking baseline measures can allow the manager to have a good set of pre- and post-measures for inclusion in the database. Which particular measurements are most useful is for the manager to decide. Some of the basic ones are incremental increases or decreases in sales of the product, number of new users captured, profitability (revenues attributed to the promotion/cost of the promotion), and changes in a number of channel distributor dimensions including such things as attitudes, satisfaction, purchase intentions, and so on. Survey data collections regarding these trade channel aspects can

TABLE 8-5 Selected Types of Sales Promotion Directed at Channel Members

Type	Characteristics	Illustration
Trade shows or meetings	One firm or a group of firms invites channel members to attend sessions where products are displayed and explained.	The annual National Hardware Show attracts more than 3,000 exhibitors and tens of thousands of attendees.
Training	A firm provides training for personnel of channel members.	Gateway trains retailers to operate and use its computers.
Trade allowances or special offers	Channel members are given discounts or rebates for performing specified functions or purchasing during certain time periods.	Channel members are given discounts or rebates for performing specified functions or purchasing during certain time periods.
Point-of-purchase displays	A firm gives channel members fully equipped displays for its products and sets them up.	Coca-Cola provides display cases with its name on them to retailers carrying minimum quantities of Coca-Cola products.
Push money	Channel members' salespeople are given bonuses for pushing the brand of a certain firm.	A salesperson in an office-equipment store is paid an extra $50 for every desk of a particular brand that is sold.
Sales contests	Prizes or bonuses are distributed if certain performance levels are met.	A wholesaler receives $2,500 for selling 1,000 microchips in a month.
Free merchandise	Discounts or allowances are provided in the form of merchandise.	A retailer gets one case of ballpoint pens free for every ten cases purchased.
Demonstration models	Free items are given to channel members for demonstration purposes.	A hospital-bed manufacturer offers demonstrator models to its distributors.
Gifts	Channel members are given gifts for carrying items or performing functions.	During one 3-month period, a book publisher gives computerized cash registers to bookstores that agree to stock a specified quantity of its books.
Cooperative promotions	Two or more channel members share the costs of a promotion.	A manufacturer and a retailer each pay part of the costs for T-shirts with the manufacturer's and the retailer's names embossed.

Source: Joel R. Evans and Barry Berman, *Marketing,* 9th ed. (Cincinnati, OH: Atomic Dog, 2005), 527.

also be gathered pre- and post-promotion. As with other marketing communications tools, data can also be measured based on any key types of information and then applied into a theoretically valid longitudinal framework to support the continued enhancement of the database for future use.

8-3d Best Case: Consumer Products Manufacturer and Channel Master— Procter & Gamble

SMC QuickLink
Procter & Gamble B2B Directory
http://www.pg.com/b2b/index.jhtml

Many people consider Procter & Gamble to be the quintessential consumer products company. The company was officially started as a partnership between William Procter and James Gamble on October 31, 1837. Since that day, the company has continued to evolve as one of the largest and most profitable consumer products companies. Recently, Procter & Gamble acquired Gillette to enhance its market and channel power in a world in which retailers like Wal-Mart had significantly impacted channel power relationships.[41] Not only is it known by the consumer for offering wide and deep lines of quality products, it is also known across the entire business community for its prowess within the channel of distribution. It is seen as a company that is a leader in the new ways of thinking about the nature of its business.[42]

8-4 Consumer Promotions

Consumer promotions are promotions that, like their sibling trade promotions, are aimed at facilitating the movement of goods/services through the channel. The difference is that these promotions are aimed directly at the final consumer. Table 8-6 provides a breakdown of the consumer promotion toolbox covered in this chapter. As with trade promotions, they should be considered to be facilitators for short-term objec-

TABLE 8-6 Consumer Promotions Toolbox

Consumer Promotions			
Coupons	Premiums	Refunds and rebates	Price-off deals
Sampling	Contests and sweepstakes	Bonus packs	

tives, not long-term objectives. Reliance on promotions for long-term product/service market strength can be a costly strategy in both brand strength and revenue.

8-4a Strategic Marketing Communications Elements

As already noted, *consumer promotions* are externally directed incentives offered to the ultimate consumer. These usually consist of offers such as coupons, premiums, rebates, and so on that are designed to gain one or more of the following: product trial; repeat usage of product; more frequent or multiple product purchases; introduction of a new or improved product; introduction of new packaging or different size packages; neutralization of competitive advertising or sales promotions; capitalization on seasonal, geographic, or special events; encouragement of consumers to trade up to a larger size, more profitable line, or another product in the line.

Some of the elements that are unique to consumer promotions are described here.

- A **bonus pack** is a special container, package, carton, or other holder in which the consumer is given more of the product for the same or perhaps even lower price per ounce or unit than in the regular container.
- A **coupon** is a printed (or electronic) certificate entitling the bearer to a stated price reduction or special value on a specific product, generally for a specified period of time. The value of the coupon is set and redeemed by the seller.
- **Coupon redemption** is the use of a seller's value certificate at the time of purchase to obtain either a lower price or greater value than normal. This term also is used to describe the act of accepting a seller's certificate by a retailer or other intermediary.
- A **contest** is a consumer promotion technique requiring the participant to use specific skills or abilities to solve or complete a specified problem to qualify for a prize or award.
- **Cross-ruff** is a consumer promotion technique in which a noncompetitive product is used as the vehicle to distribute a coupon, sample, or other sales promotion offer for another product.
- A **premium** (retailing definition) is merchandise offered at a lower price, or free, as an additional incentive for a customer to make a purchase or (sales promotion definition) an item of value other than the product itself that is given as an additional incentive to influence the purchase of a product.
- A **price-off deal** is a stated reduction in the price of a product generally offered by the manufacturer and printed directly on the product package.
- A **rebate** is a return of a portion of the purchase price in the form of cash by the seller to the buyer.
- A **referral reward** is a lead for a prospect given to the salesperson by an existing customer who is rewarded in some manner, often through cash, rebates, or gifts.
- A **refund** is a return of the amount paid for an item or some portion of the amount.
- **Sampling** is when free merchandise is given to prospective consumers to use.
- A **sweepstakes** is the offering of prizes to participants in which winners are selected by chance and no consideration is required.

bonus pack A special container, package, carton, or other holder in which the consumer is given more of the product for the same or perhaps even lower price per ounce or unit than in the regular container.

coupon A printed (or electronic) certificate entitling the bearer to a stated price reduction or special value on a specific product, generally for a specified period of time. The value of the coupon is set and redeemed by the seller.

coupon redemption The use of a seller's value certificate at the time of purchase to obtain either a lower price or greater value than normal. This term also is used to describe the act of accepting a seller's certificate by a retailer or other intermediary.

contest A consumer promotion technique requiring the participant to use specific skills or abilities to solve or complete a specified problem to qualify for a prize or award.

cross-ruff A consumer promotion technique in which a noncompetitive product is used as the vehicle to distribute a coupon, sample, or other sales promotion offer for another product.

premium In retailing, merchandise offered at a lower price, or free, as an additional incentive for a customer to make a purchase. In sales promotion, an item of value other than the product itself that is given as an additional incentive to influence the purchase of a product.

price-off deal A stated reduction in the price of a product generally offered by the manufacturer and printed directly on the product package.

rebate A return of a portion of the purchase price in the form of cash by the seller to the buyer.

referral reward (see p. 181) A lead for a prospect given to the salesperson by an existing customer who is rewarded in some manner, often through cash, rebates, or gifts.

refund (see p. 181) A return of the amount paid for an item or some portion of the amount.

sampling (see p. 181) When free merchandise is given to prospective consumers to use.

sweepstakes (see p. 181) The offering of prizes to participants in which winners are selected by chance and no consideration is required.

buy one, get one free A sales promotion offer made to either the retailer or the consumer in which purchase of one unit of the product is encouraged or rewarded by providing a second unit of the same product free of charge.

accelerated purchase A sales promotion goal achieved when consumers or channel members purchase the product before the time they normally would have bought.

cross-selling In retailing, selling between and among departments to facilitate larger transactions and to make it more convenient for the customer to do related-item shopping. In sales promotion, a consumer promotion technique in which the manufacturer attempts to sell the consumer products related to a product the consumer already uses or that the marketer has available.

continuity plan Any type of consumer promotion technique that encourages customers to purchase products on a continuing basis or over time.

SMC QuickLink
Valpak.com (coupon company site)
http://www.valpak.com

- **Buy one, get one free** is a sales promotion offer made to either the retailer or the consumer in which purchase of one unit of the product is encouraged or rewarded by providing a second unit of the same product free of charge.
- An **accelerated purchase** is a sales promotion goal achieved when consumers or channel members purchase the product before the time they normally would have bought.
- **Cross-selling** in retailing involves selling between and among departments to facilitate larger transactions and to make it more convenient for the customer to do related-item shopping. Cross-selling in sales promotion is a consumer promotion technique in which the manufacturer attempts to sell the consumer products related to a product the consumer already uses or that the marketer has available.
- A **continuity plan** is any type of consumer promotion technique that encourages customers to purchase products on a continuing basis or over time. The plan often is based on some sort of saving or accumulation scheme such as trading stamps, points, coupons, or the like.

8-4b Characteristics

The wide array of consumer promotions seen in Table 8-6 provides the marketer with any number of ways to try and "put life" into a lagging or less-than-optimally performing good/service in the consumer marketplace. Consumer promotions, like many of those from the trade side, should be regarded as short term in their application and used with care. Consumer promotions, just like trade promotions, can be a two-sided blade. While they can offer a clear positive incentive to the consumer to purchase the good/service, they also may have a negative impact once the promotion is removed that the marketing communications manager must take into account when using these tools.[43] Promotions may cause brand-switching behaviors or deterioration of brand image or simply cost the firm using it more than it gains in monetary return. In the highly competitive British newspaper market, in an attempt to stop sliding circulations, several newspapers are betting that the fairly substantial short-term costs of inserting DVDs and CDs (premiums) in their papers will pay off in the long run by keeping readers and thus attracting advertising dollars. However, some in the business liken it to a drug addiction for the newspapers.[44] If that is the case, it is another example of a consumer promotion run amok by taking on a life of its own and leaving those using it "hooked" regardless of value to the bottom line. Managers are also wise to carefully consider the viability of various promotions when the promotions are used to try and target global and subcultural segments.[45] What works with one group may not work as well or may even be counterproductive in a different cultural environment. As with the trade promotions, change is the one constant in promotions these days. SMC Marketplace Watch 8-3 suggests we are seeing the end of one long-running tradition in the grocery field.

Bonus packs are often used in the channel in an attempt to give the customer more "value" for their money. Package designs often use the "Double the Amount at the Same Price," "20 Percent Free," or similar pitches to capture consumers' attention. One study found that over 50 percent of people had purchased more than they had planned because of bonus pack offers. This "stocking up" was done mostly by females as compared to males. However, no differences were found for age, education, or shopping frequency.[46] Consumer product categories like shampoo are some of the biggest users of this type of sales promotion; its use has yielded substantial sales punch in a number of retail environments.[47] As always, though, managers throughout the channel need to evaluate the promotion as to its contribution to their operation's profitability.

It seems as though coupons have been around since the first printed materials hit the streets. We have all seen them and probably clipped them from some printed material. The coupon, however, has evolved from its early days. Along with the traditional free-standing inserts (FSIs), they are now available in a variety of forms that

SMC Marketplace Watch 8-3

Farewell to the Grocery Weekly Special

It seemed to many grocery stores that many consumers just were not willing to take the time to look for weekly specials and other deals in the marketplace. As a result, a move is underway by many of these stores to let go of promotional discounts and instead offer the everyday low prices that consumers find at places like Wal-Mart.

In 2005 the waves of change raced across several regional grocery chains that have reduced prices and stopped offering weekly bargains. This change flies against tradition. For decades, most supermarkets had tried to entice price-conscious shoppers with low-priced weekly specials and made up the lost profit by keeping other items priced substantially higher. The pervasiveness of retailers like Costco and Wal-Mart has made consumers expect inexpensive product on an everyday basis.

Supermarkets generally carry about 30,000 items. In 2004 Giant Eagle, Inc., of Pennsylvania cut the price on 4,300 items; Piggly Wiggly operator Fresh Brands, Inc., of Wisconsin cut prices on 4,000 goods; and Wegman's Food Markets, Inc., which serves parts of New York, New Jersey, and Virginia, has cut the prices of 10,000 items. In 2005 California supermarket chain Raley's reduced the daily price on 7,000 items. The price cuts are in some cases quite significant but not on every item.

The cuts may apply to no more than about 15 percent of the chain's items, but they are so-called "center-of-the-store goods" like toothpaste and toilet paper. Customers who did not "deal shop" before could take home savings, on average, of about 5 to 7 percent a shopping trip if they purchased a broad basket of goods, according to Willard Bishop Consulting, retail-marketing consultants in Barrington, Illinois. Many families could end up saving somewhere in the neighborhood of a few hundred dollars a year in grocery bills at these chains that had shifted pricing structures.

For as long as people can remember, grocery chains have been relentlessly playing with their pricing strategies. Nothing is really new with that. The move toward the everyday low price strategy is one of the most significant ones in recent memory. It is the direct result of the encroachment by stores like Wal-Mart in the grocery market. Grocery store chains such as Wal-Mart supercenters, dollar stores, and wholesale clubs controlled 31.9 percent of grocery bills last year, up from 8.9 percent in 1994. For the past few years, the nation's largest supermarket chains have been posting meager sales gains and uneven profits as they lose shoppers to these retailers.

Market forces are at play outside of the competition as well. Food prices have been rising. In 2004 they were up 3.8 percent from the year before. Coupon use is down. Consumers used 3.3 billion coupons in 2004, down from 4.5 billion in 2000. Consumers may also be getting fed up with the requirements tied to specials and coupons. For example, in the United States, about one of every four coupons requires multiple-item purchases. Customers also complained about having to drive around looking for specials.

The pricing changes could have significant impacts both within and beyond the grocery industry. Stores are driving a harder bargain with suppliers to offset the hit from the lower prices. Stores could also reduce the pages of promotional advertising they buy in local newspapers, thus impacting a significant revenue source for local newspapers.

Value pricing as an everyday strategy has not always worked in retail, though. Just ask Kmart. It did away with its in-store "BlueLight" specials and started a "BlueLight Always" program meant to lower everyday prices. The discount retailer filed for Chapter 11 bankruptcy law protection, a move that was contributed to by that failed strategy.

As of the summer of 2005, Giant Eagle, with 221 stores, reports that its sales and market share have increased—this since it lowered the price of 3,000 items in November 2004. In April 2005, the chain cut the price of another 1,300 items.

Source: Adapted from Janet Adamy, "Grocery Stores Cut Out the Weekly Special; Under Pressure from Discounters, Chains Lower Everyday Prices on a Range of Popular Staples," *Wall Street Journal,* July 20, 2005, D-1.

---

include on-packaging, electronic, in store displays, and kiosks. In 2004 over 250 billion coupons were distributed on everything from shampoo to restaurant meals and vacations. That number was up 7.7 percent from the year before. Translated into potential dollar saving per person in the United States, that worked out to about $1,000.[48] A portion of the money that had been spent on the traditional FSI coupons now goes into the electronic and in-store outlets. This type of coupon dispensing also allows a better control over coupon fraud, which can be a problem for issuers.[49]

Exhibit 8-4

Keeping Up with the MINI Owner

MINI tries to keep a strong relationship with its owners by frequent contacts about contests, promotions, and other MINI events.

Source: Reprinted by permission of BMW of North America, LLC

SMC QuickLink

ContestListings.com
http://www.contestlistings.com

Web-based successes in a number of industries have started to lead more of the mainline retailers in grocery and sundries to consider e-coupons as either an alternative to or complementary tool to be used with direct mailers and FSIs in Sunday newspapers.[50] As with direct marketing, coupon impact can be tracked fairly tightly when combined with a good database. The level of offer should be one that imparts clear value to the consumer. It also should not require a great deal of work and thought to use it. Issuers should consider the coupon offer as it relates to the market strength and purchase frequency of the brand.[51] In regard to the performance of coupons on different types of products, coupons seem to have about the same amount of impact on purchasing behavior by consumers when they are buying either consumer products or services.[52]

As seen in the definitions given previously, contests and sweepstakes differ in that one requires the consumer to have some skill or to carry out a task to be eligible to win (contests) and the other just requires participation (sweepstakes). In reality, though, consumers and the media often use the terms interchangeably. Differences aside, these promotions are used to heighten involvement and create "buzz" for goods and services. These promotions can be targeted as exclusives that involve only current consumers of a given product or service or can be aimed at a much wider and general audience. An example of the first type would be the chance given to United 1K members (the top elite level of United's frequent-flier program requiring flying 100,000 miles or more each year) to win a Round the World Cruise by having their names entered in the contestant pool each time they take a trip on United. MINIUSA is constantly sending contests by email to MINI car owners that offer the chance to win "cool" trips and prizes (see Exhibit 8-4). An example of the latter type of more general execution would be along the lines of Kellogg's and Cartoon Network teaming with marketers like AT&T or Wireless and Microsoft's Xbox for a "Toon Tour of Mysteries." The execution featured DVD-ROMs in 100 million packages of Kellogg's kids' products and a prize-laden sweepstakes. Cartoon Network supported the endeavor with Scooby-Doo spots—this, while Kellogg's ran 2 weeks of dedicated television advertisements and provided in-store point-of-purchase materials. Consumers could enter at eetandern.com or by text messaging on their AT&T wireless phone. The prizes included a Mazda minivan, Xbox systems and games, Dell computers, and even a vacation for the family. The advertisement had a bit more "buzz" that keeps on giving—the minivan will be customized by the Cartoon Network to look just like the Scooby-Doo Mystery Machine from the television cartoon show.[53]

The use of contests and sweepstakes types of promotions can be found across a wide variety of different products and media environments. Television superstation and WB network member WGN (based in Chicago) has done really well running locally sponsored trivia-based advertising sales promotions. The station's management sells the contest idea to advertisers as a way to increase their market visibility and give the marketer "an invaluable link to the viewing public, their consumers." An example was a summer promotion that linked up Dodge as a sponsor for a "Pepsi Smash" promotion. Viewers of the television concert series entered by filling out online entry forms that named the last act on each week's program. Winning contestants got tickets to attend a Destiny's Child show at Chicago's House of Blues, a $500 shopping spree, and a trip for two to another concert in Utah.[54] Sports at both the major league and minor league levels of competition often employ the contest or sweepstakes as a way to put people in the seats.[55] A last thing to consider is the increasing role that insurance coverage of such promotions is playing as liability for a host of issues is at play.[56]

Premiums can add significant value to the product/service for the consumer. The use of premiums has long been part of the promotion mix aimed at children. Toys were often inserted into the cereal boxes of the 1950s. McDonald's promotion efforts have long used premiums, starting with the action figures of Ronald and other characters included in the Happy Meals. These types of premiums are part of the fast-food landscape.[57] McDonald's in 2003 upped the ante for premiums when

Exhibit 8-5

Offering a Premium for a Magazine Subscription

The offer of two free books and four free trial issues from *The Economist* adds value to this subscription offer that makes it more difficult to resist.

Source: Used with permission from *The Economist*.

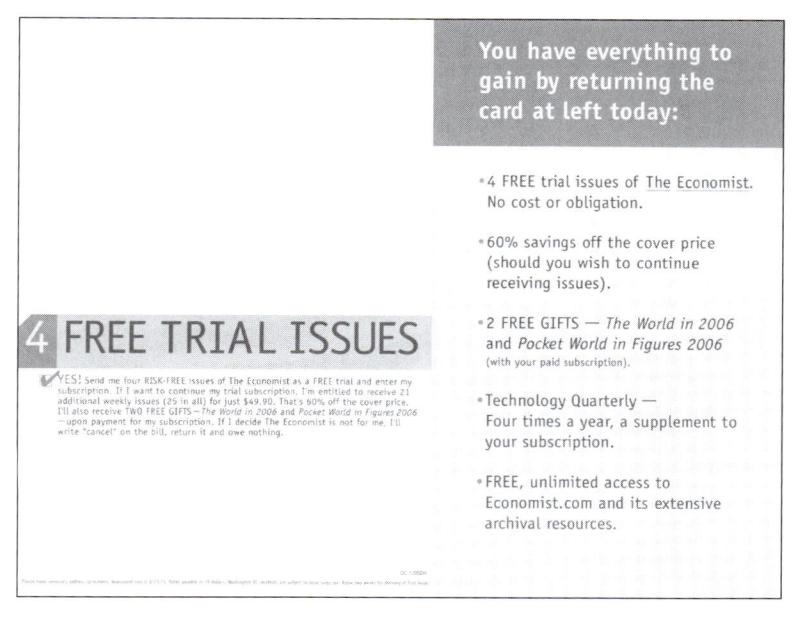

they linked up with Sega to give away video games.[58] On a more adult level, premiums can also be effective (see Exhibit 8-5). Sometimes, they can be quite extensive and expensive as well. Recent premium giveaways have included iPods. Such types of premiums and the consumer's perception of value (both for the iPod and other premiums) can really provide a strong incentive for the consumer to act on the marketer's offer. As one marketing analyst notes, though, the cost of such premiums can be prohibitive. Coupled with an increasingly savvy consumer, it may take unique and even ground-breaking products to actually make such expensive premiums pay off.[59] In addition, premiums can also overrun the product and purchasing behavior, as noted in the British newspaper example given at the beginning of this section.

Rebates and refunds offer consumers a chance to get money back from their purchase. Usually these refunds and rebates involve the consumer having to complete a refund or rebate form, but that is not always the case. The use of mail-in rebates is quite common in a number of consumer product categories and can run the gamut from shampoos to electronics. Cell phone manufacturers and other communications suppliers are common users of the promotion.[60] When a mail-in rebate is used, only about 50 percent of the eligible consumers actually end up filing to receive the rebate.[61] For something like a $50.00 cell phone rebate, a sizable portion of the eligible consumers not sending in the request is a windfall for the company offering the rebate. As a consequence, the cost to those who tender the rebate offer is significantly lowered, making the use of the promotion more appealing. The use of the Internet as a redemption outlet has become somewhat common for retailers as it offers a much reduced handling cost environment for the manufacturer or retailer offering the incentive. In some studies, it has also been shown to increase redemption rates.[62]

Rebates have also been used creatively by such diverse groups as credit card companies (Discover) and automobiles. Discover uses the "cash back" on total purchases as a way to differentiate itself from the Visa, Mastercard, and American Express cards. While the consumer may view Discover as "the rebate card," Visa, Mastercard, and American Express all have their own rebate card offers, and some are rated as quite superior to the Discover card on the rebate dimension.[63] The automotive industry used rebates to clean out year-end inventory for years. Chrysler was the first to use the rebate on a wide-scale basis years ago. There is a real danger of relying on rebates as part of a long-term strategy. Consumers can quickly learn to wait for the rebates and hold off buying until the next round of rebates is offered. In the automotive industry, rebate usage now can also signal a problem with inventory and market desires for

SMC QuickLink
Start Sampling
http://www.startsampling.com

the type of vehicle being offered. In 2004 U.S. auto manufacturers began to significantly increase rebates for SUVs as sales in the lucrative market began to slow.[64]

Sampling is all about getting the product to the consumer to try. The entire idea behind it is, "If they try it, they will buy it." A great deal of information may be had from sampling beyond the simple thought to boost sales. Getting product out to consumers for trial can also raise brand awareness and generate a great deal of usable data for research and product communications that can help maintain and grow sales farther down the line. It is also the perfect manner in which to test new products, variants, or package configurations and/or sizes.[65] Sampling is used extensively in the consumer product categories of personal care products. Shampoos, lotions, soaps, and cosmetics of all types are given out as samples for the consumer to try. The consumer can acquire these samples in a variety of manners. They are widely available and can be had at the retail outlet, in the mall, at the airport, by mail, in newspaper sleeves delivered to your door, in magazine inserts, and from street personnel, among others. Sampling is a tried and true way of getting consumers to become converts from one brand to another, especially for low-involvement types of goods when the consumer is buying brand based on simple inertia. The impact of sampling has also been shown to have some staying power for the brand as well. A study from 2004 suggested that free samples can produce measurable long-term effects on sales that can be observed as much as 12 months after the promotion.[66]

The success of sampling has also led some products that have long been thought of as inappropriate for sampling campaigns to make their way into the mix. In London, Trojan condoms began a taxicab condom-giveaway campaign aimed at late-night "clubbers." The campaign was designed to increase awareness of safe-sex practices while at the same time clearly targeting the at-risk group for sexually transmitted diseases. The campaign slogan was "The Trojan War on STIs" (sexually transmitted infections) and was backed up with FM radio promotion spots. A public relations firm cut a deal with local cab company Brighton & Hove Radio Cabs to handle the giveaways.[67] Although sampling exhibits real "star power" as a sales promotion tool, the

Sampling a Beverage at London Gatwick Airport

The sign above the booth says it all about the reasons that marketers will employ sampling.

Source: Photo by Don Rahtz.

marketing communications manager needs to recognize that its success can still be highly variable. Research shows that the effectiveness of free-sample promotions can vary widely, even between brands in the same product category.[68]

Price-off deals differ from coupons and rebates in that the price reduction is marked on the product package itself. As with a number of the other promotions, price-off promotions often relate to excess inventory. For example, car dealers mark the sticker price down by a certain margin at the end of the year to get rid of the remaining cars. In 2004 the employee pricing promotion used by GM and other automobile manufacturers led to price-off deals showing up in the used-car market. High-value used luxury cars especially were being marked down to the lowest levels in at least 2 years.[69] The use of price-off deals may be more of a standard practice than a true promotional tool in a number of industries, such as the recording industry and the book publishing industry. Most large retailers will offer a significant price-off discount on all new book releases. Chains such as Wal-Mart heavily discount suggested retail prices. Barnes & Noble's policy is to discount bestsellers by 30 percent.[70] Table 8-7 provides a summary of the types of sales promotions that are directed at the consumer market by marketers. As with the trade promotions discussed earlier, marketers will often use a combination of these techniques when putting together a strategic marketing plan.

8-4c Measurement

As noted with trade promotions, one of the appealing aspects about promotions is the short-term nature of the promotion. There is usually a well-defined starting and ending point of the promotion. Taking baseline measures can allow the manager to have a good set of pre- and post-measures for inclusion in the database. Which particular measurements are most useful is for the manager to decide. One article suggests six evaluation criteria for use by managers regarding the bonus pack promotion: repurchase delays, consumer loyalty, new category consumption, stocking up, brand switching, and administrative costs.[71] However, most managers agree

TABLE 8-7 Selected Types of Sales Promotion Directed at Consumers

Type	Characteristics	Illustration
Coupons	Firms advertise special discounts for customers who redeem coupons.	P&G mails consumers a 50-cents-off coupon for Sure deodorant, which can be redeemed at any supermarket.
Refunds or rebates	Consumers submit proofs of purchase (often to the manufacturer) and receive an extra discount.	First Alert provides rebates to consumers submitting proofs of purchase for its fire alarms.
Samples	Free merchandise or services are given to consumers, generally for new items.	America Online offers a free trial of its services.
Contests or sweepstakes	Consumers compete for prizes by answering questions (contests) or filling out forms for random drawings of prizes (sweepstakes).	Publishers Clearing House sponsors annual sweepstakes and awards cash and other prizes.
Bonus packs	Consumers receive discounts for purchasing in quantity, or multipacks	A furniture store runs a "buy one, get one free" sale on desk lamps.
Shows or exhibits	Many firms cosponsor exhibitions for consumers.	The Auto Show is annually scheduled for the public in New York.
Point-of-purchase	In-store displays remind customers and generate impulse purchases.	*TV Guide* sales in supermarkets are high due to checkout counter displays.
Special events	Firms sponsor the Olympics, fashion shows, and other activities.	Visa USA is a worldwide sponsor of the Olympics.
Gifts	Consumers get gifts for making a purchase or opening a new account.	Savings banks offer gifts for consumers opening new accounts or expanding existing ones.
Frequent-shopper	Consumers get gifts or special discounts, based on cumulative purchases. Points are amassed and exchanged for gifts or money.	Airline travelers accumulate mileage and receive free trips or gifts when enough miles are earned.

Source: Joel R. Evans and Barry Berman, *Marketing,* 9th ed. (Cincinnati, OH: Atomic Dog, 2005), 528.

that a number of basic ones are usually of interest. These are: incremental increases or decreases in sales of the product, number of new users captured, profitability (revenues attributed to the promotion/cost of the promotion), and changes in a number of consumer dimensions including such things as attitudes, satisfaction, purchase intentions, and so on. Survey data collections regarding these consumer psychological aspects should also be gathered pre- and post-promotion. As with other marketing communications tools, data can also be measured based on any set of demographic or other types of information collected via the contact point using a longitudinal framework to support the continued enhancement of the database for future use.

8-4d Best Case: Driving Home a Deal—General Motors Employee Discounts

SMC QuickLink
General Motors
http://www.gm.com

General Motors stirred up the automotive industry in 2005 when it launched the "Employee Discount Pricing" promotion. The program, which de-emphasized the traditional "haggling" at the automobile dealer, scored big for GM. It was viewed by GM as a "bridge" to the company's new "Total Value Proposition" strategy that the company is putting in place for the long term. In June 2005, GM had its best sales month in the United States in 19 years. Ford and Chrysler matched the promotion with their own employee discounts. Overall, U.S. car and light-truck sales in June jumped 16 percent from the year before. The seasonally adjusted annual sales pace for the month went to 17.5 million cars and light trucks up from a 15.4-million-vehicle pace in 2004. GM drove away with a winning 47 percent increase.[72] The promotion also saw a number of consumers trading in non-GM products for those in the GM line. Known in the industry as "conquesting," GM management estimated that the promotion had netted more than 200,000 customers from competitors than it would have if the employee-discount program had not been in place.[73] The success of the GM employee discount promotion started a number of similar promotions by retailers outside the automotive industry as well.[74]

Summary

In the SMC portfolio, the three components that are regularly used to facilitate the movement of product through the entire marketing channel between the manufacturer/service provider and the final consumer are personal selling, trade promotions, and consumer promotions; Table 8-1 summarizes the elements of each. Our discussion treats the second of these as reseller support, because the role of the trade promotion is to support the reseller of a given product through a variety of activities and incentives provided by the manufacturer/service provider in the channel. As with the other chapters in Part Two of this book, the examination highlights what these components may have to offer from an SMC manager's perspective when building an SMC plan. The examination of personal selling, trade promotions, and consumer promotions points out that combinations of these and other tools (shown in Chapters Five to Seven) are often used together in the executions of an SMC plan. Throughout this book, we argue that an SMC approach allows the marketing communications manager to find combinations of these various tools to allow greater synergy in the application of these tools and optimize overall performance within the marketing system.

This is the last chapter in Part Two. The chapters here are brief and not intended to provide in-depth coverage of each of the presented SMC elements. As the summaries before this have suggested, you may wish to spend some time on the sites that are listed in the "Additional QuickLinks" section. These sites represent trade and consumer associations and firms that work in these fields. We do not endorse any particular company or organization but, rather, want to allow you to visit a few of the many sites that are out there. A few of these sites have some good summary listings; and most of these sites offer additional information about personal selling, trade promotions or reseller support, consumer promotions, and so on, as well as what these SMC portfolio elements can offer to a marketing communications manager. Again, as noted in the previous chapters, you will be able to learn many more details about the various elements here than was possible in this chapter, given our space restraints and the strategic nature of this book. As previously noted, you have now completed the last of the SMC portfolio chapters. The book now turns to the strategic aspects and application of SMC.

Discussion Questions

Choose a consumer brand of your choice. Your boss has asked you to conduct a full marketing communications audit on your channel relationships and final consumer promotions. In putting together your assessment of the SMC portfolio elements you will need to answer a number of questions that relate to that audit.

1. What are the aspects of each of the elements? In other words, what types of properties does each of the tools possess?
2. What options for facilitation are currently being used? Which are best suited for your product?
3. Which would be your first choice for use? Why?
4. Can any of these be used in combination for better performance? Why or why not?
5. How could you measure their contribution to facilitating the movement of your product/service in the channel?
6. If you were to develop a database for assessing their performance, what would be in that database?
7. What information do you want in your database related to product information?
8. What information related to your channel members would you want and/or need?
9. What information related to the consumer would you want and/or need? Usage information? Demographic information? Others?
10. Can your direct-marketing elements be integrated with other traditional advertising approaches from Chapter Five?
11. Can your direct-marketing elements be integrated with other public relations approaches from Chapter Six?
12. Can your direct-marketing elements be integrated with other direct-marketing approaches from Chapter Seven?

Practice Quiz

Note: You can find the correct answers to these questions by taking the quiz and then submitting your answers in the Online Edition. The program will automatically score your submission. If you miss a question, the program will provide the correct answer, a rationale for the answer, and the section number in the chapter where the topic is discussed.

1. The _____ industry is associated with a short distribution channel.
   a. beverages
   b. automobile
   c. aircraft
   d. books and periodicals

2. The _____ definition defines an agent as a company or individual that represents a company in a particular market.
   a. sales
   b. global marketing
   c. retailing
   d. manufacturer's

3. In personal selling, the _____ assumes no title risks, does not usually have physical custody of products, and is not looked upon as a permanent representative of either the buyer or seller.
   a. manufacturer's agent
   b. selling agent
   c. salesperson
   d. broker

4. The _____ is the least complex personal sales presentation involving a memorized script that does not change from customer to customer.
   a. need-satisfaction approach
   b. canned sales presentation
   c. selling formula approach
   d. consultative selling approach

5. In order taking, the order taker services an account. This situation is commonly referred to as a "straight rebuy." What does it imply?
   a. The manufacturer tries to get the best price for the order.
   b. Channel members "stock up" at the lower price.
   c. The order does not change much.
   d. The order taker tries to buy the product at a discount.

6. _____ calls for introducing new products and programs to both current and potential customers.
   a. Missionary sales work
   b. Creative selling
   c. Order taking
   d. Straight rebuy

7. _____ is a danger associated with trade promotions that occurs when channel members "stock up" at the lower price.
   a. Straight rebuy
   b. Accumulation
   c. Off deal
   d. Forward buying

8. _____ is a particular type of advertising that involves sharing of expenses between the retailer and other previous marketing channel members.
   a. Ingredient-sponsored cooperative advertising
   b. Vertical cooperative advertising
   c. Horizontal cooperative advertising
   d. Lateral cooperative advertising

9. _____ refers to a form of trade promotion in which the retailer is offered a discount on the purchase of the product at a particular point in time.
   a. Buying allowance
   b. Slotting allowance
   c. Promotional allowance
   d. Retail allowance

10. _____ is a consumer promotion technique in which a company uses a noncompetitive product as the vehicle to distribute a coupon, sample, or other sales promotion offer for another product.
    a. Sampling
    b. Cross-ruff
    c. Rub-off
    d. Referral

Web Exercise

Servicing Different Markets Differently—Web Contact Points

Visit brand websites from four different product categories. First see if you can find different pages or links on the websites for general consumers and business or channel customers. For example, the Procter & Gamble website offers a distinct link for business-to-business marketing. Evaluate the emphasis that the websites put on the different support activities related to consumer promotions, trade promotions (reseller support), and personal selling. Are there differences across the different types of product manufacturers? Do you consider each of the individual brands' use of the different elements appropriate for the type of product it is? Next, visit a competitor's website. Compare the two. Do they do things differently? Which seems more successful to you? Why?

Additional QuickLinks

American Management Association
http://www.amanet.org/index.htm

American Marketing Association
http://www.ama.org

Association of Coupon Professionals
http://www.couponpros.org

British Promotional Merchandise Association
http://www.bpma.co.uk

Canadian Professional Sales Association
http://www.cpsa.com

Catalina Marketing Corporation
http://www.catmktg.com

Foodservice Sales & Marketing Association
http://www.fsmaonline.com/home.cfm?refr=index

Global Trade Show and Event Summary EventsEye
http://www.eventseye.com

Hospitality and Sales and Marketing Association International
http://www.hsmai.org

Incentive Marketing Association
http://www.incentivemarketing.org

Institute of Sales Promotion (United Kingdom)
http://www.isp.org.uk

Manufacturers' Agents National Association
http://www.manaonline.org

National Association of Pharmaceutical Sales Representatives
http://napsronline.org

National Sales Network: An African American Sales Organization
http://www.salesnetwork.org

Professional Sales Association (United Kingdom)
http://www.salespeople.org.uk/index.shtml

Promotion Marketing Association
http://www.pmalink.org

Promotion Summary Link Site
http://www.commerce-database.com/sales-promotion.htm

Sales and Marketing Executives International
http://www.smei.org

Technical Sales Organization
http://www.technicalsalesassociation.org

Trade Promotion Management Association
http://www.tradepromo.org

Trade Show Exhibitors Association
http://www.tsea.org

Trade Show Resource Summary
http://www.tsnn.com

Tradeshow Week
http://www.tradeshowweek.com

Suggested Readings

Blattberg, Robert C. 1996. *Sales promotion: Concepts, methods, and strategies.* Upper Saddle River, NJ: Pearson Prentice Hall.

Clark, Shawn. 2000. *The co-marketing solution: Strategic marketing through better branding, improved trade relationships, superior promotions, effective fact-based selling, accurate ROI of trade spending.* Chicago: NTC Business Books/American Marketing Association.

Coe, John. 2003. *The fundamentals of business-to-business sales & marketing.* New York: McGraw-Hill.

Dalrymple, Douglas J., William L. Cron, and Thomas E. DeCarlo. 2003. *Sales management.* Hoboken, NJ: John Wiley & Sons.

Manning, Gerald L., and Barry L. Reece. 2004. *Selling today: Creating customer value,* 9th ed. Upper Saddle River, NJ: Pearson Prentice Hall.

Moncrief, William C., and Shannon Shipp. 1997. *Sales management.* Upper Saddle River, NJ: Pearson Prentice Hall.

Schultz, Don E., William A. Robinson, and Lisa A. Petrison. 1998. *Sales promotion essentials: The 10 basic sales promotion techniques . . . and how to use them,* 3rd ed. Chicago: NTC Business Books.

Spiro, Rosann, William J. Stanton, and Greg A. Rich. 2003. *Management of a sales force,* 11th ed. New York: McGraw-Hill/Irwin.

Stevens, Ruth P. 2005. *Trade show & event marketing: Plan, promote & profit.* Mason, OH: South-Western Educational Publishers.

Notes

1. As with earlier chapters, these definitions, and a number of the subsequent definitions in this chapter are taken from the American Marketing Association (AMA) list of definitions (http://www.marketingpower.com/mg-dictionary.php) and are used with AMA's permission.
2. For a *Wall Street Journal* article about the role of leasing companies in the airline industry, see Scott McCartney, "The Middle Seat: Aircraft-Leasing Firms Able to Drive a Hard Bargain; Demand for Planes Is Up As Overseas Markets Open; Pushing U.S. Costs Higher," *Wall Street Journal,* March 15, 2005, D-5.
3. There are a variety of introductory marketing, personal selling, and channels textbooks that offer an in-depth look at the variety of options available regarding sales personnel. See, for example, Joel R. Evans and Barry Berman, *Marketing, 9e: Marketing in the 21st Century* (Cincinnati: OH: Atomic Dog, 2005).
4. Mary Donato, "The Win-Win Sales Call," *Sales and Marketing Management* 157, no. 6 (2005): 21.
5. Michele Marchetti, "The Big Picture," *Sales and Marketing Management* 156, no. 12 (2004): 14.
6. William Perreault Jr. and E. Jerome McCarthy, *Essentials of Marketing: A Global-Managerial Approach,* 10th ed. (New York: McGraw-Hill, 2006).
7. Ibid.
8. Robert Brenner, "Ask the Right Questions," *Sales and Marketing Management* 156, no. 8 (2004): 16.
9. Thayer C. Talor, "A Letup in the Rise of Sales Call Costs," *Sales and Marketing Management,* February 25, 1980, 24.
10. U.S. Department of Labor website: http://www.bls.gov/oco/ocos119.htm#earnings.
11. Katrina C. Arabe, "The Changing Face of B-to-B Sales and Marketing," *Industrial Market Trends,* October 20, 2003. Available at http://news.thomasnet.com/IMT/archives/2003/10/the_changing_fa.html.
12. Michele Marchetti, "What a Sales Call Costs," *Sales and Marketing Management* 152, no. 9 (2000): 80.
13. See note 11.
14. Brian Yeado, "Net Worth," *Sales and Marketing Management* 155, no. 8 (2003): 32.
15. Vanessa O'Connell, "Some Retailers Are Cutting Ad Spending," *Wall Street Journal,* August 21, 2001, B-4.
16. U.S. Department of Labor website: http://www.bls.gov/oco/ocos121.htm#earnings.
17. Michael Schrage, "Lessons from Retail," *Sales and Marketing Management* 156, no. 12 (2004): 20.
18. Meg Major, "Celebration," *Progressive Grocer* 84, no. 6, April 15, 2005, 100–101.
19. "Abbott Laboratories: Profit Rises 38% to $877 Million with Help of Drug, Device Sales, *Wall Street Journal,* July 14, 2005, B-2.
20. "Mass Channel Tops in Managing Private Label Star Power," *DSN Retailing Today* 43, no. 20, October 25, 2004, 36–37.
21. Colin Grimshaw, "Star Alliance Appoints GroupM to 136m Task," *Marketing,* May 19, 2004, 2.
22. David Silver, "Marketing Is a Group Effort," *Chain Store Age* 81, no. 7 (2005): 130.

23. Beth Snyder Bulik, "Intel New Strategy Demands New Partner," *Advertising Age* 76, no. 11, March 14, 2005, 4.
24. Kate Maddox, "IBM Rolls Out ISV Ad Program," *B to B* 90, no. 2, February 14, 2005, 12.
25. Julie Ruth and Bernard L. Simonin, "Brought to You by Brand A and Brand B: Investigating Multiple Sponsors' Influence on Consumers' Attitudes toward Sponsored Events," *Journal of Advertising* 32, no. 3 (Fall 2003): 19–31.
26. "Phillip Morris Raises Prices on Cigarettes," *Wall Street Journal*, December 13, 2004, 1.
27. "How Retailer Power Changes Marketing," *Advertising Age* 74, no. 29, July 21, 2003, 16.
28. "Slotting Allowances—A Good Thing," *Chain Store Age* 81, no. 5 (2005): 43.
29. Timothy J. Richards and Paul M. Patterson, "Slotting Allowances As Real Options: An Alternative Explanation," *Journal of Business* 77, no. 4 (October 2004): 675–96.
30. Jeff Cioletti, "The Air in There," *Beverage World* 123, no. 1739, June 15, 2004, 52.
31. *Tradeshow Week* website: http://www.tradeshowweek.com/info/CA386164.html.
32. Srinath Gopalakrishna, Gary Lilien, Jerome D. Williams, and Ian K. Sequeria, "Do Trade Shows Pay Off?" *Journal of Marketing* 59 (July 1995): 75–83.
33. Bill Owens, "Are Trade Shows Worth the Visit?" *printWriter.com*, August 27, 2005, http://www.printwriter.com/articles/09_TradeShowPerspective.htm.
34. See note 31.
35. "Show Offers Total Package," *Printing Impressions* 48, no. 3 (August 2005): 40–41.
36. William H. Murphy, Peter A. Dacin, and Neil M. Ford, "Sales Contest Effectiveness: An Examination of Sales Contest Design Preferences of Field Sales Forces," *Journal of the Academy of Marketing Science* 32, no. 2 (Spring 2004) 127–44.
37. John Hechinger, "Morgan Stanley to Face Civil Charges for Sales Incentives," *Wall Street Journal*, June 18, 2004, C-1.
38. Kate Bertrand, "New Product Marketing: Stumping for New Technology Products," *Business Marketing* 75, no. 4 (1990): 48.
39. James E. Swickland, "Alteon Training, a Boeing Subsidiary, Will Offer," *Business and Commercial Aviation* 94, no. 1 (2004): 28.
40. Emily Nelson, "The Art of the Sale—How the Beauty-Counter Staff Gets Shoppers to Buy More Than They Bargained For," *Wall Street Journal*, January 11, 2001, B-1.
41. Robert Barker, "P&G's $57 Billion Bargain," *BusinessWeek*, no. 3942, July 25, 2005, 26.
42. "A Creative Corporation Toolbox," *BusinessWeek*, no. 3945, August 1, 2005, 72.
43. Marcel Zeelenberg and Marijke van Putten, "The Dark Side of Discounts: An Inaction Inertia Perspective on the Post-Promotion Dip," *Psychology and Marketing* 22, no. 8 (2005): 611–22.
44. Aaron O. Patrick, "British Newspapers Try Free DVDs, CDs to Boost Readership," *Wall Street Journal*, August 3, 2005, B-1.
45. Nelson Oly Ndubisi and Chiew Tung Moi, "Customers' Behaviourial Responses to Sales Promotion: The Role of Fear of Losing Face," *Asia Pacific Journal of Marketing and Logistics* 17, no. 1 (2005): 332–49.
46. Larry J. Seibert, "What Consumers Think About Bonus Pack Sales Promotions," *Marketing News*, February 17, 1997, 9.
47. Liz Parks, "Value-Prices Bonus Packs Revive Limp Hair Care Segment," *DSN Retailing Today* 41, no. 8, April 22, 2002, 19–20, 22.
48. Noreen O'Leary, "Dealing with Coupons," *Adweek* 46, no. 8, February 21, 2005, 29.
49. Stephanie Thompson, "The Scoop on Coupons," *Brandweek* 38, no.11, March 17, 1997, 34 (6 pages).
50. Catherine Field, "Surfing for Savings," *Chain Store Age* 81, no. 7 (2005): 64.
51. Wayne Mouland, "Coupon Convenience," *Marketing* 110, no. 17, May 9, 2005, 16.
52. Gail Ayala Taylor, "Coupon Response in Services," *Journal of Retailing* 77, no. 1 (Spring 2001): 139.
53. Sonia Reyes, "'Toon Tour Mystery' Is Solved," *Brandweek* 45, no. 7, February 16, 2004, 6.
54. Sheree R. Curry, "Contests No Trivial Pursuit," *TelevisionWeek* 23, no. 29, July 19, 2004, 16.
55. Derek DeCloet, "The Man Who Invented Goofball," *Canadian Business* 73, no.7, April 17, 2000, 66–67.
56. Gloria Gonzalez, "Contests' Popularity Increases Demand for Prize Indemnity Cover," *Business Insurance* 39, no. 7, February 14, 2005, 10–11.
57. Andy Battaglia, "Quick-Service Operators Prosper through Toy Promotions," *Nation's Restaurant News* 33, no. 26, June 28, 1999, 118 (3 pages).
58. Kenneth Hein, "McDonald's, Sega Will Get Happy Over High-End Videogame Giveaway," *Brandweek* 44, no. 17, April 28, 2003, 6.
59. Pip Brooking, "Power Premium Revival," *Promotions and Incentives* (March 2005): 41 (3 pages).
60. Peter Lewis, "Let (Cordless) Freedom Ring," *Fortune* 152, no. 4, August 22, 2005, 120.
61. Wayne Mouland, "Rebates Rule!" *Marketing* 109, no. 33, October 18, 2004, 35.
62. Bob Holloway, "Internet to the Rescue," *Pharmaceutical Executive* 23, no. 7 (2003): 106.
63. Joan Goldwasser, "Best of the Cash-Back Cards," *Kiplinger's Personal Finance Magazine* 53, no. 4 (1999): 60.
64. Sholnn Freeman and Sharon Silke Carty, "Auto Makers Increase SUV Rebates: Cash Back on Large Vehicles Signals Trouble for Detroit in the Lucrative Market," *Wall Street Journal*, May 27, 2004, A-8.
65. James Thorton, "Why Trial Matters," *Promotions and Incentives* (November–December 2004): 5A.
66. Kapil Bawa and Robert Shoemaker, "The Effects of Free Sample Promotions on Incremental Brand Sales," *Marketing Science* 23, no. 3 (Summer 2004): 345–63.
67. "Trojan Plans Brighton Cabs Sampling Drive," *Marketing Week*, June 30, 2005, 6.
68. See note 66.
69. Jennifer Saranow, "Where the Real Deals Are: Luxury Used Cars; Employee Discount Triggers a Glut of Trade-Ins; $3,000 Off a Cadillac," *Wall Street Journal*, August 11, 2005, D-1.
70. "A Discount Extravaganza," *Publishers Weekly* 251, no. 26, June 28, 2004, 5.
71. Larry Seibert, "Are Bonus Packs Profitable for Retailers?" *Chain Store Age* 72, no. 12 (1996): 16–18.
72. Karen Lundegaard and Joseph B. White, "A New Approach to Selling Cars; After GM's Sales Jump by 47% in June, Rivals Weigh Matching Employee-Discount Offer," *Wall Street Journal*, July 5, 2005, D-1.
73. Sholnn Freeman, "Car Buyers Get New Round of Discounts; Strong July Sales Prompt Ford, GM, and Chrysler to Extend Employee Pricing Offer," *Wall Street Journal*, August 3, 2005, D-1.
74. Jennifer Saranow, "Employee Discounts Move Beyond Cars: Spurred by Auto Makers' Success, Many Retailers Extend Worker Price Breaks to All Shoppers," *Wall Street Journal*, August 24, 2005, D-1.

Strategy Development: A Hierarchical Perspective

Part Three

Strategic planners specialize in gathering intelligence and filtering relevant information to key decision makers. These people have expertise gathering intelligence through cyberspace or online information services and providing in-depth analysis and broad-based assessments of how these data will affect strategy development. Strategic planners work on either the client side or the agency side. At client companies, many strategic planners work in marketing departments. On the agency side, many people who become strategic planners used to hold account management positions. In either setting, the focus is on managing information that can aid managers in planning and executions. Databases now offer the ability to integrate these data with various analysis and planning frameworks. In turn, the effective use of these tools can aid managers in thinking both creatively and strategically. Armed with data and insights from these frameworks and wells of knowledge, managers can immerse themselves in the task of identifying appropriate brand strategy and then communicating it to all those who work with different facets of marketing communications.

9 The Corporate Level: Analysis and Planning for Corporate Strategy and Tactics

10 The Marketing Level: Analysis and Planning for Marketing Strategy and Tactics

11 The Marketing Communications Level: Analysis and Planning for Marketing Communications Strategy and Tactics

Consider the following IMC case of the Indiana Middle Grades Reading Program.[1] Back in December 1989, Dr. Jack Humphrey, the Director of Reading Services for the Evansville-Vanderburgh School Corporation in Evansville, Indiana, hired a marketing communications agency (the Keller-Crescent Company) to develop a marketing communications campaign. The goal of the campaign was to reinforce the importance of reading to children. Two market segments were targeted: Indiana youth in grades 6 through 9 who attended school in the fifty-three targeted school corporations; and teachers, parents, and all other residents who lived in the area of the fifty-three school corporations. A project team was assembled from account service, creative, research, public relations, and the production departments of the agency. Originally, the focus was to develop public service announcements for television and radio. Then the focus shifted from one of a traditional advertising campaign to a comprehensive communications program. The theme for the campaign reflected the idea that reading opens doors to the imagination and that a child's imagination is much more powerful than any video game. This led to the use of the metaphor of the "theater of the mind." Therefore, all communications had a closing line: "Enter the theater of the mind. Read, because only reading makes it real." The logo used on all forms of communications was: "Only reading makes it real." The television commercial used interesting visual effects. The children were shown in color against a black-and-white background. The background scene was varied as a function of the story the child was reading creating the impression of imagination or "the theater of the mind." The print advertisements and the outdoor posters were also designed in the same manner. The radio commercial used the audio portion of the television commercial creating the feeling that the books had come to life. Collateral materials such as press releases and press kits featured the same logo and tag line. All materials were on display at the news conference, and special logo boards were prominently featured on speaker podiums.

The campaign started with public relations activities in the form of direct mail and personal selling (phone conversations with media representatives, state officials, and programming directors). The direct-mail campaign was directed to the principals of the 144 schools in the 53 targeted school corporations. The letters requested the school principals to get involved by asking teachers to select students to be involved as characters in the advertising campaign. The student casting event was heavily publicized through the use of the wire services and extensive distribution of press releases and press kits to twenty-seven television stations, two hundred radio stations, and five hundred newspapers. Fifteen students were selected from the casting sessions from four hundred who auditioned. The names of the finalists were then publicized around the state. The production of the advertising campaign was also well publicized. A few months later, the public service announcements on television were aired and ran for 2 years. The public service announcements were publicized in the major television, radio, and newspaper media throughout the state.

> **SMC QuickLink**
> Becoming a Community of Readers: A Blueprint for Indiana
> http:// www.acsc.net/klsipes/ARTICLE2.htm

This IMC campaign illustrates the importance of analysis, planning, strategies, and tactics in an IMC campaign. What was the corporate strategy? It was to increase children's reading activities. What was the marketing strategy? It was to position reading as an effective means to opening doors to children's imagination. What was the communications strategy? It was an affective strategy designed to instill positive feelings in the act of reading. What communications tools were used? Advertising and public relations were used in implementing the marketing communications strategy. The three chapters in this part of the book will help you develop specific skills in identifying strategies and tactics at the corporate, marketing, and marketing communications levels. You will be able to come up with answers to questions regarding strategy and tactics using well-established analytical models.

Specifically, Part Three presents the core of the systems model, namely, strategy and tactics that are derived from analyses and planning frameworks. Strategy and tactics are viewed as a process hierarchy or what some systems people call a *decision tree*. Marketing communications programs (advertising, sales promotion, reseller support, direct marketing, public relations, and word-of-mouth communications) are elements of the marketing communications mix and are selected and guided by an overall marketing communications strategy—informative, affective, habit formation, and self-satisfaction. Marketing communications strategy is viewed as an element of the marketing mix (product, price, distribution, and marketing communications), which in turn is selected and guided by an overall marketing strategy—product-focus, price-focus, place-focus, and prospects-focus

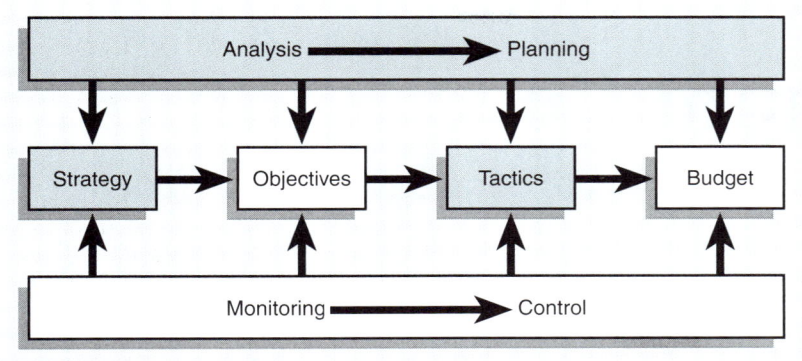

Figure 1
Analysis/Planning, Strategy, and Tactics

strategies (operationalized through fifteen alternative positions, e.g., positioning by product attribute, positioning by intangible factor, positioning by customer benefit, etc.). Similarly, marketing strategy is viewed as an element of the corporate mix (marketing, manufacturing, R&D, engineering, accounting, finance, employee relations, etc.), which in turn is selected and guided by corporate strategy (grow, maintain, harvest, innovate, and divest). These concepts are developed in this section of the book. See Figure 1.

Note

1. Diana L. Haytko, "Integrated Marketing Communication in a Public Service Context: The Indiana Middle Grades Reading Program," in *Integrated Communication: Synergy of Persuasive Voices,* ed. Esther Thorson and Jeri Moore, 233–42 (Mahwah, NJ: Erlbaum, 1996).

The Corporate Level:
Analysis and Planning for Corporate Strategy and Tactics

Chapter Nine

Chapter Outline

9-1 **Introduction**

9-2 **Corporate Strategies and Tactics**
- 9-2a The Growth Strategy and Corresponding Tactics
- 9-2b The Maintain-Position Strategy and Corresponding Tactics
- 9-2c The Harvest Strategy and Corresponding Tactics
- 9-2d The Innovation Strategy and Corresponding Tactics
- 9-2e The Divestment Strategy and Corresponding Tactics

9-3 **The Use of Situation Analysis in Corporate Strategy Selection**
- 9-3a The Boston Consulting Group (BCG) Matrix
- 9-3b The Multifactor Portfolio Matrix

Summary
Discussion Questions
Practice Quiz
Web Exercise: Analysis and Planning for Strategic Decision Making in the Airline Industry
Suggested Readings
Notes

Key Terms

barriers of entry (p. 212)
capital intensity (p. 212)
competitive analysis (p. 205)
competitive structure (p. 212)
corporate image (p. 210)
customer analysis (p. 204)
demand cyclicity (p. 212)
environmental analysis (p. 205)
experience curve effects (p. 210)
external situation analysis (p. 204)
internal situation analysis (p. 205)
maintain-position strategy (p. 201)
market analysis (p. 204)
portfolio models (p. 205)
product life cycle (p. 205)
strategic business unit (SBU) (p. 199)
value added (p. 210)

Define your business goals clearly so that others can see them as you do.

—**George Burns** (1896–1996), American comedian

9-1 Introduction

In 1995 IBM Corporation was attempting a hostile takeover of Lotus Development. CorpIBM was using all means at its disposal to publicize the event, including the Internet. IBM went all out on a public relations media blitz to convince the public that it was in the best interest of Lotus to have IBM acquire it. IBM wanted to buy it for $3.3 billion. IBM had set up a home page on the World Wide Web of the Internet to explain its move. More than 23,000 people accessed the IBM website after it announced the hostile bid.[1] At the same time, Hewlett-Packard Development Company was stepping up a marketing campaign to grab more of the corporate PC market. Compaq Computer Corporation was introducing a number of new products and was growing quickly. Meanwhile, CompUSA had cut costs and begun a marketing push into the home market.[2]

In 2004 the airline industry was undergoing significant market fluctuations. Some airlines ceased operations or sold off many of their gates at major airports and cut operations (i.e., ATA) while others sought protection in bankruptcy. Two of the latter airlines, US Airways and United Airlines, were both reorganizing to emerge from bankruptcy as two very different types of airlines. US Airways' aim was to remake itself as a low-cost carrier to compete with the discount carriers such as Southwest and Jet Blue who had made significant inroads into the market routes long dominated by US Airways flights. United Airlines, on the other hand, focused on expanding its long-haul transcontinental and international market routes and upgrading seating and meals for its business and full-fare fliers. Both US Airways and United Airlines used an extensive array of marketing communications (email; direct mail; website announcements; public relations; event marketing; aircraft livery changes; personal appearances before a variety of interested parties including frequent fliers,

Different Strategies for Different Airlines in a Competitive Market

(a) United Airlines chose to focus on its international long-haul flights and offer upgraded seating and service, while (b) US Airways focused on reinventing itself as a low-cost carrier. The US Airways strategy was further developed when it merged with low-cost carrier America West in 2005.

Source: AP/Wide World Photos.

(a)

(b)

SMC Marketplace Watch 9-1

Corporate Strategy at US Airways—Transformation

US Airways is still in the red and is struggling to get out from under. Low-fare carriers, such as Southwest Airlines, are undermining US Airways by launching new shuttle services. The recent Philadelphia shuttle is an example. US Airways is a long-term solution to a near-term problem. The solution is "transformation," a strategy to reduce costs beyond what it achieved through its 2004 Chapter 11 bankruptcy reorganization.

The strategy also has a revenue-generation component. US Airways is now fighting to gain market share in a growing low-fare market. The transformation strategy calls for offering low fares on certain high-traffic routes such as those from and to Philadelphia. To implement this strategy, the company is planning to replace Airbus narrowbodies at the Charlotte and Pittsburgh hubs with seventy-seat regional jets (RJs), moving the mainline aircraft to Philadelphia. Turboprops will be replaced with the seventy-seat RJs, and these RJs will get increased emphasis over fifty-seaters. Over time, the company will try to boost aircraft utilization beyond 10 hours per day. Through Chapter 11, US Airways managed to secure an agreement from its Air Line Pilots Association unit on a scope clause allowing much greater use of RJs by regional subsidiaries and affiliates. The company then quickly ordered RJs from both Embraer and Bombardier. It had 123 RJs on March 31, 2005—thirteen of them new.

The transformation strategy is built around rebuilding the airline to carry more passengers at lower average yield. Increasing aircraft size usually reduces unit costs—the trip cost of a larger aircraft does not usually increase by the same percentage as the number of seats. Delta did the same in 2004 when it replaced its old Express operation's 737s with Song's 757s.

US Airways has also abandoned the airline-within-an-airline strategy, which is currently in use today by United's Ted as well as Delta's Song. US Airways tried that approach with little success after Southwest moved into the eastern United States in 1993. Of course, the strategy of increasing capacity is risky. Increasing revenue and covering costs are dependent on flying the larger aircraft even fuller than the smaller ones.

> **SMC QuickLink**
> US Airways
> http://www.usairways.com

Source: Adapted from David Bond. "US Airways 'Transforms'; Having Failed to Beat Its Low-Fare Competition, the No. 7 U.S. Carrier Will Try—Again—to Join Them," *Aviation Week & Space Technology* 160, no. 18 (New York), May 3, 2004, 44.

---

employees, politicians, and the media) to make a case for their new strategies—strategies designed to survive in the current world of increased competition and high fuel costs (among other things) that continue to be civil aviation in the new millennium. SMC Marketplace Watch 9-1 is about analysis and planning at US Airways to reformulate strategy dealing with a very turbulent environment.

These events from 1995 and 2004 represent corporate decisions—decisions to grow, to diversify, to divest, to maintain position, to retrench, and so on. These are decisions made at the highest superordinate level of the organization. Any marketing program—particularly a marketing communications program—involves decisions and actions taken in an attempt to carry out strategies decided upon at the corporate level. Therefore, one cannot do justice to marketing strategy—and marketing communications strategy, in particular—without first understanding corporate decisions. This chapter is designed to help you understand both how corporate decisions are made and how these decisions provide the foundation for marketing action (see Figure 9-1). Specifically, the chapter examines the questions that follow:

- What is a strategic business unit or product/market?
- What is corporate strategy and how is it conceived?
- What strategic tools are available to the corporate-level decision makers?
- How is the corporate mix assembled as a direct function of corporate strategy?

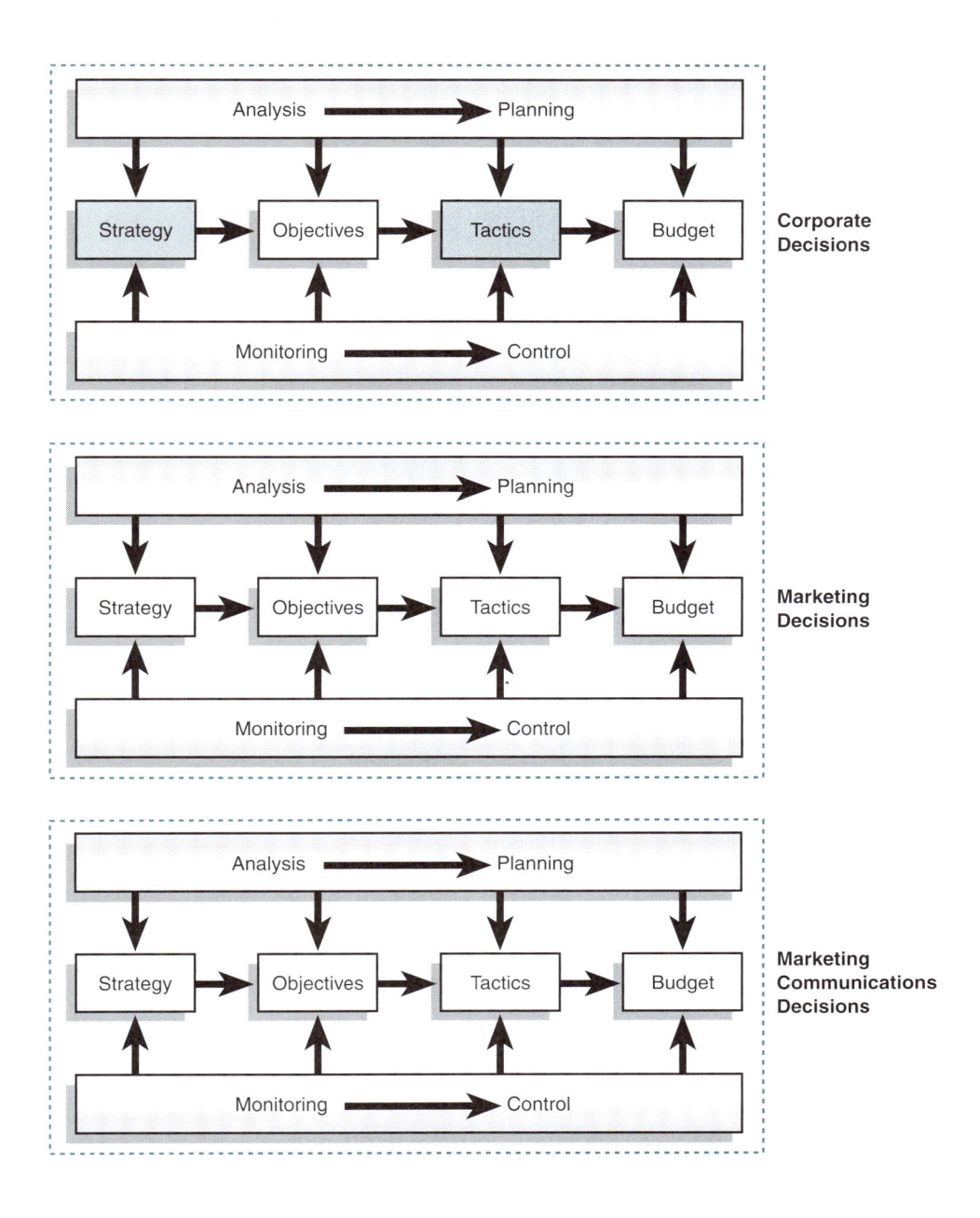

Figure 9-1
Corporate Strategy and Tactics

9-2 Corporate Strategies and Tactics

To understand corporate strategies and tactics, one has to first understand **strategic business units (SBUs)** or *product/market*. An SBU or a product/market is a unit of analysis focusing on a particular product or service in a definable market. This is because most corporate strategies and tactics are directly related to product/markets that the particular business entity is attempting to serve. Many business firms operate several "businesses." For example, a firm such as General Electric is involved in many businesses, forty-nine SBUs to be exact. A strategic business unit has three characteristics: (1) it is a single "business" that can be planned separately from other businesses of the firm; (2) the "business" has its own set of competitors; and (3) the "business" has a manager who is responsible for its planning and management.[3]

Corporate strategies are conceived and articulated in relation to corporate SBUs. In that vein, we describe several corporate strategies and tactics: grow, maintain, harvest, innovate, and divest.

strategic business unit (SBU) A product/market unit—a specific product related to a specific customer group. For example, a mercury-based thermometer needed in cooking and directed to restaurants is an SBU. A mercury-based thermometer designed to measure atmospheric temperature and directed to households is another SBU.

TABLE 9-1   Corporate Strategy, Tactics, and Objectives

Corporate Strategy	Corporate Tactics (Strategic Mix)	Corporate Objectives
Grow R&D Engineering Manufacturing Personnel Finance Accounting	*Marketing*	Maximize sales and market share
Maintain position Engineering Manufacturing *Personnel* Finance Accounting	Marketing R&D	Minimize negative percentage change in sales and market share
Harvest R&D Engineering *Manufacturing* *Personnel* Finance *Accounting*	Marketing	Maximize profit
Innovate Manufacturing Personnel Finance Accounting	*Marketing* *R&D* Engineering	Establish or increase sales and gain market leadership (through high market share)
Divest R&D Engineering Manufacturing Personnel *Finance* Accounting	Marketing	Maximize cash flow

Note: Strategic mix elements that are in italics reflect major focus or emphasis.

9-2a The Growth Strategy and Corresponding Tactics

In implementing the *growth strategy*, the *marketing, research and development (R&D)*, and *engineering* functions are likely to be viewed as important elements of the strategic mix. This is because growth usually entails expanding the scope of operations through establishing new distribution outlets, encroaching on new geographic markets, and introducing new product variations to the market. Establishing new distribution outlets and encroaching on new geographic markets are goals that can be achieved through marketing. Introducing new product variations is a goal that can be met through R&D and engineering with the guidance of marketing. See Table 9-1.

Implicit in this discussion are the corporate objectives that are corresponding to the growth strategy. Examples of corporate objectives directly related to the growth strategy are:

- Establish ___ (level of) sales by ___ (date).
- Increase sales by ___ (amount) by ___ (date).
- Establish ___ (level of) market share by ___ (date).
- Increase market share by ___ (amount) by ___ (date).

When a firm is aspiring to expand and grow in its operations, the implicit corporate strategy can be viewed as growth. Implementing this strategy generally entails treating the marketing, R&D, and engineering functions within the firm as more important than the other functional units. More resources are allocated to marketing, R&D, and engineering to help accomplish the growth goals. Furthermore, the growth goal is likely to be closely monitored, and the performances of marketing, R&D, and engineering programs are likely to be evaluated in relation to the growth goal. Control is likely to be exerted if the marketing, R&D, and engineering departments fail to deliver. In many instances, growth *tactics* (operationalized through marketing, R&D, and engineering) can take on the following goals:

- Increase the number of new distribution outlets by ___ (amount) by ___ (date).
- Penetrate geographic markets ___ (names) by ___ (date).
- Introduce to the market product variations ___ (names of product variations) by ___ (date).

We use a fictional medium-size advertising agency as an example to illustrate these points. This hypothetical advertising agency is focusing on a specific product/market offering its skills in creating high-end, interactive, full-service home pages on the World Wide Web. The target market is business firms. The agency's plan is to grow in interactive advertising. What would be the agency corporate objectives? An example of an objective congruent with the growth strategy is to establish around eight satellite offices in key metropolitan areas within a 400-mile radius in the next 2 years. These satellite offices will comprise the following: one account executive who will sell interactive advertising to local businesses; two creative people who will be responsible for creating client-tailored interactive content; and an office manager who will act as receptionist and bookkeeper and will coordinate the activities of the account executive and the creative staff. This strategic move requires the deployment of marketing, R&D, and engineering. The marketing personnel at the agency would oversee the recruitment of the key account executives and train them. The R&D personnel would work hard at perfecting the science of interactive advertising. The engineering personnel, who in this case may also involve the creative director at the agency, would help set up the necessary technologies at the satellite offices.

9-2b The Maintain-Position Strategy and Corresponding Tactics

With respect to the **maintain-position strategy,** the *marketing, engineering,* and *personnel* functions are likely to be viewed as important process elements of the strategic mix. The corporate objective corresponding to the maintain-position strategy may be stated as, *Minimize negative percentage change of sales and market share.* Achieving this stability goal entails treating the marketing, engineering, and personnel functions within the firm as more important than the other functional units. This is because marketing has to increase its efforts to offset threats from encroaching competitors. Engineering has to ensure that product quality is held to standards. The firm cannot afford any significant mistakes. A few poorly produced products can cause a great deal of damage to the company. Personnel has to do a better job of keeping employees motivated and satisfied with their jobs while keeping employee compensation and fringe benefits at bay. Also, the personnel department has to recruit qualified people in case of replacements (see Table 9-1).

Let us illustrate this strategy using another advertising agency as an example. Suppose this agency is becoming keenly aware of other competitor agencies serving

maintain-position strategy A corporate strategy that guides the corporate executive to set corporate objectives in terms of maintaining current levels of sales and market share. The intent here is to defend the firm's position against offending competitors.

the local business market with traditional mass-media advertising. This agency has been the market leader for many years and wants to maintain its leadership position. The goal is articulated by the president of the agency: The goal for next year is to maintain the twenty largest accounts, which produce 80 percent of the billings. How can this be accomplished? The president realizes that marketing has to play a bigger role in meeting this objective. Marketing has to ensure that these twenty accounts are satisfied customers and are not likely to be tempted by the encroaching competition. Thus, marketing has to work harder than ever to meet this challenge. It may need a larger budget.

Additionally, the personnel department has to work hard to prevent employee turnover. Employees who quit are likely to be hired by competitors. These employees are likely to take with them certain accounts, maybe even key accounts. Therefore, the personnel department needs to ensure that the core people at the agency, possibly the creative people and account executives, are happy with their jobs. Also, personnel needs to ensure that the creative people and account executives feel committed to the agency. This is a tough challenge. Therefore, personnel may need additional resources to meet this important goal.

Furthermore, this maintenance goal needs all the help it can get from the engineering people. At the agency, the engineering person is essentially the creative director. This person has to do a better job ensuring quality control. Since the agency cannot afford to lose key accounts, it becomes imperative that product quality is always maintained. The creative director has to work harder at quality control.

9-2c The Harvest Strategy and Corresponding Tactics

With respect to the *harvest strategy,* the *manufacturing, personnel,* and *accounting* functions are likely to be important. The corporate objective corresponding to the harvest strategy is to *maximize profit.* That is, a firm implementing a harvest strategy needs to be cost-efficient in its operations. Carrying out this strategy entails treating the manufacturing, personnel, and accounting functions within the firm as more important than the other functional units. This is because minimizing costs to increase profit is a goal that can be accomplished through cost-efficiency programs. These programs should be directed at manufacturing and personnel and overseen by accounting (see Table 9-1).

We illustrate this situation using the medium-size advertising agency example again and focusing on a specific product/market—newspaper advertising. The president realizes that this product/market is declining for the advertising agency business because many businesses now have their own graphics and design capabilities through desktop publishing software. Businesses can design their own newspaper advertisements with very little effort. Even if they cannot, any business can approach the newspaper's advertising department and the newspaper itself will design the execution for the client. This is because all newspaper advertising departments have adopted desktop publishing technology. As a result, media organizations now provide their clients with the additional service of advertisement design for little or no added cost. So what can the agency do? *Harvest* this product/market. What does this mean? The idea is to not pour any money into marketing the newspaper advertising part of the business. Actually, the harvest strategy should lead the president to cut down on any promotion effort related to this part of the business. Therefore, marketing decreases in importance. The personnel department has to cut down on the creative staff specializing in newspaper advertising, perhaps by layoffs or by eliminating vacant positions. Accounting has to pay close attention to cost control, especially in relation to personnel and tasks related to newspaper advertising. The goal is to reduce the cost of goods related to producing newspaper advertising. This step, in turn, would maximize gross profits and reduce overhead costs (and thus maximize net profits).

9-2d The Innovation Strategy and Corresponding Tactics

With respect to the *innovation strategy,* the *marketing* and *R&D* functions are likely to be important process elements because both marketing and R&D are the primary means for carrying out the innovation strategy. The corporate objectives corresponding to the innovation strategy are *to establish a certain level of sales* and *to gain market leadership* (through high market share). That is, given that the firm is aspiring to be first to market a given product, the firm's strategy can be implicitly recognized as an innovation strategy. Carrying out this strategy entails treating the marketing and R&D functions as more important than the other functional units. Specifically, the innovation strategy can be operationalized in terms of a new product introduction (see Table 9-1).

Let us apply the innovation strategy to the medium-size advertising agency again. The product/market is a form of cellular communication that is combined with a global positioning system (GPS) that allows an advertiser to target its message to any group of cellular telephone users who happen to be at a given event. This advertising medium can easily be used by businesses that are in the service area of cellular telephones. Advertising agencies can use this new advertising medium to better serve certain clients who wish to target attendees at the given type of event. The market for this product includes all businesses that have products that may interest that select group of event attendees. For a sporting event, this could include restaurants and parking lots in the area as well as sports memorabilia and paraphernalia types of firms.

Let us say the president of the advertising agency decides to introduce this advertising medium to certain clients. To do this, the R&D people must fully develop and test this technology and develop a rate card showing prices with discounts proportionate to the number of purchases. The account executives have to be involved too. They would help tailor the technology and the rate card to meet the demands of the agency's clients or prospective clients. The president may target a very specific date to offer this new advertising medium to the local clients and prospects. He or she would monitor the progress of this new product development, thus paving the way for its introduction. The president must also closely monitor performance of the people assigned to this project and take corrective action if the product development deviates from course toward the goal. Sufficient resources must be allocated to carry out this task. We address the question of resource allocation and control in some detail in the third part of this book.

9-2e The Divestment Strategy and Corresponding Tactics

Finally, for the *divestment strategy,* the *finance* function is likely to be the most important process element of the strategic mix. This is because the finance people are likely to be directly involved in implementing the divestment decision. The corporate objective corresponding to the divestment strategy may be *to maximize cash flow.*

When the corporation is trying to minimize financial losses and bring in some badly needed cash, a divestment strategy is deployed. Implementing this strategy entails treating the finance function within the firm as more important than other functional units in minimizing the firm's losses (see Table 9-1).

Going back to the advertising agency example, suppose the advertising agency is structured as follows. The president oversees the operations of several separate groups or departments: television and radio advertising production; print advertising production; interactive advertising production; bulletin board and transit advertising production; interactive advertising production; collateral services; media planning and placement; marketing and advertising research; and account executives (see Figure 9-2).

The president realizes that the bulletin board/transit advertising department has not been profitable for a while. It is very difficult to keep costs down, especially below the cost of other outdoor advertising companies competing in the same geographic area and targeting the same business clients. The president decides to divest this organizational unit. Perhaps one way to achieve this is to offer to sell the entire

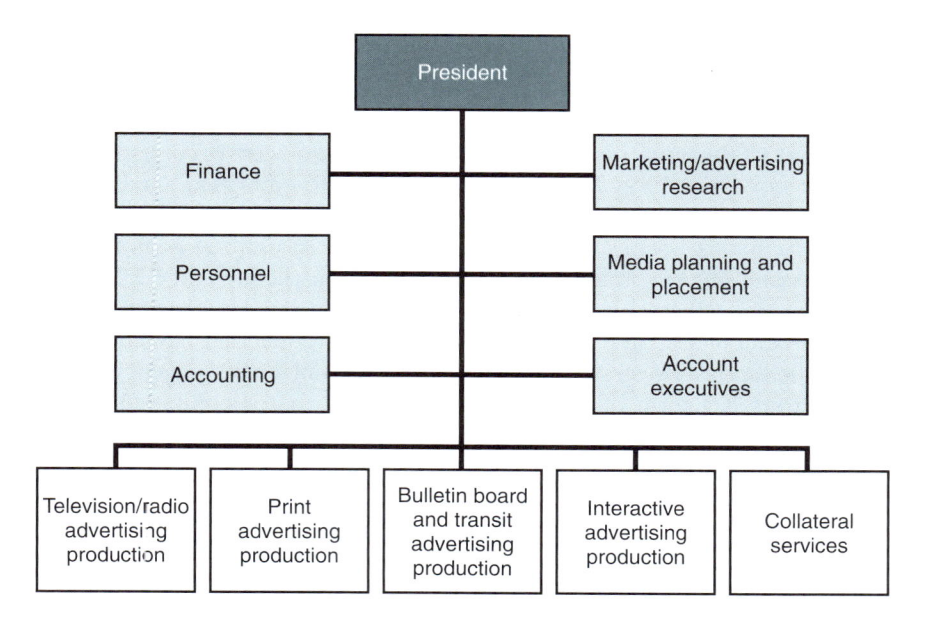

Figure 9-2
Organizational Structure of the Advertising Agency

department to the people who are presently employed in that department. The goal here is to obtain a return that is at or above market value and to bring in some badly needed extra cash. This task is likely to be effectively handled by the finance people. The president gives this charge to the finance staff and monitors their progress toward divesting this unit at or above market value. Certain resources that the finance staff needs to accomplish this task are provided.

9-3 The Use of Situation Analysis in Corporate Strategy Selection

Remember that all corporate decisions discussed from this point on are constrained to a specific SBU. That is, corporate decisions are *not* made in a vacuum. They are made in relation to specific products in specific markets. Keeping this in mind as the discussion moves forward, we first take a look at a few of the environmental assessment tools that are available for those setting the corporate strategy. These assessments, at the highest level of the system, are going to affect the marketing communications manager's ability to truly integrate his or her decisions throughout the firm by outlining the issues and problems present at the highest decision point within the system.

What this points up is the complexity of the process and the need to have a solid framework in which to make optimal decisions. A crucial part of that process is integrating existing data and information that are relevant to the entire process. This part of the chapter is about starting that process through analysis and planning. Using analysis and planning, the marketing communications manager conducts an analysis of the situation, which allows him or her to make effective decisions. Managers traditionally refer to analysis and planning as *situation analysis,* sometimes *strategic analysis.* Marketing communications managers often study a variety of factors internal and external to the firm for the purposes of gathering information that would assist them in decision making.

Traditionally, **external situation analysis** includes the analyses described here:

- **Market analysis** is gathering information about the size and geographic distribution of the market.
- **Customer analysis** is dividing the market into customer segments and establishing a demographic, psychographic, and media habits profile of each segment.

external situation analysis The process in which certain factors external to the organization are analyzed to help marketers with strategic planning. These external factors include the competition, the market, customers, and the environment.

market analysis The process of estimating the size and geographic distribution of the market for a particular product.

customer analysis The process in which the market is divided into customer segments and selected segments are profiled in terms of demographics, psychographics, and media habits.

- **Competitive analysis** is discovering the marketing profile of each major competitor—that is, the products that each competitor provides to consumers, the price of each product, the channel of distribution used by each competitor, and the elements of the communications mix used by each competitor—and the amount of resources allocated to the entire communications budget and its various elements.
- **Environmental analysis** includes information about changes in technology, culture, consumption habits, political structures, laws and regulations, and/or the economy that are likely to affect the market.

Internal situation analysis refers to analysis conducted in relation to factors internal to the organization, such as plotting sales trends from accounting data and determining those factors that affected changes in sales over time or developing a sales forecasting model from data on past sales and communications expenditure levels.

The information obtained from situation analysis is used to make a host of decisions. Specifically, situation analysis may help marketing communications managers select corporate, marketing, and marketing communications strategies. How do marketing communications managers assist in the selection of a corporate strategy (grow, maintain position, harvest, innovate, or divest)? What factors should the manager consider in selecting the most effective corporate strategy? These decisions should be the drivers of the lower marketing and marketing communications strategies (discussed in the later chapters). Again, you must look at the process in terms of the entire system (see Figure 9-3). The situation analysis is conducted to help the manager make three decisions: (1) which corporate strategy to select, (2) what corporate objectives to set, and (3) how to allocate resources. In this section, we concentrate only on strategy selection.

At the corporate level, many corporate strategists employ **portfolio models** as a prerequisite to strategy selection. Two popular portfolio models that are well accepted in the corporate strategy literature can provide you with a good understanding of how to select a corporate strategy. These are: (1) the Boston Consulting Group Matrix and (2) the multifactor portfolio matrix.

9-3a The Boston Consulting Group (BCG) Matrix

The Boston Consulting Group (BCG) matrix is commonly used to select the best mix of businesses or SBUs to maximize the long-term earnings growth of the firm.[4] It helps determine the potential value of a particular SBU for the firm. This assessment is based on how a particular product/market stands in relation to market share and market growth[5] (see Figure 9-4).

As shown in the figure, a product/market in a high-growth market but with low market share is called a "problem child." Successful competition transforms a "problem child" into a "star." Thus, a "star" is a business unit that is in a high-growth market and has high market share. The corporate strategy used to transform a "problem child" into a "star" is called the "gain-share strategy."

Implicit in the logic of the BCG matrix is the notion of the **product life cycle.** SBUs starting out in a high-growth market are the "problem children." They compete against others in a high-growth industry. The result of this competition produces winners and losers. The winners in a high-growth market are "stars." These are the SBUs that attain high levels of market share. Then market growth levels off and decreases over time. During this period, a "star" attempts to maintain its high market share in a mature market. With full market maturation, the "star" turns into a "cash cow." In this situation, the rate of return is high for the product, but the market is at low levels of growth. When a "star" starts to make good profit, it becomes a "cash cow." A "cash cow" makes a high level of profit because of experience effects. The business unit cuts costs by learning to become highly efficient. After lowering costs, the profit margin increases and the business unit generates the highest level of profit.

Further movement of the product comes from loss of sales and market share. Thus, a "cash cow" eventually turns into a "dog." A business unit classified as a "dog" has a poor competitive position and is in a declining market. Most firms select

---

competitive analysis The process in which competitors are identified and selected competitors are profiled in terms of their product offerings, the prices of their products, the channels of distribution of their products, promotional messages, and the media carrying these messages.

environmental analysis The process in which certain factors are identified that may have an impact on the size and geographic distribution of the market. Such factors may involve technology, economy, culture, media, politics, and so on.

internal situation analysis The process in which certain factors internal to the organization are analyzed to help marketers with strategic planning. These internal factors include the firm's past sales, past profit, past media expenditures, past promotional messages, and so on.

portfolio models Strategy models designed to help managers select among alternative corporate strategies. Examples of alternative strategies at the corporate level include growth, maintain position, harvest, innovation, and divestment.

product life cycle The stages that a product (product category, not a single product brand) goes through, from the early stages of inception and commercialization to eventual decline and extinction. The stages are usually referred to more specifically as introduction, development, early maturity, late maturity, and decline.

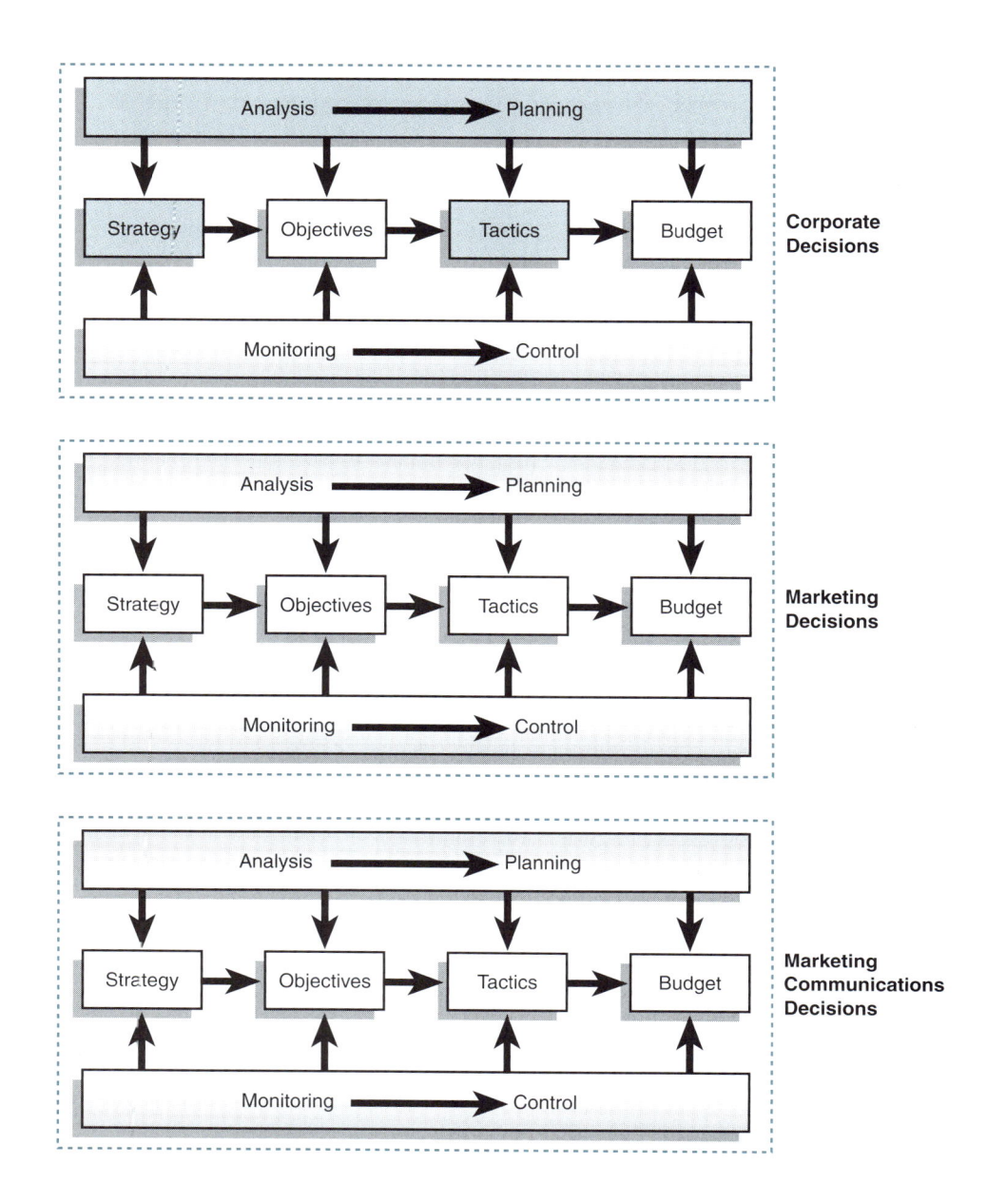

206 Part Three Strategy Development: A Hierarchical Perspective

Figure 9-3
Analysis and Planning: Guiding Corporate Strategy and Tactics

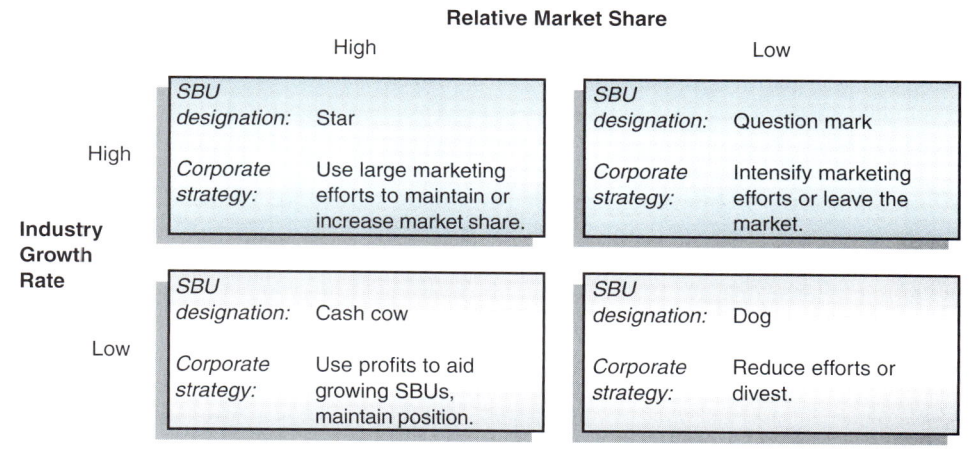

Corporate Decisions: Analysis → Planning; Strategy → Objectives → Tactics → Budget; Monitoring → Control

Marketing Decisions: Analysis → Planning; Strategy → Objectives → Tactics → Budget; Monitoring → Control

Marketing Communications Decisions: Analysis → Planning; Strategy → Objectives → Tactics → Budget; Monitoring → Control

Figure 9-4
The Boston Consulting Group Matrix

Source: Adapted from Bruce D. Henderson, "The Experience Curve Reviewed: IV. The Growth Share Matrix of the Product Portfolio" (Boston: Boston Consulting Group, 1973), *Perspectives*, no. 135.

Relative Market Share

Industry Growth Rate	High (Relative Market Share)	Low (Relative Market Share)
High	*SBU designation:* Star *Corporate strategy:* Use large marketing efforts to maintain or increase market share.	*SBU designation:* Question mark *Corporate strategy:* Intensify marketing efforts or leave the market.
Low	*SBU designation:* Cash cow *Corporate strategy:* Use profits to aid growing SBUs, maintain position.	*SBU designation:* Dog *Corporate strategy:* Reduce efforts or divest.

Relative market share is an SBU's market share in comparison to the leading competitors in the industry. Industry growth rate is the annual growth of all similar businesses in the market (such as sugarless gum).

one of two strategies when they realize that a "cash cow" is moving toward a "dog" position. One strategy is to *innovate*. This strategy focuses on turning the product around by making a new and improved version. Thus, through innovation, the product is resuscitated into a "problem child" and starts a new product life cycle of its own. The other strategy is to *harvest*. For the harvest strategy, the manager stops expending resources to nourish and sustain the product. The manager acknowledges that the end for the product is near. Thus, the firm should try to make the best out of a bad situation. It should not spend money to save the product; instead, the firm should make as much profit as possible from the product and then let it fade into extinction. When the product starts losing money, a *divestment* strategy is selected. The divestment strategy entails selling off the business unit. The company divests it from its product portfolio.

9-3b The Multifactor Portfolio Matrix

The BCG matrix is a very popular and well-accepted model in the corporate strategy field. However, it has been criticized for being *too narrow* in its focus. This is because it employs only two factors (market share and market growth) as a guide to strategy selection. In the real world, many businesses do not even know what their market share is. Market growth is also not easy to assess. Some managers consider return on investment as a more appropriate consideration for investment purposes than market share and cash flow. These difficulties have led companies such as GE and the Shell Group to adopt a portfolio model that allows a multifactor approach to assess market share and market growth.[6]

Figure 9-5 illustrates the multifactor portfolio matrix. The matrix has two dimensions: (1) company position, or business strength, and (2) market position, or industry or market attractiveness. *Company position* can be viewed as an equivalent construct to that of market share but broader in scope.[7] Similarly, *market position* can be viewed as equivalent to market growth but broader in scope.

The multifactor portfolio matrix shown in Figure 9-5 recommends that the organization invest in products assessed as high to medium in strength of company or market position. These products have good growth potential. The organization should harvest or divest products assessed as medium to low in strength of company or market position. Products assessed as medium should be managed very "selectively" to enhance earnings.

But how does the marketing communications manager assess company position (or business strength) and market position (or industry attractiveness)? General Electric developed the multifactor portfolio matrix, which uses the following factors to assess and operationalize company position: (1) market position operationalized by indicators such as 3-year average market share (total dollars) and 3-year average international market share; (2) competitive position operationalized by indicators of product quality, technological leadership, manufacturing/cost leadership, and distribution/marketing leadership; and (3) relative profitability operationalized by a 3-year average SBU return on sales (ROS) less the average ROS pertaining to the largest three competitors.

		Company Position (Business Strength)		
		High (positive)	Medium	Low (negative)
Market Position (Industry Attractiveness)	High (positive)	Invest/grow	Invest/grow	Security/earnings
	Medium	Invest/grow	Security/earnings	Harvest/divest
	Low (negative)	Security/earnings	Harvest/divest	Harvest/divest

Figure 9-5
The Multifactor Portfolio Matrix

TABLE 9-2 Assessing Company Position

Factors

$E_i \times I_i = E_j$
$E_j \times I_j = E_k$

Market Factors

Sales	5 × .50 = 2.50
Customer satisfaction	3 × .10 = .30
Brand loyalty	4 × .20 = .80
Corporate image	4 × .20 = .80
	100% 4.40 × .20 = .88

Profit Factors

Gross profit/margin	5 × .40 = 2.00
Net profit/margin	3 × .60 = 1.80
	100% 3.80 × .20 = .76

Competitive Factors

Market share	4 × .40 = 1.60
Value added	4 × .20 = .80
Brand preference	3 × .20 = .60
Experience curve effects	2 × .20 = .40
	100% 3.40 × .20 = .68

Marketing Factors

Product effectiveness	4 × .10 = .40
Price competitiveness	5 × .20 = 1.00
Distribution effectiveness	3 × .10 = .30
Mktg. comm. effectiveness	5 × .20 = 1.00
Sales effectiveness	2 × .00 = .00
Marketing organization	5 × .40 = 2.00
	100% 4.70 × .40 = 1.88
	100% 4.20

Notes: The company position is evaluated in relation to each of the subfactors *(i)* on a scale varying from 1 (poor) to 5 (excellent). These are shown in the table as E_i. These evaluations are derived through subjective judgments made by the marketing communications manager. The E_i scores are weighted by importance weights (I_i), which are also subjective judgments made by the marketing communications manager. The sum of the $(E_i \times I_i)$ scores of a given factor makes up the E_j score of that factor, which in turn is weighted by importance weights for that factor (I_j), producing the factor evaluation (E_k) scores. The sum of the E_k scores produces an overall evaluation score varying from 1 (poor) to 5 (excellent). The hypothetical example here shows that the company position is good to excellent (4.20 rating out of 5).

The factors used by GE to assess market position are (1) market size operationalized by a 3-year average served industry market dollars, (2) market growth operationalized as the market growth rate of a 10-year constant dollar average, (3) industry profitability operationalized by indicators such as the 3-year average return on sales of the three largest competitors, (4) cyclicity operationalized by the average annual percentage variation of sales from a trend, (5) inflation recovery operationalized by the 5-year average ratio of combined selling price and productivity change to change in cost due to inflation, and (6) importance of non-U.S. markets operationalized by the 10-year average ratio of international to total market.[8] However, marketing scholars have expanded the list of factors that can be considered in the assessment of both business strength and industry attractiveness.[9] Table 9-2 shows the list of factors that can be used to assess company position strength, and Table 9-3 shows the factor list in relation to market position.

TABLE 9-3 Assessing Market Position

Factors

$E_i \times I_i = E_j$
$E_j \times I_j = E_k$

Financial Factors

Sales	5 × .50 = 2.50
Market sales	5 × .40 = 2.00
Rate of growth (sales)	4 × .30 = 1.20
Profit margin	4 × .30 = 1.20
	100% 4.40 × .30 = 1.32

Competitive Factors

Number of competitors	2 × .40 = .80
Competitive structure	3 × .20 = .60
Capital intensity	3 × .20 = .60
Barrier of entry	4 × .20 = .80
	100% 2.80 × .20 = .56

Customer Factors

Market size	4 × .30 = 1.60
Rate of growth (market size)	4 × .20 = .80
Demand cyclicity	3 × .10 = .30
Availability of substitutes	2 × .20 = .40
Concentration of customers	3 × .20 = .60
	100% 3.70 × .25 = .93

Supply Factors

Availability of supplies	4 × .30 = 1.20
Availability of suppliers	5 × .40 = 2.00
Concentration of suppliers	3 × .30 = .90
	100% 4.10 × .25 = 1.03

Environmental Factors

Economy	4 × .25 = 1.00
Government regulations	5 × .25 = 1.25
Changes in technology	3 × .25 = .75
Labor market	5 × .25 = 1.25
	100% 4.25 × .10 = .43
	100% 4.27

Notes: The market position is evaluated in relation to each of the subfactors (*i*) on a scale varying from 1 (poor) to 5 (excellent). These are shown in the table as E_i. These evaluations are derived through subjective judgments made by the marketing communications manager. The E_i scores are weighted by importance weights (I_i), which are also subjective judgments made by the marketing communications manager. The sum of the ($E_i \times I_i$) scores of a given factor makes up the E_j score of that factor, which in turn is weighted by importance weights for that factor (I_j). The sum of the ($E_j \times I_j$) scores produce an overall evaluation score varying from 1 (poor) to 5 (excellent). The hypothetical example here shows that the market position or its relative attractiveness is good to excellent (4.27 rating out of 5).

Assessing Company Position

Table 9-2 shows that company position can be assessed using four major factors: (1) market factors, (2) profit factors, (3) competitive factors, and (4) marketing factors.[10] We discuss each of these factors here.

1. *Market factors:* A company is in a good position when the company's sales are high and the rate of growth (in sales) is high, too. Furthermore, a company is strong if the customers are loyal to the company product. Another indicator of

corporate image The evaluation of a firm's goodwill in the minds of certain stakeholders such as customers, employees, distributors, suppliers, government, and so on.

value added A common term used by marketers to refer to the consumers' perception of a significant advantage of one or more product features added to the firm's brand.

experience curve effects The cost saving gained as a direct result of learning, business experience, and the use of economies of scale.

company position is **corporate image.** Does the organization have a good image among customers? The rule is, The more positive the corporate image, the better the company position.

2. *Profit factors:* The company position is positive if the product generates a high level of *gross and net profit* and a high level of profit margin. That is, the higher the company's level of profitability, the more positive is its position in the market.

3. *Competitive factors:* The company is said to be in good position if the product has a high market share. Also, if the product has **value added** relative to the competition, then the company is in good position. If market research shows that customers *prefer* the company brand to competitor brands, then the company is in good position. Finally, the company is said to be in good position if it has achieved high levels of cost efficiencies as a direct function of **experience curve effects.**

4. *Marketing factors:* Marketing factors are also used as indicators of business strength. Specifically, the higher the effectiveness of product, price, distribution, and promotion, the better the company's position. Also, the company may be judged as in good position if it has a marketing organization (the corporate culture that reflects customer service throughout the entire organization) and if it has a high level of organizational synergy.

Product effectiveness can be measured through indicators such as product quality, the breadth of the product line, number of products manufactured, timeliness of product development, capacity and productivity, R&D advantage, and cost efficiency in product manufacturing. *Price competitiveness* can be measured in terms of consumers' perceived value. The higher the perceived value, the greater the price competitiveness. Also, price competitiveness may be suggested by the extent to which consumers perceive the price to fall within the acceptable price range (within the upper and lower price limits). Furthermore, the company is in good position when consumers perceive the product as significantly different and better than the leading competitor product. *Distribution effectiveness* can be measured in terms of consumers' access to the product in question. The greater the access, the better the company position. Just-in-time delivery is another distribution goal. The company is in good position if it delivers the product to the consumer when it is needed and where it is needed. *Promotion effectiveness* can be measured in terms of the extent to which the target consumers are aware of the product; are familiar with the product benefits; have a positive attitude toward the product; make a decision to buy the product; and, after purchase and trial, would feel committed to the product.

Marketing organization, as a factor to assess company position, refers to the extent to which the organization is structured to reflect marketing dominance. Table 9-4 contrasts different types of organizations—organizations dominated by manufacturing, sales, and technology versus organizations dominated by marketing.

General managers who are marketing oriented tend to be unconstrained by functional boundaries (departments such as marketing, manufacturing, engineering, R&D, accounting, finance, personnel, etc.). Thus, a marketing organization typically does the following:[11]

- Identifies specific markets for each of its products, that is, identifies several product/markets
- Monitors profitability for each product/market
- Conducts research to determine the needs, wants, and preferences of the consumers in each product/market
- Assesses the strengths and weaknesses of the major competitors in relation to each product/market
- Assesses the impact of environmental trends on each product/market
- Prepares and uses an annual marketing plan
- Understands and practices "marketing investment" (money spent on marketing is considered as an investment that pays off sooner or later)

TABLE 9-4	Organizations Dominated by Different Functional Units			
	Manufacturing	**Sales**	**Technology**	**Marketing**
Typical Strategy	Lower cost	Increase	Push research	Build share profitability
Normal Structure	Functional	Functional or profit centers	Profit centers	Market or product or brand; decentralized profit responsibility
Key Systems	Plant profit and loss statements Budgets	Sales forecasts Results versus plan	Performance tests R&D	Marketing plans
Traditional Skills	Engineering	Sales	Science and engineering	Analysis
Normal Focus	Internal efficiencies	Distribution channels Short-term sales results	Product performance	Consumers Market share
Typical Response to Competitive Pressure	Cut costs	Cut price Sell harder	Improve product	Consumer research Planning Refining
Overall Mental Set	"What we need to do in this company is to get our costs down and our quality up."	"Where can I sell what we make?"	"The best product wins the day."	"What will the consumer buy that we profitably make?"

- Has organization members who all assume the responsibility of making the business successful and profitable
- Has organization members who all "talk" marketing
- Has top executives who are marketing people

Assessing Market Position

Like assessing company position, assessing market position is multifaceted. We consider financial, competitive, customer, and environmental factors.[12]

Financial Factors Managers consider several financial factors in assessing the attractiveness of a specific market: market sales, sales growth rate, and profit margin. Here the marketing communications manager should identify current *sales* (in dollars and in units) of the entire market and project these sales into the future. The higher the current and forecasted sales, the more attractive the market. The marketing communications manager also should compute sales growth (percentage of change from one year to the next) and project the rate of growth into the future. The higher the rate of past, current, and forecasted sales growth, the more attractive that market becomes. Similarly, the manager identifies the average profit margins as reported by all the companies in that market. Also, given the means, the manager extrapolates future profit margins. The higher the past, current, and forecasted industry profit margin, the more attractive the market.

Competitive Factors The manager considers a variety of competitive factors, such as the *number of competitors*, the *industry competitive structure, capital intensity*, and *barriers of entry*. The more competitors, the less attractive the market. However, in many situations, the market is not attractive even with zero competitors. This situation is common with new product introductions, especially the kinds of products that require consumers to change existing habits. In this situation, it is very difficult to build primary demand through the efforts of only one firm. The efforts of several firms help build primary demand for the product. Therefore, one can describe the relationship between attractiveness and number of competitors as follows: market attractiveness is very low when there are no competitors; the market is highly attractive when there are a few competitors; the market becomes decreasingly attractive as more competitors enter the market (see Figure 9-6).

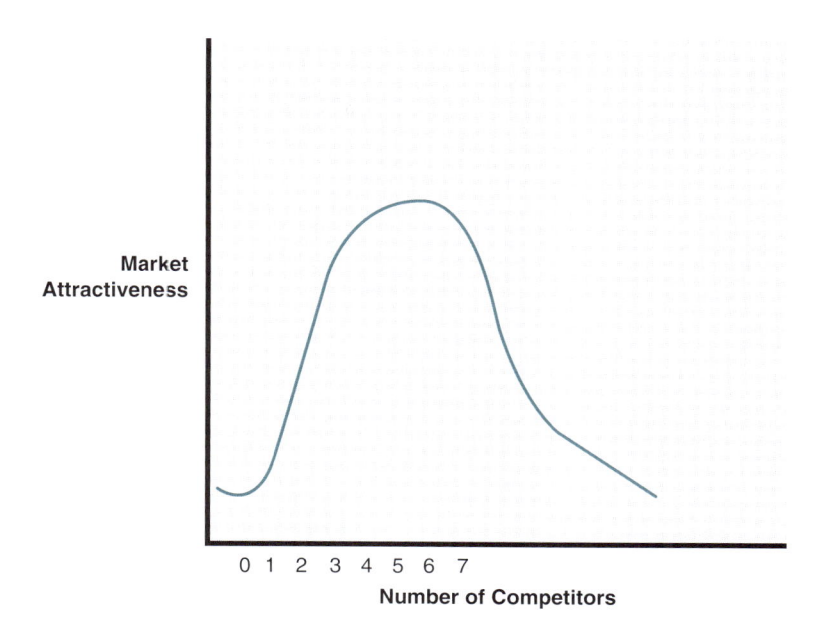

Figure 9-6
The Relationship between Number of Competitors and Market Attractiveness

[Graph: Market Attractiveness vs. Number of Competitors (0–7), showing a curve that rises from near zero, peaks around 3–4 competitors, and declines toward 7.]

competitive structure The nature of competition among firms within a given industry. Competition can be characterized as monopolistic (the market is controlled mostly by one large firm), oligopolistic (the market is controlled by several large firms), and purely competitive (the market is composed of many small firms who are "equally" competing for resources).

capital intensity This concept refers to the situation in which the firms in that market have invested a great deal of capital in land, equipment, and machinery.

barriers of entry Hurdles or obstacles for a firm to penetrate a given industry. Some industries have high barriers (e.g., aviation industry) while others have low barriers (e.g., local janitorial business).

demand cyclicity Seasonal fluctuations in product demand. Some products, such as sunblock lotion, are seasonal and, therefore, are said to have high demand cyclicity.

In assessing market position, the *competitive structure* of the industry is another significant factor. The **competitive structure** of any industry can be described in terms of a dimension varying from complete monopoly to pure competition. The first gradient is a monopolistic industry in which one large firm has complete control of the market; followed by monopolistic competition in which there is one leader and many small and insignificant competitors; followed by an oligopoly in which there are several large firms competing head-to-head and many smaller firms; all the way to pure competition, in which the industry has many small- to medium-size firms. Market attractiveness is highest in situations resembling pure competition and least attractive in monopolies. This is because it is very difficult to compete against giant monopolies and less so against oligopolies; and, by the same token, it is easiest to compete in markets approaching pure competition.

Capital intensity refers to the situation in which the firms in that market have invested a great deal of capital in land, equipment, and machinery. The higher the capital intensity in the industry, the lower its attractiveness. This is because higher levels of capital intensity usually lead firms to be ineffective in countering changes in the environment. Also, when the going gets tough, the firms become fierce and ugly competitors. On the other hand, an industry having very low levels of capital intensity is also considered unattractive. This is because the low **barriers of entry** encourage many new competitors to enter the market. A moderate barrier is often deemed desirable.

Customer Factors In assessing the attractiveness of a market, managers consider factors such as market size, market growth size, demand cyclicity, availability of substitutes, and concentration of customers. Here, the marketing communications manager should estimate the number of people that can be characterized as "customers" in the designated market. Past and current figures are identified and future projections estimated. The bigger the *size of the market* is and is likely to be in the future, the more attractive the market.

With respect to the *rate of market growth*, managers compute changes in the size of the market from year to year and make future projections, too. Managers look for stability in the rate of growth. If many change coefficients are negative, this may signal instability that makes the market in question "unstable."

Related to rate of growth is **demand cyclicity.** Many markets are besieged by cyclical demand. That is, demand tends to fluctuate significantly, perhaps as a direct function of seasonal demand or the business cycle. The greater the demand cyclicity, the less attractive the market.

Availability of substitutes is a factor that, if relevant to a market, makes the market unattractive. For example, the cable technology is rapidly evolving to the extent that consumers of video rentals are increasingly ordering the pay movies offered by cable networks. Pay movies are a substitute to video rentals. The increasing availability and demand for this substitute make the video rental market unattractive.

Concentration of customers has nothing to do with how dispersed the customers are in a certain geographic region. Concentration of customers is a power construct. It refers to the extent to which customers have bargaining power over the seller firms. For example, in the military aviation market, the entire industry is subject to the whims of the defense departments of the United States and of other allied countries. A few customers wield enormous power over the sellers. Such a situation is not attractive because losing key customers may mean the demise of key players in the industry and, perhaps, the industry as a whole. The converse situation is attractive—one in which there are many customers and these customers are not organized to transact with industry players with one voice.

Supply Factors Managers usually consider at least three supply factors in assessing market attractiveness: availability of supplies, availability of suppliers, and concentration of suppliers. *Availability of supplies* refers to the situation in which adequate raw materials are available for the industry to manufacture, distribute, and promote the product. Consider a foreign market such as Albania (next to former Yugoslavia). A company may consider entering the coffee maker manufacturing business. The plant needs a continuous water supply and uninterrupted electric power to run the equipment. But Albania's infrastructure is in shambles. Water and power are scarce commodities. Therefore, the Albania market is considered unattractive.

The same can be said about *availability of suppliers*. Even if the parts and raw materials are available, are there suppliers to sell and deliver the supplies? The more suppliers, the more attractive the market because more suppliers generate greater competition among suppliers, which in turn serves to reduce the price of supply and/or enhance its quality.

However, if the suppliers are organized and attempt to sell their products through price collusion, the buyers of this supply are not likely to benefit significantly. This is because *concentration of suppliers* enhances the bargaining power of suppliers to the detriment of the organizations needing that supply. This situation makes the market unattractive. For example, in the early 1970s, many manufacturing industries relying heavily on oil as a major source of supply were hurt by the OPEC oil cartel. OPEC decided to restrict the flow of oil to the United States because of the U.S. support of Israel in the 1973 Arab-Israeli war.

Environmental Factors Managers consider many environmental factors in assessing the relative attractiveness of a given market or industry. Among the important factors are the economy, government regulations, changes in technology, and the labor market. For example, if the *economy* is anticipated to take a downturn, it may adversely affect the market. Thus, marketing communications managers should consider the effects of the economy on the market. Consider a scenario involving doing business in a country such as Mexico. Could the fall of the peso have been forecasted? The fall of the peso has made many markets in Mexico look very unattractive. This is because the devaluation of the peso has adversely affected consumer demand for many products.

Government regulation is an important factor in assessing the attractiveness of a market. A market that is besieged by all kinds of government regulations is considered unattractive, while markets that have little or no regulation are attractive. Consider the tobacco industry. That industry has all kinds of government regulations. For example, tobacco managers cannot advertise on television or radio. In

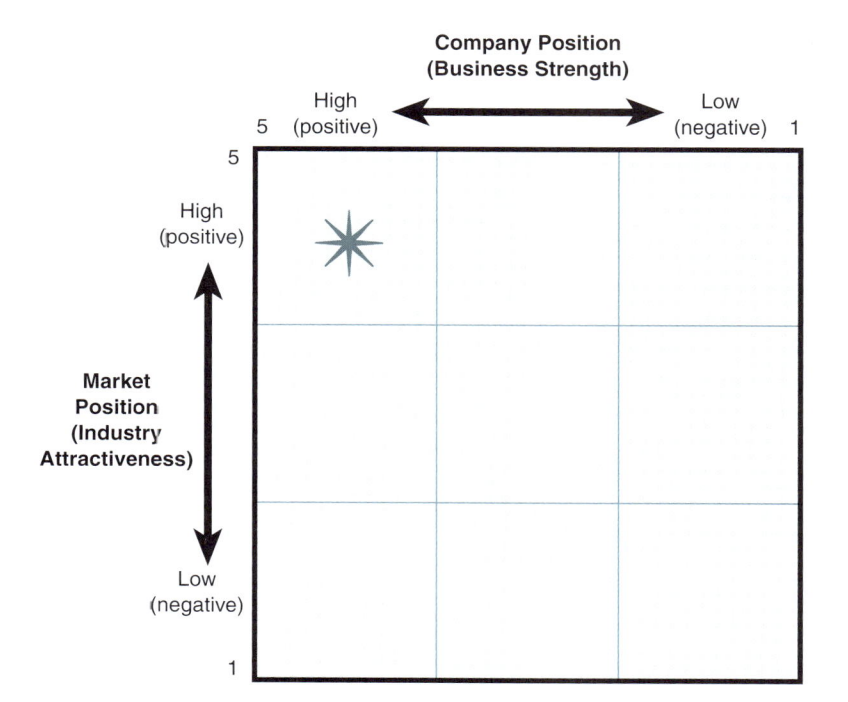

Figure 9-7

An Illustration of the Use of the Multifactor Portfolio Matrix

Note that this indicates the location of the product/market as derived from the assessments shown in Table 9-2 and Table 9-3, which means that this product/market is assessed as being strong in business strength and is in a very attractive market or industry. The recommendation is to invest in this product/market and nurture its growth.

print advertisements, they cannot show a person in the act of smoking. All kinds of warning labels have to be included in the advertisement. Also, government regulations are expected to be exacerbated in the future, making managers in that industry feel that the tobacco and cigarettes market has increasingly lost its luster.

The extent to which changes in technology are likely to affect any aspect of the industry impacts upon attractiveness. For example, an advertising agency assesses the market and examines the changing role of computer technology. Many advertisers have been establishing in-house advertising departments assisted by sophisticated graphics and design software packages. These firms do not need advertising agencies as much as they did in the past. Also, many media firms have adopted computer technology, allowing an advertiser to produce an advertisement directly through the media firm, thereby bypassing the advertising agency. This is an example of how change in computer technology has adversely affected the attractiveness of the market for advertising agencies.

The *labor market* is another important environmental factor managers pay close attention to. Is there a shortage or surplus of qualified personnel to man the manufacturing plants? What is management's relationship with unions within the industry at large? Is there an amicable relationship? Is it likely to turn sour? How is the relationship likely to affect developing the product in time? Will the labor market be adequate to manufacture the desired number of units, to deliver the promised product quality, and to maintain a certain price for the product? These considerations are important because they impact directly and indirectly on the level of attractiveness of the market.

Having illustrated how business strength (company position) and industry attractiveness (market position) can be determined (as illustrated in Table 9-2 and Table 9-3), we are ready to plug these numbers back into the multifactor portfolio matrix and ascertain the exact position of the hypothetical product/market in question. Figure 9-7 shows the result. The figure shows that both the company and market positions of the hypothetical product/market fall in the high/high quadrant, which signals that the product/market should be nurtured to growth and that the firm ought to invest in this product/market to allow it to realize its full growth potential.

Also note that there are many situations in which the application of the multifactor portfolio matrix may show that the product category is significantly discrepant

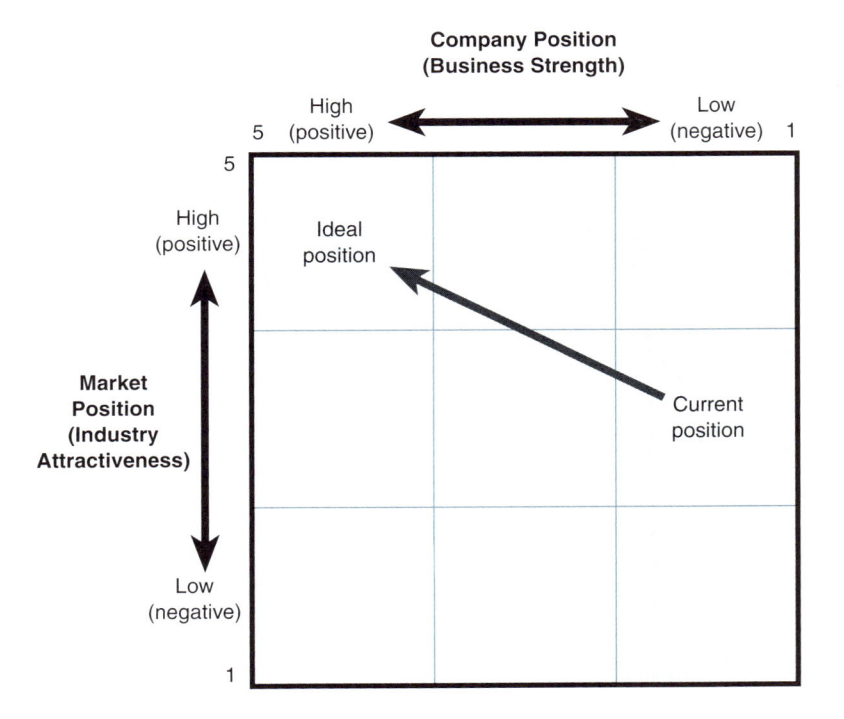

Figure 9-8
Strategic Gap: Current Position in Relation to Ideal Position

from the ideal position (see Figure 9-8). In these situations, the marketing communications manager may attempt to articulate a strategy projecting a trajectory from the current position in the direction of the ideal position. This trajectory may take a variety of forms as a direct function of the current position.

Summary

This chapter introduces conceptual tools related to corporate strategy and tactics and describes how analysis and planning help managers select the most appropriate corporate strategies and tactics. Our purpose is not to teach you how to become an expert in making corporate decisions but, instead, only to provide you with some degree of familiarity with the topic. This is because marketing communications managers are not likely to make corporate decisions directly. Instead, they are likely to influence these decisions. Also, they need to make sure that marketing communications decisions are consistent with marketing and corporate decisions.

The chapter illustrates how corporate-level decision makers define a strategic business unit and a product/market. Knowing the exact product/market units (strategic business units) of an organization is extremely important because most corporate decisions are made in relation to each definable product/market.

The various corporate strategies are discussed, including the corporate decisions to grow, maintain position, harvest, innovate, and divest. Each strategic alternative has a corresponding objective. For example, the growth strategy may aim at an increase in sales and market share. Each strategic alternative is carried out through a unique configuration of the strategic mix. The elements of the corporate strategic mix include manufacturing, engineering, marketing, R&D, personnel, accounting, and finance. A strategic alternative such as growth is implemented through the deployment of certain elements of the strategic mix. For instance, the elements of the corporate mix that are likely to be deployed for growth may be marketing, R&D, and engineering. The deployment of specific elements of the strategic mix entails the allocation of resources to those elements. Similarly, the performance of those deployed elements is monitored and deviations from the objectives are noted, triggering corrective action. Chapter Ten, our next chapter, stays at the corporate level but moves the corporate process down to the analysis and planning level.

How is corporate strategy selected? This chapter introduces two models of corporate strategy selection: the Boston Consulting Group matrix and the multifactor portfolio matrix. Both are used to help corporate executives select suitable strategies as a function of a variety of industry/market factors and factors related to their own business. Situation analysis is used to assess these factors and apply the models, the result of which is a selection of an effective corporate strategy. We recommend the multifactor portfolio matrix because of its conceptual strength.

Discussion Questions

1. What is a strategic business unit? Product/market? How do marketers identify product/markets? Illustrate with examples.
2. What is corporate strategy? Describe at least three alternative corporate strategies. Illustrate with examples.
3. Identify corporate objectives associated with each alternative corporate strategy. Illustrate with examples.
4. Identify the corporate strategic mix needed to implement each alternative corporate strategy. Illustrate with examples.
5. Suppose you are an owner of a local restaurant that has sales revenues of approximately $2 million a year. The restaurant is located in a university town and specializes in deli sandwiches. It also has a game room (pool, billiards, darts, etc.) and a staging area used at night for live band and comedy shows. Define the various strategic business units of this restaurant.
6. Still assuming that you are the owner of that restaurant, think of expanding the restaurant to make more money. In other words, your corporate strategy is to grow. How would you implement this growth strategy? Decide which specific tactics may be viable in expanding the operations. Which of the following functional units become more central to the growth strategy: marketing, R&D, engineering, manufacturing, personnel, finance, or accounting?
7. Still assuming that you are the owner of that restaurant, you become aware that another deli-type restaurant (with a nightclub setting) is now directly competing with your business. Your strategy is now to maintain market share. How would you go about implementing this strategy? What are those corporate strategic elements that you are likely to deploy? Be specific.
8. Still assuming that you are the owner of that restaurant, you realize that you can no longer compete with two or three other deli-type restaurants in town. You are now thinking of harvesting the deli operation and channeling your energy into the nightclub operation. How would you go about doing this? Which functional units of the restaurant will become more central and which less central? Explain.
9. Still assuming that you are the owner of that restaurant, you realize that the only way to effectively compete with the two or three new deli-type restaurants is to be innovative. You have to come up with something new, a new gimmick that will attract patrons to your restaurant. What could this be? Think of a new gimmick and think about how you would go about implementing it.
10. Consider the following situation. A software company called Lintronics has been recently established and manned by three people. The company developed its first software, called Apple Pie Music. The product is a CD-multimedia software that contains an encyclopedia of music and a history of music in the United States. The three partners are very excited about the launch of this software and have high hopes for it. They decide to focus on the school library market and launch a marketing communications campaign directed to that market. Use this case to select appropriate strategies. Apply the Boston Consulting Group matrix to Apple Pie Music. Recommend a corporate strategy as a direct function of this application.
11. Regarding the same situation, now apply the multifactor portfolio matrix to Apple Pie Music. Recommend a corporate strategy as a direct function of this application.

Practice Quiz

Note: You can find the correct answers to these questions by taking the quiz and then submitting your answers in the Online Edition. The program will automatically score your submission. If you miss a question, the program will provide the correct answer, a rationale for the answer, and the section number in the chapter where the topic is discussed.

1. The implementation of the _____ strategy views the marketing, R&D, and engineering functions as important elements of the strategic mix.
   a. maintain-position
   b. growth
   c. harvest
   d. innovation

2. Corporate objectives such as "increase sales by 30 percent by June 2006" and "increase market share by 10 percent by January 2007" would be associated with the _____ strategy.
   a. maintain-position
   b. growth
   c. harvest
   d. innovation

3. The _____ strategy views the marketing, engineering, and personnel functions as important process elements of the strategic mix and aims to minimize negative percentage change of sales and market share.
   a. maintain-position
   b. growth
   c. harvest
   d. divest

4. With respect to the harvest strategy, which of the following functions are likely to be important?
   a. marketing, engineering, and accounting
   b. marketing, R&D, and engineering
   c. manufacturing, personnel, and accounting
   d. marketing, engineering, and personnel

5. What functions are likely to dominate the innovation strategy?
   a. marketing and R&D
   b. marketing, R&D, and engineering
   c. manufacturing and R&D
   d. R&D, engineering, and personnel

6. Identify the most important process and the corporate objective for the divestment strategy.
   a. accounting; minimizing negative percentage change of sales
   b. personnel; maximizing profits
   c. finance; maximizing cash flow
   d. marketing; maximizing cash flow

7. Internal situation analysis refers to _____.
   a. gathering information about the size of the market
   b. dividing the market into customer segments
   c. gathering information about changes in technology
   d. plotting sales trends from accounting data

8. A "gain-share strategy" transforms a "_____" into a "_____."
   a. dog; cash cow
   b. dog; star
   c. problem child; star
   d. problem child; cash cow

9. The two strategies that firms commonly use when they realize that a "cash cow" is moving toward a "dog" position are the _____ and the _____ strategies.
   a. growth; innovate
   b. innovate; harvest
   c. growth; divest
   d. maintain-position; innovate

10. The two dimensions employed in a multifactor portfolio matrix are _____.
    a. business strength and market share
    b. market growth and market position
    c. company position and market position
    d. market share and market growth

Web Exercise

Analysis and Planning for Strategic Decision Making in the Airline Industry

Visit the websites of Virgin Atlantic Airlines (http://www.virgin-atlantic.com), United Airlines (http://www.united.com), British Airways (http://www.britishairways.com), and Icelandair (http://www.icelandair.com).

Put yourself in the position of the CEO for one of those airlines. Conduct a situation analysis of the external and internal factors that are relevant for you. From that position, how do you see your company's position in the trans-Atlantic marketplace? What implications do you see for maintaining or changing your corporate strategy? Why and how would this ultimately influence possible marketing- and communications-level strategies?

Suggested Readings

Collis, David J., and Cynthia A. Montgomery. 2004. *Corporate strategy: A resource-based approach.* Columbus, OH: McGraw-Hill/Irwin.

Ferrell, O. C., George H. Lucas Jr., and David Luck. 1994. *Strategic marketing management.* Cincinnati, OH: South-Western Educational Publishers.

Ghemawat, Pankaj, David J. Collis, Garry P. Pisano, and Jan W. Rivkin. 1999. *Strategy and the business landscape.* Reading, MA: Addison-Wesley.

Goold, Michael, Andrew Campbell, and Marcus Alexander. 1994. *Corporate-level strategy: Creating value in the multibusiness company.* New York: John Wiley & Sons.

Johnson, Gerry, Kevan Scholes, and Richard Whittington. 1993. *Exploring corporate strategy,* 7th ed. London: Prentice Hall International.

Kaplan, Robert S., and David P. Norton. 2004. *Strategy maps: Converting intangible assets into tangible outcomes.* Boston, MA: Harvard Business School Publishing.

Prahald, Hamel. 1994. *Competing for the future.* Boston, MA: Harvard Business School Press.

Notes

1. Associated Press, "The Internet Is Newest Corporate Battleground," *Roanoke Times and World News,* June 9, 1995, A15, A17.
2. Gary McWilliams, "At Compaq, A Desktop Crystal Ball," *Business Week,* March 20, 1995, 96–98; Larry Armstrong, Ira Sager, Kathy Rebello, and Peter Burrows, "Home Computers: Sales Explode As New Uses Turn PCs into All-Purpose Information Appliances," *BusinessWeek,* November 28, 1994, 88–96; Peter Burrows, "It's All Starting to Compute Now," *BusinessWeek,* March 13, 1995, 94.
3. Philip Kotler, *Marketing Management,* 8th ed. (Englewood Cliffs, NJ: Prentice Hall, 1994), 69.
4. Bruce D. Henderson, "The Product Portfolio" (Boston, MA: The Boston Consulting Group, Inc., 1970), *Perspectives* No. 66; Philippe Haspeslagh, "Portfolio Planning: Uses and Limits," *Harvard Business Review* (January–February 1982): 60, 73.
5. George Day, "Diagnosing the Product Portfolio," *Journal of Marketing* (April 1977): 29–38; Donald C. Hambrick and Ian C. MacMillan, "The Product Portfolio and Man's Best Friend," *California Management Review* (Fall 1982): 84–95; Philippe Haspeslagh, "Portfolio Planning: Uses and Limits," *Harvard Business Review* (January–February 1982): 60, 73; Yoram Wind and Vijay Mahajan, "Designing Product and Business Portfolios," *Harvard Business Review* (January–February 1980): 155–65; Yoram Wind, Vijay Mahajan, and Donald J. Swire, "An Empirical Comparison of Standardized Portfolio Models," *Journal of Marketing* (Spring 1983): 89–99.
6. Francis J. Aguilar and Richard Hamermesh, "General Electric: Strategic Position: 1981," Harvard Business School Case 9-381-174, 25; Subash C. Jain, *Marketing Planning and Strategy* (Cincinnati, OH: South-Western Educational Publishers, 1994), 271–86.
7. See note 5.
8. *Organizing and Managing the Planning Function* (Fairfield, CT: GE Company, n.d.); Francis J. Aguilar and Richard Hamermesh, "General Electric: Strategic Position: 1981."
9. William E. Rothschild, *Putting It Together* (New York: AMACOM, 1976).
10. See note 5.
11. Subash C. Jain, *Marketing Planning and Strategy,* 4th ed. (Cincinnati, OH: South-Western Educational Publishers, 1993), 183; Benson P. Shapiro, "What the Hell Is 'Market Oriented'?" *Harvard Business Review* (November–December 1988): 119–25; Gordon Canning Jr., "Is Your Company Marketing Oriented?" *Journal of Business Strategy* (May–June 1988): 34–36.
12. See note 5.

The Marketing Level:
Analysis and Planning for Marketing Strategy and Tactics

Chapter Ten

Key Terms

brand symbols (p. 251)
competition (p. 251)
consumer decision making (p. 247)
consumer experience (p. 249)
consumer involvement (p. 249)
country of origin (p. 250)
customer benefits (p. 240)
customer or brand loyalty (p. 249)
market (p. 225)
market selection (p. 225)
marketing strategy (p. 221)
needs (p. 226)
positioning (p. 220)
positioning by brand-distributor tie-in (p. 236)
positioning by celebrity or spokesperson (p. 245)
positioning by competitors (p. 231)
positioning by country of origin (p. 232)
positioning by customer benefit or problem (p. 241)
positioning by distributor location (p. 237)
positioning by distributor's serviceability (p. 239)
positioning by intangible factor (p. 230)
positioning by lifestyle or personality (p. 246)
positioning by low price (p. 234)
positioning by product attribute (p. 229)
positioning by product class (p. 228)
positioning by relative price (p. 234)
positioning by use or application (p. 242)
positioning by user or customer image (p. 243)
price consciousness (p. 248)
price-quality relationship (p. 250)
primary demand (p. 252)
product differentiation (p. 224)
product functionality versus value-expressiveness (p. 250)
product-market matrix (p. 226)
product users versus nonusers (p. 250)
prospects (p. 221)
reputation of the distributor (p. 252)
selective demand (p. 252)
strategic place focus (p. 225)
strategic price focus (p. 224)
strategic product focus (p. 224)
strategic prospects focus (p. 225)
technologies (p. 226)
variations in quality perceptions (p. 252)

Chapter Outline

10-1 Introduction

10-2 Marketing Strategies and Tactics
    10-2a Strategic Product Focus and Corresponding Strategies and Tactics
    10-2b Strategic Price Focus and Corresponding Strategies and Tactics
    10-2c Strategic Place Focus
    10-2d Strategic Prospects Focus

10-3 The Use of Situation Analysis for Marketing Strategy Selection
    10-3a Consumer-Related Factors
    10-3b Product-Related Factors
    10-3c Market-Related Factors

Summary
Discussion Questions
Practice Quiz
Web Exercise: Cruising on the Web
Suggested Readings
Notes

Marketing is merely a civilized form of warfare in which most battles are won with words, ideas, and disciplined thinking.
—Albert W. Emery, U.S. advertising agency executive

10-1 Introduction

The death of *Pepsi Edge*, described in SMC Marketplace Watch 10-1, shows the outcome of a poor positioning strategy. There was simply no market segment to match up with where this product had been positioned. Good positioning is all about creating a virtual space in the consumer's mind as to "exactly" where that product fits, and this positioning meets a significant need.

The California Milk Processor Board was behind some of the most successful positioning advertisements in recent history. In their "Got Milk?" campaign, a number of advertisements are executed around a powerful "deprivation message." In relaying that message, viewers are consistently put into situations that they can relate to as "users" of the product. Specifically, for the "Got Milk?" campaign, viewers watched people put in those familiar situations in which the lack of milk in the use of a complementary product was most unpleasant—in fact, some would consider the lack of milk "hellish." The classic "Heaven" commercial for the California Milk Processor Board shows a person who has been run over by a truck and now is in what he believes must be heaven. In heaven, he eats a huge chocolate chip cookie. His trip to hell is about to unfold. Something is missing! Milk. This commercial is designed to reinforce the association that eating cookies goes with drinking milk and, when eating cookies, there is only one beverage that "does the job." The marketer is positioning milk (the advertised product) with a specific use or application (consumption of cookies). This chapter introduces you to a marketing strategy called *positioning by use or application*.

It is estimated that about 9 million people from North America took a sea cruise in 2004.[1] What is the appeal? Escape? Relaxation? A few years ago, a commercial ran for the Norwegian Cruise Line that focused on the American market in a very American way. The commercial shows a woman experiencing sensual pleasure and adventure. The advertisement uses an analogy to articles in the Constitution, which guarantees certain rights to U.S. citizens. The point is that people are entitled to get away from work and experience sensual pleasure, relaxation, and a little adventure. The marketing strategy behind this commercial is called *positioning by customer benefit*. The marketer of the Norwegian Cruise Line is attempting to highlight customer benefits such as sensual pleasure, relaxation, and adventure with the cruise line.

In this chapter, we discuss this strategy and many other similar marketing strategies that guide marketing communications. These others include positioning by: product attribute, intangible attribute, relative price, low price, user or customer, celebrity or person, lifestyle or personality, product class, competitors, and country of origin. Thus, this chapter introduces you to a variety of marketing strategies that are operationalized through **positioning.** Positioning refers to highlighting, emphasizing, and communicating particular aspects of the brand to target consumers. We also discuss how each of the positioning strategies can be operationalized through marketing research and how appropriate models can be used to guide this research. See Figure 10-1.

positioning   The same as a *message strategy*. That is, the marketing communications manager translates corporate and marketing strategies in terms of a specific message to be communicated to target consumers. For example, a growth strategy at the corporate level may translate into a differentiation strategy at the marketing level, which further translates into positioning by intangible factor such as quality. That is, the marketing communications manager may believe that a message about product quality may be most effective in differentiating the firm's product from competitor products, which in turn may be an effective way to grow.

SMC Marketplace Watch 10-1

The Market Failure of Pepsi Edge

PepsiCo has just killed its Pepsi Edge, "mid-calorie cola" concept, launched a year ago. Consumers did not seem to understand how it differed from the company's other diet products. The product was designed to compete against Coca-Cola's C2, which targets those who want both taste and low calories. The market segment of consumers who choose cola drinks by taste is sizable; the same can be said for the segment of consumers who choose low calories. Although there seems to be a segment of consumers who want both, that segment does not seem to be significantly large enough to sustain the marketing of yet a different brand. PepsiCo has Diet Pepsi and Pepsi One for consumers interested in zero-calorie diet colas. PepsiCo now admits there was not a clear market. Company officials acknowledged that consumers are more interested in zero-calorie diet colas than mid-calorie diet colas.

So what is the history behind this fiasco? The company introduced Pepsi Edge based on research that indicates that 60 percent of consumers are "dual users"—those who switched between full-calorie and diet colas to help control their calorie intake but do not like the taste of diet drinks. Pepsi Edge was designed to capture that market. As already noted, Pepsi Edge was also designed to compete against Coca-Cola's C2. C2's market performance was equivocal at best. Coca-Cola sold twenty-five million cases of the mid-calorie cola in the United States in 2004, well below other introductions. Yet it was nearly three times the 8.6 million cases of Pepsi Edge sold in the same period.

Although PepsiCo is pulling the plug on Pepsi Edge, rival Coca-Cola is not ready to pull the plug on its C2 brand. Coca-Cola has been consistent in its support for its C2 despite negative publicity of the demise of Pepsi Edge and its own parade of diet line extensions including Diet Coke Sweetened with Splenda and Coke Zero. In fact, to add to this support, Coca-Cola recently rolled out C2 2-liter bottles and twelve packs and is currently working on a new branding initiative to target younger consumers.

Earlier this year, Pepsi relaunched its Pepsi One brand with Splenda and packaging made to appeal to males. The question that some analysts are asking now is, Can Coca-Cola sustain interest for C2 amid the marketing buzz for Coke Zero, or will it meet the same fate of Pepsi Edge?

Source: Adapted from Kate MacArthur, "PepsiCo Kills Pepsi Edge: Acknowledges Product's Failure," *AdAge.com* (Chicago), http://www.adage.com/news.cms?newsId=45071 (accessed May 19, 2005).

10-2 Marketing Strategies and Tactics

The marketing communications manager attempts to identify an overall marketing strategy guiding the marketing mix. This is a strategic decision at the marketing level. We call this **marketing strategy.** The marketing literature has so many models of marketing strategy. The most popular is Porter's model of competitive strategy.[2] The model identifies three major marketing strategies: (1) differentiation, (2) cost leadership, and (3) focus. In some ways, Porter's model guides us to think that marketing strategy is nothing more than a way to emphasize different elements of the marketing mix. His differentiation strategy typically emphasizes the product element of the marketing mix, the cost leadership strategy emphasizes the price element, and the focus strategy emphasizes the prospect element. Note that the marketing mix can be viewed as having five major elements (instead of four), namely, product, price, place, promotion, and **prospects.** We are all familiar with the traditional four Ps. We are adding the "prospects" element to the four Ps, making them "five Ps." The prospects element of the marketing mix deals with marketing efforts and programs to customize and tailor the four Ps to needs, desires, and preferences of the prospects (prospective buyers). It drives the marketing research function. The outcome of this research is usually captured in terms of market segmentation and target marketing.

marketing strategy
A decision made by the marketing manager (or a firm's executive) to allocate (or shift the allocation of) organizational resources (capital and/or human resources) to emphasize any one or combination of elements of the marketing mix (the four Ps of marketing: product, price, place, and promotion.

prospects Potential customers of a firm.

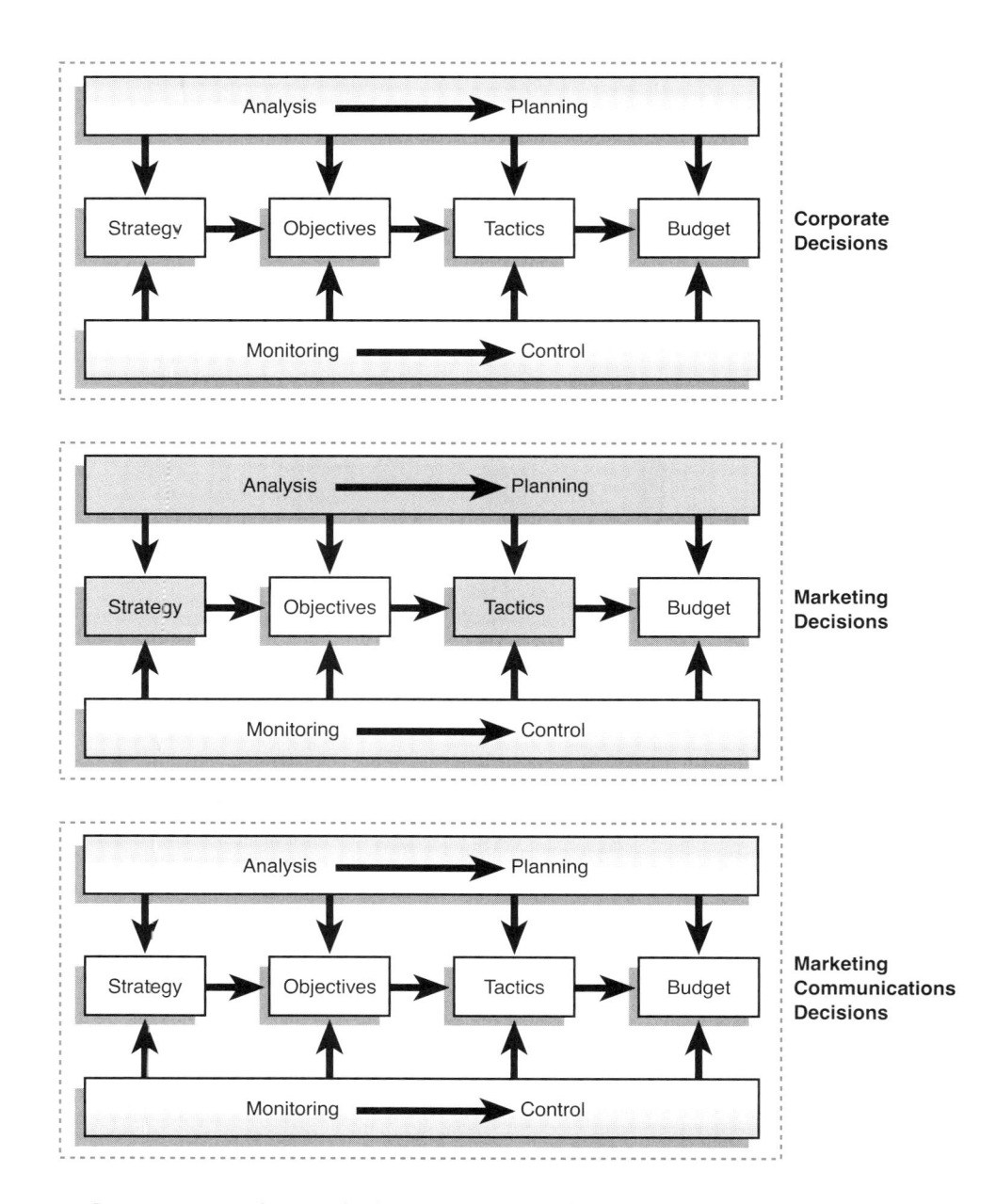

Figure 10-1
Marketing Strategy, Tactics, and Analysis

One can argue that marketing strategy is nothing more than allocating additional resources to emphasize one or more elements of the marketing mix above and beyond the remaining elements. Therefore, we can talk about marketing strategy in terms of a product strategic focus, a price strategic focus, a place strategic focus, a promotion strategic focus, and a prospects strategic focus. However, since this book is about marketing communications, we cannot fathom a product strategic focus implemented without an equal emphasis on promotion. Promotion, by definition, cannot and should not be treated as an independent strategic focus. You cannot promote just for the sake of promotion. You promote if you have something substantial to promote, something pertaining to the other elements of the marketing mix. Any promotion campaign can be effective if it informs targeted consumers about an aspect of its product, price, distribution, and/or customers that targeted consumers think may be beneficial—providing value added. Based on this reasoning, we identify four marketing strategies as a direct function of combining promotion with (1) product, (2) price, (3) place, and (4) prospects. We call them *strategic product focus, strategic price focus, strategic place focus,* and *strategic prospects focus*. We describe these four strategies in some detail.

TABLE 10-1 Marketing Strategies, Tactics, and Objectives

Marketing Strategy	Marketing Tactics (Strategic Mix)	Marketing Objectives
Strategic product focus	*Product* Price Place Promotion Prospects	Establish, increase, or brand association with facet *x*
Strategic price focus	Product *Price* Place Promotion Prospects	Establish, increase, or maintain brand association with price facet *x*
Strategic place focus	Product Price *Place* Promotion Prospects	Establish, increase, or maintain brand association with service facet *x*
Strategic prospects focus	Product Price Place Promotion *Prospects*	Establish, increase, or maintain brand association with prospects facet *x*

Note: Italics indicate corresponding marketing tactics (elements of the marketing strategic mix).

Examine Table 10-1. It shows the four marketing strategies in the left column with their corresponding marketing tactics (elements of the marketing strategic mix) and their deduced objectives. However, before we discuss these strategies, tactics, and objectives, we need to give you some more information regarding the concept of *positioning*. Once a firm selects its target market(s), it must identify the image it desires to instill in the minds of the consumers of that target market. For example, IBM promotes an image of reliability, service, range of software applications, and product variety. Apple promotes an image of ease of use, graphics, desktop publishing, and innovativeness. Dell promotes an image of made-to-order products, range of accessories carried, and direct-marketing experience. Promoting a specific brand image in the minds of targeted consumers is what positioning is about. Positioning is an attempt by a firm to occupy a niche in the minds of consumers through a distinct image. When consumers think about a particular brand, they conjure up an image. If that image is the same image that the firm has tried to instill in the minds of consumers, then we can say that the firm has successfully positioned its brand. Conversely, if consumers cannot conjure up an image at all or if they think of the brand in different terms—different from the image that the firm is trying to promote—then we can say that the firm's positioning attempts have been unsuccessful.

The concept of positioning asserts that marketing performance can be enhanced if the product is unique in the industry along some dimension widely valued by consumers. Uniqueness may be based on product (e.g., product design, service, options), price (e.g., price connoting status and prestige), distribution (e.g., excellent customer service available at each distributor), and prospects (e.g., the product is associated with a celebrity spokesperson that targeted consumers idealize). Promoting (another element of the marketing mix) a brand based on a unique and valued marketing mix dimension is referred to as *positioning*. Specifically, *positioning* is using the promotion element of the marketing mix to communicate a unique configuration of the remaining elements of the marketing mix (product, price, place, and prospects).[3]

Positioning scholars have developed an extensive repertoire of positioning techniques. Among the significant ones are: product attribute, intangible factor, customer benefits, relative price, low price, use/application, user/customer, celebrity/person, lifestyle/personality, product class, competitors, and country/geographic area.[4] Each positioning technique reflects a specific emphasis on selected elements of the marketing mix (product, price, distribution, marketing communications). Therefore, we group the various positioning techniques according to the element of the marketing mix most emphasized, as shown in Table 10-2.

Marketing scholars assert that firms attempt to position their brands in the minds of targeted consumers by emphasizing a brand facet related to the product itself, a facet dealing with the product's price, a facet related to the serviceability of the product, or a facet that has something to do with the targeted consumers, that is, customers. These reflect four different marketing strategies: product differentiation, cost leadership, service, and focus. **Strategic product focus** involves promoting a specific facet of the product itself. Therefore, the elements of the marketing mix considered strategic are the product and promotion elements. A typical objective reflecting this strategy is to establish, increase, or maintain a brand association with a facet related to the product itself. For example, Ford promotes many of its car models using the concept of "Ford Quality." That is, the emphasis of its promotion campaign is to instill in the minds of targeted consumers the notion that its cars are of high quality. This is an example of **product differentiation**—that is, positioning the brand by associating the brand with an image dealing with a specific product characteristic such as product quality.

Strategic price focus, on the other hand, deals with positioning along a price facet. For example, Wal-Mart has been very successful creating an image in the minds of bargain shoppers that their stores offer the best price deals in town. That is, Wal-Mart marketers positioned the store by associating low prices with Wal-Mart. This is the image Wal-Mart management wants to create in the minds of bargain shoppers in

strategic product focus
Promoting a specific facet of the product.

product differentiation
The state in which a particular brand is perceived to be distinct and different from competitor brands.

strategic price focus
Positioning along a price facet of the market.

TABLE 10-2	Positioning Strategies Grouped by Marketing Mix Elements

Positioning Strategies Emphasizing the *Product*
- Positioning by product class
- Positioning by product attribute
- Positioning by intangible factor
- Positioning by competitor
- Positioning by country of origin

Positioning Strategies Emphasizing *Price*
- Positioning by relative price
- Positioning by low price

Positioning Strategies Emphasizing *Place*
- Positioning by brand-distributor tie-ins
- Positioning by distributor location
- Positioning by distributor service

Positioning Strategies Emphasizing *Prospects*
- Positioning by customer benefit or problem
- Positioning by use or application
- Positioning by user or customer image
- Positioning by celebrity or spokesperson
- Positioning by lifestyle or personality

every town and neighborhood in the United States (and outside of the United States, too). The strategic elements of this marketing strategy are both price and promotion elements. In other words, the cost leadership strategy is operationalized through a heavy promotion campaign emphasizing an aspect dealing with the brand's price.

Strategic place focus is another marketing strategy that emphasizes a unique feature of the place (or distribution) element of the marketing mix. Service is typically rendered through a retail outlet (or through other facets of the channel of distribution). Positioning the brand in terms of service entails heavy promotion of aspects dealing with service to the customers. An objective related to this strategy is to establish, increase, or maintain a brand association with an aspect dealing with the distribution element of the marketing mix such as quality service, dependable service, no-hassle service, or convenient service, among others. Many of the upscale clothing boutiques position themselves in terms of high-quality service to customers, which translates to salesclerks giving personal attention to each and every patron.

Finally, **strategic prospects focus** guides the marketer to emphasize aspects related to the targeted consumers. The goal is to have targeted consumers believe that the advertised product is designed to serve people like them, that is, similar people. The goal is to get targeted consumers to identify with the typical customers of the product. They form an image of the product as consumed by the kind of people they can identify with or relate to, people just like them. A good example of this strategy is Nike shoes. Much of Nike's marketing communications campaign focuses on appealing to women who are athletic, highly active, independent, competitive, and full of life and energy. It is a campaign that speaks to these women directly in an intimate and personal way.

Before discussing the four marketing strategies and tactics in some detail, we address the concepts of market segmentation, market selection, and target marketing. Marketers typically think of marketing strategy in terms of target marketing and positioning. As we already know, positioning is about creating, reinforcing, or changing a brand image in the minds of "targeted consumers." Notice what we just said "targeted consumers." That is, before thinking about positioning, we first need to select consumer segments and decide to target them. Therefore, before immersing ourselves in positioning strategies, let us first make some decisions about market selection and target marketing.

Michael Porter, a Harvard Business School professor and a management guru, has long argued that ruthless specialist firms are likely to be successful in today's market conditions. Specialist firms are those that tailor all their activities to serve narrow market segments in ways that cannot be easily imitated by competitors. For example, Jiffy Lube specializes in oil and filter changes and therefore serves a narrow segment. Similarly, Southwest Airlines provides frequent flights at low cost between pairs of cities—again, a very narrow market compared to most airlines that have a worldwide hub-and-spoke network that can take air travelers from somewhere to anywhere. According to Professor Porter, a focus strategy entails tailoring every facet of the business to serve a narrow market segment. By doing so, focus-driven firms gain a competitive advantage over competitor firms who try to be all things to all people.[5]

Market selection involves identifying all the possible markets for the firm's product(s) and then making a deliberate decision to go after certain markets while ignoring others. In doing so, the manager attempts to segment the market using certain segmentation criteria and analyzes the viability of each segment. Market selection is thus a decision based on prioritizing the identified markets and targeting the most viable ones. What is a **market**? Here are some definitions of "market" by marketing scholars:

- An aggregate demand by potential buyers of a product or service[6]
- People with needs to satisfy, the money to spend, and the willingness to spend it[7]
- The interrelated class of brands or products whose relations of substitution and competition are powerful enough so that the sales of each are strongly influenced by the sales of the other[8]

strategic place focus Positioning in a special distribution market.

strategic prospects focus Promoting aspects related to the targeted consumers.

market selection Identifying all of the possible markets for a product and then promoting to chosen markets while ignoring others.

market A segment of the population that purchases a specific good or service.

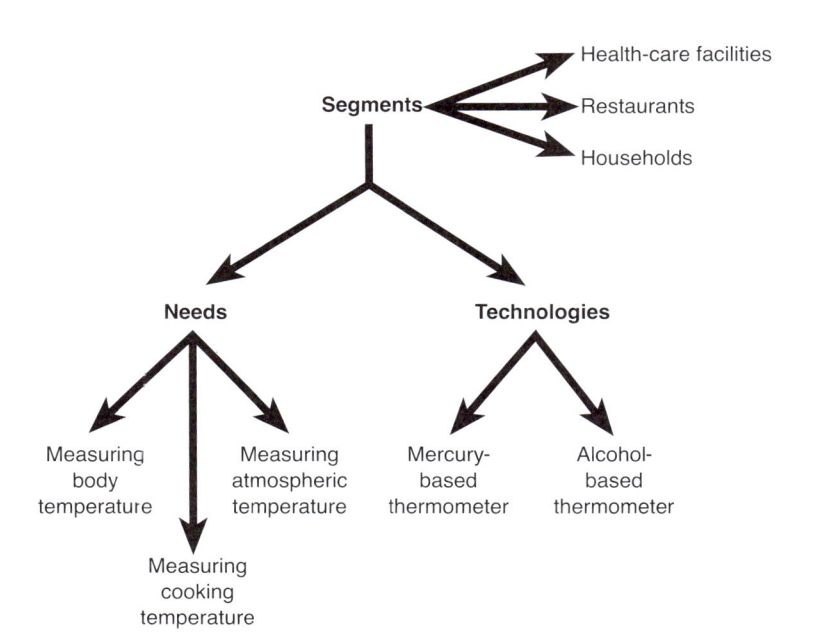

Figure 10-2

Product/Market Based on Typology of Segments, Needs, and Technologies

needs A term typically used in relation to customers. The focus in marketing is to configure the marketing mix in ways to deliver a good or service to prospective buyers to meet their expectations, desires, and wants above and beyond competitor offerings.

technologies This concept refers to specific aspects of a good or service that are typically manipulated by engineers.

product-market matrix A matrix specifying each business unit that is the basis of all subsequent corporate, marketing, and marketing communications decisions.

A typical market-segmentation model involves potential customer groups, customer needs, and technologies. Customer groups are "homogeneous" sets of buyers. A customer group can be viewed as an identifiable group of customers with the same generic need. For example, a thermometer manufacturer may have the capability to cater to three market segments: (1) health-care facilities, (2) restaurants, and (3) households. **Needs** are the functions or purposes a product serves for customers. For example, thermometers can serve three customer functions: (1) measuring body temperature, (2) measuring cooking temperature, and (3) measuring atmospheric temperature. **Technologies** refer to those particular products that can be defined and distinguished from other products through technological features. For example, there are two types of thermometers, technologically speaking—one that is mercury based and another that is alcohol based. See Figure 10-2.

By articulating different segments by different needs and by different technologies, we can construct a **product-market matrix.** See Figure 10-3. The product-market matrix specifies each business unit that is the basis of all subsequent corporate, marketing, and marketing communications decisions. The product-market matrix shows the possibility of ten different business units. Focusing on the household segment, we can identify six product-markets: (1) households using mercury-based thermometers to measure body temperature as a symptom of illness, (2) households using alcohol-based thermometers to measure body temperature as a symptom of illness, (3) households using mercury-based thermometers to measure cooking temperature in preparing oven-cooked meals, (4) households using alcohol-based thermometers to measure cooking temperature in preparing oven-cooked meals, (5) households using mercury-based thermometers to measure atmospheric temperature to figure out how warmly to dress, and (6) households using alcohol-based thermometers to measure atmospheric temperature to figure out how warmly to dress.

Restaurants use thermometers mostly for one purpose, namely, to measure cooking temperature. The thermometer can be mercury based or alcohol based. Health-care facilities use mercury- or alcohol-based thermometers to measure body temperature as a diagnostic medical tool. It may be that mercury-based thermometers are more appropriate than alcohol-based ones for certain markets. If so, certain cells within the matrix would make up the possible business units.

How do marketers identify various possible market segments and needs? It is beyond the scope of this book to delve into the huge amount of literature concerning segmentation, but it may suffice to point out that segmentation criteria are highly

	Markets				
	Households			Restaurants	Health-care facilities
Products	Body temperature	Cooking temperature	Atmospheric temperature	Cooking temperature	Body temperature
Mercury-based thermometer					
Alcohol-based thermometer					

Figure 10-3
The Resulting Products/Markets

TABLE 10-3	Segmentation Criteria Commonly Used by Consumer and Business-to-Business Marketers

Segmentation Criteria Used by Consumer Marketers
- Demographic factors (gender, income, education, etc.)
- Sociocultural factors (social class, family life cycle, social integration, opinion leadership, etc.)
- Geographic factors (local, regional, international, etc.)
- Psychographic factors (activities, interests, opinions, personality, self-concept, lifestyle, etc.)
- Motivational factors (benefits, needs, wants, etc.)
- Consumption factors (product usage, brand loyalty, etc.)

Segmentation Criteria Used by Business-to-Business Marketers
- End use (Standard Industrial Classification code)
- Customer size (number of employees, annual sales, etc.)
- Geographic factors (local, regional, international, etc.)
- Motivational factors (benefits, needs, wants, etc.)
- Consumption factors (product usage, brand loyalty, etc.)
- Channel type (type of wholesaler, type of retailer, etc.)
- Personal selling method (deals, allowances, co-op advertising, etc.)

varied. Representative segmentation criteria that are traditionally used by consumer and industrial marketers are shown in Table 10-3.

10-2a Strategic Product Focus and Corresponding Strategies and Tactics

In this section, we discuss the positioning strategies reflected through the strategic product focus and how they are implemented. The popular positioning strategies related to strategic product focus are shown in Table 10-2. We discuss them in some detail.

Positioning by Product Class

Some brands can be positioned at the product-class level, that is, by using product-class associations. To understand the concept of product class, you have to understand the distinction between *product category, product form,* and *brand*. A product category is the highest level of abstraction of a given product. For example, we can talk about automobiles as a product category. Within the product category are various product forms. For instance, cars can be differentiated as sports cars, compact economy cars, pickups, jeeps, station wagons, vans, minivans, and so on. All these are forms of the automobile. Within a product form are product brands. Thus, in relation to sport utility vehicles (SUVs), we may have a Ford SUV, a Chrysler SUV, and so on. Product-class association means connecting the brand to a particular benefit related to either the product form or the category itself. See Exhibit 10-1. For example,

228 PART THREE Strategy Development: A Hierarchical Perspective

Exhibit 10-1
Positioning by Product Class
Source: Coca-Cola, the Dynamic Ribbon Device, the Contour Bottle design, and mycokemusic are registered trademarks of The Coca-Cola Company. Reprinted by permission.

SMC QuickLink
Johnson Diversey Products (Caress soap)
http://www.jdbrands.com/main_ie.asp

positioning by product class
A message strategy that focuses on creating a mental association between the firm's brand and the product class. For example, 7UP soft drink is essentially a product class that subsumes a variety of noncola soft drinks.

7UP soft drink positioned itself as the logical alternative to the "colas" but with better taste. Because of the advertising campaign, 7UP became known as the "uncola." Caress hand soap positioned itself apart from other brands of soap by associating its brand with bath oil (a product that is different from soap).[9]

How is the **positioning-by-product-class** strategy operationalized? That is, what are the tactics associated with that strategy? Or, put simply, what are the mix elements used to implement the positioning-by-product-class strategy? Specifically, resources have to be allocated to do the following:

1. Conduct product research to identify the extent to which most of the target consumers are satisfied or dissatisfied with their current product. If the majority of the target consumers are dissatisfied with their current product, then the next step is to determine why and in what situations. If the majority of the target consumers are satisfied with their current product, then the marketer should determine new product opportunities. For example, if consumer research indicates that women who use moisturizers are dissatisfied with the current moisturizer products that can be used when taking a bath or shower, the marketing communications manager would position Nivea Shower and Bath as a moisturizer for use when taking a bath or shower.

2. Communicate selected situations reflecting dissatisfaction with the current product or satisfaction with the new product.

Positioning by Product Attribute

The most popular of all positioning strategies is the **positioning-by-product-attribute** strategy. Here, the marketer attempts to link certain important product features to the brand in question. See Exhibit 10-2. These product features are concrete and specific. For example, Crest toothpaste is associated with fluoride; Hewlett-Packard LaserJet printers are associated with excellent resolution on computer printouts. Advertisements for Viva paper towels emphasize the paper's absorbency.[10]

Operationalizing the positioning-by-product-attribute strategy entails that the element of the marketing mix that has to be mobilized is the product element. That is, resources have to be allocated (or reallocated) so that the marketing communications manager can do the following:

1. Conduct product research to ascertain the most effective product attribute(s). For example, in the case of a GIS sales software program, perhaps research may

positioning by product attribute A message strategy that focuses on creating a mental association between the firm's brand and an important product attribute. For example, Crest toothpaste indicates that fluoride is perceived to be an important attribute in toothpaste.

SMC QuickLink
Kleenex Viva Towels
http://www.vivatowels.com

Exhibit 10-2
Positioning by Product Attribute
Source: Reprinted by permission of Wal-Mart.

show that the visual clarity of the map is the most important feature of a sales-tracking software.

2. Work with the firm's product engineers to redesign the product to make the selected product attribute central to the product; or perhaps the marketer can display that attribute on the product itself and/or the package. For the GIS sales software, the marketer should work closely with the software-development engineers to guide them into developing the maplike visual features that are likely to be most appealing to sales managers (target consumers).

3. Communicate to the target consumers the fact that the brand has the desired product attribute. The marketing communications manager for the GIS brand has to launch a marketing communications campaign in which the visual clarity of the maps is demonstrated. All elements of the marketing communications mix work together to highlight the visual-clarity feature of the software.

Positioning by Intangible Factor

An *intangible factor* is a general attribute that serves to capture a host of important attributes.[11] In contrast to product attributes that are concrete and objective, intangible factors are abstract and subjective. For example, product quality, technological leadership, value, and so on are all intangibles. Ford had an ongoing "Quality is Job 1" advertising campaign focusing on the overall concept of "quality." Not much is said about particular car models. The marketing communications manager was trying to associate Ford automobiles with high quality across all car makes and models.

Consider the following study that demonstrated the power of an intangible attribute. Subjects were shown two camera brands; they were told that one was more technically sophisticated and the other easier to use. Furthermore, detailed information was provided to the subjects clearly showing that the easier-to-use brand had the superior technology. After a couple of days, subjects did not remember much of the detailed information; they merely relied on how the brand was presented, that is, "easier to use" versus "technically sophisticated." Although the easier-to-use brand was first recognized as technically superior, subjects identified the brand that was presented to them as "technically sophisticated" as the high-technology brand. This study shows that consumers rely on intangible attributes to store brand information in memory, not detailed specifications about the brand.[12]

The element of the marketing mix that is used to operationalize the **positioning-by-intangible-factor** strategy is the product element (see Exhibit 10-3). Resources have to be allocated toward the following tasks:

1. Conduct product research to identify the product's strengths and associated intangible factors. Take an example such as Siemens. Here, the marketer should conduct a product analysis. A thorough product analysis may reveal several strengths; perhaps one of them is found to be technological innovation, the intangible factor that can be used as a focus of a marketing communications campaign.

2. Communicate to the target consumers the fact that the brand has the intangible factor because the results of product research show that the intangible factor may play a salient role in the purchase decision. That is, the Siemens marketing communications manager would conduct a study to ascertain the importance of the intangible factor of technological innovation as a criterion in buying corporate stock. Given that technological innovation is found to be an important decision criterion for stockholders, the marketing communications manager can use this intangible factor as a basis for a marketing communications campaign.

Positioning by Competitors

Some brands are positioned in direct association with leading competitor brands. This is usually done when the leading competitor has a well-established image in the

---

SMC QuickLink
Ford
http://www.ford.com

positioning by intangible factor A message strategy that focuses on creating a mental association between the firm's brand and a general attribute that captures a host of important attributes. For example, Ford positions itself in terms of quality. Quality is an intangible factor that relies on a host of tangible factors, such as materials, construction, design, and so on.

Exhibit 10-3
Positioning by Intangible Factor
Source: General Motors Corp. Used with permission, GM Media Archives.

minds of the target consumers. Here, in the **positioning-by-competitors** strategy, a brand follower tries to capitalize on this well-established image by anchoring its brand next to the well-established brand in the minds of the target consumers (see Exhibit 10-4). Claiming better performance than the leading brand may result in consumers making positive inferences about the brand. The widely cited example of Avis—"We're number two; we try harder"—is the epitome of this positioning strategy. The message is that Hertz is the leading company in car rentals. Avis is positioned next to Hertz as a major car-rental option.[13] Another example is Aleve, the nonprescription pain reliever. Aleve tries to position itself directly against Tylenol, Advil, and Bayer.

The element of the marketing mix used to operationalize the positioning-by-competitors strategy is, again, the product element. Specifically, resources have to be allocated to do the following:

1. Conduct product research to ascertain consumers' perception of the product's strengths and weaknesses in relation to selected competitors, preferably the leading competitors. For example, the marketer of Aleve would conduct consumer research using a sample of consumers who have used Aleve, Tylenol, Advil, and Bayer. These consumers would be asked to compare Aleve to the competitors along a set of criteria. The findings may show that Aleve is perceived as longer lasting and gentler to the stomach than the three leading competitors and that

positioning by competitors
A message strategy that focuses on creating a mental association between the firm's brand and a specific attribute that the brand possesses that makes it appear superior to competitor brands. For example, Aleve, the nonprescription pain reliever, is positioned as having a longer-lasting effect than Tylenol, Advil, or Bayer.

SMC QuickLink
Alleve
http://www.aleve.com/index.cfm

Exhibit 10-4
Positioning by Competitors
Source: Reprinted by permission of Beiersdorf USA.

SMC QuickLink
Walkers Shortbread
http://www.walkersshortbread.com

positioning by country of origin A message strategy that focuses on creating a mental association between the firm's brand and a specific country that has a good reputation for making the product. For example, Walkers cookies are positioned as being made in Scotland, where this cookie recipe originated.

longer lasting and gentler to the stomach are criteria that consumers weigh heavily in their decision to buy a pain reliever.

2. Work with product engineers to correct noted product weaknesses and enhance strengths. If Aleve is found weak in relation to Tylenol, Advil, and Bayer along an important attribute, then the marketer should provide this data to the pharmaceutical engineers and R&D personnel to correct the problem.

3. Set prices likely to be perceived by target consumers as more appealing than those of competitors. Set a price for Aleve that is likely to be acceptable in light of the prices of Tylenol, Advil, and Bayer.

4. Distribute the product using the same channels as the leading brands. For example, Aleve should be distributed in drugstores and supermarkets where Tylenol, Advil, and Bayer are also found.

5. Communicate to target consumers information concerning strengths and/or information showing how weaknesses are being addressed to satisfy customers. The advertisement pertaining to Aleve shows the product's strength in relation to competitor brands.

Positioning by Country of Origin

Certain countries are known for producing certain high-quality products. For example, Japan is associated with high-quality automobiles and electronic gadgets; France is associated with high-quality perfumes and fashion; Italy is associated with high-quality shoes and leather goods; Germany is associated with high-quality beer and automobiles; Russia is associated with high-quality vodka; and so forth.

Many studies called "country-of-origin" studies have documented the effectiveness of brand positioning by certain countries.[14] However, note that consumers' reactions to imports could vary considerably. In general, people tend to rate products from industrialized countries more favorably than those from developing countries. Recent evidence suggests that country-of-origin information serves to stimulate consumers' interest in the product. Consumers, thus, do more thinking about products in which country of origin is presented and evaluate them more carefully than when country-of-origin information is not presented.[15] See Marketplace Watch 10-2.

Are you familiar with Walkers cookies? This brand of cookies is positioned using a country or geographic-region approach. The country or region in the Walkers cookies advertisement is Scotland, particularly the Scottish Highlands. People in the Scottish Highlands have been known for decades for making the finest shortbread cookies. The association with Scotland and the Scottish Highlands is made in every advertisement using a variety of creative cues, such as the picture of the package that is highly "Scottish."

The marketing mix element used to operationalize the **positioning-by-country-of-origin** strategy is, again, product. Specifically, resources have to be allocated to do the following:

1. Conduct product research to ascertain consumers' perception of product quality as a direct function of manufacturing the product in selected countries, and identify countries that are perceived to generally produce quality product. Select a set of countries for possible manufacture based on this analysis, and pass the recommendation to corporate executives for future action. In the case of Walkers cookies, market research could be done to ascertain the extent to which Walkers cookies would be perceived as high quality if consumers knew that the recipe is a long-cherished Scottish tradition.

2. If the product is then manufactured in countries to which target consumers attribute product quality, then the marketer should communicate to target consumers the fact that the product is manufactured in the designated country. The example of Walkers cookies advertising illustrates how a message that is grounded in a country-of-origin position can be created in print advertising.

SMC Marketplace Watch 10-2

Positioning "Proud to Be American"

Source: © 2006 JupiterImages Corporation.

According to a recent Gallup poll (conducted in June 2002), 65 percent of respondents say that they are "extremely" proud to be American, up from 55 percent in January 2001. This rise of American patriotism has caused marketers to take advantage of this sentiment in their marketing efforts. For example, Sears Portrait Studios introduced a new line of patriotic greeting cards and backgrounds at its one thousand stores nationwide. General Motors launched the "Let's Keep America Rolling" campaign immediately after 9/11.

However, consumers are not responding favorably to businesses using patriotic messages, signs, and emblems. According to recent polls conducted by *American Demographics*/Ipsos Reid polls (conducted in two waves—in 2001 and 2002), most consumers do not endorse the notion that business should focus on contributing to the nation's patriotic spirit through advertising. *American Demographics* (http://www.demographics.com) reporter Alison Stein Wellner asks, "If personal levels of patriotism gained strength over the past year, why wasn't there a parallel increase in support for businesses that affiliate themselves with patriotic word and deed?" Three probable explanations follow. The first explanation may be that Americans' patriotic sentiment has shot up as a direct function of 9/11 and then came back to "normal." The second explanation is the backlash Americans may feel about perceived infringements of civil freedoms. The third explanation is that consumers are becoming numb to flag waving because so many companies have taken advantage of it.

The same surveys also show that women are more likely to be patriotic than men; older people are more patriotic than young people; and retired and less-educated people are the most likely to be influenced by patriotic advertisements. People who are unemployed are also more likely to support patriotic spirit in advertising.

Patriotism also plays an important role in the "buy American products" campaigns. Data from 2002 *American Demographics*/Ipsos Reid polls show that 69 percent of the respondents say that companies should focus on making it clear that their products are "made in America," up from 64 percent in 2001. However, a much smaller share of consumers—around 7 percent—make purchases based on the belief that the product is "made in the U.S.A." This result comes from an online survey of one thousand American adults conducted in May 2002 by Euro RSCG.

These results affirm the fact that consumers' purchase decisions are multifaceted and driven by many factors, one being "made in the U.S.A." Marketers should be able to better understand how this decision criterion interacts with other decision criteria in affecting purchase decisions of their target consumers.

Source: Adapted from Alison Stein Wellner, "The Perils of Patriotism," *American Demographics* (September 2002): 49–51.

3. Positioning by country of origin may be used when the marketing communications manager has little concrete evidence to claim high quality for his or her product. For example, if the marketing communications manager has more substantial evidence of quality, such as quality ratings by *Consumer Reports*, he or she should use that evidence. Only in the absence of such evidence should the country-of-origin cue be used as a symbol for quality.

10-2b Strategic Price Focus and Corresponding Strategies and Tactics

Positioning efforts reflecting a strategic price focus involve two key strategies, namely, positioning by relative price and positioning by low price (see Table 10-2).

positioning by relative price
A message strategy that focuses on creating a mental association between the firm's brand and quality based on price. For example, the Mercedes automobile is positioned as a luxury car and therefore highly priced. The high price communicates luxury and quality.

SMC QuickLink
Motel 6
http://www.motel6.com

Positioning by Relative Price

Positioning by relative price refers to a brand being positioned in terms of its price relative to the price of other product brands. Many products have brands that are perceived along a price/quality hierarchy with certain brands of lower price/quality, others with mid-range price/quality, and still others of higher price/quality. Consider how hotels/motels are perceived in the minds of many consumers. The budget hotels/motels (low price/quality) may include hotels/motels such as Motel 6, Econolodge, McSleep, Days Inn, Hampton Inn, and Comfort Inn. Mid-range hotels/motels may include Courtyard, Ramada, and Holiday Inn. Luxury ones may include the Marriott, Renaissance, Clarion, Hyatt Regency, Westin Hotels, Embassy Suites, and so on.[16]

Marketing communications managers choose to position their product at the higher end of the price dimension to connote high quality. For example, the advertisement for Jaguar's XJ Super V8 in Exhibit 10-5 illustrates the positioning-by-relative-price strategy. By using such descriptives as "burl walnut," "lambswool rugs," and "stunning performance," Jaguar is establishing that its car is highly priced and of high quality.

The major marketing element that is deployed to carry out relative-price positioning is price. Specifically, resources have to be allocated to do the following:

1. Conduct research to ascertain if price is associated with quality. Consider the example of Jaguar's XJ Super V8. Are business executives more likely to perceive the XJ Super V8 as being a high-quality sedan if it is labeled as a luxury car and priced at a level comparable to other luxury sedans? If so, follow Steps 2 and 3.
2. Set a price level that would be associated with the desirable level of quality.
3. Communicate to the target consumers the price level and corresponding quality.

Positioning by Low Price

In contrast to positioning by relative price, many marketers utilize **positioning by low price.** Entire marketing communications campaigns are designed around price reductions and promotional deals. Consumers react to price reductions and promotional deals as a direct function of motivations.[17] The first motivation is related to stockpiling. Some customers who are committed to the brand may decide to take advantage of the price discount and stockpile. The second motivation is to receive an incentive for switching brands. Finally, experimentation may be a motive. Consumers

positioning by low price
A message strategy that focuses on creating a mental association between the firm's brand and a lower price than products of most or certain other competitors. For example, Wal-Mart is positioned as a low-price discount store.

Cosmetics and Brand Switching
Many consumers using cosmetic products such as lipstick tend to switch from one brand to another. Switching behavior can be easily induced by price reductions and discounts.
Source: © 2006 JupiterImages Corporation.

Exhibit 10-5
Positioning by Relative Price
Source: Reprinted by permission of Aston Martin Jaguar Land Rover North America.

who have not yet consumed the product category may decide to try the product by buying the brand with the reduced price. This is a way to reduce their risk in the product. If they do not like the product, they would not feel too bad because they have not invested too much money buying it. Consider the example of HealthMax, a treadmill brand. This brand is promoted using the positioning-by-low-price strategy. The advertisement shows that the HealthMax is significantly lower in price than the NordicTrack treadmill.

The major element of the marketing mix that is deployed to carry out the positioning-by-low-price strategy is price (see Exhibit 10-6). Specifically, resources have to be allocated to do the following:

1. Conduct pricing research to ascertain the price level that would set the firm's brand apart from competitor brands and would be perceived as a bargain by most of the target consumers. Using the HealthMax treadmill example, the question becomes, At what level below the price of the NordicTrack treadmill will the perception of a bargain be created? A $50 differential? A $100 differential? A $200 differential? A $300 differential? A $400 differential? A $500 differential? Research may show that the perception of a bargain can be established somewhere between a $300 and a $400 differential.

2. Set a price level that would be associated with the desirable level of value to be perceived as a bargain. The example of the HealthMax treadmill shows a price of $299. This price level may create the perception of value relative to the price of $669 of the NordicTrack treadmill.

3. Communicate to the target consumers the price level and corresponding value. The typical advertisement about the HealthMax treadmill shows women who exercise regularly at home and may be thinking of buying a treadmill. They can save $370 by buying the HealthMax treadmill instead of the NordicTrack treadmill.

SMC QuickLink
HealthMax Pro
http://healthfxamerica.com

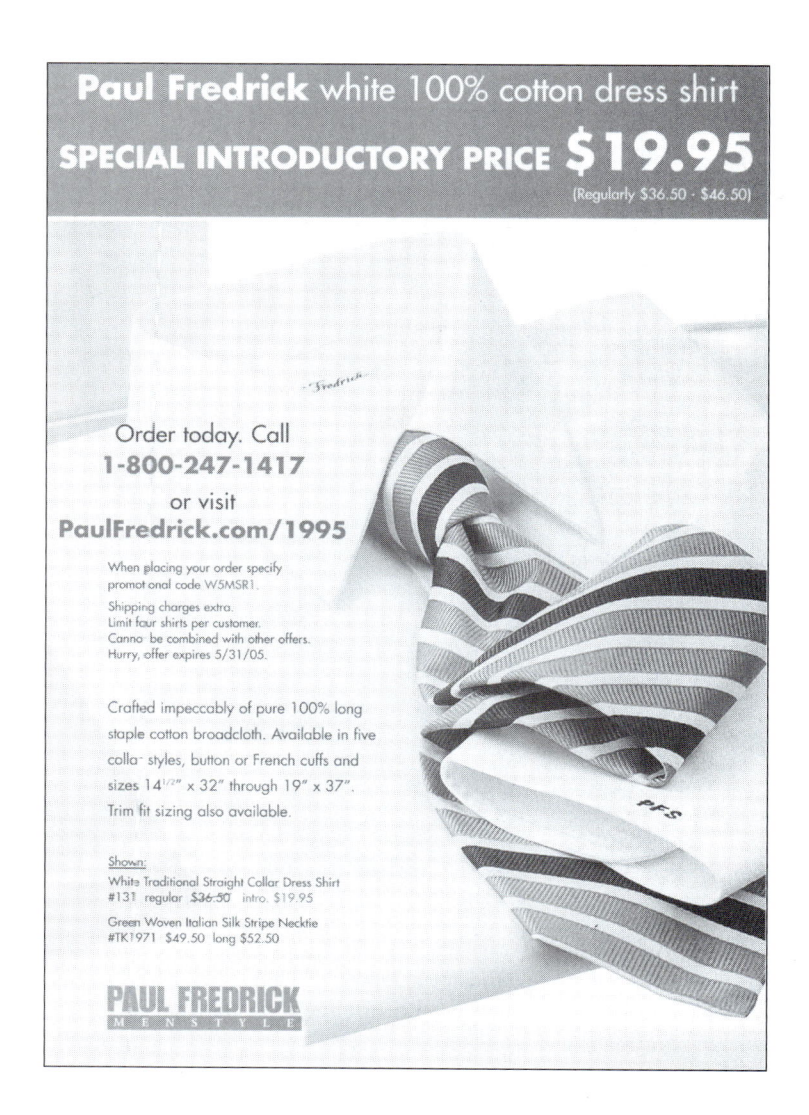

Exhibit 10-6

Positioning by Low Price

Source: Reprinted by permission of Paul Fredrick Menstyle, 2005, www.paulfredrick.com.

positioning by brand-distributor tie-in A message strategy that focuses on creating a mental association between the firm's brand and a credible and reputable distributor, or vice versa. For example, Sears advertises heavily the fact that it carries Kenmore appliances. Both Sears and Kenmore appliances benefit from this tie-in.

SMC QuickLink

Sears
http://www.sears.com

10-2c Strategic Place Focus

Strategic place focus is typically translated in terms of three positioning strategies: (1) positioning by brand-distributor tie-in, (2) positioning by distributor location, and (3) positioning by distributor's serviceability (see Table 10-2).

Positioning by Brand-Distributor Tie-In

The **positioning-by-brand-distributor-tie-in** strategy asserts that marketing success is likely to be assured by creating a brand association with a credible and reputable distributor (see Exhibit 10-7). For example, Sears has a very strong reputation in kitchen and laundry appliances with its Kenmore brand. A new manufacturer of washing machines may strike a deal with Sears to carry its product line. Based on this deal, the new washing machine can be effectively positioned by associating it with Sears. The reverse situation is also commonplace. That is, distributors attempt to create tie-ins with credible and reputable manufacturers. Sears now carries a wide variety of major brands in most of its product categories. Sears has also purchased the Lands' End brand to bolster its overall position in the market. Here we have a reverse situation in which the "distributor" uses a credible and reputable "manufacturer" to position itself effectively.

The way to implement this positioning strategy is as follows:

1. If you are a manufacturer, conduct research to identify all possible distributors. You should then contact these distributors and ascertain the possibility of doing business with them and select a set of distributors that have better offers. If you

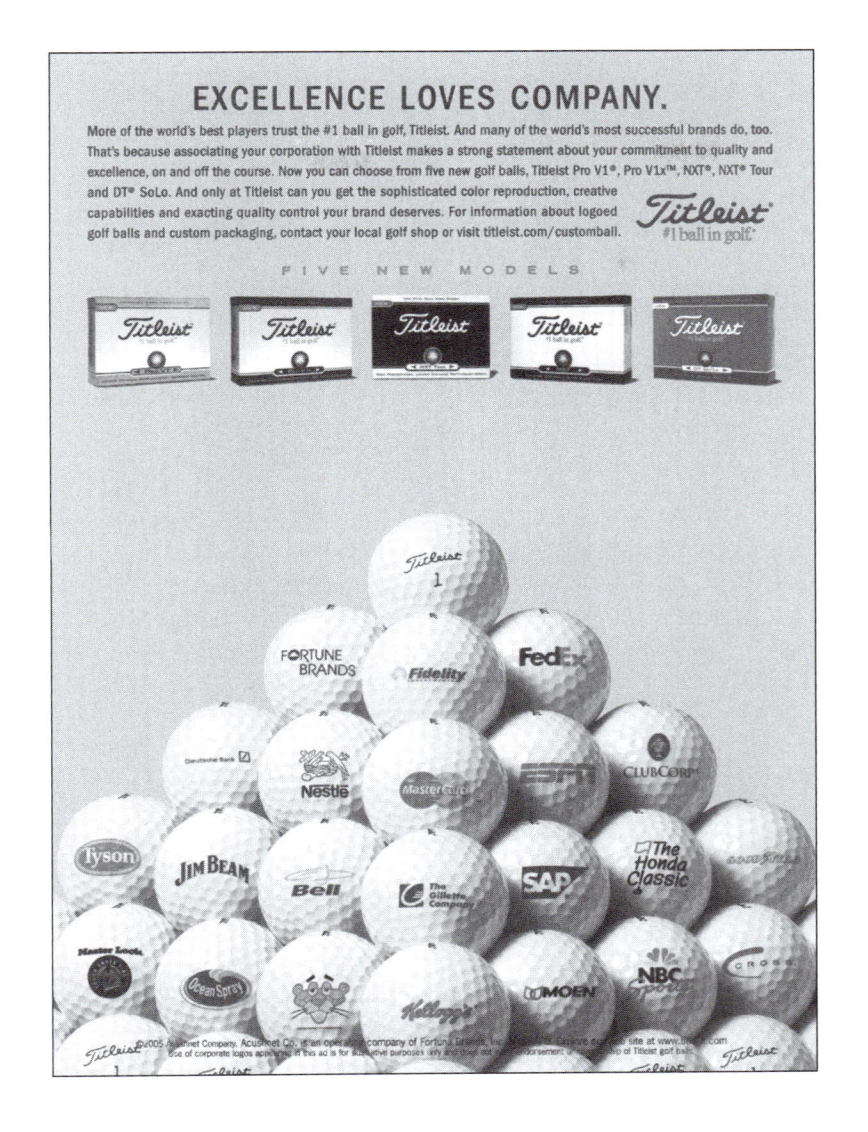

Exhibit 10-7
Positioning by Brand-Distributor Tie-in
Source: © 2004 Acushnet Company. Reprinted with permission.

are a distributor, do the reverse; conduct research to identify all possible manufacturers whose products you may want to distribute; and so on.

2. Now focus on this set of optional distributors or manufacturers. Administer a consumer survey to measure the image favorableness of each distributor or manufacturer. If these distributors are retail outlets, consult the retailing literature about store image and how measures of store image can help you select the distributor having the most favorable image in the minds of the ultimate consumers. If these are manufacturers, then tap into the measurement literature concerning corporate image. Of course, before attempting to conduct your own study, see if past studies have been conducted regarding the alternative distributors or manufacturers. Most large distributors and manufacturers conduct their own image surveys, and they can provide you with this information without you having to gather it yourself.

3. Based on the image research, select a distributor or manufacturer with the most favorable image and create the tie-in with that distributor or manufacturer.

4. Develop a communications message to target consumers emphasizing and highlighting the brand-distributor tie-in.

Positioning by Distributor Location

The **positioning-by-distributor-location** strategy posits that location, location, location is a very important decision criterion in purchase (see Exhibit 10-8).

positioning by distributor location A message strategy that focuses on creating a mental association between the firm's brand and easy access to the product through specific channels and retail outlets. For example, many companies are advertising their home pages to allow target consumers to access their products and services directly and more conveniently.

Exhibit 10-8

Positioning by Distributor Location

Source: Used with permission of Eastman Kodak Company.

SMC QuickLink

Chick-fil-A
http://www.chickfila.com/home.asp

Therefore, showing consumers how to access the product in the most convenient way is likely to improve marketing performance. For example, the marketing success of most fast-food restaurants and motels is based on location. Similarly, location is significant for hospitals and health clinics. Where they erect their establishments is likely to make a big difference in terms of corporate goals such as sales, market share, profit, and cash flow.

Chick-fil-A positioned itself initially as only being in malls. As it grew in reputation and performance, it was able to move to free-standing retail outlets; but it still positions itself either in or near major shopping venues.

To implement this positioning strategy, we recommend the following tasks:

1. First find out how your product (product class or related products) is usually distributed. Is it traditionally distributed through a direct channel? If so, what form of direct channel (e.g., teleshopping, electronic shopping)? Is it traditionally distributed through indirect channels? If so, through what kind of retailers? Where are these retailers housed—a shopping mall, shopping plaza, configuration of stores next to the entrance/exit of a major highway, or so forth?

2. Conduct research to ascertain the shopping habits of the target market in relation to the product in question. Do the consumers mostly use a direct or an indirect channel? If a direct channel, then what form of direct channel is most convenient for them? If they are out shopping, do they usually go to the nearest shopping plaza, nearest shopping mall, or elsewhere? If the product is new and

there are no comparable products on the market, then consumers can be asked to evaluate the convenience of different methods of access to the product.
3. Based on this research, select a distributor based on location and convenience to the target consumers.
4. Inform target consumers how to access the product, and stress the convenience of the distribution access.

Positioning by Distributor's Serviceability

The **positioning-by-distributor's-serviceability** strategy focuses on providing customer service at the distributor level (see Exhibit 10-9). The strength of a manufacturing firm may lie in providing excellent customer service through its dealership network. Many department stores tend to position themselves as providing excellent customer service. The Acura automobile is positioned on customer service and satisfaction. The focus is to serve the customer the best way possible at the retail level. Most product manufacturers that realize the importance of distributor's serviceability to customers have their own channel of distribution. Take the example of Brooks Brothers (upscale, conservative menswear). Products are distributed solely through Brooks Brothers' own retailers. Salespeople serve as fashion advisors rather than sales personnel. They build first-name relationships with lifelong customers. This is ideal

positioning by distributor's serviceability A message strategy that focuses on creating a mental association between the firm's brand and how well it can be delivered through specific channels and retail outlets. For example, many banks have positioned themselves on customer service.

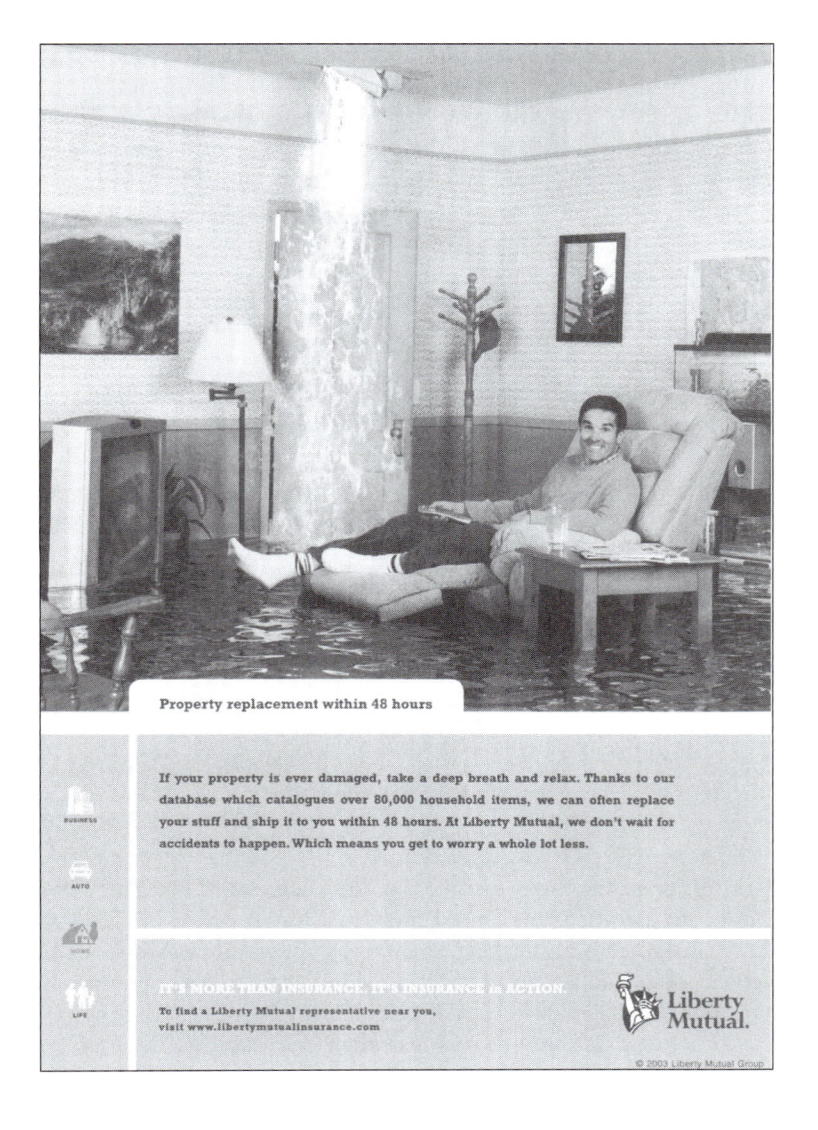

Exhibit 10-9
Positioning by Distributor's Serviceability
Source: Reprinted by permission of Liberty Mutual.

SMC QuickLink
Wachovia
http://www.wachovia.com

customer service.[18] Another example is Wachovia, one of the largest U.S. banking and financial services companies. It positions itself on service and focuses a great deal on its internal training programs in maintaining that high level of service.

How can this positioning strategy be effectively implemented? The following tasks are recommended:

1. Conduct a consumer survey of the target market to determine the relative importance of distributor's serviceability as a purchase and/or repeat-purchase criterion.
2. Given that the distributor's serviceability is found to be a very important criterion, study different ideal customer service programs housed at the retail level. Then select the program that best matches the requirements and conditions of your distributors.
3. Collaborate with the managers of the distribution outlets to set up the selected customer service program.
4. Communicate to target consumers the message that customers are entitled to the best service possible and that the distributors can best serve their needs.

10-2d Strategic Prospects Focus

Once a market segment is selected, the marketer can communicate to this segment *directly* using those marketing communications tools that can precisely target consumers in the market segment or *indirectly* through messages that are designed to speak to them, or both. The *direct* method involves selecting the marketing communications tools that have the best *reach*. For example, a direct mailing to restaurant managers obtained from a mailing-list house is likely to serve the targeting goal. However, suppose that no such lists exist and the target segment cannot be effectively reached through specific communications media. What then? In this situation, marketers typically devise communications messages that can appeal to the target consumers. For example, airing a television commercial about Ensure (nutritional drink considered as a meal substitute) on the *CBS Evening News* is likely to reach a huge audience. Part of the audience includes elderly consumers who constitute the target market for Ensure. The advertisement is designed so that elderly consumers can identify with it and realize that the commercial is "speaking" to them.

We also can talk about these message strategies in terms of positioning—as we have done in discussing differentiation. The focus is on the customer, *not* the product, price, distribution, or marketing communications. There are at least five positioning strategies here (see Table 10-2):

- Positioning by customer benefit or problem
- Positioning by user or customer image
- Positioning by use or application
- Positioning by celebrity or spokesperson
- Positioning by lifestyle or personality

Positioning by Customer Benefit or Problem

Consumer researchers distinguish between *attributes* and *benefits*. An advertising campaign can focus on one or more attributes, or it can focus on one or more benefits. **Customer benefits,** like intangible factors, are product features that can be characterized as abstract and subjective. However, in contrast to intangible factors, these product features can be easily described in terms of how the product is used by the customer and its value to the customer (see Exhibit 10-10).

customer benefits Brand attributes or features perceived by the customer as important and desirable aspects they like to have in a product.

Exhibit 10-10
Positioning by Customer Benefit or Problem
Source: Reprinted by permission of The Procter & Gamble Company.

Consider the example of an advertising campaign for a brand of shampoo that has natural protein. The marketer can translate the natural protein into customer benefits such as "It is safe to use every day" and "It is exciting and sexy." A computer with a touch-screen-entry feature (attribute) can be advertised as "easy to use" (customer benefit).[19] Have you seen the advertisement for Claussen Pickles? The product is positioned by a customer benefit, namely, a "crunchier pickle."

Similarly, an advertising campaign can appeal to certain customers having certain *problems*. For example, a financial institution wants to target business entrepreneurs who may have wonderful business ideas but cannot get any bank to lend them money to operationalize their ideas and start a business. Most banks shy away from risky investments, especially investments by entrepreneurs without collateral. Thus, the financial institution may place an advertisement in the local newspaper in the business section with a headline that reads, "If You Can't Get Your Bank to Finance a Business Venture, Then You Should Check Us Out." The financial institution may also have a web presence that comes up on searches for people looking for small business help.

How can this **positioning-by-customer-benefit-or-problem** strategy be carried out in the most effective way possible? Resources are allocated to perform the following tasks:

1. Conduct customer research to ascertain customer benefits or problems commonly perceived in relation to the product and product purchase. For example,

SMC QuickLink

Find-the-Right-Loan.com
http://www.find-the-right-loan.com

positioning by customer benefit or problem
A message strategy that focuses on creating a mental association between the firm's brand and a specific customer benefit or problem. For example, Claussen Pickles is positioned as having a crunchier pickle. Consumers perceive crunchiness as a significant benefit.

the marketing communications manager of Claussen Pickles would conduct a study to ascertain important customer benefits that pickle eaters seek in a good brand of pickles. The research may show that "crunchier pickles" is an important benefit sought by a sizable part of the pickle-eater market.

2. Work with the product, price, and/or distribution personnel and functions to enhance product attributes that are directly related to the customer benefits (or problem). That is, the marketing communications manager at Claussen should work with the engineers and manufacturing people to ensure the production of a "crunchier pickle." He or she has to price Claussen Pickles in a way that ensures the connotation of quality—crunchier than other brands of pickles. Perhaps a premium price may be consistent with this customer benefit. The manager has to ensure that the pickles are distributed in a manner to preserve the "crunchier" texture. Timing is essential in distribution to ensure freshness and, of course, "crunchiness."

3. Communicate to the target customers the most important customer benefits related to the product (or the way the product solves an important customer problem). In the case of Claussen Pickles, the marketing communications campaign has to focus on "crunchier pickles." The message should be placed in media vehicles that can reach most pickle eaters.

Positioning by Use or Application

Positioning by use or application can also be effective. In this positioning strategy, the focus is on the way the consumer uses the product or on the situation in which the consumer uses the product (see Exhibit 10-11). One study discovered nine use contexts for coffee[20] (1) to start the day, (2) between meals alone, (3) between meals with others, (4) with lunch, (5) with supper, (6) at dinner with guests, (7) in the evening, (8) to keep awake in the evening, and (9) on weekends. A marketer may decide to associate his or her brand of coffee with the most popular use or application. Campbell's Soup has been positioned as a lunchtime product; Gatorade is positioned for athletes, particularly in the summer months. Do you remember seeing the Coppertone advertisement? Coppertone is a brand of sunblock and tanning lotion. The advertisement shows a woman relaxing on the beach. The association is to use Coppertone sunblock and tanning lotion when being out in the sun at the beach for a long time.

The positioning-by-use-or-application strategy can be implemented as follows:

1. Conduct customer research to identify how the target consumers use (or can use) the product, and determine which uses or applications are most appealing or significant to the customers. For a Coppertone campaign, research may discover that many situations are equally appealing, including lying out at the beach; lying out at the swimming pool; and playing outdoor activities such as tennis, running, bicycling, sailing, canoeing, and fishing. Suppose that based on this customer research, the marketing communications manager selects *at the beach, at the swimming pool,* and *playing tennis.*

2. Work closely with the product engineers to redesign the product to make it highly conducive to one or more sets of applications that are highly appealing or significant to target customers. Suppose the marketer of Coppertone selects the beach situation. He or she would need to work closely with the product engineers to ensure that the sunblock and tanning lotion can be used in the best way possible at the beach. For example, users of Coppertone at the beach may get sandy. How does the lotion feel with sand on the body? If there is a feeling of discomfort, then can the lotion be redesigned to solve this problem? How does the lotion interact with sea breezes? Do sea breezes take away from the sunblock's durability? If so, then can the sunblock be redesigned to make it more durable given the normal sea breeze conditions? Similar questions have to be raised and addressed in relation to the swimming pool and playing tennis situations.

---

positioning by use or application A message strategy that focuses on creating a mental association between the firm's brand and a specific use of the product. For example, a brand of coffee can be positioned as highly suitable for a social get-together. Another brand may be positioned as most suitable to help people wake up and get going in the morning. Another brand may be positioned as most suitable for after meals, especially dinners.

SMC QuickLink
Coppertone
http://www.coppertone.com

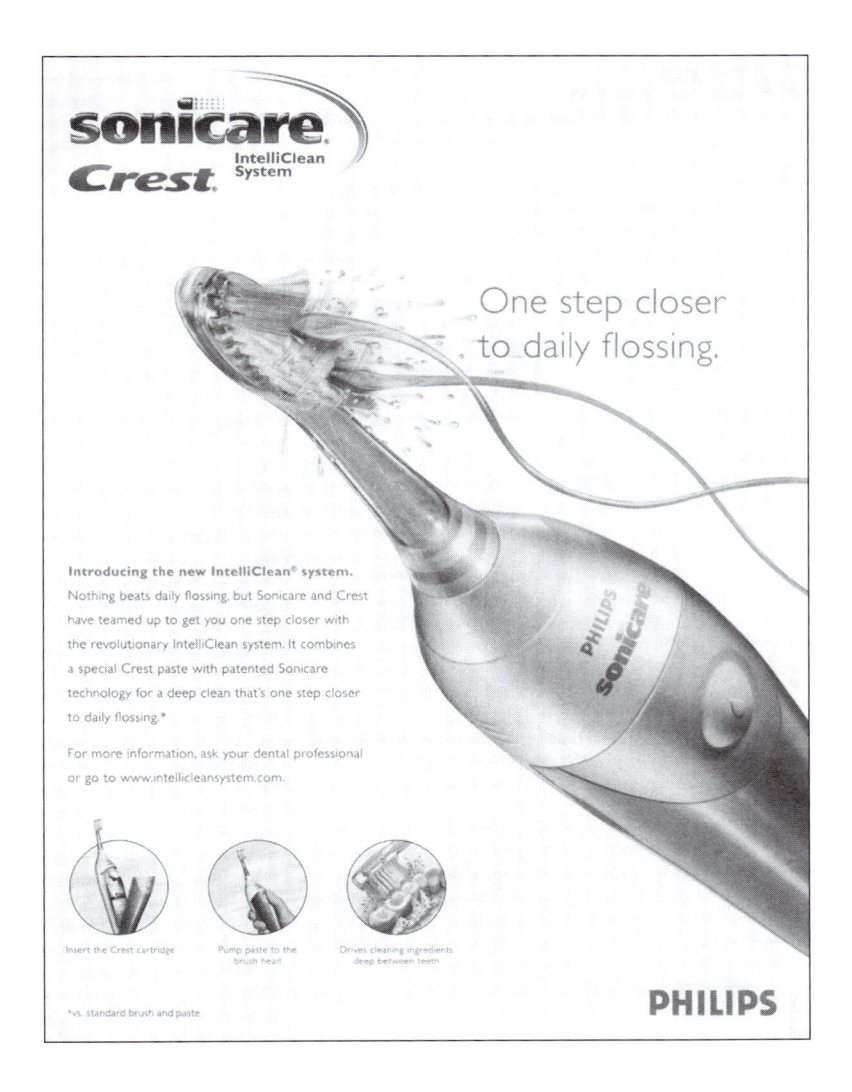

Exhibit 10-11
Positioning by Use or Application
Source: Reprinted by permission of The Procter & Gamble Company.

3. Communicate to the target customers select uses or possible applications that customers are likely to find most appealing. The Coppertone advertisement shows the use of the product at the beach. Also, suppose that Coppertone shows other advertisements reflecting the swimming pool and playing tennis situations. Therefore, the entire marketing communications campaign would involve showing the use of Coppertone sunblock and tanning lotion in three different situations—relaxing at the beach, lying out at the swimming pool, and playing tennis.

Positioning by User or Customer Image

Another effective brand-association strategy is **positioning by user or customer image.** Here the marketer associates the brand with a particular kind of person, the kind of person who typically uses the product (see Exhibit 10-12). For example, Nike traditionally associates its shoes with the serious athlete. CoverGirl (cosmetics) is associated with wholesome, healthy, young, and very attractive women. Canada Dry has positioned itself for adults, leaving Coca-Cola and Pepsi for the children's market.[21]

Think of any Nike advertisements you have seen lately (those directed to women). A typical advertisement shows an athletic-looking woman who describes herself as a "hedonist." She wants to have a good time. She wants to feel "pumped up" and "aching all over." The advertisement is designed to appeal to adult women who enjoy working out and feeling strong.

SMC QuickLink
Canada Dry
http://www.canadadry.com

positioning by user or customer image A message strategy that focuses on creating a mental association between the firm's brand and a type of product user or customer image. For example, Nike shoes are positioned for the serious athlete. The message is that if you are a serious athlete, then Nike shoes are made for you.

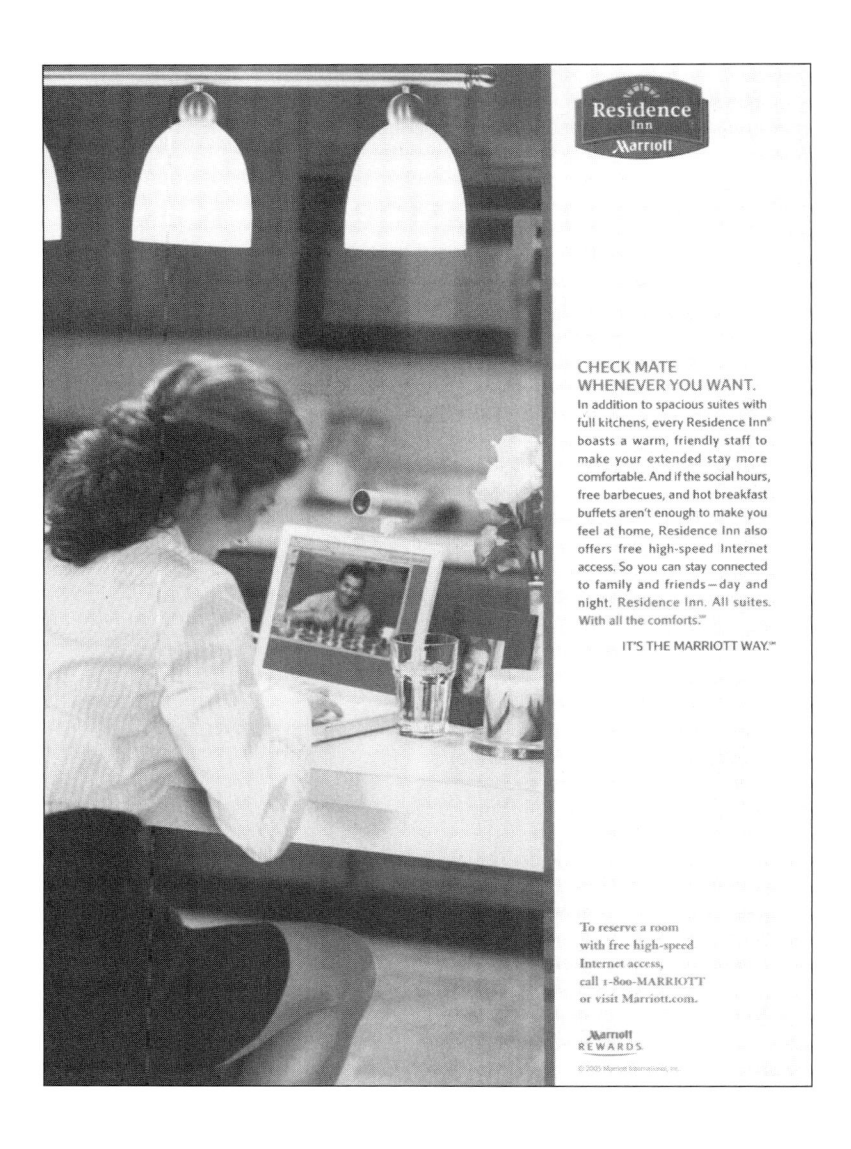

Exhibit 10-12
Positioning by User or Customer Image
Source: Provided by Marriott International, Inc.

The positioning-by-user-or-customer-image strategy can be implemented as follows:

1. Conduct customer research to identify user images associated with the product and determine which *user* images are most congruent with customers' self-concept (actual self, ideal self, social self, and/or ideal social self). Select a user image that is most congruent with target customers' self-concept. Determine which product accessories, price level, channels of distribution or retail outlets, and media categories and vehicles are associated with the selected user image. Let us use Nike shoes as an example. The Nike marketing communications manager determines how a *typical woman who likes to work out* sees herself, how she would like to see herself, how she thinks others see her, and how she would like others to see her. It may be that this woman that Nike is trying to appeal to sees herself as the kind of person who loves to work out; she loves to feel pumped up and aching after a good workout. She sees herself that way (her actual self-image); she thinks other people see her that way (her social self-image); she likes herself that way (her ideal self-image); and she likes knowing that others see her in the same light (her ideal social self-image). The Nike customer research may show several things: that special aerobic shoes with special aerobic outfits appeal most to this target segment; that this segment is willing to pay a moderate-to-premium price for a good pair of athletic shoes and sport outfits; that this segment shops for athletic shoes and outfits

in sporting goods stores and specialty outlet stores; that this segment reads magazines such as the *New Woman, Redbook,* and *McCall's;* and that this segment does not watch much television but listens to soft rock and country music on the radio.

2. Work closely with the product engineers to modify the product with accessories that are symbolic of the selected user image. For example, the Nike manager would guide the shoe designers and apparel designers to select those designs that are most appealing to the target segment, based on customers' self-concept.

3. Set a price consistent with the user image. For example, the Nike manager would price the athletic shoes and apparel at moderate and premium prices because these price levels may be most appealing to the target customers.

4. Distribute the product through channels and outlets that are associated with the selected user image. The Nike manager may place the aerobic shoes and apparel in sporting goods stores and Nike outlet stores because these stores are used most often by the target customers.

5. Develop messages with sources (spokespersons, models, characters, celebrities, etc.) that reinforce the selected user image, and place these messages in media categories and vehicles that are also associated with the user image. The Nike manager would develop advertisements and place them in media vehicles such as *New Woman* magazine.

Positioning by Celebrity or Spokesperson

In the **positioning-by-celebrity-or-spokesperson** strategy, a brand is associated with a celebrity (see Exhibit 10-13). Certain celebrities are perceived by the public as having certain personalities. Some consumers may idealize these celebrities. That is, celebrities are their role models. Consumers idealize to become these celebrities. This idealization helps establish an emotional connection between the brand image and those consumers who idealize the celebrity spokesperson. The marketer can benefit from the celebrity's personality and the cognitive and emotional responses the celebrity may elicit from the public. Marketing communications managers want some positive responses to "spill over" to the brand.

For example, when Nike developed the "pump" basketball shoes called Air Jordans (basketball shoes having a cushioning feature as pressurized-gas pockets in the soles), they used Michael Jordan (basketball celebrity). This brand was a smash success, and its success was directly attributable to the association with Michael Jordan.[22] Perhaps people felt that they could jump as high as Jordan. Perhaps the brand association was in relation to Jordan's personality as happy and friendly. Now, even a couple of years after his second retirement from the NBA, Jordan's celebrity draws consumers to new Nike brands.

To implement the positioning-by-celebrity-or-spokesperson strategy, resources have to be allocated to do the following:

1. Conduct marketing communications research to identify celebrities or spokespersons that have images matching the product and the self-concept of target consumers. Determine which media categories and vehicles are associated with the selected celebrity or spokesperson image. Consider Wendy's advertising using Dave as a spokesperson. It is possible that the image of the president of Wendy's is a humorous fatherly figure that cares about good and tasty traditional food (hamburgers made the old-fashioned way). People who prefer Wendy's may be old-fashioned, "meat-and-potato" kinds of people. Wendy's has the image of an old-fashioned hamburger joint. The image of Wendy's, the spokesperson, and Wendy's customers match, making this positioning strategy very effective.

2. Develop messages with selected celebrities or spokespersons, and place these messages in media categories and vehicles that are associated with the celebrities' or spokespersons' image. The Wendy's advertisement placed in traditional

positioning by celebrity or spokesperson A message strategy that focuses on creating a mental association between the firm's brand and a specific celebrity or spokesperson. For example, Wendy's fast-food restaurant is positioned through Wendy's father, Dave Thomas, the president of Wendy's. People associate Wendy's with this spokesperson.

SMC QuickLink
Jumpman23.com: Jordan XX
http://www.nike.com/jumpman23/home/index.jsp

Exhibit 10-13

Positioning by Celebrity or Spokesperson—Meredith Vieira

Source: Reprinted by permission of Lowe Worldwide, Inc., as agent for National Fluid Milk Processor Promotion Board.

positioning by lifestyle or personality A message strategy that focuses on a personal characteristic that consumers can relate to based on personality or lifestyle. For example, a food manufacturer marketing bakery items may focus on a personality symbol such as the "dough boy."

SMC QuickLink
Mountain Dew
http://www.mountaindew.com

women's magazines such as *Ladies' Home Journal* is a good example of how marketing communications can be guided effectively by this positioning strategy.

Positioning by Lifestyle or Personality

Over time, brands develop their own "personality." Consider the Betty Crocker personality. Research has shown that most women perceive Betty Crocker brands as honest, dependable, friendly, concerned about consumers, experts in baked goods, old, and traditional. Research also has shown that Coca-Cola has a strong, all-American, all-around image—family and flag and rural America. Pepsi, on the other hand, has a personality of being exciting, innovative, fast growing, and somewhat brash and pushy.[23] The Mountain Dew brand is an example of a soft-drink brand that has remained strong to the lifestyle approach. Even in its old persona of the "Hillbilly Drink," it instantly brought out the image of lifestyle. When Mel Torme exhorted young thrill seekers to "Do the Dew," the transformation to a youthful and rebellious lifestyle positioning began. That **positioning by lifestyle or personality** still holds today, as evidenced by Mountain Dew's connection with a variety of sponsored events built around the youthful and rebellious lifestyle.

The personality symbol used in these advertisements is of that lifestyle, and it is used consistently in all forms of marketing communications. "Skater boys" rule in the world of Mountain Dew. These kinds of advertisements reflect a positioning strategy based on lifestyle or personality. Consumers who can identify with this particular personality or lifestyle would find Mountain Dew very appealing and are very likely to adopt this brand over others.

To implement the positioning-by-lifestyle-or-personality strategy, marketers have to allocate resources to do the following:

1. Conduct marketing communications research to identify lifestyles or personalities that have desired images that can be injected into the product to establish a unique identity for the product. Select the most effective lifestyle or personality. Determine which media categories and vehicles are associated with the selected lifestyle or personality. How do marketing communications managers select lifestyle or personality symbols for their products? For example, how was the CoverGirl personality established? Such product personalities usually occur by focusing on an icon or symbol having certain cultural connotations that can be "injected" into the product. The CoverGirl symbol is seen as the epitome of youth, good looks, and a "flaunty" personality. This lifestyle personality of CoverGirl makeup is selected as a direct function of what may appeal to the target consumers. CoverGirl makeup appeals to young women who cherish good looks because CoverGirl advertising idealizes models as glamorous women who are admired by society.

2. Develop messages with the selected lifestyle or personality and place these messages in media categories and vehicles that are associated with the same lifestyle or personality symbols.

10-3 The Use of Situation Analysis for Marketing Strategy Selection

Like corporate analysis and planning, marketing analysis and planning have to be discussed in relation to marketing strategy selection. In this chapter, we have identified and discussed fifteen positioning strategies. These were classified under four key strategies (strategic product focus, strategic price focus, strategic place focus, and strategic prospects focus). Under strategic product focus, the positioning strategies include positioning by: product attribute, intangible factor, product class, competitors, and country of origin. The strategic price focus involves positioning by relative price and positioning by low price. The strategic place focus involves positioning by brand-distributor tie-in, distributor location, and distributor's serviceability. Finally strategic prospects focus involves positioning by customer benefits, user/customer, use/application, celebrity/person, and lifestyle/personality.

Strategic analysis is conducted to help the marketing communications manager determine the best marketing strategy for the situation at hand. In this section, we discuss conditions under which each marketing strategy is thought to be most effective. Analysis is therefore required to ascertain these conditions and select the most effective strategy. The factors involved in this analysis can be categorized into three major groups: consumer-related factors, product-related factors, and market-related factors (see Table 10-4).

10-3a Consumer-Related Factors

Consumer decision making is one of the most important factors marketers consider in marketing strategy selection. Understanding which decision criteria consumers are likely to use guides strategy selection. For example, *positioning by product attribute* should be used when consumers make buying decisions using one or more product attributes. Thus, the purchase of mineral water may be based on certain decision criteria. Examples of decision criteria are whether an alternative brand has attributes such as "in-between color," "nonalcoholic," and "not too sweet, less sugar." In other words, consumer analysis has to be conducted to find out the extent to which consumers

consumer decision making This concept refers to the process and outcome associated with brand selection, choice, and purchase.

TABLE 10-4 Analysis to Select Marketing Strategy

Consumer-Related Factors
- Consumer decision making
- Price consciousness
- Consumer experience
- Consumer involvement
- Customer or brand loyalty
- Product users versus nonusers

Product-Related Factors
- Product functionality versus value-expressiveness
- Country of origin
- Price-quality relationship
- Brand symbols

Market-Related Factors
- Competition
- Product life cycle
- Reputation of the distributor
- Product differentiation
- Variations in quality perceptions

regard product attributes as important and how they use these attributes in their purchase decision making.

Positioning by use or application is commonly used when consumers make purchase decisions based on the product use or application in specific contexts. For example, some consumers decide to buy a PC because they need to use it at home, at school, and at work. *Positioning by distributor location* is commonly used when consumers feel that the convenience of the distribution outlet and product access are very important criteria in purchase decisions. For example, a consumer survey indicates that the decision to patronize a fast-food restaurant such as Subway is determined not only by the restaurant's "good food" but also by the convenient access to Subway restaurants. Based on this finding, many of the Subway franchises are located inside convenience stores.

The same can be said in relation to all other marketing strategies. Each positioning approach is based on the assumption that consumers use a decision criterion to guide purchase decisions. If consumers' decision making was to be dominated by the use of product attributes, then *positioning by product attribute* should be used as the marketing strategy; similarly, if consumers' decision making was to be dominated by an intangible factor, then the *positioning by intangible factor* should be used; and so on.

Price consciousness is another consumer-related factor that marketing communications managers should consider in selecting a positioning approach. Price consciousness refers to the extent to which consumers use price to make purchase decisions. Sometime marketers talk about price elasticity of demand to mean price consciousness. Specifically, *price elasticity of demand* is a term used more by economists than by marketers, and it denotes the extent to which market demand is responsive to changes in price.

Positioning by low price is based on the fact that targeted consumers are likely to be price conscious. If so, they are likely to purchase the brand. This strategy works best when a significant segment of the target market is price or deal conscious. That is, the strategy is very effective when directed to consumers who frequently shop around

---

price consciousness This is a state of mind that motivates consumers to make purchase decisions based on the price of the product.

and are seeking good bargains. An example of a consumer segment having this profile is traditional homemakers who are bargain seekers. These consumers tend to shop around for savings. A consumer study can be conducted here to identify the extent to which target consumers are price or deal conscious.[24]

The same strategy works well when the product/market is considered price elastic. If price is not an important consideration for the average consumer in the target market, then this strategy should not be used. For example, marketing communications managers should not use this strategy if the product is women's jewelry directed to upscale clientele. These consumers are not likely to be price sensitive.[25]

Another consumer-related factor that enters into strategy selection is **consumer experience.** Marketing strategies such as *positioning by relative price* and *positioning by country of origin* assume that consumers do not have much experience with various brands in that product category. Lack of experience prompts consumers to use extrinsic cues such as price and country of origin to make a purchase decision. Consumers that have quite a bit of experience with the product category typically do not use extrinsic cues to make attributions about quality. Therefore, the use of strategies such as *positioning by relative price* and *positioning by country of origin* may not be effective for such consumers.

Other marketing strategies such as *positioning by intangible factor* may be effective for consumers with high levels of product experience. Experienced consumers may have already formed perceptions of quality based on their own experience. If the message concerning the brand's intangible factor matches the consumer's perception of the brand, then the message may serve to reinforce the consumer's perception, which in turn may further motivate the consumer to adopt the brand. See Table 10-3 on page 227.

Consumer involvement is another consumer-related factor that is used in the strategic analysis. When consumers are emotionally and cognitively involved with the purchase of a product, they are likely to process much information. Certain marketing strategies are likely to be more effective than others for consumers seeking much information. For example, *positioning by competitor* may allow the marketer to develop a marketing communications campaign to inform and educate consumers about the strengths and weaknesses of its brand in relation to key competitors. Such a strategy is conducive to the dissemination of much information compared to strategies such as a "made in the U.S.A." campaign (*positioning by country of origin* or *positioning by celebrity or spokesperson*). In other words, celebrity endorsements are likely to be effective given that the audience is not highly involved.[26] On the other hand, celebrity endorsements may serve to heighten consumers' involvement with the product and the advertised brand prompting further information processing.[27]

Customer or brand loyalty is another consumer-related factor involved in the strategic analysis. Brand loyalty refers to the state in which consumers feel good about a brand they have used and exhibit a tendency to repurchase the same brand. Traditionally, positioning by low price is employed when a significant segment of the target market consists of consumers who are "brand switchers" (the converse of "brand loyalists"). For example, many consumers using cosmetic products such as lipstick, eye shadow, and makeup tend to switch from one brand to another. Switching behavior can be easily induced by price reductions and discounts. Typically, a consumer study is conducted to determine the level of switching behavior in the product category. A measure of brand commitment or loyalty is used to measure the extent of brand switching. Various measures of brand loyalty are discussed in the objectives and performance measures chapter (Chapter Twelve).

Conversely, other positioning strategies are used given consumers who exhibit high brand loyalty. An example of an effective positioning strategy is *positioning by use or customer.* The focus of this marketing communications campaign is to reinforce the consumer's attitude toward the brand (therefore enhancing the probability of

consumer experience
The state in which consumers have much knowledge and familiarity of a product category.

consumer involvement
The state in which consumers are emotionally and cognitively involved with the purchase of a product and they are likely to process much information.

customer or brand loyalty
The state in which customers express a certain amount of commitment to a brand as in repeated purchase.

250 Part Three Strategy Development: A Hierarchical Perspective

product users versus nonusers Product users are consumers identified as using the product in question. Nonusers are identified as not using the product in question.

repurchase) by depicting the kind of customer that typically uses the brand. This depiction of the typical user or customer serves to help consumers establish self-image congruence with the brand— match between the user image and the consumer actual self-image, ideal self-image, and social self-image. This self-image congruence promotes further loyalty to the brand.

The last consumer-related factor commonly used in the strategic analysis is **product users versus nonusers.** Many marketers use *positioning by low price* to convert nonusers of the product to users. In other words, this strategy is employed when a significant segment of the target market is comprised of product nonusers, that is, people who have not yet had a chance to try the product. For example, personal computers may fall under this category. Personal computers are expensive, and there are many nonusers. But many nonusers can be persuaded to buy a PC if they find a good bargain. This possibility can be ascertained through a market potential study.[28]

10-3b Product-Related Factors

product functionality versus value-expressiveness Some products such as toothpaste and soap are referred to as functional because they serve the specific purpose of the product class: toothpaste is used to clean teeth and soap is used for washing. In contrast, value-expressive products are those that serve other goals besides functionality, goals such as expressing one's identity. For example, a sexy outfit not only provides clothing but also expresses the consumer's identity as being sexy.

Many product-related factors should be considered in selecting a positioning approach. One such factor is **product functionality versus value-expressiveness.** Marketers typically conduct consumer research to measure the extent to which the product is functional versus value-expressive.[29] Functional products are those that consumers buy only for their utility in accomplishing other goals. For example, toothpaste is purchased to accomplish goals such as fighting tooth decay, freshening breath, whitening teeth, and controlling tartar buildup. In contrast, when consumers buy a car, they do so not only because of the functional utility of the vehicle but also for the vehicle's value-expressiveness. A BMW is bought because of status and prestige, perhaps more so than because of its reliability and durability. Status and prestige are value-expressive goals, whereas product reliability and durability are functional goals.

Positioning by user or customer is commonly used when the brand is value-expressive. Examples of value-expressive products include computer notebooks, watches, clothes, cars, and magazines. Each of these reflects a user image. In other words, this strategy works best when the brand has a clear user image or when the marketing manager is willing to establish that image.[30]

Understanding the extent to which the brand is functional or value-expressive is important in marketing strategy selection. For example, *positioning by product attribute* is typically used when targeted consumers perceive the brand as highly functional and low in value-expressiveness. That is, the product serves a functional or practical purpose. For example, mineral water is a practical type of product. People consume it for practical reasons. In contrast, jewelry does not have a strong utilitarian purpose; it mostly serves to express the consumer's values. *Positioning by user image* is used when the brand is considered to be highly value-expressive.

country of origin This concept refers to the country responsible for the design and/or manufacturing of a particular economic good.

Another product-related factor in marketing analysis is **country of origin.** In many instances, consumers perceive the quality of a brand to be directly linked with a country of origin. For example, Japanese and German cars are perceived to have high quality; watches from Switzerland are also perceived to have high quality; movies from the United States are perceived to be far superior in quality than movies from other parts of the world; and so on.

Marketers typically use *positioning by country of origin* when consumers perceive quality of a brand to be directly linked with a country of origin. In other words, this strategy is used when the majority of the consumers in the target market use quality as an important criterion in evaluating product alternatives and use country of origin to make attributions about quality. For example, a Rolex watch (made in Switzerland) has a clear image of quality, which calls for the use of *positioning by country of origin*.[31]

price-quality relationship This is a psychological association between price and quality. That is, it is the belief that the higher the price of the product, the more likely that the product is of higher quality.

Price-quality relationship is yet another product-related factor in the selection of positioning strategy. Many consumers make purchase decisions based on price. They use price to make an inference about the quality of the brand. In other words, a psychological connection exists between the price of a given product and its quality: the higher the price, the higher the quality; and vice versa.

Many marketers employ a *positioning-by-relative-price* strategy based on the price-quality relationship. That is, this strategy is used when most consumers in the target market have much confidence that there is a direct correlation between price and quality and that a higher-priced product has better quality. For example, most consumers feel that the more they pay for an automobile, the better quality it is. A consumer price-quality study is recommended to make this determination.[32]

Brand symbols are other product-related factors in the strategic analysis. *Positioning by lifestyle/personality* is commonly used when the product has been associated with certain symbols that have carried certain meanings and images over an extended period. Examples include the use of CoverGirl as a symbol to identify CoverGirl cosmetics and the use of the Pillsbury dough boy as a symbol for Pillsbury baked goods, among others. Marketing communications managers can capitalize on this opportunity to clearly and forcefully reinforce this position in the minds of target consumers.

Of course, the use of brand symbols as a basis for marketing strategy necessitates the study of product and brand symbols from a consumer's point of view. A large field of study in consumer research—referred to as *semiotics* and *symbology*—focuses on the use of symbols in the marketplace.[33] Marketers who are intent on the use of symbols in their marketing communications campaigns are advised to consult with consumer semioticians and symboligists to ensure that they use the most effective symbols possible. See Table 10-4 on page 248.

brand symbols Icons associated with a brand that make a reference to something else (person, object, or event).

10-3c Market-Related Factors

Managers should consider a number of market-related factors in making a positioning decision. One is **competition.** Marketers should analyze consumers' perceptions of competitor brands vis-à-vis the focal brand. Understanding how targeted consumers perceive the focal brand in relation to the competition provides marketers ample opportunity to select a suitable marketing strategy. When the brand is competing against another that is well established in the marketplace, it is best to use *positioning by competitor* as a marketing strategy. Measuring the strength of one's brand by comparing it to the leading brand is very advantageous to the brand because it allows consumers to bring the brand into their evoked set. The *evoked set* refers to those alternative brands that consumers consider when they contemplate purchase of a given product. A situation analysis involving market share of the various brands can reveal which other brands are well established. The same marketing strategy is used when the brand is perceived by consumers to have a significant strength beyond that of the leading brand(s). This information is typically obtained from consumer surveys.

competition The state in which firms in the same market offer a good or service to the same consumer population.

However, other marketing strategies are used by considering how consumers perceive the brand vis-à-vis competitor brands. Consider an example such as fluoride in Crest. For years and years, Crest had positioned its toothpaste brand in terms of fluoride (a product attribute). A strong association exists between Crest and fluoride. Such a brand association may call for a *positioning by product attribute,* because fluoride is considered to be a product attribute.

Consider another example. The marketing manager knows that his or her target consumers perceive the brand to be marked by technological distinction, above and beyond the competition. Owners of pickup trucks perceive Ford trucks as being of higher quality than other brands of pickup trucks. As such, the Ford manager of the pickup product line may choose this intangible factor as the focus of a marketing communications campaign, that is, *positioning by intangible factor.*

The product life cycle (PLC) is yet another factor in a manager's choice of positioning strategy. The PLC describes the various stages that a product (and its constituent brands) go through from inception to death. Products and brands go through the following stages: introduction, growth, early maturity, late maturity, and decline. From the vantage point of the target market, an understanding is required of whether the product is perceived to be new in the market. If so, then *positioning by product class* may be an effective marketing strategy. In other words, this strategy is typically used under one condition—when the product is perceived to be in the early stages of its life cycle.

The Nivea shower and bath moisturizing gel is an example of a product in the early stages of the product life cycle (PLC). Thus, the focus of any marketing communications campaign pertaining to products in the introduction stage of the PLC is primary demand, not *selective demand*. For example, **primary-demand** advertising of personal computers focuses on educating consumers about personal computers and how they can be used in a variety of settings. In contrast, **selective-demand** advertising of personal computers focuses on differentiating a brand of PC from other competitor brands. This is done by showing how a given brand of PC is better in terms of product attributes or customer benefits such as portability, compatibility with certain computer environments and applications, multimedia compatibility, speed, storage capacity, and so forth. Note that in the early stages of the PC market, probably about 10 or 15 years ago, most of the PC advertising focused on primary demand. Now, much of the PC advertising can be characterized as selective-demand advertising.[34]

Positioning by use or application also is commonly used when the product is still early in its product life cycle. At this stage, many consumers have not used the product and may not be very familiar with how and why the product should be used. Personal computers are a good example here.

Another market-related factor in strategy selection is the **reputation of the distributor.** *Positioning by brand-distributor tie-in* is a strategy commonly used when the manufacturer does not have much of a reputation while the distributor has a good and solid reputation in the minds of target consumers. For example, a new brand of washing machine (called "Washer") may be manufactured by a medium-size company. This company does not have an established reputation in the washing machine industry and market. This firm contracts with a reputable retailer such as Sears to distribute its line of washing machines.[35] *Positioning by distributor's serviceability* is also dependent on consumers' perceptions of the reputation of the distributor. Specifically, such a strategy is used only and only if targeted consumers perceive the distributor to have a good reputation.

Product differentiation in the marketplace is yet another market-related factor involved in the strategic analysis. Here, product differentiation refers to consumers' perceptions that "all brands are alike" and no significant quality and price differences exist among the optional brands. An example of a marketing strategy that is effective under conditions of low product differentiation is *positioning by user or customer*. This strategy is used commonly when the market is likely to be in its mature stage, in which the market is dominated by an oligopoly and in which product differentiation between competitive brands is minimal. An example may be the economy/sports market. The market is dominated by a handful of well-established brands with little differentiation among the brands.

Conversely, when brands in a product category are highly differentiated, other strategies are recommended. For example, *positioning by product attribute* or *positioning by intangible factor* may be effective here. Of course, this is assuming that the firm may be able to build on the fact that consumers perceive at least some differentiation between the firm's brand and competitor brands in terms of a particular product attribute or intangible factor; thus, the objective of the marketing communications campaign is to accentuate these differences.

Variations in quality perceptions comprise yet another factor in strategy selection. Equally important is conducting consumer research to gauge the level of quality perceptions of the focal brand vis-à-vis the competitor brands. Faced with significant quality variations among the brands in the product category, consumers use decision heuristics to help them make a decision to select the brand with the

---

primary demand
The demand for a general product category.

selective demand
The demand for a specific brand marketed by a firm.

reputation of the distributor
The distributor is the firm that makes the manufacturer's product accessible to consumers through retail outlets. The reputation of the distributor is the consumers' image of the distributor.

variations in quality perceptions Within a product line, there may be many brands differing in their level of quality—some good and some bad.

desired level of quality.[36] Price-quality relationship and country of origin are such decision heuristics. In other words, consumers use price and/or country of origin as indicators of quality. Therefore, when consumers feel that significant quality variations exist in the product category, *positioning by relative price* and/or *positioning by country of origin* may be effective marketing strategies.

Summary

This chapter focuses on marketing strategies. Marketing strategy involves selecting among four strategies: strategic product focus, strategic price focus, strategic place focus, and strategic prospects focus. The product-focus positioning strategies are positioning by product class, positioning by product attribute, positioning by intangible factor, positioning by competitors, and by positioning by country of origin. Two price-focus strategies are positioning by relative price and positioning by low price. Three place-focus strategies are positioning by brand-distributor tie-in, positioning by distributor location, and positioning by distributor's serviceability. Finally, the five prospects-focus strategies are positioning by customer benefit or problem, positioning by user or customer image, positioning by use or application, positioning by celebrity or spokesperson, and positioning by lifestyle or personality.

We also describe the situation analysis that managers conduct to ascertain the suitability of these various strategies. In other words, we describe the various conditions and factors that managers take into account in determining the effectiveness of each of the aforementioned strategies. Furthermore, each of these marketing strategies is described as having a unique marketing mix.

Once managers know precisely what is required to implement the strategy, they can effectively allot resources to implement that strategy. Also, knowing the marketing mix helps the marketer spell out one or more objectives consistent with the strategy. Once objectives are articulated, the marketing communications manager monitors the performance of the marketing programs in relation to the stated objectives. If the objectives are not met, the manager changes the system to create future outcomes that are more aligned with the objectives.

Finally, we describe how marketing managers conduct analysis to help select among the various positioning strategies. Marketing managers consider consumer-, product-, and market-related factors in performing this analysis. Consumer-related factors include consumer decision making, price consciousness, consumer experience, consumer involvement, customer or brand loyalty, and product users versus nonusers. Product-related factors involved in the strategic analysis include product functionality versus value-expressiveness, country of origin, price-quality relationship, and brand symbols. Market-related factors include competition, the product life cycle, reputation of the distributor, product differentiation, and variation in quality perceptions.

Discussion Questions

1. Describe a communications campaign you know for which the objective is to associate the brand with an important product attribute. What is the central theme of the campaign? How are the product attributes identified through marketing research?

2. Suppose you are the marketing communications manager of a regional hospital. The hospital has just built a fitness club to further promote preventive physical health through exercise and nutrition programs. The hospital board of directors is now expecting you to effectively promote the fitness club, and you need to plot a strategy. Design a campaign strategy by identifying at least two positioning strategies that may be highly effective for the fitness center.

3. Suppose you are part of the marketing communications team working on the Cingular account. It seems obvious to you and to the rest of the team that the primary campaign objective of Cingular is to convince current and previous customers of AT&T/Cingular that Cingular is not more expensive than the competition and that it offers better service. What is this positioning strategy called? Give a general description of this strategy. Describe the optimal conditions under which to use this positioning approach. What is the appropriate marketing mix for this strategy? Give an example of an objective that is highly consistent with the strategy.

4. Suppose you are part of the marketing communications team working on the Verizon account. What is Verizon's current positioning strategy? Do you think it is effective? Why or why not?

5. Suppose you are the marketing communications manager of Nike athletic shoes. You realize that the campaign objective is to create certain kinds of associations that are powerful in inducing a long-term positive image for Nike shoes. What would these brand associations be? How would you do a study to discover these brand associations?

6. Suppose you are the marketing communications manager of the Macintosh line of personal computers. Your objective is to reinforce the positive image among Macintosh users. You realize that the typical Macintosh user perceives the Macintosh in very complex ways. Use a consumer-behavior model to map out how the Macintosh is perceived by its longtime users. Design a campaign strategy based on the findings.

7. Suppose you are the marketing communications manager of a pharmaceutical company that just produced a new pharmaceutical substance to fight gum disease, which is most common among elderly people. The substance is much more effective than the ingredients currently used by most of the major toothpaste manufacturers. The company decides to package the substance as toothpaste and penetrate the toothpaste market. You realize that you need to do some research to investigate how the various toothpaste brands are perceived and evaluated by elderly people. Your first task is to identify the toothpaste brands currently on the market. Second, use a consumer-behavior model and develop hypotheses about elderly people's perceptions and evaluation of the current brands. Third, based on the hypothetical findings, make recommendations about the optimal attribute configuration of the new brand and about how you would advertise it to appeal to a significant segment of elderly consumers in North America and Europe.

8. Suppose you are working for a large advertising/marketing communications agency and you are assigned to work with the team handling the Wendy's account (fast food). Your team is given specific instructions that the advertising campaign objective should aim to achieve a higher level of sales and market share from older consumers. That is, it is very important to get a mature person who is thinking of eating fast food out to consider Wendy's as a viable and very likely alternative. Determine a positioning strategy for Wendy's and design a marketing communications campaign for the company. Justify your decisions.

9. You are the communications manager of a large pharmaceutical company that recently has developed a new antiperspirant that is highly effective for athletically inclined women. The brand name of the new product is Sweat Free. You realize that your communications campaign objective is to instill a positive attitude about Sweat Free among women who exercise a lot. Develop a positioning strategy that can help you figure out the message of the entire campaign. Make sure to justify your decisions.

Practice Quiz

Note: You can find the correct answers to these questions by taking the quiz and then submitting your answers in the Online Edition. The program will automatically score your submission. If you miss a question, the program will provide the correct answer, a rationale for the answer, and the section number in the chapter where the topic is discussed.

1. The concept of positioning refers to _____ .
   a. targeting a segment of the overall consumer population
   b. highlighting, emphasizing, and communicating particular aspects of the brand to target consumers
   c. launching a promotion campaign that focuses on differentiating the product from the competition
   d. engaging in market research that identifies the profile of consumers likely to use the product

2. Porter's model of competitive strategy emphasizes three marketing strategies. These are _____ .
   a. differentiation, cost leadership, and low price
   b. differentiation, cost leadership, and focus
   c. target marketing, quality, and restructuring
   d. differentiation, product quality, and low price

3. Some brands are positioned by using associations at the product category. This is known as _____ .
   a. positioning by product attribute
   b. positioning by an intangible factor
   c. positioning by product class
   d. positioning by customer benefit

4. Some brands are positioned by linking certain important product features to the brand in question. This is known as _____ .
   a. positioning by product class
   b. positioning by product attribute
   c. positioning by intangible factor
   d. positioning by competitor

5. Suppose a car manufacturer positions one of its new models in terms of "quality." What kind of positioning strategy is this?
   a. positioning by product class
   b. positioning by product attribute
   c. positioning by intangible factor
   d. positioning by competitor

6. Consider how hotels/motels are perceived in the minds of many consumers. The budget hotels/motels (low price/quality) may include hotels/motels such as Motel 6, Econolodge, McSleep, Days Inn, Hampton Inn, and Comfort Inn. Midrange hotels/motels may include Courtyard, Ramada, and Holiday Inn. Luxury ones may include the Marriott, Renaissance, Clarion, Hyatt Regency, Westin Hotels, and Embassy Suites. Suppose the marketer of Ramada launches an advertising campaign by showing how Ramada Inn is in a class of hotels comparable to Courtyard and Holiday Inn in terms of price. What kind of positioning strategy is this?
   a. positioning by product class
   b. positioning by intangible factor
   c. positioning by competitor
   d. positioning by relative price

7. Consider the example of an advertising campaign for a brand of shampoo that has natural protein. The advertising campaign emphasizes two message claims: "It is safe to use every day" and "It is exciting and sexy." What kind of positioning strategy is behind this advertising campaign?
   a. positioning by product class
   b. positioning by product attribute
   c. positioning by intangible factor
   d. positioning by customer benefit or problem

8. In at least one advertising campaign, Campbell's soup focused on eating soup for lunchtime. What kind of positioning strategy is this?
   a. positioning by customer benefit or problem
   b. positioning by user or customer image
   c. positioning by use or application
   d. positioning by lifestyle or personality.

9. Nike traditionally associates its shoes with the serious athlete. CoverGirl (cosmetics) is associated with wholesome, healthy, young, and very attractive women. These are examples of _____ .
   a. positioning by customer benefit or problem
   b. positioning by user or customer image
   c. positioning by use or application
   d. positioning by lifestyle or personality

10. Betty Crocker brands are shown in most advertising as honest, dependable, friendly, concerned about consumers, experts in baked goods, old, and traditional. What kind of positioning strategy underlies most of Betty Crocker's advertising?
    a. positioning by customer benefit or problem
    b. positioning by user or customer image
    c. positioning by use or application
    d. positioning by lifestyle or personality

Web Exercise

Cruising on the Web

Visit the website of Carnival Cruise Lines at http://www.carnival.com and conduct a positioning audit that evaluates its positioning strategies for its different brands and cruises. How are they different? Which positioning strategies are being used for the various markets that you can identify? Visit other cruise line websites and conduct positioning audits for them as well. Is there a single "best" positioning strategy for cruise lines as a whole? The SMC QuickLink presented here takes you to a 2005 report on the cruise industry:

SMC QuickLink
International Council of Cruise Lines
http://www.iccl.org/clc/index.cfm

Suggested Readings

Aaker, David A. 1991. *Managing brand equity: Capitalizing on the value of a brand name.* New York: The Free Press.

Anton, Jon, and Natalie L. Petouhoff. 2002. *Customer relationship management: The bottom line to optimizing your ROI.* Upper Saddle River, NJ: Prentice Hall PTR.

Berg, Thomas L. 1971. *Mismarketing: Case histories of marketing misfires.* Garden City, NY: Anchor Books.

Breakenridge, Deirdre. 2001. *Cyberbranding: Brand building in the digital economy.* Upper Saddle River, NJ: Prentice Hall PTR.

Cagan, Jonathan, and Craig M. Vogel. 2002. *Creating breakthrough products: Innovation from product planning to program approval.* Upper Saddle River, NJ: Prentice Hall PTR.

Cespedes, Frank V. 1996. *Managing marketing linkages.* Upper Saddle River, NJ: Prentice Hall PTR.

Cross, Richard, and Janet Smith. 1995. *Customer bonding: Pathway to lasting customer loyalty.* Lincolnwood, IL: NTC Business Books.

Davis, Frank W., and Karl B. Manrodt. 1996. *Customer-responsive management: The flexible advantage.* Cambridge, MA: Blackwell.

Enrico, Roger. 1986. *The other guy blinked.* New York: Bantam Books.

Fishbein, Martin, and Icek Ajzen. 1975. *Belief, attitude, intention, and behavior: An introduction to theory and research.* Reading, MA: Addison-Wesley.

Hatton, Angela. 2000. *The definitive guide to marketing planning.* Upper Saddle River, NJ: Prentice Hall PTR.

Johnson, Michael D. 1998. *Customer orientation and market action.* Upper Saddle River, NJ: Prentice Hall.

Osenton, Tom. 2002. *Customer share marketing.* Upper Saddle River, NJ: Prentice Hall.

Porter, Michael E. 1980. *Competitive strategy.* New York: The Free Press.

Reichheld, Frederick F. 1996. *The loyalty effect: The hidden force behind growth, profits, and lasting value.* Cambridge, MA: Harvard Business School Press.

Ries, Al, and Jack Trout. 1982. *Positioning: The battle for your mind.* New York: Warner.

Wind, Yoram, and Vijay Mahajan, with Robert E. Gunther. 2002. *Convergence marketing: Strategies for reaching the new hybrid consumer.* Upper Saddle River, NJ: Prentice Hall PTR.

Woodruff, Robert B., and Sarah F. Gardial. 1996. *Know your customer: New approaches to understanding customer value and satisfaction.* Cambridge, MA: Blackwell.

Notes

1. "Cruise Vacation Industry Report" (May 2005). Available from International Council of Cruise Lines website: http://www.iccl.org/clc/index.cfm.
2. Michael E. Porter, *Competitive Strategy* (New York: The Free Press, 1980).
3. Al Ries and Jack Trout, *Positioning: The Battle for Your Mind* (New York: Warner Books, 1982); David Aaker and J. Gary Shansby, "Positioning Your Product," *Business Horizons* (May–June 1982): 56–62.
4. David A. Aaker, *Managing Brand Equity: Capitalizing on the Value of a Brand Name* (New York, The Free Press, 1991), Chapter 5.
5. Jill Dutt, "Hedging Your Bets in 1997: Diversify to Survive Markets' Ups and Downs," *The Washington Post*, December 29, 1996, H1, H4.
6. W. J. Stanton, M. S. Sommers, and J. B. Barnes, *Fundamentals of Marketing*, 2nd Canadian ed. (Toronto: McGraw-Hill Ryerson, 1977).
7. Philip Kotler, *Marketing Management: Analysis, Planning, and Control*, 2nd ed. (Englewood Cliffs, NJ: Prentice Hall, 1976), 7.
8. Frank Bass, C. W. King, and E. A. Pessemier, *Applications of the Sciences in Marketing Management* (New York: John Wiley, 1968), 252.
9. David A. Aaker, *Managing Brand Equity*, 127.
10. David A. Aaker, *Managing Brand Equity*, 114–15.
11. David A. Aaker, *Managing Brand Equity*, 116.
12. Joseph W. Alba and J. Wesley Hutchinson, "Dimensions of Consumer Expertise," *Journal of Consumer Research* 13 (March, 1987): 411–54.
13. See note 9.
14. David A. Aaker, *Managing Brand Equity*, 128–29; C. Min Ha and Vern Terpstra, "Country-of-Origin Effects for Uni-National and Bi-National Products," *Journal of International Business Studies* 19 (Summer 1988): 242; N. G. Papadopoulos, L. A. Heslop, F. Garby, and G. Avlonitis, "Does Country-of-Origin Matter?" (working paper, Marketing Science Institute, 1987).
15. Richard Ettenson, Janet Wagner, and Gary Gaeth, "Evaluating the Effect of Country of Origin and the 'Made in the U.S.A.' Campaign: A Conjoint Approach," *Journal of Retailing* 64 (Spring 1988): 85–100; C. Min Ha and Vern Terpstra, "Country-of-Origin Effects for Uni-National and Bi-National Products," 235–55; Michelle A. Morganosky and Michelle M. Lazarde, "Foreign-Made Apparel: Influences on Consumers' Perceptions of Brand and Store Quality," *International Journal of Advertising* 6 (Fall 1987): 339–48; Gary M. Ericksen, Johnny K. Johansson, and Paul Chao, "Image Variables in Multi-Attribute Product Evaluations: Country-of-Origin Effects," *Journal of Consumer Research* 11 (September 1984): 694–99; Sung-Tai Hong and Robert S. Wyer Jr., "Effects of Country-of-Origin and Product-Attribute Information on Product

Evaluation: An Information Processing Perspective," *Journal of Consumer Research* 16 (September 1989): 175–87; Marjorie Wall, John Liefeld, and Louise A. Heslop, "Impact of Country-of-Origin Cues on Consumer Judgments in Multi-Cue Situations: A Covariance Analysis," *Journal of the Academy of Marketing Science* 19, no. 2 (1991): 105–13.

16. David A. Aaker, *Managing Brand Equity*, 120–22; Stuart Agres, *Emotion in Advertising: An Agency's View* (New York: The Marschalk Company, 1986).
17. M. M. Moriarity, "Retail Promotional Effects on Intra- and Interbrand Sales Performance," *Journal of Retailing* (Fall 1985): 27–47; B. E. Kahn and D. C. Schmittlein, "The Relationship Between Purchase Made on Promotion and Shopping Trip Behavior," *Journal of Retailing* (Fall 1992): 294–315; K. Helsen and D. C. Schmittlein, "How Does a Product Market's Typical Price-Promotion Pattern Affect the Timing of Households' Purchases?" *Journal of Retailing* (Fall 1992): 316–38.
18. G. Bruce Boyer, "The Man (and the Woman) in the Brooks Brothers Shirt," *Town and Country* (May 1981): 58–66.
19. David A. Aaker, *Managing Brand Equity*, 120; Stuart Agres, *Emotion in Advertising*.
20. Glen L. Urban, Philip L. Johnson, and Hohn R. Hauser, "Testing Competitive Market Structures," *Marketing Science* 3 (Spring 1984): 83–112.
21. David A. Aaker, *Managing Brand Equity*, 123–24.
22. David A. Aaker, *Managing Brand Equity*, 125; Tom Murray, "The Wind at Nike's Back," *Adweek's Marketing Week*, March 27, 1986, 28–31.
23. David A. Aaker, *Managing Brand Equity*, 126; Roger Enrico, *The Other Guy Blinked* (New York, Bantam Books, 1986).
24. For a good measure of price or deal consciousness, see Donald R. Lichtenstein, Richard G. Netemeyer, and Scott Burton, "Distinguishing Coupon Proneness from Value Consciousness: An Acquisition, Transaction Utility Theory Perspective," *Journal of Marketing* 54 (July 1990): 54–67.
25. Marketing researchers traditionally measure price sensitivity through price elasticity of demand. This is a mathematical measure of percentage change in quantity demanded divided by percentage change in price.
26. John C. Mowen and Stephen W. Brown, "On Explaining and Predicting the Effectiveness of Celebrity Endorsers," in *Advances in Consumer Research*, vol. 8, 437–41 (Ann Arbor, MI: Association for Consumer Research, 1981); Charles Atkin and M. Block, "Effectiveness of Celebrity Endorsers," *Journal of Advertising Research* 23, no. 1 (February–March 1983): 57–61.
27. For a measure of consumer involvement, see Gilles Laurent and Jean-Noel Kapferer, "Measuring Consumer Involvement Profiles," *Journal of Marketing Research* 22 (February 1985): 41–53.
28. For a method to determine market potential, see Philip Kotler, *Marketing Management: Analysis, Planning, Implementation, and Control*, 8th ed. (Englewood Cliffs, NJ: Prentice Hall, 1981), 245–54.
29. For those who want to conduct a consumer study and measure the level of functionalism (utilitarianism) and value-expressiveness of the product in question, see M. Joseph Sirgy, J. S. Johar, A. Coskun Samli, and C. B. Claiborne, "Self-Congruity Versus Functional Congruity: Predictors of Consumer Behavior," *Journal of the Academy of Marketing Science* 19 (Fall 1991): 363–75.
30. For a measure of value-expressiveness, see M. Joseph Sirgy, J. S. Johar, and Michael Wood, "Determinants of Product Value-Expressiveness: Another Look at Conspicuousness, Differentiation, and Common Usage," in *Developments in Marketing Science*, vol. 9, ed. Naresh Malhotra, 35–39 (Atlanta, GA: Academy of Marketing Science, 1985).
31. For measures of country image, see Richard Ettenson, Janet Wagner, and Gary Gaeth, "Evaluating the Effect of Country of Origin and the 'Made in the U.S.A.' Campaign: A Conjoint Approach," *Journal of Retailing* 64 (Spring 1988): 85–100; and Sung-Tai Hong and Robert S. Wyer Jr., "Effects of Country-of-Origin and Product-Attribute Information on Product Evaluation," 175–87.
32. For methods to measure the price-quality relationship, see Gary M. Ericksen and John K. Johansson, "The Role of Price in Multi-Attribute Product Evaluations," *Journal of Consumer Research* (September 1985): 195–99; and George J. Szybillo and Jacob Jacoby, "Intrinsic Versus Extrinsic Cues As Determinants of Perceived Product Quality," *Journal of Applied Psychology* (February 1974): 74–78.
33. For an excellent article introducing the study of consumer semiotics and symbolic consumption, see David Glen Mick, "Consumer Research and Semiotics: Exploring the Morphology of Signs, Symbols, and Significance," *Journal of Consumer Research* 14 (September 1986): 196–213.
34. If you want to know more about the product life cycle (PLC) and know of methods and ways to measure the stage of your product in its PLC, see Chester R. Wasson, *Dynamic Competitive Strategy and Product Life Cycles* (Austin, TX: Austin Press, 1978); John A. Weber, "Planning Corporate Growth with Inverted Product Life Cycles," *Long Range Planning* (October 1976): 12–29; and Peter Doyle, "The Realities of the Product Life Cycle," *Quarterly Review of Marketing* (Summer 1976): 1–6.
35. If you want to conduct a consumer study to ascertain the strength of the company image, the following measure is recommended: David W. Cravens, Gerald E. Hills, and Robert B. Woodruff, *Marketing Decision Making: Concepts and Strategy* (Homewood, IL: Richard D. Irwin, 1976), 234; the same measure appears in Philip Kotler, *Marketing Management*, 8th ed., Englewood Cliffs, NJ: Prentice Hall, 1996), 568.
36. Valerie Zeithaml and Merrie Brucks, "Price As an Indicator of Quality Dimensions" (paper presented at the 1987 Association for Consumer Research Annual Conference, October 9–11, Cambridge, MA); Kent B. Monroe and Akshay R. Roa, "Testing the Relationship Between Price, Perceived Quality, and Perceived Value" (paper presented at the 1987 Association for Consumer Research Annual Conference, October 9-11, Cambridge, MA).

The Marketing Communications Level:
Analysis and Planning for Marketing Communications Strategy and Tactics

Chapter Eleven

Chapter Outline

- **11-1 Introduction**
- **11-2 An Analytic/Planning Model**
  - 11-2a High Involvement/High Thinking: Informative (Thinker) Strategy
  - 11-2b High Involvement/High Feeling: Affective (Feeler) Strategy
  - 11-2c Low Involvement/Low Thinking: Habit-Formation (Doer) Strategy
  - 11-2d Low Involvement/Low Feeling: Self-Satisfaction (Reactor) Strategy
- Summary
- Discussion Questions
- Practice Quiz
- Web Exercise: Marketing Communications Strategies and Website Congruity
- Suggested Readings
- Notes

Key Terms

- absolute cost (p. 264)
- attribute sensory modality (p. 264)
- bounce-back coupon (p. 279)
- electronic coupons (p. 279)
- event sponsorship (p. 275)
- geographic selectivity (p. 266)
- gross reach (p. 269)
- group selling (p. 283)
- instant coupon (p. 279)
- in-store advertising (p. 284)
- interactive advertising (p. 277)
- intermedia selection (p. 264)
- intramedia selection (p. 264)
- media habits (p. 267)
- media selectivity (p. 267)
- one-to-one selling (p. 283)
- press conference (p. 275)
- press release (p. 272)
- production flexibility (p. 264)
- referral system (p. 273)
- reseller support (p. 271)
- seasonal usage in media (p. 267)
- self-liquidating premiums (p. 283)
- specialty advertising (p. 281)
- teleshopping (p. 283)
- videotext (p. 283)
- word-of-mouth (WOM) communications (p. 273)

The meaning of a communication is the result you get.
—R. Bandler, American linguist

11-1 Introduction

For the first time ever, the Discovery Channel ranked as the number one consumer brand for overall quality in the United States, according to the Spring 2002 EquiTrendSM Study. The same study named the Discovery Channel as the number one television brand for the tenth straight year. These groundbreaking results were echoed in the influential 2002 Beta Research Study, in which viewers ranked the network first in program quality among major networks for the fourteenth straight year. The current success of the Discovery Channel can be traced back to a large marketing communications budget—$20 million annually—that laid the groundwork for this success in the 1990s. Chris Moseley, senior vice president of marketing and communications of the Discovery Channel, devised an effective marketing communications strategy that involved a mix of communications elements, including using moving LED signs on telephone kiosks; using the new multimedia, theatrical, and even retail venues; and making buys on competing cable channels.[1] The Discovery Channel is an example of how diverse elements of marketing communications can be integrated effectively to meet marketing objectives such as brand association. In this case, the Discovery Channel is associated with learning.

In contrast, IBM in the 1990s had a different kind of problem. It was advertising in twenty-four different magazines, and each advertisement had a different image of IBM Corporation. To correct this problem, Abby Kohnstamm, IBM's vice president of corporate marketing, fired around eighty advertising agencies around the globe and gave its account to Ogilvy & Mather Worldwide. Kohnstamm also unified the look of the company's packaging and brochures. She pulled together IBM divisions' scattered booths at trade shows to present a consistent image of IBM. Years later the goal is pretty much the same—that is, to create a unified image for IBM. To meet this challenge, the various elements of marketing communications must be integrated and the disparate communications must be viewed as components of a system.[2]

These two scenarios exemplify the challenges of making marketing communications decisions and integrating these decisions into the big picture. This chapter highlights some of the issues related to meeting these challenges. Specifically, this chapter introduces you to marketing communications decisions. Having gotten a good feel for corporate and marketing strategy and tactics, you must now be ready to appreciate how marketing communications decisions can be effectively made within the greater system of the corporate and marketing decision framework. Like corporate and marketing decisions, marketing communications decisions involve selecting a marketing communications strategy, determining the optimal marketing communications mix to implement the strategy, setting concrete and quantifiable marketing communications objectives that reflect the overall thrust of the strategy and tactics, allocating resources for the marketing communications mix, and engaging in monitoring and control to ensure effectiveness over time. In this chapter, we concentrate only on marketing communications strategy and tactics and the analysis managers conduct to select the most effective marketing communications strategy. See Figure 11-1 and SMC Marketplace Watch 11-1.

SMC QuickLink
The Discovery Channel
http://www.discoverychannel.com

SMC QuickLink
IBM
http://www.ibm.com

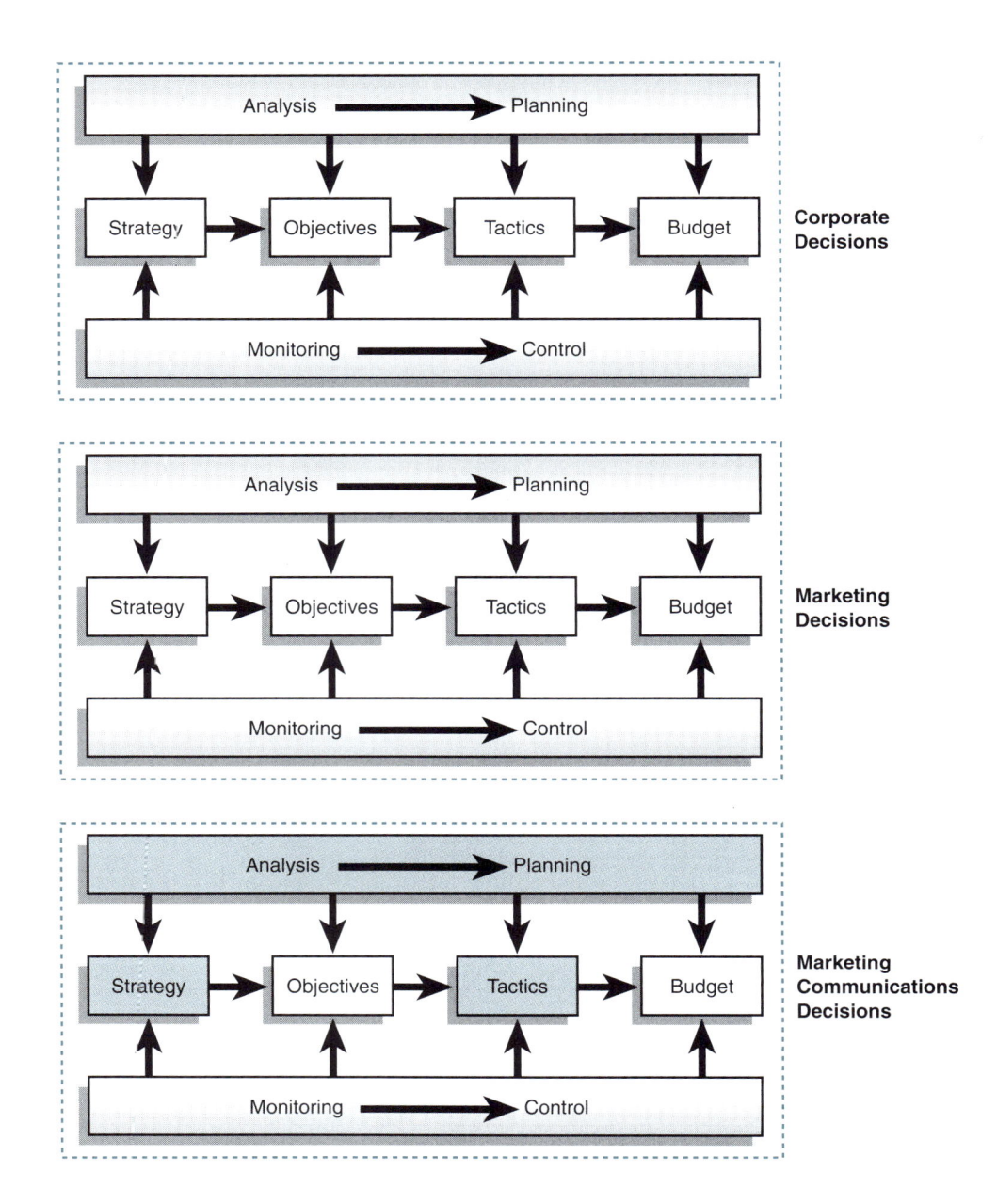

Figure 11-1
Marketing Communications Strategy, Tactics, and Analysis

11-2 An Analytic/Planning Model

In one of his Marketing News columns, Professor Schultz (an expert on IMC) gave advice to marketing communications practitioners as to how to allocate expenditures across the various elements of the marketing communications mix (e.g., advertising, PR, sales promotion, and direct marketing). He advised practitioners to have the customers determine the value of these different communications elements. That is, practitioners should ask customers and prospects how they would like to receive information or materials.[3] He used Lexus as an example of this selection strategy. When a person purchases a Lexus, a short questionnaire asks how he or she would like to receive information. Would he or she like to receive information through direct mail? A telephone call from the dealership? Should the telephone call be directed to the home or to the office? And, if so, what are the most convenient times? And so on. The idea here is to let the customer or prospect tell you his or her preferences and to then use this customer or prospect input to select the appropriate mix of marketing

SMC Marketplace Watch 11-1

Disney Begins to Migrate to Consumer-Controlled Media

Research has documented the fact that consumers are migrating from traditional mass media (e.g., watching television programs on the four major television networks—ABC, NBC, CBS, and FOX) to consumer-controlled media (e.g., video on demand). In response to this media migration, Walt Disney Co. President and Chief Operating Officer Bob Iger indicated that the company has made video on demand (VOD) and digital advertising formats a high priority. Iger said the company was involved in a number of new media initiatives, including discussions with advertisers about how to embed their message in content that would be digital video recorder (DVR)–proof. Disney plans to make content available in VOD formats—such as *Desperate Housewives* or *Good Morning America*—that have the potential to excite and attract consumers through additional unseen footage. The model that Disney is trying to emulate is ESPN. ESPN provides live sportscast and interactive games through broadband online channel ESPN 360. ESPN also has ESPN Mobile, its own branded cell phone.

Disney's Iger is negotiating with Time Warner Cable and Comcast about VOD program distribution starting as early as 2006. Disney rolls out first-season DVDs in September of its two hits, *Desperate Housewives* and *Lost*. The shows have also been licensed around the world.

Source: Adapted from Claire Atkinson, "Disney Chief Cites 'Great Migration' to Consumer Control: Says New Media Initiatives Are a Company Priority," *Advertising Age,* June 08, 2005, http://adage.com/news.cms?newsId=45248.

communications tools. Although this selection method is highly intuitive and plausible, it ignores corporate/marketing/marketing communications strategies and objectives. Our position is that the elements of the marketing communications mix should be assembled as a direct function of marketing communications strategy (informative, affective, habit formation, or self-satisfaction), which in turn is guided by marketing strategy (product focus, price focus, place focus, or prospect focus), which in turn is guided by corporate strategy (grow, maintain position, harvest, innovate, or divest). In this section, we show how specific elements of the marketing communications mix go hand in hand with certain marketing communications strategies, which in turn are selected to meet marketing and corporate goals.

Some purchase decisions demand a great deal of thought; others are dominated by feelings. Some are made through force of habit; others are made consciously. Both advertising scholars and managers alike have embraced an analytic/planning model referred to as the Foote, Cone, & Belding model (it is also referred to as the learn-feel-do model).[4] The model is shown in Figure 11-2. It involves a simple matrix that attributes consumer choices to information (learn), attitude (feel), and behavior (do) issues. Shown in the figure, the matrix has four quadrants, each specifying a major promotion goal: to be informative, to be affective, to be habit forming, or to promote self-satisfaction. Thinking and feeling are represented as a continuum—some decisions involve one or the other, and many involve elements of both. Over time, there is movement from thinking toward feeling. The high- and low-product importance variables are also shown on a continuum, and over time importance can diminish.

This model was first envisioned in the context of advertising, but it clearly can be adapted to marketing communications at large. The model allows all the intramedia elements that are part of an SMC portfolio to be better coordinated in their executions. The next section introduces you to the four marketing communications strategies—namely, informative (thinker), affective (feeler), habit formation (doer), and self-satisfaction (reactor)—and how they fit into the larger system of the SMC integrated framework. The intent here is to show how these four marketing communications strategies can be actually implemented at the tactical level and be truly integrated throughout the entire SMC system.

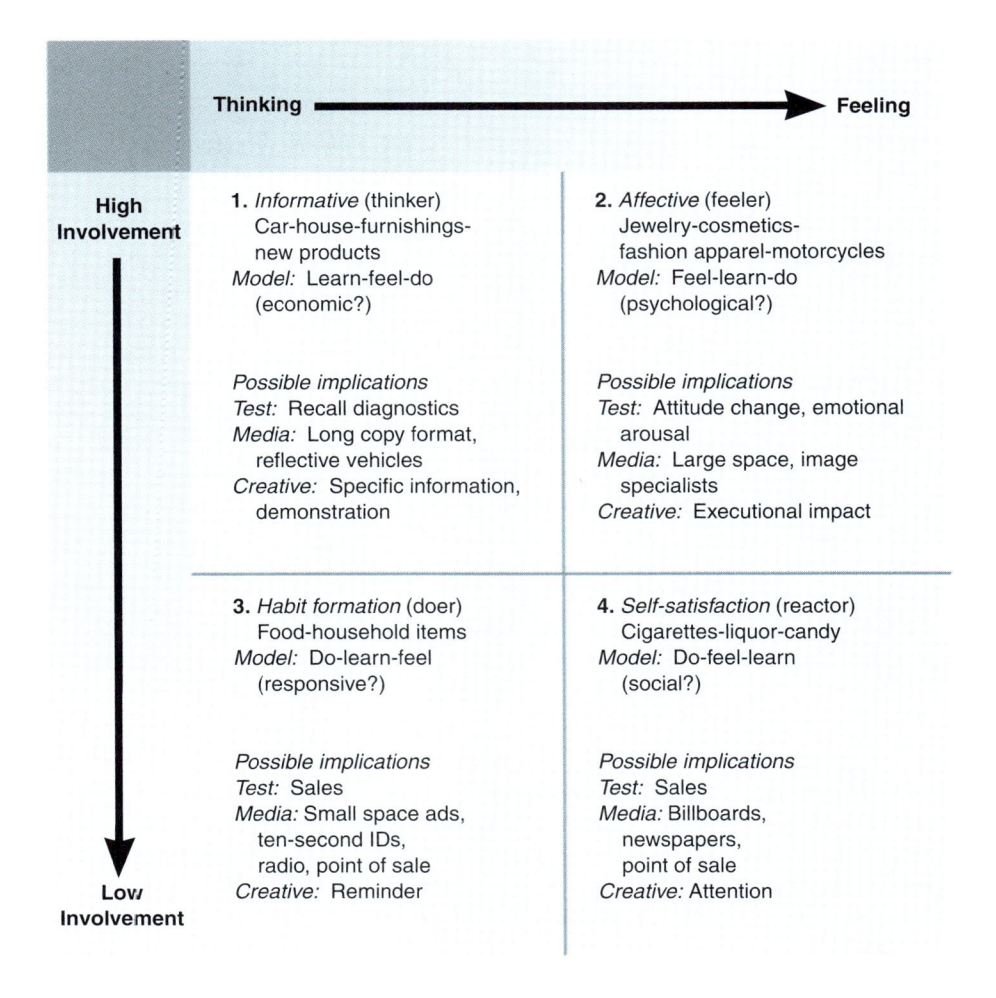

Figure 11-2
The Foote, Cone, and Belding Model (the Learn-Feel-Do Model)

This simple matrix attributes consumer choices to information (learn), attitude (feel), and behavior (do) issues. Thinking and feeling are represented as a continuum—some decisions involve one or the other, and many involve elements of both.

Source: Adapted from "The Consumer Mind: How to Tailor Ad Strategies" by Richard Vaughn. Reprinted with permission from the June 9, 1980 issue of *Advertising Age.* Copyright, Crain Communications, 1980.

	Thinking →	Feeling
High Involvement	**1.** *Informative* (thinker) Car-house-furnishings-new products *Model:* Learn-feel-do (economic?) *Possible implications* *Test:* Recall diagnostics *Media:* Long copy format, reflective vehicles *Creative:* Specific information, demonstration	**2.** *Affective* (feeler) Jewelry-cosmetics-fashion apparel-motorcycles *Model:* Feel-learn-do (psychological?) *Possible implications* *Test:* Attitude change, emotional arousal *Media:* Large space, image specialists *Creative:* Executional impact
Low Involvement	**3.** *Habit formation* (doer) Food-household items *Model:* Do-learn-feel (responsive?) *Possible implications* *Test:* Sales *Media:* Small space ads, ten-second IDs, radio, point of sale *Creative:* Reminder	**4.** *Self-satisfaction* (reactor) Cigarettes-liquor-candy *Model:* Do-feel-learn (social?) *Possible implications* *Test:* Sales *Media:* Billboards, newspapers, point of sale *Creative:* Attention

There is the whole issue of the product itself and its relationship with the consumer. Product factors are considerations related to product characteristics. For example, consider how you buy and "think about" a variety of products in your life. You probably evaluate some products in a very cognitive, "thinking" manner; with others, you "just feel" that they are the right product for you. Understanding whether the product is a "thinking" type of product or a "feeling" type may make a difference in selecting an appropriate communications strategy. The level of product involvement may also make a difference.

As noted, products can be classified as the "thinking type" or the "feeling type." The distinction between *thinking* and *feeling* products is based on the distinction between right- and left-brain information processing. The left brain processes semantic information through "rational" or cognitive thinking. The right brain, in contrast, processes information that is more spatial and visual in nature. The right brain engages in the affective or feeling functions. Consumers tend to process information about cars, houses, furnishings, new products, and household items more with the left brain than with the right brain. Information processing for these products is more cognitive or rational than emotional. These products are characterized as "thinking products." From the product involvement side, let's face it, there are products that you "really care about" every aspect and then some you "just buy." This is the issue of product involvement. Nondurable products of low value and frequently purchased products requiring routine decision making are low-risk products and therefore are not highly involving for consumers. Cars, music, fashion, the college you choose to attend, and other high-ticket items generally are considered high-

TABLE 11-1 Marketing Communications Strategies, Tactics, and Objectives

Strategies	Tactics	Objectives
Informative (thinker)	Advertising (mostly print)	To generate maximum brand awareness and learning
	Reseller support (training and trade shows)	
	Public relations (press release and publicity)	
	Word-of-mouth (WOM) communications (stimulating WOM communications through advertising and sampling, referral system)	
Affective (feeler)	Advertising (mostly broadcast)	To generate maximum brand awareness and positive attitude (liking)
	Reseller support (cooperative advertising)	
	Public relations (press conference, corporate advertising, and event sponsorship)	
	WOM communications (simulating WOM communications through advertising)	
Habit formation (doer)	Advertising (mostly print and interactive)	To induce trial purchase and learning from product use (first-time users) and to reinforce learning (repeat users)
	Direct marketing (direct mail, newsletter, direct-response advertising)	
	Sales promotion (coupons, sampling, refunds and rebates, bonus packs, and price-off deals)	
	Reseller support (trade allowances)	
	Public relations (publicity)	
Self-satisfaction (reactor)	Advertising (outdoor and specialty)	To induce trial purchase and brand liking from product use (first-time users) and to reinforce positive attitude (repeat users)
	Direct marketing (catalogs, direct-response advertising, telemarketing, and direct selling)	
	Sales promotion (premiums and contests, sweepstakes)	
	Reseller support (contests and incentives, in-store advertising, POP displays, and personal selling)	
	Public relations (corporate advertising, event sponsorship, and placement of product in movies and on television)	

involvement products. The obvious here for the communications manager is that "Size does matter" when "size" is the amount of effort and shopping behavior that goes into a product. The next sections examine the development of marketing communications strategies and tactics that consider this and other relevant factors.

The various communications strategies, their tactics, and objectives are all shown in Table 11-1. The table shows four marketing communications strategies, namely, informative (thinker), affective (feeler), habit formation (doer), and self-satisfaction (reactor).

11-2a High Involvement/High Thinking: Informative (Thinker) Strategy

Consumers buying goods and services in this quadrant have a high need for information, both because of the importance of the product and because of the thinking issues related to it. Major purchases such as cars, houses, and furnishings qualify, along with almost any new product that needs initially to convey its function, price, and availability. The strategy model is *learn → feel → do*. Marketers provide salient information to build consumers' attitudinal acceptance and lead to purchase.

An *informative (thinker) strategy* seeks to expose a target to the messages and to educate target consumers about the product's important costs and/or benefits. For example, a firm selling dormitory room lofts (a loft is a high bed that stands on four poles allowing possibly a desk to be placed under the bed) to college students at the beginning of the fall semester may launch a marketing communications campaign with the objectives of making students aware of the availability of these lofts and educating them about the benefits of buying a loft instead of a regular bed.

Once the marketing communications manager selects a marketing communications strategy, the elements of the communications mix have to be assembled. Table 11-1 shows elements of the marketing communications mix that can be effectively employed to meet the requirements of the informative (thinker) strategy—namely, advertising, reseller support, public relations, and word-of-mouth (WOM) communications. These communications tools help achieve the maximum brand awareness and learning possible. The other elements of the marketing communications mix (direct marketing and sales promotion) are not likely to be as effective.

Advertising

Advertising is a marketing communications tool that focuses on the mass media. That is, messages are placed in impersonal types of media such as television, radio, newspapers, and magazines, among others. Advertising is an excellent communications tool to generate the highest brand awareness possible. To accomplish this, the marketing communications manager should select the appropriate mix of media categories—**intermedia selection**—and the appropriate mix of media vehicles—**intramedia selection,** then compute the net reach of the media schedule and adjust the media components to achieve the maximum reach.

Intermedia Selection Examine Table 11-2, which shows advertising to involve the use of a variety of media. The major media include television, radio, newspapers, magazines, outdoor, and transit, among others. Within each medium are different forms of media. For example, within television, the various types of media are network, spot, local, and syndicated programs.

Factors that influence intermedia selection are divided into two groups: (1) eliminating criteria and (2) discriminating criteria. The manager has to consider the eliminating criteria first to eliminate media categories that do not meet the company's requirements and then make discriminating judgments among the media categories not eliminated (see Table 11-3).

Eliminating criteria include attribute sensory modality, production flexibility, absolute cost, geographic selectivity, and legal requirements. **Attribute sensory modality** refers to the sensory component associated with information processing of a particular medium. Certain messages have to be communicated in a medium with a certain sensory modality. The sensory modalities of television, for example, are greater than those of radio, newspapers, magazines, and so on. This is because television relies on the visual and auditory sensory modalities. Radio strictly relies on the auditory sensory modality; newspapers and magazines rely on the visual static modality. Even newspapers and magazines differ in sensory modality in that newspapers rely mostly on black-and-white photography (and dull colors) while magazines use glossy colors. For example, if one is trying to advertise a graphics software program, one needs to select an advertising medium that allows the display of color graphics in the most vivid way possible. The sensory modalities of television, magazines, and outdoor may fit the message requirements of this product. Newspapers and radio advertising may be easily ruled out.

Another possible eliminating criterion is **production flexibility.** Managers often do not have the luxury of time. They may be forced to select certain media simply as a function of production flexibility. Radio advertising is the most flexible timewise followed by newspapers. Outdoor, magazine, and television placements are usually the least flexible. Magazines have "closing dates," dates by which the advertisement must arrive at the publisher to make a particular issue—sometimes 8 weeks ahead of the "cover date" or the time when the issue is actually on sale.

With respect to **absolute cost,** in many cases managers do not have the luxury of a large media budget and are forced to select certain media simply as a function of

---

intermedia selection
The decision to select among media categories such as television, radio, magazines, newspapers, billboards, transit advertising, interactive advertising, and so on.

intramedia selection
The selection of the appropriate mix of media vehicles.

attribute sensory modality
The sensory component associated with information processing of a particular message. For example, an advertisement shown in a magazine is processed through the visual sense, and a radio commercial is processed through the auditory sense.

production flexibility
The ability of certain media to accommodate the scheduling demands of advertisers. For example, radio advertising is highly flexible; radio script can be easily modified, and changes can be easily made to within the last few days of the airing of the radio commercial.

absolute cost The total amount of money needed to purchase advertising in certain media. The term *absolute cost* is used in contrast to *relative cost* in media planning. Media costs can be compared in relation to one another, and therefore media are selected in relation to their relative costs. However, certain media are selected or eliminated from consideration based on the total dollar cost needed for advertising because the total costs are too high and prohibitive in an absolute sense.

TABLE 11-2 Advertising Media Categories

Television Advertising
- Network television
- Spot television
- Local television
- Cable television

Radio Advertising
- Network radio
- Spot radio
- Local radio
  - —Regular :30/:60 advertisements
  - —Live/on-site advertising

Newspaper Advertising
- National and daily newspapers
  - —Display advertising
  - —Classified advertising
  - —Reading notice
  - —Inserts
  - —Supplements
- Weekly newspapers
- Special audience newspapers

Magazine Advertising
- International and national magazines
  - —Consumer magazines
    - Regular print advertisements (B&W/4C, different sizes)
    - Back cover (inside of front/back cover)
    - Fold-out
    - Talking advertisements (5-second play)
      - Anaglyphic images (three-dimensional materials that are viewed with colored glasses)
      - Lenticular images (color images printed on finely corrugated plastic that seem to move when tilted)
      - Singing advertisements
    - Heat/pressure-sensitive ink (images that change color on contact)
  - —Business magazines
    - Regular print advertisements (B&W/4C, different sizes)
    - Back cover (inside of front/back cover)
    - Fold-out
    - Talking advertisements (5-second play)
  - —Farm magazines
    - Regular print advertisements (B&W/4C, different sizes)
    - Back cover (inside of front/back cover)
    - Fold-out
  - —Academic and trade journals
    - Regular print advertisements (B&W/4C, different sizes)
    - Back cover (inside of front/back cover)
    - Fold-out
- Regional magazines
  - —Regular print advertisements (B&W/4C, different sizes)
  - —Back cover (inside of front/back cover)
  - —Fold-out

Out-of-Home Advertising
- Outdoor advertising
  - —National and local outdoor advertising
    - Poster panels
    - Painted bulletins
    - Spectaculars
- Transit advertising
  - —Mobile advertising
    - Inside cards
    - Outside posters
    - Taxi exteriors
  - —Immobile advertising (station/terminal posters)
    - Aerial advertising
    - Mobile billboards
    - Miscellaneous outdoor media (e.g., parking meters, automatic teller machines, trash cans, ski-lift poles, restroom walls, public phones)

Specialty Advertising

Directory Advertising
- Yellow pages advertising
- Specialized directories

Interactive Advertising

In-Store Advertising

In-Flight Advertising

Movie Theater Advertising

Video Advertising

TABLE 11-3 Criteria to Select among Advertising Media Categories as a Way to Implement the Brand-Awareness Strategy

Eliminating Criteria
- Attribute sensory modality
- Production flexibility
- Absolute cost
- Geographic selectivity
- Legal requirements

Discriminating Criteria
- Media habits
- Media selectivity
- Ethical considerations

---

absolute cost. For example, placing an advertisement on network television usually requires a large media budget. Newspaper and radio advertising can be selected with a meager budget. Table 11-4 shows some figures to give you a sense of typical unit costs in national advertising.

The manager considers not only the absolute cost of media but also the production costs within the different media categories. Production costs do not include the cost of running an advertisement. Costs incurred in producing an advertisement may include hiring actors and directors for television advertisements, paying copy editors

TABLE 11-4 Typical Costs for Selected National Advertising Buys, 2004

Network Television
Prime time (M–F, 8 P.M.–11 P.M.), 30-second spot: $192,400
Daytime (M–F, 10 A.M.–4 P.M.), 30-second spot: $28,055

Network Radio (Adult 18+ CPRP)*
Drive time (M–F, 6 a.m.–10 a.m.), 30-second spot: $2,833
Drive time (M–F, 3 p.m.–7 p.m.), 30-second spot: $2,621

Newspapers (B&W Full Page)
The Wall Street Journal: $184,562
USA Today: $98,900

Magazines (Four-Color Full Page)
Time: $234,000
Business Week: $106,500
Sports Illustrated: $279,450
Spin: $48,483
Farm Journal: $57,880

Source: *Mediaweek: Marketer's Guide to Media 2005,* vol. 28 (New York: VNU Business Publications, 2005).
*CPRP = Cost per rating point (cost of 30-second spot/network audience rating)

geographic selectivity
The targeting of select geographic areas, commonly used in media planning to help select media.

for magazine and newspaper advertisements, and so on. For example, a 30-second commercial on prime-time network television can cost hundreds of thousands of dollars to produce and hundreds of thousands of dollars more to run on television, while a one-page, four-color advertisement in *Reader's Digest* may be able to be executed for under $5,000 and the full page bought in a single issue for about $240,000 (in 2005). Alternatively, an advertiser can produce advertisements for cable television, radio, or local newspapers at a very small fraction of those costs. Often a local car dealer or similar business can self-produce very low budget advertisements that can run under $500 in production costs. While some of us may laugh at the production quality, these "cheap" advertisements may deliver the needed information to the particular target market to facilitate the desired attitude or behavior change.

What about **geographic selectivity** as an eliminating criterion? In many cases, managers are automatically constrained to promote the assigned product within a specific geographic territory. Hence, they are forced to select certain media categories that target the chosen area. In this situation, placing an advertisement on network television is inconceivable not only because it usually requires a large media budget but also because it provides more coverage than is needed. For example, suppose a marketing communications manager is trying to promote a new brand of ice cream that is presently being distributed within a 300-mile radius from the manufacturer's location. This marketing communications manager is automatically constrained to specific media categories such as spot television, cable television, spot radio, local newspapers, regional editions of consumer magazines, regional magazines, and outdoor media.

What about legal requirements? In some cases, marketing communications managers are automatically constrained by legal rulings or laws prohibiting the use of certain media. For example, tobacco companies are prohibited by law from advertising on television, *period*. Hard liquor advertisements have never been legally banned but did not appear on television through a "gentleman's agreement" between the producers and the government. That agreement now has evolved into one that keeps the advertisements on programming and in time slots that are not likely to be seen by underage viewers.

Once the eliminating criteria have been evaluated, the discriminating criteria must be examined. One of the most important factors in selecting media categories to implement the informative (thinker) strategy is **media habits.** The term *media habits* refers to the extent to which a certain audience is exposed to a particular media category. Some people tend to watch more television than others. Some listen to the radio more than others. Some subscribe to magazines, while others do not. Usually, secondary data sources, such as Simmons National Consumer Survey with Choices 3, provide data about consumers' media habits.

Another important discriminating factor is **media selectivity,** which refers to the extent to which a particular media category targets a specific or unique audience that can be clearly identified demographically and/or psychographically. If the marketing communications manager is dealing with a general audience (e.g., all adults), then nonselective media such as network television, newspapers, newspaper supplements, and outdoor advertising are appropriate. However, if the marketing communications manager is trying to reach a highly select target market that can be clearly identified demographically or psychographically, then magazines and cable television are likely to be better choices because specific media vehicles within magazines or cable television can match the demographic or psychographic profile of the target market.

Still another important discriminating factor in intermedia selection is **seasonal usage in media.** Different media categories are used more or less frequently at different times of the year. For example, most people watch network television during fall and early spring. Network television viewing declines in late spring and the summer months. The opposite is true for radio. Radio listenership peaks in the summer months. Advertisers (such as retailers) who direct their advertising campaigns to general audiences usually consider the seasonal usage of specific media. To maximize their reach, they advertise heavily on network television during the fall and winter seasons and switch to radio and magazines in the summer months.

Finally, the advertiser may consider any ethical ramifications of using a specific media. Some products or advertisements may irritate or offend the general public. Examples include feminine-hygiene products, medicinal products such as hemorrhoid medicines, contraceptives such as condoms, liquor and cigarette advertisements, advertisements with strong sexual overtones, and so on. Marketing communications managers of products that are likely to offend certain people are advised not to use general media such as network television or outdoor advertising. They should use those media that are targeted to certain populations, thereby reducing the extent of spillover to the general population. For example, although Viagra is used for treating a very prevalent male medical problem, there are certain groups that may question the widespread use of advertising for the brand (and competing brands) in public places (such as ballparks and other sporting venues) where such advertisements are viewable by both adults and children.

So far the discussion has centered on the implementation of the informative (thinker) strategy through advertising only in relation to brand awareness and learning. Specifically, the discussion centers on how advertising media categories and vehicles can be selected to maximize awareness. In relation to intermedia selection, the focus is on a set of eliminating and discriminating criteria. These same criteria also apply to brand learning and knowledge. The informative (thinker) strategy guides the marketing communications manager in selecting a media category that lends itself to an informational message. Audience learning is maximized if the informational message is placed in a print medium. For example, when target consumers are likely to demand more information, then it is imperative to place the advertisement in a print or more highly involving medium rather than in a broadcast medium. While this is not to say that all print advertisements focus on large amounts of information, print media executions generally allow marketing communications managers to design advertisements with much information if they so choose.

media habits Consumers' frequent use of certain media classes and vehicles. Market researchers typically develop profiles of the media habits of target consumers.

media selectivity Reaching a consumer group through highly select media. For example, avid cyclists can best be reached through cyclists' magazines. Cyclists' magazines are considered highly select media.

seasonal usage in media This refers to seasonal variation in the use of certain media. For example, radio is listened to more frequently in the summer months than during other times. Prime-time television is typically watched more frequently during mid-fall and winter than during other times of the year.

Intramedia Selection Once the broader advertising media categories are selected (network television, spot television, local television, cable television, network radio, and so on), the marketing communications manager then has to select specific media vehicles within the broader range of media categories. For example, if network television was selected, then the next decision is which network television programs should be selected to maximize reach? Because each media category has a large pool of media vehicles, the marketing communications manager must choose a manageable set of media vehicles. How can this be done? This is done by using a set of eliminating criteria such as media ratings and cost per thousand.

With respect to media ratings, media vehicles are usually rated by rating services such as Nielson and Arbitron. As with reach, typical ratings are stated as a percentage of the target market. For example, *60 Minutes* on CBS may have a rating of 20. This means that 20 percent of television households (TVHH) in the United States would be tuned into the show at some point between 7 and 8 P.M. Eastern Time Sunday evenings. Secondary data pertaining to media ratings can be easily obtained through Standard Rate and Data Service (SRDS).

In addition to media ratings, marketing communications managers compute a cost per thousand (CPM) for a variety of possible vehicles and then may select vehicles that are found to have low CPMs. A CPM figure of a certain vehicle denotes its cost in reaching a thousand people. As noted in Part Two, the precise CPM index is computed as follows:

Cost per thousand (CPM) = (cost of the media unit/audience delivery) × 1,000

For example, what is the CPM of the following three magazines? For the purposes of demonstration, let us assume the cost of a half-page advertisement is $108,800 for *Reader's Digest* (*RD*), $89,300 for *TV Guide* (*TVG*), and $69,245 for *Good Housekeeping* (*GH*). Suppose that we are interested in the adult women population in the United States that we assume totals approximately one hundred million. The ratings of these three magazines are 26.6, 25.4, and 20.8 (target market of adult women). Therefore:

$$\text{CPM}(RD) = [(\$108{,}800) / (100{,}000{,}000 \times .266)] \times 1{,}000 = \$4.09$$
$$\text{CPM}(TVG) = [(\$89{,}300) / (100{,}000{,}000 \times .254)] \times 1{,}000 = \$3.52$$
$$\text{CPM}(GH) = [(\$69{,}245) / (100{,}000{,}000 \times .208)] \times 1{,}000 = \$3.33$$

As we see from the CPM figures of the three potential media vehicles, *Good Housekeeping* magazine is the most cost-efficient. The second most cost-efficient vehicle is *TV Guide*, and the third is *Reader's Digest* (see SMC Marketplace Watch 11-2).

Remember that brand awareness/learning is the marketing communications goal. In making an *intramedia* selection, the marketing communications manager should consider two additional factors, namely, the *image of the media vehicle* and *its attention level*. To effect maximum learning, the selected media vehicles have to be perceived as credible. Lack of media credibility affects message credibility, which in turn affects message acceptance. For example, consider placing a political message in a tabloid magazine such as *National Enquirer*. *National Enquirer* is perceived as a magazine that exploits sensationalism and would not hesitate to print stories and accounts based on fiction rather than fact. Placing a political message in such a media vehicle is likely to render the message incredible. Furthermore, for learning to take place, the audience has to attend to the vehicle and its programming (or editorial) content. Some media vehicles may have high rating points but low attention levels. Compare *CBS Evening News* to *The Late Show with David Letterman*. Most people tend to be attentive watching the news but are getting ready to go to bed watching *The Late Show*. One program draws a high level of attention; the other does not. As a result, learning is likely to be enhanced for advertisements in media vehicles having high levels of attention. Market research services such as Simmons provide data concerning attention levels of national television programs.

SMC QuickLink
SRDS Media Solutions
http://www.SRDS.com

SMC QuickLink
Simmons
http://www.smrb.com

SMC Marketplace Watch 11-2

Rising CPMs of Network Television and Daily Newspapers

Mass marketing is based on low cost per thousand (CPM). In the days of yesteryear, advertising on television provided advertisers a golden opportunity to reach millions of consumers at relatively low prices. During the golden age of network television, from the 1950s through the mid-1970s, the size of CBS, NBC, and ABC's prime-time audience grew, and so did prices charged for 30-seconds spots. In other words, the CPMs remained relatively stable. Starting in the early 1980s, ratings and advertising rates began to diverge. By 2002, networks' average CPM had soared to $16.79 in prime time, compared with $1.96 in 1972.

At a CPM of $10, a packaged-goods firm had to sell only four or five units per one thousand viewers to cover the costs of a television advertisement. The range of prime-time advertising has narrowed greatly over the years. Only four industries can afford the rising CPMs of prime-time network television: the automobile, pharmaceutical, telecommunications, and movie industries. This is because those industries target the mass market.

Similarly, readership of daily newspapers fell to 55 percent of households in 2002, from a high of 81 percent in 1964. As with broadcast television, the cost of newspaper advertising per unit of circulation has increased tenfold since the mid-1960s.

Source: Adapted from Anthony Bianco, "The Vanishing Mass Market: New Technology. Product Proliferation. Fragmented Media. Get Ready: It's a Whole New World," *Business Week,* July 12, 2004, 65–66.

Computing the Net Reach of the Media Mix and Making Adjustments

While reach of single media choices is pretty straightforward, the *net reach*—that is, what nonduplicated percentage of the target market was reached by a combination of media vehicles—gets a bit more complex. Now the question becomes, How do we compute the nonduplicated or net reach of this combination of selected media vehicles? Table 11-5 shows how to compute the net reach of selected media vehicles

The table shows a hypothetical example of three media vehicles and their combined reach. Three media vehicles are proposed (X, Y, and Z). Vehicle X is estimated to reach 8,000, while vehicles Y and Z reach 5,000 and 3,000, respectively. Therefore, the combined vehicles can reach a *gross audience* of 16,000 (8,000 + 5,000 + 3,000) and the **gross reach** is 80 percent (16,000 consumers reached by the combined vehicles out of 20,000 consumers in the target market). We refer to the 16,000 reach as *gross audience* because this estimate does not take into account the duplication between/among the different vehicles. For example, the table shows that 1,000 consumers are likely to be exposed to both X and Y vehicles. This is a *paired audience*. So the goal here is to start by figuring out the reach from a certain vehicle (Vehicle X). Then we account for the duplication between the reach of that vehicle (Vehicle X) and another program (Vehicle Y). Then we add the extent of unduplicated reach of the other vehicle (Vehicle Y) to the reach of the base program (Vehicle X). We do this by (1) estimating the paired audience and (2) obtaining a *net ratio,* which is the audience figure of the other vehicle (Vehicle Y) minus the paired audience, divided by the audience figure. The example in the table shows that Vehicle X reaches 8,000 target consumers. Vehicle Y reaches 80 percent of 5,000 consumers who cannot be reached through Vehicle X. Therefore, the net added audience of Vehicle Y is 4,000 consumers.

Now let us count the added reach of Vehicle Z after taking into account the paired audience (or duplication) between Vehicle Z and the two preceding vehicles (X and Y). In this case, we have to partial out the duplication between Z and Y and Z and X. That means we need to estimate the net ratio of both $Z + X$ and $Z + Y$ and then get the cumulative net ratio of these two by multiplying them. Once the cumulative net ratio is obtained, then the net added reach of Z (after partialling out the duplication between Z and X and between Z and Y) becomes the cumulative net ratio

gross reach A measure commonly used by media planners to assess the effectiveness of a media schedule in terms of its maximum reach of a target market. It is computed by adding the percentages of reach of all media vehicles without taking into account the duplication among the vehicles. For example, a 90 percent gross reach is the ability of a combination of media vehicles to reach 90 percent of the target market, assuming that there is no audience duplication among the media vehicles. *Net reach* is computed by subtracting audience duplication from gross reach and therefore is considered to be a more accurate index of media schedule effectiveness than gross reach.

TABLE 11-5 How to Compute the Net Reach of a Number of Media Vehicles

Media Vehicle	Audience Figure	Paired Audience	Net Ratio	Cumulative Net Ratio	Net Added
X	8,000				8,000
Y	5,000	1,000 (Y + X)	.8	.8	4,000
Z	3,000	500 (Z + X)	.83		
		700 (Z + Y)	.77	.64	1,900
	16,000				13,900

Total market = 20,000
Gross audience = 16,000
Net audience = 13,900
Net reach = 13,900/20,000 = .7 or 70 percent

times the audience figure pertaining to Z alone. This figure is 1,900. Therefore, the net audience reached by the combined media vehicles is 13,900 (8,000 + 4,000 + 1,900). Dividing this figure by the estimate of the total market (20,000) produces the net reach, which is 70 percent (13,900/20,000). That is, the combined effect of these three vehicles is to reach 70 percent of the target consumers. Assume that vehicles X, Y, and Z are three different magazines. By accounting for the individual effects of these programs, we may be misled into believing that the total reach of these three vehicles is 16,000 or 80 percent of the total market. However, after partialling out the duplication among the three vehicles, the marketing communications manager can accurately calculate that the advertisement reaches 13,900 (or 70 percent) of the target market, not 16,000 (or 80 percent) as originally postulated. The goal of this exercise is to put together a set of media vehicles that is likely to maximize net reach, that is, reach the most people in the target market. The questions then become, Is 70 percent reach good enough? Can the marketing communications manager do any better through an alternative set of vehicles? Which vehicles might these be?

You may wonder where these estimates come from. The audience figures pertaining to each vehicle are derived by analyzing the individual vehicles. The paired audience figures are estimated through primary or secondary research. A marketing communications manager does primary research on his or her own for the specific purpose of deriving these estimates. Secondary research is conducted by research firms and sold to whoever needs the data. Examples of secondary data include the data from Nielsen, Simmons National Consumer Survey with Choices 3, MarketFacts, and Arbitron, among others. Thus, to compute the net reach of a set of media vehicles, the marketing communications manager needs to have estimates of the audience reached by each individual vehicle and the duplication between each pair of vehicles. The rest of the figures shown in Table 11-5 are arithmetic derivations.

Creative Aspects in Advertising

To achieve maximum brand awareness, certain creative decisions have to be made. The most important decision is to select the kind of advertising that draws audience attention. For example, in network television, the marketing communications manager should be very creative in developing an advertisement that can capture attention and stand out from the clutter of other advertising. This may be done through an emotional appeal or possibly an out-of-the-ordinary concept or event. Radio advertising must likewise draw attention. Radio has a unique tool, live/on-site advertising. This method of advertising is very powerful in drawing attention and creating brand awareness. In newspaper advertising, the use of provocative display advertisements can do the trick. Classified advertising, reading notices, inserts, and supplements are less likely to be as effective. In magazine advertising, the use the back-cover advertise-

Exhibit 11-1
High Visual Impact and Brand Recall

Purina found a funny and meaningful visual to express the misery caused by different dog foods. It is both attention-getting and relevant, creating high visual impact and brand recall for Purina.

Source: Reproduced by permission of Carl Furuta Studio, Inc., Los Angeles, CA.

ments, fold-outs, talking advertisements, anaglyphic images (images of ornaments sculptured or embossed in low relief, as a cameo), lenticular images (images that are biconvex), singing advertisements, and heat/pressure-sensitive ink are all methods that can capture readers' attention. Similarly, in outdoor advertising, the use of spectaculars (large-scale displays) can be very effective in creating brand awareness. Transit advertising has to be very creative to draw attention. Aerial advertising and mobile billboards are likely to draw attention by the mere fact that they are out of the ordinary. Similarly, any new form of advertising placed in a new, unfamiliar media is likely to draw attention and create brand awareness. Therefore, marketing communications managers seeking to create maximal brand awareness should be very creative in their advertising efforts because the greater the creativity, the higher the brand awareness (see Exhibit 11-1).

When the goal is brand learning, creativity plays a different role. Here the advertisement has to be designed to be informative, rational, and utilitarian. The novelty and emotional aspects of the advertisement should draw attention, but much of the copy should be informative. An advertisement that is too emotional should not be used because it may distract the audience from the true goal, fully processing the content of the message.

Reseller Support

Reseller support is a marketing communications tool that is directed to "resellers" or distributors. It is also known as *trade promotion*. Table 11-6 shows a listing of the various elements or tools involved in reseller support. These tools are used only by business-to-business marketing communications managers or manufacturer-to-retailer

reseller support An element or tool of marketing communications that involves promotional activities by distributors such as contests and incentives, trade allowances, in-store displays, point-of-purchase materials, training programs, trade shows, cooperative advertising, and personal selling. It is often called *trade promotion*.

TABLE 11-6	Reseller Support (Trade Promotion) Tools and Techniques

Contests and incentives
Trade allowances
- Buying allowances (free goods)
- Promotional allowances
- Slotting allowances

In-store displays and point-of-purchase materials
Training programs
Trade shows
Cooperative advertising
- Horizontal cooperative advertising
- Ingredient-sponsored cooperative advertising
- Vertical cooperative advertising

Personal selling

promotions and include contests and incentives, trade allowances, in-store displays and point-of-purchase materials, training programs, trade shows, and cooperative advertising. Not all of these reseller support tools effectively implement the informative (thinker) strategy. Some work better than others. The ones that can be used to implement the informative (thinker) strategy include sales training programs and trade shows.

Training is a form of manufacturer-sponsored educational program. For example, in the medical equipment industry, manufacturers usually offer to both train physicians and health-care personnel (the buyers) how to best use the equipment and also educate them about the product's benefits. Trade shows are also very effective in educating potential customers about the product benefits. Trade show sellers get a chance to interact with potential buyers and educate them about the product's benefits and its various applications.

Public Relations

Public relations is a marketing communications tool that is used to promote the goodwill of the firm as a whole. Many marketing communications scholars recognize the effectiveness of public relations as an information tool, as a tool to educate consumers about the product benefits. However, its use is mostly limited to newsworthy events such as the introduction of new product, the new use or application of existing products, product improvements, and so on. There are many tools of public relations. These are shown in Table 11-7.

Public relations tools include press releases, press conferences, exclusives, interviews, publicity, corporate advertising, event sponsorship, and product placements in movies, games, and television. The tools that serve the informative (thinker) strategy and objectives the best are the press release and publicity. The **press release** is information about the company and/or its products sent to the news media for dissemination. Of course, for the news media to disseminate information about a product or its company, the information has to be newsworthy. *Publicity,* on the other hand, is information about the company and/or one or more of its products that originates from sources beyond the control of the company. The information may be either positive or negative. The marketing function comes in when the company attempts to react to publicity. For example, J.D. Power and Associates is a reputable marketing research firm that conducts customer satisfaction surveys in the automobile industry. If J.D. Power and Associates rates Lexus as having the highest customer satisfaction, the Lexus marketing communications manager could turn around and use this information in an advertising campaign. The Lexus advertisement would boast about its high customer satisfaction ratings.

press release Information about the company and/or its products that is sent to the news media for dissemination.

TABLE 11-7	Public Relations Tools and Techniques

- Press releases
- Press conferences
- Exclusives
- Interviews
- Publicity
- Corporate advertising
- Event sponsorship
- Product placements in movies and television

Word-of-Mouth (WOM) Communications

Just as publicity does not originate with the company itself, **word-of-mouth (WOM) communications** involve information about the company and/or one or more its products that originates from customers. The information can be either positive or negative. Customers talk to other potential customers about their experience with the company's product(s), and they recommend for or against purchase. These recommendations are powerful because they do indeed influence potential customers' purchase decisions. So what can marketing communications managers do about WOM communications? Can they influence WOM communications to the company's advantage? The answer is, *possibly*. Word-of-mouth communications can be induced and influenced in at least three ways: (1) through advertising, (2) through sampling, and (3) by creating a referral network. All of these tools can be effective in achieving maximum learning.

Stimulating WOM communications *through advertising* can be accomplished by creating a message that encourages the audience to talk about the advertised product. For example, consumers are offered a reward if they refer a friend or relative to try the product. Each referral would entitle them to a price discount or some premium or bonus.

In contrast, stimulating WOM communications *through sampling* relies on opinion leadership. Some product users are more likely to be opinion leaders than others. Opinion leaders are those who have a certain expertise about a product category and therefore are more likely to give advice to others about the product and the various brands of that product. For example, business professors each year receive numerous samples of business magazines and software. Business professors are considered opinion leaders because their advice and opinions are sought by students and professionals in the business community. Think of all the business students that pass through a major university each year. If professors form a favorable opinion of the product, then they are likely to communicate to others favorable information about the product to hundreds, if not thousands, of students each year.

The final way to stimulate WOM communications, *by creating a* **referral system,** is a major effort but nevertheless can be a very worthwhile effort in some industries. A referral system can be established by a certain company to provide customers and potential customers with information about the myriad of products and services available to the consumer. For example, most health-maintenance organizations (HMOs) in the United States have their own referral system. A patient within the geographic boundaries of the HMO can call the Physician Referral Office to get information and advice about which physician within the HMO network has the proper background and expertise to treat specific health problems. Also, the Physician Referral Office provides callers with information about the many educational seminars that are related to specific medical conditions and are offered by the HMO. Referral systems can also be created at the industry level. For example, the automobile industry can set up a referral system in which each automobile company provides information about all its cars, prices, and options. Potential buyers then can

word-of-mouth (WOM) communications An element or tool of marketing communications that focuses on consumers communicating among themselves about the firm's product. WOM communications involve both controllable and uncontrollable forms of communications. Controllable forms of WOM communications include stimulating WOM through advertising and sampling, simulating WOM communications through advertising, and using a referral system.

referral system An information network in which consumers refer other consumers to a specific good or service.

SMC QuickLink
Carmax.com: The Online Auto Superstore
http://www.carmax.com

contact the referral system to obtain information about the options of specific car forms (e.g., alternative sports cars within a certain price range) and which models may be available through which dealers within a specific geographic radius. The Internet is particularly suited to the building of such a referral system. CarMax has an extensive referral system that is constantly accessed by used- and new-car buyers in search of automobiles.

11-2b High Involvement/High Feeling: Affective (Feeler) Strategy

The affective (feeler) product decision is involving, but information is less important than feeling in inducing purchase. Typical purchases tied to self-esteem—jewelry, cosmetics, and apparel—may fall here. The strategy model is *feel → learn → do*. Marketers provide emotional appeals that encourage consumers to find out more about the product or service and ultimately lead to purchase.

The affective (feeler) strategy involves the application of marketing communications tools to generate maximum awareness and create the most positive attitude toward the brand. Examples of statements of objectives reflecting this strategy include: "We need to get the target consumers to become fully aware of our brand and develop a preference for it." "We want the marketing communications campaign to increase brand preference by 20 percent in the next 6 months." "We want 70 percent of the target consumers to feel good about our product by the end of next month." "Our goal is to strengthen positive attitudes toward the product by increasing brand attitude from the current 50 percent to 70 percent by the end of this year."

According to Table 11-1, the affective (feeler) strategy can be most effectively implemented through advertising, reseller support, public relations, and WOM communications, the same communications tools used to implement the informative (thinker) strategy but with some variations.

Advertising

In relation to *intermedia* selection, we discussed a set of eliminating and discriminating criteria applied to the informative (thinker) strategy. Now we want to focus on a certain criterion that should be closely examined in implementing the affective strategy through advertising. This criterion is *message valence*. We previously recommended that the marketing communications manager should use the print media mainly because print allows the audience to process more easily the technical and detailed information describing the product and brand benefits. That is, audience learning is maximized if the informational message is placed in a *print* medium. However, given an affective (feeler) strategy, the marketing communications manager should use the *broadcast* medium because the broadcast medium is more effective in inducing emotion and creating affect.

In making an *intramedia* selection, the same criteria employed in the informative (thinker) strategy also apply in the implementation of the affective (feeler) strategy. In relation to the *creative aspects of the advertisement*, marketing communications managers are advised to use emotional rather than rational appeals. Examples of emotional appeals include the use of humor, sex, fear, love, romance, and nostalgia, among others. These emotional appeals can be effective in building positive affect toward the product.

Reseller Support

Table 11-6 lists the various elements or tools involved in reseller support. In discussing the implementation of the informative (thinker) strategy, we recommended the use of sales training programs and trade shows. In implementing the affective (feeler) strategy, we recommend the use of the same tools with the addition of cooperative advertising. Of course, the idea of cooperative advertising is to associate one's product with a reseller for which the target consumers have positive feelings. Intel Inside plays on the value of the Intel chip to prospective buyers of a variety of PC manufacturers. By doing so, the positive affect transfers or spills over to the manufacturer's product, thereby achieving the goals of the affective (feeler) strategy.

Public Relations

In the section pertaining to the informative (thinker) strategy, we discussed the use of the press release and publicity. Of course, these same public relations tools should also be used to implement the affective (feeler) strategy. However, uniquely suited to the affective (feeler) strategy are other public relations tools such as the press conference, interviews, exclusives, corporate advertising, and event sponsorship (see Table 11-7).

With respect to the **press conference,** the topic, of course, has to be of major interest to the news media. For example, holding a press conference about the Super Bowl is likely to draw the attention of news organizations. Here the marketing communications manager contacts the various local offices of the news media and alerts them about the date, time, and place of the press conference and the topic to be addressed. The news media send in their news reporters to cover the event and elicit more responses from the spokesperson by asking pointed questions. The press conference is an effective tool in accomplishing the goals of the affective (feeler) strategy, because the topic and the public attention devoted to the product or issue are usually emotionally charged to begin with. Thus, the audience is likely to experience certain emotions while viewing (listening to or reading about) the press conference. These emotions, although uncontrolled by marketing communications managers, can be positively charged, resulting in the building or strengthening of a positive attitude toward the product or the company. The same can be said in relation to *interviews* and *exclusives.*

Corporate advertising and *event sponsorship* are public relations programs designed to build and strengthen a positive attitude toward the firm at large and all its products. *Corporate advertising* is image-based advertising in which the company is shown in a positive light. It is formally defined as "the provision of assistance either financially or in kind to an activity by a commercial organization for the purpose of achieving commercial objectives."[5] DuPont ran a series of advertisements that focused on the commitment of its employees to finding breakthroughs in the development of products that contributed to solving a variety of problems that the world faces. The idea here is to build positive feelings about the company. **Event sponsorships,** on the other hand, are programs in which a marketing communications manager shares the cost of an event that customers or potential customers attend or, perhaps, an event that is picked up by a communications medium such as television. For example, a local bank may sponsor a community baseball game. The bank's name and logo appear on the baseball program to indicate sponsorship of the event. People attending the baseball game are likely to develop positive feelings about the bank, knowing that it sponsored the event.

press conference A form of public relations in which a company spokesperson provides newsworthy information about a company event to reporters and responds to reporters' questions.

event sponsorship A form of public relations program designed to build and strengthen a positive attitude toward the firm at large and all its products. It is done by having the firm sponsor a specific community event.

Word-of-Mouth (WOM) Communications

As already noted, three key WOM communications tools can be used to implement the informative (thinker) strategy. These tools are stimulating WOM communications through advertising, stimulating WOM communications through sampling, and creating a referral system. I believe that these tools are not likely to be effective given the affective (feeler) strategy, that is, to build positive affect for a product. Another form of WOM communications is likely to be effective in carrying out the affective (feeler) strategy, and this is *simulating* WOM communications mostly through advertising.

Simulating WOM communications is commonly used in television advertising in which a typical advertisement shows a simulation in which two consumers are talking about the product and one consumer is recommending another particular brand based on certain benefits. The consumer who is recommending the brand describes the benefits of the brand over competitor brands. The actor who recommends the brand to others is usually selected to reflect the profile of an opinion leader for that product category. For example, suppose a company is trying to market a business magazine to college students majoring in business. Market research indicates that a significant segment of business students watch CNN and they do look up to business professors; business professor are considered to be opinion leaders in relation to business magazines. So a television commercial is made showing a young, vibrant, and intelligent business professor interacting with several of his students. The actors playing the role of students are shown to revere the professor and hold him in high esteem. One student notices that the business professor has *Business Magazine X* in his briefcase. The briefcase is sitting on the professor's table in the classroom, and this interaction occurs immediately after a business class. The student asks the professor about the business magazine. The professor discusses the virtues of the magazine and makes an explicit recommendation to the students about how the magazine is likely to help them with their business classes and also help them establish their business careers. This is a good example of using WOM communications through simulation in television advertising.

Everyone has no doubt received something like the following direct-mail piece. The envelope has your name typed on it and a postage stamp. It looks like a person (not a company) mailed the letter. Inside the envelope is a newspaper article that looks as though it was cut out from a management magazine. The article addresses the use of trend analysis in making better management decisions. The two-page article (back to back) has a yellow Post-it sticker that says in this particular case, "Joseph, try this. It's really good!" It is signed "J." It looks like a handwritten note from someone that you know. The end of the article has information about how to subscribe to this magazine. After reading the article and closely examining the Post-it note, you realize that this is merely a clever way to make you believe a friend referred this product. The letter is actually a direct-mail advertisement. Here we have an example in which the marketer of this magazine used advertising (more specifically, direct mail) to create the illusion of WOM communications. Please note that this marketing communications method that simulates WOM is highly unethical and perhaps even illegal and is not recommended.

11-2c Low Involvement/Low Thinking: Habit-Formation (Doer) Strategy

The habit-formation (doer) product decision requires minimal involvement or thought, tending to result from habitual buying. Most food and staple packaged goods belong here. Over time, almost any product can fall into this category. Information, to the extent that it plays a role, consists of any point of difference from competitors that the marketer can meaningfully exploit. Brand loyalty may result simply from habit, but it is quite likely that most consumers have several acceptable brands. The strategy model is *do → learn → feel*. It suggests that simply inducing trial through coupons or free samples can generate subsequent purchase more readily than product information.

For the habit-formation strategy, marketing communications tasks aim to maximize product trial and purchase and learning from experience for first-time users. With respect to repeat users, the goal is to enhance repeat purchase and reinforce brand learning. Examples of statements of objectives reflecting this strategy include: "We need to get 35 percent of the target market to express a purchase intention for our advertised product by the year's end." "We want to induce trial and direct experience of our product so that at least 30 percent of the target market will have experienced the product by 6 months' time." "We need to get our old customers to do more business with us." Table 11-1 shows that the habit-formation (doer) strategy can be implemented mostly through direct marketing, sales promotion, and reseller support.

Advertising
Advertising does an effective job of reminding consumers to buy. Therefore, when consumers need to purchase a given type of product, they are more likely to consider

brands that are in their *evoked set* (top-of-the-mind awareness) than brands that are not. Advertising does an effective job of maintaining a brand name in the consumers' evoked set. Thus, the same tactical aspects of advertising discussed in the context of the informative (thinker) strategy also apply here. However, it should be noted that this "reminder" advertising may be somewhat different in that shorter advertisements or commercials can be used. Recently, **interactive advertising** has been used to encourage customers to repeat purchase. This advertising constantly updates descriptions and explanations of a product line and any information to help customers maintain their commitment to the firm. These updates are posted on a home page through a computer online website.

> **interactive advertising** Advertising that constantly updates descriptions and explanations of a product line or any information that helps to keep customers loyal.

Direct Marketing

Direct marketing is addressed as a marketing communications tool used in the context of direct forms of distribution. Table 11-8 shows the various tools and techniques of direct marketing: direct mail, catalogs, telemarketing (telephone in and telephone out), direct-response advertising (broadcast and print), new electronic media (teleshopping and videotext), and direct selling (repetitive person-to-person selling, nonrepetitive person-to-person selling, and party plans).

To reiterate, direct-marketing tools and techniques are limited to businesses that promote their products through direct channels. In other words, the company products cannot be distributed to resellers (wholesalers and retailers) who in turn sell the products to the ultimate consumers. Direct marketing involves promotion to the ultimate consumers *directly*. Firms that market their products through intermediaries and resellers should use the tools and techniques of sales promotion and reseller support. We discuss these, too, but for now we turn our attention to the tools and techniques of direct marketing that are considered most effective in implementing the habit-formation (doer) strategy: direct mail and direct-response advertising.

Direct mail is the most prevalent form of promotion by direct-marketing communications managers. Consumers refer to it as "junk mail"—the unsolicited mail consumers find in their mailboxes. We now get this both in paper and in email. Direct-marketing communications managers who use direct mail start out by developing their own database of actual and potential customers using a variety of sources. Those who do not have their own database of target consumers purchase mailing lists from mailing-list houses. Direct-marketing communications managers use the Standard Rate and Data Service (SRDS) to identify the various mailing-list companies and compare prices. Direct-marketing communications managers can order a mailing list that can target highly select groups of consumers. These are usually defined in terms of where they live (through their ZIP codes); demographics (e.g., income, occupation, age, and gender); and, to a certain extent, lifestyles (e.g., bikers, skiers,

TABLE 11-8 List of Direct-Marketing Tools and Techniques

Direct mail	New electronic media
Catalogs	• Teleshopping (home shopping channels)
Telemarketing	• Videotext (electronic shopping)
• Telephone in	Direct selling
• Telephone out	• One-to-one selling
Direct-response advertising	• Group selling
• Broadcast	
—The one-minute commercial	
—Infomercials	
• Print media	

and fitness enthusiasts). Most mailing-list houses identify consumers' lifestyles through past purchases of related products. For example, golfers are identified through recent purchases of golf-related materials in golf specialty shops and sporting goods stores. This information is bought from retailers and used to develop the mailing lists of "golfers." In many instances, mailing-list houses buy information about consumers from various sources and merge them into a comprehensive database. Direct mail can encourage consumers to respond immediately by offering them special incentives to act immediately. Offers such as special discounts are also common.[6]

In terms of enhancing repeat purchase, the use of a newsletter is also very effective. The newsletter would contain news and information about the marketing communications manager's product line, updates, any favorable publicity cited from other sources, and possibly endorsements and testimonial from certain customers. The newsletter may also contain information about employees who have won certain awards for quality work, updates about industry trends, and so on.

Direct-response advertising is also an effective direct-marketing tool designed to achieve the goals of a habit-formation (doer) strategy. Part of the message in direct-response advertising is information about how to order the product directly from the manufacturer (or distributor). Direct-response advertising is usually done through media such as broadcast, Internet, or print. In the broadcast medium, direct-response advertising sometimes takes the form of *infomercials* (long commercials). In these commercials, a sales response is elicited immediately. Many products, such as Soloflex fitness equipment and the NordicTrack machine, are promoted through 1- or 2-minute commercials. Infomercials, on the other hand, can range from 3 to 60 minutes. The 30- and 60-minute infomercials are designed as television programs (regular television shows). The purpose is to induce an immediate purchase response by having the audience dial an 800 or 900 number to place an order on the spot. An example is *Ron Popeil's Showtime* that promotes kitchenware.

SMC QuickLink
Ronco
http://www.ronco.com

Sales Promotion

Sales promotion is a marketing communications tool specifically designed to provide consumers with some incentive inducing an immediate response, possibly in the form of purchase. Table 11-9 shows a list of sales promotion tools and techniques: coupons (printed and electronic), sampling, premiums, contests and sweepstakes, refunds and rebates, bonus packs, and price-off deals.

Coupons are still a widely used sales promotion tool. A *coupon* is a printed document that allows the holder to get a price discount for the purchase of a product. We all are familiar with pizza coupons. Most pizza places use coupons to entice pizza eaters to purchase their pizza. Coupons are printed in display advertisements in newspapers or magazines. They are mailed directly to target consumers. They are also mailed through promotion firms specializing in that type of service. An example

TABLE 11-9   Sales Promotion Tools and Techniques

Coupons
- Printed coupons
- Electronic coupons

Sampling

Premiums
- Free premiums (e.g., an inexpensive gift in a cereal box)
- Self-liquidating premiums (related products offered at cost only to customers)

Contests and sweepstakes

Refunds and rebates

Bonus packs

Price-off deals

is Valpak. In many tourist locations, coupons are placed in tourist guides and brochures. Sometimes they are placed on the product package itself. The coupon that encourages an immediate purchase response is called an **instant coupon.** Usually it is pasted on top of the package. The consumer sees it and may be motivated to use it to purchase the product on the spot. A common form of coupon designed to encourage a product trial is called the *cross-ruff coupon*. This is placed inside or outside of the package of a related product, a product usually sold by the same company. For example, Kellogg's may come up with a new brand of cereal. To encourage product trial, Kellogg's may place a coupon in Kellogg's Corn Flakes. The cross-ruff coupon may encourage those who purchase and use Kellogg's Corn Flakes to try the new Kellogg brand.

A special form of coupon that is used to elicit repeat response is called a **bounce-back coupon.** This is a coupon that is placed inside or outside of the product package. The coupon is redeemable for the next purchase of the same brand. Have you ever ordered a pizza and gotten a bounce-back coupon taped on the pizza box? The idea is to encourage you to make a repeat purchase of the same brand. **Electronic coupons** are also designed to encourage repeat purchase. Think back to your last visit to the supermarket or mass merchandiser. When you paid the bill at the cash register, you got the receipt. The back of the receipt may have had coupons that could be redeemed for certain products. Product selection is determined by what you have purchased. If you have purchased Philadelphia Cream Cheese, you may get a coupon for that brand to encourage you to buy the same brand of cream cheese on your next visit to the supermarket.

In designing a coupon, the marketing communications manager typically shows a picture of the product; a very brief message (reflecting the positioning of the product) usually in the form of a slogan; the firm's logo, address, and phone number; and the terms of the coupon. Usually at the bottom of the coupon, coupon constraints are spelled out, for example, "coupon may not be combined with any other offer." The expiration date is usually spelled out, too. Coupons are an effective means to motivate consumers to purchase.[7]

Sampling is another sales promotion tool commonly used to induce product trial and purchase (see Exhibit 11-2). For example, Procter & Gamble has always used sampling to get homemakers to try a new brand of detergent. It mails a sample to adult females in households across the United States. Sampling is also very common

instant coupon A form of coupon that encourages an immediate purchase response; it is usually pasted on top of the package.

bounce-back coupon A coupon placed inside or outside of the product package that is redeemable for the next purchase of the same brand.

electronic coupons A form of sales promotion involving coupons; however, the coupons are electronic and are typically printed on the back of the customer invoice or receipt.

Exhibit 11-2
Volvic Water Sampling in Frankfurt
Source: Photo by Don Rahtz.

with food items. The consumer tries a sample; he or she likes it; he or she ends up buying it.

Rebates are also another sales promotion technique. A rebate is usually used to entice a potential consumer to purchase the manufacturer's brand. Once the purchase is made, the consumer provides proof of purchase and gets a partial refund. Many car manufacturers use rebates to entice consumers to buy in certain periods. Likewise, *refund* offers are often used to encourage repeat purchase. Marketing communications managers require consumers to send in proof of purchase as a condition to receiving the refund. Many firms offer consumers special discounts and premiums with more purchases in order to encourage their customers to remain loyal. For example, many airlines use the frequent-flier program to reward fliers who stick with one airline. The nature of the reward varies from free tickets for future flights to special discounts on car rentals and hotels/resorts.

Bonus packs provide an extra amount of the product at regular price. Consumers may feel motivated to switch from one brand to another brand if the other brand offers a bonus pack. Thus, marketing communications managers use this sales promotion tool to induce consumers to purchase their brand or switch from competitor brands.

Price-off deals differ from coupons in that the price reduction is marked on the product package itself. Many retailers use this sales promotion tool to get rid of extra inventory. For example, car dealers mark the sticker price down by a certain margin at the end of the year to get rid of the remaining cars sitting on the lot, thus making room for the new cars for the beginning of the year. Marketing communications managers seeking repeat purchase may mail notices to past customers reminding them to take advantage of price-off deals. This form of sales promotion may be combined with other promotional materials sent to the customers through direct mail.

Reseller Support

Reseller support tools are used only by business-to-business marketing communications managers or manufacturer-to-retailer promotions and include contests and incentives, trade allowances, in-store displays and point-of-purchase materials, training programs, trade shows, and cooperative advertising (see Table 11-6). We addressed some of these in the context of the informative (thinker) strategy, namely, training programs and trade shows. We also argued that the same programs are effective in achieving affective goals and added cooperative advertising to the list. In relation to the habit-formation (doer) strategy, we recommend the use of *trade allowances* as the most effective communications tool.

Trade allowances are most commonly used for trade promotion. They usually involve some form of a discount or deal to encourage the reseller to carry, promote, and display the product. There are three types of trade allowances—buying allowances, promotional allowances, and slotting allowances. A *buying allowance* is a price discount offered to resellers. The resellers can take advantage of this allowance only during the fixed period in which the allowance is offered. Another form of a buying allowance is a deal in which resellers get to have more free products if they buy immediately. A *promotional allowance*, on the other hand, is a price reduction given if the reseller agrees to promote the product. This may be in the form of advertising or displaying the product more visibly than the competing brands. Slotting allowances are somewhat related to promotional allowances. *Slotting allowances* involve the payment of a certain fee for shelf space. Slotting allowances are therefore viewed as a reward for resellers who agree to carry and devote shelf space to a manufacturer's products. The higher the slotting fee, the more the shelf space.

Public Relations

Public relations is an important tool to maintain a positive image of the firm in the minds of customers to enhance repeat patronage. The most common use of public relations tools to achieve goals of the habit-formation (doer) strategy is *publicity*. Publicity is important because it is most credible. Any favorable publicity about the product and/or the company has to be fully exploited. We previously talked about how this information can be used as news items in a newsletter to customers. Favorable publicity can also be used in all forms of advertising to strengthen the positive image of the product and the company

11-2d Low Involvement/Low Feeling: Self-Satisfaction (Reactor) Strategy

The self-satisfaction product decision is triggered primarily by the need to satisfy personal tastes, many of which are influenced by self-image. Cigarettes, liquor, candy, and movies all fall here, along with such products as beer and soft drinks. Group influences are often apparent in the purchase of these items. The strategy model is $do \rightarrow feel \rightarrow learn$. The consumer is reacting to social pressures or to situations—loyalty will be hard to hold or short-lived. (See SMC Marketplace Watch 11-3.)

The *self-satisfaction (reactor)* strategy can be viewed as the application of marketing communications tasks designed to maximize trial and repeat purchases while also increasing positive feelings about the firm's brand. Examples of statements reflecting objectives derived from this strategy include: "We want to increase trial purchase by 40 percent by the end of next year." "We need to get at least 80 percent of those who tried our brand to express liking for it." "We need to increase the number of purchases per individual consumer. Approximately 80 percent of our target consumers are purchasing our product once a month and 20 percent twice a month. We want to get 50 percent to purchase the product twice a month by the end of next year." "We need to reinforce commitment to the brand, so by the end of next year at least 60 percent of our customers should express their loyalty to our brand." Table 11-1 indicates that all of the elements of the marketing communications mix can be effectively used to achieve the goals of the self-satisfaction (reactor) strategy, except for WOM communications.

Advertising

Advertising does an effective job of reminding consumers of certain brands. Thus, the same tactical aspects of advertising discussed in the context of the affective (feeler) strategy also apply here. However, it should be noted that this "reminder" advertising may be somewhat different in that shorter advertisements or commercials can be used. Furthermore, other forms of advertising can be used besides broadcast. Here, *outdoor advertising* can be effective in reminding consumers to repeat purchase. Also, *specialty advertising* does an effective job of reminding current customers of previous transactions, thus enhancing customer loyalty. **Specialty advertising** involves giving consumers inexpensive items such as calendars, pens, pen sets, and paper holders on which is inscribed the name of the marketing communications manager's firm, its logo and slogan, and address and phone number.

specialty advertising A form of advertising that employs gadgets (e.g., pens, mugs, calendars, T-shirts) as a medium to advertise the brand's name and slogan.

Direct Marketing

Direct-marketing tools are direct mail, catalogs, telemarketing (telephone in and telephone out), direct-response advertising (broadcast and print), new electronic media (teleshopping and videotext), and direct selling (repetitive person-to-person selling, nonrepetitive person-to-person selling, and party plans). Of these, the most effective tools that can be used to carry out the self-satisfaction (reactor) strategy are catalogs, direct-response advertising, telemarketing, and direct personal selling.

Catalogs are a traditional method of direct marketing. Many companies like Sears, Nordstrom, and JCPenney sell directly through catalogs. These catalogs are usually distributed on site or can be mailed directly to consumers when consumers request them. Other catalogs (the ones that are not too expensive to produce) are classified as part of a direct-mail campaign. Catalogs help consumers make decisions on the spot and therefore are viewed as effective in achieving product trial and purchase as well as repeat purchase.

Direct-response advertising is also an effective direct-marketing tool designed to achieve the goals of the self-satisfaction (reactor) strategy. For example, the broadcast

SMC Marketplace Watch 11-3

The Challenge of Targeting College Students or the "Millennials"

Marketers refer to the college student generation as "millennials" because they are coming of age in the new millennium. This generation was raised in a world jam-packed with information and entertainment. The millennials were born between 1979 and 1994. There are sixty million of them. These consumers grew up with the Internet, which made them regard information as something they can control. The millennials consume globs of digital fare. They also master tech tools to customize their own programming. Television commercials are either bypassed through channel surfing or zapped with the push of a button on the TiVo Inc. remote. Pop-up advertisements online? They are nixed by a pop-up blocker. Four out of five college students have broadband connections and cell phones. They play video games, chat online, and send text messages by phone. Millennials are renowned for multitasking, regarded as hard sell on brands, and skeptical on advertising.

Lesson One in this world is that the customer, with his finger on the zapper, the mouse, or the remote, wields control as never before. This means that marketers have to come up with advertisements and promotional messages that this generation values. Those messages may reach this generation; but, if so, they will do so through websites, channels, video games, and even billboards.

Lesson Two is to pump promotions into programming. Avon Products, Inc., for example, not only sponsors the NBC soap opera *Passions* but also has paid to have one of the lead characters work on the show as a sales representative for its youth line of cosmetics. Advertisers pepper sports programming with a blitz of sponsored spots, with digital billboards even popping up on the hallowed brick walls of Chicago's Wrigley Field.

Lesson Three is to develop advertisements and promotional messages that make good first impressions. The millennials call the shots. Anyone who bores them will be getting blocked, zapped, and tuned out for years to come.

Source: Adapted from Anthony Bianco, "The Vanishing Mass Market: New Technology. Product Proliferation. Fragmented Media. Get Ready: It's a Whole New World," *Business Week*, July 12, 2004, 70–72.

---

medium can be used to appeal to consumers in a very emotional way, which is befitting of the self-satisfaction (reactor) strategy. Direct-response advertising sometimes takes the form of *infomercials* (long commercials). Examples are all the weight-control shows that promote a given diet program. Dieting is a highly emotional area in which a television infomercial can be highly effective in inducing consumers to act and act repeatedly.

Telemarketing is another direct-marketing promotional tool. It requires the use of telephones. Two forms of telemarketing are used: telephone in and telephone out. *Telephone in* refers to situations in which consumers dial an 800 number to place an order. Usually the 800 number is advertised or promoted through other sources such as direct-response advertising. A new form of telephone in is increasing in popularity and is called *telemedia* or *audiotext*. This tool involves the use of an 800, 900, or 976 number to promote a certain product. Most telemedia systems are interactive in that the consumer dials in and interacts with a computer. For example, a new audiotext system is being developed to allow health-care providers to call a computer that can help diagnose the medical condition of patients. The system interacts with the caller and guides the caller to respond to questions by pressing numbers on the dial. The outcome is a medical diagnosis. This system is less typical than those designed to promote a specific product. A more common example is an audiotext used by a restaurant to promote its menu. Callers dial in to find out what is on the menu for what days. Most systems are automated. *Telephone out*, on the other hand, involves the use of the telephone by a salesperson to call on current and potential customers in order to persuade them to make an immediate purchase.

Direct-marketing communications managers are now increasingly using new forms of *electronic media* to promote their products and elicit an immediate purchase response. For example, **teleshopping** is now widespread. The use of certain television channels that are exclusively devoted to selling products directly is now commonplace. Most of us know about the Home Shopping Network (HSN) and QVC. Consumers watch these cable channels; and, if they like whatever product is being advertised, they pick up the telephone and place an order on the spot through an 800 number. Similarly, electronic shopping is now becoming a fad. It is called **videotext.** Consumers can shop electronically through their personal computers. Most online services such as America Online, Compuserve, and Prodigy offer consumers a link to many manufacturers and resellers, allowing consumers to place an order directly.

Finally, we have direct personal selling as another tool of direct marketing. In direct selling, a salesperson presents and demonstrates the product to consumers and elicits an immediate sales response. There are two forms of direct selling: one-to-one selling and group selling. **One-to-one selling** involves having a salesperson interact with an individual consumer. The salesperson explains and demonstrates the product to that consumer. Most industrial marketing communications managers use this form of direct marketing. They send their sales representatives to visit potential customers at the job site. In many cases, one-to-one selling is difficult and costly. In these situations, group selling is attempted. **Group selling** involves assembling potential consumers in a group and presenting and demonstrating the product to them in one location. For example, many investment brokers send out invitations to prospective clients and invite them to attend a seminar on investment and to discuss the various services that the firm offers. Another form of group selling is the "party plan." For example, Mary Kay Cosmetics typically uses this sales technique.

Sales Promotion

Two sales promotion tools are especially well suited to the self-satisfaction (reactor) strategy. These are premiums and contests and sweepstakes. There are two forms of *premiums*—free and self-liquidating ones. *Free premiums* are inexpensive gifts placed in the product package. For example, in many children's cereal boxes, marketing communications managers place inexpensive toys. These are free premiums. Have you ever seen a child exerting pressure on his or her mother to buy a certain brand of cereal that contains a toy? The child is eager to get the gift. **Self-liquidating premiums,** on the other hand, are "gifts" that require the consumer to pay some or all of the premium plus the costs of handling and mailing. For example, local fast-food restaurants may sell beverages in containers with logos of local sports teams. These are sold to the fast-food patron at cost only.

Premiums are also commonly used to encourage repeat purchase. Premiums are a method to reward customers for purchasing a certain brand. This reward strengthens positive feelings toward the firm and its products, enhancing the likelihood of future purchases. Similar to premiums are bonus packs. They operate the same way. Because they receive more of the product at the regular price, customers feel rewarded for doing business with a specific firm and the bonus pack is seen as the reward.

Contests and sweepstakes are another popular form of sales promotion. A *contest* is a game in which consumers compete for prizes or money on the basis of a specific skill. Many radio stations use contests by challenging listeners to answer trivia questions. The first caller who gives the right answer wins the prize. If there is more than one winner, then a lottery drawing may be used to pick the winner. A *sweepstakes,* on the other hand, is a game based on chance. McDonald's over the years has run (and rerun every so often) the Monopoly game. With every purchase of certain products, the customer receives a sticker that allows him or her to purchase a piece of land on the Monopoly board. Once the customer collects an entire set of a particular color of property, he or she wins a prize. Contests and sweepstakes also reinforce customers' involvement with the marketing firm. This enhanced involvement increases repeat patronage.

teleshopping The use of certain television channels that are exclusively devoted to selling products directly.

videotext A form of electronic shopping in which consumers can place an order directly with the firm.

one-to-one selling A form of direct personal selling in which a salesperson interacts with an individual consumer. The salesperson explains and demonstrates the product to that consumer.

group selling A form of direct personal selling in which the salesperson assembles potential consumers in a group and demonstrates the product to them in one location.

self-liquidating premiums "Gifts" to consumers, provided they pay some or all of the premium plus the cost of shipping and handling.

Reseller Support

Contests and incentive programs are promotions that manufacturers use to stimulate sales. These contests are often directed to the managers and purchasing managers of the reseller firms. For example, an incentive for resellers may be in the form of free merchandise or a bonus for having met a sales quota. Although the goal of the contests and incentive programs is to encourage purchase of the manufacturer's product, it should be noted that learning is also enhanced. These contests and incentives motivate the resellers to learn more about the manufacturer's product and therefore are effective in implementing the learning communications strategy.

In-store advertising and point-of-purchase displays are also special types of incentives that encourage resellers to buy and stock manufacturers' products. A manufacturer that can set up point-of-purchase displays and promote its products within the store is very attractive to the reseller. This is because in-store advertising and point-of-purchase displays help move the manufacturer's products, thus allowing the store to do more selling. The more selling, the more profit for the reseller.

Personal selling is also commonly used in the context of reseller support. In this context, there are three types of personal selling jobs, namely creative selling, order taking, and missionary sales representatives.[8] *Creative selling* involves the following personal selling tasks: prospecting, assessing needs, recommending a means of satisfying needs, demonstrating the capabilities of the firm, and closing the sale. Here, the salesperson is the "point person" who establishes the initial contact and has the major responsibility for completing the transaction. *Order taking* is very different from creative selling. The order taker services an account. This situation is commonly referred to as a "straight rebuy." That is, the order does not change much. For example, a food manufacturer's salesperson may call on wholesale food companies and present them with a list of food products to sell. The *missionary sales representative* type of personal selling involves a combination of creative selling and order taking. The position calls for introducing new products and programs to both current and potential customers.

Public Relations

Public relations helps enhance repeat patronage by maintaining a positive image of the firm in the minds of customers. The most common public relations tools to achieve goals of the self-satisfaction (reactor) strategy are corporate advertising, event sponsorship, and product placements in television programs and movies. Corporate advertising is usually affectively based. That advertising serves to maintain and enhance the company's image in the minds of customers and other publics.[9] Have you seen corporate advertising on television lately? The Dow Chemical commercials? The DuPont commercials? The General Electric commercials? These are all affectively based, and none of them provide much information about their respective companies. They are simply designed to reinforce positive feelings about the company.

The same can be said for event sponsorship. Many companies sponsor specific sports events. For example, DuPont has had a long tradition sponsoring Tour DuPont—a bicycle race that is internationally known. Many companies, such as McDonald's, sponsor the Olympics. These sponsorships do not communicate a specific message about the company and its product line. The communications are affectively based rather than cognitive. Positive affect is transferred in the minds of consumers from the sporting event to the sponsoring company.[10]

A much more subtle way of inducing positive feelings about a product is to work out a deal with a popular movie in which the product appears and is used by favored characters. Because the audience has positive feelings about the movie character, positive affect transfer is a likely result. That is, the positive feelings the audience may have for the movie character would transfer to the product, too. This technique is referred to as *product placements in movies and television*. For example, the launch of the BMW Z3 was centered on its role in a James Bond movie. In today's world, many of the comedy shows on television have a variety of products appear in the background. In many shows, the product is shown to be used in explicit ways by the actors and actresses on the show.

---

in-store advertising A form of sales promotion in which consumers are provided with special types of information about product availability in the context of the store.

Summary

This chapter introduces ideas to help you conceptualize the marketing communications subsystem. Four different communications strategies are identified within the marketing communications subsystem: (1) informative (thinker), (2) affective (feeler), (3) habit formation (doer), and (4) self-satisfaction (reactor). For each strategy, you are shown a method of implementing the strategy, that is, assembling the appropriate elements of the marketing communications mix.

In relation to the informative (thinker) strategy, we recommend the use of certain forms of advertising (mostly print advertising), certain forms of reseller support programs (mostly training programs and trade shows), certain forms of public relations programs (press releases and publicity), and word-of-mouth (WOM) communications (stimulating WOM through advertising and sampling and creating a referral system).

In relation to the affective (feeler) strategy, we recommend the use of certain forms of advertising (mostly broadcast advertising), certain forms of reseller support programs (mostly cooperative advertising), certain forms of public relations programs (press conferences, corporate advertising, and event sponsorship), and WOM communications (stimulating WOM through advertising and sampling).

In relation to the habit-formation (doer) strategy, we recommend the use of advertising (mostly in the form of print and interactive advertising), direct marketing (mostly through direct mail, newsletter, and direct-response advertising), sales promotion programs (coupons, sampling, refunds and rebates, bonus packs, and price-off deals), reseller support programs (mostly in the form of trade allowances), and public relations (mostly in the form of publicity).

Finally, in relation to the self-satisfaction (reactor) strategy, we recommend the use of certain forms of advertising (such as outdoor and specialty advertising), certain forms of direct marketing (catalogs, direct-response advertising, telemarketing, and direct selling), sales promotion (the use of premiums and contests and sweepstakes), reseller support programs (contests and incentives, in-store advertising, point-of-purchase displays, and personal selling), and certain forms of public relations (corporate advertising, event sponsorship, and placement of the product in movies and television).

The four strategies and their applications as outlined previously provide a framework in which one can carry out execution of the SMC campaign and maintain its integration throughout the entire system. These discussions were designed to provide examples of tactical development as guided by the four overarching marketing communications strategies. In providing these examples, we show you a template upon which a manager can better link the tactical decisions made at this level back up throughout the entire SMC system of the firm. The examples show the use of the marketing communications strategies from Table 11-1 in an applied manner to allow you to develop a clearer understanding of how the SMC system works at this level. The discussion is also an introduction to the way in which the elements in the middle column of Table 11-1, the marketing communications portfolio components from Part Two of this book, can be used in building an optimal SMC mix. The following major section of the book, Part Four, provides you with an examination of all the important dimensions related to operationalizing the SMC program. It focuses the execution side of things by looking at how one can set objectives and measure, monitor, and assess the SMC executions.

Discussion Questions

1. Describe a model that offers a set of marketing communications strategies. Describe these strategies.
2. Describe the objectives associated with each of the marketing communications strategies.
3. Suppose you are a marketing communications manager of a new chain of restaurants that specializes in Middle Eastern food. You are beginning to plan the marketing communications campaign. What is your first priority? That is, what is the most important goal during the first year of the campaign? What is the appropriate strategy here? What elements of the marketing communications mix will be used to implement the selected strategy? Explain.
4. Now you are 6 months into the campaign for this Middle Eastern national restaurant. What should be the campaign goal? Should you now change your strategy? What elements of the marketing communications mix would you use? Explain.
5. Now you are one full year after the launch of the campaign. Again, should your goal and strategy change? If you now choose a new strategy, how will you go about implementing this strategy?
6. This is now the end of the second year. Upper management is now exerting pressure on you to show a high level of sales. Will you change your marketing communications strategy? From what to

what? What are your goals now? How will you go about implementing the new strategy?

7. After a couple of years, you have now built a patron base. A majority of people in the United States have tried your restaurant at least several times. Your goal is to make sure that these patrons come back and come back often. Articulate your marketing communications goals. What is your strategy? What marketing communications tactics would you use to carry out the strategy?

Practice Quiz

Note: You can find the correct answers to these questions by taking the quiz and then submitting your answers in the Online Edition. The program will automatically score your submission. If you miss a question, the program will provide the correct answer, a rationale for the answer, and the section number in the chapter where the topic is discussed.

1. The Foote, Cone, & Belding model involves a simple matrix that attributes consumer choices to _____, _____ and _____ issues.
   a. knowledge, approach, ethics
   b. information, attitude, behavior
   c. information, approach, attributes
   d. information, conception, application

2. Products can be classified as the "thinking type" or "feeling type." The distinction between thinking and feeling products is based on the distinction between _____.
   a. cognitive thinking and the emotional quotient (EQ)
   b. product factors and product characteristics
   c. right- and left-brain information processing
   d. high-involvement and high-thinking processing

3. _____ seeks to expose a target to the messages and to educate target consumers about the product's important costs and/or benefits.
   a. Transit advertising
   b. Information (knowledge) marketing
   c. An intermedia selection
   d. An informative strategy

4. Factors that influence intermedia selection are divided into two groups. Identify these two groups.
   a. low involvement and high involvement
   b. eliminating criteria and discriminating criteria
   c. media habits and media selectivity
   d. geographical reach and product selection

5. The affective (feeler) strategy involves _____.
   a. the application of marketing communications tools to generate maximum awareness and create the most positive attitude toward the brand
   b. exposing a target to the messages and educating target consumers about the product's important costs and/or benefits
   c. creating a message that encourages the audience to talk about the advertised product
   d. information about the company and/or one or more of its products that originates from customers

6. _____, formally defined, is "the provision of assistance either financially or in kind to an activity by a commercial organization for the purpose of achieving commercial objectives."
   a. Advertising
   b. Reseller support
   c. Corporate advertising
   d. Marketing

7. _____ are used only by business-to-business marketing communications managers or manufacturer-to-retailer promotions.
   a. Bonus packs
   b. Reseller support tools
   c. Trade allowances
   d. Habit-formation (doer) strategies

8. Which of the following is not a description of the "millennials"?
   a. This generation was raised in a world jam-packed with information and entertainment.
   b. The millennials were born between 1969 and 1984.
   c. The millennials consume globs of digital fare.
   d. Millennials are renowned for multitasking, regarded as hard sell on brands, and skeptical on advertising.

9. Two sales promotion tools are especially well suited to the self-satisfaction (reactor) strategy. These are _____ and _____ .
   a. premiums and contests, sweepstakes
   b. one-to-one selling, group selling
   c. in-store advertising, point-of-purchase displays
   d. telemarketing, teleshopping

10. Prospecting, assessing needs, recommending a means of satisfying needs, demonstrating the capabilities of the firm, and closing the sale, are all part of _____ .
    a. in-store advertising
    b. point-of-purchase displays
    c. personal selling
    d. creative selling

Web Exercise

Marketing Communications Strategies and Website Congruity

Using the FCB planning model quadrants, select four products/services you think would match with each of the four quadrants. Visit the websites of those different companies (or ones mentioned in this chapter—e.g., Ronco's http://www.ronco.com). Evaluate the way in which they provide information to the person who visits the website. Are they assuming that the individual is approaching the product from a certain perspective? If you were the webmaster, how would you redesign the website to better fit with the FCB quadrant classification that you had thought the product best fit into?

Suggested Readings

Barban, Arnold M., Donald W. Jugenheimer, and Peter B. Turk. 1989. *Advertising media sourcebook*, 3rd ed. Lincolnwood, IL: Crain Books/NTC Business Books.

Blattberg, Robert C., and Scott A. Nelson. 1990. *Sales promotion: Concepts, methods, and strategies.* Englewood Cliffs, NJ: Prentice Hall.

Block, Tamara Brezen, and William A. Robinson, eds. 1994. *Sales promotion handbook*, 8th ed. Chicago: Dartnell Press.

Bogart, Leo. 1984. *Strategy in advertising*, 2nd ed. Lincolnwood, IL: Crain Books/NTC Business Books.

Kaatz, Ron. 1995. *Advertising and marketing checklists*, 2nd ed. Lincolnwood, IL: Crain Books/NTC Business Books.

Lancaster, Kent M., and Helen E. Katz. 1992. *Strategic media planning*. Lincolnwood, IL: Crain Books/NTC Business Books.

Lodish, Leonard M. 1986. *The advertising & promotion challenge: Vaguely right or precisely wrong.* New York: Oxford University Press.

McGann, Anthony F., and J. Thomas Russell. 1988. *Advertising media: A managerial approach*, 2nd ed. Homewood, IL: Irwin.

Nelson, Carol. 1991. *The new road to successful advertising: How to integrate image and response.* Chicago: Bonus Books.

Parente, Donald, Bruce Vanden Bergh, Arnold Barban, and James Marra. 1996. *Advertising campaign strategy: A guide to marketing communication plans.* Fort Worth, TX: Dryden Press.

Schultz, Don, and Beth Barnes. 1993. *Strategic advertising campaigns*, 4th ed. Lincolnwood, IL: Crain Books/NTC Business Books.

———. 1999. *Strategic brand campaigns.* Lincolnwood, IL: Crain Books/NTC Business Books.

Schultz, Don E., Stanley I. Tannenbaum, and Robert F. Lauterborn. 1994. *Integrated marketing communications: Pulling it together & making it work.* Lincolnwood, IL: NTC Business Books.

Stone, Bob. 1994. *Successful direct marketing methods*, 5th ed. Lincolnwood, IL: NTC Business Books.

Thorson, Esther, and Jeri Moore. 1996. *Integrated communication: Synergy of persuasive voices.* Mahwah, NJ: Lawrence Erlbaum Associates.

Vaughn, Richard. 1980. How advertising works: A planning model. *Journal of Advertising Research* 20 (October): 27–33.

———.1986. How advertising works: A planning model revisited. *Journal of Advertising Research* 26 (February–March): 57–66.

Wall, Robert W. 1987. *Media math: Basic techniques of media evaluation.* Lincolnwood, IL: Crain Books/NTC Business Books.

Wilson, Laurie J., and Joseph Ogden. 2000. *Strategic communications planning: For effective public relations and marketing,* 4th ed. Dubuque, IA: Kendall/Hunt.

Yale, David R. 1995. *The publicity handbook.* Lincolnwood, IL: NTC Business Books.

Notes

1. Joe Mandese, "Chris Moseley: Discovery Channel," *Advertising Age,* June 26, 1995, S-4.
2. Bradley Johnson, "Abby Kohnstamm: IBM," *Advertising Age,* June 26, 1995, S-4.
3. Don E. Schultz, "Customers Determine Value of Your Marketing Tactics," *Marketing News,* October 7, 1996, 7.
4. Richard Vaughn, "The Consumer Mind: How to Tailor Ad Strategies," *Advertising Age,* June 9, 1980; Richard Vaughn, "How Advertising Works: A Planning Model." *Journal of Advertising Research* 20 (October 1980): 27–33; Richard Vaughn, "How Advertising Works: A Planning Model Revisited," *Journal of Advertising Research* 26 (February–March 1986): 57–66.
5. John Meenaghan, "Commercial Sponsorship," *European Journal of Marketing* 7, no. 7 (1983): 9; also see John Meenaghan, "Sponsorship—Legitimizing the Medium," *European Journal of Marketing* 25, no. 11 (1991): 5–10.
6. Martin S. Bressler, "Mainstream Companies Find Direct Mail Profitable," *Marketing News,* July 29, 1996, 7.
7. Note that Procter & Gamble, the maker of hundreds of staples including Tide, Pampers, and Folgers Coffee, is undergoing an experiment to eliminate coupons. P&G has realized that the long-run use of coupons has a negative effect on brand equity. Instead of coupons, P&G will lower price. "Procter & Gamble to Try Clipping Coupons—Out," *Knight-Ridder/Tribune,* appeared in the *Roanoke Times,* January 12, 1996, A9.
8. Thayer C. Talor, "A Letup in the Rise of Sales Call Costs," *Sales & Marketing Management,* February 25, 1980, 24.
9. David Schumann, Jan M. Hathcote, and Susan West, "Corporate Advertising in America: A Review of Published Studies on Use, Measurement, and Effectiveness," *Journal of Advertising* 20, no. 3 (1991): 35–56.
10. Howard Thomas, "Sponsorship—An Advertiser's Guide," *International Journal of Advertising* 4 (1985): 319–26; William L. Shanklin and John R. Kuzma, "Buying That Sporting Image," *Marketing Management* (Spring 1992): 59–67; Christian Ryssel and Eric Stamminger, "Sponsoring World-Class Tennis Players," *European Research* (May 1988): 110–16.

Building, Executing, and Assessing Your Integrated Marketing Communications Plan

Part Four

Executing an effective marketing communications program should entail an effective system for implementation, control, and monitoring. The firm has to articulate its goals clearly and quantitatively. It has to determine the exact amount of resources that are needed to accomplish the stated goals. It has to identify the tests or measures needed to assess performance and use these tests or measures to collect data. It has to ascertain deviations between desired and actual levels and take corrective action. To businesses that operate in a world that has become home to global products and huge multinational firms, the need to be an effective system is clear.

12 Setting Objectives and Assessing Performance: Setting Goals and Measuring Performance of the Strategic Marketing Communications System

13 Analysis Guiding Objective Setting: Linking Strategies and Tactics to Objectives and Performance Measures

14 Strategic Allocation of Resources: Budgeting in the Strategic Marketing Communications System

15 Takeaways from the Strategic Marketing Communications Process: Lessons in Monitoring, Control, and Integration

In 2004 Procter & Gamble had $51 billion in sales and an impressive 25 percent growth in net income over the previous year; sixteen of its brands like Bounty and Pampers had over a billion dollars in sales themselves. Jim Stengel, P&G's global marketing officer (GMO) of consumer products oversees an annual marketing budget of $5.5 billion and manages a global workforce of thirty-five hundred marketers and three hundred brands. Stengel is very aware, though, that today's global environment has led to major changes in the marketplace. There is an increasing awareness all across the industry that there is a crucial need for being able to better understand and respond to the consumer. Stengel strongly believes that the consumer is much more in control now. Companies cannot simply put advertisements together in the old ways and pummel the consumers until they buy the brand. In today's world, it is all about strategy embracing a more holistic-based approach to thinking, one that is guided by constant market analyses based on a better measurement and monitoring system for development of products and marketing programs and the subsequent allocation of resources. One author refers to Stengel as an obsessive measurer and quotes the executive's view on the subject of today's market. "Unless you are vigilant, and unless you are extremely clear as a leader about what is important in marketing, it gets diffuse. Making sure that a worldwide marketing organism is thinking the same way, motivated by the same things, and working toward the same goals. If that happens it's a powerful dynamic."[1]

The chapters in Part Four offer a discussion related to the various elements of the system that are needed if that powerful dynamic is to be operating effectively. Chapter Twelve examines the issue of measurement and performance within the SMC system. Chapter Thirteen's discussion focuses on the links of strategies and tactics discussed in Part Three to executions in the system. The system's budgeting and allocation of resources are examined in Chapter Fourteen. Finally, Chapter Fifteen ends the section with a look back at the entire system and how it needs to be considered in an integrative and holistic manner.

Note

1. John Galvin and Jack Neff, "The World on a String," *Advertising Age* (February 2005): 13.

Setting Objectives and Assessing Performance

Setting Goals and Measuring Performance of the Strategic Marketing Communications System

Key Terms

affective brand attitude (p. 310)
aided-recall measures (p. 304)
associative strength (p. 307)
attitude toward brand purchase (p. 315)
brand acceptance (p. 313)
brand attitude (p. 310)
brand awareness objective (p. 295)
brand do objective (p. 296)
brand feel objective (p. 296)
brand learn objective (p. 296)
brand loyalty (p. 319)
brand preference (p. 314)
brand profit (p. 296)
brand purchase (p. 317)
brand recall (p. 308)
brand recognition (p. 309)
brand repeat objective (p. 296)
brand sales (p. 296)
brand satisfaction (p. 318)
brand-as-an-animal-or-thing test (p. 306)
brand-as-a-person test (p. 306)
brand-listing procedure (p. 314)
brand-user test (p. 306)
cash flow (p. 301)
cognitive brand attitude (p. 310)
cognitive-structure index (p. 304)
decision-process test (p. 306)
entrenched loyalty (p. 320)
favorability measure of attitude toward purchase (p. 316)
free-association test (p. 306)
how-brand-is-different test (p. 306)
image measure (p. 304)
multiattribute attitude index (p. 310)
mushiness index (p. 312)
paired-comparison method (p. 315)
percentage-of-purchase measure (p. 318)
personal-values test (p. 307)
picture-interpretation test (p. 306)
profit (p. 300)
projective measures (p. 313)
purchase intention (p. 316)
ranking method (p. 314)
recognition measures (p. 303)
repeat purchase (p. 317)
semantic differential measure of attitude toward purchase (p. 316)
thought-elicitation procedure (p. 312)
top-of-mind awareness (p. 308)
tracking studies (p. 317)
unaided self-report questions (p. 314)
use-experience test (p. 306)

Chapter Twelve

Chapter Outline

12-1 Introduction

12-2 Advantages of Stating and Quantifying Objectives

12-3 Setting Objectives
- 12-3a Identifying Campaign Execution Objectives
- 12-3b Identifying Appropriate Measures for Each Objective
- 12-3c Identifying Desired Levels and Appropriate Time Frames for Each Objective

12-4 Examples of Objectives
- 12-4a Corporate Objectives
- 12-4b Marketing Objectives
- 12-4c Marketing Communications Objectives

12-5 Measures of Corporate Objectives
- 12-5a Profit and Cash Flow
- 12-5b Brand Sales and Market Share

12-6 Measures of Marketing Objectives
- 12-6a Recognition Measures of Brand Knowledge
- 12-6b Aided-Recall Measures of Brand Knowledge
- 12-6c The Image Measure of Brand Knowledge
- 12-6d The Cognitive-Structure Index
- 12-6e The Belief-Strength Measure
- 12-6f Projective Measures of Brand Associations
- 12-6g Associative-Strength Measures of Brand Awareness

12-7 Measures of Marketing Communications Objectives
- 12-7a Brand Awareness *(Aware)*
- 12-7b Brand Attitude *(Feel)*
- 12-7c Brand Trial or Purchase *(Do)*
- 12-7d Repeat Purchase *(Repeat)*

Summary
Discussion Questions
Practice Quiz
Web Exercise: Let Me Count the Ways—Measurement of Communications
Suggested Readings
Notes

If you can't measure it, you can't manage it.

—**George Odiorne,** American management guru (1920–1992)

12-1 Introduction

The Weather Channel attracts people who tend to be very interested about the content of the programming. An executive at the network calls Weather Channel viewers "passionate and action-oriented." It seems that this passion also transfers to their interaction with clients who purchase spots on the channel. A 2004 survey of 1,250 adults ages 12 to 64 found that advertisements on the Weather Channel had a 50 percent higher recall rate than advertisements that were viewed on other news networks. Advertisements that focus on a local advertiser (local tag) were 38 percent higher than a regular 30-second spot. Additionally, if a spot was specifically set up to be triggered by a local weather condition, that advertisement had a phenomenal 125 percent higher recall than a regular advertisement on the channel.[1] These numbers point to the complexity of what seems to be a simple media buy on a cable network. If one simply examined "exposure," the true value of the interaction toward ultimately achieving a given corporate objective would be lost. Marketers cannot simply assume that their corporate, marketing, or marketing communications objectives are likely to be met by looking at a simple, single, cross-sectional measure of exposure. They have to measure performance explicitly using reliable and valid measures of performance dimensions. A recent Australian study found that firms that better managed their marketing communications through a higher level of integration were more likely to see a better brand performance in the marketplace.[2] The management of the integrative system is only possible when there is a fully integrated, theoretically sound measurement system in place as well. This chapter is about research and measurement. We need to be very clear and specific about the objectives that we set for a given marketing communications campaign and monitor progress and performance within the system.

This chapter introduces you to marketing communications objectives, their conceptualizations, and the particular methods and measures used to tap them. All marketing communications decisions are designed to meet particular objectives. These are designated as brand awareness (brand recognition, recall), brand learn (brand knowledge, association, image, comprehension), brand feel (brand affect, attitude, preference, acceptance), brand do (purchase intention, trial purchase, actual purchase), repeat purchase (brand satisfaction, brand loyalty, brand commitment), brand sales (brand market share), and brand profit (cash flow) objectives; and decision outcomes are evaluated against these goals (see Figure 12-1). Before we describe these objectives and their measures, let us first discuss the advantages of specifying objectives that are quantifiable and measurable. See SMC Marketplace Watch 12-1.

12-2 Advantages of Stating and Quantifying Objectives

Advertising agency and marketing communications managers have always used a variety of research methods over the years to assess the effectiveness of advertising campaigns. One study from the 1980s found that the percentage of organizations that

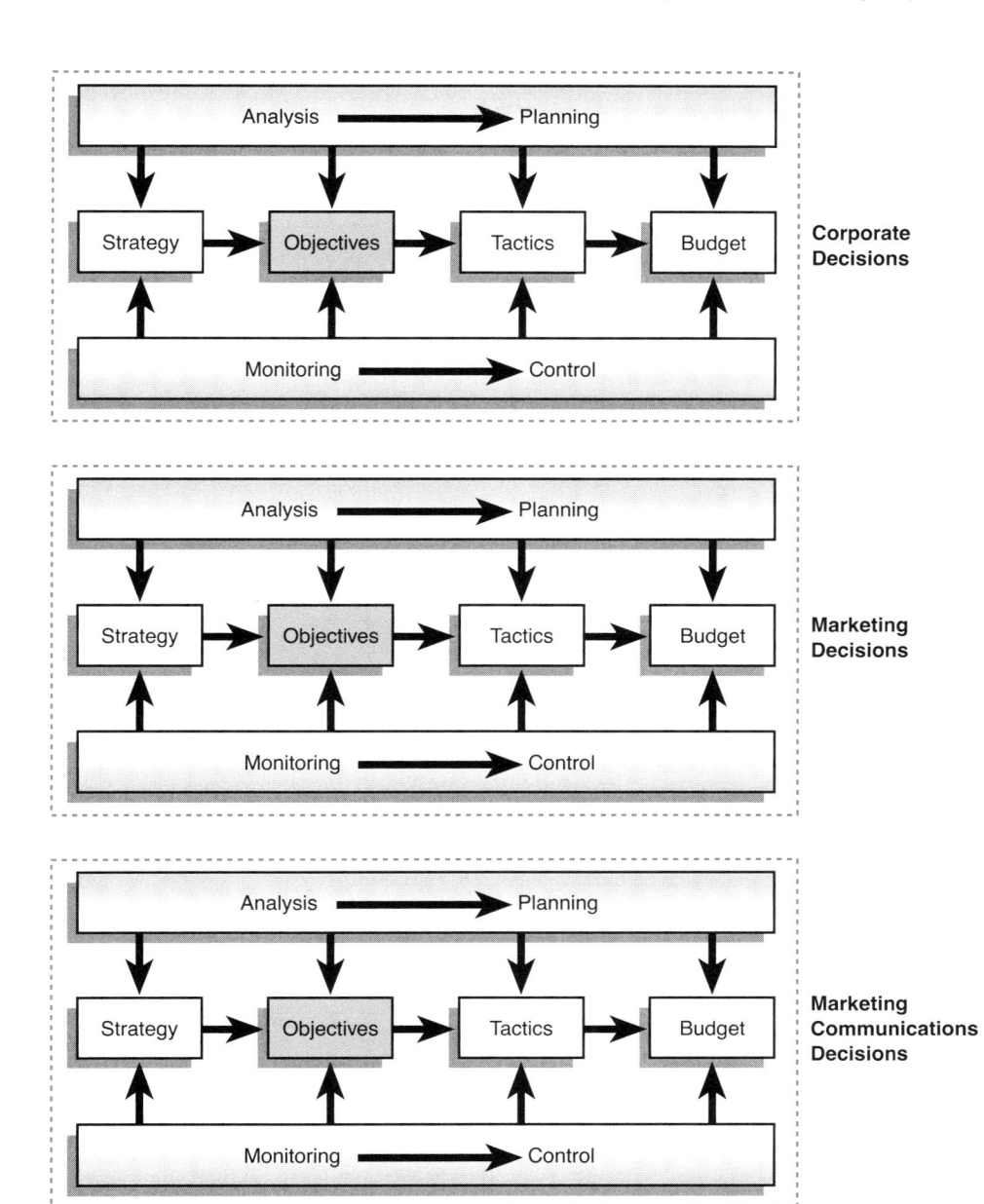

Figure 12-1
Corporate, Marketing, and Marketing Communications Objectives

evaluate television advertising campaigns is very high.[3] Specifically, 87.5 percent responded that marketing/advertising research was used to test the effectiveness of television campaigns (with 94.9 percent of advertising agencies concurring and 83.6 percent of advertisers concurring). In today's world, measurement continues to be crucial. More recently, Stienberg noted that all forms of advertising-impact measurement from Nielsen's television ratings to simple newspaper circulation numbers are "under keen scrutiny."[4] As an example of the measurements that are being touted by a variety of firms, he cites a product placement example of Procter & Gamble's Crest on *The Apprentice,* a reality show. Using the tracking company's (iTVX) measurement scheme, the Crest product placement scored a 10.8—a score that, according to iTVX, indicated the placement was worth 10.8 commercials on the show, or $4.2 million.[5] However, the question left unanswered by such a rating is, What was the ultimate objective of Procter & Gamble regarding the brand and its placement in the show?

SMC Marketplace Watch 12-1

Changes in Media Habits Create Challenges for New Ways of Measuring Media Habits

The 2005 Annual Conference of the American Advertising Federation was a big extravaganza. It was attended by twelve hundred advertising professionals who saw a glimpse of how rapidly new technologies are fueling the shift in media habits. The pace of change in consumers' adoption of media technology in the household is progressing far faster and more dramatically than many understand. What are those household communications devices that have contributed to a shift in media habits? These include wireless networking to 3-D movies, television, DVD, podcasts, and other on-demand media. Marketing representatives from AOL and Yahoo made the case that broadband is not only increasing the time consumers spend on the Internet but also changing how they are using it.

The adoption of broadband on the Internet is also revolutionizing music marketing. A marketing representative from Warner Bros. Music said that "placing songs into commercials is becoming more important because it's now easier for consumers to find the musicians behind the songs." Furthermore, radio stations that traditionally defined format lines through their playlists are increasingly having to respond to consumer tastes for songs they learn about elsewhere (i.e., on the Internet and satellite radio). A representative from OMD (a media-buying agency specializing in radio spots) indicated that stations have increase playlists from a few hundred songs to twelve hundred.

In the film world, technology is now allowing local theaters to replace film projectors with digital ones, bringing with it the bonus of 3-D movies; 3-D sound is already possible from existing televisions using special techniques that make the stereo sound seem as if it's coming from all over a room.

Source: Adapted from Ira Teinowitz, "Pace of Household Technology Change Increases: AAF Conference Speakers Emphasize Sweeping Impact," *Advertising Age,* June 16, 2005. AdAge.com QwikFIND ID: AAQ65U.

Any marketing communications campaign cannot be effectively planned and executed without specific objectives. Using marketing communications objectives addresses the following concerns:

1. Without marketing communications objectives, a company cannot determine the effectiveness of a marketing communications campaign. This is because it would not know which measurement instruments to use for assessing campaign effectiveness. Effectiveness measures are numerous and varied. To find out which measures to use to assess effectiveness, we first need to know what we are supposed to be measuring, which is very much dependent on the exact objectives the marketing communications campaign was designed to accomplish. For example, suppose we have a pharmaceutical company advertising a brand of an analgesic pain reliever. The advertising campaign addresses the benefits of the company's analgesic relative to the leading brand of analgesics. How can we assess the effectiveness of the advertising campaign? Should we look at brand sales? How about measuring consumers' purchases? Purchase intention? How about preference for the analgesic brand in relation to the leading brand? Satisfaction with the brand? Extent of repeat purchase? How about brand awareness? The list can go on and on. The idea here is that every marketing communications campaign is designed to accomplish some very specific objectives. It may be that the pharmaceutical company developed the advertising campaign to increase consumers' preference for its brand over the leading brand by a certain margin. Suppose that the preference for the company's brand of analgesic was 10 percent before the advertising campaign. The company wanted to increase the preference to 20 percent by launching the campaign. At the end of the campaign period, the company would assess the effectiveness of the advertising campaign by measuring the consumers' preference for the analgesic brand. Suppose the preference effectiveness measure indicates 15 percent. This means that the advertising campaign was moderately effective in that it increased preference

from 10 percent to 15 percent. However, the objective was 20 percent. In other words, the campaign fell short by 5 percent.

2. Without specific marketing communications objectives, the marketing communications manager is not likely to know what marketing communications tactics or programs to use. There is an ever-increasing number of elements in the marketing communications mix to choose from in developing a communications campaign. Specifically, the manager is very much concerned with the questions, What is the best configuration of the marketing communications mix to accomplish the marketing communications objectives? Should the marketing communications manager develop a campaign through advertising? Print? Television? Cable? Radio? How about a mix between advertising and personal selling? How about a mix of direct marketing and sales promotion? How much should be allocated to website-based interactive games? What role should a word-of-mouth viral marketing program play? What about automated instant messaging (AIM) on the Internet or on cellular telephones? In the marketing communications environment of today, the list from which to choose the ultimate configuration is staggering. We need to know marketing communications objectives first and foremost before we can select the right tools to accomplish the stated objectives. Think of the toolbox as an analogy. A toolbox has many tools. Each tool is designed to accomplish something, something concrete and specific. Similarly, the elements of the marketing communications mix are like tools. Without marketing communications objectives, we would not be able to effectively choose the appropriate mix. The selection of a marketing communications mix is partly guided by marketing communications objectives. At the same time, the consumer is becoming more savvy to the channels of choice, so the question of what comprises the optimal mix is critical for target market influence and budget development.

3. Without marketing communications tactics, the marketing communications manager cannot figure out an optimal budget to develop a marketing communications campaign. A very common question is: How much should we spend on a communications campaign? The marketing communications manager does not want to overspend or underspend. To figure out exactly how much to spend, the manager needs to define what he or she is trying to accomplish. Once the marketing communications manager has clearly defined what he or she is trying to accomplish through marketing communications, it is much easier to figure out the tools needed to accomplish the objectives *and* the cost of using these tools.

12-3 Setting Objectives

Setting objectives is an organizational task involving three key processes: (1) identification of one or more objective dimensions, (2) identification of the measures used to gauge outcomes related to each objective, and (3) identification of the desired level and time frame associated with each objective dimension. Let us discuss each of these tasks in some detail and provide illustrations.

12-3a Identifying Campaign Execution Objectives

Here, the marketing communications manager tries to select appropriate goals or objectives. The objectives are such things as *brand awareness* (brand recognition, recall), *brand learn* (brand knowledge, association, image, comprehension), *brand feel* (brand affect, attitude, preference, acceptance), *brand do* (purchase intention, trial purchase, actual purchase), *repeat purchase* (brand satisfaction, brand loyalty, brand commitment), *brand sales* (brand market share), and *brand profit* (cash flow).

- The **brand awareness objective** is the goal to achieve a certain level of brand awareness in the minds of a target market. For example, a pizza restaurant in a college

brand awareness objective
A marketing communications goal. It describes a situation in which target consumers recognize or recall the brand name as related to a product category.

town launches a marketing communications campaign directed to college students. The owner states his objective as "I want 95 percent of college freshman students to become aware of my pizza place in the next 3 months."

- A **brand learn objective** is the goal to achieve a certain level of learning, knowledge, association, image, and/or comprehension related to the product's benefits. "We need to get target consumers to understand what our product is all about." The owner of the pizza place may say, "I want at least 60 percent of the college freshman students to know that my pizza tastes better because of the special tomato sauce I use. I want them to know this in the next 3 months."

- A **brand feel objective** is the goal to achieve a certain level of positive attitude (affect, preference, or acceptance) toward the product. Statements reflecting this objective are: "We need to get the target consumers to develop a preference for our product." "We want the communications campaign to increase brand preference by 20 percent in the next 6 months." The pizza place owner may say, "I want at least 40 percent of all college students to prefer my pizza place over the other pizza places we have in town."

- A **brand do objective** is the goal to induce a certain level of the target market to purchase (or at least to make plans to purchase) the product. Statements reflecting this objective are: "We need to get 35 percent of the target market to express a purchase intention of our product by the year's end." The owner of the pizza place may say, "I want at least 40 percent of the college freshman students to try my pizza at least once in the next 3 months."

- A **brand repeat objective** is the goal to achieve a certain level of purchases in a given period of time as a direct function of the campaign (repeat purchases, brand satisfaction, brand loyalty, brand commitment). "We need to increase the number of purchases per individual consumer. Approximately 80 percent of our target consumers are purchasing our product once a month and 20 percent twice a month. We want to get 50 percent to purchase the product twice a month by the end of next year." The pizza place owner may say, "I want 80 percent of my college student patrons to express a great deal of satisfaction with my pizza and to indicate that they will eat pizza in my place again when they want to eat pizza in the next few weeks."

- **Brand sales** (actual sales, market share, etc.) and **brand profit** (gross profit, net profit, cash flow, ROI, etc.) are goals that focus on the financial bottom line. The pizza place owner may say, "We need to increase sales by 20 percent by the end of next quarter."

The challenge is to identify the appropriate objectives that are consistent with the selected strategy and its strategic mix. This was the subject of the preceding chapter. Having read Part Three of the book, we now know what objective dimensions go with what strategies and what elements of the strategic mix go with what strategy and what objective. The point is: *Select the appropriate objectives that closely match the selected strategy and its strategic mix.*

Let us revisit how the different strategies help the marketing communications manager select objectives. Table 12-1 lists strategies and objectives for each level of the organization.

12-3b Identifying Appropriate Measures for Each Objective

Once one or more objective dimensions are specified, the marketing communications manager has to identify and select valid and reliable measures that are well established in the industry for each selected objective. In addition, the norms pertaining to that measure must be identified. For example, suppose we select a brand awareness objective. We must examine alternative measures of brand awareness and select a suitable method and measure.

---

brand learn objective
The goal to achieve a certain level of learning, knowledge, associations, image, and/or comprehension related to the product's benefits.

brand feel objective
The goal to achieve a certain level of positive attitude (affect, preference, or acceptance) toward the product. A statement reflecting this objective is: "We need to get the target consumers to develop a preference for our product."

brand do objective The goal to induce a certain level of the target market to purchase (or at least to make plans to purchase) the product.

brand repeat objective
The goal to achieve a certain level of purchases in a given period of time as a direct function of the campaign (repeat purchases, brand satisfaction, brand loyalty, brand commitment).

brand sales A goal that focuses on the financial bottom line; includes actual sales, market share, and so on.

brand profit A goal that focuses on the financial bottom line; includes gross profit, net profit, cash flow, ROI, and so on.

TABLE 12-1 Strategies and Objectives by Organization Level

The Corporate Level

- Growth strategy → *Objective:* Maximize sales and market share.
- Maintain-position strategy → *Objective:* Minimize negative percentage change in sales and market share.
- Harvest strategy → *Objective:* Maximize profit.
- Innovation strategy → *Objective:* Establish or increase sales and gain high market share.
- Divestment strategy → *Objective:* Maximize cash flow.

The Marketing Level

- Strategic product focus → *Objective:* Build a psychological association between brand and product attribute *x*, intangible factor *x*, product class, leading competitor *x*, or country of origin *x* in the minds of targeted consumers.
- Strategic price focus → *Objective:* Build a psychological association between brand and relative price or low price in the minds of targeted consumers.
- Strategic place focus → *Objective:* Build a psychological association between brand and distributor *x*, distributor location *x*, or distributor *x*'s service ability in the minds of targeted consumers.
- Strategic prospects focus → *Objective:* Build a psychological association between brand and customer benefit *x*, customer image *x*, or specific product use *x* in the minds of targeted consumers.

The Marketing Communications Level

- Informative (thinker) strategy → *Objective:* Generate maximum brand awareness and learning in the minds of targeted consumers.
- Affective (feeler) strategy → *Objective:* Generate maximum brand awareness and positive attitude toward the brand in the minds of targeted consumers.
- Habit-formation (doer) strategy → *Objective:* Induce trial purchase and learning from product use (first-time users) and reinforce learning (repeat users) in the minds of targeted consumers.
- Self-satisfaction (reactor) strategy → *Objective:* Induce trial purchase and brand liking from product use (first-time users) and reinforce positive attitude toward the brand (repeat users).

Next we examine the norms of that measure. Are there previous studies using this measure with our product, a comparable product, a comparable target market, and a comparable marketing communications campaign? Suppose our product is a brand of deodorant soap. We are planning an affective (feeler) strategy to be implemented through a television advertising campaign that should last 6 months. Our target consumers are adult women ages 12 to 34. Now suppose we find several studies that deal with a comparable market, product, and advertising campaign. Now let us say that based on these studies, the average increase in brand awareness after 6 months of television advertising seems to hover around 50 percent. Now we are in a position to go to the next step and identify the desired level associated with the selected objective.

12-3c Identifying Desired Levels and Appropriate Time Frames for Each Objective

Knowing the norms of the measure that will be used to gauge the performance of our advertising campaign, we are now positioned to identify the goal of the communications campaign in a very concrete and quantitative way. Should the marketing communications manager set his or her goal to reflect the norm, above the norm, or below the norm? If a 50 percent increase in brand awareness is the norm should the goal be 50 percent, greater than 50 percent, or less than 50 percent?

Setting the objective above the norm is possible when the marketing communications manager knows that his or her communications campaign is likely to be more effective than the campaigns of "comparable" products. Conversely, if the marketing communications manager believes that his or her campaign is not likely to be as effective, perhaps setting objectives below the norm is better. In the absence of strong feelings one way or the other, the marketing communications manager should set objectives at a level reflecting the norm.

Note that the time frame must also match comparability with previous studies to be guided by the norms of these previous studies. For example, if most of the previous studies conducted with comparable products and communications campaigns involve a time frame of 6 months (duration of the entire advertising campaign), then the time frame of the planned campaign should also be 6 months.

The manager considers factors such as the firm's past and forecasted performance, the competition's past and anticipated performance, anticipated changes in the industry and marketplace, and anticipated changes in the firm itself. At all times, the manager needs to be cognizant of how his decisions regarding a particular execution can be linked back into the entire corporate system.

12-4 Examples of Objectives

Some examples of exactly how those decisions can be integrated within the larger corporate system may be useful. What follows are integrated objectives developed by a software company named MapLinX. MapLinX has since been acquired by Microsoft and is known now as MapPoint. However, for demonstration purposes, the following examples use the company's independent brand status of *MapLinX*. Examples are presented at the three levels of corporate, marketing, and marketing communications and are followed by an extended discussion of each of these types of objectives. The possible objectives for MapLinX (the software program keeps track of sales data using geographic plots) are stated in terms of next quarter (the next 3 months), the second quarter (the 3 months after next quarter), and the third quarter (the 3 months after the second quarter). (You can learn more about the product by accessing the SMC QuickLink.)

SMC QuickLink
Microsoft MapPoint
http://www.microsoft.com/mappoint/default.mspx

12-4a Corporate Objectives

Objectives for next quarter: MapLinX will be introduced at the beginning of next quarter. Therefore, the goal is to establish *sales* of MapLinX by capturing 2 percent of the global market. This translates into 100,000 units sold by the end of next quarter.

Objectives for the second quarter: Capture another 5 percent of the global market. This translates into 250,000 additional unit sales by the end of the second quarter. The total units sold at the end of the second quarter should be 350,000.

Objectives for the third quarter: Capture another 10 percent of the global market. This translates into 500,000 additional unit sales by the end of the third quarter. The total units sold at the end of the third quarter should be 850,000.

12-4b Marketing Objectives

Objectives for next quarter: Establish an *association* between MapLinX (brand) and the visual clarity of the maps (product attribute) so that at least 7 percent of sales managers in the global market (or 350,000 sales managers out of the entire population of 5 million) will come to describe MapLinX by referring to its visual clarity. This should be accomplished by the end of next quarter.

Objectives for second quarter: Increase the *association* between MapLinX (brand) and the visual clarity of the maps (product attribute) so that at least 15 percent of sales managers in the global market (or 750,000 sales managers out of the entire population of 5 million) will come to describe MapLinX by referring to its visual clarity. This should be accomplished by the end of the second quarter.

Objectives for third quarter: Increase the *association* between MapLinX (brand) and the visual clarity of the maps (product attribute) so that at least 30 percent of sales managers in the global market (or 1.5 million sales managers out of the entire population of 5 million) will come to describe MapLinX by referring to its visual clarity. This should be accomplished by the end of the third quarter.

12-4c Marketing Communications Objectives

Objectives for next quarter: Establish *brand awareness* of MapLinX so that at least 10 percent of sales managers in the global market (or 500,000 sales managers out of the entire population of 5 million) will recognize MapLinX as a sales management software. This should be accomplished by the end of next quarter. Establish brand association between MapLinX (brand) and the visual clarity of the maps (product attribute) so that at least 7 percent of sales managers in the global market (or 350,000 sales managers out of the entire population of 5 million) will come to describe MapLinX by referring to its visual clarity. This should be accomplished by the end of the next quarter. Establish brand preference for MapLinX so that at least 5 percent of sales managers in the global market (or 250,000 sales managers out of the entire population of 5 million) will come to express liking and preference for MapLinX by the end of next quarter. Establish brand trial for MapLinX so that at least 3 percent of sales managers in the global market (or 150,000 sales managers out of the entire population of 5 million) will come to order it on a trial basis by the end of next quarter.

Objectives for the second quarter: Increase brand awareness of MapLinX so that at least 20 percent of sales managers in the global market (or 1 million sales managers out of the entire population of 5 million) will recognize MapLinX as a sales management software. This should be accomplished by the end of the second quarter. Increase the brand association between MapLinX (brand) and the visual clarity of the maps (product attribute) so that at least 15 percent of sales managers in the global market (or 750,000 sales managers out of the entire population of 5 million) will come to describe MapLinX by referring to its visual clarity. This should be accomplished by the end of the second quarter. Increase brand preference for MapLinX so that at least 10 percent of sales managers in the global market (or 500,000 sales managers out of the entire population of 5 million) will come to express liking and preference for MapLinX by the end of the second quarter. Increase brand trial for MapLinX so that at least 7 percent of sales managers in the global market (or 350,000 sales managers out of the entire population of 5 million) will come to order it on a trial basis by the end of the second quarter.

Objectives for the third quarter: Increase brand awareness of MapLinX so that at least 40 percent of sales managers in the global market (or 2 million sales managers out of the entire population of 5 million) will recognize MapLinX as a sales management software. This should be accomplished by the end of the third quarter. Increase the brand association between MapLinX (brand) and the visual clarity of the maps (product attribute) so that at least 40 percent of sales managers in the global market (or 2 million sales managers out of the entire population of 5 million) will come to describe MapLinX by referring to its visual clarity. This should be accomplished by the end of the third quarter. Increase brand preference for MapLinX so that at least 20 percent of sales managers in the global market (or 1 million sales managers out of the entire population of 5 million) will come to express liking and preference for MapLinX by the end of the third quarter. Increase brand trial for MapLinX so that at least 13 percent of sales managers in the global market (or 650,000 sales managers out of the entire population of 5 million) will come to order it on a trial basis by the end of the third quarter.

The corporate, marketing, and marketing communications objectives are summarized in Table 12-2.

TABLE 12-2 Examples of Corporate, Marketing, and Marketing Communications Objectives

	Next-Quarter Objective (Percentage)	Second-Quarter Objective (Percentage)	Third-Quarter Objective (Percentage)
Corporate			
Sales	2	5	10
Marketing			
Brand association	7	15	30
Marketing Communications			
Brand awareness	10	20	40
Brand preference	5	10	20
Brand trial	3	7	13

Note: The size of the target consumer population is 5 million. For example, the 2 percent sales objective for the next quarter means that the goal is to capture 2 percent of the market in sales by the end of next quarter, which amounts to 100,000 units (2 percent × 5 million). The 7 percent brand association for next quarter means that the goal is to establish a mental association between the brand and an important feature so that least 7 percent of the market will come to describe the brand in terms of that feature, and this has to be accomplished by the end of next quarter. The 10 percent brand awareness objective for next quarter means that the goal is to make 10 percent of the target consumers aware of the brand by the end of next quarter. The 5 percent brand preference for next quarter means that the goal is to make 5 percent of the target consumers prefer the brand in question over competitor brands, and this should be accomplished by the end of next quarter. The 3 percent brand trial for next quarter means that the goal is to make 3 percent of the market order the product on a trial basis by the end of next quarter.

12-5 Measures of Corporate Objectives

Corporate objectives are usually classified as either long-term or short-term objectives. Long-term marketing objectives involve measurable standards such as brand sales and market share. Short-term objectives usually involve measures of profit and cash flow. Usually, short-term marketing effectiveness is judged at the corporate level in terms of profits. In this section, we show you how marketing communications managers conceptualize and measure profit, cash flow, brand sales, and market share and how they conduct market tests (see Table 12-3).

12-5a Profit and Cash Flow

The most common measures of short-term marketing effectiveness are profit and cash flow. **Profit** is the difference between the company's sales revenue and the cost of producing and selling the good.[6] Mathematically formulated,[7]

$$Z = R - C$$

where

Z = product's profit
R = product's revenue
C = product's costs

in which

$$R = P' \times Q$$

where

P' = product's net price
Q = quantity sold

where

$$P' = P - k$$

profit A corporate performance standard, traditionally measured in terms of a product's revenues minus costs for a given time period.

TABLE 12-3 Measures of Corporate Objectives and Performance

- Profit
- Cash flow
- Sales
- Market share

in which

P = product's list price

k = unit allowance representing freight, commissions, and/or discounts

where

$$C = cQ + F + M$$

in which

c = unit variable nonmarketing costs (e.g., labor costs, delivery costs)

F = fixed costs (e.g., salaries, rent, electricity)

M = marketing costs (e.g., advertising, sales promotion)

Therefore,

$$Z = [(P - k)Q] - (cQ - F - M)$$

Cash flow, on the other hand, is nothing more than a figure that indicates how much cash the firm has in hand. Usually a profit/loss statement is generated after the completion of a project or periodically, such as every quarter, every year, and so on. A cash-flow statement can be generated any time to indicate how much cash is available, whether the firm has enough cash to pay its bills this month, next month, and so on.

cash flow A corporate performance standard traditionally measured in terms of cash availability after a given time.

12-5b Brand Sales and Market Share

A common way to measure marketing effectiveness is to plot sales figures over time and to overlap the plot with marketing communications expenditures and the different types of marketing communications that have been used over the same period. The graphs may clearly show that changes in sales are being influenced by changes in marketing communications type and expenditure levels. For example, the graph may show that sales peaked at a time when marketing communications expenditures were highest. The inference then is that high expenditures are likely to drive up sales.

The market share measure is a variation of the brand sales measure in that it accounts for the company's brand sales in relation to competitor brand sales within the same period (e.g., last quarter). We focus on two popular forms of measuring brand sales and market share. These are the *proportion of sales method* and the *market test method*.

Market Share as a Proportion of Sales Relative to Competitor Sales

Market share is usually formulated as

$$M_1 = S_1 / (S_2 + S_3 + S_4 + \ldots S_n)$$

where

M_1 = market share belonging to Brand 1

S_1 = sales belonging to Brand 1

S_2 = sales belonging to Brand 2

S_3 = sales belonging to Brand 3

S_4 = sales belonging to Brand 4

S_n = sales belonging to Brand n

Market Tests

The focus of a market test is to select a representative geographic area and conduct a periodic survey to measure the level of sales over time. Changes in sales are interpreted to be a function of the marketing communications campaign over time. In particular, market tests are employed to test the viability of a new brand before its introduction at the national or international level. High levels of brand sales (and/or market share) in the test market are taken as an indication of the effectiveness of the marketing communications campaign.

Another use of the market test method is to test the effectiveness of different marketing communications campaigns. For example, suppose that three different marketing communications campaigns are selected. The campaigns are implemented in different test markets, and brand sales (and/or market share) are monitored in each of the test markets. The test market that records the highest levels of sales (and/or market share) signifies a successful marketing communications campaign.

12-6 Measures of Marketing Objectives

Let us review what we talk about in Chapter Eleven, the marketing strategies and tactics chapter. We describe several marketing strategies and the objectives of each of these strategies. The strategies and objectives all sought to positively influence brand equity, brand associations, brand knowledge, or brand image. Brand image is a learning outcome of knowing something about the brand; its performance features; and other features such as reliability, durability, quality, price, stereotypic image of the user, and so on. A major goal of any marketing program is to mold the right image of the brand in the minds of the target consumers. This means that the marketing communications manager has to educate the consumer about certain attributes of the brand.

Consumer researchers usually show brand knowledge as a connection between a node representing the brand and other nodes representing attributes (see Figure 12-2). For example, "Crest toothpaste whitens teeth" is a brand belief. This belief links the brand, Crest, with an attribute, "whitens teeth." Each belief can be characterized in terms of strength and valence. The strength of a belief reflects the strength of the linkage between the brand node and the attribute node. Looking at Figure 12-2, we can see that the belief strength of "Crest toothpaste has nice color" is the strongest

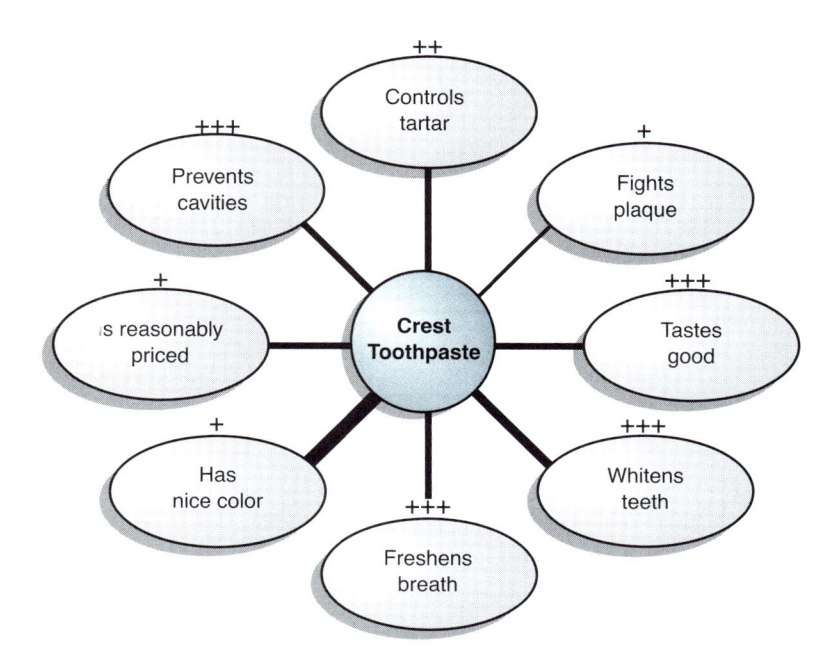

Figure 12-2

A Schematic Representation of Belief/Knowledge in a Consumer's Mind about Crest Toothpaste

The plus signs (+) indicate the level of desirability for each attribute. The strength/thickness of the line linking the brand node and the attribute node reflects the strength of the link between the brand and that attribute.

belief; the second strongest is "Crest toothpaste whitens teeth"; the weakest belief is "Crest toothpaste fights plaque."

The valence property of a belief reflects the desirability of that belief in relation to other beliefs. For Crest toothpaste, note that in the mind of that particular consumer, the consumer regards the attributes of "whitens teeth," "freshens breath," "tartar control," and "has nice color" to be highly desirable (three positive signs). The desirability of "fight cavities" is moderate, while "tastes good," "cavity prevention," and "is reasonably priced" are somewhat desirable.

The marketing communications manager's task is to identify strengths and weaknesses within the brand belief/knowledge structure. An attribute that is considered highly desirable but may not be strongly linked with the brand in the minds of the target consumers signals a weakness, or a strategic gap. The marketing communications manager, thus, can set a marketing objective to strengthen a weak belief of a highly desirable attribute (e.g., tartar control) by formulating a communications campaign aimed at strengthening this belief in the minds of the target consumers. Of course, the communications claims about the attribute have to be substantiated.

Strategic opportunities also are identified based on strengths. In other words, instead of formulating a campaign to address a weak belief and attempt to strengthen it, the focus can be on strong beliefs with desirable attributes. By focusing on established beliefs related to desirable attributes (e.g., fights cavities), the marketing communications manager thus can capitalize on positive characteristics and further reinforce these. One approach is corrective action; the other is reinforcement.

Marketing communications researchers use measures of brand knowledge not only to ensure that the target consumers have formed the "right" beliefs about the brand in question but also to understand which beliefs are most related with brand purchase. For example, suppose you are a marketing communications manager of a new brand of toothpaste. Your brand has been advertised to emphasize the following benefits: tartar control, plaque prevention, tooth decay prevention, teeth whitening, fresh breath, good taste, and pump dispenser. Suppose research reveals that brand purchase among teenagers, the target market, is directly related to the following benefits: whitens teeth, freshens breath, and tastes good. That is, brand purchase may be determined by consumers' beliefs about these benefits; hence, these particular benefits should be treated as more important than others. Future marketing communications efforts thus can be adjusted to emphasize the benefits that are directly related to purchase behavior (and to de-emphasize those that are not directly related to behavior).

In subsequent sections, we discuss and review common measures of marketing objectives (see Table 12-4).

12-6a Recognition Measures of Brand Knowledge

Recognition measures of brand knowledge deal with the recognition of specific aspects (mostly product benefits) formed about the brand in question. For example, Johnson Controls, Inc., is an industrial company that introduced a total building automation system permitting all automatic building systems to be monitored,

recognition measures
Methods to capture brand awareness by presenting sample respondents with an advertisement without the brand name and asking respondents if they recognize the brand name.

> **TABLE 12-4** Measures of Marketing Objectives and Performance

- Recognition measures of brand knowledge
- Aided-recall measures of brand knowledge
- The image measure of brand knowledge
- The cognitive-structure index
- The belief-strength measure
- Projective measures of brand associations
- Associative-strength measures of brand awareness

SMC QuickLink
Johnson Controls
http://www.johnsoncontrols.com

coordinated, and operated by a single computer. The company was advertised in *The Wall Street Journal* for 6 months. The company may wonder what kind of impression potential customers have formed about the company after the 6-month advertising campaign in *The Wall Street Journal*. Johnson Controls's goal was to instill certain beliefs about the company, namely, that the company can install the building automation system and that the building automation system can monitor, coordinate, and operate all automated aspects of the building. Measuring brand knowledge in this case is a matter of asking respondents whether they recognize that the company offers these benefits.

Responses are usually coded as "yes" or "no," and a percentage frequency of those who said "yes" is determined by each belief statement (e.g., the total building system can monitor all automatic building systems; the total building system can coordinate all automatic building systems; the total building system can operate all automatic building systems; Johnson Controls can install the total building system, etc.). Of course, like all tests and measures testing the effectiveness of the marketing program, the before-the-campaign scores are compared with the after-the-campaign scores. This measure of brand knowledge is highly suitable to assess the effects of marketing communications campaigns guided by any of the fifteen positioning strategies described in Chapter Ten.

12-6b Aided-Recall Measures of Brand Knowledge

aided-recall measures
Methods to capture what consumers remember about the advertisement, the brand name, and the benefits and costs of the brand by asking subjects to recall the information without giving them memory cues.

Aided-recall measures usually involve asking a sample of consumers from the target market in an open-ended manner to list everything they know about the brand in question.[8] The open-ended responses are then analyzed, and brand beliefs statements are identified and tabulated. This is done before and after the launch of the communications program. The percentage of subjects identifying a certain brand attribute before the communications campaign is then compared to the percentage of subjects identifying the same attribute after the campaign. Like the recognition measure, this measure too can be used to assess the effects of all fifteen positioning strategies.

12-6c The Image Measure of Brand Knowledge

A very popular instrument that has been commonly used to measure beliefs or knowledge of a particular brand is a modified version of the semantic differential scale. Figure 12-3 shows an example of a profile of beliefs/knowledge pertaining to two brands of beer.

image measure A method that captures respondents' perceptions of the benefits, costs, and/or other attributes of the brand.

The **image measure** involves a certain configuration of beliefs represented on bipolar scales, such as something special/just another beer; relaxing/not relaxing; little aftertaste/lots of aftertaste; strong/weak, aged a long time/not aged a long time, and so forth. The respondent evaluates a certain brand of beer in relation to other brands of beer by marking a response somewhere between the polar extremes of each of the bipolar scales. The responses for each attribute dimension are averaged across all respondents. The result is a belief/knowledge profile of the brand in question contrasted with belief/knowledge profiles of the competing brands.

As in all tests and measures of marketing program effectiveness, premeasures and postmeasures are administered and the effectiveness of the communications campaign is judged in terms of the degree of change in the brand image profile. This measure is particularly suitable to assess the effectiveness of the following positioning strategies: *positioning by attribute, positioning by intangible factor, positioning by customer benefits*, and *positioning by distributor's serviceability*.

12-6d The Cognitive-Structure Index

cognitive-structure index
A method that captures brand knowledge; it is typically an inventory of items in which respondents rate the likelihood of the brand having or not having certain features on a 7-point rating scale varying from "very unlikely" to "very likely."

The **cognitive-structure index** is constructed from items asking subjects to indicate their level of agreement with brand attribute statements For example, items for a set

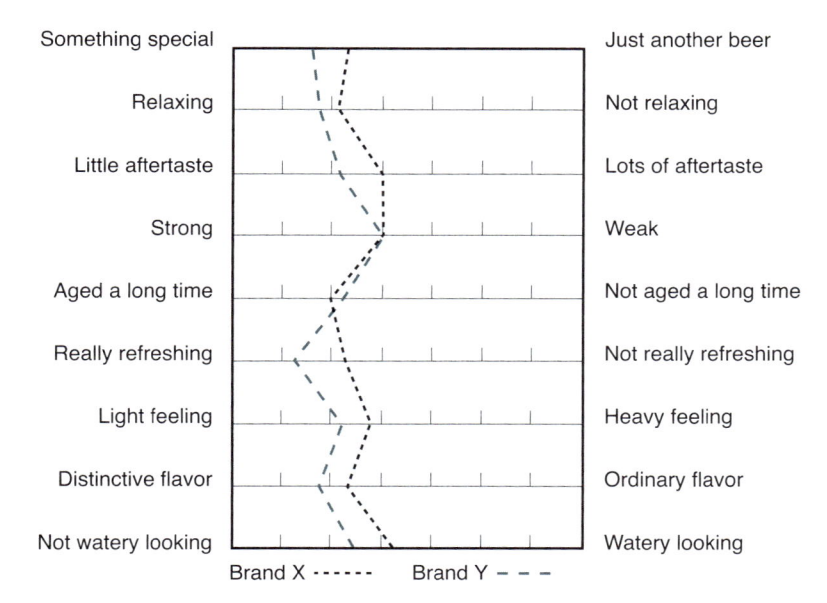

Figure 12-3
A Semantic Differential Comparison of Branded Beers

of Bose headphones may include: "delivers high-quality sound," "is small and lightweight," and so on. These perceptions are measured on seven-point scales anchored by "extremely unlikely" (−3) and "extremely likely" (+3).[9]

To judge the effectiveness of a marketing campaign in terms of brand knowledge, the precampaign average score pertaining to each belief item is compared with its corresponding postcampaign score. For example, the precampaign average score pertaining to the belief that the Bose brand of headphones "delivers high-quality sound" is +1.2, whereas the postcampaign score is +2.8. Therefore, the campaign has changed the belief that the brand delivers high-quality sound from a +1.2 to a +2.8, an average change of +1.6 units. This measure, like the image measure of brand knowledge, is particularly suitable to assess the effectiveness of the following positioning strategies: *positioning by attribute, positioning by intangible factor, positioning by customer benefits,* and *positioning by distributor's serviceability.*

12-6e The Belief-Strength Measure

Belief strength is measured by asking subjects, "How likely do you think it is that (the brand) has (attribute *x*)?" Responses are plotted on a six-point scale labeled from "zero likelihood" to "certain" (coded 1 to 7).[10] The idea here is that the communications campaign is responsible for increasing the certainty or strength of certain beliefs about the brand (the belief that the brand has attribute *x*). The campaign effectiveness is judged by comparing the average belief strength score of each attribute dimension derived before the launch of the campaign with those derived after the launch of the campaign. This measure may be particularly suitable to assess the effectiveness of the following positioning strategies: *positioning by relative price, positioning by low price, positioning by use or application, positioning by competitors, positioning by country of origin, positioning by brand-distributor tie-in,* and *positioning by distributor's location.*

12-6f Projective Measures of Brand Associations

In many instances, consumers feel uncomfortable or may be unable to elicit associations stored in their memories, perhaps because these associations are buried in the subconscious memory. Also, many of the self-report tests and measures of brand knowledge may bias respondents toward logical/rational responses, while in actuality the brand associations that may matter the most are those that are not logical or rational. In these instances, projective measures are effective to tap brand associations.

Typical projective tests include free-association tests, picture-interpretation tests, describing-the-brand-as-a-person tests, describing-the-brand-as-an-animal tests, in-depth examination of the person's use experience with the brand, dissection of the decision process, description of the brand user, description of how brands are different from one another, and discovery of personal values driving choice:[11]

- A **free-association test** involves word associations. Subjects are presented with a list of objects including the brand in question and asked to provide the first set of words that comes to mind.

- The **picture-interpretation test** involves presenting subjects with a picture of a scene in which the brand is somewhat embedded in the picture. For example, a brand association test involving BMW may show a person standing in front of the car and looking at it. The subject is asked what this person is thinking and feeling.

- The **brand-as-a-person test** instructs subjects to select from a set of fifty personality-related words to describe the brand in question. For example, in a study conducted at Young & Rubicam (one of the largest advertising agencies in the world), Holiday Inn was described as "cheerful, friendly, ordinary, practical, modern, reliable, and honest"; Atari was described as "youthful"; Oil of Olay was described as "gentle, sophisticated, mature, exotic, mysterious, and down to earth."[12]

- The **brand-as-an-animal-or-thing test** involves asking subjects to think of animals or animal characteristics that come to mind when thinking about a certain brand. For example, in a study conducted at Young & Rubicam advertising agency, subjects were given a list of twenty-nine animals and were asked: "If each of these brands was an animal, what one animal would it be?" They asked similar questions for twenty-five different activities, seventeen fabrics, thirty-five occupations, and twenty nationalities. The results showed that Oil of Olay was associated with mink, France, secretaries, silk, swimming, and *Vogue* magazine. Kentucky Fried Chicken was associated with Puerto Rico, a zebra, a housewife dressed in denim, camping, and reading *TV Guide*.[13]

- The **use-experience test** is an in-depth interview with consumers who have a history of using the brand in question. The discussion focuses on past experience with the product. The subject is encouraged to open up, to remember and express feelings and situations in which the brand was used. Ernest Dichter, a psychologist who was once very popular for using projective measures to uncover hidden motives associated with the use of products and brands, reported the following encounter with Ivory soap. He interviewed more than one hundred users of Ivory soap, allowing them to express themselves about their bathing habits. One finding was that young women would take an unusually thorough bath before going out on a date. This finding resulted in the advertising theme: "Be smart, get a fresh start with Ivory soap."[14]

- The **decision-process test** involves tracking a consumer's decision process. This is traditionally done through an in-depth personal interview. The interviewer starts from the decision to purchase and probes backward to understand the dynamics and the reasons the consumer has made that decision.

- The **brand-user test** is a simple procedure in which subjects are asked to describe the typical brand user. More specifically, subjects are asked how a user of one brand is different from the user of another brand and how the needs and motivations of the users of the two brands differ. For example, a classic study showed that people perceive the brand user of Maxwell House drip-grind coffee to be very different from the user of Nescafé instant coffee. The instant-coffee woman was perceived as a lazy, bad homemaker; whereas the woman buying the drip-grind coffee was perceived as an industrious, good homemaker.[15]

- The **how-brand-is-different test** asks subjects to distinguish between various brands in a particular product category. Specifically, this test uses a pairwise comparison. Two brands at a time are shown to a subject, and the subject is asked to

---

free-association test A test that involves word associations. Subjects are presented with a list of objects including the brand in question and asked to provide the first set of words that comes to mind.

picture-interpretation test A test that involves presenting subjects with a picture of a scene in which the brand is somewhat embedded in the picture.

brand-as-a-person test A test that instructs subjects to select from a set of fifty personality-related words to describe the brand in question.

brand-as-an-animal-or-thing test A test that asks subjects to think of animals or animal characteristics that come to mind when thinking about a certain brand.

SMC QuickLink
Olay
http://www.olay.com

use-experience test An in-depth interview with consumers who have a history of using the brand in question.

SMC QuickLink
Ivory
http://www.ivory.com

decision-process test A test that involves tracking a consumer's decision process. This is traditionally done through an in-depth personal interview. The interviewer starts from the decision to purchase and probes backward to understand the dynamics and the reasons the consumer has made that decision.

brand-user test A simple procedure in which subjects are asked to describe the typical brand user.

how-brand-is-different test A test that asks subjects to distinguish between various brands in a particular product category.

point to differences between the two brands. Subtle differences among the different brands may be uncovered using this method, and these differences may play a significant role in brand purchase.

In a more sophisticated version of this method, similarity judgments (judgments of the extent to which two brands are similar) are used in a multidimensional scaling algorithm. The multidimensional scaling procedure produces spatial maps in which the different brands are plotted in two- or three-dimensional space. The distance between any two brands represents the perceptual similarity/differences between them. Thus, the closer two brands are on the map, the more similar they are in the judgment of consumers.

- The **personal-values test,** sometimes referred to as the "laddering technique," involves using in-depth interviews to uncover the person's motivation to purchase and use a specific brand. Here the subject is asked to describe the brand attributes. For each attribute, the interviewer probes the personal significance of the attribute through a series of "why" questions. Probing why a certain concrete attribute is important to the individual may result in an abstract attribute, which may reveal functional consequences, psychosocial consequences, and personal values, respectively.

For example, a consumer may describe a certain brand of car as receiving 45 miles per gallon (concrete attribute), which is interpreted as "high" miles per gallon (abstract attribute). The reason this product attribute is important to the individual may be because it helps him save money (functional consequence). He thinks that his parents would approve of his buying an economy car (psychosocial consequence). Saving money makes the consumer feel good because he sees himself as responsible and disciplined (instrumental value), which in turn enhances his self-esteem (terminal value). See Figure 12-4 for an example of how this technique is used on Nike shoes.

Projective measures and methods can be effectively employed to assess the more "subtle" positioning strategies, such as *positioning by user or customer, positioning by lifestyle or personality,* and *positioning by brand-distributor tie-ins.*

12-6g Associative-Strength Measures of Brand Awareness

Associative strength is defined as the strength of the association in memory between the product category and the brand.[16] One study identified two direct measures of

SMC QuickLink
Nescafé
http://www.nescafe.com

personal-values test A test, sometimes referred to as the "laddering technique," that involves using in-depth interviews to uncover the person's motivation to purchase and use a specific brand.

SMC QuickLink
Nike
http://www.nike.com

associative strength The strength of the association in memory between the product category and the brand.

Researcher: You said that a shoe's lacing pattern is important to you in deciding what brand to buy. Why is that important to you?
Consumer: A staggered lacing pattern makes the shoe fit more snugly on my foot. *[physical attribute and functional consequence]*
Researcher: Why is it important that the shoe fit more snugly on your foot?
Consumer: Because it gives me better support. *[functional consequence]*
Researcher: Why is better support important to you?
Consumer: So I can relax and enjoy the run. *[psychological consequence]*
Researcher: Why is it important for you not to worry while running?
Consumer: Because it gets rid of tension I have built up at work during the day. *[psychological consequence]*
Researcher: Why is it important to you to get rid of tension from work?
Consumer: So I can go back to work in the afternoon. I can perform better. *[instrumental value—high performance]*
Researcher: Why is it important that you perform better?
Consumer: I feel better about myself. *[terminal value—self-esteem]*
Researcher: Why is it important that you feel better about yourself?
Consumer: It just is! *[the end!]*

Figure 12-4
An Example of a Laddering Interview

associative strength. One measure involves assessing how early a brand was named in response to a directive to list all the members of a given product category. The other measure tests the time it takes consumers to identify correctly a brand name belonging to a given product category. Specifically, subjects are presented with a product category name (e.g., toothpaste) on a monitor, followed by a brand name (e.g., Crest) that is either a member or nonmember of that product category. Subjects press either a "yes" or "no" button to indicate as rapidly as possible whether the brand is a member of the specified product category. Associative strength is measured in terms of response latency (how long it took the subject to respond).

Associative-strength measures are used to assess the effectiveness of a marketing communications campaign in significantly increasing brand awareness. This is done by administering an associative-strength test before the launch of the campaign and another after a period of time. The assumption is that if the campaign is successful in significantly increasing brand awareness, then consumers will more readily associate the brand in question with the product category. Note that this method is most suitable to assess the effectiveness of positioning by product class.

12-7 Measures of Marketing Communications Objectives

We organize the discussion of the marketing communications measures based on the five objective dimensions—namely, *aware* (brand awareness), *learn* (message comprehension), *feel* (attitude toward the brand), *do* (brand trial or purchase), and *repeat* (brand loyalty). Note that the *learn* or brand comprehension dimension is essentially the same as brand knowledge, the objective dimension used to identify and describe the various objective measures pertaining to marketing performance. This is because positioning strategies focus on brand associations, brand image, or brand knowledge. Because the preceding section related to measures of marketing objectives covered these measures, they are not repeated here. The various constructs of marketing communications objectives and their measures are shown in Table 12-5.

12-7a Brand Awareness *(Aware)*

Brand awareness is very important because without awareness the consumer cannot travel up the hierarchy. That is, the consumer is not likely to learn about the brand features, feel positive about the brand, make a preference decision, or feel convicted to purchase the product. In other words, the consumer has to be aware of the brand before feeling any desire or conviction to use it.

Brand awareness is the ability to recall or recognize a certain brand as being a member of a certain product class; thus, this objective fits well with the positioning-by-product-class strategy. Consider the following brands of housewares: Rubbermaid, General Electric, Corning, Cannon, Corelle, Ecko, Visions, Sunbeam, Black & Decker, and Libbey. Some consumers may be aware of Corning, for example, as a brand of houseware, while others may fail to recognize the connection. Aaker views brand awareness as a hierarchy consisting of five layers.[17] At the bottom of the hierarchy are the consumers who are unaware of the brand. These people simply do not recognize the brand as belonging to a given product class. The next layer includes those who have brand recognition. Brand recognition is the minimum level of awareness. **Brand recall** is the layer above it. The brand recall layer includes consumers who can retrieve information from memory concerning the various brands belonging to a product class. Finally at the top of the hierarchy we have the **top-of-mind awareness.** These consumers recall the brand first and foremost. The brand name is on the "top of their minds." When asked about a certain product, the brand in question is evoked quickly and with relative ease compared to other brands.[18]

brand recall A way to capture brand awareness that involves asking subjects about what they remember in relation to a brand in question.

top-of-mind awareness A state of mind in which consumers can easily recall the brand. The brand name is on the "top of their minds." When asked about a certain product, the brand in question is evoked quickly and with relative ease compared to other brands.

TABLE 12-5 Measures of Marketing Communications Objectives and Performance

Brand Awareness (Aware)
- The recognition measure of brand awareness
- Aided-recall measure of brand awareness

Brand Attitude (Feel)
- Cognitive brand attitude
  - The multiattribute attitude index
  - The thought-elicitation procedure
  - The mushiness index
- Affective brand attitude
  - The semantic differential measure of brand attitude
  - Projective measures of brand attitude
- Brand acceptance
  - The brand-listing procedure
  - Unaided self-report questions
- Brand preference
  - The ranking method
  - The paired-comparison method

Brand Trial or Purchase (Do)
- Attitude toward brand purchase
  - The semantic differential measure of attitude toward purchase
  - The favorability measure of attitude toward purchase
- Purchase intention
  - A measure of purchase intention given product need
  - A planned purchase measure
- Brand purchase
  - Tracking studies
  - Purchase incentive measures

Repeat Purchase (Repeat)
- Repeat purchase
  - Repurchase measures
  - Percentage-of-purchase measures
- Brand satisfaction
- Brand loyalty
  - A multivariate measure of brand loyalty
  - A measure of entrenched loyalty

Note the difference between recognition measures of brand awareness and brand knowledge. Brand awareness recognition measures deal mostly with the recognition of the brand name, while recognition measures of brand knowledge deal with the recognition of specific aspects (mostly product benefits) of the brand in question. The purpose of awareness measures is to tap consumers' memory about the product over a specific time. More specifically, brand awareness tests and measures tap whether consumers remember the brand name before and after the implementation of a marketing program. We cover two popular measures of brand awareness: the recognition method and the aided-recall method.

The Recognition Measure of Brand Awareness

Here is an example of a **brand recognition** measure that was used to gauge the level of brand awareness before and after an advertising campaign. We have already discussed an industrial company—Johnson Controls—that introduced a total building automation system that permits all automatic building systems to be monitored, coordinated, and operated by a single computer. The company wanted to make key people *aware* of the new system, specifically people who make major decisions regarding buildings. So the company ran an advertising campaign in *The Wall Street Journal*. They measured brand awareness before the campaign and 6 months after the advertising campaign had been launched. Sample consumers were asked before the launch of the advertising campaign whether they recognized the brand or its name. Responses were coded as "yes" or "no," and the percentage of those who said "yes" was determined. Before the launch of the advertising campaign in *The Wall Street Journal*, the brand awareness of the total building automation system was close to 0 percent among the decision makers. After 6 months of the advertising campaign,

brand recognition A way to capture brand awareness that involves exposing subjects to certain stimuli (e.g., an advertising slogan) and then a series of brand names. Subjects are then asked if they can recognize the correct brand name.

the same recognition measure of brand awareness was administered to another sample of the target population. The results indicated that brand awareness increased to 63 percent for the same target population. In other words, because all other promotion and marketing elements were held constant, the 63 percent change in brand awareness may be attributed to the advertising campaign.[19]

Aided-Recall Measures of Brand Awareness

Aided-recall measures usually involve asking a sample of consumers from the target market to list the names of different brands of the product in question. Aided-recall measures are used in tracking studies. Tracking studies use the same measure over a period of time to "track" changes or shifts in a behavioral phenomenon. (In this case, the behavioral phenomenon is brand awareness measured through an aided-recall testing procedure.)

Some researchers argue that the recognition-type measures are more realistic than aided-recall measures. This is because when faced with a buying decision, consumers are exposed to different brands (as in the supermarket). This exposure to the different brands may serve to facilitate the recognition of the brand in question.[20]

12-7b Brand Attitude *(Feel)*

brand attitude A marketing communications objective; marketing communications managers not only try to educate target consumers about the brand itself; they also try to do so in such a way that the brand image will result in an overall liking toward the brand.

Brand attitude is another major marketing communications objective. Marketing communications managers not only try to educate target consumers about the brand itself; they also try to do so in such a way that the brand image will result in an overall liking toward the brand. Marketing scholars distinguish between two types of brand attitude—cognition-based and affect-based brand attitude. They also make a distinction between brand attitude and brand acceptance.

Cognitive Brand Attitude

cognitive brand attitude A marketing communications goal that describes a desirable situation in which target consumers establish a favorable attitude toward the firm's brand. The attitude is formed based on "rational" beliefs and cognitions.

affective brand attitude A marketing communications goal that describes a desirable situation in which target consumers establish a favorable attitude toward a firm's brand. The attitude is based on an emotional response.

Cognitive brand attitude refers to the overall positive or negative opinion consumers have about the brand based on "rational" beliefs and cognitions. We define "rational" beliefs and cognitions as the kind of beliefs that are generated by conscious thought. To fully understand the concept of cognitive brand attitude, we need to distinguish cognitive brand attitude from "affective brand attitude." **Affective brand attitude** refers to the overall positive or negative opinion consumers may have about the brand based on emotional considerations. In other words, consumers may form an overall judgment of the goodness or badness of the brand based on some good reasoning, the kind of reasoning that they may be conscious of and that allows them to articulate the "reasons why" they like or dislike the brand. Thus, a brand attitude formed as a result of well-articulated cognitions (e.g., one's belief that Crest toothpaste is reasonably priced, has a nice color, whitens teeth, and has tartar control) is a cognition-based brand attitude. In contrast, if a consumer forms an overall opinion of the brand based on an association with an attractive celebrity and the consumer is not conscious of the underlying reason, the brand attitude is said to be affective. That is, the consumer's attitude is not based on conscious reasoning. If we ask the consumer why he or she likes or dislikes the brand, he or she may not be able to respond accurately because the information processing occurred at a basic, subconscious, emotional level.

Three methods for assessing cognition-based brand attitude are described here. These are the multiattribute attitude index, the thought-elicitation procedure, and the mushiness index.

multiattribute attitude index A measure that captures attitude by taking into account many benefits and costs of brand.

The Multiattribute Attitude Index Many marketing researchers use a **multiattribute attitude index** to establish brand attitude scores that are firmly embedded in "reasons why" consumers may like or dislike the brand. The typical multiattribute attitude index takes the following form:

$$A = \Sigma\, B_i I_i$$

where

A = cognitive-type attitude score toward the brand
B_i = belief that the brand has attribute i
I_i = importance of attribute i in relation to the other attributes

For example, suppose the communications campaign is directed to college students. The goal is to convince the local residents who are college students of large universities to stick around in the summer and take summer courses at the community college. That is, the focus of the advertising campaign is to persuade the local residents to attend the community college during the summer by educating them about the college's lower tuition costs, proximity to home, academic reputation of the faculty, party atmosphere, and summer athletic program. Before the launch of the campaign, a sample of local residents who attend large universities outside of their community would respond to a survey questionnaire in which they are asked the extent to which they believe the local community college has lower tuition costs (compared to the large state universities), is indeed conveniently located, has a good academic reputation, is the kind of place where students would have a good time at parties and other social events, and has a good summer athletic program. These questions are in essence the belief-strength (B_i) measures. An example of a measure follows.

Indicate your agreement or disagreement with the following statement: Community College *X* has a good summer athletic program.

(−3)	(−2)	(−1)	(0)	(+1)	(+2)	(+3)
Highly disagree	Moderately disagree	Slightly disagree	Neither agree nor disagree	Slightly agree	Moderately agree	Highly agree

Traditionally, belief-strength measures are comparative. That is, the subject responds to the belief-strength questions pertaining to the focal brand (Community College *X*) in relation to competitive brands (State University *Y* and *Z*). The importance weights (I_i) are usually assigned by instructing respondents to rank the attributes (tuition costs, proximity, academic reputation, party atmosphere, summer athletic program) in terms of importance. The greater the importance, the higher the rank. Here is an example. "Rank these decision criteria in order of importance (use the following scale: 5 = 1st most important criterion, 4 = 2nd most important criterion, 3 = 3rd most important criterion; 2 = 4th most important criterion; and 1 = 5th most important criterion)." See Table 12-6.

Each belief-strength agreement score is then multiplied with its corresponding importance weight rank score. The resulting scores pertaining to each attribute are then summed across all attributes. The higher the total score (in the positive direction), the more favorable the attitude based on the designated attributes (the reasons why). At a specific time after the launch of the campaign, the same survey is re-administered and the attitude of the local residents who attend the state universities is re-assessed. The campaign is deemed effective (based on a cognitive brand attitude objective) if the postcampaign attitude scores are significantly higher than the precampaign scores.

TABLE 12-6 Example of Ranking Decision Criteria

Decision Criterion	Rank
Tuition costs	4
Proximity	3
Academic reputation	5
Party atmosphere	2
Summer athletics	1

Note: The higher the score, the more important the decision criterion.

thought-elicitation procedure A method designed to measure the consumer's attitude toward the brand by capturing the kind of thoughts articulated by the respondent about the brand.

The Thought-Elicitation Procedure The **thought-elicitation procedure** is another test of brand attitude (the cognitive component). Subjects are presented with the actual brand (or a description of it in words and/or pictures). They are then asked to evaluate the brand strengths and weaknesses (possibly in relation to competitive brands) and to record their thoughts in writing. A variation of this procedure is to request the subject to think out loud and record the verbal expressions on a tape recorder. Trained judges then analyze the thoughts. They identify favorable and unfavorable thoughts about the brand and record their frequency.

A subject's brand attitude score is computed in terms of a simple arithmetic difference by subtracting the number of negative thoughts from the number of positive thoughts. Of course, the test is administered before the onset of the campaign and after the advertising campaign. The effectiveness of the advertising campaign is judged in terms of the extent to which it is able to generate more positive than negative thoughts about the brand.

mushiness index A measure capturing attitude strength.

The Mushiness Index Attitude strength can be measured through different methods. One method that is gaining popularity in advertising/public opinion literatures is Yankelovich, Skelly, and White's mushiness index.[21] The **mushiness index** was specially designed to determine the firmness of an attitude. The measure contains four items. Two example items are shown in Table 12-7.

Note that the mushiness score is not used exclusively as a measure of the cognitive component of brand attitude. The mushiness score is used with some other measures of brand attitude that capture the valence of the attitude. As with other tests and measures of campaign effectiveness, a survey is done before the launch of the campaign and the attitude strength and valence scores are computed. Another survey is conducted using the same measures after a specified period of time, and attitude strength and valence scores are computed again. The precampaign score is then compared with the postcampaign score to judge effectiveness.

Affective Brand Attitude

The focus here is on attitude, the kind of attitude that is formed or changed as a direct function of subtle and emotional factors. For example, consider a communications program involving an advertisement that employs a very attractive celebrity (one who is considered a sex symbol). The target consumers are likely to form a positive attitude toward the advertised brand mostly because of the celebrity. Here the attitude is formed (or changed) not because consumers thought about the brand, its benefits, its costs, and so on but because of uncontrollable factors operating in the subcon-

---

TABLE 12-7 Examples of Mushiness Index Items

"On some issues, people feel that they really have all the information they need in order to form a strong opinion on that issue, while on other issues they would like to get additional information before solidifying their opinion. On a scale of 1 to 5, where 1 means that you feel you definitely need more information, where would you place yourself?"

| Definitely need more information | 1 | 2 | 3 | 4 | 5 | Do not need more information |

"People have told us that on some issues they come to a conclusion and they stick with that position, no matter what. On other issues, however, they take a position but they know that they could change their minds easily. On a scale of 1 to 5, where 1 means that you could change your mind very easily on this issue and 5 means that you are likely to stick with your position no matter what, where would you place yourself?"

| Could change your mind very easily | 1 | 2 | 3 | 4 | 5 | Likely to stick with your position no matter what |

scious. In this section, we describe two tests or measures of affectively based brand attitude. These are the semantic differential scale and projective measures.

The Semantic Differential Measure of Brand Attitude Measuring the effects of a marketing campaign on brand attitude usually involves testing a given sample of consumers regularly over a period of time with the same test to see if there is any change in their attitudes toward the product. The test most often used is the semantic differential, which uses adjectives about the product.[22] Examples of adjectives used in the semantic differential measure of brand attitude are shown in Table 12-8.

An average composite is computed from the before-the-campaign survey and pitted against the average composite from the after-the-campaign survey. The advertising campaign is expected to significantly raise the average composite score.

Projective Measures of Brand Attitude **Projective measures** are research tests that avoid the pitfalls of direct questioning such as "Do you like this brand?" Projective measures permit subjects to indirectly project their feelings. Examples of indirect questions include: "What thoughts come to your mind when you think of Brand *X*?" "What do you think of the person who buys Brand *X*?" "What motives, needs, or desires does this product serve?"

Some projective tests involve sentence completion or drawing pictures. For example, researchers at McCann-Erickson used a projective technique to investigate why women continued to buy a brand of roach killer in canned sprays even though they admitted that the little plastic toys (which do not require spraying) were more effective. Women subjects were asked to draw pictures of roaches and write stories about their sketches. The results indicated that roaches in the pictures were all male roaches. The interpretation was that these male roaches symbolized men who had abandoned the women subjects and left them feeling poor and powerless. Killing the roaches with a bug spray and watching them squirm and die allowed the women to express their hostility toward the men who abandoned them.[23]

The effectiveness of a marketing program using projective measures is judged using the before-after campaign method.

projective measures
Methods used to capture respondents' perceptions, thoughts, and feelings about a brand in very indirect ways. For example, the respondent is asked to draw a picture of the brand; the interpretation of the drawing provides the researcher with an indicator of how well the respondent likes the brand.

Brand Acceptance

Marketing researchers have distinguished between brand attitude and "brand acceptance." **Brand acceptance** refers to the psychological process involving information assimilation about the brand leading to the judgment that the advertised brand is an acceptable alternative. Brand acceptance is considered highly important from a marketing point of view because it is a precursor to brand choice and purchase. That is, acceptable brand alternatives are pitted against each other in decision

brand acceptance
A marketing communications goal that describes a desirable situation in which target consumers recognize the firm's brand as an acceptable choice for the product category.

TABLE 12-8 An Example of Semantic Differential Scales Used to Measure Brand Attitude

	4 3 2 1	
Very appealing	___ ___ ___ ___	Very unappealing
Very good	___ ___ ___ ___	Very bad
High preference	___ ___ ___ ___	Low preference
Very beautiful	___ ___ ___ ___	Very ugly
Very special	___ ___ ___ ___	Not special
Very happy	___ ___ ___ ___	Very unhappy
Very much like	___ ___ ___ ___	Very much dislike
Very favorable	___ ___ ___ ___	Very unfavorable

making, leading to brand choice and purchase. Acceptable brands are evoked from memory for further consideration. Therefore, an advertising campaign can be developed for the purpose of making a brand acceptable to target consumers. Two tests or measures are described as research techniques operationalizing brand acceptance. These are the brand-listing procedure and unaided self-report questions.

The Brand-Listing Procedure For the **brand-listing procedure,** respondents are asked at the moment of purchase to indicate the brand they chose in a given situation, as in the moment of purchase. The interviewer comes up to the consumer in the supermarket (or some other retail outlet) and asks the consumer to grant an interview about the brand choice he or she has just made. Next, respondents are asked to list the names of any other brands they considered while making their choice. They are usually given 30 seconds for the brand-listing task.[24]

The effectiveness of a marketing communications program can be judged by running the brand-listing procedure twice, once before the launch of the program and a second time after a specified period of time. An effective program will significantly increase the percentage of respondents listing the brand in question.

Unaided Self-Report Questions Consideration set content (the set of brands considered for purchase) is measured by subject response to **unaided self-report questions.**[25] Examples of questions include:

1. What brands are you willing to buy?
2. What brands do you consider acceptable for purchase?
3. What brands would you consider buying?
4. What brands did you find acceptable for purchase the last time you purchased the product?
5. What brands did you consider buying the last time you purchased the product?

A percentage of respondents listing the brand in question is derived from responses to any of these questions. A marketing communications program is deemed effective if it was instrumental in raising the percentage score.

Brand Preference

Brand preference refers to the liking consumers have for that brand over competitor brands in the product category. Brand preference is different from brand attitude in the sense that a consumer may have a positive attitude toward the brand but may feel the same way about other brands. From the vantage point of the marketing communications manager, brand liking, therefore, is not good enough. The marketing communications manager needs to ensure that the positive feelings consumers have toward the brand are such that the consumer will prefer the brand over alternative brands. Similarly, brand acceptance merely indicates to the marketing communications manager that consumers will consider the brand when they need to purchase the product category. Marketing communications managers need to know whether the brand is preferred over competitors' brands because preference is very likely to lead to brand purchase. Two tests or measures of brand preference are described here. These are the ranking method and the paired-comparison method.

The Ranking Method For the **ranking method,** respondents judge their liking of a specific brand by ranking it in relation to other brands. For example, suppose we have five brands. The subjects are asked to express their liking of each brand by ranking each from 1 to 5, 1 being the brand that is most preferred and 5 being the brand that is least preferred. This method is commonly used when the number of brands to be judged is small, usually less than six. The viability of this method declines dras-

| TABLE 12-9 | The Paired-Comparison Method |

	\multicolumn{8}{c}{Referent Brands}	Total Score
	A	B	C	D	E	F	G	H	
Brand A		yes	no	yes	yes	no	no	no	3/7
Brand B			yes	yes	yes	yes	yes	yes	7/7
Brand C				no	no	no	no	yes	2/7
Brand D					yes	no	yes	no	4/7
Brand E						yes	yes	yes	4/7
Brand F							no	no	2/7
Brand G								yes	4/7
Brand H									4/7

Notes: A "yes" response means that the brand is liked better than the referent brand, for example, the "yes" response for Brand A in relation to Brand B (referent brand) means that Brand A is preferred over Brand B.

The total score for each brand per subject is derived by summing all the "yes" responses for that brand. For example, Brand A received a total preference score of 3/7. This means that Brand A was preferred in relation to three other brands. Brand F was preferred in relation to two other brands. This score is computed by adding all the "yes" responses going down the Brand F vertical column and across the Brand F horizontal row.

The results of this matrix show that the particular respondent indicates that he or she prefers Brand B the best, followed by a tie among brands D, E, G, and H, followed by Brand A. Brands C and F are the least preferred.

tically when the subject has to rank more than six brands. When a large pool of brands must be judged, the paired-comparison method is used.

The Paired-Comparison Method The **paired-comparison method** involves instructing the subjects to indicate whether they like or dislike a given brand in relation to another brand. For example, if the marketing communications manager's brand is *A*, and there are seven other alternatives, *B, C, D, E, F, G,* and *H*, then subjects indicate their liking of each brand in relation to all other brands (see Table 12-9).

paired-comparison method A method that induces respondents to indicate their preference of a particular brand by comparing it with other brands.

12-7c Brand Trial or Purchase *(Do)*

Brand trial or purchase refers to the extent to which consumers have psychologically committed themselves to trying the product and therefore buying it. This commitment may be in the form of an intention to purchase the brand given the right circumstances, such as on the next shopping trip or when the current brand is worn out or depleted. A number of concepts that marketing communications managers usually refer to are highly related to brand conviction. These are *attitude toward brand purchase, purchase intention,* and *brand purchase.*

Attitude Toward Brand Purchase
Attitude toward brand purchase refers to the attitude a consumer may have not about the brand itself and its attributes but toward the purchase and use of the brand. Many studies in social and consumer psychology have made the distinction between attitude toward the object versus attitude toward the act because attitude toward the act is a better predictor of behavior than attitude toward the object.[26] For example, if we play the role of scientists trying to predict purchase of Crest toothpaste, we will do better if we know how the consumers feel about the purchase of Crest (attitude toward the act) than if we know how consumers feel about Crest (attitude toward the object). In other words, attitude toward brand purchase is the next best thing to brand purchase intention in predicting brand purchase.

attitude toward brand purchase A marketing communications goal that describes a desirable situation in which target consumers have established a positive attitude toward the act of purchasing the firm's brand.

purchase intention
A marketing communications goal that describes a desirable situation in which target consumers have formed a behavioral intention to purchase the firm's brand.

semantic differential measure of attitude toward purchase A method that induces respondents to indicate their preference of a particular brand by rating the brand along a set of bipolar dimensions.

favorability measure of attitude toward purchase A method that induces respondents to indicate their preference of a particular brand by rating it on a scale that has "very unfavorable" on one end and "very favorable" on the other end.

Attitude toward brand purchase is defined as the consumer's disposition to purchase the brand given the need for the product category. This is different from purchase intention in that **purchase intention** is defined as the extent to which the consumer plans to purchase the brand in the foreseeable future. Two measures of attitude toward brand trial or purchase are briefly described here: the semantic differential measure and the favorability measure.

The Semantic Differential Measure of Attitude Toward Purchase

Attitude toward purchase is traditionally measured by asking subjects to indicate their feelings about buying Brand X using the bipolar adjectives shown in Table 12-10, which demonstrate the **semantic differential measure of attitude toward purchase.**

These items have been demonstrated to have high internal consistency and are therefore very reliable.[27] An average composite is computed. This average composite is derived twice, once before the marketing campaign and again after a specified period of time. A successful campaign should be responsible for a significant shift in the attitude composite score.

The Favorability Measure of Attitude Toward Purchase

Another rather simple measure of attitude toward purchase follows. Subjects are asked to evaluate the act of purchasing the brand in question on a 6-point scale anchored by "very favorable" and "very unfavorable."[28] This **favorability measure of attitude toward purchase** is administered in the context of a survey, which is taken before the launch of the communications campaign and again after a specified period of time. An effective campaign should produce a higher average score for attitude toward purchase after the designated time.

Purchase Intention

Purchase intention refers to the decision to purchase the brand given the need for the product category. That is, consumers decide that when they go shopping next time to purchase the product in question, they intend to buy the designated brand. Two measures of purchase intention are described here, one in which consumers consider the hypothetical situation of needing the product or shopping for the product category and another in which consumers indicate the likelihood of purchase within an upcoming period of time.

A Measure of Purchase Intention Given Product Need Purchase intention is usually measured by a question such as: "If you were in the market today shopping for product x, how likely would you be to buy Brand A?"[29] Response scales are of the semantic differential variety. Examples are shown in Table 12-11.

A mean composite score is computed before and after the campaign. Significant positive changes in the mean purchase intention composite scores are taken as an indication that the advertising campaign was effective in changing consumers' purchase intention toward the brand.

The Planned Purchase Measure An equally popular measure of purchase intention involves asking respondents to indicate whether they plan to purchase Brand X dur-

TABLE 12-10 The Semantic Differential Measure of Attitude Toward Purchase

Good	__ __ __ __ __ __ __ __ __	Bad
Foolish	__ __ __ __ __ __ __ __ __	Wise
Pleasant	__ __ __ __ __ __ __ __ __	Unpleasant
Unsafe	__ __ __ __ __ __ __ __ __	Safe
Punishing	__ __ __ __ __ __ __ __ __	Rewarding

TABLE 12-11	Response Scales for the Measure of Purchase Intention, Given Product Need

Very unlikely	__ __ __ __ __ __	Very likely
Very improbable	__ __ __ __ __ __	Very probable
Very impossible	__ __ __ __ __ __	Very possible
Very nonexistent	__ __ __ __ __ __	Very existent

ing the next x days (months, years). Responses are coded on one or more semantic differential scales comparable to the scales used in the measure of purchase intention given product need. Two average composites are computed, one before the launch of the advertising campaign and the other after the launch. The campaign effectiveness is judged in terms of the positive shift in the mean planned purchase score.

Brand Purchase

Brand purchase refers to a one-time purchase. It can refer to a brand trial, in which the consumer buys the brand in order to try it out. Two measures of brand purchase are described here, one that uses tracking studies and another that provides sample consumers with purchase incentives.

Tracking Studies

Tracking studies are conducted to track the behaviors of consumers at the supermarket checkout counter. Consumer panel participants are given a card (similar to a credit card) that identifies their household and the household demographics. The households are split into matched groups, with one group receiving the marketing communications, the other not. The purchases of these consumer panelists are recorded from the bar codes of the product bought. Exposure to the marketing communications is also measured using a diary method. Communications exposures are then correlated with brand purchases.

Popular firms in tracking studies include:

- BehaviorScan by Information Resources (http://www.infores.com/public/us/default.htm)
- Yankelovich Monitor (http://www.yankelovich.com)
- Claritas (http://www.claritas.com)
- ACNielsen (http://www2.acnielsen.com/site/index.shtml)

Advantages of tracking studies include control and the ability to measure the effects of the advertisements on sales as directly as possible. Disadvantages include the focus on short-term sales and the high cost of data collection.[30] (See Table 12-12.)

Purchase Incentive Measures Subjects are recruited to participate in a marketing study. The subjects are told: "As a participant in this study, you may purchase (same brand) for (certain cents or dollars) per package. [The price is heavily discounted.] If you want to buy any, please provide your name and the number of packages below." Purchase is coded as the number of packages requested. The assumption is that the more packages requested, the greater the motivation to purchase the brand in general.[31] This type of study is conducted before and after the marketing communications campaign. The precampaign score for the average number of packages of the brand requested is compared with the postcampaign score.

12-7d Repeat Purchase *(Repeat)*

Repeat purchase refers to the situation in which the consumer purchases the same brand over and over again. Every time the need arises for the product, the consumer

brand purchase A marketing communications goal that describes a desirable situation in which target consumers have actually purchased the firm's brand.

tracking studies A method that monitors the performance of the brand through actual purchases and sales.

repeat purchase A marketing communications goal that describes a desirable situation in which target consumers have purchased the firm's brand repeatedly over time.

TABLE 12-12	Factors Making or Breaking Tracking Studies

1. Properly defined objectives
2. Alignment with sales objectives
3. Proper sampling—for example, random sampling
4. Consistency through replication of the sampling plan
5. Evaluative measures related to behavior
6. Asking critical evaluative questions early to reduce bias from response to early questions
7. Measures of competitors' performance
8. Using "moving averages" to spot long-term trends and avoid seasonality
9. Reporting data in terms of relationships rather than as isolated facts
10. Relating variables such as advertising expenditures, price changes, introduction of new brands, and so on with brand and product sales

Source: Adapted from Fred Cuba, "Fourteen Things That Make or Break Tracking Studies," *Journal of Advertising Research* 25, no. 1 (February–March 1985): 21–23.

buys the same brand. Also, the same construct refers to brand satisfaction and brand loyalty. We discuss the measures of all three constructs in this section.

Repeat Purchase

Two repeat purchase measures are discussed here, one based on anticipated repeat purchase and the other based on past repeat purchase.

Repurchase Measure The repurchase measure of brand loyalty involves ascertaining what percentage of the owners of the brand go on to purchase the same brand on their next product purchase.[32] The precampaign repurchase average score is compared to the repurchase score after the campaign. The greater the change in the repurchase scores, the more effective the communications campaign.

percentage-of-purchase measure A method that induces respondents to indicate the percentage of times the respondent purchased the same brand during a certain time span.

Percentage-of-Purchase Measure The **percentage-of-purchase measure** involves asking users of the product class questions such as, "Of the last [number of] purchases, what percentage went to Brand X, Brand Y, and Brand Z?"[33] The higher the average percentage that went to the brand in question, the higher the repeat purchase of that brand. Of course, the effectiveness of the communications campaign in terms of repeat purchase is judged by the difference between the percentage-of-purchase score before and after the campaign.

Brand Satisfaction

brand satisfaction
A marketing communications goal that describes a desirable situation in which target consumers feel satisfied with the firm's brand after purchase and use.

Brand satisfaction refers to the positive (or negative) feelings consumers may have about the brand after using it. In other words, after brand purchase, consumers evaluate the brand against their expectations. If they perceive that the brand did better than expected, they may have high brand satisfaction. If the brand is perceived to do as expected, then they are likely to have moderate levels of brand satisfaction. Similarly, if consumers perceive the product to do worse than expected, they may have low levels of satisfaction. Hence, brand satisfaction refers to the psychological process leading to brand evaluation after purchase and usage. Brand satisfaction is traditionally measured through a variety of rating scales.[34] Examples are shown in Table 12-13.

Professors Peterson and Wilson[35] have shown that the preceding self-reports of consumer satisfaction invariably have frequency distributions that are skewed toward the high-satisfaction end of the scale, reflecting a "positivity bias." In other words, most people tend to indicate inflated levels of satisfaction, perhaps more than they actually felt. Peterson and Wilson discussed other methodological problems:

TABLE 12-13　Examples of Satisfaction Scales

Completely satisfied	1 2 3 4 5 6 7	Completely dissatisfied

Satisfaction percentage:
91–100
81–90
71–80
61–70
51–60
41–50
31–40
21–30
11–20
1–10

Very satisfied	Somewhat satisfied	Somewhat dissatisfied	Very dissatisfied	Uncertain

Very satisfied	Somewhat satisfied	Unsatisfied	Very unsatisfied	

Completely satisfied	Very satisfied	Fairly satisfied	Somewhat dissatisfied	Very dissatisfied

Very satisfied	Quite satisfied	Not very satisfied	Not at all satisfied	

Very satisfied	Somewhat satisfied	Completely unsatisfied		

response rate bias, data collection mode bias, problems with question form, problems with question context, measurement timing, response styles, and mood. Marketing communications managers must take these methodological shortcomings into account when evaluating such self-reports. The effectiveness of a communications campaign in terms of increasing brand satisfaction is judged by comparing the precampaign satisfaction scores against the postcampaign satisfaction scores.

Brand Loyalty

With respect to **brand loyalty,** Professor Aaker has conceptualized this construct in terms of a five-layer hierarchy varying from the nonloyal buyer (bottom layer) to the committed buyer (top layer).[36] At the bottom layer are the brand nonloyal consumers who are completely indifferent to the brand. They do not buy out of loyalty for the brand. Perhaps factors such as price and convenience are important motivators. The second layer of the brand loyalty hierarchy includes the satisfied consumers. These are the habitual buyers. They buy the brand not necessarily out of a sense of loyalty and commitment but merely because of habit. They do not have a reason to change the brand. The third layer includes a different type of satisfied consumers. What distinguishes these consumers from the layer below them is the fact that these people cannot think of switching brands because of the high cost of switching. These people are "financially stuck" with the brand; they simply cannot afford to switch to another brand. The fourth layer involves those who like the brand. They consider the brand a friend. There is an emotional/feeling attachment to the brand. Finally, on top of the hierarchy are the committed consumers. They are proud of being users of

brand loyalty A marketing communications goal that describes a desirable situation in which target consumers feel psychologically committed to the firm's brand after purchase and use.

the brand. The brand is important to them functionally and/or in the way the brand expresses their identity. We discuss two measures of brand loyalty here, one referred to as the multivariate measure of brand loyalty and the other referred to as the measurement of entrenched loyalty.

A Multivariate Measure of Brand Loyalty One of the more popular measures of brand loyalty is the multivariate measure.[37] The multivariate measure is comprised of several questions:

1. Did you repurchase the old brand? Yes ___ No ___
2. If you answered "Yes" to Question 1, how many brands did you think of at the outset of decision process? Many ___ Few ___ One ___
3. If you answered "One" to Question 2, did you think mainly of the old brand? Yes ___ No ___
4. If you answered "Yes" to Question 3, did you seek any brand-related information? Yes ___ No ___

Brand loyalty is estimated as the percentage of consumers who respond affirmatively to all of these four questions. As with other tests and measures of the effectiveness of a communications campaign, these measures are used before and after the campaign.

entrenched loyalty A state of mind in which respondents indicate a high degree of commitment to the brand.

A Measure of Entrenched Loyalty Another measure of brand loyalty involves asking target consumers, "Which other brands (or options) would you consider if your favorite were not available?" **Entrenched loyalty** is revealed when the answer is something like, "None—I will shop no further. I will wait until the brand becomes available."[38]

Summary

This chapter introduces you to tests and measures of campaign effectiveness. Campaign effectiveness tests and measures are grouped in terms of the hierarchy-of-effects components—brand awareness, brand knowledge, brand attitude, brand trial and purchase, and repeat purchase. We further examine the same hierarchy-of-effects components in greater detail and discuss common tests and measures used to operationalize these constructs. These tests and measures are used to assess effectiveness of any marketing communications campaign.

In assessing the effectiveness of a marketing communications campaign, marketing researchers traditionally employ a pre/post experimental design. That is, before the launch of the communications campaign (considered here as the experimental treatment), measures of selected components of the hierarchy of effects (e.g., brand awareness, purchase intention) are taken. These measures are administered on a sample of target consumers. These are referred to as "premeasures." After the launch of the campaign, the same measures are administered to either the same sample or a comparable sample. The measures administered to assess the effectiveness of the advertising campaign are referred to as "postmeasures." Campaign effectiveness is judged by examining the magnitude of change between the premeasure scores (for example, on brand awareness) and the postmeasure scores. The greater the change (e.g., reflecting greater brand awareness) the more likely the campaign will be judged as "effective."

Discussion Questions

1. Assume that you are working for a major pharmaceutical company. The company develops a nicotine patch that cigarette smokers stick on their shoulder to emit nicotine directly through the skin into the bloodstream. The nicotine patch helps cigarette smokers stop smoking by preventing or reducing the nicotine craving. The product has been branded as "Nicofit." You, the vice president of marketing communications, are planning a major advertising campaign. The objectives of the advertising campaign involve (1) getting cigarette smokers who are trying to quit to know the benefits of the nicotine patch, (2) getting cigarette smokers to become aware of the brand name,

Nicofit, (3) getting cigarette smokers to believe that the use of Nicofit can significantly help only if accompanied by other therapeutic techniques dealing with the psychological addiction, and (4) getting cigarette smokers to develop a positive attitude toward Nicofit as a direct function of its primary benefit of being able to reduce the craving for nicotine. Now is the time to plan how you will assess the effectiveness of the advertising campaign. You need to get together with the research people and select suitable tests and measures. Review the different tests and measures associated with the objectives of the advertising campaign, and select one test/measure for each objective. Defend your selection.

2. Suppose you are the vice president of marketing communications in a multinational cosmetics company. The R&D department has just developed a new cologne for men. The cologne has the kind of fragrance that is said to "drive women crazy." The company is now counting on you and your people to launch a major advertising campaign for this new cologne, branded as "Crazy." The market research people at your company are convinced that men in their 20s who are fashion conscious are likely to find this cologne very appealing and purchase it. Therefore, the advertising campaign is directed at young men in their 20s who are fashion conscious. The objective of the advertising campaign is to have these men develop a positive attitude toward (and preference for) Crazy. You have a meeting with the research people tomorrow to talk about possible effectiveness measures for this advertising campaign. You need to prepare some ideas about the suitability of certain tests and measures to assess the effectiveness of the advertising campaign against the campaign objective. Generate some ideas in preparation for this meeting.

3. Suppose you are working for one of the fastest growing fast-food restaurant chains in the country and you just have been promoted to the position of advertising manager within the marketing department. This position became available after the current advertising manager was lured by another company to become its vice president of marketing. He gave you a big file on the current advertising campaign and, right before he said his good-byes, dropped a hint that the advertising campaign may be in trouble. He pointed to the brand acceptance figures, and the figures showed a constant decrease in acceptance over the last 3 years. After staring at the figures for awhile, it dawns on you that the objective of the advertising campaign should be repeat purchase, not brand acceptance. You start thinking about coming up with a marketing communications strategy to enhance repeat purchase. You come up with some ideas that you will bounce against the creative people in the next few days. Now you start to think about effectiveness measures. How are you going to show that your strategy will work by the next quarter? Think about the various options of tests and measures for repeat purchase. Which test and/or measure would you suggest for the research people? How do you think they will react to your suggestions?

4. Consider the pro-life advertising campaign sponsored by the Moss Foundation. The advertising campaign shows how parents are happy with their children whose births were neither planned nor wanted by the parents and how the children relish their own lives. The message is that life is a gift and that we should not consider abortion as a viable option just because the pregnancy is unplanned or ill timed. What do you think is the objective of this advertising campaign? Explain.

5. Suppose you are the marketing communications manager of Adidas athletic shoes. The market research people tell you that there is a niche for Adidas shoes among mature consumers (ages 40 to 60) who are health conscious and tend to wear athletic shoes for casual occasions. These people purchase and use athletic shoes but are not involved with Adidas. You are now preparing a plan for the forthcoming advertising campaign. What campaign objectives would you set for the campaign? Explain.

6. You are an advertising manager for Procter & Gamble. The research and development department has just developed a new laundry detergent that has the power of removing extremely tough stains. The advertising campaign is to be directed to housewives in blue-collar families. What kind of advertising campaign would you come up with? What kind of campaign objectives would be advisable for this type of advertising campaign?

7. Suppose you are the advertising manager of RCA. RCA is competing against many others in the television market. The television market is in the mature stage of the product life cycle. The competition is fierce, and RCA's televisions have lost their differentiation advantage. In other words, the RCA brand does not seem to be significantly differentiated from most of the competitor brands of televisions. RCA has just changed advertising agencies, providing you with an opportunity to strongly influence the creative people of the new agency. What would be the major thrust of the new advertising campaign? In other words, what would

you say to the creative people of the new agency about the goals of the RCA advertising campaign?

8. Have you seen DuPont advertisements showing college students who are highly motivated to make a difference in improving the quality of life on this planet? This advertising campaign is classified as a corporate-image campaign or institutional advertising. What do you think DuPont is trying to accomplish with this advertising campaign? Explain.

9. "If target consumers are highly involved and knowledgeable about the product, the advertising campaign should be designed to. . . ." Complete this sentence. Provide an example of a product that the target consumers are highly involved with and are knowledgeable about. Develop an advertising campaign for this product, and explain how the advertising campaign is designed to meet the advertising objectives.

Practice Quiz

Note: You can find the correct answers to these questions by taking the quiz and then submitting your answers in the Online Edition. The program will automatically score your submission. If you miss a question, the program will provide the correct answer, a rationale for the answer, and the section number in the chapter where the topic is discussed.

1. The brand awareness objective
    a. is the goal to achieve a certain level of brand awareness in the minds of a target market.
    b. is the goal to achieve a certain level of learning, knowledge, association, image, and/or comprehension related to the product's benefits.
    c. is the goal to achieve a certain level of positive attitude (affect, preference, or acceptance) toward the product.
    d. is the goal to induce a certain level of the target market to purchase (or at least to make plans to purchase) the product.

2. A _____ objective is the goal to achieve a certain level of purchases in a given period of time as a direct function of the campaign (repeat purchases, brand satisfaction, brand loyalty, brand commitment).
    a. brand awareness
    b. brand repeat
    c. brand feel
    d. brand do

3. _____ is the difference between the company's sales revenue and the cost of producing and selling the good.
    a. Profit
    b. Cash flow
    c. Sales
    d. Market share

4. _____ are not considered to be measures of marketing objectives and performance.
    a. Recognition measures of brand knowledge
    b. Aided-recall measures of brand knowledge
    c. Associative-strength measures of brand awareness
    d. Projective measures of brand attitude

5. The _____ involves using in-depth interviews to uncover the person's motivation to purchase and use a specific brand. Here the subject is asked to describe the brand attributes. For each attribute, the interviewer probes the personal significance of the attribute through a series of "why" questions.
    a. free-association test
    b. picture-interpretation test
    c. personal-values test or "laddering technique"
    d. brand-as-a-person test

6. Subjects are presented with a product category name (e.g., toothpaste) on a monitor, followed by a brand name (e.g., Crest) that is either a member or nonmember of that product category. Subjects press either a "yes" or "no" button to indicate as rapidly as possible whether the brand is a member of the specified product category. Associative strength is measured in terms of response latency (how long it took the subject to respond). Such a measure is designed to capture _____.
    a. brand liking
    b. brand awareness
    c. brand satisfaction
    d. brand loyalty

7. _____ is another test of brand attitude (the cognitive component). Subjects are presented with the actual brand (or a description of it in words and/or pictures). They are then asked to evaluate the brand strengths and weaknesses (possibly in relation to competitive brands) and to record their thoughts in writing. A variation of this procedure is to request the subject to think out loud and record the verbal expressions on a tape recorder. Trained judges then analyze the thoughts. They identify favorable and unfavorable thoughts about the brand and record their frequency.
   a. The multiattribute index
   b. The thought-elicitation procedure
   c. The mushiness index
   d. The semantic differential measure of brand attitude

8. The subjects are told: "As a participant in this study, you may purchase (same brand) for (certain cents or dollars) per package. [The price is heavily discounted.] If you want to buy any, please provide your name and the number of packages below." Purchase is coded as the number of packages requested. What does this measure capture?
   a. learn
   b. feel
   c. do
   d. None of the preceding are correct.

9. _____ refers to the positive (or negative) feelings consumers may have about the brand after using it.
   a. Brand awareness
   b. Brand satisfaction
   c. Brand recognition
   d. Brand loyalty

10. A measure of _____ involves asking target consumers: "Which other brands (or options) would you consider if your favorite were not available?" _____ is revealed when the answer is something like, "None—I will shop no further. I will wait until the brand becomes available."
    a. brand awareness
    b. brand liking
    c. brand recognition
    d. brand loyalty

Web Exercise

Let Me Count the Ways—Measurement of Communications

Using your favorite search engine, conduct a search for measurement of marketing communications. Type in the word "measurement" and then the SMC portfolio elements one at a time and request a search. Start with "advertising AND measurement," followed by "public relations AND measurement," and so forth. What did you find? Are the companies and articles that you find consistent? How many companies are out there that deal with measuring the effectiveness of these elements?

Suggested Readings

Aaker, David A. 1991. *Managing brand equity: Capitalizing on the value of a brand name.* New York: The Free Press.

Ajzen, Icek, and Martin Fishbein. 1980. *Understanding attitudes and predicting social behavior.* Englewood Cliffs, NJ: Prentice Hall.

Axelrod, Joel N., and Hans Wybenga. 1985. Perceptions that motivate purchase. *Journal of Advertising Research* (June–July): 19–22.

Bagozzi, Richard P. 1981. Attitudes, intentions, and behavior: A test of some key hypotheses. *Journal of Personality and Social Psychology* 41 (October): 606–27.

Barry, Thomas E. 1987. The development of the hierarchy of effects: An historical perspective. *Current Issues and Research in Advertising* 10 (2): 251–95.

Bartos, Rena. 1986. Ernest Dichter: Motive interpreter. *Journal of Advertising Research* (February–March): 15–20.

Britt, S. H. 1969. Are so-called successful advertising campaigns really successful? *Journal of Advertising Research* 9 (June): 3–9.

Broadbent, Simon, ed. 1984. *The Leo Burnett book of advertising*. London: Business Books, 86–98.

Brown, Juanita J., and Albert R. Wildt. 1992. Consideration set measurement. *Journal of the Academy of Marketing Science* 20 (Summer): 235–43.

Colley, R. H. 1961. *Defining advertising goals for measured advertising results*. New York: Association of National Advertisers.

———. 1971. *Defining advertising goals in modern marketing management*, ed. R. J. Lawrence and M. J. Thomas, 282–92. New York: Penguin Books.

Colman, Stephen, and Gordon Brown. 1983. Advertising tracking studies and sales effects. *Journal of the Market Research Society* 25 (2): 165–83.

Corkingdale, David. 1976. Setting objectives for advertising. *European Journal of Marketing* 10 (3): 109–26.

Haire, Mason. 1950. Projective techniques in marketing research. *Journal of Marketing* (April): 649–56.

Kruegel, Dave. 1988. Television advertising effectiveness and research innovation. *Journal of Consumer Marketing* 5, no. 3 (Summer): 40–50.

Krugman, E. H. 1975. What makes advertising effective. *Harvard Business Review* 53 (March–April): 96–103.

Lang, Annie, ed. 1994. *Measuring psychological responses to media messages*. Hillsdale, NJ: Erlbaum.

Lavidge, Robert J., and Gary A. Steiner. 1961. A model for predictive measurements of advertising effectiveness. *Journal of Marketing* (October): 59–62.

Lipstein, Benjamin, and James P. Neelankavil. 1984. Television advertising copy research: A critical review of the state of the art. *Journal of Advertising Research* 24, no. 2 (April–May): 112–25.

Lucas, D. B., and S. H. Britt. 1963. *Measuring advertising effectiveness*. New York: McGraw-Hill.

Majaro, S. 1970. Advertising by objectives. *Management Today* (January): 71–73.

Moriarity, Sandra Ernest. 1983. Beyond the hierarchy of effects: A conceptual framework. *Current Issues and Research in Advertising* 6 (1): 45–55.

Nedungadi, Prakash. 1990. Recall and consumer consideration sets: Influencing choice without altering brand evaluations. *Journal of Consumer Research* 17 (December): 263–76.

Palda, Kristian S. 1966. The hypothesis of a hierarchy of effects: A partial evaluation. *Journal of Marketing Research* 3 (February): 12–24.

Peterson, Robert A., and William R. Wilson. 1992. Measuring customer satisfaction: Fact and artifact. *Journal of the Academy of Marketing Science* 20 (Winter): 61–72.

Ray, Michael L., Alan G. Sawyer, Michael L. Rothschild, Roger M. Heeler, Edward C. Strong, and Jerome B. Reed. 1973. Marketing communications and the hierarchy of effects. In *New models for mass communications research*, ed. Peter Clarke. Beverly Hills, CA: Sage.

Reynolds, Thomas J., and Jonathan Gutman. 1984. Advertising is image management. *Journal of Advertising Research* 25 (February–March): 29–37.

Schwartz, D. A. 1969. Measuring the effectiveness of your company's advertising. *Journal of Advertising* 33 (April): 20–25.

Smith, Robert E., and William P. Swinyard. 1988. Cognitive response to advertising and trial: Belief strength, belief confidence and product curiosity. *Journal of Advertising* 17 (3): 3–13.

Notes

1. Jon Lafayette, "Weather Channel Making Split-Run Spots Available," *Television Week* 23, no. 17 (Chicago), April 26, 2004, 22.
2. Mike Reid, "Building Strong Brands Through the Management of Integrated Marketing Communications," *International Journal of Wine Marketing* 14, no. 3 (Patrington, 2002): 37–52.
3. Benjamin Lipstein and James P. Neelankavil, "Television Advertising and Copy Research: A Critical Review of the State of the Art," *Journal of Advertising Research* 24 (April–May 1984): 112–25.
4. Brian Steinberg, "Product-Placement Pricing Debated; Deutsch Launches Firm to Gauge Exposure's Value Against a Paid Commercial," Wall Street Journal (Eastern Edition), November 19, 2004, B.3. Retrieved December 20, 2004, from ABI/INFORM Global database. (Document ID: 738465591)
5. Ibid.
6. Gary L. Lilien and Philip Kotler, *Marketing Decision Making* (New York: Harper & Row, 1983).
7. Philip Kotler, *Marketing Management: Analysis, Planning, Implementation, and Control*, 8th ed. (Englewood Cliffs, NJ: Prentice Hall, 1994), 112–13.

8. E. H. Krugman, "What Makes Advertising Effective?" *Harvard Business Review* 53 (March–April 1975): 96–103.
9. Scott B. MacKenzie and Richard J. Lutz, "An Empirical Examination of the Structural Antecedents of Attitude Toward the Ad in an Advertising Pretesting Context," *Journal of Marketing* 53 (April 1989): 412–65; Darrel D. Muehling, Russell N. Laczniak, and Jeffery J. Stoltman, "The Moderating Effects of Ad Message Involvement: A Reassessment," *Journal of Advertising* 20 (June 1991): 29–38.
10. Robert E. Smith and William P. Swinyard, "Cognitive Response to Advertising and Trial: Belief Strength, Belief Confidence and Product Curiosity," *Journal of Advertising* 17, no. 3 (1988): 3–14.
11. David A. Aaker, *Managing Brand Equity: Capitalizing on the Value of a Brand Name* (New York: The Free Press, 1991), 136–46.
12. Ibid.
13. Ibid.
14. Ibid.
15. Ibid.
16. Russell H. Fazio, Paul M. Herr, and Martha C. Powell, "On the Development and Strength of Category-Based Associations in Memory: The Case of the Mystery Ads," *Journal of Consumer Psychology* 1, no. 1 (1992): 1–14.
17. David A. Aaker, *Managing Brand Equity*.
18. Ibid.
19. J. Thomas Russell, Glenn Verrill, and Ronald Lane, *Kleppner's Advertising Procedure*, 10th ed. (Englewood Cliffs, NJ: Prentice Hall, 1988), 134.
20. See note 8.
21. Karyln H. Keene and Victoria A. Sackett, "An Editor's Report on the Yankelovich, Skelly, and White's Mushiness Index," *Public Opinion* (April–May 1981): 50–51.
22. Kathleen Debevec and Jean B. Romeo, "Self-Referent Processing in Perceptions of Verbal and Visual Information," *Journal of Consumer Psychology* 1, no. 1 (1992): 83–102.
23. Ronald Alsop, "Advertisers Put Consumers on the Couch," *Wall Street Journal*, section 2, May 13, 1988, 21.
24. Prakash Nedungadi, "Recall and Consumer Consideration Sets: Influencing Choice without Altering Brand Evaluations," *Journal of Consumer Research* 17 (December 1990): 263–76.
25. Juanita J. Brown and Albert R. Wildt, "Consideration Set Measurement," *Journal of the Academy of Marketing Science* 20 (Summer 1992): 235–43.
26. Icek Ajzen and Martin Fishbein, *Understanding Attitudes and Predicting Social Behavior* (Englewood Cliffs, NJ: Prentice Hall, 1980).
27. Chris T. Allen, Karen A. Machleit, and Susan Schultz Kleine, "A Comparison of Attitudes and Emotions As Predictors of Behavior at Diverse Levels of Behavioral Experience," *Journal of Consumer Research* 18 (March 1992): 493–504; Richard P. Bagozzi, "Attitudes, Intentions, and Behavior: A Test of Some Key Hypotheses," *Journal of Personality and Social Psychology* 41 (October 1981): 606–27.
28. Chris T. Allen, Karen A. Machleit, and Susan Schultz Kleine, "A Comparison of Attitudes and Emotions as Predictors of Behavior at Diverse Levels of Behavioral Experience."
29. See note 22.
30. Dave Kruegel, "Television Advertising Effectiveness and Research Innovation," *Journal of Consumer Marketing* 5, no. 3 (Summer 1988): 40–50.
31. See note 10.
32. See note 11.
33. Ibid.
34. Robert A. Peterson and William R. Wilson, "Measuring Customer Satisfaction: Fact or Artifact," *Journal of the Academy of Marketing Science* 20 (Winter 1992): 61–72.
35. Ibid.
36. See note 11.
37. Joseph W. Newman and Richard A. Worbel, "Multivariate Analysis of Brand Loyalty for Major Household Appliances," *Journal of Marketing Research* (November 1973): 404–8.
38. James F. Engel, Roger D. Blackwell, and Paul W. Miniard, *Consumer Behavior*, 6th ed. (Chicago: Dryden Press, 1990), 33.

Analysis Guiding Objective Setting

Linking Strategies and Tactics to Objectives and Performance Measures

Chapter Thirteen

Chapter Outline

13-1 Introduction

13-2 Using Situation Analysis to Set Corporate Objectives
- 13-2a Industry Average in Relation to Sales, Market Share, Profit, and Cash Flow
- 13-2b Forecasted Sales, Market Share, Profit, and/or Cash Flow
- 13-2c Past Sales, Market Share, and Profit of Key Competitors
- 13-2d Anticipated Profit, Sales, and/or Market Share of Key Competitors
- 13-2e Anticipated Market Changes That May Affect Future Sales, Market Share, and/or Profit
- 13-2f Anticipated Changes within the Firm That May Affect Future Sales, Market Share, Profit, and/or Cash Flow

13-3 Using Situation Analysis to Set Marketing Objectives
- 13-3a Industry Average in Relation to the Use of This Particular Measure of Brand Association
- 13-3b Forecasted Changes in the Brand Association in Question
- 13-3c Past Brand Association of Key Competitors
- 13-3d Anticipated Brand Association of Key Competitors
- 13-3e Anticipated Market Changes That May Affect the Brand Association in Question
- 13-3f Anticipated Changes within the Firm That May Affect the Brand Association in Question

13-4 Using Situation Analysis to Set Marketing Communications Objectives
- 13-4a The Industry Average in Relation to the Use of the Selected Measure of the Communications Objective
- 13-4b Forecasted Changes in the Selected Measure of the Communications Objective
- 13-4c Past Performance of Key Competitors along the Selected Measure of the Communications Objective
- 13-4d Anticipated Performance of Key Competitors along the Selected Measure of the Communications Objective
- 13-4e Anticipated Market Changes That May Affect Communications Objectives
- 13-4f Anticipated Changes within the Firm That May Affect Communications Objectives

Summary
Discussion Questions
Practice Quiz
Web Exercise: Is Image Everything?
Suggested Readings
Notes

Key Terms

corporate objectives (p. 327)
marketing communications objectives (p. 335)
marketing objectives (p. 332)
referents (p. 331)
reliable and valid measures (p. 328)

The two words "information" and "communication" are often used interchangeably, but they signify quite different things. Information is giving out; communication is getting through.
—Sydney J. Harris (1917–1986), American journalist and writer

13-1 Introduction

Consider the following case. Dell Inc., the world's largest personal computer maker, reported that its net income surged 28 percent in its first quarter in 2005 and issued an optimistic outlook for its next quarter. Its net income was $934 million for the first quarter, compared with a net of $731 million a year earlier. Revenue rose 16 percent to $13.39 billion from $11.54 billion. On the other hand, rival PC manufacturers were moving, too. In 2005 Lenovo, a Chinese PC manufacturer, acquired IBM's PC business division for $1.25 billion. At Hewlett-Packard Development Company, CEO Carleton S. Fiorina was ousted and the company was seeking a stronger initiative to lead the company in another direction.[1]

Now imagine yourself in the shoes of Michael Dell, the founder and CEO at Dell. Armed with the information just discussed, can you set sales or revenue objectives for next year? Would you set an objective increase at the level of last year? Would you go higher? Lower? Why? What information would you use to set your sales and revenue objectives? Why? This chapter is designed to sensitize you to the kind of analysis and planning that can be done to help managers—especially marketing communications managers—set objectives.

Note that the situation analysis discussed in earlier chapters pertains to strategy selection—selection of strategy at the corporate, marketing, and marketing communications levels. Situation analysis can also be conducted to assist marketers in setting objectives and allocating resources. This chapter starts out by discussing situation analysis that focuses on setting objectives at the corporate level, then proceeds to discuss situation analysis at the marketing and marketing communications levels (see Figure 13-1).

13-2 Using Situation Analysis to Set Corporate Objectives

As previously stated, situation analysis can be conducted to help the manager make three decisions. One is how to select corporate strategy; the second major decision is what corporate objectives to set; and the third decision is related to budgeting or the allocation of resources to achieve those goals (see Figure 13-2). **Corporate objectives** are typically set in relation to four performance dimensions: (1) sales, (2) market share, (3) profit, and (4) cash. Remember that all corporate objectives, like corporate strategy and tactics, are constrained to a very specific strategic business unit (SBU). We previously recommended that objectives be set using a three-stage process: (1) identification of one or more objective dimensions, (2) identification of the measures used to gauge outcomes related to each objective, and (3) identification of the desired level and time frame associated with each objective dimension. This discussion focuses on how situation analysis can assist in the third stage of this

corporate objectives Formal statements that represent concrete and precise desired states of affairs articulated at the corporate level. Corporate objectives are usually stated in terms of sales, market share, profit, and cash flow in relation to a given strategic business unit (SBU).

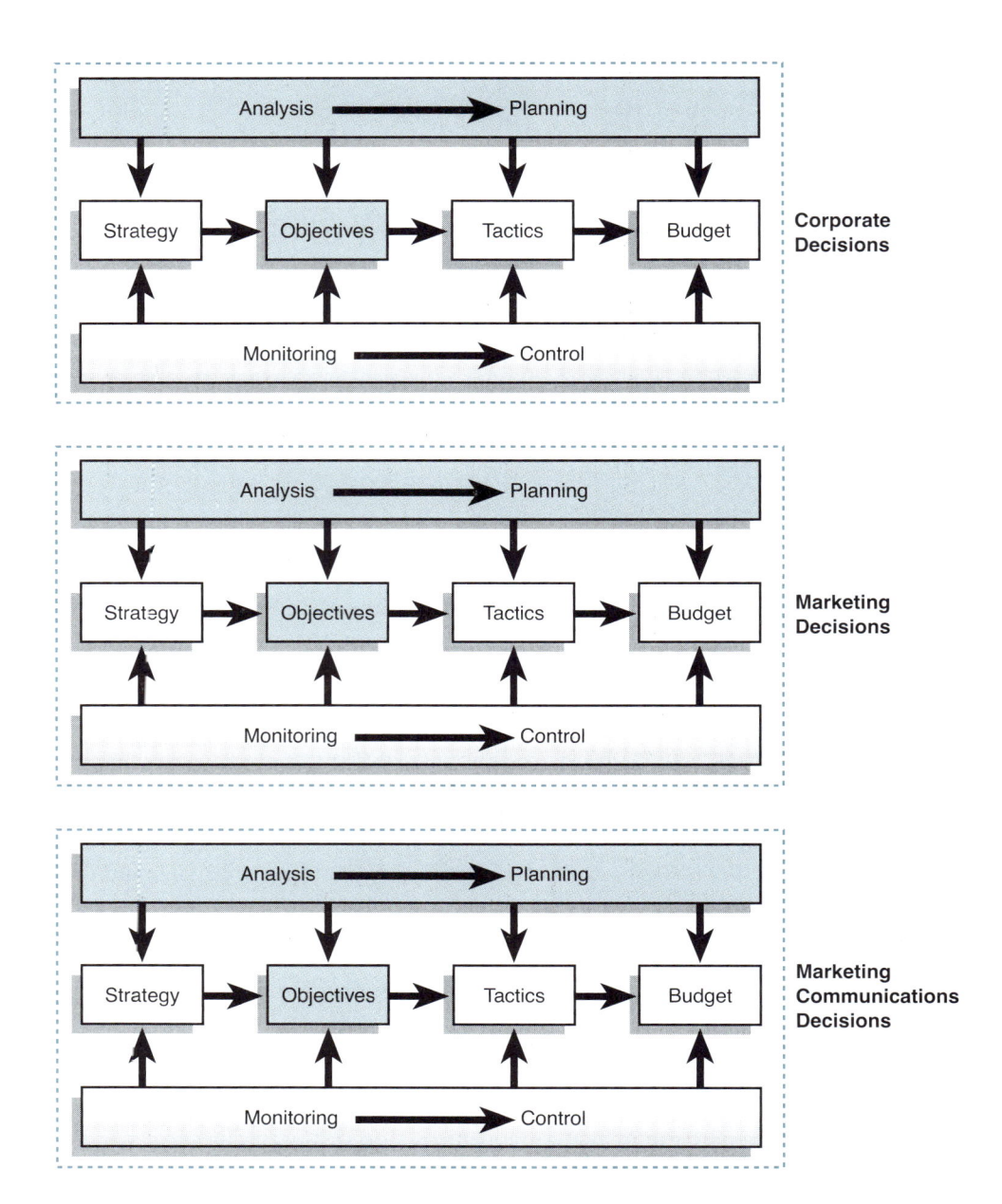

Figure 13-1
The Use of Analysis and Planning in Setting Corporate, Marketing, and Marketing Communications Objectives

reliable and valid measures
Performance assessment instruments that capture the core essence of the phenomenon in question and do so consistently with multiple measures or methods.

three-stage decision model, the identification of the desired level and time frame of the selected objective dimension.

Earlier in the book, we emphasize that the objective dimensions have to be selected as a direct function of the selected strategy. In other words, knowing what the strategy is helps the manager determine (at least partly) possible objective dimensions. For example, sales and market share are usually most consistent with a growth strategy. On the other hand, a harvest strategy may lead the manager to select a profit objective. An innovation strategy entails a sales objective. A divestment strategy focuses on cash flow.

In order to set objectives quantitatively and concretely, the manager has to work with **reliable and valid measures** of sales, market share, profit, and cash flow. Managers must use objective measures that are based on sound accounting principles. The accounting calculus used to measure sales, market share, profit, and cash flow must be well established and accepted by the accounting profession because the manager has to gather data pertaining to the norms of the measure, especially in relation to past performance and the performance of other firms in the industry. The

SMC Marketplace Watch 13-1

Corporate Ideals to Execution

Recently, Estée Lauder signed a multiyear contract with actress Gwyneth Paltrow to star in global advertisements for a number of its fragrance and makeup collections. The company's objective is to increase sales and market share significantly for its 10-year-old Pleasures fragrance this holiday season. Pleasures is the fourth-largest fragrance brand in the world and ranks in the top ten fragrances in the United States. Estée Lauder president John Demsey wants to change the image of the brand from fusty to fashionable. Furthermore, Demsey intends to develop a product line. He just signed a deal with former Gucci designer Tom Ford to develop products for the line.

Demsey believes that Gwyneth Paltrow is a perfect fit for the Estée Lauder brand. She not only is a very popular actress and a fashion icon but also personifies the image of the Estée Lauder brand—the image of aspiration and style. The plan is to feature Paltrow in print and television advertisements to support the fragrance during holiday 2005 and follow with appearances for other Estée Lauder fragrances and makeup categories yet to be announced.

Source: Adapted from Stephanie Thompson, "Estée Lauder Signs Gwyneth Paltrow: Company Turns to Actress Rather Than Model for New Face," *Advertising Age,* May 23, 2005, http://adage.com/news.cms?newsId=45131.

Figure 13-2
Analysis for Objective Setting

norms of these measures are very important in determining the desired level and time frame associated with each objective.

After determining the norms of the objective measure (e.g., average yearly sales of comparable competitor brands), then the manager sets the desired level (and the time frame) in relation to past profit, sales, and/or market share. For example, suppose a company is in the retail wireless telephone business. The average yearly retail sales for the company in question have been determined to be $1.5 million per store. The store manager then sets a sales objective for the next year in direct relation to the $1.5 million. Should it be $1.5 million? Should it be greater than or less than $1.5 million? At least six factors should be considered in setting corporate-level objectives. These are shown in Table 13-1 and are discussed in some detail in the following sections.

> **TABLE 13-1** Factors Considered in Setting Corporate Objectives
>
> 1. Industry average in relation to profit, sales, and/or market share
> 2. Forecasted profit, sales, and/or market share
> 3. Past profit, sales, and/or market share of key competitors
> 4. Anticipated profit, sales, and/or market share of key competitors
> 5. Anticipated market changes that may affect future profit, sales, and/or market share
> 6. Anticipated changes within the firm that may affect future profit, sales, and/or market share

13-2a Industry Average in Relation to Sales, Market Share, Profit, and Cash Flow

The industry average of sales, market-share, profit, and/or cash-flow figures can help the manager determine whether the desired level of the selected objective should be at, above, or below the firm's own norm (past profit, sales, and/or market share). For example, if the industry at large has an average gross profit margin of 35 percent and the firm has averaged 30 percent gross margin for the past 5 years, then next year's gross margin objective should be set at a higher level than 30 percent, perhaps somewhere between 30 and 35 percent.[2]

13-2b Forecasted Sales, Market Share, Profit, and/or Cash Flow

Similarly, forecast figures can help the manager figure out whether the desired level of the objective(s) should be set at, above, or below the firm's norm. For example, if the firm's sales forecast is very positive (e.g., a forecast of 5 million units to be sold next year, a jump from 3.9 million sold this year), then the sales objective should be set at a level between 3.9 and 5 million.[3]

13-2c Past Sales, Market Share, and Profit of Key Competitors

Many managers select key competitors and gather as much data as possible about these companies. Usually, the key competitors are "comparable" competitors. These competitors may be looked at as "role models" to be emulated in most respects. If the manager knows the past sales data of a key competitor, then the manager's sales objective for next year may be somewhat influenced by the competitor's past sales. For example, if a key competitor had a market share of 25 percent and the firm in question had a market share of 20 percent, then next year's market-share objective is likely to be somewhere between 20 and 25 percent.[4]

13-2d Anticipated Profit, Sales, and/or Market Share of Key Competitors

Similarly, the anticipated profit, sales, and/or market share of key competitors can be quite valuable. For example, if the manager finds out that the anticipated market share of a key competitor is 30 percent and the firm in question had a last-year market share of 20 percent, then next year's market-share objective is likely to be somewhere between 20 and 30 percent.[5]

13-2e Anticipated Market Changes That May Affect Future Sales, Market Share, and/or Profit

The focus here is on market changes. Suppose the firm acquires information about an industry study that indicates that the market is likely to increase by 5 percent. This new information should help the manager set sales objectives for next year.[6]

13-2f Anticipated Changes within the Firm That May Affect Future Sales, Market Share, Profit, and/or Cash Flow

Changes within the firm can certainly affect corporate-level performance and, therefore, future objectives.[7] Imagine the following scenario. A corporate-level executive of a Fortune 500 firm is told that a new vice president for marketing has agreed to join the company. This new vice president comes from another Fortune 500 company and has much experience in the industry of the recruiting firm. Knowing this, the corporate executive is likely to feel quite optimistic in setting the sales and market-share objectives for next year.

Table 13-2 shows how setting corporate-level objectives can be done in a quantitative and mathematical way. Note that we first need to start out with some baseline. The best baseline is the firm's past performance on the objective dimension. The example shown in Table 13-2 involves average unit sales from the past 5 years (5,000 unit sales). If the product is new, the manager may examine comparable products and their past performance in the first year of product launch. The five factors we have discussed (industry norms, forecasted performance, past performance of key competitors, anticipated performance of key competitors, anticipated market changes that may affect the firm's performance, and anticipated changes within the firm that may affect the firm's performance) are used to estimate other performance **referents.** Note that each of these referents is assigned an importance weight. In other words, the manager may have higher confidence in certain referents than others and, therefore, is likely to weigh these referents more heavily. An average referent is then computed (7,100 unit sales). Then an average is computed between the firm's past performance (5,000) and the weighted average referent (7,100). The unit sales objective is therefore determined to be 6,050. Of course, if one wishes to obtain a weighted average rather than a simple average, then both the firm's past performance

referent A standard of comparison used in performance assessment to help interpret performance ratings.

TABLE 13-2 An Example of Setting Unit Sales Objectives

Factor	Estimated Unit Sales		Importance Weight		Weight Score
Average unit sales of industry at large	4,000	×	10%	=	400
Sales forecast	6,000	×	25%	=	1,500
Past sales of key competitor	8,000	×	20%	=	1,600
Anticipated sales of key competitor	9,000	×	10%	=	900
Anticipated market changes that may affect sales	7,000	×	10%	=	700
Anticipated changes within the firm that may affect sales	8,000	×	25%	=	2,000
The firm's unit sales based on analysis			100%		7,100
Final objective unit sales for next year (average of past unit sales and unit sales based on analysis)					6,050

and the average referent can be similarly weighted by importance scores, and a weighted average can be similarly derived.

13-3 Using Situation Analysis to Set Marketing Objectives

Like corporate analysis and planning, marketing analysis and planning have to be discussed in relation to strategy selection, objective setting, and resource allocation. Here, we concentrate on the use of situation analysis to set effective marketing objectives. Remember what **marketing objectives** are? They are typically set in relation to specific brand associations and are directly related to the type of positioning strategy selected. For example, a positioning-by-product-attribute strategy automatically leads the marketing manager to focus on the association between the marketer's brand and a significant product attribute, an important product feature that is unique to the marketer's brand. Similarly, the positioning-by-intangible-factor strategy guides the marketer to focus on establishing, maintaining, or reinforcing an association between the brand and an intangible factor. That intangible factor is supposed to be a significant criterion in the consumer purchase decision. Note that identification of the objective dimension is predicated on the selected positioning strategy. Knowing the positioning strategy automatically allows the marketing manager to identify the objective dimension.

However, as stated in the section in this chapter on setting corporate objectives, the manager has to work with reliable and valid measures of brand association. Managers must use objective measures that studies have shown to be reliable and valid. The manager has to gather data pertaining to the norms of the measure, especially in relation to past performance and the performance of other firms in one's industry, and the norms of these measures are very important in determining the desired level and time frame associated with each objective.

Once the norms of the objective measure to be used are determined (e.g., recognition of Brand X as part of Product Class Y using Measure Z), then the manager sets the desired level and time frame in relation to past data on brand association. For example, suppose the firm that markets a toothpaste to teenagers—let us call it "Bright Smile"— wants to reinforce a brand association with the benefit of "a sexy smile." That is, the firm wants to assert, "If you brush your teeth with Bright Smile brand of toothpaste, you will have a bright and sexy smile." Suppose that through a consumer survey it has been determined that only 30 percent of the teenagers in the United States recognize the brand name and its key benefit of "making one's smile brighter and more sexually appealing." The brand manager then sets the objective for next year: *Increase recognition of the brand name and its key benefit of sexually appealing smile by 200 percent by the end of next year*. In other words, the goal is to have 90 percent of all teenagers in the United States recognize the brand and its key benefit of a sexy smile by the end of next year; but how did the manager come up with 90 percent or an increase of 200 percent? Actually, once the referent is determined, how much to increase (or decrease) from the referent can be determined by taking into account several factors, shown in Table 13-3. These are discussed in some detail in the sections that follow.

marketing objectives
Formal statements that represent concrete and precise desired states of affairs articulated at the marketing level. Marketing objectives are usually stated in terms of brand equity or brand associations. An example of a marketing objective is "Establish an image of quality for Brand X."

> **TABLE 13-3** Factors Considered in Setting Marketing Objectives

1. The industry average in relation to the use of this particular measure of brand association
2. Forecasted changes in the brand association in question
3. Past brand associations of key competitors
4. Anticipated brand associations of key competitors
5. Anticipated market changes that may affect the brand association in question
6. Anticipated changes within the firm that may affect the brand association in question

13-3a Industry Average in Relation to the Use of This Particular Measure of Brand Association

Marketing communications managers should gather information about the norms of brand association measures and especially the norms of the measure that they use to gauge brand association performance. The industry average of brand association performance can help marketers determine whether the desired level of the selected objective should be stated at, above, or below the brand's past performance.[8] For example, if the industry at large has an average brand association of 50 percent using Brand Association X and the brand in question has averaged 30 percent over the past year, then next year's brand association objective should be set at a higher level than 30 percent, perhaps somewhere between 30 and 50 percent.

13-3b Forecasted Changes in the Brand Association in Question

Similarly, forecast figures can help marketing communications managers figure out whether the desired level of the objective(s) should be set at, above, or below the firm's norm.[9] For example, one study indicated that at least 60 percent of all teenagers in the United States will come to believe that all brands of toothpaste can make their smiles more sexually appealing. This may be due to the collective industry advertising that implies that all brands of toothpaste can produce sexy smiles. This collective industry effort is likely to cause more teenagers to believe that Bright Smile brand of toothpaste, as well as others, enhances smiles by making them look sexually appealing. If the consumer survey conducted last year revealed (1) that 30 percent of all teenagers believed that Bright Smile toothpaste enhanced their bright smile and (2) that approximately 60 percent of the same population are expected to believe in the same benefit next year, then what should the objective be? Perhaps it should be somewhere between 30 and 60 percent.

13-3c Past Brand Association of Key Competitors

Many marketers select key competitors and gather as much data as possible about these competitors. Usually the key competitors are "comparable" competitors. If marketers have data about past brand associations of a key competitor, then the marketers' brand association objectives for the next year may be somewhat influenced by the competitor's past brand associations.[10] For example, if the association with Bright Smile of a key competitor—let us call it X—was 25 percent among all teenagers, then next year's brand association objective is likely to be somewhere between 25 and 30 percent. See SMC Marketplace Watch 13-2 for another example.

13-3d Anticipated Brand Association of Key Competitors

Similarly, the anticipated brand association of key competitors can be quite valuable.[11] For example, if the marketing communications manager of Bright Smile finds out that the anticipated association with a sexually appealing smile of a key competitor X is likely to be 40 percent next year and the firm in question had a last-year association of 30 percent, then next year's brand association objective is likely to be somewhere between 30 and 40 percent.

13-3e Anticipated Market Changes That May Affect the Brand Association in Question

The focus here is on market changes. Suppose the Bright Smile manager acquires information about an industry study indicating that there is a market trend among teenagers toward adopting products that make them look and feel sexually appealing. This new information should help the marketer of Bright Smile toothpaste set the brand association objective for next year, right? The answer is obviously "yes." If

SMC Marketplace Watch 13-2

Cialis: Qualitative Research Guides Development and Execution of an Advertising Campaign

Paula Garrett, a marketing executive at Eli Lilly and Company, conducted some research to gauge consumer reaction to a new drug (Cialis—the name is derived from the French *"ciel,"* or sky) aimed at treating erectile dysfunction. The nature of the research was *focus group* (qualitative research). The lights went back on in a conference room where three women had been viewing a prospective television commercial for Cialis. The focus-group members, whose husbands all suffered from impotence, had watched attentively as a male voice-over gently advised: "Introducing Cialis. You can take Cialis anytime and have up to 36 hours to respond to your partner, without planning or rushing." Garrett observed from the other side of a one-way mirror as the group's moderator said, "Tell me specifically, what is it you like about Cialis?" One of the women leaped out of her chair. She was about 60 years old and looked like a Sunday school teacher. "Thirty-six hours!" she exclaimed, raising her arms like she was doing the wave at a ballgame. "Yeah!" Garrett was amused. In her 15-year career in brand marketing, she has monitored hundreds of focus groups—for Procter & Gamble; Coca-Cola; and, since early 2001, Lilly as U.S. consumer marketing manager for Cialis. Yet she says she cannot recall ever seeing anyone get this excited about a product.

Clinical trials have shown that, while Cialis, Viagra, and Levitra all make muscles in the penis relax allowing increased blood flow for an erection, some crucial differences were noted. For one, unlike Viagra, Cialis as well as Levitra remained effective even if the user ate or had a drink. While both Viagra and Levitra enabled men to have an erection anytime from a half-hour to 4 hours after swallowing the pill, Cialis provided that advantage up to 36 hours. The research question was: Would consumers perceive that to be a valuable benefit to their mating rituals? The answer seemed clear enough from the reaction of focus-group participants.

With a promising point of differentiation, the next challenge for Eli Lilly was to identify effective ways to communicate this point of differentiation to consumers. Lilly's consumer researchers detected sharp differences in the way men perceived Cialis and Viagra. In one-on-one interviews in mid-2000, Viagra users who had been informed of the attributes of both drugs were given a stack of objects and asked to sort them into two groups, one for Viagra and the other for Cialis. Red-lace teddies, stiletto-heeled shoes, and champagne glasses were assigned to Viagra; while fluffy bathrobes and down pillows belonged to Cialis. The implication: Viagra was for studs, Cialis for romantics.

The dichotomy was reinforced in one-on-one sessions with partners of men with impotence problems. Women often confessed that they felt under the gun to perform with Viagra. "It feels like there are three of us in bed," Garrett recalls one saying. "Me, him, and the pill." On the other hand, women typically said that from what they had heard about Cialis, they could be more natural and wait to have sex until both of them were in the mood.

Based on the results of patient and partner interviews and focus groups, Lilly and its advertising agency, Grey Worldwide, opted for an advertisement with scenes of couples snuggling and slowly caressing to emphasize cozy, tender, or playful moments. A soundtrack of easy, laid-back jazz was used. The scenes in the advertisement created the impression that with Cialis there is no hurry. The slogan? "When a tender moment turns into the right moment, you'll be ready."

Source: Adapted from Michael Arndt, "Is Viagra Vulnerable? Eli Lilly's Cialis Lasts for 36 Hours—and a $100 Million Ad Blitz Will Spread the Word," *BusinessWeek*, October 22, 2003.

---

past brand association with a sexually appealing smile was 30 percent, then next year's objective should be set at a level definitely higher than 30 percent, perhaps 40 percent.[12]

13-3f Anticipated Changes within the Firm That May Affect the Brand Association in Question

Changes within the firm can certainly affect brand association performance and, therefore, the setting of future objectives.[13] Imagine the following scenario. The marketing communications manager of Bright Smile toothpaste has successfully recruited a new advertising specialist. This person has much experience with developing advertising for products directed at teenagers. Knowing this, the marketing manager is likely to feel quite optimistic in setting next year's brand association objective.

13-4 Using Situation Analysis to Set Marketing Communications Objectives

Just as we have discussed analysis and planning at both the corporate and marketing levels, we now address analysis and planning with respect to **marketing communications objectives**: *aware, learn, feel, do,* and *repeat*. However, because we have argued that *learn* goals constitute the marketing objectives, we only concentrate on the goals of *aware, feel, do,* and *repeat*.

As stated in the section on setting corporate and marketing objectives in this chapter, the manager has to work with reliable and valid measures of brand awareness, brand attitude, brand purchase, and repeat purchase. Managers must use objective measures that studies have demonstrated to be reliable and valid. The manager has to gather data pertaining to the norms of the measure, especially in relation to past performance and the performance of other firms in one's industry. The norms are crucial in determining the desired level and time frame associated with each objective.

Once the norms of the objective measure to be used are determined (e.g., brand name recognition using Measure X), then the manager sets the desired level and time frame. Let us go back to the example of the firm that markets the Bright Smile toothpaste to teenagers. Suppose the marketing communications goal is to reinforce a positive brand attitude. Suppose that through a consumer survey it has been determined that only 50 percent of the teenagers in the United States like this brand. The marketing communications manager then sets the following objective for next year: Increase positive brand attitude by 50 percent by the end of next year. In other words, the goal is to have at least 75 percent of all teenagers in the United States feel good about Bright Smile toothpaste by the end of next year; but how did the manager come up with 75 percent, or an increase of 50 percent? Actually, once the referent is determined, knowing how much to increase (or decrease) from the referent can be determined by taking into account several factors that are shown in Table 13-4. These are discussed in some depth in the following sections.

marketing communications objectives Formal statements that represent concrete and precise desired states of affairs articulated at the marketing communications level. Marketing communications objectives are usually stated in terms of increases in brand awareness, learning about the benefits and costs of the brand, establishing positive attitude or liking toward the brand, and inducing trial purchase.

13-4a The Industry Average in Relation to the Use of the Selected Measure of the Communications Objective

Marketing communications managers should gather information about the norms of brand awareness (and/or brand attitude, brand purchase, and repeat purchase) measures and especially the norms of the measure that they use to gauge communications performance.[14] Knowing the industry average of communications performance can help the manager determine whether the desired level of the selected objective should be at, above, or below the brand's past performance. For example, if the industry at large usually attains an average brand attitude of 40 percent using a certain measure and the brand in question has averaged 50 percent as indicated by

TABLE 13-4 Factors Considered in Setting Marketing Communications Objectives

1. The industry average for the selected measure of the communications objective
2. Forecasted changes in the selected communications measure
3. Past performance of key competitors along the selected communications measure
4. Anticipated performance of key competitors along the selected communications measure
5. Anticipated market changes that may affect the selected communications objective
6. Anticipated changes within the firm that may affect the selected communications objective

a consumer survey conducted last year, then next year's brand attitude objective should be set at a lower level than 50 percent, perhaps somewhere between 40 and 50 percent.

13-4b Forecasted Changes in the Selected Measure of the Communications Objective

Similarly, forecast figures can help marketing communications managers figure out whether the desired level of the communications objective should be set at, above, or below the firm's norm.[15] For example, one study may indicate that at least next year's brand attitude toward Bright Smile toothpaste may increase by 25 percent, perhaps due to a social contagion effect. That is, the more teenagers use the product, the more they talk about it and the more they feel good about it. If the consumer survey conducted last year revealed that 50 percent of all teenagers have a positive attitude toward Bright Smile toothpaste, then what should the objective be? Perhaps it should be somewhere between 50 and 67.5 percent. Good research that has been integrated into the broader system should clarify that question.

13-4c Past Performance of Key Competitors along the Selected Measure of the Communications Objective

Many marketing communications managers select key competitors and gather as much data as possible about these competitors. Usually the key competitors are "comparable" competitors. Suppose that in the same survey conducted last year consumers were asked to indicate their brand preference and the marketer's brand was included among a list of key competitor brands. Thus, the marketing communications manager would have an idea how the brand in question stands in relation to key competitors along a communications performance dimension such as brand awareness, brand attitude, brand purchase, and repeat purchase. This information may be very helpful to the marketing manager in setting communications objectives for next year.[16] For example, if a comparable competitor brand called Close-Up toothpaste was preferred by 60 percent among all teenagers, then next year's attitude objective for Bright Smile toothpaste is likely to be somewhere between 50 and 60 percent.

13-4d Anticipated Performance of Key Competitors along the Selected Measure of the Communications Objective

Similarly, the anticipated communications performance of key competitors can be quite valuable.[17] For example, the marketing communications manager of Bright Smile may find out that teenagers' attitude toward Close-Up is likely to increase by 10 percent because the marketing communications manager of Close-Up toothpaste fired the firm's advertising agency and gave this account to another agency that has a reputation for great creative advertising. The Bright Smile manager thus surmised that because of the new advertising campaign that is currently being developed, brand attitude toward Close-Up is likely to increase by at least 10 percent next year, bringing it to a level of 66 percent brand preference. Based on this information, the marketing communications manager of Bright Smile toothpaste decides to set the brand attitude objective for next year somewhere between 50 and 66 percent.

13-4e Anticipated Market Changes That May Affect Communications Objectives

Suppose the Bright Smile communications manager becomes informed of an industry study that reveals a market trend toward sexiness and sensuality among the teen population. This new information should help the marketer of Bright Smile toothpaste set the brand attitude objective for next year, right? Perhaps. If past brand attitude toward Bright Smile was 50 percent last year, then next year's objective may be set at a level higher than 50 percent as a direct function of this market trend.[18]

13-4f Anticipated Changes within the Firm That May Affect Communications Objectives

Changes within the firm can certainly affect the performance of any communications objective and, consequently, the setting of future communications objectives.[19] Imagine the following scenario. The marketing communications manager of Bright Smile toothpaste finds out that several outstanding, key creative people at the advertising agency that services the Bright Smile account have left the agency and joined the agency that services the Close-Up account. This is bad news that may dampen any high expectations in relation to next year's communications performance. Knowing the situation, the manager is likely to feel pessimistic in setting next year's brand attitude objective.

Summary

How are objectives set? Corporate objectives? Marketing objectives? Marketing communications objectives? This chapter introduces you to situation analyses that can be performed to help managers set objectives at the corporate, marketing, and marketing communications levels. The basic situation analysis model calls for gathering information about past performance in relation to the selected objectives to establish a baseline. Once a baseline is established using past performance data, then new data should be gathered in relation to several referents. These referents include industry norms, forecasted changes, past performance in relation to key competitors, anticipated performance in relation to key competitors, anticipated market changes, and anticipated changes within the firm. These referents are compared against the baseline parameter (established based on past performance), and the baseline parameter is adjusted in the direction of these referents.

Discussion Questions

Study the following case:

The marketing plan of a certain bank—let us call it United States Bank—calls for operating in the mid-Atlantic states. The bank offers the traditional banking services plus consumer and business loans, home mortgage loans, and its own credit card. The bank wants to make greater inroads in the mid-Atlantic states. The marketing plans call for a growth strategy. The bank's present market share in the mid-Atlantic states is only 2 percent. There is a plethora of banks in the mid-Atlantic states, and the average market share seems to hover around 6 percent. The United States Bank regards First States Bank as a key competitor. First States Bank has a market share of 12 percent in the designated states. An article about banking in the mid-Atlantic states reveals that First States is planning to launch an aggressive marketing campaign to significantly increase its market share to 15 percent in the next year or two. A situation analysis revealed that major strengths of the United States Bank are its consumer and business loan divisions. These divisions have aggressively marketed themselves as providing fast, low-interest loans with top-notch service. A recent consumer survey reveals that 68 percent of the bank customers rated the bank as excellent in terms of fast loans, low-interest loans, and top-quality service in relation to loans. The same survey also revealed that 85 percent of the bank customers have positive feelings toward the bank and 60 percent intend to use the bank to obtain loans when the need arises. An industry study has shown that most banks achieve an average of 45 percent of their customers indicating "excellent" on the dimensions of fast-speed loans, low-interest loans, and high-quality service in relation to loans. The same study also indicated that there is a trend away from traditional banking. Many consumers are increasingly using specialized financial services, and a significant segment is also beginning to bank using online computer services. Respond to the following questions.

1. What would be a reasonable corporate objective for the United States Bank for the next 2 to 3 years? Explain the logic you used to set the objective.

2. What would be a reasonable marketing objective for the United States Bank for the next 2 to 3 years? Explain the logic you used to set the objective.

3. What would be a reasonable marketing communications objective for the United States Bank for the next 2 to 3 years? Explain the logic you used to set the objective.

Practice Quiz

Note: You can find the correct answers to these questions by taking the quiz and then submitting your answers in the Online Edition. The program will automatically score your submission. If you miss a question, the program will provide the correct answer, a rationale for the answer, and the section number in the chapter where the topic is discussed.

1. Corporate objectives are typically set in relation to four performance dimensions. _____ is not a dimension.
   a. Sales
   b. Cash
   c. Profit
   d. Tactic

2. It was previously recommended that corporate objectives be set using a three-stage process. _____ is one of the stages of this process.
   a. Identification of cash flow and revenue
   b. Identification of the measures used to derive the outcomes
   c. Identification of the desired level and time frame associated with each objective dimension
   d. Identification of the resource and the manpower required to fulfill the objectives

3. After determining the norms of the objective measure, then the manager _____ in relation to past profit, sales, and/or market share.
   a. sets the desired level
   b. forecasts profit
   c. anticipates market changes
   d. anticipates changes within the firm

4. Many managers select key competitors and gather as much data as possible about these companies. Usually, the key competitors are _____ competitors.
   a. higher profit making
   b. comparable
   c. superior
   d. nonthreatening

5. _____ are typically set in relation to specific brand associations and are directly related to the type of positioning strategy selected.
   a. Competitor objectives
   b. Marketing objectives
   c. Marketing positions
   d. Tangible factors

6. _____ can help marketers determine whether the desired level of the selected objective should be stated at, above, or below the brand's past performance.
   a. The industry average of brand association performance
   b. The positioning strategy
   c. The marketing objectives within the positioning strategy
   d. All of the preceding answers are correct.

7. The marketing communications manager of Bright Smile toothpaste has successfully recruited a new advertising specialist. This person has much experience with developing advertising for products directed at teenagers. Knowing this, the marketing manager is likely to feel quite optimistic in setting next year's brand association objective. What does this example depict?
   a. anticipated market changes that may affect the brand association in question
   b. anticipated brand association of key competitors
   c. past brand association of key competitors
   d. anticipated changes within the firm that may affect the brand association in question

8. If the industry at large usually attains an average brand attitude of 40 percent using a certain measure and the brand in question has averaged 50 percent as indicated by a consumer survey conducted last year, then next year's brand attitude objective should be set at a lower level than 50 percent, perhaps somewhere between 40 and 50 percent. What does this example represent?
   a. the industry average in relation to the use of the selected measure of the communications objective
   b. forecasted changes in the selected measure of the communications objective
   c. past performance of key competitors along the selected measure of the communications objective
   d. anticipated performance of key competitors along the selected measure of the communications objective

9. The marketing communications manager would have an idea how the brand in question stands in relation to key competitors along a communications performance dimension such as brand awareness, brand attitude, brand purchase, and repeat purchase. How does this information help the marketing manager?
   a. This information may be very helpful to the marketing manager in setting revenue budgets for next year.
   b. This information may be very helpful to the marketing manager in setting communications objectives for next year.
   c. This information may be very helpful to the marketing manager in setting corporate strategies for next year.
   d. This information may be very helpful to the marketing manager in predicting revenue outflow for next year.

10. The marketing communications manager of Bright Smile toothpaste finds out that several outstanding, key creative people at the advertising agency that services the Bright Smile account have left the agency and joined the agency that services the Close-Up account. What is the likely reaction of a manager given this scenario?
    a. The manager may not view this as a major setback.
    b. Based on this information, the marketing communications manager of Bright Smile toothpaste may decide to set the brand attitude objective for next year somewhat higher.
    c. The manager is likely to feel pessimistic in setting next year's brand attitude objective.
    d. All of the preceding are likely outcomes.

Web Exercise

Is Image Everything?

Visit the websites of cosmetic companies from around the world. Estée Lauder is just one. What is their web presence meant to accomplish? Seek out the stores and advertisements that these companies use to market their products. Can you purchase these products online? If so, are they heavily discounted? Do the companies you selected truly have an integrated image in everything they do? How would you better that image to fit what you think are corporate objectives?

Suggested Readings

Bogart, Leo. 1984. *Strategy in advertising,* 2nd ed. Lincolnwood, IL: Crain Books/NTC Business Books.

Ferrell, O. C., George H. Lucas Jr., and David Luck. 1994. *Strategic marketing management.* Cincinnati, OH: South-Western Educational Publishers.

Ghemawat, Pankaj, David J. Collis, Garry P. Pisano, and Jan W. Rivkin. 1999. *Strategy and the business landscape.* Reading, MA: Addison-Wesley.

Goold, Michael, Andrew Campbell, and Marcus Alexander. 1994. *Corporate-level strategy: Creating value in the multibusiness company.* New York: John Wiley & Sons.

Johnson, Gerry, Kevan Scholes, and Richard Whittington. 1993. *Exploring corporate strategy,* 7th ed. London: Prentice Hall International.

Kaplan, Robert S., and David P. Norton. 2004. *Strategy maps: Converting intangible assets into tangible outcomes.* Boston: Harvard Business School Publishing.

Lancaster, Kent M., and Helen E. Katz. 1992. *Strategic media planning.* Lincolnwood, IL: Crain Books/NTC Business Books.

Lodish, Leonard M. 1986. *The advertising and promotion challenge: Vaguely right or precisely wrong.* New York: Oxford University Press.

McGann, Anthony F., and J. Thomas Russell. 1988. *Advertising media: A managerial approach,* 2nd ed. Homewood, IL: Irwin.

Nelson, Carol. 1991. *The new road to successful advertising: How to integrate image and response.* Chicago: Bonus Books.

Parente, Donald, Bruce Vanden Bergh, Arnold Barban, and James Marra. 1996. *Advertising campaign strategy: A guide to marketing communication plans.* Fort Worth, TX: Dryden Press.

Prahald, Hamel. 1994. *Competing for the future.* Boston: Harvard Business School Press.

Schnaars, Steven P. 1991. *Marketing strategy: A customer-driven approach.* New York: Free Press.

Schultz, Don, and Beth Barnes. 1993. *Strategic advertising campaigns,* 4th ed. Lincolnwood, IL: Crain Books/NTC Business Books.

———. 1999. *Strategic brand campaigns.* Lincolnwood, IL: Crain Books/NTC Business Books.

Schultz, Don E., Stanley I. Tannenbaum, and Robert F. Lauterborn. 1994. *Integrated marketing communications: Pulling it together and making it work.* Lincolnwood, IL: NTC Business Books.

Thorson, Esther, and Jeri Moore. 1996. *Integrated communication: Synergy of persuasive voices.* Mahwah, NJ: Lawrence Erlbaum Associates.

Wilson, Laurie J., and Joseph Ogden. 2000. *Strategic communications planning: For effective public relations and marketing,* 4th ed. Dubuque, IA: Kendall/Hunt.

Notes

1. Gary McWilliams, "Dell Net Jumps As Optimism Grows: PC Maker's View Reflects Upbeat Industry Forecasts; Some Skepticism Persists," *Wall Street Journal,* May 13, 2005, A3; Steve Hamm, with Andrew Park and Ben Elgin, edited by Ira Sager, "A Lemon For Lenovo?" *BusinessWeek,* February 21, 2005; Ben Elgin, Cliff Edwards, and Peter Burrows in San Mateo, California, with Michael Arndt in Chicago, "Handicapping the HP Hopefuls: Techdom's Top Names Are Popping Up As the Search to Replace Carly Hits Overdrive," *BusinessWeek,* March 21, 2005.
2. George Day, "Diagnosing the Product Portfolio," *Journal of Marketing* (April 1977): 29–38; Donald C. Hambrick and Ian C. MacMillan, "The Product Portfolio and Man's Best Friend," *California Management Review* (Fall 1982): 84–95; Philippe Haspeslagh, "Portfolio Planning: Uses and Limits," *Harvard Business Review* (January–February 1982): 60, 73; Yoram Wind and Vijay Mahajan, "Designing Product and Business Portfolios," *Harvard Business Review* (January–February 1980): 155–65; Yoram Wind, Vijay Mahajan, and Donald J. Swire, "An Empirical Comparison of Standardized Portfolio Models," *Journal of Marketing* (Spring 1983): 89–99.
3. Ibid.
4. Ibid.
5. Ibid.
6. Ibid.
7. Ibid.
8. O. C. Ferrell, George H. Lucas Jr., and David Luck, *Strategic Marketing Management* (Cincinnati, OH: South-Western Educational Publishers, 1994); Steven P. Schnaars, *Marketing Strategy: A Customer-Driven Approach* (New York: The Free Press, 1991).
9. Ibid.
10. Ibid.
11. Ibid.
12. Ibid.
13. Ibid.
14. Leo Bogart, *Strategy in Advertising,* 2nd ed. (Lincolnwood, IL: Crain Books/NTC Business Books,1984); Kent M. Lancaster and Helen E. Katz, *Strategic Media Planning* (Lincolnwood, IL: Crain Books/NTC Business Books, 1992); Leonard M. Lodish, *The Advertising and Promotion Challenge: Vaguely Right or Precisely Wrong* (New York: Oxford University Press, 1986); Anthony F. McGann and J. Thomas Russell, *Advertising Media: A Managerial Approach,* 2nd ed. (Homewood, IL: Irwin, 1988); Carol Nelson, *The New Road to Successful Advertising: How to Integrate Image and Response* (Chicago, IL: Bonus Books, 1991); Donald Parente, Bruce Vanden Bergh, Arnold Barban, and James Marra, *Advertising Campaign Strategy: A Guide to Marketing Communication Plans* (Fort Worth, TX: The Dryden Press, 1996); Don Schultz and Beth Barnes, *Strategic Advertising Campaigns,* 4th ed. (Lincolnwood, IL: Crain Books/NTC Business Books, 1993); Don Schultz and Beth Barnes, *Strategic Brand Campaigns* (Lincolnwood, IL: Crain Books/NTC Business Books, 1999); Don E. Schultz, Stanley I. Tannenbaum, and Robert F. Lauterborn, *Integrated Marketing Communications: Pulling It Together and Making It Work* (Lincolnwood, IL: NTC Business Books, 1994); Esther Thorson and Jeri Moore, *Integrated Communication: Synergy of Persuasive Voices* (Mahwah, NJ: Lawrence Erlbaum Associates, 1996); Laurie J. Wilson and Joseph Ogden, *Strategic Communications Planning: For Effective Public Relations and Marketing,* 4th ed. (Dubuque, IA: Kendall/Hunt, 2000).
15. Ibid.
16. Ibid.
17. Ibid.
18. Ibid.
19. Ibid.

Strategic Allocation of Resources
Budgeting in the Strategic Marketing Communications System

Chapter Fourteen

Key Terms

all-you-can-afford method (p. 350)
budgeting (p. 342)
competitive-parity methods (p. 346)
experimental method (p. 347)
historical-statistical method (p. 348)
match or outspend competitors (p. 347)
match-industry-norms method (p. 346)
objective-task method (p. 350)
percentage-of-anticipated-sales method (p. 345)
percentage-of-past-sales method (p. 345)
percentage-of-unit-anticipated-sales method (p. 345)
percentage-of-unit-past-sales method (p. 345)
previous-budget method (p. 351)
ratio-to-sales methods (p. 345)
return-on-investment (ROI) method (p. 348)
share-of-voice/market method (p. 346)

Chapter Outline

14-1 Introduction
14-2 Ratio-to-Sales Methods
    14-2a Percentage of Anticipated Sales
    14-2b Percentage of Unit Anticipated Sales
    14-2c Percentage of Past Sales
    14-2d Percentage of Unit Past Sales
14-3 Competitive-Parity Methods
    14-3a Match Industry Norms
    14-3b Share of Voice/Market
    14-3c Match or Outspend Competitors
14-4 Quantitative Methods
    14-4a Experimental
    14-4b Historical Statistical
14-5 Return-on-Investment (ROI) Method
14-6 Objective-Task Method
14-7 All-You-Can-Afford Method
14-8 Previous-Budget Method
14-9 A Strategic Marketing Communications Budgeting Method
    14-9a Determine the Corporate Objectives
    14-9b Determine the Corporate Mix to Achieve the Stated Objective
    14-9c Determine the Marketing Strategy to Achieve the Corporate Objective
    14-9d Determine the Marketing Objective That Operationalizes the Marketing Strategy
    14-9e Determine the Marketing Communications Strategy to Achieve the Marketing Objective
    14-9f Determine the Marketing Communications Objective That Operationalizes the Marketing Communications Strategy
    14-9g Determine the Marketing Communications Mix to Achieve the Marketing Communications Objective
    14-9h Determine the Cost of Implementing the Selected Marketing Communications Programs
    14-9i Adjust the Marketing Communications Budget as a Function of Monitoring/Control and Analysis/Planning
14-10 Analysis for Budgeting Decisions
    14-10a Organizational Factors
    14-10b Industry Factors
    14-10c Product Factors
    14-10d Customer Factors
Summary
Discussion Questions
Practice Quiz
Web Exercise: An Exercise of Dollars and Cents
Suggested Readings
Notes

The trouble with a budget is that it's hard to fill up one hole without digging another.

—**Dan Bennett,** American author and essayist

14-1 Introduction

In 2004 Colgate-Palmolive's advertising spending rose 10 percent to an all-time record level, $1.063 billion. Have you ever wondered how these giant companies allocate resources? How does a company like Colgate-Palmolive determine how to allocate an annual advertising budget of $1.063 billion? This budget, however, pales in comparison to the two giants of the industry, Procter & Gamble and Unilever. (Access the SMC QuickLink to see Unilever's brands.) The results of an *Advertising Age* study from 2004 pegged the spending of these two multinational consumer products companies in 2003 at $5.76 billion and $3.54 billion respectively.[1]

The entire focus of this book has been on treating integrated marketing communications (IMC) decisions from a strategic standpoint. At the end of the day, strategic marketing communications (SMC) is about providing optimal "value" in decisions as they relate to the well-being of not only a given brand but also the entire corporate system. As the Unilever website demonstrates, each brand has a place within the greater system that is Unilever. Each of those brands requires a certain amount of resources to perform well in its respective competitive environment. At the same time, however, only a certain amount of resources are available within the Unilever system to allocate to the entire brand portfolio. In today's world of limited resources and for the survival of both the brand and the firm, managers at all levels of a firm must be strategic in their use of those resources. When you "drill down" to the basics, allocating resources to the elements of the strategic mix is a **budgeting** decision. The marketing communications manager must decide what resources are needed to implement the selected strategy and its respective strategic mix. For example, given the decision to advertise the product through the web and television in a combined campaign, the manager determines the amount of money needed to launch a combined web- and television-based advertising campaign to achieve a certain level of brand awareness. The managers higher up in the system have to decide if the requests for resources at that level are justified, given the marketing and corporate-level resource pool and demands from other components in the entire system. Assessments are made in the context of the competitive environment at all levels for the firm. Change in that competitive environment is generally the only constant (see SMC Marketplace Watch 14-1).

While we believe that an SMC approach to budgeting is the optimal choice, it is not always the choice in the "real world." A number of approaches to budgeting have been used in the past and continue to be applied in today's competitive environment. A manager needs to understand all the options that are available for use in allocating resources—even those approaches that may be less than optimal in nature. In some cases, they can be integrated within the SMC approach, or used as one's own fall-back strategy. An examination of all available approaches can also allow the manager to gain insight into the budget-setting practices of a current or potential competitor who is known to use one of the particular approaches. So that you get a

SMC QuickLink

Unilever
http://www.unilever.com/ourbrands

budgeting The process of allocating resources to a certain organization activity.

SMC Marketplace Watch 14-1

Budget Allocations Are Changing—More Money Is Going to the Internet

The Chrysler Corporation is reintroducing its muscle car, the 2006 Dodge Charger, and is planning to promote it heavily on the web. To do so, the automaker beefed up its online advertising spending in 2005 by 20 percent over 2004. In 2004 the Chrysler Corporation spent $1.6 billion on marketing communications; $36.1 million was allotted for online advertisements.

The crux of the web campaign is the use of a desktop toolbar as a way to point users to Charger advertising messages all over the Internet, not just at one website. The campaign is dubbed "Unleash Your Freak." The Internet is the lead medium for the campaign.

Consumers can do a bunch of exciting things once they download the toolbar. The toolbar allows them to access regular news, sports, and business updates. They can earn "muscle points" to spend on ring tones, screen savers, wallpapers, or music. They can also download a game for Sony's PlayStation Portable; and consumers can peruse photos, information, and video clips of the Charger. An online scavenger hunt sends web users in search of the four major attributes of the car. These are personified by animated characters: the control freak, the speed freak, the style freak, and the power freak. Players search the web for video advertisements that feature the freaks, who hang from key chains dangling from the advertisements. When users click on a freak, they are transported to a microsite (one for each type of freak), where they try to engage their key in a virtual ignition. Those that start an engine win a Charger.

Source: Adapted from Jean Halliday and Kris Oser, "Dodge Charges Online for Charger: Desktop Toolbar Puts Muscle Car Ad Messages across Web," *Advertising Age,* July 07, 2005, AdAge.com QwikFIND ID: AAQ72Z.

---

sense of the myriad of approaches, this chapter offers a look at a number of the alternative approaches to the SMC method.

An example of one often-used budgeting method in advertising is the "buildup approach." Sometimes this budgeting method is also referred to as the "objective-task method." This approach works within the context of a greater system approach to the setting of budgets, albeit slightly differently than the SMC approach discussed later in the chapter. Using the buildup approach, resource allocation is determined by a two-stage process: First, the manager identifies the subordinate tasks needed to implement the superordinate task and accomplish its goals (e.g., the television programs and number of insertions needed to meet a stated objective of brand awareness). Then, he or she sums up the total costs related to the implementation of the subordinate tasks (see Figure 14-1).

Managers commonly use many other methods to allocate resources at the corporate, marketing, and marketing communications levels. However, because the focus of this book is on the marketing communications level, little purpose would be served to thoroughly review and address budgeting methods at either the corporate or marketing levels. Nevertheless, as already noted, the integrative nature of the SMC budgeting process must be recognized to show how corporate and marketing strategies and tactics influence the budget at the marketing communications level. The process by which corporate and marketing strategies and tactics influence the marketing communications budget can be referred to as a top-down ("build-down") process. Before discussing the build-down process of resource allocation and its use within the SMC context, we first discuss some of the other traditional methods of budgeting.

Many methods are traditionally used in allocating communications expenditures. Among the popular methods are ratio-to-sales methods, competitive-parity methods, quantitative methods, the return-on-investment (ROI) method, the objective-task method, the all-you-can-afford method, and the previous-budget method.[2] We discuss these in some detail (see Table 14-1).

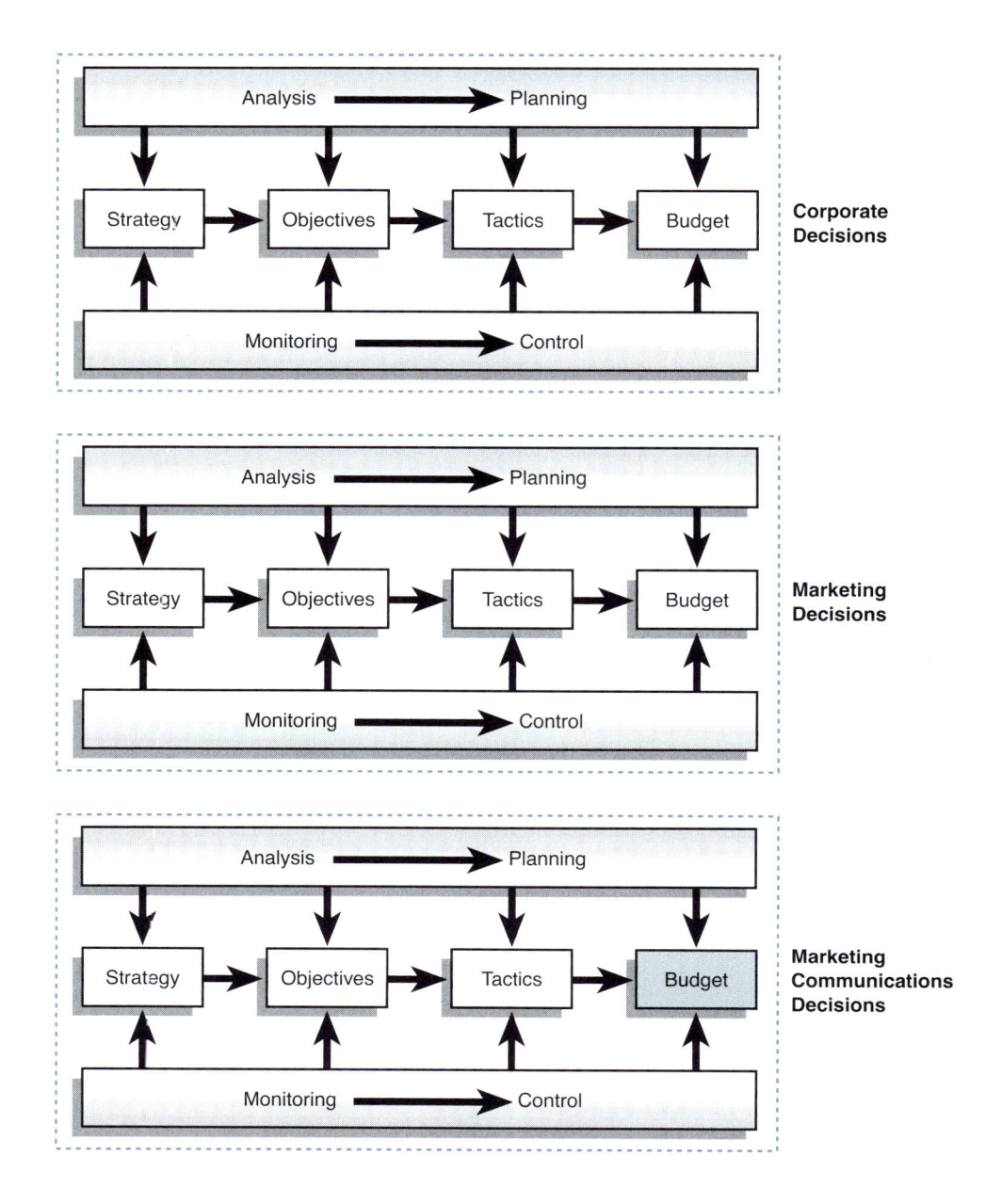

Figure 14-1
Allocating Marketing Communications Resources (Budget)

TABLE 14-1	Traditional Budgeting Methods of Marketing Communications
Ratio-to-Sales Methods	
• Percentage of anticipated sales	• Percentage of past sales
• Percentage of unit anticipated sales	• Percentage of unit past sales
Competitive-Parity Methods	
• Match industry norms	• Match or outspend competitors
• Share of voice/market	
Quantitative Methods	
• Experimental	• Historical statistical
Return-on-Investment (ROI) Methods	
• Objective-task method	• Previous-budget method
• All-you-can-afford method	

14-2 Ratio-to-Sales Methods

Ratio-to-sales methods calculate a budget based on *percentage of anticipated sales, percentage of unit anticipated sales, percentage of past sales,* and *percentage of unit past sales*. The marketing communications budget thus becomes a percentage of past sales or projected sales or a percentage of past unit sales or projected unit sales. These methods rely heavily on industry norms and customs. Many communications scholars have argued that relying too much on past sales or forecasted sales is not an effective method of budgeting because if sales were down last year, the marketing communications budget for next year is likely to be smaller. This smaller budget may weaken the effectiveness of marketing communications, which, in turn, will likely cause further decreases in sales. The various ratio-to-sales methods are described in the following sections.

ratio-to-sales methods Budgeting methods that allocate resources based on percentage of anticipated sales, percentage of unit anticipated sales, percentage of past sales, and percentage of unit past sales.

14-2a Percentage of Anticipated Sales

The **percentage-of-anticipated-sales method** states that a marketing communications budget can be determined as a percentage of forecasted sales. For example, suppose a marketing communications manager of a software package such as Microsoft Office has traditionally allocated 3 percent of sales to marketing communications. Sales are expected to increase by 10 percent in the next 12 months. Assume that sales of Microsoft Office for 2004 were $75 million. The sales forecast for 2005, therefore, is $82.5 million. The marketing communications manager allocates 3 percent of the $82.5 million (sales forecast), not the $75 million (past sales). Therefore, the marketing communications budget for Microsoft Office for 2005, based on the percentage-of-anticipated-sales method, is $2.48 million.

percentage-of-anticipated-sales method Budgeting method based on a percentage of forecasted sales.

14-2b Percentage of Unit Anticipated Sales

The **percentage-of-unit-anticipated-sales method** states that a marketing communications budget can be determined as a percentage of unit cost. In the Microsoft example, suppose each Microsoft Office unit is expected to be sold next year at $550. Suppose Microsoft expects to sell 10 million units next year. The tradition has been to allocate 2 percent of the unit sales to marketing communications. Therefore, the marketing communications budget is determined as $110 million ($550/unit × 10 million units to be sold × .02).

percentage-of-unit-anticipated-sales method Budgeting method determined as a percentage of unit cost.

14-2c Percentage of Past Sales

The **percentage-of-past-sales method** states that a marketing communications budget can be determined as a percentage of last year's sales. The only difference between this method and the percentage-of-anticipated-sales method is the source of the sales figure. The sales figure in the percentage-of-anticipated-sales method is based on a sales forecast, while this method relies on past sales, perhaps last year's sales.

percentage-of-past-sales method Budgeting method determined as a percentage of last year's sales.

14-2d Percentage of Unit Past Sales

The **percentage-of-unit-past-sales method** states that a marketing communications budget can be determined as a percentage of the unit price for last year's sales. Again, the only difference between this method and the percentage-of-unit-anticipated-sales method is the source of the sales figure. The sales figure in the percentage-of-unit-anticipated-sales method is based on a sales forecast assuming a certain price level, while this method relies on past sales based on a fixed price.

percentage-of-unit-past-sales method Budgeting method determined as a percentage of the unit price for last year's sales.

14-3 Competitive-Parity Methods

competitive-parity methods Budgeting methods that focus on some aspect of what and how the competition is spending on promotion.

At least four budgeting methods are known as **competitive-parity methods:** *match industry norms, match competitors, outspend competitors,* and *share of voice/market*. All of these methods are based on a basic assumption, namely, that the competition's level of expenditure is effective and is based on well-articulated logic. The problem with this method is that marketing communications managers cannot rely on a major competitor to determine their own budget. It is hard to justify that a major competitor "knows best" and should be an industry guide for followers. Too many factors are unique to different firms within a product/market, with each factor requiring special considerations in budget formulation.

14-3a Match Industry Norms

match-industry-norms method Budgeting method based on the industry average or "norm."

The **match-industry-norms method** states that an effective marketing communications budget is equivalent to the industry average or "norm." Marketing communications managers who rely on this method seek and fund studies to gather data establishing the industry norms. For example, a 5-year study examined how industrial marketing communications managers set their advertising budgets.[3] The study involved sixty-six industrial products from twelve firms. The study objective was to establish marketing expenditure norms for industrial marketing communications managers. The study found that most industrial marketing communications managers spend 6.9 percent of the previous year's budget on marketing tasks, with a range from 3 percent to 14 percent. With respect to advertising expenditures, the norm was that industrial marketing communications managers spend 9.9 percent (range 5 to 19 percent) of their marketing budgets on advertising or 0.6 percent of total sales (range 0.1 to 1.8 percent). The same study also found that most industrial marketing communications managers allocate their advertising budget in the following manner:

- 41 percent on print medium advertising (trade, technical press, and house journals)
- 24 percent on direct mail (leaflets, brochures, catalogs, and other direct-mail pieces)
- 11 percent on shows (trade shows and industrial films)
- 24 percent on promotion (sales promotion)

A study from the mid-1990s conducted for the American Marketing Association in business-to-business (biz-to-biz) marketing showed that biz-to-biz firms devoted an average of 3.49 percent of their sales to marketing.[4] The marketing budget is broken down as follows: 2.14 percent of sales have gone to direct selling (this includes sales staff salaries, bonuses, commissions, travel, and entertainment); .88 percent of sales went to marketing communications (defined as print advertisements, direct mail, trade shows and exhibits, radio, television, out-of-home media, public relations, catalogs/directories, literature, coupons, point-of-purchase materials, and dealer and distributor materials); .37 percent of sales went to marketing support (marketing/advertising planning, advertising salaries, and presentations); .07 percent of sales went to market research; and .03 percent of sales went to telemarketing. In today's world, we have seen a shift of resources toward the web as that media choice continues to prove itself as a strong business-to-business tool (see SMC Marketplace Watch 14-2).

14-3b Share of Voice/Market

share-of-voice/market method Budgeting method based on the examination of the firm's market share in relation to the major competitors in the product/market.

The **share-of-voice/market method** entails the examination of one's market share in relation to the major competitors in the product/market. What do the major competitors spend on marketing communications? The rule of thumb is that the marketing communications manager's budget for marketing communications should be in direct proportion to past and desired market share.

For example, suppose we are in the motel business. We are marketing a motel chain, say, Hampton Inn. Let us say, hypothetically speaking, that Hampton Inn's

SMC Marketplace Watch 14-2

More Spending on Internet Communications

Advertising spending on the Internet continues to break records. Analysts at the Interactive Advertising Bureau (IAB)—an association of over two hundred leading interactive companies—report spending online totaled more than $2.8 billion for the first quarter of 2005, making this the highest reported quarter in nine consecutive quarters of growth. The 2005 first-quarter spending was a 26 percent increase from the $2.2 billion spent during the same period in 2004, and it increased 4.3 percent from the fourth-quarter 2004 figure of $2.7 billion.

What accounts for the increased spending on Internet communications? Analysts at the IAB point to several factors. One reason is the increased trend in audience fragmentation. Much research has documented the fragmentation of television viewers. Another reason is greater access to broadband. More and more consumers have adopted broadband connections. Yet another factor accounting for more spending on Internet communications is the growth of the Internet audience in general.

Many of the spending figures are published in *The Advertising Revenue Report* (analysis conducted by the media group of PricewaterhouseCoopers but initiated back in 1996 by the IAB). The report includes data from all companies that report meaningful online advertising revenue. Information is collected from revenue from websites, commercial online services, free email providers, and other companies selling online advertising.

Source: Adapted from Kris Oser, "First-Quarter Online Ad Spending Up 26 Percent from Last Year: Marketers Continue to Shift Money onto Web," *Advertising Age*, June 8, 2005. AdAge.com QwikFIND ID: AAQ63W.

---

market share last year was 20 percent. The major competitor that Hampton Inn is directly competing against is Holiday Inn, which reported a market share of 30 percent last year. We know that Holiday Inn spent $20 million on marketing communications last year. Suppose that Hampton Inn's market share objective is to increase market share by 5 percent (from 20 percent to 25 percent). How much money should Hampton Inn allocate for marketing communications? The answer is $16.67 million ($20 million multiplied by 25 percent, the product of which is divided by 30 percent).

14-3c Match or Outspend Competitors

Most industries have access to published figures showing marketing communications expenditures as a percentage of sales, which are used as a guide by many marketing communications managers. For example, a marketing communications manager may read that a major competitor has allocated 20 percent of the dollar sales from this year to cover marketing communications costs for next year. The manager may then decide to outspend the competition by allocating 23 percent; or the manager may simply match the competition by allocating 20 percent. Typically, firms such as automobile manufacturers and oil companies rely on published data to figure out what certain competitors are doing and make decisions either to **match or outspend competitors.**

match or outspend competitors Budgeting method guided by the notion that optimal spending is to match or outspend the firm's major competitors.

14-4 Quantitative Methods

Two common types of empirical methods are used to determine the optimal level of communications expenditures—the experimental method and the historical-statistical method.

14-4a Experimental

The **experimental method** states that an effective way to determine an optimal amount of expenditures is to experiment with different amounts and observe the effects. For example, a firm may set its rate for communications based on its most current information about the sales-response function. In Market *A*, it may have

experimental method Budgeting method based on experimental studies.

spent X amount on communication; in Market B, it may have spent Y amount; and in Market C, it may have spent Z amount. Which level of expenditure produced a significantly higher sales response? Thus, an optimal level of expenditure is chosen.[5] An example of the use of this method involves a DuPont study. DuPont Paint Division divided fifty-six sales territories into high, average, and low market-share territories. Across these territories, DuPont spent a "normal" amount of advertising in one-third of the territories, two and one-half times as much in another third of its territories, and four times as much in another third of the territories. At the end of the designated period, sales were estimated. The question was: How much extra sales were created by higher levels of advertising expenditures? The study revealed that higher advertising expenditure increased sales at a diminishing rate and that the sales increase was weaker in the high market-share territories.[6]

Another common experimental method is an industry study in which communications expenditures and sales data are collected from as many firms as possible within the industry in relation to a particular time period (e.g., the last 2 years). From this data, an attempt is made to estimate the elasticity coefficients of various communications tools. The tool that is found to have the greatest elasticity warrants the highest level of expenditure. For example, one study estimated the sales effectiveness of three communications tools used in the pharmaceutical industry.[7] The study showed that journal advertising had the highest long-run advertising elasticity at .365; samples and literature had an elasticity of .108; and direct mail had an elasticity of only .018. Thus, firms in that industry should allocate expenditures to the various communications tools as a direct function of the elasticity coefficients.

14-4b Historical Statistical

historical-statistical method Budgeting method based on statistical data from the company's archives.

In the **historical-statistical method,** statistical data from the company's archives are manipulated. The goal is to build a regression model in which sales are predicted by past sales, communications expenditure levels, and other factors. The hope is that the variable pertaining to communications expenditure levels turns out to be a significant predictor of sales and that the entire regression equation (involving all the predictors) accounts for a large percentage of the variance in the criterion variable (i.e., the sales variable). Given a statistically valid regression model, the marketing communications manager experiments with different expenditure levels to identify the level of expenditure increment that accounts for the highest level of sales increase.[8]

For example, one study focused on the effect of advertising expenditures on the sales of Lydia Pinkham's Vegetable Compound between 1908 and 1960.[9] The study found that marginal advertising dollars increased sales by only $.50 in the short term. However, the long-term marginal sales effect was three times as large. The marginal rate of return on company advertising was estimated to be 37 percent over the whole period.

14-5 Return-on-Investment (ROI) Method

return-on-investment (ROI) method Budgeting method guided by the assumption that money spent today is an investment that is likely to pay off in sales tomorrow.

The **return-on-investment (ROI) method** has received a lot of attention in recent years. Advertisers have demanded to have advertising agencies show them "what they actually bought" for the dollars they invested in advertising. This method assumes that money spent today is an investment that is likely to pay off in sales tomorrow. Implementing this budgeting method requires payout planning. For example, launching a new product is likely to result in higher levels of expenditures on communications the first year or two. In the first year, sales are not likely to be high and profits are likely to be in the red. This picture may begin to change in the second year. Sales are likely to pick up, and profit is likely to be still in the red or close to breakeven. The third year may be quite different, and the payoff (i.e., the return on investment) starts to become evident. Sales may be high, and profits are likely to grow. See SMC Marketplace Watch 14-3 for an interesting analysis of ROI ratings of various media and promotion tools.

SMC Marketplace Watch 14-3

Rating Media for Their Accountability

The groundswell of marketer demand for methods to measure the value of advertising has hit an unprecedented level. *Advertising Age* asked Aegis Group's Marketing Management Analytics to rate the measurability for ROI of various marketing media (refer to Table 1).

TABLE 1 Return-on-Investment Measurability Rating for Various Marketing Media

Medium	The Measurement Challenge	ROI Measurability Rating
Direct response	Direct mail, telemarketing, and other forms are the most measurable of media listed here. Direct can have a synergistic effect, especially for pharmaceutical, telecommunications, and financial services.	5
Sales promotion	Offers such as coupons and discounts generate a lot of consumer response and therefore a bounty of data. The data lend themselves to measurement, especially for package goods via syndicated scanner data. Free-standing inserts generate much valuable data.	5
Internet	The Internet can be very influential for big-ticket purchases like cars. The Internet is very measurable, with the cautionary note that "Internet is a very broad net," ranging from search engines to advertisements in content to websites such as in the auto market, where such marques as Saab get lots of hits, and all should be looked at separately. The goal is to understand how the consumer is interacting online with the brand.	5
Television	While promotions have very pronounced, short-term effects that allow precise measurement, television has a more subtle and gradual effect that may show greater variability. But ROI can be measured with a high degree of accuracy, and there's no excuse for television not to show a measurable effect.	4
Print	The experts can slice and dice print by weekly versus monthly publications, by targeted versus general market, by promotional advertisements versus equity building. Print promotional materials, like free-standing inserts, are a separate—and much more measurable—matter. As with all other media, accuracy and timing of the data are crucial in determining how measurable the medium is. Print can play a strong role in expanding the reach of the media mix.	4
Public relations	There are companies that specialize in the measurement of PR campaigns' quality; they can measure the number of impressions delivered—via positive or negative PR—for a brand name or category. PR can have a measurable impact on sales (think trans fats in food). The problem: Many marketers are not buying these PR data.	4
Video games	Whether the game is played online or offline is crucial. An advertisement embedded in a game cartridge is very hard to measure because there is no way to know how often it is played, though there is no denying "True Crime's" Nick Kang is a big hit. With online games, great data are available through the Internet.	Online: 4 Offline: 1
Radio	The available data typically are not as strong as those for its traditional-media colleagues of television and print, and this hampers radio.	3
Cinema	Movie advertising can be measured by the number of impressions delivered, much like outdoor or kiosk advertising would be measured.	3
Sponsored events	Measurability depends on whether sponsorship is likely to spark short-term effect. A major recurring event like the Olympics is very measurable. Others can be difficult to measure short term. Measurement can be complex because events have so many pieces, including how the event is advertised, the PR buzz, signage, and the recollection of the event itself.	3
Product placement in content	There are companies that measure quality of placement as well as the quantity of exposures. It is treated much like television advertising, with the caveat that not every product placement is the same. Fox's *American Idol* is a great example: AT&T Wireless's tie-in, which involves voting by text message, is interactive—even part of the entertainment—while Paula Abdul drinking from a Coca-Cola cup is not. So the question becomes, How do you score the quality of placement?	3

continued

TABLE 1	Continued	
Medium	**The Measurement Challenge**	**ROI Measurability Rating**
Outdoor	Available data are limited due to the nature of outdoor advertising; there is no syndicated vendor that sells the needed data on outdoor. Outdoor lacks "variance"—the billboard is up X number of months and is seen by an unchanging X number of people each day.	2
Guerilla marketing	This is hard to measure if the variable you are using is sales. If 10,000 people at an event get free T-shirts, it is difficult to measure the effect of the 400,000 people living in that market. Because guerilla can encompass so many different kinds of tactics, getting useful data can be a problem—it depends on how measurable the response is. Marketers' ROI expectations for guerilla are lower than for other media, so the urgency to measure is less—not to mention that they spend a lot less on guerilla than on traditional media like television.	1

Source: "Media Scorecard: How ROI Adds Up" by Dan Lippe. Reprinted with permission from the June 20, 2005 issue of *Advertising Age*. Copyright, Crain Communications Inc., 2005.

Although ROI is a very reasonable budgeting method, the problem lies with implementation. The marketing communications manager still does not know exactly how much to spend on communications tools the first year, the second year, and so on. Because this method lacks specificity, many marketing communications managers work with the method more implicitly than explicitly.

14-6 Objective-Task Method

objective-task method
Budgeting method based on a precise account of how much money is needed to build a marketing communications campaign that will meet certain communications, marketing, and/or corporate objectives.

The **objective-task method** of allocating expenditures for marketing communications is considered to be the ideal method—but also the most tedious. It is tedious because it is based on a precise account of how much money is needed to build a marketing communications campaign that will meet certain communications, marketing, and/or corporate objectives. That is, the method calls for marketing communications managers to develop their marketing communications budgets by defining their objectives clearly, determining the marketing communications programs (tasks) to achieve these objectives, and estimating the costs of these programs.[10] Here is an example involving a direct-response campaign:

> ... [F]or a lead generation program, we might set a campaign objective of 1,000 sales, determine the average close ratio (leads to sales) to be 30 percent, and determine the number of qualified leads needed to generate 1,000 sales (4,000 responses). Then determine how much it will cost to bring in 4,000 qualified leads. That equals your budget. If past response is 1 percent, then 400,000 pieces need to be mailed out to yield 4,000 qualified leads. For print, if past response is 0.2 percent, then a reach of 2 million is needed to yield 4,000 qualified leads. You then price a 400,000-piece direct mail campaign or a print campaign that reaches 2 million readers. If you can't run a campaign that mails this many pieces or reaches this many readers due to budget constraints, then your objectives need to be modified.[11]

14-7 All-You-Can-Afford Method

all-you-can-afford method
Budgeting method that is quite arbitrary and is based on the notion that a good marketing communications budget is as much as the firm can afford to spend.

The **all-you-can-afford method** is quite arbitrary and states that a good marketing communications budget is as much as the firm can afford to spend. Small businesses usually use this method because of resource scarcity. They usually cannot or refuse to borrow money to finance a marketing communications campaign. They feel the risk is high. In contrast, some medium and large businesses use this method, thinking that marketing communications are a form of investment. The more one spends, the bigger the investment. Since marketing communications pay off in the long run, whatever the firm can afford, the firm will spend. Of course, this method of budgeting for marketing communications is ineffective because it ignores the role of marketing communications as an investment and the impact of marketing communications on corporate and marketing objectives.

14-8 Previous-Budget Method

The **previous-budget method** is not really an analytical method to determine communications expenditures. It is very simple. It states that an effective budget is the previous budget, possibly with some adjustments. Many marketing communications managers in large companies that have rich and long histories tend to rely on tradition. They do not want to "rock the boat." They think that there is a good reason that the company has spent certain amounts of money on marketing communications in the way it did in the past. The company has survived and prospered. Therefore, previous efforts at budgeting should be considered successful and previous budgets can be used to set new ones.

Of course, the logic of this method is not very defensible. One can argue that the company could have done even better with a different budget; or, perhaps the company has survived and prospered despite the "faulty" budget.

previous-budget method
Allocating resources based on the previous budget, possibly with some adjustments.

14-9 A Strategic Marketing Communications Budgeting Method

Is there such a thing as an optimal budgeting method? Yes, and we recommend that a marketing communications budget be determined using the procedure described in subsequent subsections and shown in Table 14-2.

14-9a Determine the Corporate Objectives

The first step is to determine the corporate objectives in terms of sales, market share, profit, and/or cash flow. As a refresher, review Chapter Twelve, which deals with objectives and measurement. Consider the following example throughout this discussion. A software company is now ready to launch a new product. The software is a comprehensive and interactive music encyclopedia that covers all the genres of

TABLE 14-2 Recommended Budgeting Method

1. Determine the corporate objective.
2. Determine the corporate mix to achieve the corporate objective.
3. Determine the marketing strategy to achieve the corporate objective.
4. Determine the marketing objective that operationalizes the marketing strategy.
5. Determine the marketing communications strategy to achieve the marketing objective.
6. Determine the marketing communications objective that operationalizes the marketing communications strategy.
7. Determine the marketing communications mix to achieve the marketing communications objectives.
8. Determine the cost of implementing the selected marketing communications programs.
9. Adjust the marketing communications budget as a function of monitoring/control and analysis/planning.

music. Such an encyclopedia has never been available before in either hard copy or online for download. This is a truly innovative interactive software that allows online access to a comprehensive web-based experience that will allow students to select any type of music and explore all aspects of the genre including video interviews with artists, past performances, downloads of music, and even online discussion groups for any music topic. Music teachers and professors have the ability to post interactive assignments and guide students through customized learning environments based on course requirements. The next quarterly goal is to increase sales of this software by 50 percent.

14-9b Determine the Corporate Mix to Achieve the Stated Objective

The second step is to develop a corporate mix that is capable of achieving the stated objective (e.g., the sales objective). As a refresher, review Chapter Nine, which deals with corporate strategy and tactics. We can implement the *growth* strategy through an aggressive marketing effort. Therefore, we need to allocate more resources to marketing to match the increased effort. In other words, the marketing function is viewed as playing a key role in achieving the goals of the growth strategy. All eyes are now focused on marketing. The marketing communications manager is now charged with developing a marketing plan that can achieve the sales objective of a 50 percent increase in the quarter. Let us say a 50 percent increase in sales translates to the sale of an additional 50,000 units.

14-9c Determine the Marketing Strategy to Achieve the Corporate Objective

The third step is to develop a marketing strategy that is capable of achieving the stated corporate objective (e.g., the 50 percent increase in sales of the music encyclopedia software). Review Chapter Ten, which deals with marketing strategy and tactics. The marketing manager determines that a prospect strategy is likely to be most effective. This software can be easily used in high school and college music courses. Therefore, the strategy is to focus on music teachers and professors and convince them that this software can be highly instrumental in their teaching of music to their students. Market analysis indicates that there are a minimum of 250,000 music high-school teachers and college professors in the United States. Thus, a positioning by user or customer is likely to be most effective here.

14-9d Determine the Marketing Objective That Operationalizes the Marketing Strategy

The idea here is to figure out an exact marketing objective that captures the essence of the marketing strategy and ties it back to the corporate objective. In other words, the marketing communications manager has to come up with a marketing objective that is most likely to result in the attainment of the corporate objective too. The marketing objective is *to establish an association between this software brand and the typical music teacher or professor*. A possible goal is to successfully position the product in the minds of at least 20 percent of this population. The likely result would be sales of 50,000 units, thus achieving the objective of 50 percent increase in sales.

14-9e Determine the Marketing Communications Strategy to Achieve the Marketing Objective

The focus here is to figure out the best marketing communications strategy to convince 20 percent of high-school teachers and college professors to adopt this software for classroom use by the end of next quarter. The decision is to use an *informative (thinker)* communications strategy. This strategy is likely to be more effective than other communications strategies such as the affective (feeler), habit-formation (doer), and self-satisfaction (reactor) strategies.

14-9f Determine the Marketing Communications Objective That Operationalizes the Marketing Communications Strategy

The goal here is to figure out those exact marketing communications objectives that reflect the selected marketing communications strategy and to link these objectives with the superordinate marketing objectives. In the context of the software company, the question becomes, What communications objectives reflect an effective implementation of the informative (thinker) communications strategy? These objectives may be stated in the form of the specific sequence of objectives related to *learn → feel → do*. Perhaps the total marketing communications campaign can be broken into three phases, the first phase reflecting the *learn* component, the second phase reflecting the *feel* component, and the third phase reflecting the *do* component. Specifically, the most effective implementation of the informative (thinker) strategy that is likely to achieve the marketing objective of 20 percent brand association may be a 60 percent brand awareness/learning. That is, if the company can get 60 percent of all high-school music teachers and college professors to become aware of the music software and learn something about it in the next quarter, 20 percent are likely to realize that this software is most used by people like them. This should be the focus of the first phase of the marketing communications campaign (the *learn* phase). The objective of the second phase of the campaign should focus on the *feel* component. A possible objective would be to ensure that at least 40 percent of the teachers and professors who have been exposed to the software by now will form a positive attitude toward the software. The objective of the third phase of the campaign should focus on the *do* component. A possible objective would be to ensure that at least 25 percent of the teachers and professors who now have formed a positive attitude toward the software will purchase the software at least on a trial basis (see Table 14-3).

14-9g Determine the Marketing Communications Mix to Achieve the Marketing Communications Objective

This step involves selecting the best marketing communications tools or programs that are capable of achieving the stated marketing communications objective. As a refresher, review Chapter Eleven, which deals with marketing communications strategy and tactics. For the music encyclopedia software, the best communications tool is advertising in both electronic and hard copies of trade and academic journals that music teachers and professors commonly read. The first phase of the campaign should involve informative direct-response advertisements placed in the trade and academic journals. The second phase of the campaign should involve variations of the first informative direct-response advertisements but with less information and more

TABLE 14-3 Setting Marketing Communications Objectives as a Direct Function of the Informative (Thinker) Strategy

	Learning about the Software	Liking the Software	Purchasing the Software
First phase of the campaign	60%	20%	5%
Second phase of the campaign	70%	40%	10%
Third phase of the campaign	80%	50%	25%

Note: The consumer population is music high-school teachers and college professors.

emotional cues (vivid pictures of emotional events or characters). The third phase of the campaign may involve a variation of the advertisements of the second phase, but an economic incentive is offered to induce purchase.

14-9h Determine the Cost of Implementing the Selected Marketing Communications Programs

The next step is to determine the cost of the selected marketing communications programs. Suppose that advertising in three magazines/journals (in combination with a direct-mail campaign) is the most effective in attaining the stated marketing communications objectives. Also, the manager determines that twelve insertions in these weekly magazines/journals would be sufficient to generate the desired levels of awareness/learning, attitude, and purchase. Suppose that advertising this software in these three magazines/journals, with three advertisement insertions each in the next three issues, will cost $100,000; also, suppose that the cost for creative production of the advertisements is $5,000.

14-9i Adjust the Marketing Communications Budget as a Function of Monitoring/Control and Analysis/Planning

This marketing communications budget is then adjusted as a direct function of monitoring/control and analysis/planning. As Figure 14-1 shows, budgeting at the marketing communications level is determined by considering three factors: (1) marketing communications tactics, (2) marketing communications monitoring and control, and (3) marketing communications analysis and planning. The previous discussion shows how the marketing communications manager can set the marketing communications budget by assessing the cost of the tactics (programs) needed to implement the marketing communications strategy. Chapter Fifteen describes how the marketing communications budget can be adjusted by trial-and-error experience, that is, monitoring and control. The manager adjusts the budget based on past marketing communications expenditures and the goals achieved with these expenditures. For example, past experience dealing with the music teachers' and professors' market may suggest that two advertisement insertions in three issues can achieve a high level of awareness/learning. Hence, three advertisement insertions in the next three issues may be too much. The marketing communications manager may adjust the budget as a direct function of past experience. Analysis and planning work the same way. The manager adjusts the budget after considering factors likely to affect marketing communications performance. Suppose that by conducting a competitive analysis, the manager realizes that a key competitor is likely to target music teachers and professors using the same trade and academic journals. Because of this, the manager decides that more advertisement insertions are needed to offset the competition. This should increase the budget by another $15,000 to $20,000. The marketing communications manager then requests a budget of approximately $110,000 from the marketing manager or vice president of marketing.

14-10 Analysis for Budgeting Decisions

Consider the following case: The focus is on the photo industry. The product is an advanced photo system. This is the hottest new photo technology in years. The system does not allow any errors—no more pictures that are poorly exposed, no more pictures that are poorly colored, and no more pictures that are printed badly. A consortium of industry leaders, such as Fuji Photo Film U.S.A. Inc. and Eastman Kodak Company, has jointly developed the product. The product is expected to raise industry sales by at least 10 percent in 1996. These industry leaders are expected to spend at least $150 million on marketing support in 1996. The marketing communications

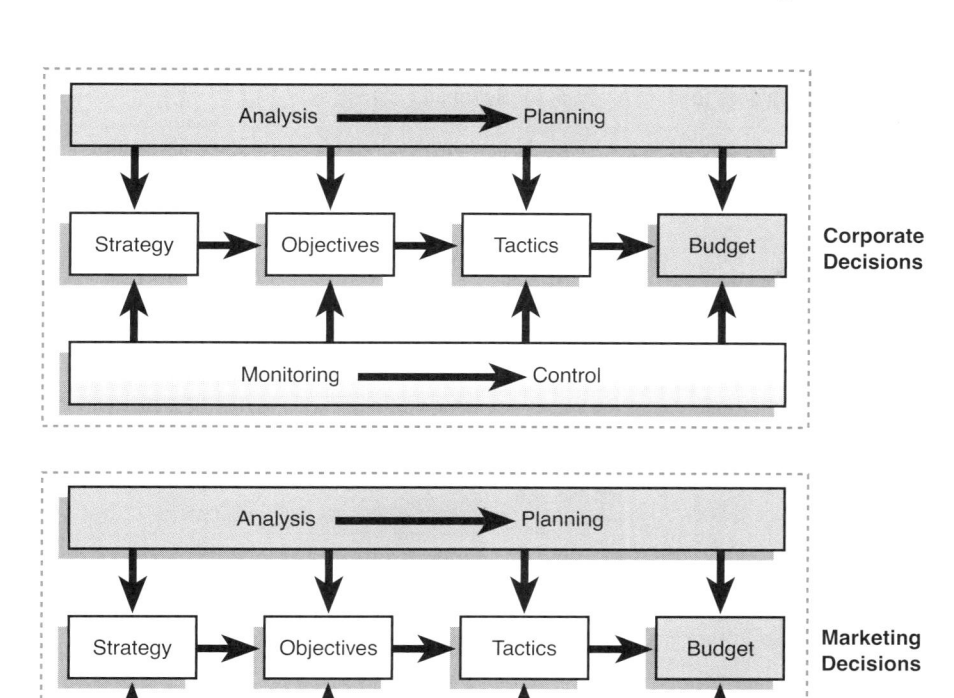

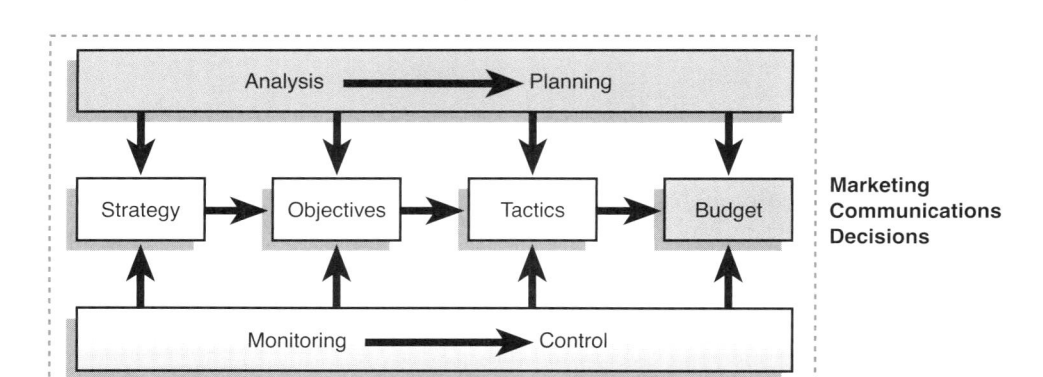

Figure 14-2
Analysis for Budget Decision Making

campaign will focus on consumer education. Fuji, which spent $6.5 million on measured media in 1994, is expected to spend twice this amount in 1996. Kodak spent $65.4 million in the United States on its brand last year; Canon spent $10.3 million on media in 1994; Nikon spent $9 million; and Minolta spent $5.1 million. Film sales hit 864 million units in 1994.[12]

Now imagine that you are a marketing communications executive at Kodak. Your goal is to determine an effective marketing communications budget for 1996 and 1997. How would you use this information? Or would you use this information at all? Would you want to gather additional information? What kind and why? This section explains how marketing communications managers can use analytic techniques in making budgeting decisions (see Figure 14-2).

Note that we are not interested in how to allocate resources for all functions at the corporate level. We are only interested in allocating the portion of marketing resources that will ultimately go toward marketing communications and its elements. In the preceding sections, we describe methods for IMC budgeting. In this section, we describe those factors that the marketing communications manager should

| TABLE 14-4 | Factors Guiding Analysis for Budgeting Decisions |

Organizational Factors		
• Objectives	• Strategy and tactics	• Control

Industry Factors		
• Industry norm	• Product life cycle	• Market growth
• Competition	• Market size	• Market potential

Product Factors		
• Product involvement	• Brand differentiation	• Product newness

Customer Factors		
• Purchase frequency	• Consumer familiarity	• Customer demand of the product
• Consumer involvement	• Growth in customer base	

consider in making budgeting decisions. The manager needs to gather information about organizational, market, product, and customer factors and then analyze the information to guide decision making. These factors are shown in Table 14-4 and discussed in some depth in this section.

14-10a Organizational Factors

Organizational factors involve objectives, strategy and tactics, and control. We describe the effects of these factors on budgeting in some detail.

Objectives

At the corporate level, the rule is, the higher the market share objective, the greater the marketing budget and, possibly, the larger the marketing communications budget.[13] Research has shown that firms with large market share have an advantage over smaller firms. Although they spend more money on marketing and communications, they get better returns for the money. This may be due to economies of scale.[14] In contrast, an objective to significantly increase profit may not necessarily mean a significantly larger marketing or marketing communications budget. This is because increasing profits tends to be a goal consistent with a harvest strategy, which specifically prohibits increases in expenditures in whatever form.

Therefore, increases or decreases in the marketing budget should closely match changes in corporate objectives. If sales and market-share objectives increase, then proportional increases in the marketing budget may be justified. For example, marketing expenditures as a percent of past sales or profit can be easily computed. Suppose that the corporate objective is to increase sales by 50 percent in the next year. This would call for a corresponding 50 percent increase in the marketing budget. Therefore, the marketing communications manager needs to keep track of changes in corporate objectives to see if increases or decreases in the marketing budget are consistent with changes in the corporate objectives.

At the marketing level, the same rule applies. That is, the higher the brand association objective, the larger the marketing communications budget. Consider these two scenarios. The first scenario involves a new product, let us say a new dental device designed for consumers to remove plaque without having to go to the dentist. The marketing objective is to create an association between the brand, called The Plaque Remover, and the major product class, namely, dental products designed to remove plaque. The marketing objective is to establish a brand association with the benefit of removing plaque. In one year, 50 percent of the U.S. consumers between the ages of 40 and 60 should learn about this new product. Now compare this scenario to the scenario involving Interplak. This is an electric toothbrush that is also designed to remove plaque, but it is less effective than the new device. Interplak has been around for a number of years. Currently, 60 percent of U.S. consumers between the ages of 40 and 60 are aware of Interplak and its major benefit. The marketing objective is to increase this brand association to 80 percent next year. Which marketing program is likely to require a higher level of marketing communications expenditure? Obviously, the program for the new product would cost more because the marketing objective is much more ambitious than the objective for Interplak, which has been around for a few years.

The same rule also applies at the marketing communications level. Increases in certain marketing communications objectives may warrant proportional increases in resources for certain elements of the marketing communications mix. For example, if the goal is to increase brand trial and purchase by 50 percent in the next 6 months and we know that telemarketing is a suitable communications tool to achieve this objective, then a 50 percent proportional increase in resources allocated to telemarketing may be warranted, too.

A caveat: Note that an increase (or decrease) in an objective at a superordinate level may not necessarily mean a proportional increase (or decrease) at a subordinate level. For example, if the sales objective at the corporate level is increased by 40 percent, should every element of the marketing communications mix (e.g., coupons) be proportionately increased? The answer is a resounding "No!" Perhaps the use of coupons as a marketing communications tool is deemed to be ineffective in this situation. Perhaps a combination of other tools was selected.

Strategy and Tactics

Different strategies call for different approaches to resource allocation. For example, market-share objectives tend to go along with a growth strategy, which in turn places much emphasis on the marketing function. Resources are shifted so that the marketing department is provided with more resources to carry out the growth strategy and achieve the higher market-share objectives. However, a maintain-share strategy may not entail an increase in the marketing and marketing communications budgets. Actually, resource allocation may depend on the fierceness of the competition. A harvest strategy dictates decreasing marketing communications expenditures for the exact purpose of increasing profit. An innovation strategy may entail assigning more resources to help launch the new product. A divestment strategy, on the other hand, requires that the marketing communications budget be significantly reduced or perhaps cut off.

The marketing communications manager should know the corporate strategy in place and the role of the marketing department in achieving the goal of the corporate strategy. If the marketing budget is inadequate for the goal, the marketing communications manager should point this out to top management and ask for a budget increase.

At the marketing and the marketing communications levels, the same logic holds. Specific brand association objectives tend to go along with specific positioning strategies, which in turn may place increased or decreased emphasis on the marketing communications function. Resources may need to be shifted so that the marketing communications department is provided with more resources to carry out the positioning strategy. For example, a positioning strategy such as positioning by celebrity is likely to require more marketing communications than, say, positioning by product class. Therefore, more resources are allocated to the marketing communications function as a direct function of the nature of the positioning strategy and its communications requirements.

Control

Control can be viewed as learning from experience. Some managers are very good at learning from experience. This experience may be personal (data stored qualitatively in their memories) or quantitative (data stored in the firm's accounting archives). Budgeting decisions can be partly guided by the lessons of experience. Here is an example of how budgeting decisions can be made based on past experience. Suppose through the company archive, a manager is able to develop a regression equation. The regression equation has a criterion variable of sales and predictor variable of marketing expenditures. Sales data are dated from 1945 to 1995, that is, fifty observations. The regression coefficient turns out to be statistically significant and accounts for 75 percent of the variance in sales scores. This regression equation is ideal because it allows the manager to manipulate potential increases or decreases in the marketing budget and observe the effect of these increases or decreases on sales. Thus, an optimal marketing budget is selected based on a regression simulation. The regression equation indicates that a 5 percent increase in the marketing budget is likely to increase sales by 8 percent, but further increases in the marketing budget above 5 percent are not likely to generate significant increases in sales. Thus, the manager chooses to increase the marketing budget by 5 percent.

This quantitative method described in Section 14-4b as the *historical-statistical method* is a traditional method commonly used in budgeting. It can be easily used here as one of the many factors that the marketing communications manager should consider in making budgeting decisions.

Note that expenditures and performance dimensions at different levels should not be mixed. That is, expenditures on an element of the marketing communications mix (e.g., trade shows) should not be used as a predictor of sales. Sales is a performance dimension at the corporate level, whereas a trade show is a tactical program belonging to the marketing communications level. This is an important caveat.

A more qualitative version of the use of control to allocate expenditures is the percentage-of-past-sales-or-profit method (or previous-budget method). This method is described in Section 14-2c. Managers commonly set a marketing (or a marketing communications) budget as a percentage of sales, perhaps 5 percent. When asked, "Why 5 percent?" they may say something to the effect that 5 percent of sales has worked well in the past. Why change?

14-10b Industry Factors

At least six industry factors are likely to influence communications budgeting decisions at the corporate level: industry norm, competition, product life cycle, market growth, market size, and market potential.

Industry Norm

Most industries publish expenditure norms. Many trade journals of specific industries conduct industry studies and publish norms such as average marketing (and marketing communications) expenditures as a percentage of sales. For example, *Advertising Age* usually publishes advertising dollars as percentage of sales of industry categories. For example, the category "automobiles" is 4.4 percent, "bottled and canned soft drinks" is 6.5 percent, "personal computers" is 12.4 percent, "dairy products" is 5.7 percent, and "movies" is 9.5 percent, while "perfumes, cosmetics, and toiletries" is 9.4 percent.[15]

Many managers seek out these data and rely on industry norms to increase or decrease the marketing budget in the direction of industry norms. For example, if a firm has spent 5 percent of its sales on marketing and the industry average is 3 percent, top management may be motivated to decrease next year's marketing budget to make it more consistent with the industry norm. Studies are also conducted to find out average expenditures in relation to the various elements of the marketing communications mix. These data are used as a guide to determine future expenditure level.

Competition

In discussing the effect of corporate strategy on allocating resources to marketing and marketing communications, we note that a maintain-share strategy may or may not entail an increase in the marketing budget. It depends on the competition. If the competition is fierce, the corporate executives may recognize the need for a larger marketing communications budget to prevent the competition from "stealing" market share. Competitors may take away customers by using effective marketing communications methods in the form of sales promotion. In order to combat the competition, the firm has to counteract the sales promotion by matching and possibly outmatching its monetary incentives. This may call for a bigger marketing budget (and also a proportional increase in the marketing communications budget). In general, the greater the competition, the greater the need to combat the competition with marketing communications with greater marketing (and marketing communications) resources.

Consider the recent case of Revlon, the cosmetics giant that is number one in market share. Back in the mid-1990s, Revlon competitors had been developing new cosmetic products and were spending a lot more on marketing communications in an attempt to derail Revlon. Specifically, Maybelline, the second largest cosmetics manufacturer (ranked number two in market share at 18.4 percent), spent $30 million or 60 percent of its media budget to introduce The Greats, a product line involving a collection of makeup products. The Greats was a defense against Revlon's ColorStay eye makeup and foundation and ColorStay Lash Color mascara. Proctor & Gamble spent $20 million on U.S. media advertising Factor, which had a market share of 7.3 percent in December 1995, up from 6.1 percent at the start of 1995. CoverGirl, which had a market share of 23.5 in 1995, spent $15 million of 1996's $40 million–plus media budget on Continuous Wear foundation. Also, Simply Powder, a lightweight powder that acts like a foundation, was launched supported by $15 million in media advertising.[16] How did Revlon react to this kind of competition? Did it raise its media budget to counteract the competition?

Review the discussion of the competitive-parity methods as traditional budgeting methods earlier in this chapter. We describe the share-of-voice/market method and the match-or-outspend-competitors method. These methods underscore the importance of competition, and top management should consider this factor in determining the marketing budget. To use these methods, the marketing communications manager has to gather information about key competitors and their marketing and marketing communications expenditures. This can provide them with ammunition to make a case for increases or decreases in the marketing and marketing communications budget.

Product Life Cycle

As a product ages through its product life cycle (PLC), marketing budgets decline proportionately.[17] Specifically, in the introduction stage of the PLC, extra resources are allocated to the marketing function (and, therefore, to marketing communications, too). The marketing budget decreases as the product enters into its growth stage and decreases significantly during the late maturity and decline stages. Why? This is because in the early stages of the PLC, resources are allocated to create brand awareness and educate consumers. In the later stages of the PLC, the objective is to get consumers to switch from competitor brands or to maintain loyalty and encourage repeat purchase. The resources needed for marketing communications tasks to create awareness and educate consumers are likely to be significantly higher than the resources needed to, say, encourage repeat purchase.

Hence, the marketing communications manager should have a good understanding of the product and the stage of the product in its overall life cycle. Such understanding may help the marketing communications manager make a case to top management for increases (or decreases) in the marketing budget.

Market Growth

The higher the customer growth rate, the greater the marketing need to exploit the market growth opportunity. This need, of course, necessitates higher levels of marketing and marketing communications expenditures.[18] For example, the growth of the telecommunications market is phenomenal. More opportunities are available today than ever before. One telecommunications product is the cellular phone. Cellular phone marketers are recognizing the growth in this market and are increasing their marketing communications expenditures to exploit this emerging opportunity. Again, by having this kind of information, the marketing communications manager can make a justifiable case to top management for increases in the marketing budget.

Some managers use quantitative models to forecast sales by taking into account changes in trends related to technology, law, society, culture, environment, economics, and so on. They develop these sales models to forecast market growth and brand sales. They then allocate a certain percentage of the forecasted sales to marketing or marketing communications. That percentage of sales may be based on the industry norm. This method is described in Section 14-2a as the percentage of anticipated sales. We recommend the use of this method to provide the marketing communications manager with additional information based on another potentially significant factor. The idea is not to rely on one factor alone but to take into account as many factors as possible.

Market Size

The size of the market is an important factor. Small and concentrated markets are easier to communicate to, while communication with larger and more disperse markets is more difficult. Larger and more disperse markets warrant higher levels of marketing communications expenditures.[19] Consider the case of the computer software company Microsoft and its marketing of Windows 95. Microsoft developed a marketing program and a marketing communications campaign that covered the world. Such a campaign required enormous amounts of resources.

Market Potential

The focus here is potential. If the difference between actual and potential sales is large, much of the market remains underserved. This situation warrants a significant increase in communications expenditures. How about Microsoft's latest Windows version? After a year or two, Microsoft will compare its sales to market potential. If a significant discrepancy still remains between market penetration and market potential, another aggressive marketing communications effort should be launched. This new effort would require significantly more resources.

14-10c Product Factors

At least three product factors are likely to influence the proportion of the total marketing budget assigned to marketing communications: product involvement, brand differentiation, and product newness.

Product Involvement

The higher the product involvement, the less need for marketing communications and, therefore, the lower the marketing communications budget. This is because products that create involvement are likely to motivate consumers to seek information about the product. When they are exposed to any information about the product, they will process it. Marketers do not need to launch an extensive marketing communications campaign with many repeated exposures to achieve the goals of a positioning strategy. For example, compare the marketing of two products that vary significantly in their capacity to elicit involvement in message processing. One is an automobile; the other is candy. Consumers who are shopping around for a sports car are likely to actively seek and process most messages related to sports cars. In contrast, consumers who want to purchase candy are not likely to feel highly involved in processing most messages related to candy. This is because automobiles are more involving than candy. Marketing communications messages about products that elicit more consumer involvement are more likely to be attended to and processed than messages about products that elicit less involvement.

Brand Differentiation

If the marketer's brand is highly differentiated from competitor brands, then the opportunity is present to communicate the differential uniqueness of the brand to consumers. On the other hand, if the marketer's brand is not at all differentiated, then perhaps marketing communications is not likely to be effective and, therefore, a large budget may not be warranted. Similarly, if the basis for differentiating a brand is hidden and cannot be readily judged at the time of the purchase, then more money should be spent on marketing communications to make consumers aware of the hidden benefit.[20]

Product Newness

It takes substantially more money to communicate a new product than to communicate an established brand.[21] This is because consumers need to be educated about new products. Communication involving new products involves many message repetitions and the placement of the message in different media. This effort requires money, lots of money, compared to communicating an established brand.

14-10d Customer Factors

Four customer factors can be used to help the marketing manager allocate a marketing communications budget: purchase frequency, consumer involvement, consumer familiarity, and customer demand of the product.

Purchase Frequency

The higher the purchase frequency of a given product, the greater the need for marketing communications. For example, conducting a marketing communications campaign for staple products such as food items commonly found in supermarkets and convenience stores may require more resources than a marketing communications campaign for a durable good such as a kitchen appliance.[22]

Consumer Involvement

What is the difference between product involvement and consumer involvement? When marketing scholars talk about product involvement, they refer to the fact that consumers become involved in a certain product more than another, mostly because of the characteristics of the product. For example, most people get more involved in the purchase of an automobile than in the purchase of a staple good such as toothpaste. An automobile tends to be perceived by most consumers as a risky purchase, whereas toothpaste is not. There the involvement comes from the product, not the consumer per se. In contrast, consumer involvement refers to the kind of involvement that comes mostly from the consumer, not the product per se. Design engineers, by virtue of their occupation, tend to be more involved with computers than homemakers are, for example.

The higher the consumer involvement, the less need for marketing communications and, therefore, the lower the marketing communications budget; because consumers who care greatly about a product will probably seek more information about the product. They will naturally pay close attention to any information about the product. Marketers can achieve the goals of a positioning strategy without launching an extensive marketing communications campaign with many repeated exposures. Imagine launching a marketing communications campaign to sell a sophisticated software design package to design engineers. Most of these people are highly involved with design software because it is a vital tool in their profession. Any message directed to them would be readily processed. Now compare the design engineers to other lay people. Perhaps the firm decides to target parents of teenagers who have a design proclivity. Many more resources are needed to conduct this marketing campaign because, compared to design engineers, the parent consumers are not likely to be highly involved with design software.

Consumer Familiarity

If the marketer's product and brand are well known to consumers, then the need for marketing communications is less pressing and, therefore, less marketing communications resources are required. Going back to the design engineers example, we can easily surmise that design engineers are likely to be more familiar with design software and various software brands than the parents of teenagers who may be interested in design are. A substantially more costly marketing communications campaign is needed to communicate with the parents market than the design engineers market. Because the parents are not familiar with the product and the various design software brands, a campaign involving a more compelling message with a high level of message repetition has to be used.

Customer Demand of the Product

If the product class in general is in high demand, it is easier to stimulate brand preference through advertising and other means of marketing communications.[23] That is, when there is primary demand for the product, there is also the opportunity to use marketing communications to attain higher levels of sales, profit, market share, and cash flow. Consider the case of many small- and medium-size businesses in industrializing countries. These entrepreneurial enterprises are motivated to become economically efficient and realize that the use of computers in operating their business would help to achieve efficiency. The demand for PCs is high. In this situation, PC marketers can take advantage of this situation and launch a marketing communications campaign targeting these potential customers.

Growth in Customer Base

As the customer base grows, the marketing communications budget should grow proportionately. Increases in resource allocations are needed to continue reaching a larger number of customers.[24] This typically occurs with technological innovations. In time, the general population increasingly accepts a technological innovation, thereby increasing the customer base for the firm's product. For example, the customer base of the home computer market has been increasing in the last decade or so. Computer companies targeting the home market spend more than ever to communicate to that market.

Summary

This chapter introduces you to traditional budgeting methods of marketing communications. They are discussed in terms of ratio-to-sales methods, competitive-parity methods, quantitative methods, the objective-task method, the return-on-investment method, the all-you-can-afford method, and the previous-budget method. The shortcomings of these methods are discussed. Finally, an SMC approach is recommended to allow a much better integration of the process. It is a systematic approach that integrates the budgeting method based on the traditional objective-task method. The presentation also suggests that many of the other traditional methods can actually be subsumed in the recommended method.

What kind of situation analysis can the marketing communications manager perform to assist in making budgeting decisions at the corporate, marketing, and marketing communications levels? We discuss several organizational, industry, product, and customer factors that are highly related to marketing and marketing communications expenditures. Organizational factors include objectives, strategy and tactics, and control. Industry factors include industry norms, competition, the product life cycle, market growth, market size, and market potential. Product factors include product involvement, brand differentiation, and product newness. Customer factors include purchase frequency, consumer involvement, consumer familiarity, and growth in customer base. We discuss how information about these factors should assist the manager in determining a suitable budget for marketing, marketing communications, and the various elements of the marketing communications mix.

Discussion Questions

Scenario 1: You are a corporate executive in the Ritz-Carlton Resort of Naples, Florida. Recently, upper management decided to aggressively pursue the business conference market, that is, corporate businesses that have educational seminars and workshops throughout the United States. Determine a marketing communications budget for next year using ratio-to-sales methods. The following figures are available. Assume that Ritz-Carlton spent $350,000 on marketing communications last year. Their sales from last year were $150 million, of which only $30 million came from the business conference market. A recent study projected a 25 percent industry increase in sales due to increasing demand for business conferences. Assume the major competitor of Ritz-Carlton is the Hyatt in Naples. The Hyatt has 70 percent of the business conference market compared to 25 percent for Ritz-Carlton. Hyatt spent approximately $700,000 on marketing communications costs last year. It was determined that an aggressive marketing communications campaign can increase the use of business conference facilities at the hotel by at least 20 percent, which can generate a 25 percent increase in revenues. This goal can be accomplished by hiring three additional sales representatives with good experience in recruiting corporate business to hotels. The cost of these three representatives is expected to be $70,000 a person, with approximately $10,000 needed for additional sales materials and miscellaneous expenses (phone, mailing, etc.).

1. Describe ratio-to-sales methods and discuss their disadvantages. Examine the Ritz-Carlton scenario and determine a marketing communications budget for next year using the ratio-to-sales methods.
2. Describe the competitive-parity methods and discuss their disadvantages. Examine the Ritz-Carlton scenario and determine a marketing communications budget for the next year using a competitive-parity method.
3. Describe the objective-task method. Examine the Ritz-Carlton scenario and determine a marketing communications budget for the next year using the objective-task method.

Scenario 2: Study the following case about the advanced photo system that we discussed earlier in the chapter. The product raised industry sales by at least 10 percent in 1996. Kodak and Fuji spent at least $150 million on marketing support in 1996. Fuji spent $6.5 million on measured media in 1994 and spent twice this amount in 1996. Kodak spent $65.4 million in the United States on its brand in 1995; Canon spent $10.3 million on media in 1994; Nikon spent $9 million; and Minolta spent $5.1 million. The strategic alliance between Fuji and Kodak captured a large chunk of the market share in this new product market in 1996. Suppose that Kodak executives recall that they spent approximately $10 million on marketing communications when they marketed a comparable but less-sophisticated product years ago with outstanding results. Kodak was able to achieve a 70 percent brand awareness. Say that in relation to this new photo system, both Kodak and Fuji felt that they needed to achieve a 70 percent brand awareness in the next 6 months. Both Kodak and Fuji may have expected sales revenues to exceed $100 million the first year of operation. From projected sales, Kodak had traditionally allocated 3 percent of sales to marketing support, whereas Fuji's marketing support traditionally amounts to 5 percent. Suppose you were the marketing communications manager for this advanced photo system back then. How would you have made the following decisions?

1. Describe those organizational factors that you should have taken into account in determining an optimal marketing communications budget for the advanced photo system. How might these factors may have affected the budget?
2. Describe those industry factors that you should have considered in determining an optimal marketing communications budget for the advanced photo system. How might these factors have affected the budget?
3. Describe those product factors that may have been relevant to determining an optimal marketing communications budget for the advanced photo system. How might these factors have affected the budget?
4. Describe those customer factors that might have affected the planning of an optimal marketing communications budget for the advanced photo system. How might these factors have affected the budget?

Practice Quiz

Note: You can find the correct answers to these questions by taking the quiz and then submitting your answers in the Online Edition. The program will automatically score your submission. If you miss a question, the program will provide the correct answer, a rationale for the answer, and the section number in the chapter where the topic is discussed.

1. The _____ is a budgeting method that allocates resources based on percentage of anticipated sales, percentage of unit anticipated sales, percentage of past sales, and percentage of unit past sales.
   a. ratio-to-sales method
   b. competitive-parity method
   c. quantitative method
   d. return-on-investment method

2. The _____ is a budgeting method based on a percentage of sales anticipated for the next year.
   a. return-on-investment method
   b. percentage-of-anticipated-sales method
   c. percentage-of-unit-anticipated-sales method
   d. objective-task method

3. The _____ is a budgeting method based on a percentage of the unit price for last year's sales.
   a. return-on-investment method
   b. percentage-of-anticipated-sales method
   c. percentage-of-unit-anticipated-sales method
   d. objective-task method

4. Suppose a marketing communications manager of a software package such as Microsoft Office has traditionally allocated 3 percent of sales to marketing communications. Sales are expected to increase by 10 percent in the next 12 months. Assume that sales of Microsoft Office for 2004 was $75 million. The sales forecast for 2005, therefore, is $82.5 million. The marketing communications manager allocates 3 percent of the $82.5 million (sales forecast), not the $75 million (past sales). Therefore, the marketing communications budget for Microsoft Office for 2005 is $2.48 million. This budgeting method is commonly referred to as the _____ method.
   a. percentage-of-anticipated-sales
   b. return-on-investment
   c. percentage-of-unit-anticipated-sales
   d. objective-task

5. Suppose we are in the motel business. We are marketing a motel chain, say, Hampton Inn. Let us say, hypothetically speaking, that Hampton Inn's market share last year was 20 percent. The major competitor that Hampton Inn is directly competing against is Holiday Inn, which reported a market share of 30 percent last year. We know that Holiday Inn spent $20 million on marketing communications last year. Suppose that Hampton Inn's market-share objective is to increase market share by 5 percent (from 20 percent to 25 percent). How much money should Hampton Inn allocate for marketing communications? The answer is $16.67 million ($20 million multiplied by 25 percent, the product of which is divided by 30 percent). This budgeting method is commonly referred to as the _____ method.
   a. ratio-to-sales
   b. share-of-voice/market
   c. objective-task
   d. return-on-investment

6. Consider the following example of resource allocation. A marketing communications manager may read that a major competitor has allocated 20 percent of the dollar sales from this year to cover marketing communications costs for next year. The manager may then decide to outspend the competition by allocating 23 percent. This budgeting method is called the _____ method.
   a. percentage-of-past-sales
   b. match-or-outspend-competitors
   c. objective-task
   d. all-you-can-afford

7. DuPont Paint Division divided fifty-six sales territories into high, average, and low market-share territories. Across these territories, DuPont spent a "normal" amount of advertising in one-third of the territories, two and one-half times as much in another third of its territories, and four times as much in another third of the territories. At the end of the designated period, sales were estimated. The study revealed that higher advertising expenditure increased sales at a diminishing rate and that the sales increase was weaker in the high market-share territories. DuPont relied on this study to develop its promotion budget. This budgeting method is commonly referred to as the _____ method.
   a. experimental
   b. quantitative
   c. historical-statistical
   d. objective-task

8. The historical-statistical method is a budgeting method
   a. based on examining past and anticipated sales.
   b. that relies on statistical data from the company's archives.
   c. based on examining what the competition is doing.
   d. based on objectives of the promotion plan and the cost to implement those objectives.

9. The _____ method assumes that money spent today is an investment that is likely to pay off in sales tomorrow.
   a. percentage-of-anticipated-sales
   b. return-on-investment
   c. percentage-of-unit-anticipated-sales
   d. objective-task

10. The SMC budgeting method recommended in this chapter has the following major sequential steps:
    a. corporate objectives → corporate mix → marketing strategy → marketing objectives → marketing mix → marketing communications strategy → marketing communications objectives → marketing communications mix → marketing communications budget
    b. marketing communications budget → corporate objectives → corporate mix → marketing strategy → marketing objectives → marketing mix → marketing communications strategy → marketing communications objectives → marketing communications mix
    c. corporate objectives → corporate mix marketing communications budget → marketing strategy → marketing objectives → marketing mix → marketing communications strategy → marketing communications objectives → marketing communications mix
    d. marketing communications mix → marketing communications objectives → marketing communications strategy → marketing mix → marketing objectives → marketing strategy → corporate mix → corporate objectives → marketing communications budget

Web Exercise

An Exercise of Dollars and Cents

Pick one of your favorite brand categories (e.g., soft drinks, beer, sportswear). Conduct a web search on two specific brands (e.g., Caffeine Free Diet Coca-Cola, Caffeine Free Diet Pepsi) from the brand category. See if you can identify what role the specific brand plays in the firm. What does it contribute in revenues to the firm? What is its budget for the past year? How does it compare to the second brand you have selected? What is your assessment of how the company allocates resources to that specific brand? Is it one of the approaches discussed in this chapter?

Suggested Readings

Aaker, David A., and James M. Carman. 1982. Are you overadvertising? *Journal of Advertising Research* 22, no. 4 (August/September): 57–70.

Aaker, David A., and John G. Myers. 1987. *Advertising management*, 3rd ed. Englewood Cliffs, NJ: Prentice Hall, Chapter 3.

Blasko, Vincent J., and Charles H. Patti. 1984. The advertising budgeting practices of industrial marketers. *Journal of Marketing* 21 (Fall): 104–10.

Broadbent, Simon. 1988. *The advertiser's handbook for budget determination*. Lexington, MA: Lexington Books.

Eastlack, Joseph O. Jr., and Ambar G. Rao. 1986. Modeling response to advertising and pricing changes for V-8 cocktail vegetable juice. *Marketing Science* 5, no. 3 (Summer): 245–59.

Gilligan, Colin. 1977. How British advertisers set budgets. *Journal of Advertising Research* 17 (February): 47–49.

Herremans, Irene, John K. Ryans Jr., and Raj Aggarwal. 2000. Linking advertising and brand value. *Business Horizons* 43, no. 3 (May–June): 19–26.

Jones, John P. 1990. Ad spending: Maintaining market share. *Harvard Business Review* (January–February): 314–42.

———. 1992. *How much is enough? Getting the most from your advertising dollar.* New York: Lexington Books.

Lancaster, Kent M., and J. A. Stern. 1983. Computer-based advertising budgeting practices of leading U.S. consumer advertisers. *Journal of Advertising* 12 (4): 4–9.

Little, John D. C. 1966. A model of adaptive control of promotional spending. *Operations Research* 14 (November–December): 175–97.

Patti, Charles, and Vincent Blasko. 1981. Budgeting practices of big advertisers. *Journal of Advertising Research* 21 (December): 23–29.

Piercy, Nigel. 1987. Advertising budgeting: Process and structure as explanatory variables. *Journal of Advertising* 16 (2): 34–40.

Ray, Michael L. 1982. *Advertising and communication management.* Englewood Cliffs, NJ: Prentice Hall.

Rossiter, John R., and Peter J. Danaher. 1998. *Advanced media planning.* Norwell, MA: Kluwer Academic Publishers.

Schroer, James C. 1990. Ad spending: Growing market share. *Harvard Business Review* (January–February): 44–48.

Notes

1. R. Craig Endicott, "Top Marketers Spend $83 Billion," *Advertising Age,* November 8, 2004, 30.
2. George E. Belch and Michael A. Belch, *Introduction to Advertising and Promotion: An Integrated Marketing Communications Perspective,* 5th ed. (Chicago: Irwin, 2001), 232.
3. Gary L. Lilien and John D. C. Little, "The ADVISOR Project: A Study of Industrial Marketing Budgets," *Sloan Management Review* (Spring 1976): 17–31; Gary L. Lilien, "ADVISOR 2: Modeling the Marketing Mix Decision for Industrial Products," *Management Science* (February 1979): 191–204.
4. Cyndee Miller, "Marketing Industry Report: Who's Spending What on Biz-to-Biz Marketing," *Marketing News,* January 1, 1996, 1, 7.
5. John D. C. Little, "A Model of Adaptive Control of Promotional Spending," *Operations Research* (November 1966): 1075–97.
6. Robert D. Buzzell, *Mathematical Models and Marketing Management* (Boston: Division of Research, Harvard Business School, 1964), 166.
7. David B. Montgomery and Alvin J. Silk, "Estimating Dynamic Effects of Market Communications Expenditures," *Management Science* (June 1972): 485–501.
8. Gary L. Lilien, Philip Kotler, and K. Sridhar Moorthy, *Marketing Models* (Englewood Cliffs, NJ: Prentice Hall, 1992), Chapter 6.
9. Kristian S. Palda, *The Measurement of Cumulative Advertising Effect* (Englewood Cliffs, NJ: Prentice Hall, 1964), 87.
10. G. Maxwell Ule, "A Media Plan for 'Sputnik' Cigarettes," in *How to Plan Media Strategy,* 41–52 (American Association of Advertising Agencies, 1957 Regional Convention).
11. "Direct-Response Skills for the 21st Century" by Karen J. Marchetti in *Marketing News,* July 29, 1996, p. 5. Copyright © 1996. Reprinted by permission of American Marketing Association.
12. Michael Wilkie, "New Photo Tech Ready for '96 Flash," *Advertising Age,* December 4, 1995, 36.
13. See note 3.
14. Randall S. Brown, "Estimating Advantages to Large-Scale Advertising," *Review of Economics and Statistics* 60 (August 1978): 428–37; Kent M. Lancaster, "Are There Scale Economies in Advertising?" *Journal of Business* 59, no. 3 (1986): 509–26; Johan Arndt and Julian Simon, "Advertising and Economies of Scale: Critical Comments on the Evidence," *Journal of Industrial Economics* 32, no. 2 (December 1983): 229–41.
15. *Advertising Age,* October 24, 1988, 51.
16. Pat Sloan, "Cosmetics Competitors Try to Slap Down Revlon," *Advertising Age,* December 4, 1995, 38.
17. See note 3.
18. Ibid.
19. Michael L. Ray, *Advertising and Communication Management* (Englewood Cliffs, NJ: Prentice Hall, 1982), 161–62.
20. Ibid.
21. Ibid.
22. Ibid.
23. Ibid.
24. Ibid.

Takeaways from the Strategic Marketing Communications Process

Lessons in Monitoring, Control, and Integration

Chapter Fifteen

Chapter Outline

15-1 Introduction

15-2 Monitoring and Control of Marketing Communications
- 15-2a Failing to Meet Marketing Communications Objectives
- 15-2b Failing to Meet Marketing Objectives
- 15-2c Failing to Meet Corporate Objectives

15-3 Integrating the Marketing Communications System
- 15-3a The Link between Strategy, Objective, and Tactics
- 15-3b The Link between Strategy-Objective-Tactics and Budget
- 15-3c The Link between Monitoring and Control
- 15-3d The Link between Monitoring-Control and Strategy-Objective-Tactics
- 15-3e The Link between Monitoring-Control and Objectives
- 15-3f The Link between Monitoring-Control and Budget
- 15-3g The Link between Analysis and Planning
- 15-3h The Link between Analysis-Planning and Strategy-Objective-Tactics
- 15-3i The Link between Analysis-Planning and Objectives
- 15-3j The Link between Analysis-Planning and Budget

Summary
Discussion Questions
Practice Quiz
Web Exercise: Brand Unity and Marketing Communications Assessment
Suggested Readings
Notes

Make your work to be in keeping with your purpose.
—**Leonardo da Vinci** (1452–1519), Italian genius; leading artist, scientist, architect, and military engineer of his time

15-1 Introduction

At one point in time, one of the authors helped a small publishing company that specializes in Appalachian history. This publisher had an extensive line of books dealing with the history of the region, its geography, and its culture. The publisher had been established for 20 years or so and was essentially a two-person operation (the owner/publisher and a copy editor). The owner expressed her frustration over her failure to do a good job promoting the book line. She was convinced that there is a sizable population in and surrounding the Appalachian Mountains that is highly interested in books related to the history, geography, and culture of the region. This interest was indicated by the many college courses and community noncredit courses on the subject offered in the Appalachian region. For the prior 5 years, the publisher had sold approximately three thousand books a year. Most of the books used in the college courses and noncredit community seminars were published by major publishers, but none of those publishers had a book line on Appalachian studies. She thought that she had an advantage over the competition. She also thought that she could do a whole lot better than three thousand books a year, perhaps at least double this amount.

At first glance, it seemed that her marketing communications efforts were "all over the place." That is, her communications efforts lacked a sense of cohesion. Things were done rather haphazardly without any plan or systematic effort on her part. The corporate strategy seemed to be growth, as indicated by her statement of her objective; however, the more she talked, the more it became clear that she had become very frustrated trying to grow the business. She had contemplated selling the business several times in the past. When she was queried as to her marketing, it came out that she was selling her books very cheaply. In other words, she was competing by positioning the book line as a bargain. This is a cost-leadership strategy. Further questioning led her to acknowledge that many of her customers would have paid a great deal more for her books. She was very reluctant to change her pricing strategy for fear that a change would make matters worse. Cost-leadership strategy was not the best marketing strategy to meet her sales objectives. I asked her about her marketing objective. She did not understand! I asked her about her promotion strategy and goals. She did not understand! She responded that she had tried a variety of communications tools such as direct mail using a mailing list of households in several selected towns in the Appalachian Mountains. Once in awhile she had advertised in the regional newspapers and, especially, in the classified section of the newspaper. She pulled out several newspaper articles that had been written about her company and book line, and she seemed very proud of this exposure. She also indicated that she has small Yellow Page advertisements in the phone books of a number of Appalachian towns that she kept renewing year after year. She admitted that she did not know which communications method was best. She did not keep track of the effectiveness of any of them. Moreover, each year she spent whatever she could afford on promotion and this amount varied from year to year.

While this may be an extreme example, this is a common situation regarding the lack of system integration in marketing communications. In many small to medium enterprises run by businesspeople who are not well trained in the managerial sciences, it is very common. In larger firms, surprisingly, it is still not uncommon to run across a similar type of situation.

At the Appalachian publishing company, individual components in the overall marketing communications system did not seem to be linked even slightly with other components as our systems model shows they should be. There was no systematic method for making marketing communications decisions, and each decision did not seem to be guided or influenced by other decisions. *The system lacked strategic integration.*

In this chapter, we end our discussion of SMC by revisiting and sensitizing you to the issues surrounding monitoring, control, and integration of marketing communications. The message of this chapter is very simple: Monitoring, control, and integration come about by establishing strong links among the system components (see SMC Marketplace Watch 15-1). We have already seen how this is done throughout the entire book. This chapter emphasizes the importance of the system's integrity and connections.

15-2 Monitoring and Control of Marketing Communications

A 1996 *Fortune* magazine article on Kmart documented its business ills. Kmart's market share dropped from approximately 5.2 percent in 1990 to 4.7 percent in 1995, while Wal-Mart's market share increased from approximately 5.2 percent in 1990 to 10 percent in 1995. Kmart's stock price plummeted from $15/share in 1990 to $6/share in 1995. In an interview, Floyd Hall, CEO of Kmart, showed that he did not have a thorough understanding of either Kmart's customers or its competitors and that he did not have a corporate strategy. The challenge of saving Kmart was indeed formidable. In 1990 Kmart was the world's biggest discount retailer. In 1995 it was about one-third of Wal-Mart. There were problems everywhere, in merchandise selection, service, and value. There were often stockouts of items on sale. Employees' morale was down in the dumps. The previous CEO, Joseph Antonini, employed a diversification strategy, getting involved in other ventures such as OfficeMax, the Sports Authority, and Builders Square. Wal-Mart, Kmart's key competitor, focused on its core discount store and used a growth strategy to achieve ambitious sales, market share, and profit goals. Hall said that Kmart's typical shopper was a 55-year-old consumer who had no kids at home and had less than $20,000 in income. Independent marketing researchers consulted by *Fortune* magazine indicated that Kmart's typical shopper was very much like Wal-Mart's. To better serve Kmart's shoppers, Hall was planning to install large sections up-front carrying cheap consumables like laundry soap, snacks, cereals, and dog food. These items were likely to be appealing to the low-income shoppers. Also, he was planning to build more supercenters, which combine the general discount store with a supermarket. However, Wal-Mart was well ahead of Kmart in this area.[1]

Here we have a company that desperately needed a good job of what we call "monitoring and control." Kmart needed to assess its performance not only at the corporate level but also at the marketing and communications levels. It needed to determine how discrepant performance (at the corporate, marketing, and communications level) was from what it considered acceptable goals. It needed to exert control by reassessing its strategies, its tactics, the way resources were allocated, and so on. In this chapter, we start to grasp the complex issues involved with monitoring and control.

SMC Marketplace Watch 15-1

Integrated Marketing Communications—Company Examples

Texas Instruments

Texas Instruments (TI), a Dallas-based company of semiconductors, was losing business to foreign semiconductor rivals in the 1980s. Part of the problem was the corporate culture. Most of the TI executives viewed the company as a technology leader—the focus was on creating new technological products to be on the leading edge. However, this was done without paying much attention to customer needs. The company took corrective action by changing its culture—from that of technology to being customer focused. The company started to shift from a technology-driven company to one driven by customer needs. The person behind this transformation was John Tammaro, senior strategy manager in corporate marketing communications and design. Tammaro created TI's "Virtual University," a program of marketing communications courses and workshops for marketing professionals and product managers. The curriculum was centered around integrating marketing communications and marketing management.

Lane Bryant

Lane Bryant, a clothing retailer and a division of The Limited, Inc., of Columbus, Ohio, employed an IMC campaign to penetrate the African-American market with its oversized women's clothing. This eight-hundred-store chain designed and implemented several highly coordinated promotional campaigns: a mailing campaign, in-store events, five-city mall tour orchestrated by *Essence* magazine, advertising in *Essence*, radio advertisements in local markets, and publicity.

Acxiom

Acxiom, a fast-growing data-management company, has developed an IMC campaign to establish brand awareness and a consistent image in the firm's target markets. The company's product was decision support capabilities based on customer information. This product has a strong market demand among major retailers, publishers, financial service organizations, and others. Acxiom developed a centralized messaging function so that everything the firm says and does communicates a common theme and a unified image of the company. This was done through advertising, public relations, direct mail, trade shows, and direct contact between Acxiom salespeople and customers.

The Sunday School Board

The Sunday School Board, an agency of the Southern Baptist Convention, sells ministry products through sixty-four retail bookstores from Los Angeles to Fort Lauderdale. The firm does this through direct mail, continuity programs, trade sales, churches and institutions, and conferences. In the past, each retail bookstore—as well as the publishing division that produces books, magazines, textbooks, Bibles, and hymnals—maintained its own transaction systems and managed its own marketing communications programs. The organization adopted an IMC plan and built a data-

---

At any given level of the process hierarchy, the decision maker is faced with a set of organizational tasks:[2] (1) deciding on a strategy and assembling the strategic mix, (2) allocating resources to the elements of the strategic mix, (3) setting objectives, and (4) monitoring performance and exerting control. This chapter concentrates on the last system component—that is, monitoring and control (see Figure 15-1). Also, because this book is about marketing communications, we address monitoring and control issues strictly from the vantage point of the marketing communications manager.

The control function involves the use of a feedback mechanism. A feedback mechanism generates a stress signal when a specific measured outcome is significantly below the stated objective. For example, a marketing communications objective may be a 50 percent increase in brand awareness as measured by a brand recognition method 6 months after the launch of the communications campaign. After 6 months, the marketing communications manager assesses the outcome using the designated method and finds out that brand awareness inched up only 10 percent. That is, a negative deviation of 40 points from the goal is detected. Significant negative deviations "raise red flags" and motivate the manager to make adjustments.

base-marketing system that provided support to all the board's divisions. The database-marketing system allowed the organization to gather information about the needs of ministries. A profile is developed for each customer. The customer is identified by life stage. The database had to be cleaned because 39 percent of the board's 8.4 million individual mail pieces never made it to their destinations. Cleaning the database helped recover 300,000 lost customers. Customers were treated as the asset, and the database-marketing system was used to track the value of each and every customer.

VisionTek

VisionTek, a privately held manufacturer of computer memory modules and peripheral products, based in Chicago, developed an IMC campaign to tie together all its disparate promotional programs. The firm does business in memory upgrades for desktop personal computers, for central processing units (CPUs), and for memory and hard drives for notebook computers. Its market is strictly business-to-business: its customers are resellers, computer system integrators, distributors, and catalogers throughout the world. More specifically, VisionTek wanted to attract and create partnerships with resellers who were interested in more than short-term, one-time sales. VisionTek's marketing communications objective was two-pronged: to "push" its computer memory boards and peripherals among chief information officers (CIOs) and information system (IS) specialists, and to "pull" the larger resellers and computer system integrators into stocking more of its products. The company created a multimillion-dollar campaign that ran in computer trade magazines (*PC Week*, *Computer World*, and *Interactive Week*) and on the Internet. The trade magazine program was designed to express compassion for top-level people who influenced or sat on a standards committee or those who were responsible for the day-to-day technology operations. A third set of advertisements targeted the resellers, system integrators, catalogers, and distribution agents who deal with everyday problems such as missed shipments. To reach this segment, advertisements were created and placed in magazines such as *VAR Business* and *Computer Reseller News*. Other aspects of the IMC campaign included a new tagline, a new logo for corporate communications, spec sheets, business papers, direct-marketing material, and an Internet website. That new look was implemented also on materials used in trade shows. To measure the effectiveness of the IMC campaign, the company conducted marketing research testing aided and unaided awareness to establish benchmarks before the launch of the campaign. Then they used the same measures to test changes in awareness throughout the campaign.

Sources: Adapted from Janet Smith, "Integrated Marketing," *American Demographics* (November–December 1995); and Scott Hample, "A Test of Memory," *American Demographics* (November–December 1997).

These adjustments may involve one or more of the following: (1) change the strategy and/or tactics, (2) change budget, and/or (3) change the objective. We illustrate how the monitoring and control system works at the three different levels—corporate, marketing, and marketing communications.

The control aspect of marketing communications comes into play when the marketing communications manager conducts marketing research to ascertain the extent to which the explicitly stated objectives at the marketing communications level, as well as at the marketing and corporate levels, have been met. We use the MapLinX software package as an example to illustrate the control dynamics related to marketing communications. MapLinX is a software program that keeps track of sales data using geographic plots.

Suppose the *corporate objective* of MapLinX has been stated as follows:

Increase sales and market share of MapLinX software by 25 percent in relation to the U.S. market. The current sales are 5,500 units, and the market share was 58 percent all of last year. Specifically, the goal is to raise unit sales to 6,875 and to achieve a market share of 72.5 percent by the end of next year.

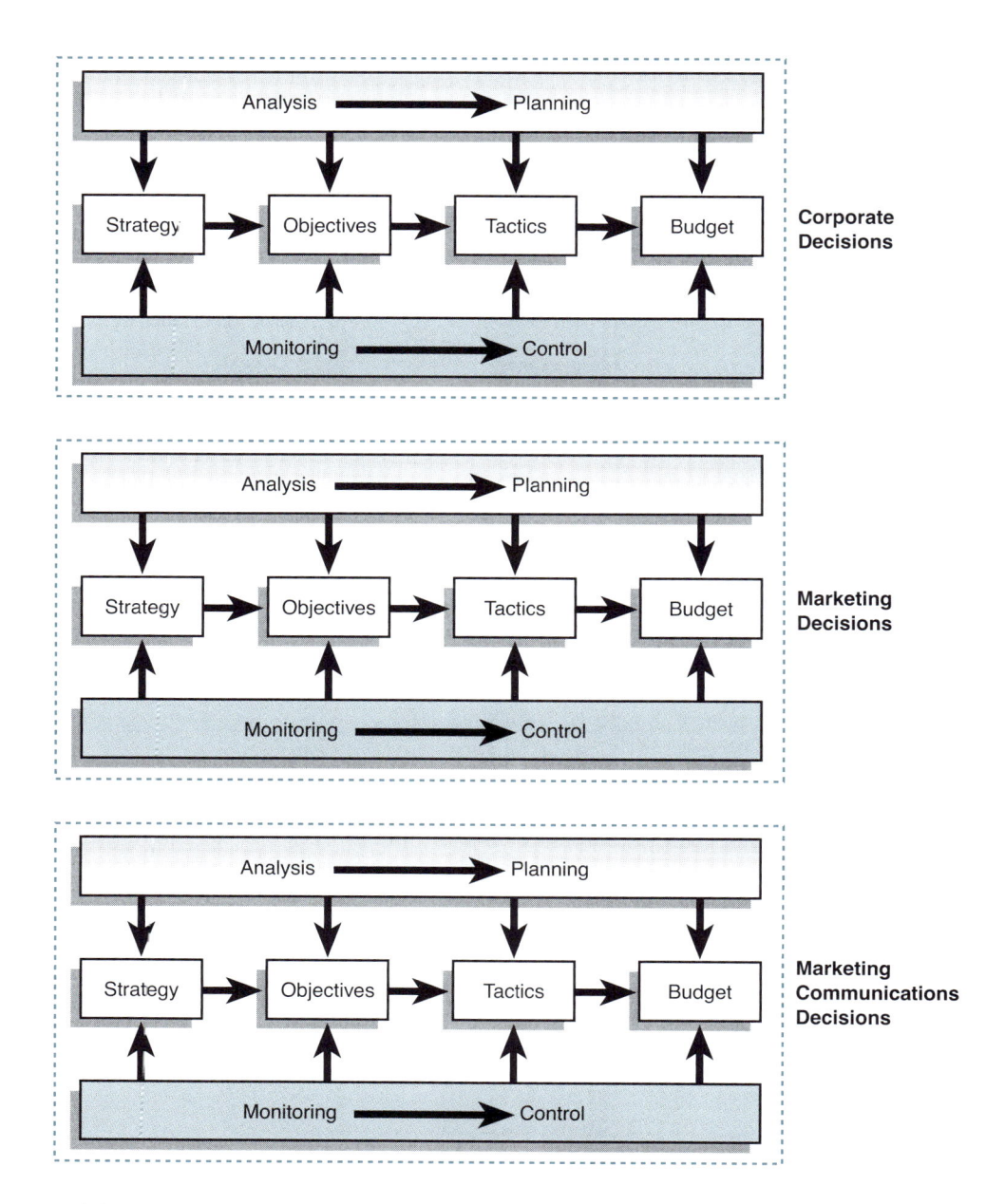

Figure 15-1
Corporate, Marketing, and Marketing Communications Control

The corporate strategy is to *gain market share (or grow)*. The president is taking an aggressive posture because of the perceived quality and superiority of the software over several key competitor brands.

Suppose the *marketing objective* has been stated as follows:

Increase the association between MapLinX and visual mapping clarity by 40 percent in the next 12 months. Currently, 50 percent of sales managers in the United States describe MapLinX by referring to its visual mapping clarity. The goal is to have 70 percent of sales managers describe MapLinX by making reference to its visual mapping clarity. This should be accomplished by the end of the next 12-month period.

The marketing strategy is differentiation by positioning MapLinX as having "visual mapping clarity," that is, *positioning by product attribute*. This product attribute was chosen because it is the most distinct feature that differentiates MapLinX from other sales-tracking software on the market and because the same attribute is found to be an important decision criterion in the purchase of sales-tracking software.

Suppose the marketing communications objective pertaining to MapLinX software has been stated as follows:

TABLE 15-1	Possible Corrective Actions When Failing to Meet Marketing Communications, Marketing, and Corporate Objectives

Failing to Meet Marketing Communications Objectives

- Reassess the marketing communications strategy.
- Reassess the marketing communications mix.
- Reassess the implementation of each element of the marketing communications.
- Reassess the extent of coordination among the elements of the marketing communications mix.
- Reassess the realism of the marketing communications objectives.
- Reassess the amount of resources that have been allocated toward the elements of the marketing communications mix and their implementation.

Failing to Meet Marketing Objectives

- Reassess the marketing strategy.
- Reassess the marketing mix.
- Reassess the implementation of each element of the marketing mix.
- Reassess the extent of coordination between the marketing strategy and the strategies pertaining to the other elements of the marketing mix.
- Reassess the realism of the marketing objectives.
- Reassess the amount of resources that have been allocated toward the elements of the marketing mix and their implementation.

Failing to Meet Corporate Objectives

- Reassess the corporate strategy.
- Reassess the corporate mix.
- Reassess the implementation of each element of the corporate mix.
- Reassess the realism of the corporate objectives.
- Reassess the amount of resources that have been allocated toward the elements of the corporate mix and their implementation.

Increase brand trial by 30 percent. Last year we had approximately 4,000 units that were sent out on a trial basis, and 97 percent of them were ultimately purchased. Next year we want to increase brand trial to 5,200.

Here the marketing communications strategy involves a habit-formation (doer) strategy. That is, sales managers (potential customers) are to be encouraged to try the software package and either pay the invoice or return the software. Personally trying the software would allow sales managers to readily learn about the software and its key benefit, the clarity of visual mapping. With a high rate of satisfaction, the majority of brand trials are likely to translate into brand purchase and sales.

After the end of the designated period, the marketing communications manager conducts research to ascertain the extent to which the marketing communications programs have been successful in increasing brand trial by 30 percent, brand association by 40 percent, and sales and market share by 25 percent. The performance assessment may show that the objectives at the three levels (corporate, marketing, and marketing communications) have been met. This state of affairs signifies that the selected strategies and tactics have been successful. However, what happens when corporate, marketing, or marketing communications performance fail to meet their stated objective? We address this situation next (see Table 15-1).

15-2a Failing to Meet Marketing Communications Objectives

What happens if the research results show that marketing communications objectives were not met? What should the company do in a situation like this? For example, what if the research findings signal a significant shortfall from the stated marketing communications objectives such that brand trial only increased from 4,000 to 4,200, the stated goal being 5,200? In this situation, the marketing communications manager can exert control by doing any one or more of the following assessments and/or corrective actions.

Reassess the Marketing Communications Strategy
The selected communications strategy for MapLinX was a habit-formation (doer) one. Is it possible that this strategy was not effective? Is it likely that a different communications strategy would produce better results? Perhaps so much emphasis had been placed on the habit-formation (doer) strategy because the company assumed that most sales managers are aware of MapLinX. Perhaps a strategy that would emphasize learning (i.e., informative [thinker] strategy) could be employed.

Reassess the Marketing Communications Mix
Perhaps the marketing communications mix used to implement the marketing communications strategy was not the most effective to meet the marketing communications objectives. The marketing communications mix may have to be reconfigured. Suppose the MapLinX software had been advertised in airline magazines and general business magazines. Perhaps these two elements of the marketing communications mix are not effective. Perhaps a direct-mail campaign to sales mangers accompanied by advertising in several key sales management magazines would be more effective.

Reassess the Implementation of Each Element of the Marketing Communications Mix
Was each element of the marketing communications mix implemented effectively? Were there problems in the implementation? Can these implementation problems be corrected? For example, although the designated number of insertions were bought in the airline magazines, only half of them were actually printed in the magazines. Perhaps the creative people at the advertising agency failed to meet the magazine publication deadlines.

Reassess the Extent of Coordination among the Elements of the Marketing Communications Mix
Perhaps there was a coordination problem. The elements of the marketing communications mix may have been successful on an individual basis, but perhaps the problem was with the coordination among the elements. Perhaps different logos, slogans, colors, copy styles, and illustrations could be used in the airline magazines than in the general business magazines. The lack of consistency may have missed reinforcement opportunities.

Reassess the Realism of the Marketing Communications Objectives
Perhaps an expected increase of 30 percent in brand trial is unrealistic given the short period of time allotted to achieve the objective. Perhaps a more realistic objective would be an increase of 15 percent instead of 30 percent.

Reassess the Amount of Resources That Have Been Allocated toward the Elements of the Marketing Communications Mix and Their Implementation
Examples of questions that the marketing communications manager asks here include: Was the budget for creating the magazine advertisement sufficient? Could the agency develop a better advertisement given more resources? Was the person who was responsible for placing the print advertisement in the airline magazines competent? Could media placement be improved by hiring a more experienced person for more pay?

15-2b Failing to Meet Marketing Objectives
What happens if the research results show that marketing objectives were not met? For example, what if the research findings signal a significant shortfall from the stated

marketing objectives such that the brand association with visual clarity only increased from 50 percent to 55 percent, the stated goal being 70 percent? In this situation, the marketing communications manager can exert control by doing any one or more of the following assessments and/or corrective actions.

Reassess the Marketing Strategy
Perhaps the differentiation strategy involving positioning by the product attribute of visual mapping clarity was not the best marketing strategy to meet the marketing objectives. Perhaps another marketing strategy would be more effective. Perhaps sales managers are more sensitive to the price of the software than they are to visual mapping clarity. Perhaps other sales-tracking software packages are selling for a significantly lower price than MapLinX. If so, a *cost-leadership* strategy may be more effective. The price should be reduced.

Reassess the Marketing Mix
Perhaps the marketing mix used to implement the marketing strategy was not the most effective to meet the marketing objectives. The marketing mix may have to be reconfigured. Suppose too much emphasis was placed on the communications element without much regard to the pricing of MapLinX. A better pricing program should be conceptualized and implemented. For example, a pricing program could be implemented in which sales managers could purchase or lease the product. Perhaps the company could offer a lease arrangement that leads to purchase after a number of lease payments. Credit financing could be arranged.

Reassess the Implementation of Each Element of the Marketing Mix
Was each element of the marketing mix implemented effectively? Were there problems in the implementation? Can these implementation problems be corrected? Perhaps there were disk-related problems. Several customers called and complained that some of the installation disks were damaged. Perhaps there was a problem with a virus infection. How were these problems handled and were they handled effectively? How can the marketing communications manager work closely with the other managers to prevent a recurrence of these problems?

Reassess the Extent of Coordination between the Marketing Strategy and the Strategies Pertaining to the Other Elements of the Marketing Mix
Perhaps there was a coordination problem. The marketing strategy may have been successful, but perhaps the shipping department failed to handle the surplus of orders on time—a failure that caused the shortfall in the expected brand trial.

Reassess the Realism of the Marketing Objectives
Perhaps the marketing objective of increasing the association of MapLinX with visual clarity by 40 percent is unrealistic. Brand association only edged up from 50 percent to 55 percent, an increase of only 5 percent, while the objective was a 20 percent increase (the goal was to increase brand association with visual mapping clarity from 50 percent to 70 percent). Perhaps the best that can be achieved is 10 percent.

Reassess the Amount of Resources That Have Been Allocated toward the Elements of the Marketing Mix and Their Implementation
Examples of questions that the marketing communications manager may ask here include: Was the budget allocated for marketing communications at large sufficient? Could the agency have developed a better marketing communications plan given more resources? Was the person who was responsible for developing the strategic communications plan competent? Could a better plan be developed by hiring a more experienced person for more pay?

15-2c Failing to Meet Corporate Objectives

What happens if the research results show that corporate objectives were not met? For example, the research findings signal a significant shortfall from corporate objectives—sales dipped from 5,500 units to 5,100 units, and market share changed from 58 percent to 53 percent. The objective was to increase sales and market share by 25 percent. Specifically, the goal was to raise unit sales to 6,875 and market share to 72.5 percent by the end of the year. Here the marketing communications manager can exert control by doing any one or more of the following assessments and/or corrective actions.

Reassess the Corporate Strategy

Perhaps the growth strategy was not well thought out. Perhaps a maintain-share strategy would be more effective because certain key competitors are able to produce and market comparable software with the same quality of visual mapping clarity at a lower price. Perhaps when the growth strategy was selected as *the* corporate strategy, the firm did not know much about the competition and its capabilities. In this situation, the marketing communications manager should attempt to convince corporate executives to change the corporate strategy.

Reassess the Corporate Mix

Perhaps the corporate mix used to implement the corporate strategy of growth was not the most effective to meet the corporate growth objectives of sales and market share. The corporate mix may have to be reconfigured. Suppose too much emphasis was placed on the R&D and engineering elements without much regard to the marketing aspects. The R&D and engineering people were calling the shots. The software was developed and given to marketing, which in turn was charged with selling it. The marketing communications manager may believe that the R&D and engineering people have to be led and guided by the marketing people to develop the product that meets customers' specifications. Who is better equipped to know customers' specifications than the marketing people within the firm?

Reassess the Implementation of Each Element of the Corporate Mix

Was each element of the corporate mix implemented effectively? Were there problems in the implementation? Can these implementation problems be corrected? For example, the accounting department had significant problems with its staff. Numerous invoices were not sent out on time; some were not sent out at all. Correctable returns (software packages that were sent back because of disk damage) were not followed up. Periodic sales reports were not generated. In this situation, an element of the corporate mix that is not marketing related may have caused the dip in sales and market share. The dip may have very little to do with marketing, although the marketing communications manager may be blamed for failing to achieve the stated sales and market-share objectives. By investigating the source of the problem, the marketing communications manager may be able to point to the source and exert pressure to have the problem corrected.

Reassess the Realism of the Corporate Objectives

Perhaps the corporate objective of increasing sales and market share by 25 percent is not realistic. Perhaps maintaining the same level of sales and market share is more realistic because the competition was not part of the equation when the corporate objectives were set. Note that the data show that sales dipped from 5,500 units to 5,100 units and market share changed from 58 percent to 53 percent. In this situation, the marketing communications manager may be able to account for the performance shortfall by showing the gains made by the competition and may then work closely with corporate executives to set more realistic sales and market-share goals for the near future.

Reassess the Amount of Resources That Have Been Allocated toward the Elements of the Corporate Mix and Their Implementation

Examples of questions that the marketing communications manager may ask here include: Was the budget allocated for marketing at large sufficient? How about the other departments? Were they able to function effectively given the resources made available? Could the marketing department develop a better marketing plan given more resources? Was the person who was responsible for developing the strategic marketing plan competent? Which department can use more resources, and how will the department use the resources to increase sales and market share?

15-3 Integrating the Marketing Communications System

Having gotten a feel for working dynamics of the marketing communications system, you are now in a position to appreciate the lessons in system integration. As briefly discussed in Chapter Three, the systems concepts chapter, system integration can be effectively managed by ensuring strong links between the system components. Specifically, the system can be effectively integrated by ensuring strong links among the system components. These links are shown in Table 15-2 and are discussed in some detail in the following sections (also see Figure 15-2).

15-3a The Link between Strategy, Objective, and Tactics

Systems tend to break down and become ineffective when there is no clear logic between a given strategy, the way this strategy becomes a goal guiding tactics, and the way tactics are formulated to achieve the objective. For a system to be effectively integrated, strategy has to be translated into a quantifiable objective, and tactics have to be developed to achieve the stated objective. Each tactic, in turn, becomes a strategy or a goal to guide subordinate-level tactics, and so on. This is a necessary but not sufficient principle of system integration.

At the corporate level, a corporate strategy has to be operationalized in terms of a quantifiable goal. If the corporate strategy is "growth and expansion into new markets," then this strategy has to be articulated concretely as a goal to guide corporate tactics. Should the goal be an increase in sales and market share? If so, what percentage increase is to be expected? What is the logic supporting this expectation? How will the corporate objective of a specified level of sales and market-share increase help guide corporate tactics? Corporate tactics, in this instance, would be implemented by the various functional departments of the organization—marketing, finance, personnel, operations, engineering, R&D, and so on. How does a certain percentage increase in sales

TABLE 15-2 System Links That Need to Be Strengthened to Ensure Integration

- Link between strategy, objective, and tactics
- Link between strategy-objective-tactics and resource allocation
- Link between monitoring and control
- Link between monitoring-control and strategy-objective-tactics
- Link between monitoring-control and objectives
- Link between monitoring-control and resource allocation
- Link between analysis and planning
- Link between analysis-planning and strategy-objective-tactics
- Link between analysis-planning and objectives
- Link between analysis-planning and resource allocation

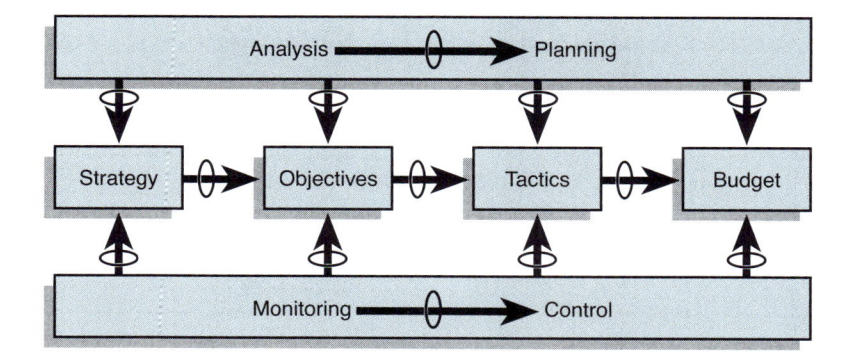

Figure 15-2
Reinforcing System Links = System Integration

and market share (corporate objective) guide the strategy in the context of the various departments? Will the vice president of marketing, for instance, have to come up with a new marketing strategy to meet the new challenge? What changes in the marketing plan have to be effected to achieve the desired level of sales and market share? Perhaps the marketing manager decides that a focus strategy can be highly instrumental in accomplishing the corporate objective of increased sales and market share. How should this marketing strategy be operationalized and quantified in terms of a goal (i.e., marketing objective)? Perhaps the marketing manager figures that targeting specific consumers with a highly select psychographic profile should do the trick. Thus, the marketing objective can be stated in terms of establishing or reinforcing brand association in the minds of the target consumers. In other words, the objective is to get a certain percentage of the target consumers to identify with the firm's brand.

What marketing tools (elements of the marketing mix) should be deployed to achieve this new marketing objective? Does the product need to be redesigned to appeal to the target consumers (product tactics)? If so, how? Does the price have to be changed to increase target consumers' willingness to buy (price tactics)? If so, how? Should the product be distributed to the target consumers using a unique channel or distributor (place tactics)? If so, what channel or distributor? How should the product be communicated to target consumers (promotion tactics)? What marketing communications strategy is likely to be most effective for target consumers? See SMC Marketplace Watch 15-2 for an interesting exposition of consumer trends and how they may be monitored to revise and update the marketing plan.

Perhaps the marketing communications manager decides that a self-satisfaction (reactor) strategy is likely to be most effective in achieving the marketing objective of establishing a certain level of brand association in the minds of target consumers. The marketing communications manager thinks that getting target consumers to buy the product first is likely to get them to experience self-identification with the product. Once they experience it, they are likely to develop a strong preference for it and to buy it again. Now the question becomes, How should the self-satisfaction (reactor) strategy be translated in terms of concrete and quantifiable goals (i.e., marketing communications objectives)? How should the marketing communications objectives be stated? Here the objectives have to be stated in terms of percentage increases in brand trial and preference. This is because the self-satisfaction (reactor) strategy dictates the use of these objective dimensions. Once concrete marketing communications objectives are set, the marketing communications manager has to assemble the most effective communications mix to achieve the stated marketing communications objectives. What would be the most effective communications mix? What forms of advertising should be used? How big of a web presence will be efficient? Perhaps interactive forms of advertising are likely to be most effective. Perhaps premiums and a contest can get target consumers to buy and experience the product.

Note that this exercise is extremely important as a first step of system integration. The corporate strategy has to be strongly linked with corporate objectives. Corporate objectives have to be strongly linked with marketing strategy. Marketing strategy has to

SMC Marketplace Watch 15-2

Consumer Trends

Pamela Danziger wrote the book *Why People Buy Things They Don't Need,* which highlighted several consumer trends:

- A shift from buying things to buying experiences
- A shift to realism and naturalism
- Increasing emphasis on time
- A shift in retail outlet selection.

Danziger argues that as the Baby Boomers age, their needs will change from *things* to *experiences.* The majority of the Baby Boomers are going through a "midlife-crisis" stage. This transition into maturity gets them to buy services that meet emerging needs. They begin to face mortality. In doing so, they become motivated to experience aspects of life they never had. Examples include travel, health, personal development, aesthetics, knowledge, languages, and cooking, among others. Organizations providing these services are likely to prosper, as are manufacturers of goods related to those experiences. For example, automobile manufacturers focus on providing recreational vehicles that can satisfy the need for adventure for the Baby Boomer generation. The Baby Boomers will experience their second adolescence—their first was during the 1960s when they lashed out against society and against materialism and established traditions and customs. After lashing out, they got married, settled down, and fell back to the pursuit of material possessions. Now that they have aged, they are ready to exchange their material possessions with adventure. They may travel to China or hike the Appalachian trail, take a French cooking class, or cross-country travel on a Harley.

A second trend involves a shift toward realism and naturalism. Today's world has become more digital. The Internet is playing an increasingly important role in people's lives. Reality is becoming "virtual." Cyberspace is taking over real space. Danziger argues that because of the level of saturation of computers and cyber technologies in people's lives, many feel the need to get back to reality. Reality, in this case, may translate into nature and history. Therefore, people may become increasingly motivated to escape virtual reality and experience natural reality by visiting parks, going on hikes, experiencing nature and wildlife, and visiting historical sites and destinations. People may do more gardening as they try to get closer to nature; build garden pools; and populate their habitats with birds, frogs, and nature's friendly animals and pets.

A third trend is people's increasing emphasis on time. They are becoming very conscious of time—how they use it and how they waste it. They realize that they have a finite amount of time to do things, especially the kinds of things they like to do. They are becoming acutely aware of their aging process and impending mortality. Therefore, according to Danziger, they seek to allocate time wisely to get much more out of life. This translates into seeking products and services that are time-efficient. To save time, consumers are increasingly shopping at mega stores. Doing so allows them to save time from shopping so they can spend more time on other more pleasurable activities. Consumers do more shopping per shopping trip to save time, too. They turn to the Internet for shopping because Internet shopping is more time-efficient.

As a result of consumers emphasizing time-efficient shopping, they shop less and less at traditional department stores and more at mass merchants, discounters, and warehouse marts. Examples include Wal-Mart, Target, Kmart, Costco, and Sam's Club. Nonstore retailers (such as catalogers, mail-order marketers, television shopping networks, direct-sales companies, party-plan marketers, and e-tailers) experience more business. Danziger also argues that large national specialty chains (Bed Bath & Beyond, Linen 'n Things, Pier 1, Pottery Barn, Williams-Sonoma, Restoration Warehouse, Home Depot, Lowe's, and so forth) will increasingly benefit from this trend. Consumers are shopping in these national specialty stores to satisfy their need for high-quality "specialty" products. The national specialty chains with their brand equity signal to consumers high quality, and consumers are increasingly flocking to these stores and away from local specialty stores.

Source: Adapted from Pamela N. Danziger, *Why People Buy Things They Don't Need* (Ithaca, NY: Paramount Market Publishing, Inc., 2002). Available from http://www.paramountbooks.com.

---

be strongly linked with marketing objectives. Marketing objectives have to be strongly linked with marketing communications strategy. Marketing communications strategy has to be strongly linked with marketing communications objectives. Finally, marketing communications objectives have to be strongly linked with the selection and implementation of certain elements of the marketing communications mix (see Figure 15-3).

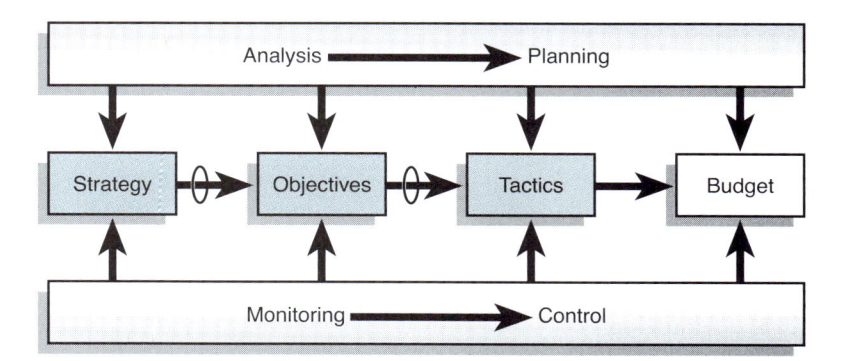

Figure 15-3
Reinforcing the Strategy-Objective-Tactics Link

15-3b The Link between Strategy-Objective-Tactics and Budget

The marketing communications system lacks integration when marketing communications resources are allocated in a manner that has little to do with the resource requirements of the selected marketing communications programs. In many instances, top management allocates resources (e.g., 5 percent of last year's sales) using methods that do not take into account the resource requirements to accomplish the goals of certain strategies. Such misallocation of funds can put the marketing communications system in jeopardy (see Figure 15-4).

For example, examine the hypothetical case of a relatively new alternative business magazine called *Buzz World* that has been developed and marketed by one the mainstream publishers in the United States. The idea has been to use this magazine (both print and electronic versions) to fill the need for a magazine that provides managerial information concerning issues in the new alternative media field. The CEO of the publishing house decides that the corporate strategy for *Buzz World* is to grow in new markets. This strategy was translated in terms of a 15 percent increase in sales and market for next year. It was determined that a product-focus strategy can effectively achieve the 15 percent increase in sales and market share. Specifically, the marketing manager decides to position the product by creating a psychological tie-in with an Internet online portal like Yahoo! The goal was articulated as establishing brand association with the selected distributor so that 80 percent of readers of buzz management-related magazines would associate *Buzz World* with Yahoo! by the end of next year. The marketing communications manager decides to use a habit-formation (doer) strategy. She feels that this strategy is likely to be highly instrumental in achieving the goal of getting target consumers to adopt the magazine on a trial basis. The corresponding objective is to increase product trial by 30 percent in the next year. She knows that such an objective will require at least two targeted email and two mass direct-mailing campaigns to Yahoo! users and would cost approximately $100,000. However, top management has traditionally allocated a marketing communications budget based on 2 percent of forecasted sales. The sales forecast is $4 million, and 2 percent of $4 million allocates $80,000. The marketing communications manager needs at least $100,000

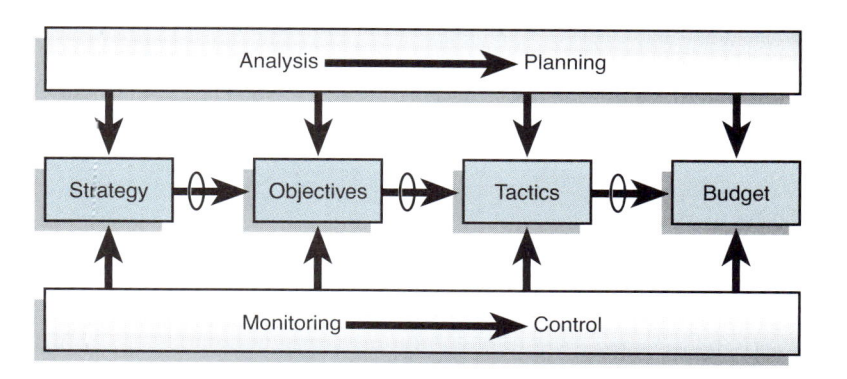

Figure 15-4
Reinforcing the Link between Strategy-Objective-Tactics and Budgeting

to accomplish the goals of the communications strategy and its stated objective. There is a very real problem here! The resources allocated do not mesh with the required strategies and the cost of the program required to achieve the goal of the strategy.

15-3c The Link between Monitoring and Control

A lack of system integration in marketing communications may also occur when performance monitoring at any level (corporate, marketing, or marketing communications) is not followed by control. In other words, a manager at any hierarchical level may monitor system performance based on certain well-thought-out objective dimensions, but no control is exerted. The manager may fail to observe deviations from desired states. The manager may fail to respond by taking corrective action. Corrective action may be completely dissociated from monitoring (see Figure 15-5).

For example, suppose the marketing communications manager observes that the email and direct-mail campaign designed to increase product trial by 30 percent in the next 6 months has failed. She does nothing! There is no corrective action! There is no learning from mistakes! Failure is imminent! Effective organizations learn and adapt behaviors from trial and error. Effective organizations take corrective action to improve future performance. If the link between monitoring and control is weak, then the organization does not learn. Here the marketing communications manager should take some corrective action. An example of corrective action may be to investigate the cause of the failure by focusing on the marketing communications tactics (or programs) that have been put in place to achieve the 30 percent product trial. In this case, the marketing communications program is the email and direct-mail campaign. Perhaps a combination email and direct-mail campaign is less effective than direct-response advertising in a magazine that targets the "right" consumers. Perhaps the email and direct-mail campaign was not implemented effectively. Perhaps the email and mailing lists used were outdated. A significant percentage of the mailings went to no-longer-used email addresses and postal addresses. This happens quite frequently. What can the manager learn from this so that the same mistake will not reoccur in future email and direct-mail campaigns?

15-3d The Link between Monitoring-Control and Strategy-Objective-Tactics

The focus here is how monitoring and control are exerted to change strategy-objective-tactics links, which is part of the monitoring and control functions. If the marketing communications system fails to meet certain performance objectives, corrective action can be instituted by changing the strategy, its objective, and the corresponding tactics (supporting programs) at any of the three levels (corporate, marketing, and marketing communications). The system lacks integration if the monitoring and control functions fail to reassess the strategy-objective-tactics link in the face of negative feedback (see Figure 15-6).

Let us focus on the email and direct-mail example used in the preceding section. The marketing communications objective was set as 30 percent brand trial in 6 months.

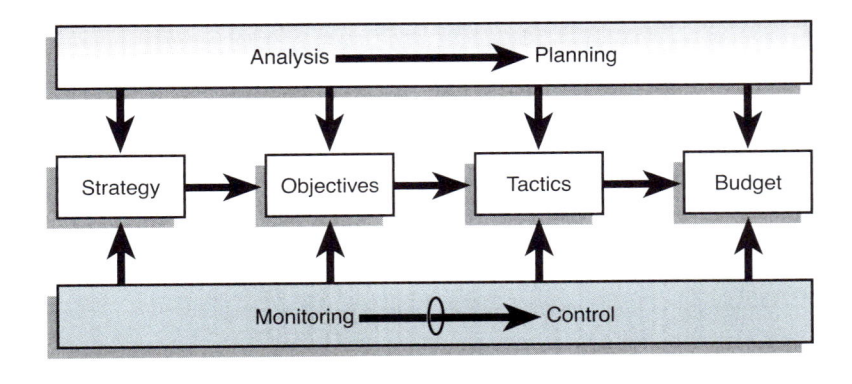

Figure 15-5
Reinforcing the Link between Monitoring and Control

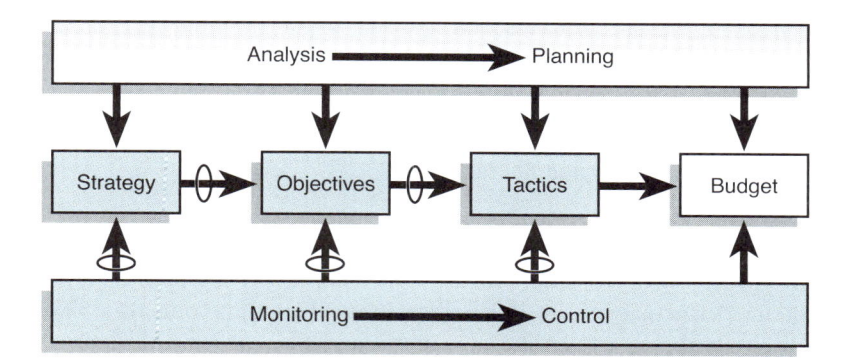

Figure 15-6

Reinforcing the Link between Monitoring-Control and Strategy-Objective-Tactics

Let us assume that after 6 months we find that only 10 percent ordered the product on a trial basis. This is a negative deviation of 20 percent, which is highly significant. What should we do? In the previous section, we talked about examining the link between the marketing communications objective and the use of the direct-mail campaign and possible problems with the implementation of the direct-mail campaign. The focus was on the link between the marketing communications objective and marketing communications tactics. The same examination and evaluation are needed for superordinate links, that is, the link between the marketing communications strategy and the objective, the link between the marketing objective and the marketing communications strategy, the link between the marketing strategy and the corporate objective, and the link between the corporate objective and the corporate strategy. In other words, any of the strategy-objective-tactics links can be faulty and should be reassessed.

15-3e The Link between Monitoring-Control and Objectives

The focus here is how the monitoring and control functions serve to make changes to the stated objectives. The desired level of an objective is reassessed in light of failure. The manager asks whether the objective was set unrealistically high and whether it should be adjusted to reflect the system's true capabilities. The system lacks integration if the manager fails to reassess the objectives in light of performance outcomes reflecting significant deviations from those objectives (see Figure 15-7).

For example, suppose an advertiser such as Nike is running an advertising campaign trying to create awareness of a new model of basketball shoes. The objective is to create 90 percent awareness of the new shoes in the minds of those who are athletically inclined after 6 months of the campaign. After 6 months, Nike finds out that only 60 percent of the target consumers became aware of the new-model shoes. That is, a negative deviation of 30 percentage points is detected. Why did the advertising campaign not reach its objective of 90 percent awareness? Was it because the 90 percent awareness objective was too inflated and unrealistic to begin

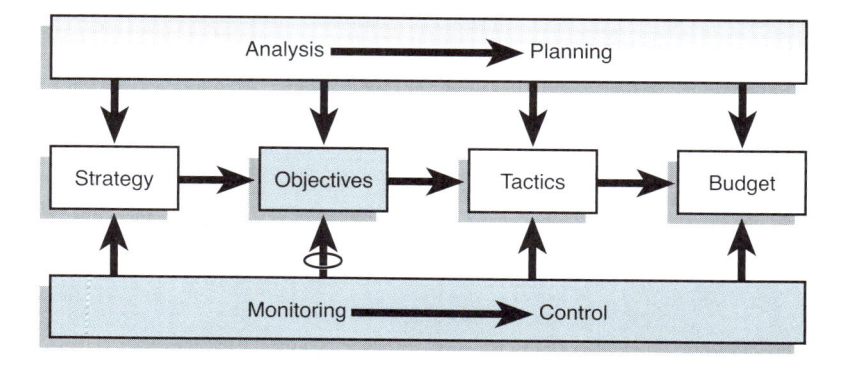

Figure 15-7

Reinforcing the Link between Monitoring-Control and Objectives

with? A 60 percent awareness objective should have been set from the beginning. Perhaps the way the manager set the 90 percent objective was faulty to begin with!

15-3f The Link between Monitoring-Control and Budget

The monitoring and control functions serve to motivate the marketing communications manager to reassess the appropriateness of the resources allocated. Given failure, the manager asks whether failure may be attributed to lack of resources or the misallocation of resources. If so, changes in resource allocations are recommended as corrective action. Failure to reassess the method and outcomes of resource allocation when a program does not succeed is a signal of system breakdown or lack of system integration (see Figure 15-8).

Let us go back to our Nike example. Nike is running the advertising campaign to create 90 percent awareness of a new model of athletic shoes. The goal is to accomplish this in 6 months. About $20 million was allotted to run this advertising campaign in general sports magazines such as *Sports Illustrated* and *ESPN Magazine*, nationwide. After 6 months, Nike finds out that only 60 percent of the target consumers became aware of the new-model shoes. That is, a negative deviation of 30 percentage points is detected. Why did the advertising campaign not reach its objective of 90 percent awareness? Was it because the $20 million budget did not go far enough? Was more money for a wider media buy needed to achieve the 90 percent awareness objective? Perhaps more insertions in these magazines were needed. Perhaps the reach of these magazines was more limited to the target group than originally thought. Therefore, more targeted magazines like *Hoop* and *Dime* may be needed to extend the reach into a more basketball-involved group within the targeted population. Perhaps more of a web advertising presence is needed? These things would require additional resources.

SMC QuickLink
Dime Magazine
http://www.dimemag.com

SMC QuickLink
NBA Inside Stuff
http://www.nba.com/inside_stuff/index.html

15-3g The Link between Analysis and Planning

Lack of integration in the marketing communications system may be due to a lack of a strong link between analysis and planning. Many managers engage in research; they set up elaborate intelligence apparatus; they hire consultants and gather enormous amounts of data. But the same managers fail to use this information in decision making. Most business, marketing, and marketing communications textbooks show managers how to conduct all kinds of analyses—about the competition, about the market, about the environment. Managers commission consumer-behavior studies to establish demographic and psychographic profiles of consumers. Markets are segmented into groups and elaborate profiles are established. Sales data are analyzed and fancy regression models are developed. Is there much sophistication in information gathering? Yes! The failure is in how much of this information is used. Textbooks usually provide very little guidance in this area. A breakdown between analysis and planning is a strong sign of a lack of system integration (see Figure 15-9).

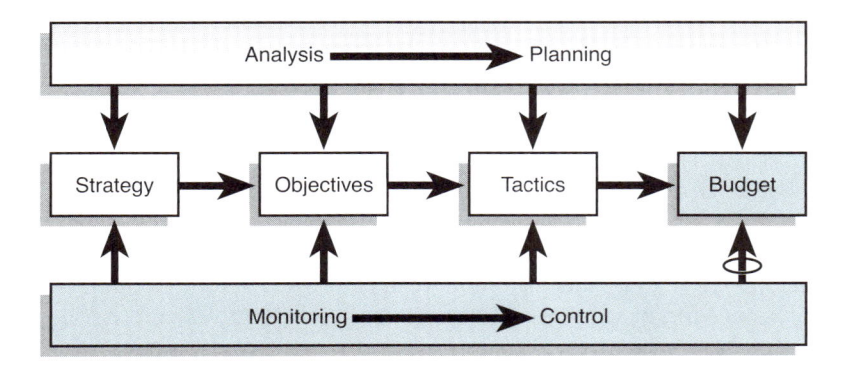

Figure 15-8
Reinforcing the Link between Monitoring-Control and Budgeting

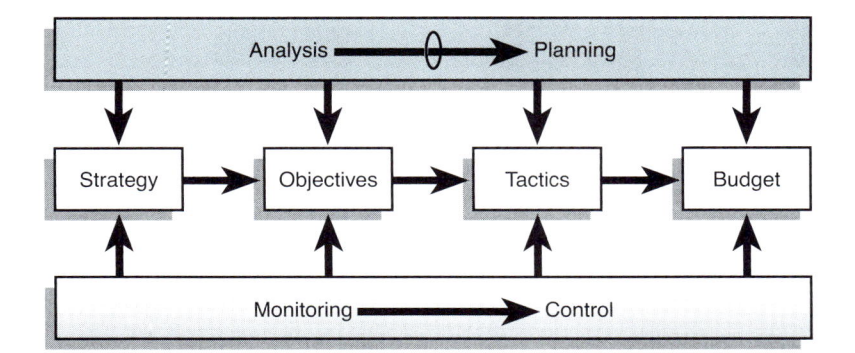

Figure 15-9
Reinforcing the Link between Analysis and Planning

```
Analysis ──────▶ Planning
   │      │         │      │
   ▼      ▼         ▼      ▼
Strategy → Objectives → Tactics → Budget
   ▲      ▲         ▲      ▲
   │      │         │      │
Monitoring ──────▶ Control
```

Let us use Nike as an example to illustrate the breakdown between analysis and planning. Suppose that Nike has conducted a consumer survey of those who are athletically inclined. The survey was rather extensive. Questions were asked about demographics and lifestyle. That is, respondents were asked about their activities, interests, and opinions regarding all kinds of sports activities. Terrific information, right? Not really. The marketing communications manager needs appropriate information to make a host of decisions. Let us focus on strategy selection. The manager has a choice among four strategies: informative (thinker), affective (feeler), habit-formation (doer), and self-satisfaction (reactor). He or she needs information that would assist in making this decision. What kind of information is needed? According to the FCB planning model, two key factors may help the manager decide on the best strategy. Specifically, these factors relate to product involvement and thinking versus feeling. That is, the manager needs to find out whether Nike shoes are a high- or low-involvement item for athletically inclined consumers. Are these consumers likely to be highly involved in processing messages about the new Nike shoes? What is their extent of involvement? The consumer survey should include questions, items, and measures about consumer involvement with the product so that the manager can be in a better position to make a strategic selection than if he or she were to make a decision based on sheer guessing. The same can be said in relation to the thinking versus feeling factor. The manager needs to find out whether Nike shoes are a thinking or feeling product for the targeted market. The same consumer survey may have included a measure about this factor. Are messages about this Nike shoe likely to be processed mostly through the right brain (indicating that the product is a feeling-type product) or left brain (indicating a thinking-type product)? Again, hard information is better than guessing. All the information about demographics and lifestyle is not really helpful. Remember that analysis is supposed to empower the marketing communications manager to plan. If the link between analysis and planning is not strong, the system cannot be effectively integrated. See SMC Marketplace Watch 15-3 for more on the athletic shoe industry and related marketing communications campaigns. See SMC Marketplace Watch 15-4 to learn how analysis of market demand can lead to good planning.

15-3h The Link between Analysis-Planning and Strategy-Objective-Tactics

Analysis and planning are used to help marketing communications managers plot strategy, articulate objectives from strategy, and formulate tactics guided by objectives. Analysis and planning are imperative. Strategy selection (at the corporate, marketing, and marketing communications levels) that is not guided by a thorough analysis of the situation can lead to ineffective decisions. If the wrong strategy is selected, then the wrong objectives are articulated and the wrong tactics are deduced. Analysis and planning are aids to the marketing communications manager, aids assisting in strategy selection, setting of objectives, and developing tactics. The literature on marketing strategy, marketing management, and marketing communi-

SMC Marketplace Watch 15-3

It Is More Than "Spend the Big Money" for And 1 Strategy

By June of 2004 over 216 million pairs of athletic shoes had been purchased for the year. Spending was up over 5 percent from the year before to $7.7 billion dollars. Basketball shoes accounted for almost 35 percent of that market. As a driving force, footwear deals with NBA players were generally controlled by Nike (over 50 percent), Adidas (15 percent), Reebok (7 percent). And 1, an upstart company was focusing on increasing its presence in the NBA footwear market to drive market sales. And 1 said that it would have about 20 percent of the NBA players wearing its shoes to start the 2004–2005 NBA season.

The launch of its new shoe Uprise Mid (suggested retail price $85) was headed for retail shelves. A print campaign that built on the I Ball campaign from the previous year was being launched using *ESPN, Dime,* and *Slam* magazines. Point-of-purchase support also rolled out at Foot Locker, FootAction, and Champs. These chains also were stocking Uprise colors that are exclusive to their stores. And 1 spent a great deal less on advertising than its bigger rivals ($3 million in 2003) but effectively reached its target audience with its Mix Tape tour. (Check out the SMC QuickLink; by the way, Mountain Dew is there, too.)

The advertisements are about linking the street courts with the NBA courts. The audience is all about street ball and the image of the players in the advertisement and "having street game." They feature Stephen Marbury (New York Knicks), Ben Wallace (Detroit Pistons), Jason Williams (Memphis Grizzlies), and Rafer Alston (Toronto Raptors). The link to the street is built in the visual by a street scene and with the text that plays up the connect to the ultimate target market of street ballers and related audiences. That text is: "I have street game and hardwood fame. I control the game at both ends of the court. I'm a lottery pick and an undrafted phenom. I'm living out my dream. I ball."

> **SMC QuickLink**
> And 1
> http://www.and1.com/

Source: Adapted from Barry Janoff, "And 1 Has an NBA Uprising; Favre Adds Chapter to Career," *Brandweek* 45, no. 36, October 11, 2004, 10.

---

cations is very rich with models that allow managers to determine what strategies are effective under what conditions. Failure to use these analytic models may lead the manager to make misguided decisions, leading to disintegration of the marketing communications system (see Figure 15-10).

Let us go back to the Nike example used in the previous section. The marketing communications manager needs to select one of the four strategies: informative (thinker), affective (feeler), habit formation (doer), and self-satisfaction (reactor). The manager gathers information about the extent to which the product in question induces consumer involvement and the extent to which the product is a thinking or feeling type. Situation analysis reveals that the Nike shoes in question are a high-involvement product and more of a thinking-type product than a feeling one. Therefore, an informative (thinker) strategy is selected based on this analysis. Now the question is how to set an objective that directly reflects the goal of the informative

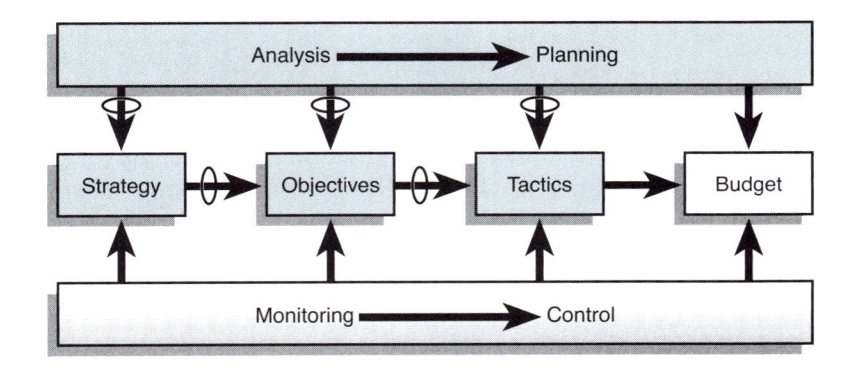

Figure 15-10
Reinforcing the Link between Analysis-Planning and Strategy-Objective-Tactics

SMC Marketplace Watch 15-4

A Look at the Crystal Ball—The Year 2020

Cultural Product and Services

The American population is likely to become more ethnically diverse in the year 2020. The Hispanic and Asian population will be higher than ever before. The size of the white/Anglo consumers will shrink even more. Therefore, there will be a greater need for cultural products and services related to Hispanic and Asians people (e.g., ethnic food, ethnic music, and ethnic movies). This trend is likely to be accentuated by the growing realization that maintaining one's ethnicity and cultural heritage is something to be celebrated rather than shunned.

Housing

Immigration will be the key factor that will significantly increase the size of the American population. Immigration from Latin America is likely to continue at a higher rate than before. As a result, there will be high demand for housing, especially for Hispanic people.

Services for Elderly People

Because the Baby Boom generation will reach full maturity in the year 2020, they will need more services. Many of the Baby Boomers are likely to be unmarried and come from smaller families. Therefore, there will be less informal care available to them that will be compensated for by formal services.

Signaling Devices

Information technology will allow people to know where things and people are at any time. This is because signaling devices will be installed in many products, animals, and humans (e.g., infants).

Small Business

Information technology will allow more people than ever to establish and manage their own business.

Energy Products and Services

There will be large changes in the energy industry due to technological innovations. New forms of energy creation will lead the way to a host of new products and services.

Real Estate Development

There will be an emergence of "micropolitan" area growth. These are satellite micro areas outside of major metro areas. The cost of real estate in these areas is likely to be lower than in the metro areas.

Product Obsolescence

Technological speed accelerates change. The rate of technological innovation will shorten the product life cycle of many technological products.

Hedonic Products and Services

The American consumer will become more fixated on material things and gratification that comes from goods and services. Consumers will seek sensory gratification more than ever before, and technological innovations will deliver sensory gratification to meet market demand.

Distance Learning

Distance education will become commonplace by the year 2020. Traditional brick-and-mortar campuses will be replaced by distance learning. Anyone in the world can enroll and attend a class on the Internet. This technology will allow universities and other institutions of higher learning to offer highly specialized courses. A lot of classes will be recorded and stored; if students miss a class, they will be able to access it via the Internet.

Source: Adapted from Noah Rubin Brier, David Myron, and Christopher Reynolds, "Foresight is 20/20," *American Demographics* (July–August 2004): 33–39.

(thinker) strategy. We know that the objective dimension should be brand awareness and learning; but then the manager needs to determine those marketing communications tools that are most effective in maximizing the stated objectives. Should he or she decide to work with advertising? What form of advertising? How about public relations? What form? How about sales promotion? What form? Which marketing communications tools or programs are likely to be most effective in achieving the objective of 90 percent awareness? Here the marketing communications manager needs information to help him or her make tactical decisions. What does he or she

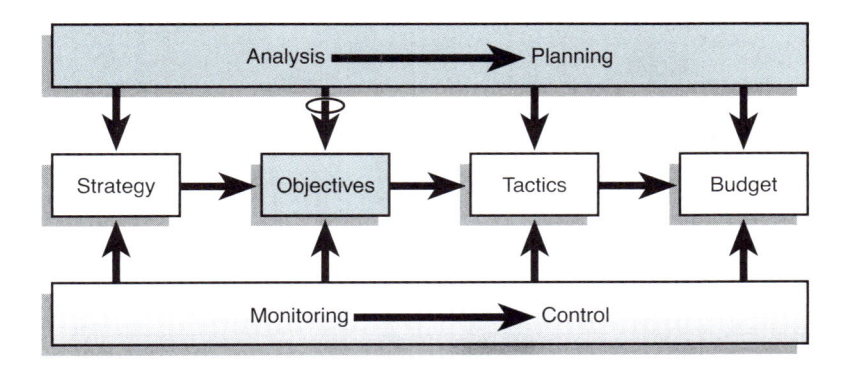

Figure 15-11
Reinforcing the Link between Analysis-Planning and Objectives

know about the relative effectiveness of each tool under various conditions? How do these conditions translate in the context of the situation at hand? This kind of analysis and planning is very helpful in making effective decisions. Lack of a strong link between analysis-planning and strategy-objective-tactics is indicative of a lack of system integration, a situation that must be corrected.

15-3i The Link between Analysis-Planning and Objectives

In the preceding section, we address analysis and planning in relation to the links between strategy, objective, and tactics. Part of the discussion includes objectives. Here, we focus exclusively on objectives and how analysis and planning are used to help managers set effective objectives. Objective setting that is not guided by situation analysis may lead managers to set unrealistic and unreasonable objectives. This is again symptomatic of a lack of system integration (see Figure 15-11).

This discussion has looked at how analysis and planning assist the Nike manager in selecting a marketing communications strategy and how this strategy leads to the specification of objective dimensions, which in turn guide the formation of marketing communications tactics. But the important question still unanswered is: What level of brand awareness and learning should be set? The manager has to conduct additional analyses to be able to determine a desired level of brand awareness and learning. The manager may gather information from past marketing communications campaigns to see what has been achieved in the past. He or she may gather information about the norms of brand awareness and learning measures to be used. What level of performance did most "comparable" products register on the brand awareness and learning measures? This information can be vital in forming reasonable expectations.

15-3j The Link between Analysis-Planning and Budget

Analysis and planning also assist managers in allocating resources effectively. Remember how the marketing communications budget is determined—through the objective-task method. In other words, the manager examines the marketing communications tasks (elements) needed to achieve the stated marketing communications objectives and determines the costs of the tasks. The sum of these costs makes up the marketing communications budget. However, we also discussed the importance of monitoring and control as well as analysis and planning in making adjustments to the budget. Failing to make these adjustments, which may be at least partly due to failure to conduct adequate analysis and planning, may contribute to system disintegration (see Figure 15-12).

The Nike example helps illustrate the importance of analysis and planning in resource allocation. The marketing communications objective is to create 90 percent awareness of the new shoes in the minds of those who are athletically inclined after

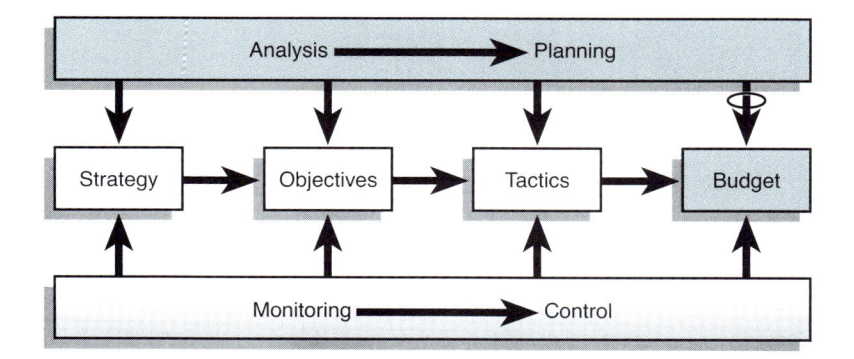

Figure 15-12
Reinforcing the Link between Analysis-Planning and Resource Allocation (Budget)

6 months of the campaign. About $20 million was allotted to run this advertising campaign in athletic magazines nationwide. In other words, it was determined that $20 million was needed to place a certain number of advertisements in so many magazines over a 12-month period. The reach and the number of insertions in these magazines were thought to be highly instrumental in achieving the 90 percent awareness objective; then, through situation analysis, the marketing communications manager began to understand that the costs of placing the specified number of advertising insertions in the selected magazines were expected to increase by at least 8 percent. Knowing this, the manager has to adjust the marketing communications budget by 8 percent to reflect the information about the expected increase in media costs. If the manager has failed to do a thorough analysis of the situation, he or she will not be able to take this factor into account and develop an effective marketing budget, a budget capable of achieving the designated objectives.

Summary

In this chapter, you are exposed to the concepts of monitoring and control. Monitoring and control are discussed from the vantage of the marketing communications manager. The manager assesses marketing communications performance in relation to communications objectives (e.g., brand awareness, brand liking, brand trial/purchase, repeat purchase) and also in relation to marketing objectives (e.g., brand association with a product attribute) and corporate objectives (e.g., sales, market share, and profit). Negative deviations between performance and the objective should prompt the marketing communications manager to take corrective action at three different levels—communications, marketing, and corporate. Corrective action can be in the following forms:

- Reassessment of the selected strategy
- Reassessment of the strategic mix (or tactics)
- Reassessment of the extent of coordination among the elements of the strategic mix
- Reassessment of the implementation of each element of the strategic mix
- Reassessment of the realism of the stated objectives
- Reassessment of the amount of resources allocated toward the elements of the strategic mix

This chapter also highlights the importance of strengthening links between the system components as a means to enhance system integration. Specifically, system integration can be effectively managed by ensuring that the links among the following system components remain strong: (1) the link between strategy, objective, and tactics; (2) the link between strategy-objective-tactics and resource allocation; (3) the link between monitoring and control; (4) the link between monitoring-control and strategy-objective-tactics; (5) the link between monitoring-control and objectives; (6) the link between monitoring-control and resource allocation; (7) the link between analysis and planning; (8) the link between analysis-planning and strategy-objective-tactics; (9) the link between analysis-planning and objectives; and (10) the link between analysis-planning and resource allocation.

Discussion Questions

Scenario 1: Consider the case of Kmart that is discussed at the beginning of this chapter. You probably have been exposed to Kmart's advertising and other forms of marketing communications. You probably have also visited Kmart on a number of occasions. You probably have visited its key competitor, Wal-Mart. Respond to the following questions by relying on your own knowledge of Kmart and Wal-Mart.

1. Describe the typical Kmart advertising message. Compare it with Wal-Mart's.
2. What communications objectives do you think Kmart is trying to achieve with its advertising? How about Wal-Mart?
3. Do you think that Kmart's advertising campaign is effective? Comment on the effectiveness of Kmart's advertising campaign in relation to what you think may be Kmart's advertising objectives.
4. Do you think that Wal-Mart's advertising campaign is effective? Comment on the effectiveness of Wal-Mart's advertising campaign in relation to what you think may be Wal-Mart's advertising objectives.
5. If you think Kmart's advertising campaign is not effective, then would you recommend that Kmart change its marketing communications strategy? From what to what?
6. Would you recommend changes in Kmart's marketing communications mix? Explain.
7. Would you recommend changes in Kmart's marketing strategy? What is Kmart's current positioning strategy? Do you think it is an effective strategy? If not, what other positioning strategy is likely to be more effective for Kmart?
8. Would you recommend changes in Kmart's marketing mix? Explain.
9. What is Kmart's current corporate strategy? Do you think it is an effective strategy? If not, what other corporate strategy is likely to be more effective for Kmart? Would you recommend changes in the corporate mix? Explain.

Scenario 2: Let us revisit the small publishing company that we first talked about at the beginning of this chapter. Remember that the company specializes in Appalachian history. This publisher has an extensive line of books dealing with the history of the region, its geography, and its cultural. The publisher has been around for the last 20 years or so and is a two-person operation (the owner/publisher and a copy editor). Now respond to the following questions.

1. Develop an overall marketing communications plan that spells out the corporate strategy. Make sure that the corporate objectives are strongly linked with the corporate strategy. What do you think is an effective marketing strategy? Connect the marketing strategy with the corporate objective. Now translate the marketing strategy into a marketing objective. Explain the logic of the link. What is an effective marketing communications strategy? Why did you select that strategy and how is it linked with the marketing objective? Explain. What is a reasonable marketing communications objective? How is this tied to the marketing communications strategy? What communications tools and programs are best here? Why? Explain how these communications programs can achieve the stated marketing communications objective.
2. How much do you think this company should spend on marketing communications annually? How can you go about figuring out the best way to develop a marketing communications budget? Is the budget linked to strategy, objectives, and tactics? Explain.
3. Is there a problem with monitoring and control? Explain. What would you advise the publisher?
4. If you focus on the link between strategy-objective-tactics and monitoring and control, what do you have to say about this publisher? Come up with a script that will educate the publisher about the importance of this system link. Happy scripting!
5. Now focus on the link between monitoring-control and objective setting. Use what you have learned from this chapter and previous ones to educate the publisher about how she should set her corporate, marketing, and marketing communications objectives.
6. Do the same thing in relation to the monitoring-control–resource-allocation link. That is, come up with a script to educate the publisher about the importance of feedback and trial and error to figure out an effective budget over the long haul.
7. Now focus on analysis and planning. What advice would you give this publisher about analysis and planning? What kind of analysis should she do and how can this analysis be used in planning marketing communications campaigns?
8. What kind of information should the publisher gather to help her with determining the best strategies

at the corporate, marketing, and marketing communications levels? Explain.

9. What kind of information should the publisher gather over time to help her set reasonable objectives? Explain.

10. What kind of information should the publisher gather over time to help her figure out the best marketing communications budget possible? Explain.

Practice Quiz

Note: You can find the correct answers to these questions by taking the quiz and then submitting your answers in the Online Edition. The program will automatically score your submission. If you miss a question, the program will provide the correct answer, a rationale for the answer, and the section number in the chapter where the topic is discussed.

1. Increase sales and market share of MapLinX software by 25 percent in relation to the U.S. market. The current sales are 5,500 units, and the market share was 58 percent all of last year. Specifically, the goal is to raise unit sales to 6,875 and to achieve a market share of 72.5 percent by the end of next year. This is an example of _____.
   a. a marketing communications objective
   b. marketing objectives
   c. a corporate objective
   d. None of the preceding answers are correct.

2. What happens if the research results show that marketing communications objectives were not met? What should the company do in a situation like this? The marketing communications manager can exert control by doing any one or more of the following:
   a. reassess the marketing strategy
   b. reassess the corporate marketing communications mix
   c. reassess the implementation of each element of the corporate mix
   d. None of the preceding answers are correct.

3. Reinforcing the strategy-objective link means _____.
   a. assessing performance in light of the stated objectives
   b. selecting objectives that are aligned with the stated strategy at the same hierarchical level
   c. allocating resources to meet the stated objectives
   d. selecting a strategy at a hierarchical level aligned with the objectives of the lower-level subsystem

4. Reinforcing the link between strategy-objective-tactics and budget means _____.
   a. assessing performance in light of the stated objectives
   b. selecting objectives that are aligned with the stated strategy at the same hierarchical level
   c. allocating resources to meet the stated objectives
   d. selecting a strategy at a hierarchical level aligned with the objectives of the lower-level subsystem

5. Reinforcing the link between monitoring and control means _____.
   a. assessing performance in light of the stated objectives
   b. selecting objectives that are aligned with the stated strategy at the same hierarchical level
   c. engaging in corrective action as a direct result of a negative variance between the stated objectives and performance outcomes
   d. selecting a strategy at a hierarchical level aligned with the objectives of the lower-level subsystem

6. Reinforcing the link between monitoring-control and strategy-objective-tactics means _____.
   a. assessing performance in light of the stated objectives
   b. selecting objectives that are aligned with the stated strategy at the same hierarchical level
   c. engaging in corrective action as a direct result of a negative variance between the stated objectives and performance outcomes
   d. ensuring that the negative variance between the stated objectives and performance outcomes can be remedied by selecting another strategy, modifying the stated objectives, and/or modifying the tactics at the same hierarchical level

7. Reinforcing the link between monitoring-control and objectives means _____.
   a. ensuring that the negative variance between the stated objectives and the performance outcomes can be sufficiently reduced by restating the objectives
   b. selecting objectives that are aligned with the stated strategy at the same hierarchical level
   c. engaging in corrective action as a direct result of a negative variance between the stated objectives and performance outcomes
   d. ensuring that the negative variance between the stated objectives and performance outcomes can be remedied by selecting another strategy, modifying the stated objectives, and/or modifying the tactics at the same hierarchical level

8. Reinforcing the link between monitoring-control and budget means _____.
   a. ensuring that the negative variance between the stated objectives and the performance outcomes can be sufficiently reduced by reallocating resources
   b. selecting objectives that are aligned with the stated strategy at the same hierarchical level
   c. engaging in corrective action as a direct result of a negative variance between the stated objectives and performance outcomes
   d. ensuring that the negative variance between the stated objectives and performance outcomes can be remedied by selecting another strategy, modifying the stated objectives, and/or modifying the tactics at the same hierarchical level

9. Reinforcing the link between analysis-planning and objectives means _____.
   a. ensuring that the stated objectives are consistent with the results of strategic analysis
   b. selecting objectives that are aligned with the stated strategy at the same hierarchical level
   c. engaging in corrective action as a direct result of a negative variance between the stated objectives and performance outcomes
   d. ensuring that the negative variance between the stated objectives and performance outcomes can be remedied by selecting another strategy, modifying the stated objectives, and/or modifying the tactics at the same hierarchical level

10. Reinforcing the link between analysis-planning and budget means _____.
    a. ensuring that the stated objectives are consistent with the results of strategic analysis
    b. selecting objectives that are aligned with the stated strategy at the same hierarchical level
    c. engaging in corrective action as a direct result of a negative variance between the stated objectives and performance outcomes
    d. ensuring that the allocation of resources is consistent with the results of the strategic analysis

Web Exercise

Brand Unity and Marketing Communications Assessment

Visit the website of a brand of your choice. Carefully go through the layers of the website to visit each of the brands and products that your brand offers. Assess the unity that exists regarding the brand and all its elements and related products/brands on the website. Now using the search engine of your choice, conduct a webwide search for articles and blogs about the brand and how it communicates with its customers and relevant stakeholders. What did you find? Does the company create unity of message in all its communications portfolio elements? What does the market think? From your analysis, what actions might you suggest for management to undertake immediately? Long term?

Suggested Readings

Baumler, J. 1971. Defined criteria of performance in organizational control. *Administrative Science Quarterly* (September): 340.

Cavaleri, Steven, and Krzysztof Obloj. 1993. *Management systems: A global perspective.* Belmont, CA: Wadsworth.

Churchman, C. W. 1968. *The systems approach.* New York: Dell.

Flamholtz, E. 1979. Organizational control systems as a managerial tool. *California Management Review* 22 (2): 50–59.

Katz, D., and R. Kahn. 1966. *The social psychology of organizations.* New York: John Wiley.

Lerner, A. Y. 1972. *Fundamentals of cybernetics.* London: Chapman and Hall.

Miller, James G. 1978. *Living systems.* New York: McGraw-Hill.

Morell, R. W. 1969. *Management: Ends and means.* San Francisco: Chandler.

Powers, W. T. 1973. *Behavior: The control of perception.* Chicago: Aldine.

———. 1990. Control theory: A model of organisms. *Systems Dynamics Review* 6 (1): 1–20.

Rahmation, S. 1985. The hierarchy of objectives: Toward an integrating construct in systems science. *Systems Research* 2 (3): 237–45.

Richardson, G. 1991. *Feedback thought in social science and systems theory.* Philadelphia: University of Pennsylvania Press.

Robb, F. F. 1985. Cybernetics in management thinking. *Systems Research* 1 (1): 5–23.

Simon, Herbert A. 1965. *Administrative behavior.* New York: The Free Press.

Sirgy, M. Joseph. 1984. *Marketing as social behavior: A general systems theory.* New York: Praeger.

———. 1988. Strategies for developing general system theories. *Behavioral Science* 33 (1): 25–37.

———. 1989. Toward a theory of social organization: A systems approach. *Behavioral Science* 34:272–85.

———. 1990. Self-cybernetics: Toward an integrated model of self-concept processes. *Systems Research* 7 (1): 19–32.

———. 1990. Toward a theory of social relations: The regression analog. *Behavioral Science* 35 (4): 195–206.

Notes

1. Patricia Seller, "Kmart Is Down for the Count," *Fortune*, January 15, 1996, 102–3.
2. J. Baumler, "Defined Criteria of Performance in Organizational Control," *Administrative Science Quarterly* (September 1971): 340; C. W. Churchman, *The Systems Approach* (New York: Dell, 1968); E. Flamholtz, "Organizational Control Systems As a Managerial Tool," *California Management Review* 22, no. 2 (1979): 50–59; D. Katz and R. Kahn, *The Social Psychology of Organizations* (New York: John Wiley, 1966): A. Y. Lerner, *Fundamentals of Cybernetics* (London: Chapman and Hall, 1972); W. T. Powers, *Behavior: The Control of Perception* (Chicago: Aldine, 1973); G. Richardson, *Feedback Thought in Social Science and Systems Theory* (Philadelphia: University of Pennsylvania Press, 1991); F. F. Robb, "Cybernetics in Management Thinking," *Systems Research* 1, no. 1 (1985): 5–23; M. Joseph Sirgy, "Toward a Theory of Social Organization: A Systems Approach," *Behavioral Science* 34 (1989): 272–85.

An IMC Plan for Cable & Wireless Using the Systems Approach

Case A

This case describes an IMC plan for Cable & Wireless plc and is based on the systems approach of IMC. This approach ensures the consistency of the promotional message at all levels of the organization: corporate, marketing, and marketing communications (see Figure A-1). Within each level, the plan describes the following functions:

1. Develop strategy.
2. Create objectives.
3. Develop tactics used to reach these objectives.
4. Allocate resources, that is, budgeting.
5. Monitor and control.

A-1 History of Cable & Wireless

The beginning of the existence of Cable & Wireless plc stems back to the early 1800s. Sir John Pender was born in Scotland in 1815 and was the telecommunications entrepreneur whose foresight led to the creation of the world's largest telecommunications network. He invested in the Anglo-Irish Magnetic Telegraph Company, which was the first step in his involvement with international telecommunications. In 1856 Pender became a director of the Atlantic Telegraph Company and later founded or cofounded the following major telecommunications companies: the Telegraph Construction and Maintenance Company, the Anglo-American Telegraph Company, the British Indian Submarine Telegraph Company, and the Eastern Telegraph Company. Pender was CEO of Eastern Telegraph Company until he died in 1896.

Cable & Wireless plc is the successor organization to Sir John Pender's telecommunications empire. Cable & Wireless has been a world leader in developing and providing telecommunications solutions around the world for more than 125 years. It is a global carrier providing a complete portfolio of Internet, data, voice, and messaging communications. Today the company has seventeen million customers in more than seventy countries, with annual revenues of about $14 billion. The stock is traded on the London, New York, Hong Kong, and other major stock exchanges around the world. It is known as the first communications company to own and operate a global network, known as the *Global Digital Highway.*

Incorporated in March 1975 in Washington, D.C., Cable & Wireless USA has been a wholly owned subsidiary of Cable & Wireless plc since 1977. Cable & Wireless USA is headquartered in Vienna, Virginia, and has more than four thousand

Source: This case was adapted from a case written by Jay and Kristin Mulkerin in partial fulfillment of requirements of a marketing communications class taught by Professor Joe Sirgy during the fall semester of 2000.

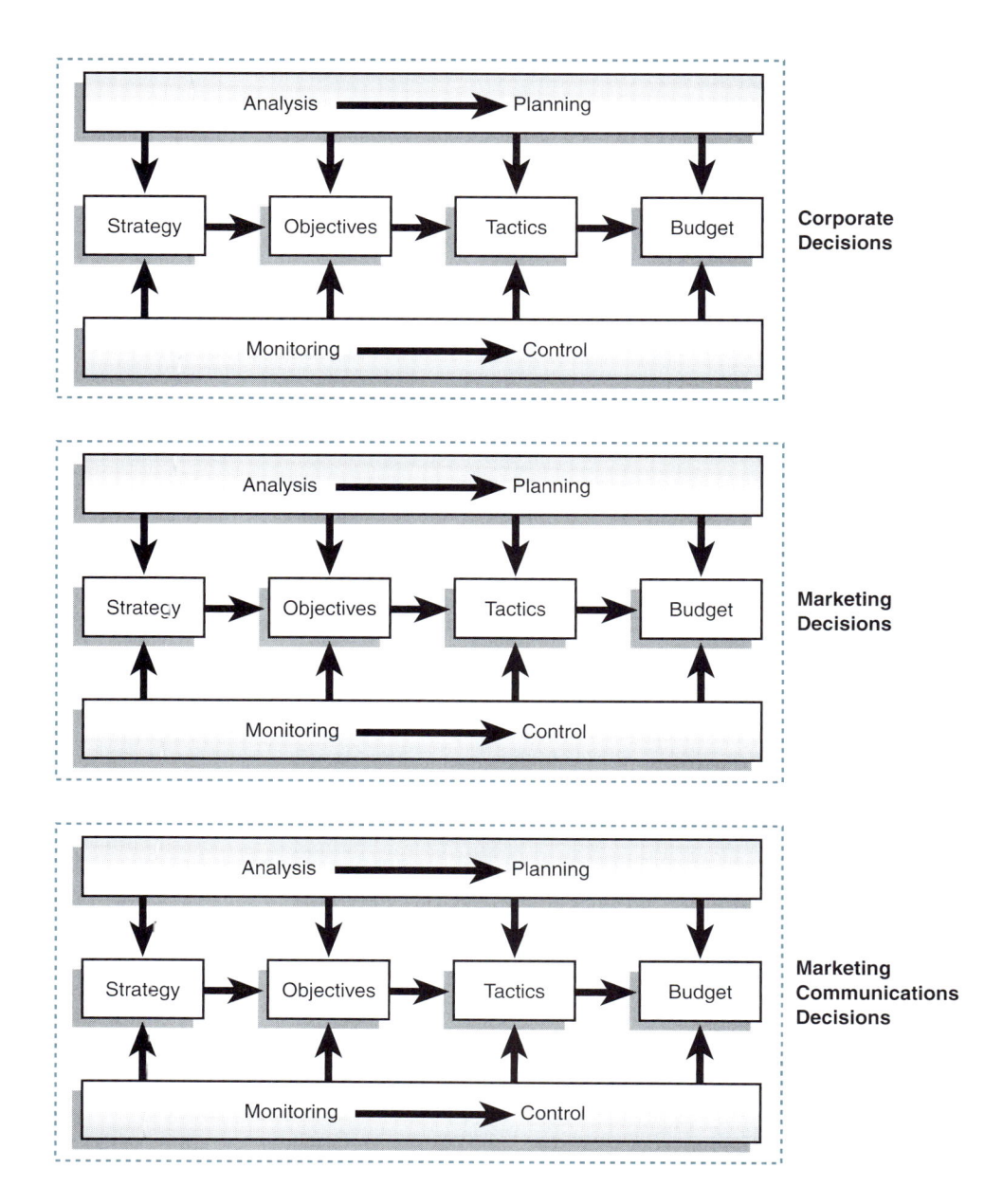

Figure A-1
Corporate, Marketing, and Marketing Communications Decisions

employees and over fifty sales offices nationwide. It goes far beyond the competition in delivering communications services that meet the specific needs of the business customers. Cable & Wireless USA provides Internet, data, and voice long distance services to its customers. The Internet backbone it owns carries 28 percent of all Internet traffic. It uses a consultative approach to understanding customers' objectives and then carefully tailors solutions to achieve their goals. Cable & Wireless is known throughout the industry as customer intimate by continuing to build strong relationships with its existing customers.

A-2 Current Situation and the Need for an IMC Plan

Currently, sales at Cable & Wireless are down, and the company is losing market share. The company is struggling with name recognition, which may be part of the problem related to poor sales. Many of the people who know the company associate

Cable & Wireless with voice long distance services. The people who have not heard of the company tend to think Cable & Wireless is either a cable television company or provider of wireless phone services, neither of which is accurate.

Another reason for the need for an IMC plan is the fact that Cable & Wireless's competitors do much more advertising and promotion than it does. For example, UUNet is an inside sales organization (phone sales) and advertises heavily in magazines, newspapers, and television; PSINet owns a stadium and invests heavily in mass media advertising.

Paradoxically, Cable & Wireless is ranked as the number two Internet service provider (ISP) in the world in terms of powerful backbones. It may be the best kept secret in town.

A-3 Information from Cable & Wireless

An interview was conducted with the senior marketing manager at Cable & Wireless. Based on this interview, it seems that the corporate strategy is well defined. Cable & Wireless defines two goals as part of its mission for the fiscal year 2001. One goal is to become the number one network service provider (NSP) for small/medium-size enterprises (SMEs) in target geographies by achieving a market share of 25 to 40 percent, and the other goal is to become one of the top two providers of communications services to United States–based multinational companies (MNCs) in target industry segments by achieving a market share of 15 to 20 percent. The strategy for Cable & Wireless to achieve these goals is by establishing the company as a leader in integrated communications.

Becoming the number one NSP is to be achieved by the following strategic initiatives: establishing solid brand identity, becoming one of the top two providers of communications services to United States–based multinational companies (MNCs) in target industry segments, and continuing to focus on customer relationships. Increasing market share is to be achieved by the following: cross-selling Internet Protocol (IP) into existing customer base, building a list of the top 100,000 prospects, telemarketing, selling through Customer Care (the user support group), creation of compelling IP/data/voice product bundles, and leading with IP technology. In addition, Cable & Wireless plans to focus on deep industry and technical expertise, the creation of compelling IP/data/voice application suites (product and service information), leading with innovations in IP, and by sharing of local and global expertise through synchronization between sales, customer service, and marketing.

Cable & Wireless plans to achieve these goals and objectives by doing the following:

- *Best-in-class service:* Customer-first responsiveness and service delivery, order to provisioning time for all products less than 30 days
- *Superior network performance:* Leader in high bandwidth, speed, reliability and security
- *Compelling product bundles and application suites:* Leading with IP number one provider of IP backbone services—top provider to ISPs and Internet content providers

In quantifiable terms, Cable & Wireless plans to achieve best-in-industry, overall revenue growth of 30 percent, with IP growth of 70 percent, voice growth of 10 percent, and data growth of 25 percent.

Cable & Wireless assigns departments and individuals responsible for certain objectives. These individuals are responsible for updating the status of their respective objectives. One of the objectives is to establish synchronization between the sales force, customer service, and marketing. A group or person is identified as having responsibility to achieve the specific task, and information about the extent to which the task is completed is published every 2 weeks on the company's internal website for all employees to see.

The strategy for marketing is to help achieve new business by focusing on two separate groups: existing customers and new customers who are to be acquired. The customer-retention side (existing customers) strives to develop loyalty between Cable & Wireless and its customers. The acquisition side focuses on gaining market share and acquiring "new logos."

Objectives for the two different groups involve retention and acquisition. In relation to retention, the company focuses on reducing the attrition rate. The specific objective is to maintain the industry average of attrition, which is 4 percent. Another objective is to maximize revenue by selling additional services to existing customers. "Maximizing revenue" is not defined as a measurable goal. Maximizing revenue is merely kept in mind when marketers develop new products and programs.

In relation to the acquisition objective, the focus is on gaining market share and selling new products. One way of achieving this is to further develop the partner programs and agent programs in which non–Cable & Wireless employees refer business to the company or actually sell products and services themselves.

These objectives are achieved on a per-program basis. An example of a program may be a relaunch of a product that is not doing well. Again, the tactics are left to each program manager to define, and there is no kind of continuity between tactics. Each program manager defines specific tactics related to his or her program, and there does not seem to be a common goal. The goal is to do "good," but "good" is not defined.

The budget for all retention and acquisition programs is based on past budgets. This is very similar to how the federal government establishes budgets: if you don't use it, you lose it. Both the retention and acquisition groups forecast a budget; they are provided with resources based on the forecast and historical data. If a new program is developed that needs funding but is not in the budget, then the respective groups can develop a business case for the "unexpected" program and additional monies may or may not be granted. The director of marketing indicates that this is a defined weakness and that the company is always quick to cut the marketing budget in order to allocate funds to engineering or other more critical groups.

The monitoring of objectives is done through monthly reports from the field. Marketing managers tally up the results of sales, and this information is then communicated to the marketing directors. There are no severe consequences for underachievement or objectives not being met. In reality, year-end is when the actual numbers are tallied; the monthly reports are just a way to take a snapshot of what is currently going on. The marketing managers do have part of their compensation based on achieving certain objectives, but the evaluation criteria are more subjective than quantitative because no real measurable criteria are assigned to the objectives.

At the end of the year, objectives are defined as either being met or not met. If they are not met, the marketing managers take a monetary hit but not a severe one. The marketing group then "learns from its mistakes" and develops new strategies and objectives for the following year based on the past performance. No real accountability is in place.

At the marketing communications level, the strategy is to achieve brand awareness, grow market share, and sell new products to existing and new customers by increased advertising. Because Cable & Wireless operates in a business-to-business environment, the focus is to enhance awareness in the business world. Therefore, mass media forms of advertising are considered ineffective.

No formal objectives are stated for achieving brand awareness, growing the market share, and selling new or additional products. Marketing managers at Cable & Wireless stated they wished to improve brand awareness through advertising, but there are no formal objectives defined such as selling an additional three hundred Internet connections once an advertisement in *DataComm* is run.

Marketing communication is done by promoting Cable & Wireless's products and services through business magazines, trade magazines, radio advertisements, trade show participation, direct mail, and newspaper advertisements. Specifically, Cable & Wireless has advertisements printed in the following newspapers, magazines, and journals: *The Wall Street Journal, Business Week, The Washington Post*, and *DataComm Magazine*. In addition to Cable & Wireless paying to have advertisements published, the company is written up in many trade magazines when the magazines are evaluating top Internet service providers (ISPs), backbone performance of ISPs, and other "comparison-type" articles. Cable & Wireless attends all major trade shows across the country including ISPCon, InterOp, and so on. Radio commercials have been aired in the Baltimore/Washington Metropolitan area at the time of the interview. Direct-mail campaigns are launched frequently, but the sentiment among marketing managers is that direct mail is a "waste of money."

Cable & Wireless also uses marketing "slicks" for the sales force to distribute to both potential and existing customers. The glossy, one-page promotional brochure provides valuable information about the company and its products and services. Sales representatives are constantly performing cold calling and knocking door-to-door to gain new business. These slicks are personally dropped off at potential customers' sites, or they are mailed to them. Much emphasis is placed on the sales force to promote Cable & Wireless.

With respect to the budget, each marketing manager develops a budget based on past budgets and marketing programs that are known for the upcoming year. If a new program is developed that needs funding but is not in the budget, then the group in question develops a case for the need of additional resources.

What about monitoring and control? Because no formal objectives are defined, it seems that there is no formal mechanism to monitoring performance.

The interview with the marketing managers also revealed that the most important buying criteria (purchase of ISPs) are backbone performance and customer service. Backbone performance includes peering agreements with other ISPs (the way the networks are interconnected), capacity of the backbone trunks, and the physical reach of the network. Customer service includes all departments of the company that a customer would interface with: the sales force, the help desk, the billing department, the service-delivery group, and the customer-retention specialists.

A-4 An IMC Plan for Cable & Wireless

The previous section describes information provided by Cable & Wireless contacts. In this section, an attempt is made to develop an IMC plan based on the systems approach (see Figure A-1 on page 394).

A-4a Corporate Decisions—Top Level

1. *Strategy and objectives:* The corporate strategy for Cable & Wireless seems to be pretty well defined. The first strategy is to become the number one NSP (network service provider) for small/medium-sized enterprises (SMEs) in target geographies by achieving a market share of 25 to 40 percent.

    The second strategy is to become one of the top two providers of communications services to United States–based multinational companies (MNCs) in target industry segments by achieving a market share of 15 to 20 percent.

    These strategies are designed to establish the company as a leader in integrated communications. In both cases, there is a desired increase in market share. According to the systems model, Cable & Wireless appears to be pursuing a growth strategy at the corporate level.

2. *Tactics:* How will the corporate objectives be met? It seems that the aforementioned objectives will be met as follows:

    - Marketing: Cable & Wireless does not appear to emphasize marketing very much. Advertising is limited and mostly poorly done. The company does little in terms of trade shows. The sales force does not seem to be very skilled. Compensation for the sales force is below the industry average.

- Engineering: Cable & Wireless appears to spend quite a bit on engineering. This emphasis on engineering ensures that Cable & Wireless's backbone can handle the increasing demand of its customers.
- R&D: This organizational function is also emphasized. The focus is on coming up with innovative ways to utilize existing technologies.
- Personnel: Personnel at Cable & Wireless does not seem to be emphasized. Salaries for the sales staff appear to be below industry average. However, there is much emphasis on frequent training on *sales force automation systems*.

In order to properly implement a growth strategy, we suggest that Cable & Wireless put more emphasis on marketing. The company needs to launch an aggressive marketing communications campaign. The current campaign appears to be very weak. It is difficult to grow and expand if potential clients are not aware of and informed about the company's offerings.

3. *Allocate resources:* As previously mentioned, information about resource allocation at the corporate level is highly confidential and cannot be disclosed. However, based on the interviews, it seems that resources are allocated heavily to reflect the company's emphasis on engineering, R&D, and personnel. We recommend that resources should be allocated to reflect a marketing emphasis. This is much needed to implement the corporate strategy of growth.

4. *Monitor and control:* As previously mentioned, there does not seem to be a monitoring and control mechanism in place at the corporate level. It appears that Cable & Wireless keeps track of sales and market share but does not take appropriate action if the set objectives are not met. A system of incentives has to be designed to encourage managers to take forceful corrective action to ensure that the corporate objectives are met.

A-4b Marketing Decisions—Middle Level

1. *Strategy:* It appears that Cable & Wireless is pursuing a product-focus strategy. Evidence of this strategy derives from the company's promotional message that emphasizes the following:

   - Best-in-class service: Customer-first responsiveness and service delivery, order to provisioning time for all products less than 30 days
   - Superior network performance: Leader in high bandwidth, speed, reliability, and security
   - Compelling product bundles and application suites: Leading with IP, number one provider of IP backbone services, top provider to ISPs and Internet content providers

   Within the product-focus strategy, the company seems to position its offering using a *product-attribute strategy*. Both *superior network performance* and *best-in-class service* suggest positioning by *product attribute* as well as by *intangible factor*. Response times can be used to determine superior network performance (i.e., faster response times equate to superior performance). In addition, the amount of time it takes to resolve a problem captures *best-in-class service* (i.e., a support staff of one hundred people is more likely to resolve issues quicker than a support staff with ten people). Both of these examples reflect an emphasis on positioning by product attribute.

   If one asks typical information technology (IT) managers which company offers superior network performance, Cable & Wireless or DIGEX, they are likely to point to Cable & Wireless. Cable & Wireless is perceived to offer superior network performance and has a good reputation among IT experts. If this evidence is credible, then the product-focus strategy with an emphasis on positioning by product attribute and intangible factor seems warranted. The recommendation then is stay the course by maintaining the same marketing strategy.

2. *Objectives:* The interviews with the marketing managers at Cable & Wireless revealed that the company does not have established marketing objectives. There seems to be a desire to "establish solid brand identity," but it does not go any deeper than that. If Cable & Wireless were to set proper marketing-level objectives, they would have to be something similar to the following (in both cases, these objectives can be measured via marketing research):

   - Product attribute: What are some of the most important criteria IT personnel use to evaluate various Internet service providers? In most cases, the most important buying criterion is backbone performance. If so, the marketing objective should be to tie "backbone performance" to Cable & Wireless. An example would be: *Increase association of Cable & Wireless Internet service with high backbone performance by 10 percent in one year.*

   - Intangible factor: Cable & Wireless's reputation for customer service is good. As previously mentioned, many aspects of customer service are not concrete and quantifiable. Therefore, the marketing objective here is to associate superior customer service with the Cable & Wireless Internet offerings. An example would be: *Increase association of Cable & Wireless Internet service with superior customer service (intangible factor) by 10 percent in one year.*

3. *Tactics:* The interviews failed to reveal exactly how the marketing strategy (product focus through positioning by product attribute and intangible factor) is operationalized through product, price, distribution, and promotion (elements of the marketing mix). Consequently, a set of tactics is recommended without the benefit of knowing how the company has operationalized its marketing strategy:

   - Product attribute: The first step would be to determine the most critical buying factor in selecting an Internet service provider. This has to be done through marketing research. Assuming that superior backbone performance is indeed the most important product attribute (as revealed through marketing research), the next step is to work with engineering to ensure that a superior backbone is central to the company's Internet offering. This basically entails ensuring that the pipes are bigger than competitor service providers and that the backbone equipment is capable of producing high performance. The final step is to ensure that the target market realizes that Cable & Wireless offers superior backbone performance. This has to be done through an aggressive marketing communications campaign involving sales force, advertising, customer testimonial, and third party testing.

   - Intangible factor: As with product-attribute positioning, the first step is to conduct marketing research to validate the notion that superior customer service is a critical factor in selecting an ISP. Therefore, the company should promote customer service.

4. *Allocate resources:* Again, the interviews revealed very little about how resources are allocated within marketing. There is no available data providing a breakdown of marketing expenditures. However, it appears that marketing budgeting decisions are based on historical data and forecasts. How these forecasts are developed seems to be an enigma.

   Thus, we recommend that a budget should be formulated based on determining the costs of those specific marketing-related tasks implementing the product-attribute and intangible-factor positioning strategies.

5. *Monitor and control:* Based on the interviews, marketing progress seems to be monitored through monthly reports. However, because there are no formally established marketing objectives, it makes it difficult to gauge progress. This translates into no real accountability.

    Thus, we recommend that a monitor-and-control system be devised to gauge progress in relation to the two suggested objectives: (1) *Increase association of Cable & Wireless Internet service with high backbone performance by 10 percent in one year.* (2) *Increase association of Cable & Wireless Internet service with superior customer service (intangible factor) by 10 percent in one year.* A specific plan of action has to be formulated to engage in corrective action given failure to achieve the stated objectives.

A-4c Marketing Communications Decisions—Lower Level

1. *Strategy:* Let us examine how prospective clients go about selecting an Internet service provider for their business. This is a high-involvement decision. Poor performance can be costly. Many service providers tie clients by multiyear contracts. Thus, the ISP decision is based on much thinking and is highly involving. Prospective clients are likely to consider various features and components before making a selection. In other words, they are motivated to seek and process quite a bit of information about various ISPs' offerings before making a selection. Furthermore, it is easy to categorize Cable & Wireless products and services as "rational" products. Emotions are not likely to play an important role in the ISP buying decision. The decision is likely to be made based on performance or a fixed set of criteria. Examples include network response time (measured in seconds), throughput (measured in megabits per second), or minutes of network outage per year. An *informative (thinker)* strategy appears to be the best strategy for this scenario. Furthermore, examining the promotional messages of Cable & Wireless, it is our judgment that the company is currently pursuing an informative (thinker) communications strategy.

2. *Objectives:* Because we have selected the informative strategy, we realize that an effective communications campaign has to be done in the following stages: *learn → feel → do.* Cable & Wireless has not conducted its promotion campaign as such. Table A-1 and subsequent discussion provide suggested marketing communications objectives for a one-year campaign. The objectives for each component would be as follows:

First 4 months

a. Get 80 percent of the target consumers to learn about Cable & Wireless's Internet service offerings, basically educating them on Cable & Wireless offerings and the benefits of those offerings. Some of the following questions can be answered:

- Does Cable & Wireless offer its Internet service in your business locations?
- Is Cable & Wireless's Internet offering highly robust and reliable?
- Does Cable & Wireless offer high-quality customer service?

TABLE A-1 One-Year Marketing Communications Objectives

Stage	Brand Learning (*Learn*)	Brand Liking (*Feel*)	Brand Purchase (*Do*)
First 4 months	80 percent	20 percent	10 percent
Second 4 months	90 percent	50 percent	20 percent
Third 4 months	95 percent	60 percent	50 percent

b. Get 20 percent of the target consumers to begin to "like" or have good feelings toward Cable & Wireless's offerings. This can be done by offering good customer testimonials as well as by showing competitive information showing Cable & Wireless in a good light.

c. Persuade 10 percent of the target market to purchase Internet service from Cable & Wireless. Given the fact that Internet service is categorized as a thinker product in which customers often read up on the product/service before buying, this number is understandably low for the first 4 months.

Second and third 4 months

As Table A-1 shows, we recommend that the company induce more prospective clients to purchase the company's service in the later months. This is based on the assumption that we have educated these clients regarding the benefits of Cable & Wireless's Internet service. We suggest that we continue to educate the target market regarding the company's offerings.

3. *Tactics:* Cable & Wireless is currently engaging in the following marketing communication programs:

   - Advertising: Cable & Wireless advertises in business magazines, trade magazines, and newspapers. They also have radio commercials and newspaper advertisements in major cities across the United States.
   - Direct marketing: The company conducts a direct-mailing campaign.
   - Reseller support: Companies will often purchase a large quantity of dial-up accounts from Cable & Wireless. These companies will then turn around and resell this service for a profit. Cable & Wireless will often provide training for these companies (emphasizing the power of the Cable & Wireless backbone and equipment used). These companies participate in joint or cooperative advertising. Finally, Cable & Wireless participates in trade shows. The clientele of these trade shows are typically both end users and resellers. ISPcon is a trade show geared to Tier II ISPs. These ISPs typically purchase large amounts of bandwidth from Cable & Wireless.
   - Public relations: Cable & Wireless often sends out press releases. For example, in early 2000, a joint press release was sent out announcing that Nortel agreed to help Cable & Wireless implement a global optical network.
   - Word-of-mouth communications: Cable & Wireless attempts to develop good referrals from existing customers.

   Based on the systems model of IMC, it seems that the company is using the right mix of marketing communications tools to achieve the maximum amount of brand awareness and learning possible.

4. *Allocate resources:* As mentioned several times, the interviews did not result in knowing how resources are allocated at the three levels: corporate, marketing, and marketing communications levels. As suggested by the IMC systems model, it is recommended that marketing managers at Cable & Wireless allocate resources by following these steps:

   - Determine the corporate objectives: The corporate objectives are an increase in market share (aligned with the growth strategy).
   - Determine corporate mix to achieve stated objectives: The corporate mix should emphasize engineering, R&D, and marketing.
   - Determine the marketing strategy to achieve the stated objective: The marketing strategy should be *differentiation by product attribute* and *differentiation by intangible factor*. This will enable us to differentiate ourselves from the competition and allow us to increase our market share (grow).

- Determine the marketing objective that best emphasizes the marketing strategy: There are essentially two marketing objectives. The first is to build an association of high backbone performance, a product attribute, with Cable & Wireless in the minds of the target market. The second objective is to build an association of Cable & Wireless and superior customer service in the mind of the target market.
- Determine the marketing communications strategy to achieve the marketing objective: The best marketing communications strategy is the thinker strategy. This is necessary given the long duration of Internet service contracts, the complexity of the offerings, and the rational nature of Internet service offerings (mostly based on data, not feelings).
- Determine the marketing communications objectives that best emphasize the marketing communications strategy: The main objective is to get customers to learn about Cable & Wireless's offerings. Although the ultimate goal is to actually sell Internet service, the main focus is on this learning aspect.
- Determine the marketing communications mix to achieve the marketing communications objectives: It appears that the stated strategic mix (including print advertising, trade shows, reseller training, WOM communications, press releases, and reference accounts) is the best strategy for Cable & Wireless.
- Determine the cost of implementing the selected marketing communications programs: Most of these items are relatively inexpensive in comparison with mass media advertising, such as national television commercials. This is due to the fact that Cable & Wireless views the mass media advertising as geared toward the households, not business firms.
- Adjust the marketing communications budget as a function of monitoring/control and analysis/planning.

5. *Monitor and control:* Since no formal marketing communications objectives were defined, the monitoring-and-control function at Cable & Wireless seems defunct. We recommend that the company measure marketing communications performance once before the launch of the marketing communications campaign and another time a year later. This is necessary to evaluate the effectiveness of the campaign and take corrective action if needed.

A-5 Final Comments

It is our hope that this assessment of the company based on the IMC systems model can help the company plan and implement a more effective marketing communications campaign. We feel that Cable & Wireless needs to place more emphasis on marketing, especially marketing communications. The marketing department should grow in size and have sufficient resources to implement the company's corporate, marketing, and communications strategies.

Bibliography
The Cable & Wireless Marketing Department.
"IntraWorks," Cable & Wireless's internal website.
Sirgy, M. Joseph. *Integrated Marketing Communications: A Systems Approach.* Upper Saddle River, NJ: Prentice Hall, 1998.

UnitedHealth Group Roanoke Call Center: IMC Plan

Case B

B-1 Overview of UnitedHealth Group (UHG)

UnitedHealth Group (UHG) is a *Fortune* 100 company founded in 1977. It is the leading supplier of medical insurance services in the United States. In 2003 UHG had recorded revenues of over $2.6 billion. UHG has been involved in acquisitions of other health-care providers. Since 1995, UHG has ranked first or second in *Fortune* magazine's annual survey of the most admired health-care companies in America.

One of UHG's missions is to help people both by providing choices for a broad range of health care and by facilitating access to these services and resources. Another of UHG's missions is to help simplify health care and provide safe, fact-based medicine.

UHG focuses on offering four main classes of health-care products and services:

- Employer business services: Health plans for national employers
- Network-based health-care services: Health and wellness plans
- Knowledge and information services
- Specialized care services: Unique sets of health and wellness services provided by independent businesses

UHG prides itself in providing the best quality health-care services. This culture translates into recruiting the best and compensating employees for good performance. Employees at UHG cannot get in, move up, or stay in unless they are providing significant measurable value.

UHG has many divisions of health-care products and services. This case focuses specifically on Ovations. Ovations provides network-based health-care services to a very specific market: mature Americans ages 50 and up. This market is one of the major consumers of health care within the United States and is quickly growing in size as the baby boomers come of age.

Over the years, Ovations has developed a strong relationship with AARP and offers many products endorsed by AARP. Within Ovations, a specific subdivision—the call center facility in Roanoke, Virginia—is the focus of this case. Somewhat new as a recent acquisition by UHG (acquired in mid-2001), the call center is facing the very challenge of being heard within the company. To be successful and cost-effective, the Roanoke Call Center needs to promote its service to establish a good customer base (customers within the UHG network).

Because of the very complex nature of health-care services provided by UHG (information, insurance, etc.), there seems to be a need to help patients navigate

Source: This case was adapted from a report developed by Jeremy Scott Barnes in partial fulfillment of a graduate-level course (Promotion Strategy) taught by Joe Sirgy during the spring semester of 2004.

through the huge mosaic of products and services and, therefore, the need for a call center. Through its acquisition of the AARP Pharmacy Services in 2001, UHG also picked up the Roanoke Call Center as part of the acquisition. The challenge now comes for the Roanoke Call Center to educate its own company on the value it can provide and capture a market that is already satisfied by strong external competitors.

B-2 Overview of the Roanoke Call Center

The Roanoke Call Center was one subdivision of Retired Persons Services (RPS), Inc., until the summer of 2001. RPS was a nonprofit organization whose main products were the AARP Pharmacy Service and the AARP-endorsed Member Choice prescription discount card. RPS had a fulfillment center in Horsham, Pennsylvania; corporate headquarters in Alexandria, Virginia; and the telephone service center in Roanoke, Virginia. RPS's primary customers were Americans ages 50 and up, including AARP members.

RPS's culture had good and bad aspects. With respect to its negative aspects, RPS was besieged by weak management due to nepotism and internal politics. Financial performance was alarmingly low by nonprofit standards. Customer service representatives (CSRs) had no leadership and did whatever they felt necessary to appease customers. For example, to appease customers with high prescription bills, the company provided them with credit of up to $1,000 and payment plans of $5 a month. Many of its employees were either older Americans themselves or stayed with the company solely because they enjoyed interacting with customers (who were essentially their "peer group"). This was good because these CSRs were considered very sensitive to patients' special needs. However, the patience, sensitivity, and empathy of the CSRs were the only strong positive aspect of RPS before 2001.

RPS, suffering from poor management and dwindling finances, faced liquidation, and soon thereafter the company was purchased by UHG; more specifically, UHG's division Ovations acquired RPS. Immediately after purchase, UHG began to fuse its "bring in the best" and "pay for performance" philosophy into RSP. RSP was restructured and the leadership team revamped. As mentioned in the previous section, it was not long before the Roanoke leadership team discovered that there were many opportunities within UHG to bring customer service back in-house. UHG is so large with so many divisions and employees (over 30,000 in the United States) that it is essentially a market of its own. The key question Roanoke has now is, How do we reach and promote to this market?

B-3 The Call Center Environment

Customer contact centers in the United States can be described in terms of price, quality, technology and reporting, and human resources.

B-3a Price

Typically, call center services charge their clients a per-hour charge and may offer a choice of per-CSR-hour charge or a per-telephone-minute charge based on whether dedicated or semidedicated representatives are requested (see Section B-3b, "Quality"). Examples of major call center provider prices are shown in Table B-1.

B-3b Quality

Quality is very important to many clients. The manner in which a customer is treated by a customer contact center reflects directly on the client. Quality may mean consistency of service, politeness, speed, and knowledgeable CSRs. Most call centers

TABLE B-1　Call Center Provider Prices

Company	Price Per Call (Approximate)
Affina	From $0.72 to $0.80 per minute
Americall	$0.75 per minute
Call Solutions	From $0.68 to $1.00 per minute
The Connextion	From $0.72 to $1.10 per minute
The Hartford	$0.78 per minute
UHG Roanoke Call Center	From $0.72 to $0.82 per minute

TABLE B-2　Descriptions of Call Center Service-Level Metrics

Measure of Quality	Description
Percentage of calls answered within x seconds	Indicator of how long customers have to remain on hold to speak to a CSR. Higher percentages result in higher satisfaction.
Average speed of answer (ASA)	Indicates how long a customer must wait on average to speak to a CSR. Higher ASA results in lower satisfaction.
Abandonment rate	This is the percentage of calls in which the customer hangs up before a CSR picks up. Higher abandonment results in lower satisfaction.
Blocked calls	When a call center is extremely busy, it is sometimes better customer service to give a customer a busy signal—despite being annoying—than to let them wait on hold for extended periods of time. These are blocked calls. A higher amount of blocked calls results in lower satisfaction.
Occupancy	The percentage of time CSRs spend speaking to customers. Occupancy is a double-edged sword. When occupancy is too low, CSRs become bored, become rusty on skills, and are apathetic to customers. When occupancy is too high, CSRs burn out and become apathetic to customers. Typical acceptable occupancies are between 75 and 90 percent.

allow the client to define and specify quality standards such as *call center service* and *call monitoring*:

- *Call center service* consists of five major metrics: percentage of calls answered within x seconds, average speed of answer (ASA), abandonment rate, blocked calls, and CSR occupancy (see Table B-2 for details). Typically the client can specify what service is acceptable. The higher the service level, the more CSRs are needed and, thus, the higher the price.
- *Call monitoring* is the second major dimension of quality. Most call center facilities have a minimum number of quality monitoring sessions performed on each CSR per month. CSR calls are usually rated in terms of politeness; professionalism; communication skills; accuracy of information; use of technology and appropriate reference material; and, in the case of sales, technique. Furthermore, it is typical to allow clients remote access to monitor calls and computer screens. Some call centers outsource the quality monitoring service to a third party (e.g., management consulting firm). This allows for a more objective assessment of quality.

The Roanoke Call Center is considered to provide quality service, especially in the area of customer sensitivity. Coaches (supervisors) monitor CSRs regularly and provide feedback. In addition to coach monitoring, there is a third objective party that monitors CSRs—the quality assurance team. The quality assurance team monitors all CSRs a minimum of twice per month and provides management with feedback. This feedback is used to evaluate CSRs' performance.

With respect to Roanoke's quality monitoring, call quality is measured on a 100-point scale, 75 being acceptable quality and 90 and up being outstanding. A CSR can lose as many as 10 points for missing something as simple as "thank you for calling." Other sites within UHG report quality scores in excess of 95 percent regularly, while Roanoke reports scores as low as 78 percent. This may be due to the high quality expectations for the Roanoke center.

B-3c Technology and Reporting

By *technology*, we do not mean the order-entry system or customer service systems used by the CSR when serving a client's customer because access to this software is usually provided by the client, not the call center itself. The technology we are referring to involves the following: the phone system, auto-attendants, interactive voice response (IVR) systems, computer-telephony integration (CTI) technology, knowledge-base software, "front-end" call software, customer survey software, scheduling/workforce management software, quality assurance hardware/software, and computer-based training (CBT). A brief review of these items and how Roanoke compares to the industry follows.

- *The phone system:* An effective call center has a robust phone system allowing for appropriate routing, tracking, and control of calls. Roanoke currently operates on an older phone system, but it is not that far behind on the technology curve.

- *Auto-attendants and interactive voice response systems:* Auto-attendants answer the telephone, greet customers, present them with a set of options to press on their touch-tone phone, and route calls to the appropriate team of CSRs based on the caller selection. An interactive voice response (IVR) system actually *replaces* a CSR for simple functions such as placing an order, checking the status of an order, paying a bill with a credit card, and so on. An IVR system actually connects to any order management (or customer service) system, thus allowing callers to interact with the system through voice response (or through touch-tone dialing). Roanoke has a number of adequate auto-attendants as well as a good IVR system. However, the IVR system is somewhat antiquated in that it is incapable of communicating with any current client systems without some significant programming, which makes this system obsolete (it is currently not used). Not being able to use the center's IVR system places an extra burden on the CSRs. However, this situation does not seem to be a significant problem with most of the callers who are 50 or more years old; these callers prefer not to speak to a machine or are sometimes not able to do so effectively.

- *Computer-telephony integration technology:* Computer-telephony integration (CTI) technology allows telephone information (time of call, length of call, phone number origination, which 800 number was dialed) to be delivered to any active order management or customer service system instantly. This technology provides valuable information to clients about why customers call, when they call, what for, and how long each call type takes. Roanoke lacks good CTI technology.

- *Knowledge-base and "front-end" software:* Knowledge-base software is very simply an online reference tool that allows CSRs to look up information when needed. Roanoke currently has adequate knowledge-base software. Many call center service providers (e.g., Call Solutions) have software available that is typically placed on the "front end" of other order management and customer service software packages to help the CSRs. Roanoke does not have the resources to build the front-end software. However, the lack of this front-end software does not seem to be a problem because Roanoke's CSRs seem to be able to learn and manage multiple software packages.

- *Customer survey software:* Some call centers tend to conduct customer surveys regularly and employ special software to do so. Customer survey technology asks the caller if he or she would like to take a survey following the call. The

TABLE B-3 Roanoke's Technology Resources

Technology Component	Roanoke Compared to Competition	Importance to Clients
Phone system	Strong	High
Auto-attendant	Comparable	Medium
IVR	Weak	High
CTI	Very weak	Medium
Knowledge-base	Strong	Medium
"Front-end" support	Very weak	Medium
Customer survey	Very weak	Low (trending to high)
Workforce management	Very strong	Medium
Quality monitoring	Very weak	High
CBT	Comparable	Medium

CSR is unaware of this because it is conducted automatically after the CSR hangs up. Thus, the customer can evaluate the service he or she was just provided. Roanoke does not conduct customer surveys because it does not have this technology.

- *Workforce management software:* This is a software package that the management of a call center can use to forecast call volume, determine staffing and schedules necessary to meet service levels, and monitor CSR adherence to these schedules. The Roanoke center has this technology and it uses it effectively.
- *Quality assurance:* Some software packages (e.g., *Witness, e-Talk*) are designed to record all calls and all CSR screens at all times. This technology allows supervisors, clients, and quality assurance teams to check calls made any time in the past. It is used as a feedback tool to allow CSRs to review their own performance. The Roanoke center lacks a quality assurance technology.
- *Computer-based training:* Computer-based training (CBT) for CSRs is becoming an industry standard. This technology allows CSRs, at their stations, to improve their skills during down times. Roanoke has a CBT system and was considering updating the system by the end of 2004.

Table B-3 provides a brief review of Roanoke's technology resources.

B-3d Human Resources

Human resources at the Roanoke center is described in relation to quality of CSRs, use of dedicated versus nondedicated CSRs, and pool of talent in the area.

- *Quality of CSRs:* The hiring and firing practices of the call center are reflected in the quality of CSRs. The process includes proper screening, background checks, pre-established minimum requirements for employment, and management of poorly performing CSRs. Roanoke's employment practices are those of UHG's, which reflect the "bring in the best" and "pay for performance" philosophy. The Roanoke center does not consider a candidate who does not have at least a year of call center experience. UHG's pay starts out as competitive for the area; and only high-performing employees receive pay increases, bonuses, and other awards. The result is that the Roanoke center has a good record of recruiting good employees and paying them well to retain them. As previously mentioned, the very culture of the Roanoke center prompts CSRs to be sensitive and caring to older Americans (most of the callers).
- *Dedicated versus nondedicated CSRs:* When a client requests dedicated CSRs, these CSRs take calls for that client *only* and do not serve other clients of the

call center. This typically leads to a very specialized CSR with a specific focus, which translates into higher quality. Nondedicated CSRs answer telephone calls for multiple clients and use multiple software packages. Nondedicated CSRs are more cost-effective, but if the CSR is not very experienced or a not good at multitasking, quality can suffer. The Roanoke center typically provides dedicated CSRs unless there is an opportunity for synergy within UHG. For example, a CSR that sells a discount prescription card can also offer AARP catalog items based on customer needs.

- *Talent pool:* The location of any call center must have an appropriate pool of skilled CSRs. The Roanoke metropolitan area has a large population and many call center facilities—Wachovia, Orvis, Matria, Miss Utility, and Allstate, to name a few. Thus, the area has a sufficient talent pool. The Roanoke center has little difficulty maintaining a quality staff of experienced CSRs.

In this section, we have provided you with background information about the industry of call center services and how the Roanoke center compares. Now, with this background, we apply the IMC systems model to articulate an IMC plan.

B-4 The Corporate Plan

In the case of the UHG Roanoke Call Center, the different levels of the IMC plan are specific to the Roanoke center strategic business unit (SBU), not UHG in its entirety. The first question to consider is, What is the appropriate strategy for the Roanoke Call Center? Some key themes kept recurring as UHG, the Roanoke center, and the call center industry were examined. Many of these themes stressed the importance of market size—and not just for lowering costs through economies of scale.

Let us first focus on the UHG corporate mission and then trickle down to the Roanoke Call Center subdivision. UHG's mission is to simplify health care and facilitate access to health-care resources. Roanoke can help accomplish this by integrating different divisions into a single contact center. Here, different programs and services can be effectively communicated to patients and appropriate referrals can be made. Routing more customer service through UHG's in-house call center is less expensive than outsourcing. Thus, the Roanoke center has the potential to make a significant contribution to UHG's mission. The Roanoke center welcomes more business. More call volume decreases per-minute costs making it more competitive than other call centers. Larger call volume and more clients allow the Roanoke center to grow and invest in newer technology.

Now let us examine the call center using the BCG matrix and multifactor portfolio mode. First, we would identify the Roanoke center as a "problem child" in the BCG matrix. Roanoke's share of UHG's market for call center services is very low, and the potential for growth is very high. In this environment, the BCG matrix would prescribe a growth strategy to possibly move Roanoke to the next step in the cycle, a "star."

The multifactor portfolio model also points to a growth strategy. The appeal of capturing UHG's internal market is attractive. There are many benefits to growing for both the Roanoke center and UHG. Roanoke has been steadily growing since its last downsizing in 2003, including its capture of a new and very high-profile client (the Medicare-endorsed drug plan). Roanoke's performance has been strong in the past decade finding efficiencies, reducing costs, improving quality, and finding new customers. This would place Roanoke in the medium to high range of the business strength dimension. The multifactor portfolio model prescribes an investment or growth strategy for Roanoke.

Thus, the corporate strategy for 2004–2005 will be *growth*. Deciding on such a strategy should guide the Roanoke center to place much importance on educating and marketing the Roanoke center services to internal clients. With respect to corporate objectives, a challenging yet attainable objective by year-end 2005 would be to "in-source" two UHG service center services to the Roanoke site.

After a thorough analysis of the environment and goals of both UHG and the Roanoke Call Center, the corporate plan can be described as follows:

> To take advantage of customer service synergy among different UHG divisions and improve patient access to health care, the Roanoke Call Center will focus on growing its UHG clientele.
>
> The current objectives are to
> - increase the Roanoke center's UHG clientele count by two in one year and
> - increase inbound call minutes by 75 percent in one year.
>
> To accomplish these objectives at the Roanoke center, a marketing plan is needed. The marketing plan should address how a marketing program can be developed to attain the stated corporate objectives.

B-5 The Marketing Plan

The next step in the IMC process is to determine the appropriate marketing strategy and objectives to achieve the corporate growth objectives. After reviewing the environment for call center services and background on the Roanoke center, we find a few alternative strategies and tactics that could be used to market Roanoke's services. Using a mix of messages may confuse clientele about what value the Roanoke center has to offer and result in slow growth. To ensure success and faster results, a clear and consistent message must be communicated to potential clientele. Establishing the Roanoke center as superior on some dimension in comparison to other call centers is a possible strategy. Many UHG divisions currently outsource services to other centers and are satisfied with the services received. Managers of those UHG divisions may feel committed to maintaining their relationships with their own call centers. A marketing communications campaign designed to communicate the fact that the Roanoke center is superior on some dimension may be the key to switching.

First, let us see if we can rule out certain strategies. We begin by examining the price-focus strategy. The importance of price per minute in the call center industry has already been discussed. For many clients, it is the only decision criterion, especially for clients with short-term needs. Lower price could be a good strategy for capturing more internal business. However, as previously discussed, the Roanoke center is *not* a cost leader at this time. With additional business, the Roanoke center may be able to afford to lower its price, but until then attempting to position the center as a cost leader is not likely to be effective. Therefore, we rule out this strategy.

We should also rule out the place-focus strategy because we do not believe that clients are likely to contract with call centers strictly based on location. These call centers can operate from any geographic location.

With respect to a product-focus strategy, we need to analyze certain "product" attributes before deciding on whether a product-focus strategy may be effective. After reviewing Roanoke's strengths and weaknesses (in comparison to other call centers), we determine that quality, human resources, and service to the elderly are the three major strengths that can be used in a marketing communications campaign to differentiate the Roanoke center from other call centers.

The Roanoke center is proud of its high quality; however, there are obstacles here. Quality is already reported internally to UHG and, as detailed earlier, "appears" less than satisfactory. The Roanoke center has no consistent name, brand, or identity at this point. A name would need to be established before an image could be established. Establishing a brand name should be done in a manner consistent with developing a "quality image" for the center. The problems associated with quality also apply to human resources.

Historically, the Roanoke center has focused on two specific customer segments: the health-care industry and customers ages 50 and up. The service its CSRs provide has always been focused on quality, empathetic communication to those in need of health care, especially elderly people.

In contrast, a customer-focus strategy requires that the Roanoke center position itself to serving the needs of UHG and its various divisions—and only UHG. Therefore, the center's strategy of growth should be not only the health-care industry but also UHG itself. The center is well equipped and well skilled to serve health-care patients for UHG. This strategy would combine the best of a quality focus, an HR focus, and a focus on partnership within UHG to serve a common mission—UHG's mission.

Therefore, our marketing strategy is to promote the image that Roanoke is the *key* to facilitating quality patient access to UHG's health-care programs and services through consolidation and synergy of service centers, which is an integral part of UHG's corporate mission. This strategy would position Roanoke not as a general service center but as *UHG's* service center. Communications should focus on quality, economies of scale, and synergies that can be achieved by using UHG's call center.

To do this, the virtually unknown Roanoke center must create a name for itself and educate UHG executives and other employees about what that name means. Developing brand knowledge is key to success.

Based on this marketing analysis, we determine that the marketing strategy for 2005 will be as follows:

To promote growth (increase the Roanoke center's UHG clientele count by two in one year and increase inbound call minutes by 75 percent in one year), the Roanoke center should position itself as the health-care service center specifically developed and operated for and by UHG. As such, the center should

- increase brand awareness to 85 percent in one year, and
- increase brand knowledge to 50 percent in one year.

B-6 The Marketing Communications Plan

The next step in developing the IMC plan for the Roanoke center is to identify strategies, objectives, and tactics at the marketing communications level. Remember that marketing objectives call for an aggressive marketing communications campaign directed to UHG's executives and other employees to enhance brand awareness and educate them about the Roanoke center as a service center designed to support UHG's overall mission. Specifically, it has been established that the Roanoke center's strategy is to grow its internal clientele by positioning itself as a health-care service center specifically designed and operated for and by UHG. Brand awareness and knowledge must increase within UHG through a strong and clear communications strategy.

To establish the center's image, the center's brand name and its strengths must be communicated to UHG's executives and other employees multiple times through different communication media. Establishing an effective brand name for the Roanoke center is the first step. This task can be completed by assembling a management team comprised of managers from the Roanoke center and UHG. A logo has to be identified through this effort. An example of a brand name may be *United TeleService*. This brand name is comparable to the strong and conservative brand names UHG is known for (UnitedHealthcare, Ingenix, Uniprise, Americhoice). The brand name also plays on words: "United" as in "UHG" and "United" as in its mission of providing synergistic service for UHG clients. The logo could, for example, have the same leaf-embossed "*v*" in service as its parent subsidiary Ovations and display "United" in the traditional, larger-font blue and "TeleService" in the soft green, both referencing its roots.

Neither an informative nor a self-satisfaction strategy would be appropriate and easy to execute for United Teleservice (UTS). An informative strategy would force us to focus on specific attributes of UTS's service, which would be inconsistent with the selected marketing strategy. Informing UHG's executives and other employees about Roanoke's strengths in terms of quality, HR, and its effectiveness in dealing with elderly people may be good but not good enough to cause brand switching. A self-satisfaction strategy would be difficult to execute as potential clients have to use UTS on a trial basis first. This is not possible under the current circumstances.

We believe that the most appropriate marketing communications strategy is the affective approach. An affective strategy should be successful in generating a high level of brand awareness and knowledge. The goal of an affective strategy is to evoke a strong feeling of liking for a specific brand as well as creating optimal brand awareness among potential clientele. The purpose is to push clients through the process of "*feel → think → do*" or "*become aware and feel good → explore the opportunity → partner.*"

An affective message has to focus on evoking positive feelings of togetherness, wholeness, unity, and integration. That message has to be communicated to UHG's executives and other employees through broadcast media, press releases, and word-of-mouth communications. Of course, in this particular case, the customer is internal; thus, broadcast media and press releases would be inappropriate. However, the purpose is to select media that have a broad reach within UHG providing maximum exposure to the message. As such, UHG's Intranet ("Frontier") is an excellent place for executives within UHG to be exposed to UTS's message.

Currently, the Roanoke Call Center does not have its own home page. Other divisions within UHG provide regular information on leadership, performance, and product offerings. The first step to more exposure would be to arrange for a UTS website to be constructed and updated regularly with positive results and leadership quotes. This site should also have contact instructions to request more information. To bring internal people to the site, some information needs to be posted on Frontier's home page. The center's current high-profile, Medicare-endorsed card program is an excellent internal press release opportunity to expose UHG's executives to UTS's message with more information only a click away.

Word-of-mouth communication is also an important component for growth within UHG. Similar to most large companies, UHG is no exception to rampant politics from within. To stimulate word-of-mouth communications, UTS should ensure that current internal clients are satisfied. These clients are then asked to speak on behalf of UTS to other UHG executives, generating positive "buzz" about UTS. Client satisfaction can be enhanced by conducting a satisfaction survey to determine what current clients' opinions are of the Roanoke center in an attempt to increase satisfaction and decrease dissatisfaction. Ensuring that key clients and corporate players such as the *CEO of Consumer Health Products*, the *CFO of Pharmacy Solutions*, the *Senior Project Manager*, and the *CEO of Claims Services* are supportive of UTS should be an important step in that direction.

Another advertising medium that can be used to generate awareness and knowledge is direct mail of marketing material to key executives—players within UHG who use call center services. These executives can easily be identified through an internal chain of contacts. The direct mail should not be a full disclosure of UTS services but a simple promotion tool to create awareness and a positive feeling toward UTS. It should be a simple postcard with UHG's logo addressed to specific executives, with an attention-grabbing image and a brief message reflecting unity within UHG and contact information. Humor is typically appropriate for grabbing attention as well as developing liking (or positive feelings) for the brand and could be part of this communication medium. Three to four different versions should be developed and mailed in regular intervals to ensure repeated exposure.

The next step is to have more informative material available such as a booklet or pamphlet describing in more detail the leadership, HR, quality, speed of setup, and performance results. Contact information in this pamphlet should be the *VP of Customer Service* to ensure that interested clients can schedule a visit and proper sales presentation can be arranged. A sales presentation should also be designed, examined, consistently revamped, and rehearsed for these occasions. These steps are to ensure that UTS is prepared to assist potential clients who have left the "*feel*" stage and moved to "*think*." The goal, of course, is to move the client to "*do*" or partner with UTS.

To measure the ongoing success of the marketing communications strategy, short surveys can be sent to UHG employees via email (or calls) asking for a response. These surveys can measure brand awareness and attitude before and after the launch of the marketing communications campaign.

In sum, the marketing communications strategy for 2004–2005 is as follows:

To promote growth (increase the Roanoke center's UHG clientele count by two in one year and increase inbound call minutes by 75 percent in one year), the Roanoke center will position itself as the health-care service center specifically developed and operated for and by UHG. As such, the center will increase brand awareness to 85 percent and increase brand knowledge to 50 percent in one year. This is to be accomplished by providing a new identity and displaying a positive image for that identity using multiple communications media. Specifically, UTS should

- increase brand liking to 40 percent in one year.

Bibliography

Information available from http://www.UnitedHealthGroup.com.

Network Direct, Inc. "Marketing outsourcing options for UnitedHealth Group, 2003."

Pate, Cheryl. Interview and consultation, April 2004.

Sirgy, M. Joseph *Integrated Marketing Communications: A Systems Approach*. Upper Saddle River, NJ: Prentice Hall, 1998.

Hancock Rack's IMC Plan

Case C

C-1 Background

In this section, we describe the company mission statement, the company's history, the industry, growth, customers and channel members, competition, opportunities, and current marketing communications programs.

C-1a Company Mission Statement

Hancock Rack's mission is to become the largest structural rack manufacturer on the East Coast of the United States while providing significant value for its customers. The company aims to satisfy its customers with top-quality racks and first-class customer service.

C-1b History

Hancock Rack is a small business located in Salem, Virginia. It is one of several steel product–producing subsidiaries of Roanoke Electric Steel (Stock Quote: RES). Hancock Rack began operation in the fall of 1994 as a side operation of Hancock Joist. It was created to help the parent company diversify to avoid the classic construction cycles. The idea was that Hancock Rack could fill in when the joist business was not performing well, and vice versa. Hancock Rack adapted many of the Hancock Joist operating procedures, and the two divisions actually share employees and resources to this day. Both Hancock Rack and Hancock Joist rely heavily on Roanoke Electric Steel for their raw materials. Hancock Rack makes structural racks.

C-1c The Rack Industry

The rack market revolves around two types of steel products: structural rack and roll-form rack. A structural rack is considered heavy duty and is used in warehouses where the rack system is subjected to forklift abuse or extremely heavy loads. In contrast, a roll-form rack is a lighter-duty rack system that can be easily damaged by a forklift. It can be used in most warehouse applications, too. A roll-form rack dominates the retail rack environments of stores like Lowe's, Home Depot, Sam's Club, and so on.

A roll-form rack is approximately two-thirds the cost and weight of a structural rack. Customers are motivated to buy structural racks when they believe that over the long term structural racks are easier to maintain; they do not have to replace rack components as often.

Source: This case was adapted from a report developed by Luke Pugh in partial fulfillment of a graduate-level course (Promotion Strategy) taught by Joe Sirgy during the spring semester of 2004 at Virginia Tech.

The rack industry has an association, the Rack Manufacturers Institute (RMI). The RMI is composed of approximately thirty member companies that meet twice a year. The RMI collects data about the market environment and provides suggested best practices for the design and implementation of rack systems.

The RMI estimates that the roll-form rack makes up 75 percent of the total rack market at $1 billion dollars annually. The remaining 25 percent involves structural racks. Note that Hancock Rack makes structural racks only, not roll-form racks.

C-1d Growth

Hancock Rack started operation in 1994 with approximately twenty shop employees and two office employees. Annual revenues in 1994 were in the range of $700,000 to $750,000. Since then, Hancock Rack has grown to approximately 150 shop employees and ten office employees. Its current annual revenues are approximately $3 million. The revenue growth rate over the past 10 years has been approximately 14.86 percent. Its current market share of the total rack market (structural and roll form) is 0.5 percent. Its current market share of the structural rack line is 2 percent.

Management believes that the annual growth rate of the industry is at least 50 percent during the first few start-up years with growth leveling off after it is established. Therefore, management is convinced that the company has not lived up to its full potential.

C-1e Customers and Channel Members

The rack industry is composed of three types of customers: dealers, distributors, and end users/consulting groups. Dealers typically are small businesses, consisting of four to five salesmen, focusing on a regional market (20 to 100 square miles). They have much knowledge of the local environment. Dealers typically handle projects ranging from $1,000 to $50,000. They sell unbundled products and provide service agreements with the end user. Dealers are not brand loyal and typically will shop around for low prices.

In contrast, distributors tend to package the rack system with other aspects of warehouse management tools such as forklifts, mezzanines, or conveyors. Each state usually has five or six large distributors. Some states, such as Ohio and Pennsylvania, have more. Each distributor usually has a preferred line of forklifts and rack systems. They are typically involved in large contracts ($50,000 to $1,000,000). Rack firms develop strong relationships with distributors. Hancock Rack maintains relationships with at least one distributor in each of the major East Coast states (Florida, Georgia, North Carolina, Ohio, Pennsylvania, New York, and New Jersey).

Finally, end users buy racks directly from rack manufacturing firms directly with the assistance of consulting firms. Contracts tend to be in the $500,000 to $5,000,000 price range. The goal of direct purchase is to cut out the middlemen (i.e., dealers and distributors). End users hire a consulting firm to help them with the process. Some of Hancock Rack's end users include GE, Publix, Sysco, and Kroger. End users are typically brand loyal.

C-1f Competition

The rack market is very competitive and crowded. Many buyers consider racks as a commodity product and make purchase decisions mostly on price. With low barriers to entry, new entrants can commence production in 6 months with as little as a million dollars of investment. Thus, supply outweighs demand.

The largest rack manufacturers are Interlake, which is a roll-form manufacturer, and Frazier, which produces mostly structural racks. Both companies have been established for well over 40 years and have several factories strategically located throughout the country. Both companies are several times the size of Hancock Rack and have automated robots to weld rack components. In addition, both companies engage in pricing wars in attempts to gain or maintain their market share.

C-1g Opportunities

Many industry analysts believe that most firms are guilty of late deliveries, poor product quality, and poor customer service. Hancock Rack gains most of the new customers who are fed up from being mistreated by Hancock Rack's competitors. The management at Hancock Rack believes that the company is known for its on-time delivery record, quality product and service, and low price.

The rack market is projected to grow roughly 3 to 5 percent a year. As such, the firm's management believes that there is a good opportunity to grow—at least proportionately to the overall growth of the market—by educating prospective customers about the company's strengths.

C-1h Current Marketing Communications Program

Like Hancock Joist, Hancock Rack does *not* engage in advertising, personal selling, direct marketing, cyber marketing, sales promotions, or public relations campaigns. Prospective customers come to Hancock Rack by word of mouth; old customers come back for more business. Hancock Rack management realizes that the growth of the business can be achieved with an effective marketing program and an aggressive promotion campaign.

C-2 The IMC Model and Its Application to Hancock Rack

An effective IMC plan should capture strategy, objectives, tactics, analysis and planning, budgeting, and monitoring and control at the corporate, marketing, and marketing communications levels.

C-2a Strategy

Based on Hancock Rack's mission statement, the corporate strategy is to grow by providing customers with a quality product and good service. Other strategies (i.e., maintain position, harvest, innovation, and divestment) are not consistent with management views of the firm's strategic direction. The maintain-position strategy is not suitable because the firm does not have a large market share. The harvest strategy would not work because the business needs to expand before it gains economies of scale and generate high profits to "harvest." The innovation strategy is not effective because the product is essentially a commodity and there is very little room for innovation. The divestment strategy is in the opposite direction that Hancock Rack wants go as top management.

Following the systems approach to IMC, corporate growth strategy is the starting point of the IMC plan. The four marketing strategies to choose from are: product focus, price focus, place focus, and customer focus. The product-focus strategy highlights the differences between the firm's products and services and other competitors based on factors such as product attributes, intangible factors, product class, competitors, and country of origin. The price-focus strategy involves factors such as relative price and low price. The place-focus strategy involves factors such as brand-distributor tie-in and distributor serviceability. Finally, the customer-focus strategy involves factors such as customer lifestyle, customer benefits, and use of application.

An analysis of the firm's internal and external environments points to the possible effectiveness of a product-focus strategy. A small company such as Hancock Rack cannot compete strictly on low price. It does not have the economies of scale to allow it to be a cost leader. Other companies, such as Frazier or Interlake, are 10 to 20 times larger than Hancock Rack. Although the customer-focus strategy may be viable, it does not fit with the firm's mission statement. Once the firm is better established with sufficient market share, the firm may target specific customers (e.g., distributors) and attempt to cater to their specific needs. Hancock Rack has survived and prospered so far by providing on-time deliveries, quality products, and good customer service. These are the company's strengths; therefore, they should be used to differentiate the firm from its competitors to gain a competitive advantage.

At a marketing communications level, the four strategies to choose from are: informative (thinker), affective (feeler), habit formation (doer), and self-satisfaction (reactor). The informative or thinker strategy seems to be more suitable to business-to-business marketing in which customers buy a high-end product and usually evaluate alternatives. The affective or feeler strategy seeks to develop an emotional bond between the customer and product. The habit-formation or doer strategy is geared toward lower-priced items that are bought routinely over a short period. The self-satisfaction or reactor strategy is geared toward low-involvement products.

Hancock Rack's situation involves business-to-business marketing; as such, an informative strategy is likely to be most effective. This type of high-involvement purchase requires the buyer to evaluate alternatives carefully along criteria such as price, customer service, on-time deliveries, and product quality, among others.

C-2b Objectives

To develop an effective IMC plan, the planner should ensure that all objectives (across corporate, marketing, and marketing communications levels) are consistent with all corresponding strategies. At the corporate level, the strategy is to grow. Therefore, a proper objective is to build sales and market share. A reasonable goal would be to increase sales by 25 percent each year. Table C-1 shows desired levels of sales over a 10-year horizon.

At the marketing levels, the strategy is product focus, positioning the firm along factors such as product attributes and intangible factors. The attributes should be "weld quality," "craftsmanship," and "paint finish." These are the company's strengths. Most rack manufacturers try to produce as much product as possible—they focus on quantity not quality. The common results are sloppy welds with little penetration, components not constructed square, and sloppy paint jobs and drips. Hancock Rack pays attention to weld quality and craftsmanship. All of its welders are certified by the American Welding Society (AWS), and craftsmanship is high. Painting is done with a state-of-the-art powder coating process that produces a high-gloss enamel coating. The intangible factor is on-time delivery. Most customers like to have their product delivered when promised. Typically, larger rack manufacturers have poor on-time delivery records. This does not seem to be the case at Hancock Rack. Therefore, marketing objectives should focus on educating prospective customers with "weld quality," "craftsmanship," "paint finish," and "on-time deliveries."

At the marketing communications level, the most effective strategy is the informative or thinker strategy. The corresponding objectives are *learn* → *feel* → *do*. Over a period of a year, the firm should transition from brand learning to brand liking to

TABLE C-1 Desired Sales (Thousands of Dollars)

2004	2005	2006	2007	2008	2009	2010	2011	2012	2013	2014
$4,000	$5,000	$6,250	$7,813	$9,766	$12,207	$15,259	$19,073	$23,842	$29,802	$37,253

TABLE C-2	Marketing Communications Objectives		
Learn → Feel → Do	Brand Learning	Brand Liking	Brand Purchase
First 4 Months	80 percent	20 percent	10 percent
Second 4 Months	90 percent	50 percent	20 percent
Third 4 Months	95 percent	60 percent	50 percent

brand purchase. Prospective customers are essentially dealers, distributors, and end users (see Table C-2).

The firm should target 80 percent of the market with brand learning the first 4 months, then transition to 90 percent and 95 percent in subsequent months. Notice that these objectives emphasize the information aspect of the marketing communications campaign.

C-2c Tactics

To provide a consistent message, the firm must integrate tactics with strategies and objectives. At the corporate level, the strategy and its objective are to grow and increase market share, respectively. This can be accomplished by allocating more resources to the marketing function as well as to the R&D and engineering functions. Through marketing, the firm should target new geographic areas and prospective customers. The R&D and engineering functions should be devoted to process technology in the factory. The firm also should make the same quality product faster. Robotic welding and improved table jigs should be researched and developed and introduced into the production mix. Factory operations should be speeded up.

With respect to marketing tactics, the firm should spell out the meaning involved in the selected attributes and factors: "weld quality," "craftsmanship," "paint finish," and "on-time deliveries."

At the marketing communications level, the informative or thinker strategy can be implemented through advertising (mostly print), trade shows, and public relations. Advertising should focus on dealers, distributors, and end users. Research has shown that material-handling trade journals cover news-related items concerning racks, conveyors, and forklifts and are popular with prospective rack customers. These trade journals are usually published monthly with an assortment of relevant articles and an array of manufacturers' advertisements. The cost is about $5,000 for a full-page advertisement in one issue. A smaller advertisement can be purchased for $1,000. The two main trade journals are *Industrial Equipment* and *Material Handling*. During the first 4 months, the firm should run a full page advertisement in each issue to reach 80 percent of its target audience. The following 8 months, the firm should scale back and run smaller advertisements.

To support advertising, the firm should participate in material handling trade shows. There are two very popular shows in Chicago and Cleveland during February and April each year. Both shows typically last about 4 or 5 days. These shows are attended by a variety of manufacturers from the material handling industry including other major rack companies. The firm should set up a booth with product samples and literature at each event. The literature should emphasize quality and on-time delivery. The cost to participate in each trade show is approximately $20,000.

The firm also should build a sales force by hiring three new salespersons and placing them in strategic areas. Currently, the firm has only two salespersons who operate in Virginia, Ohio, and Pennsylvania. The new salespersons should be placed in Florida, Georgia, Texas, New York, New Jersey, Indiana, and Illinois. They should be able to travel to dealers, distributors, and end users in those states. They should also be able to take quotes and prepare bid packages.

TABLE C-3 IMC Annual Budget for 2005

Tactic				Cost
Advertising				
	Industrial equipment	Jan thru April (full page)	4 × $5,000	$ 20,000
		May thru December	8 × $1,000	$ 8,000
	Material handling	January thru April (full page)	4 × $5,000	$ 20,000
		May thru December	8 × $1,000	$ 8,000
			Subtotal	$ 56,000
Trade Shows				
	Chicago			$ 20,000
	Cleveland			$ 20,000
			Subtotal	$ 40,000
Personal Selling				
	Salesman #1			$ 75,000
	Salesman #2			$ 75,000
	Salesman #3 (new hire in 2005)			$ 50,000
	Salesman #4 (new hire in 2005)			$ 50,000
	Salesman #5 (new hire in 2005)			$ 50,000
			Subtotal	$300,000
			Grand Total	**$396,000**

C-2d Budgeting

To achieve the stated tactics, the firm should develop an IMC budget. Several methods are commonly used to budget: ratio-to-sales methods, previous-budget methods, competitive-parity methods, and objective-task methods. The firm should use the objective-task method. Table C-3 shows the cost breakdown of the IMC plan using the objective-task method.

To implement the stated marketing communications tactics, Hancock Rack should allocate approximately $396,000 for 2005. That amount is approximately 10 percent of total sales in 2004.

C-2e Monitoring and Control

Any system requires a feedback mechanism to ensure effective performance over time. Integrated marketing communications is no different. Steps must be taken to ensure that the objectives are measured to see if they are met. If the objectives are not met, the firm engages in corrective action. Corrective action may be in the form of changes or modifications in strategies, objectives, and tactics.

Bibliography

Hancock Rack.

Sirgy, M. Joseph. *Integrated Marketing Communications: A Systems Approach.* Upper Saddle River, NJ: Prentice Hall, 1998.

Glossary

A

absolute cost   The total amount of money needed to purchase advertising in certain media. The term *absolute cost* is used in contrast to *relative cost* in media planning. Media costs can be compared in relation to one another, and therefore media are selected in relation to their relative costs. However, certain media are selected or eliminated from consideration based on the total dollar cost needed for advertising because the total costs are too high and prohibitive in an absolute sense.

accelerated purchase   A sales promotion goal achieved when consumers or channel members purchase the product before the time they normally would have bought.

ad hoc approach   An attempt to integrate the disparate elements of marketing communications programs by arranging meetings with all the interested parties.

administrative complaint   In the event that a firm refuses to sign an FTC consent order, the FTC continues with an administrative complaint. This complaint entails a formal hearing held before an administrative law judge, and the judge makes a ruling after he or she hears testimony from the firms and the FTC.

advance dating   An arrangement by which the seller sets a specific future date when the terms of sale become applicable. For example, the order may be placed on January 5 and the goods shipped on January 10 but under the terms "2/10, net 30 as of May 1." In this case, the discount and net periods are calculated from May 1. Season dating is another name for terms of this kind.

advertising   One of the elements or tools of marketing communications for use in mass media, such as television, radio, newspaper, magazine, outdoor, transit, aerial, mobile billboards, specialty, directory, interactive, in-store, in-flight, movie theater, and videotape advertising.

advertising to children   A paid, mass-mediated attempt to persuade a certain audience, in this case, children.

advertising/display allowance   A form of trade promotion in which retailers are given a discount in exchange for either promoting the product in their own advertising or setting up a product display or both.

advocacy advertising   A type of advertising placed by businesses and other organizations that is intended to communicate a viewpoint about a controversial topic relating to the social, political, or economic environment.

affective (feeler) strategy   A marketing communications strategy that guides the marketing communications manager to elicit an affective response, a feeling that helps build a positive attitude toward the firm's brand. The focus here is on feelings, much more so than learning or inducing purchase.

affective brand attitude   A marketing communications goal that describes a desirable situation in which target consumers establish a favorable attitude toward a firm's brand. The attitude is based on an emotional response.

agent   In sales, a person who acts as a representative of a firm or individual. In retailing, a business unit that negotiates purchases, sales, or both but does not take title to the goods in which it deals; and a person agent—one who represents the principal (who, in the case of retailing, is the store or merchant) and who acts under authority, whether in buying or in bringing the principal into business relations with third parties. In global marketing, a company or individual that represents a company in a particular market. Normally an agent does not take title to goods.

aided-recall measures   Methods to capture what consumers remember about the advertisement, the brand name, and the benefits and costs of the brand by asking subjects to recall the information without giving them memory cues.

all-you-can-afford method   Budgeting method that is quite arbitrary and is based on the notion that a good marketing communications budget is as much as the firm can afford to spend.

analysis   The process of identifying factors that may assist the decision maker in selecting an effective strategy, setting objectives, determining tactics, and/or allocating resources. Once these factors are identified and specific information about the case in question is gathered (guided by the identified factors), then the decision maker is ready for planning. In other words, analysis assists the decision maker in planning.

area of dominant influence (ADI)   The geographic area over which a local television station holds domination. For example, a station from Chicago would have a dominant influence in northern Illinois until it came close to where station signals from another nearby city (e.g., Milwaukee)

Note: Some of these definitions are from the American Marketing Association (AMA) and are used with AMA's permission. [http://www.marketingpower.com/mg-dictionary.php]

dominated the area. Arbitron uses the ADI term, and Nielsen uses the DMA designation.

associative strength The strength of the association in memory between the product category and the brand.

attitude toward brand purchase A marketing communications goal that describes a desirable situation in which target consumers have established a positive attitude toward the act of purchasing the firm's brand.

attribute sensory modality The sensory component associated with information processing of a particular message. For example, an advertisement shown in a magazine is processed through the visual sense, and a radio commercial is processed through the auditory sense.

average quarter-hour (AQH) audience The number of people who are listening (tuned in) to a given program at a certain time. The measure is based on 15-minute segments (hence, the quarter hour). When this number is reported as a percentage of a given population, it becomes a *rating*.

B

barriers of entry Hurdles or obstacles for a firm to penetrate a given industry. Some industries have high barriers (e.g., aviation industry) while others have low barriers (e.g., local janitorial business).

Better Business Bureau (BBB) The Better Business Bureau, founded in 1912, is an organization based in the United States and Canada devoted to honest business. On its website, it lists its core services as: "Business Reliability Reports," "Dispute Resolution," "Truth-in-Advertising," "Consumer and Business Education," and "Charity Review."

blog A hybrid form of Internet communication that combines a column, diary, and directory. The term *blog* is short for "weblog" and refers to a frequently updated collection of short articles on various subjects with links to further resources.

bonus pack A special container, package, carton, or other holder in which the consumer is given more of the product for the same or perhaps even lower price per ounce or unit than in the regular container.

bounce-back coupon A coupon placed inside or outside of the product package that is redeemable for the next purchase of the same brand.

brand A name, term, design, symbol, or any other feature that identifies one seller's good or service as distinct from that of other sellers. The legal term for brand is *trademark*. A brand may identify one item, a family of items, or all items of that seller. If used for the firm as a whole, the preferred term is *trade name*.

brand acceptance A marketing communications goal that describes a desirable situation in which target consumers recognize the firm's brand as an acceptable choice for the product category.

brand association A marketing goal. The term is used interchangeably with terms such as *brand equity, brand image,* and *brand knowledge*. It describes a desirable situation in which target consumers associate the brand with desirable features, events, and/or people.

brand attitude A marketing communications objective; marketing communications managers not only try to educate target consumers about the brand itself; they also try to do so in such a way that the brand image will result in an overall liking toward the brand.

brand awareness objective A marketing communications goal. It describes a situation in which target consumers recognize or recall the brand name as related to a product category.

brand do objective The goal to induce a certain level of the target market to purchase (or at least to make plans to purchase) the product.

brand equity A marketing goal. The term is used interchangeably with terms such as *brand association, brand image,* and *brand knowledge*. It describes a desirable situation in which target consumers associate the brand with desirable features, events, and/or people.

brand feel objective The goal to achieve a certain level of positive attitude (affect, preference, or acceptance) toward the product. A statement reflecting this objective is: "We need to get the target consumers to develop a preference for our product."

brand identity Brand image. The perception of a brand in people's minds. The brand image is a mirror reflection (though perhaps inaccurate) of the brand personality or product being. It is what people believe about a brand—their thoughts, feelings, and expectations (AMA website: http://www.ama.org).

brand learn objective The goal to achieve a certain level of learning, knowledge, associations, image, and/or comprehension related to the product's benefits.

brand loyalty A marketing communications goal that describes a desirable situation in which target consumers feel psychologically committed to the firm's brand after purchase and use.

brand preference A marketing communications goal that describes a desirable situation in which target consumers recognize the firm's brand as preferable to competitor brands.

brand profit A goal that focuses on the financial bottom line; includes gross profit, net profit, cash flow, ROI, and so on.

brand purchase A marketing communications goal that describes a desirable situation in which target consumers have actually purchased the firm's brand.

brand recall A way to capture brand awareness that involves asking subjects about what they remember in relation to a brand in question.

brand recognition A way to capture brand awareness that involves exposing subjects to certain stimuli (e.g., an advertising slogan) and then a series of brand names. Subjects are then asked if they can recognize the correct brand name.

brand repeat objective The goal to achieve a certain level of purchases in a given period of time as a direct function of the campaign (repeat purchases, brand satisfaction, brand loyalty, brand commitment).

brand sales A goal that focuses on the financial bottom line; includes actual sales, market share, and so on.

brand satisfaction A marketing communications goal that describes a desirable situation in which target consumers feel satisfied with the firm's brand after purchase and use.

brand symbols Icons associated with a brand that make a reference to something else (person, object, or event).

brand trial A marketing communications goal. It describes a desirable situation in which target consumers have psychologically committed themselves to trying the firm's brand.

brand unity Brand consistency. How well the marketer has tied together and maintained all elements of the brand into a consistent and unified image in the mind of the consumer and target markets. This includes such things as marketing communications, promotions, product design, consumer promotions, imagery, and so on.

brand-as-an-animal-or-thing test A test that asks subjects to think of animals or animal characteristics that come to mind when thinking about a certain brand.

brand-as-a-person test A test that instructs subjects to select from a set of fifty personality-related words to describe the brand in question.

brand-listing procedure A method for capturing brand acceptance by asking respondents to indicate the brand they chose at the moment of purchase.

brand-user test A simple procedure in which subjects are asked to describe the typical brand user.

broadcasting A method of distributing television or radio signals by means of stations that broadcast (make public) signals over channels assigned to specific geographic areas.

broker A middleperson who serves as a go-between for the buyer or seller. The broker assumes no title risks, does not usually have physical custody of products, and is not looked upon as a permanent representative of either the buyer or seller.

budget The amount of monetary resources allocated to implement certain tactics (or a course of action).

budgeting The process of allocating resources to a certain organization activity.

buildup approach A method of building up the expenditure levels of various tasks to help establish an advertising budget.

Bureau of Alcohol, Tobacco, Firearms and Explosives (ATF) Government agency that rules when the sale, distribution, and advertising of alcohol and tobacco are at issue.

buy one, get one free A sales promotion offer made to either the retailer or the consumer in which purchase of one unit of the product is encouraged or rewarded by providing a second unit of the same product free of charge.

buy-back allowance A form of trade promotion in which channel members are offered an incentive to restock their store or warehouse with the product to the level in place prior to a count and recount promotion offer.

buying allowance A form of trade promotion in which the retailer is offered a discount on the purchase of the product at a particular point in time. The discount is often tied to the purchase of a particular number of units.

buzz marketing Creation of an atmosphere in which both the consumer and the media find the discussion and promotion of a particular brand to be entertaining, exciting, and newsworthy.

C

campaign continuity The situation in which all messages communicated in different media through different marketing communications tools are interrelated.

capital intensity This concept refers to the situation in which the firms in that market have invested a great deal of capital in land, equipment, and machinery.

card pack A type of cooperative mailing that is usually a number of "cards" from a variety of marketers that are included in a mailing package sent to consumers. These cards are often from companies that view the other cards included in the pack as complementary products that may increase the chance for a response or sale. Mailing costs are shared by those including cards in the pack.

cash flow A corporate performance standard traditionally measured in terms of cash availability after a given time.

catalog A publication containing the descriptions or details of a number or range of products used to increase mail-order sales, phone sales, and/or in-store traffic of the sender. Generally, all the information needed for purchase and acquisition is included. See also e-catalogs.

cease and desist order A court order that requires a firm to immediately halt the disputed advertising practice and to refrain from similar practices in the future.

channel of distribution An organized network (system) of agencies and institutions that, in combination, perform all the functions required to link producers with end customers to accomplish the marketing task.

Children's Advertising Review Unit (CARU) An organization belonging to the Better Business Bureau (BBB) that focuses on regulating the advertising industry in relation to children. CARU has strict guidelines to help firms that advertise to children to do the right thing. The guidelines address standards related to the type of appeal, product presentation and claims, disclosure and disclaimers, the use of premiums, safety, and techniques such as special effects and animation.

Children's Online Privacy Protection Act (COPPA) A congressional act to prohibit unfair or deceptive acts or practices in connection with the collection, use, or disclosure of personally identifiable information on the Internet from and about children under 13 years old. The act requires operators of websites directed to children and operators who knowingly collect personal information from children (1) to provide parents notice of their information practices and (2) obtain prior verifiable parental consent for the collection, use, or disclosure of personal information from children (with certain limited exceptions for the collection of "online contact information," such as an email address); (3) provide a parent, upon request, with the means to review the personal information collected from his or her child; (4) provide a parent with the opportunity to prevent the further use of personal information that has already been collected or the future collection of personal information from that child; (5) limit collection of personal information for a child's online participation in a game, prize offer, or other activity to information that is reasonably necessary for the activity; and (6) establish and maintain reasonable procedures to protect the confidentiality, security, and integrity of the personal information collected.

circulation Total number of issue copies sold through all channels of distribution (subscription, newsstand, bulk). Used for magazines and newspapers.

clutter A condition that exists when many advertisements and/or commercials are placed too closely together in space or time. In today's media-rich environment, this is a constant problem for advertisers.

cognitive brand attitude A marketing communications goal that describes a desirable situation in which target consumers establish a favorable attitude toward the firm's brand. The attitude is formed based on "rational" beliefs and cognitions.

cognitive-structure index A method that captures brand knowledge; it is typically an inventory of items in which respondents rate the likelihood of the brand having or not having certain features on a 7-point rating scale varying from "very unlikely" to "very likely."

competition The state in which firms in the same market offer a good or service to the same consumer population.

competitive analysis The process in which competitors are identified and selected competitors are profiled in terms of their product offerings, the prices of their products, the channels of distribution of their products, promotional messages, and the media carrying these messages.

competitive structure The nature of competition among firms within a given industry. Competition can be characterized as monopolistic (the market is controlled mostly by one large firm), oligopolistic (the market is controlled by several large firms), and purely competitive (the market is composed of many small firms who are "equally" competing for resources).

competitive-parity methods Budgeting methods that focus on some aspect of what and how the competition is spending on promotion.

conjoint analysis A multivariate statistical technique that is used by marketers to assess the consumer's relative importance and utility of levels of various attributes that a product/service possesses.

consent order An FTC order to stop illegal advertising immediately.

consideration set The group of alternatives that a consumer evaluates in making a decision (can also be referred to as the *evoked set* in a consumer behavior sense).

consumer-based integration A goal of marketing communications in which marketing communications decisions are guided by marketing strategy.

consumer decision making This concept refers to the process and outcome associated with brand selection, choice, and purchase.

consumer experience The state in which consumers have much knowledge and familiarity of a product category.

consumer information Resources that help a consumer make decisions about a purchase.

consumer involvement The state in which consumers are emotionally and cognitively involved with the purchase of a product and they are likely to process much information.

consumer promotions Externally directed incentives offered to the ultimate consumer. These usually consist of offers such as coupons, premiums, rebates, and so on that are designed to gain one or more of the following: product trial; repeat usage of product; more frequent or multiple product purchases; introduction of a new or improved product; introduction of new packaging or different size packages; neutralization of competitive advertising or sales promotions; capitalization on seasonal, geographic, or special events; encouragement of consumers to trade up to a larger size, more profitable line, or another product in the line.

consumer sovereignty The concept of how consumers' economic votes weed out bad businesses and reward good businesses.

contact management The process by which the marketer determines the time, place, or situation in which to communicate to the customer or prospect.

contest A consumer promotion technique requiring the participant to use specific skills or abilities to solve or complete a specified problem to qualify for a prize or award.

continuity plan Any type of consumer promotion technique that encourages customers to purchase products on a continuing basis or over time. The plan often is based on some sort of saving or accumulation scheme such as trading stamps, points, coupons, or the like.

control The process by which a warning signal is generated to trigger corrective action. The strength of the signal is determined by the degree of the negative deviation between an objective and a performance outcome—the greater the negative deviation, the greater the warning signal.

cooperative advertising An approach to paying for local advertising or retail advertising whereby the advertising space or time is placed by a local retail store but is partly or fully paid for by a national manufacturer whose product is featured in the advertising.

coordinated integration A goal of marketing communications in which the personal selling function is directly integrated with other elements of marketing communications (advertising, public relations, sales promotion, and direct marketing).

corporate advertising An advertising message or campaign that has the primary purpose of promoting the name, image, personnel, or reputation of a company, organization, or industry.

corporate communications Communications used to build favorable attitudes toward a particular company with competitors, consumers, the financial community, stockholders, and other publics. Can also refer to internal marketing communications that are sent throughout the organization for information dissemination or the same purpose as above.

corporate image The evaluation of a firm's goodwill in the minds of certain stakeholders such as customers, employees, distributors, suppliers, government, and so on.

corporate objectives Formal statements that represent concrete and precise desired states of affairs articulated at the corporate level. Corporate objectives are usually stated in terms of sales, market share, profit, and cash flow in relation to a given strategic business unit (SBU).

corrective advertising Advertising designed to attempt to return consumers' beliefs to those that they held before a damaging advertising campaign.

cost per rating point (CPRP) Cost of a commercial ÷ rating.

cost per thousand (CPM) The cost of a given media, or media mix, in delivering one thousand individual impressions within the target market.

count and recount promotion A trade promotion technique in which inventory is counted at the beginning of the promotion and recounted at the end of the promotion period. Discounts are then allowed based on the total quantity of product moved during the promotion period.

country of origin This concept refers to the country responsible for the design and/or manufacturing of a particular economic good.

coupon A printed (or electronic) certificate entitling the bearer to a stated price reduction or special value on a specific product, generally for a specified period of time. The value of the coupon is set and redeemed by the seller.

coupon redemption The use of a seller's value certificate at the time of purchase to obtain either a lower price or greater value than normal. This term also is used to describe the act of accepting a seller's certificate by a retailer or other intermediary.

creative selling Involves several personal selling tasks: prospecting, assessing needs, recommending a means of satisfying needs, demonstrating the capabilities of the firm, and closing the sale. Here, the salesperson is the "point person" who establishes the initial contact and has the major responsibility for completing the transaction.

cross-ruff A consumer promotion technique in which a noncompetitive product is used as the vehicle to distribute a coupon, sample, or other sales promotion offer for another product.

cross-selling In retailing, the process of selling between and among departments to facilitate larger transactions and to make it more convenient for the customer to do related item shopping. In sales promotion, a consumer sales promotion technique in which the manufacturer attempts to sell the consumer products related to a product the consumer already uses or that the marketer has available.

cume or cumulative radio audience An estimated number that is the total number of different people who listened to radio station programming for at least 5 minutes during a given daypart.

customer analysis The process in which the market is divided into customer segments and selected segments are profiled in terms of demographics, psychographics, and media habits.

customer benefits Brand attributes or features perceived by the customer as important and desirable aspects they like to have in a product.

customer or brand loyalty The state in which customers express a certain amount of commitment to a brand as in repeated purchase.

D

daily effective circulation (DEC) Average number of persons age 18 or over potentially exposed to an advertising display for either 12 hours unilluminated (6:00 A.M. to 6:00 P.M.) or 18 hours illuminated (6:00 A.M. to midnight); also called *daily impressions*.

database A compendium of information on current and prospective customers that generally includes demographic and psychographic data, as well as purchase history and a record of brand contacts. This information can be from internal or external sources and includes such items as sales reports and research studies.

database marketing Marketing communications that are directly facilitated by a large database containing relevant information about customers and prospects.

data mining The analytical process of finding new and potentially useful knowledge from data. The process includes the use of mathematical tools to find difficult patterns of intelligence. Helps to identify unforeseen patterns and behaviors.

dating In sales promotion, a type of trade promotion in which the retailer is allowed to buy a certain amount of product from the manufacturer and then pay for that product over a prolonged period of time. In retailing, the dates in which discounts can be taken or the full invoice amount is due.

dayparts Time-scheduling segments for a given day, used for television and other broadcast media.

dealer tie-in The local support by a retailer for an advertiser's promotional program through use of in-store display materials, cooperative advertising, local contests, identification in media advertisements, and so on.

decision tree   See *process hierarchy*.

decision-process test   A test that involves tracking a consumer's decision process. This is traditionally done through an in-depth personal interview. The interviewer starts from the decision to purchase and probes backward to understand the dynamics and the reasons the consumer has made that decision.

demand cyclicity   Seasonal fluctuations in product demand. Some products, such as sunblock lotion, are seasonal and, therefore, are said to have high demand cyclicity.

demographics   The characteristics of people and population segments, especially when used to identify consumer markets. Popular demographics used in media planning and buying typically include gender, age, household income, education levels, household size, and ethnicity.

designated market area (DMA)   The geographic area over which a local television station holds domination. For example, a station from Chicago would have a dominant influence in northern Illinois until it came close to where station signals from another nearby city (e.g., Milwaukee) dominated the area. Arbitron uses the ADI term, and Nielsen uses the DMA designation.

direct mail   The use of the mail delivered by the U.S. Postal Service or other delivery services as an advertising media vehicle. Direct mail can include letters, brochures, postcards, etc.

direct marketing   An element or tool of marketing communications. It involves various forms of marketing communications couched in direct channels of distribution, such as direct mail, catalogs, telemarketing, direct-response advertising, the new electronic media (e.g., teleshopping and videotext), and direct selling.

direct selling   1. (sales definition) A marketing approach that involves direct sales of goods and services to consumers through personal explanation and demonstrations, frequently in the home or workplace. 2. (retailing definition) The process whereby the firm responsible for production sells directly to the user, ultimate consumer, or retailer.

direct-broadcast commercial   A commercial that usually fits in a standard time format (e.g., 30 seconds) and that gives the listener or viewer the ability to directly respond to the commercial, via a telephone number or Internet access point, to continue the purchase process by either gaining more information or actually buying the product or service.

direct-response advertising   An approach to the advertising message that includes a method of response, such as an address or telephone number, whereby audience members can respond directly to purchase the advertised product or service. Direct-response advertising can be conveyed to members of a target market by a wide variety of advertising media, including television, radio, magazines, mail delivery, etc.

display   A special exhibit of a product at the point of sale, generally over and above standard shelf stocking.

diversity   Variety; noticeable heterogeneity.

divestment strategy   A corporate strategy that guides the corporate executive to set corporate objectives in terms of cash flow. The focus here is to generate needed cash flow by selling off the firm's least prosperous organizational entities.

E

effective net reach   A level of reach that is tied to the level of frequencies needed to achieve a given goal of exposure that is then assessed regarding nonduplication of audience. That is computed by adding the percentages of effective reach of all media vehicles minus duplication among the vehicles.

effective reach   A level of reach that is tied to the level of frequencies needed to achieve a given goal of exposure.

electronic catalogs (e-catalogs)   Like the regular hard-copy catalogs, these electronic publications offer a complete enumeration of items offered for sale by a firm or cause. Beyond simply listing all the products and their attributes, these publications generally provide instructions on how to order and acquire the products or services directly.

electronic coupons   A form of sales promotion involving coupons; however, the coupons are electronic and are typically printed on the back of the customer invoice or receipt.

electronic mail (email)   A communication format that involves sending computer-based messages over telecommunication technology. Email can include a letter-style text message or more elaborate Web-style HTML messages. Users can also attach other files to the email and transmit all elements simultaneously.

electronic newsletters (e-newsletters)   Electronic publications (usually small in relative size to a full publication) containing news of interest chiefly to a special group or community.

end-aisle display   An exhibit of a product set up at the end of the aisle in a retail store to call attention to a special offering or price.

entrenched loyalty   A state of mind in which respondents indicate a high degree of commitment to the brand.

environmental analysis   The process in which certain factors are identified that may have an impact on the size and geographic distribution of the market. Such factors may involve technology, economy, culture, media, politics, and so on.

event marketing   The development, promotion, support, and execution related to a particular event that is designed to promote a particular brand, product, service, idea, or cause. As with sponsorship, if the event involves multiple entities, the common practice is for one or more of the entities to provide financial and/or other types of support in exchange for brand promotion. See **sponsorship.**

event sponsorship   A form of public relations program designed to build and strengthen a positive attitude toward the firm at large and all its products. It is done by having the firm sponsor a specific community event.

experience curve effects The cost saving gained as a direct result of learning, business experience, and the use of economies of scale.

experimental method Budgeting method based on experimental studies.

external situation analysis The process in which certain factors external to the organization are analyzed to help marketers with strategic planning. These external factors include the competition, the market, customers, and the environment.

F

favorability measure of attitude toward purchase A method that induces respondents to indicate their preference of a particular brand by rating it on a scale that has "very unfavorable" on one end and "very favorable" on the other end.

Federal Communications Commission (FCC) An independent U.S. government agency, directly responsible to Congress. The FCC was established by the Communications Act of 1934 and is charged with regulating interstate and international communications by radio, television, wire, satellite, and cable. The FCC's jurisdiction covers the fifty states, the District of Columbia, and U.S. possessions.

Federal Trade Commission (FTC) A government agency established in 1915 whose purpose is to enforce a variety of federal antitrust and consumer protection laws. The FTC seeks to ensure that the nation's markets function competitively, vigorously, efficiently, and free of undue restrictions. It also attempts to eliminate acts or practices that are unfair or deceptive.

feedback The outcome or state of a system that may be utilized in the modification of the system's operation. This term is usually used in terms of compensation and, as such, relates to the system whereby information is obtained regarding performance versus compensation.

feedback mechanism A mechanism that generates a stress signal when a specific measured outcome is detected to be significantly below (or above) the stated objective.

feedforward Analysis that examines the future situation.

Food and Drug Administration (FDA) Government agency whose mission is to promote and protect the public health by helping safe and effective products reach the market in a timely way and monitoring products for continued safety after they are in use.

free merchandise A trade promotion technique in which an additional amount of the product is offered without additional cost as an incentive to purchase a minimum quantity. The incentive is typically offered for a limited period of time.

free-association test A test that involves word associations. Subjects are presented with a list of objects including the brand in question and asked to provide the first set of words that comes to mind.

frequency How many times an advertisement or campaign comes in contact with the target market.

functional integration A goal of marketing communications in which decisions are made as a direct function of marketing goals, such as sales and market share.

G

geographic selectivity The targeting of select geographic areas, commonly used in media planning to help select media.

goal The purpose toward which an endeavor is directed; an objective.

gross rating points (GRPs) A gross measure can be estimated based on either a percentage of target market delivery or the number of individuals. The measure based on the percentage is called gross rating points. When multiplied together, reach (not effective or net reach) and frequency will yield the measure of gross rating points.

gross reach A measure commonly used by media planners to assess the effectiveness of a media schedule in terms of its maximum reach of a target market. It is computed by adding the percentages of reach of all media vehicles without taking into account the duplication among the vehicles. For example, a 90 percent gross reach is the ability of a combination of media vehicles to reach 90 percent of the target market, assuming that there is no audience duplication among the media vehicles. *Net reach* is computed by subtracting audience duplication from gross reach and therefore is considered to be a more accurate index of media schedule effectiveness than gross reach.

group selling A form of direct personal selling in which the salesperson assembles potential consumers in a group and demonstrates the product to them in one location.

growth strategy A corporate strategy that guides the corporate executive to set corporate objectives in terms of increases in sales and market share. The aim here is to expand the market by going after new prospects and/or encouraging customers to purchase more.

guerilla marketing Unconventional marketing intended to get maximum results from minimal resources. The technique relies on quick-hitting, irregular, and often unexpected means by which to elevate the brand in the consumer's eyes and mind. It often requires marketing personnel to "think outside the box."

H

habit-formation (doer) strategy A marketing communications strategy that guides the marketing communications manager to induce purchase or an overt behavioral response. The focus here is on inducing action. Action, in turn, is likely to prompt consumers to learn about the brand's costs and benefits, and this learning is likely to facilitate the development of a positive attitude toward the brand. The positive attitude is likely to motivate consumers to purchase the brand when the need for the product arises in the future.

harvest strategy A corporate strategy that guides the corporate executive to set corporate objectives in terms of maximizing profit. The intent here is to stop investing and making improvements and thus reduce costs of doing business. Therefore, profit maximization can be achieved through cost reduction.

higher order A term used to refer to abstract ideas or constructs that are superordinate over (or comprised of) lower constructs. For example, a consumer may be said to be "highly involved with a product." To better understand what that is, the involvement construct is decomposed into two "lower-order" dimensions (or constructs), here called *product importance* and *product commitment*. Measurements are taken of these lower constructs because they are better defined than the more abstract "higher-order" construct of involvement. These lower constructs of importance and commitment, when considered together, make up the "higher-order product involvement" construct for the consumer.

historical-statistical method Budgeting method based on statistical data from the company's archives.

horizontal cooperative advertising An advertising partnership in which several retailers share the cost of a promotion.

house list A list of customers developed and maintained "in house" by the company that is marketing the products or services. A house list is often used by catalog companies that can segment the list into a variety of categories, generally based on levels of and types of purchases.

households using television (HUT) The number of television households (TVHH) that have a television "in use."

how-brand-is-different test A test that asks subjects to distinguish between various brands in a particular product category.

I

image measure A method that captures respondents' perceptions of the benefits, costs, and/or other attributes of the brand.

infomercial The use of a program-length time period to advertise products and services. Usually seen on broadcast or cable television. This approach often includes a direct-response offer to sell the advertised items directly to the public.

informative (thinker) strategy A marketing communications strategy that guides the marketing communications manager to provide target consumers with information about the firm's brand—that is, to educate consumers about the product costs and/or benefits. The focus here is on learning, much more so than eliciting an affective response or inducing purchase. The goal is that learning about the brand's costs and benefits is likely to help consumers develop a positive attitude toward the brand. In turn, these positive feelings for the brand are likely to motivate consumers to purchase the brand.

ingredient-sponsored cooperative advertising An advertising partnership in which producers of a particular ingredient or component used in a product share the cost of a promotion.

innovation strategy A corporate strategy that guides the corporate executive to set corporate objectives in terms of increases in sales. The aim here is to develop a new product to increase sales.

inserts Advertisements or promotional materials that are inserted into newspapers, magazines, or other publications as either "free inserts" (not attached) or "bound inserts" (attached).

instant coupon A form of coupon that encourages an immediate purchase response; it is usually pasted on top of the package.

instant messages (IMs) While very similar to email communication, these messages allow an immediate message exchange between parties as long as the parties stay online. Most exchanges are text only, but use of file sharing, video, and voice is growing. Cell phones are especially well-suited in today's environment for IMs, although on cell phones, such activity generally is referred to as text messaging.

in-store advertising A form of sales promotion in which consumers are provided with special types of information about product availability in the context of the store.

integrated marketing communications (IMC) A concept that recognizes the added value in a program that integrates a variety of strategic disciplines—such as general advertising, direct response, sales promotion, and public relations—and combines these disciplines to provide clarity, consistency, and maximum communications impact.

integration The state of combination or the process of combining into completeness and harmony. It is one of the hallmarks of an on-demand business, and one of the four characteristics of the on-demand operating environment.

interactive advertising Advertising that constantly updates descriptions and explanations of a product line or any information that helps to keep customers loyal.

interactive marketing A special case of direct marketing that occurs in the virtual world of cellular, Internet, or any other type of electronic-technology-enhanced environment.

intermedia selection The decision to select among media categories such as television, radio, magazines, newspapers, billboards, transit advertising, interactive advertising, and so on.

internal situation analysis The process in which certain factors internal to the organization are analyzed to help marketers with strategic planning. These internal factors include the firm's past sales, past profit, past media expenditures, past promotional messages, and so on.

Internet direct advertising Direct marketing that is limited to the Internet environment. In this setting, users are interacting with various offers that appear as banners, buttons, floaters, pop-ups, pop-unders, and transitional items on websites and search engines. The Interactive Marketing Bureau identifies them based on their Interactive Marketing Unit (IMU) specifications.

intramedia selection The selection of the appropriate mix of media vehicles.

L

Lanham act This act provides for the registration and protection of trademarks.

lifetime value A method of calculating the contribution (value) of a customer over the long term. The calculation is usually based on the yearly number of visits by a customer multiplied by the average amount of money spent per visit multiplied by the customer's average life span.

linkage The ability to establish a relationship between two or more constructs, events, or behaviors.

lower order See *higher order*.

M

maintain-position strategy A corporate strategy that guides the corporate executive to set corporate objectives in terms of maintaining current levels of sales and market share. The intent here is to defend the firm's position against offending competitors.

manufacturer's agent An independent businessperson who is paid a commission to sell a manufacturer's products or services but does not take title to the products.

market A segment of the population that purchases a specific good or service.

market analysis The process of estimating the size and geographic distribution of the market for a particular product.

market power The ability of a market participant, as a result of its control of sufficient or essential facilities, to profitably set prices above or reduce supply below that which would occur in a fully competitive market.

market selection Identifying all of the possible markets for a product and then promoting to chosen markets while ignoring others.

marketing communications objectives Formal statements that represent concrete and precise desired states of affairs articulated at the marketing communications level. Marketing communications objectives are usually stated in terms of increases in brand awareness, learning about the benefits and costs of the brand, establishing positive attitude or liking toward the brand, and inducing trial purchase.

marketing objectives Formal statements that represent concrete and precise desired states of affairs articulated at the marketing level. Marketing objectives are usually stated in terms of brand equity or brand associations. An example of a marketing objective is "Establish an image of quality for Brand *X*."

marketing strategy A decision made by the marketing manager (or a firm's executive) to allocate (or shift the allocation of) organizational resources (capital and/or human resources) to emphasize any one or combination of elements of the marketing mix (the four Ps of marketing: product, price, place, and promotion).

match or outspend competitors Budgeting method guided by the notion that optimal spending is to match or outspend the firm's major competitors.

match-industry-norms method Budgeting method based on the industry average or "norm."

materialism A cultural value that places emphasis on the role of material possessions in achieving "the good life."

means-end chains Conceptual frameworks for advertising strategy that are used to link message elements to consumers' personal values. The standard linkages will move from the attributes presented to benefits sought by the consumer, which are then leveraged to impact personal values of the individual.

media habits Consumers' frequent use of certain media classes and vehicles. Market researchers typically develop profiles of the media habits of target consumers.

media selectivity Reaching a consumer group through highly select media. For example, avid cyclists can best be reached through cyclists' magazines. Cyclists' magazines are considered highly select media.

message/media consistency Consistency of message between written and visual elements of an advertisement.

missionary sales work Involves a combination of creative selling and order taking. The position calls for introducing new products and programs to both current and potential customers.

models A set of hypotheses or theoretical propositions tied together to convey a logical point, message, or story.

monitoring The process by which performance outcomes are measured.

multiattribute attitude index A measure that captures attitude by taking into account many benefits and costs of brand.

multiattribute attitude models Theoretical models used by marketers that view attitudes as being comprised of a number of attributes (dimensions) upon which consumers build up to a total attitude. The models generally include both attribute importance and a belief regarding whether or not the brand/product/service being evaluated possesses the specific attribute. The consumer's complete attitude is then a summation of the cross-products of these importance and belief components. An example would be

$$A_1 = \sum B_i * E_i$$

where A_1 is the attitude toward the brand, B_i is the belief regarding performance on the brand attribute being evaluated, and E_i is the importance to the consumer of the attribute being evaluated regarding the brand.

multilevel marketing A strategy used by direct-selling companies to have independent agents serve as distributors and resell merchandise to other agents, who eventually make sales to consumers. This is a compensation system in which salespeople earn money from the sales of other people they recruited into the business and also from the sales of the people their recruits recruited. Sometimes negatively referred to as pyramid marketing.

mushiness index A measure capturing attitude strength.

N

narrowcasting A focused television buy versus the wider broadcast from traditional television outlets. Cable buys are often used for this purpose.

National Advertising Division (NAD) A subsidiary of the Better Business Bureau (BBB). Complaints about deceptive advertising (typically national-level advertising) are typically referred to the NAD for review. The NAD investigates the charge and determines whether the advertiser's claims are real or false. If false, the NAD negotiates with the offending firm to modify or discontinue the advertising campaign. If the NAD does not resolve the complaint or the advertiser appeals the NAD's decision, the complaint goes to the National Advertising Review Board.

National Advertising Review Board (NARB) A committee composed of advertising professionals and prominent civic leaders who decide whether a specific ad is deceptive or misleading.

National Association of Attorneys General (NAAG) A professional association whose membership is comprised of state-level attorneys general.

needs A term typically used in relation to customers. The focus in marketing is to configure the marketing mix in ways to deliver a good or service to prospective buyers to meet their expectations, desires, and wants above and beyond competitor offerings.

net reach A measure commonly used by media planners to assess the effectiveness of a media schedule in terms of its maximum reach of a target market. It is computed by adding the percentages of reach of all media vehicles minus duplication among the vehicles. For example, a 90 percent net reach is the ability of a combination of media vehicles to reach 90 percent of the target market.

O

objectives Formal statements of a strategy that serve as goals. These formal statements are precise and quantifiable and guide the formulation of tactics or action. For example, a corporate strategy of "Maintain position" can be quantified and treated as a goal to guide action as follows: "Maintain current market share for the next quarter."

objective-task method Budgeting method based on a precise account of how much money is needed to build a marketing communications campaign that will meet certain communications, marketing, and/or corporate objectives.

offensive promotion A message issued in behalf of some product or cause or idea or person or institution and is defined as "offensive" because it elicits unsavory or morally offensive feelings in the consumer.

off-invoice allowance A type of trade promotion in which the manufacturer offers the retailer a price reduction on the product price at the time of billing, generally for a limited period of time.

one-look approach An approach that attempts to create unity in all forms of marketing communications through maintaining a "single look and feel" in all executed messages including colors, fonts, visuals, logos, and so on.

one-to-one selling A form of direct personal selling in which a salesperson interacts with an individual consumer. The salesperson explains and demonstrates the product to that consumer.

order taking The order taker services an account. This situation is commonly referred to as a "straight rebuy." That is, the order does not change much. For example, a food manufacturer's salesperson may call on a wholesale food company and present it with a list of food products to sell.

outdoor advertising Made up of a number of different types of presentation formats, including such things as traditional billboards, transit boards (at stops and on equipment), aerial advertising (billboards, banners, etc.), mobile billboards (painted trucks, cars, or other derivations), and inflatables (you may have seen the giant gorilla tethered near a main thoroughfare).

outside list A list of customers developed and maintained outside of the company that is marketing the products or services. These lists are then sold to interested parties (e.g., catalog companies).

P

paid circulation Number of copies from subscription or newsstand sales.

paired-comparison method A method that induces respondents to indicate their preference of a particular brand by comparing it with other brands.

panels In outdoor advertising, standard billboard units. In the past, only a few choices were available for the size of billboards, but now many different options are available. (See *sheets*.)

percentage-of-anticipated-sales method Budgeting method based on a percentage of forecasted sales.

percentage-of-past-sales method Budgeting method determined as a percentage of last year's sales.

percentage-of-purchase measure A method that induces respondents to indicate the percentage of times the respondent purchased the same brand during a certain time span.

percentage-of-unit-anticipated-sales method Budgeting method determined as a percentage of unit cost.

percentage-of-unit-past-sales method Budgeting method determined as a percentage of the unit price for last year's sales.

permission marketing Marketing centered around getting customer's consent to receive information from a company.

personal selling Selling that involves a face-to-face interaction with the customer.

personal-values test A test, sometimes referred to as the "laddering technique," that involves using in-depth interviews to uncover the person's motivation to purchase and use a specific brand.

physical continuity The consistent use of creative elements in all marketing communications.

picture-interpretation test A test that involves presenting subjects with a picture of a scene in which the brand is somewhat embedded in the picture.

planning Making decisions related to strategy, objectives, tactics, and resource allocation that are based on information obtained through analysis.

point-of-purchase (POP) advertising Advertising usually in the form of window and/or interior displays in establishments where a product is sold to the ultimate consumer. POP can also be promotional materials placed at the contact sales point designed to attract consumer interest or call attention to a special offer. Finally, there can be both on- and off-shelf display materials or product stocking that is generally at the retail level that is used to call special attention to the featured product. This latter element of POP is sometimes referred to as *point-of-sale display.*

point-of-purchase materials/displays Promotional materials placed at the contact sales point and on- and off-shelf display material or product stocking generally at the retail level that is used to call special attention to the featured product. It is sometimes referred to as *point-of-sale display.*

portfolio models Strategy models designed to help managers select among alternative corporate strategies. Examples of alternative strategies at the corporate level include growth, maintain position, harvest, innovation, and divestment.

positioning The same as a *message strategy.* That is, the marketing communications manager translates corporate and marketing strategies in terms of a specific message to be communicated to target consumers. For example, a growth strategy at the corporate level may translate into a differentiation strategy at the marketing level, which further translates into positioning by intangible factor such as quality. That is, the marketing communications manager may believe that a message about product quality may be most effective in differentiating the firm's product from competitor products, which in turn may be an effective way to grow.

positioning by brand-distributor tie-in A message strategy that focuses on creating a mental association between the firm's brand and a credible and reputable distributor, or vice versa. For example, Sears advertises heavily the fact that it carries Kenmore appliances. Both Sears and Kenmore appliances benefit from this tie-in.

positioning by celebrity or spokesperson A message strategy that focuses on creating a mental association between the firm's brand and a specific celebrity or spokesperson. For example, Wendy's fast-food restaurant is positioned through Wendy's father, Dave Thomas, the president of Wendy's. People associate Wendy's with this spokesperson.

positioning by competitors A message strategy that focuses on creating a mental association between the firm's brand and a specific attribute that the brand possesses that makes it appear superior to competitor brands. For example, Aleve, the nonprescription pain reliever, is positioned as having a longer-lasting effect than Tylenol, Advil, or Bayer.

positioning by country of origin A message strategy that focuses on creating a mental association between the firm's brand and a specific country that has a good reputation for making the product. For example, Walkers cookies are positioned as being made in Scotland, where this cookie recipe originated.

positioning by customer benefit or problem A message strategy that focuses on creating a mental association between the firm's brand and a specific customer benefit or problem. For example, Claussen Pickles is positioned as having a crunchier pickle. Consumers perceive crunchiness as a significant benefit.

positioning by distributor location A message strategy that focuses on creating a mental association between the firm's brand and easy access to the product through specific channels and retail outlets. For example, many companies are advertising their home pages to allow target consumers to access their products and services directly and more conveniently.

positioning by distributor's serviceability A message strategy that focuses on creating a mental association between the firm's brand and how well it can be delivered through specific channels and retail outlets. For example, many banks have positioned themselves on customer service.

positioning by intangible factor A message strategy that focuses on creating a mental association between the firm's brand and a general attribute that captures a host of important attributes. For example, Ford positions itself in terms of quality. Quality is an intangible factor that relies on a host of tangible factors, such as materials, construction, design, and so on.

positioning by lifestyle or personality A message strategy that focuses on a personal characteristic that consumers can relate to based on personality or lifestyle. For example, a food manufacturer marketing bakery items may focus on a personality symbol such as the "dough boy."

positioning by low price A message strategy that focuses on creating a mental association between the firm's brand and a lower price than products of most or certain other competitors. For example, Wal-Mart is positioned as a low-price discount store.

positioning by product attribute A message strategy that focuses on creating a mental association between the firm's brand and an important product attribute. For example, Crest toothpaste indicates that fluoride is perceived to be an important attribute in toothpaste.

positioning by product class A message strategy that focuses on creating a mental association between the firm's brand and the product class. For example, 7UP soft drink is essentially a product class that subsumes a variety of noncola soft drinks.

positioning by relative price A message strategy that focuses on creating a mental association between the firm's brand and quality based on price. For example, the Mercedes automobile is positioned as a luxury car and therefore highly priced. The high price communicates luxury and quality.

positioning by use or application A message strategy that focuses on creating a mental association between the firm's brand and a specific use of the product. For example, a brand of coffee can be positioned as highly suitable for a social get-together. Another brand may be positioned as most suitable to help people wake up and get going in the morning. Another brand may be positioned as most suitable for after meals, especially dinners.

positioning by user or customer image A message strategy that focuses on creating a mental association between the firm's brand and a type of product user or customer image. For example, Nike shoes are positioned for the serious athlete. The message is that if you are a serious athlete, then Nike shoes are made for you.

preferred position Advertisers can select the section (e.g., sports, local, world, national, life, classified, real estate, food, travel, etc.) or particular page placement that fits a particular product.

premium In retailing, merchandise offered at a lower price, or free, as an additional incentive for a customer to make a purchase. In sales promotion, an item of value other than the product itself that is given as an additional incentive to influence the purchase of a product.

press conference A form of public relations in which a company spokesperson provides newsworthy information about a company event to reporters and responds to reporters' questions.

press release Information about the company and/or its products that is sent to the news media for dissemination.

previous-budget method Allocating resources based on the previous budget, possibly with some adjustments.

price consciousness This is a state of mind that motivates consumers to make purchase decisions based on the price of the product.

price-off deal A stated reduction in the price of a product generally offered by the manufacturer and printed directly on the product package.

price-quality relationship This is a psychological association between price and quality. That is, it is the belief that the higher the price of the product, the more likely that the product is of higher quality.

primary demand The demand for a general product category.

process hierarchy A *decision tree;* a hierarchy of decisions reflecting a hierarchical link between strategy, objectives, and tactics. For example, the following can be described as a process hierarchy: A corporate strategy of "Gain market share" leads the decision maker to set a corporate objective of "Increase market share by 20 percent by next quarter." Certain corporate tactics are then selected to meet this objective, such as to hold the marketing department responsible to develop a marketing program that can achieve the corporate objective.

product differentiation The state in which a particular brand is perceived to be distinct and different from competitor brands.

product functionality versus value-expressiveness Some products such as toothpaste and soap are referred to as functional because they serve the specific purpose of the product class: toothpaste is used to clean teeth and soap is used for washing. In contrast, value-expressive products are those that serve other goals besides functionality, goals such as expressing one's identity. For example, a sexy outfit not only provides clothing but also expresses the consumer's identity as being sexy.

product life cycle The stages that a product (product category, not a single product brand) goes through, from the early stages of inception and commercialization to eventual decline and extinction. The stages are usually referred to more specifically as introduction, development, early maturity, late maturity, and decline.

product placement The placing (inserting) of brands into regular entertainment, news, or other media. The intent is to create an association between the brand being placed and the audience that is interacting with the given medium. The common practice is for the placed brand to provide financial and/or other types of support in exchange for brand insertion in the regular content of the medium.

product users versus nonusers Product users are consumers identified as using the product in question. Nonusers are identified as not using the product in question.

production flexibility The ability of certain media to accommodate the scheduling demands of advertisers. For example, radio advertising is highly flexible; radio script can be easily modified, and changes can be easily made to within the last few days of the airing of the radio commercial.

product-market matrix A matrix specifying each business unit that is the basis of all subsequent corporate, marketing, and marketing communications decisions.

profit A corporate performance standard, traditionally measured in terms of a product's revenues minus costs for a given time period.

projective measures Methods used to capture respondents' perceptions, thoughts, and feelings about a brand in very indirect ways. For example, the respondent is asked to draw a picture of the brand; the interpretation of the drawing provides the researcher with an indicator of how well the respondent likes the brand.

promotional allowance In retailing, an allowance given by vendors to retailers to compensate the latter for money spent in advertising a particular item in local media or for preferred window and interior display space used for the vendor's product. In sales promotion, the payments, price reductions, or other inducements used to reward channel members for participation in advertising and/or sales promotion programs.

prospects Potential customers of a firm.

psychographics While demographics are objective characteristics of a population, psychographics are subjective lifestyle psychological characteristics that are based on consumers' responses to questions regarding their activities, interests, and opinions (AIO). These AIO variables are usually combined with demographics to get a more complete picture of consumer market segment types.

psychological continuity A consistent attitude toward a firm and its brand(s).

public relations That form of communications management that seeks to make use of publicity and other nonpaid forms of promotion and information to influence the feelings, opinions, or beliefs about the company, about its products or services, or about the value of the products or services or the activities of the organization to buyers, prospects, or other stakeholders.

publicity The non-paid-for communication of information about the company or product, generally in some media form.

puffery An exaggerated claim made by a firm in relation to one of its products or services, without making an overt attempt to deceive or mislead.

purchase intention A marketing communications goal that describes a desirable situation in which target consumers have formed a behavioral intention to purchase the firm's brand.

R

ranking method A method that induces respondents to indicate their preference of a particular brand by placing it in some order of high to low appeal.

rate base The guaranteed average issue circulation upon which a book's (magazine's) advertising rates are based.

rating point This figure is equal to 1 percent of the TVHH (or broadcast media target market) and is reported as a percentage. Consequently, if a program receives a 10 rating, that rating translates as 10 percent of the TVHH in the United States were tuned into the particular program when the measurement was taken.

ratio-to-sales methods Budgeting methods that allocate resources based on percentage of anticipated sales, percentage of unit anticipated sales, percentage of past sales, and percentage of unit past sales.

reach A percentage related to the amount of the audience who were exposed to the media vehicle.

readership The circulation of a newspaper multiplied by the estimated readers per copy.

rebate A return of a portion of the purchase price in the form of cash by the seller to the buyer.

recent reading A technique used by Mediamark Research, Inc., for determining magazine readership. Respondents to the survey are shown magazine logos and asked if they have recently read or looked into any of the publications.

recognition measures Methods to capture brand awareness by presenting sample respondents with an advertisement without the brand name and asking respondents if they recognize the brand name.

referent A standard of comparison used in performance assessment to help interpret performance ratings.

referral reward A lead for a prospect given to the salesperson by an existing customer who is rewarded in some manner, often through cash, rebates, or gifts.

referral system An information network in which consumers refer other consumers to a specific good or service.

refund A return of the amount paid for an item or some portion of the amount.

relationship marketing Marketing with the conscious aim to develop and manage long-term and/or trusting relationships with customers, distributors, suppliers, or other parties in the marketing environment.

relationship-management integration A marketing communications goal in which messages are guided not only by marketing strategy but also by corporate strategy.

reliable and valid measures Performance assessment instruments that capture the core essence of the phenomenon in question and do so consistently with multiple measures or methods.

repeat purchase A marketing communications goal that describes a desirable situation in which target consumers have purchased the firm's brand repeatedly over time.

reputation of the distributor The distributor is the firm that makes the manufacturer's product accessible to consumers through retail outlets. The reputation of the distributor is the consumers' image of the distributor.

reseller support An element or tool of marketing communications that involves promotional activities by distributors such as contests and incentives, trade allowances, in-store displays, point-of-purchase materials, training programs, trade shows, cooperative advertising, and personal selling. It is often called *trade promotion*.

return-on-investment (ROI) method Budgeting method guided by the assumption that money spent today is an investment that is likely to pay off in sales tomorrow.

Robinson-Patman Act This is an amendment to the Clayton Act that prohibits price discrimination when the effect "may be substantially to lessen competition or create a monopoly"; prohibits payments of broker's commission when an independent broker is not employed; forbids sellers to provide allowances or services to buyers unless these are available to all buyers on "equally proportional terms"; and prohibits a buyer from inducing or receiving a prohibited discrimination in price.

run of press (ROP) Buying an advertisement that can be placed anywhere in the newspaper or other print vehicle by the editorial staff of the publication; that is, the advertiser is not able to select certain a placement for his or her advertisement. (See *preferred position*.)

S

sales contest In sales, a short-term incentive program designed to motivate sales personnel to accomplish specific sales objectives. In general, a sales contest is used by firms to stimulate extra effort for obtaining new customers, promoting the sales of specific items, generating larger orders per sales call, and so on. Also in sales, a short-term incentive program designed to motivate salespeople to accomplish very specific sales objectives. Although a contest should not be considered part of the firm's ongoing compensation plan, it does offer salespeople the opportunity to gain financial as well as nonfinancial rewards. Contest winners often receive prizes in cash or merchandise or travel that have monetary value. Winners also receive nonfinancial rewards in the form of recognition and a sense of accomplishment.

salesperson A person who is primarily involved in the personal process of assisting and/or persuading a potential customer to buy a product or service to the mutual benefit of both buyer and seller. Also referred to as a *sales representative*.

sampling When free merchandise is given to prospective consumers to use.

seasonal usage in media This refers to seasonal variation in the use of certain media. For example, radio is listened to more frequently in the summer months than during other times. Prime-time television is typically watched more frequently during mid-fall and winter than during other times of the year.

segmentation The process of breaking up a larger, heterogeneous market into smaller subsegments that group around homogeneous similarities.

selective demand The demand for a specific brand marketed by a firm.

self-liquidating premiums "Gifts" to consumers, provided they pay some or all of the premium plus the cost of shipping and handling.

self-satisfaction (reactor) strategy A marketing communications strategy that guides the marketing communications manager to induce purchase. That is, the focus here is on inducing action, which in turn sparks certain positive feelings for the brand. This emotional response, in turn, is likely to motivate consumers to learn about the brand's costs and benefits. This learning is expected to help establish a positive attitude toward the brand, thereby inducing future purchase.

selling agent An agent who operates on an extended contractual basis. The agent sells all of a specified line of merchandise or the entire output of the principal and usually has full authority with regard to prices, terms, and other conditions of sales. The agent occasionally renders financial aid to the principal.

semantic differential measure of attitude toward purchase A method that induces respondents to indicate their preference of a particular brand by rating the brand along a set of bipolar dimensions.

share Number of households tuned in to a program ÷ HUT (households using television).

share-of-voice/market method Budgeting method based on the examination of the firm's market share in relation to the major competitors in the product/market.

sheets Standard billboard units. In the past only a few choices were available for the size of billboards, but now many different options are available. The most common size for an outdoor panel is 30 sheets (9′6″ high × 21′7″ wide) or 8 sheets (5′ high × 11′ wide). (See *panels*.)

showing The number of panels in a given market required to reach a fixed percentage of the population on a daily basis. For example, a 100 showing means that you have provided a gross number of impressions equal to 100 percent of the local desired population. It varies for each local. The term is only used in outdoor advertising and is generally being discarded in favor of the more common media measure of GRP.

situation analysis Another term for *strategic analysis*, situation analysis refers to the process in which certain factors internal and external to the organization are analyzed to help marketers with strategic planning. Examples of internal factors include the firm's past sales, past profit, past media expenditures, past promotional messages, and so on. Examples of external factors include the competition, the market, customers, and the environment.

slotting allowance In retailing, a fee paid by a vendor for space in a retail store. In sales promotion, the fee a manufacturer pays to a retailer in order to get distribution for a new product. It covers the costs of making room for the product in the warehouse and on the store shelf, reprogramming the computer system to recognize the product's UPC code, and including the product in the retailer's inventory system.

social stereotypes A form of media representation by which instantly recognized characteristics are used to label members of social or cultural groups. While often negative, stereotypes can contain an element of truth and are used by the media to establish an instant rapport with the audience.

spam Bulk, unsolicited email.

specialty advertising A form of advertising that employs gadgets (e.g., pens, mugs, calendars, T-shirts) as a medium to advertise the brand's name and slogan.

sponsorship A relationship executed between two or more entities that seeks to establish an association between the entities for mutual benefits. This sponsorship can exist long term or as a single event for the common promotion of a product, service, idea, or cause. The common practice is for one of the entities to provide financial and/or other types of support in exchange for brand promotion.

stakeholder-based integration The goal of marketing communications in which messages directed to target consumers, employees, suppliers, distributors, stockholders, the community, and certain government agencies are coordinated.

strategic business unit (SBU) A product/market unit—a specific product related to a specific customer group. For example, a mercury-based thermometer needed in cooking and directed to restaurants is an SBU. A mercury-based thermometer designed to measure atmospheric temperature and directed to households is another SBU.

strategic marketing communications (SMC) A systematic approach that guides the marketing communications manager to fully integrate strategies and objectives at the corporate and marketing organizational levels with all elements of the marketing communications campaign at the planning, execution, and monitoring stages.

strategic orientation An orientation that attempts to provide consistency of marketing communications strategies with product/market strategies and the organization's mission, goals, and resources in the face of relevant market environmental factors.

strategic partnering The process by which two (or more) entities, who on their own lack the resources to create the desired market offering, will come together to gain synergies and optimize resource utilization to meet performance demands of a given marketplace.

strategic partnership Cooperation strategy between companies to jointly pursue a common goal. Strategic partnerships are also referred to as *collaborative agreements* or *strategic alliances*.

strategic place focus Positioning in a special distribution market.

strategic price focus Positioning along a price facet of the market.

strategic product focus Promoting a specific facet of the product.

strategic prospects focus Promoting aspects related to the targeted consumers.

strategy A course of action that emphasizes certain elements of the strategic mix. For example, at the corporate level, a "Gain market share" strategy would manipulate the marketing element of the corporate mix in such a way as to generate a different outcome—a higher share of the market. At the marketing level, an example of a marketing strategy is "cost leadership," which is essentially a marketing strategy that manipulates the price element of the marketing mix to gain a competitive advantage. At the marketing communications level, an "informative" strategy involves manipulating certain elements of advertising (mostly print), reseller support (mostly training and trade shows), and public relations (mostly press release and publicity).

subordinate Placed in or occupying a lower class, rank, or position.

substantiation of marketing claims An FTC rule that if a company uses an endorser to make claims about product benefits, the company has to substantiate these claims based on legitimate tests performed by experts.

superordinate Superior in rank, class, or status.

superstations Powerful broadcasting stations that often have relationships with other local broadcasters and cable companies to provide their programming across a broad geographic region.

supply-side planning approach Using a system of marketing communications services that has the appearance of integration. A combination of marketing communications outlets that are put together to increase value to the buyer. Communications with a common look and theme are placed across varied media vehicles.

sweepstakes The offering of prizes to participants in which winners are selected by chance and no consideration is required.

system A set of procedures and methods for the regular, planned collection, analysis, and presentation of information for use in making marketing decisions.

system integration The extent to which the system components (strategy, objectives, tactics, budget, analysis, planning, monitoring, and control) are strongly or weakly linked. A system is said to lack integration if any one link between the system components is weak. In contrast, a system is said to be fully integrated when all of the system components are strongly linked.

T

tactics Selected courses of action guided by objectives of the superordinate level of the organization's hierarchy. For example, at the corporate level, an objective such as "Increase market share by 10 percent by next quarter" has to be implemented within the confines of each corporate department—engineering, R&D, manufacturing, marketing, accounting, finance, legal, and so on. The implementation of specific programs in relation to each corporate element reflects corporate tactics. At the marketing level, an objective of, say, "Establish reputation of quality that by the end of next quarter at least 50 percent of target consumers would recognize the brand as high quality" guides tactical action. The marketing manager has to configure a marketing program involving the four Ps in a manner to meet this objective. Similarly, a marketing communications objective such as "Increase positive affect toward the brand by 10 percent the end of next quarter" would motivate the marketing communications manager to put together a marketing communications program that can meet this objective. The elements of this program would involve selected communications tools (selected elements of advertising, public relations, sales promotion, reseller support, and direct marketing). These, in turn, become the marketing communications tactics.

technologies This concept refers to specific aspects of a good or service that are typically manipulated by engineers.

telemarketing Marketing products or services by using the telephone to contact potential buyers.

Telephone Consumer Protection Act (TCPA) A federal law that imposes restrictions on the use of automatic telephone dialing systems (also called *autodialers*), artificial or prerecorded voice messages, and fax machines to send unsolicited advertisements.

teleshopping The use of certain television channels that are exclusively devoted to selling products directly.

television households (TVHH) The number of households in the market (usually reported as the entire U.S. market) that have at least one television set.

television shopping network A network that is built around the process of showing, discussing, and selling products and services directly to viewers. Viewers often call in to be part of the shows, while hosts of certain shows can obtain celebrity-like status to buyers.

theme-lines or "matchbooks" approach Used by marketers who attempt to coordinate all supporting forms of marketing communications around an advertising theme. The goal is to use nonadvertising forms of marketing communications to trigger consumers to remember the advertising message.

theoretical framework A framework within which various suppositions and questions can be examined using the scientific method of empirical testing (See *theory*.)

theory A hypothesis that has withstood extensive testing by a variety of methods and in which a higher degree of certainty may be placed. A theory is *never* a fact but, instead, is an attempt to explain one or more facts. A strict definition refers to a theory as a systematically related set of statements, including some lawlike generalizations, that are empirically testable.

thought-elicitation procedure A method designed to measure the consumer's attitude toward the brand by capturing the kind of thoughts articulated by the respondent about the brand.

through the book A technique used by the Simmons Market Research Bureau (SMRB) to estimate total readership of publications. Respondents are asked to examine a stripped-down issue of any magazine that they have read or looked into recently. Initially, they are asked whether they have read or looked into the specific issue previously. Those who answer "yes" are counted as readers of the magazine.

top-of-mind awareness A state of mind in which consumers can easily recall the brand. The brand name is on the "top of their minds." When asked about a certain product, the brand in question is evoked quickly and with relative ease compared to other brands.

tracking studies A method that monitors the performance of the brand through actual purchases and sales.

trade allowances Short-term special offers made by marketers to channel members as incentives to stock, feature, or in some way participate in the cooperative promotion of a product.

trade promotions Marketers' activities directed to channel members to encourage them to provide special support or activities for the product or service. Also called *seller support*.

trade regulation ruling An FTC ruling designed to implicate an entire industry of unfair or deceptive practices and force the industry to correct these practices.

trade show In sales, an exhibition in which a number of manufacturers display their products. In sales promotion, a periodic gathering at which manufacturers, suppliers, and distributors in a particular industry or related industries display their products and provide information for potential buyers (retail, wholesale, or industrial).

U

unaided self-report questions Questions asked to induce respondents to indicate the brands they consider when they are getting ready to buy a certain product.

United States Postal Service (USPS) Government agency that watches over all mail-type marketing materials and investigates mail fraud schemes and other fraudulent marketing practices.

unity The state or quality of being in accord; harmony. There is a combination or arrangement of parts into a whole. There is a singleness or constancy of purpose or action.

use-experience test An in-depth interview with consumers who have a history of using the brand in question.

V

value added A common term used by marketers to refer to the consumers' perception of a significant advantage of one or more product features added to the firm's brand.

variations in quality perceptions Within a product line, there may be many brands differing in their level of quality—some good and some bad.

vertical cooperative advertising Advertising in which the retailer and other previous marketing channel members (e.g., manufacturers or wholesalers) share the cost.

videotext A form of electronic shopping in which consumers can place an order directly with the firm.

viral marketing A marketing phenomenon that facilitates and encourages people to pass along a marketing message; nicknamed *viral* because exposing people to a message mimics the process of passing a virus or disease from one person to another.

W

websites A collection of interconnected electronic "pages" on the Internet and used to provide information about a company, organization, cause, or individual. The website is often a crucial IMC component in building and maintaining a consistent brand image in the eyes of the consumer.

Wheeler-Lea Amendment An amendment to the Federal Trade Commission Act that added the phrase "unfair or deceptive acts or practices in commerce are hereby declared unlawful" to the Section 5 prohibition of unfair methods of competition in order to provide protection for consumers as well as competition.

word-of-mouth (WOM) communications An element or tool of marketing communications that focuses on consumers communicating among themselves about the firm's product. WOM communications involve both controllable and uncontrollable forms of communications. Controllable forms of WOM communications include stimulating WOM through advertising and sampling, simulating WOM communications through advertising, and using a referral system.

Index

Note: Page numbers in italics identify illustrations. An italic *t* next to a page number (e.g., 241*t*) indicates information that appears in a table. An italic *n* and number following a page number (e.g., 241*n*13) indicates information that appears in an end-of-chapter note and the number of the note where the material can be found.

A

Aaker, David A., 40*n*28, 116, 224*n*4, 225*n*8, 227*n*9, 228*n*11, 231*n*13, 232*n*14, 234*n*16, 241*n*19, 244*n*21, 245*n*22, 246*n*23, 256, 306*n*11, 306*n*12, 306*n*13, 306*n*14, 306*n*15, 308*n*17, 308*n*18, 318*n*32, 318*n*33, 319*n*36, 323, 365
Abbott Laboratories, 170–71
Absolute costs of media, 264–66
Absolut vodka, 105
Accelerated purchases, 182
Acceptance of brands, 314
Accounting functions, strategies emphasizing, 202
ACNielsen tracking studies, 317
Acquisitions, 15, 396
Acura automobiles, 239
ACUVUE contact lens, 6
Acxiom, 370
Adamy, Janet, 156*n*45
Ad hoc approach, 17–18
Administrative complaints, 35
Advance dating, 173
Advanced photo system, 354–55
Advertising
  with affective strategies, 274
  basic elements, 93–96
  broadcast media overview, 97–103
  budgeting for (*see* Budgeting)
  to children, 34, 37, 41–43
  cooperative, 172, 173, 174–76, 274–75
  corporate or institutional, 122–23, 275, 284
  corrective, 35
  direct-response, 152, 278, 281–82, 349*t*
  growing costs in mass media, 13–15
  with habit-formation strategies, 276–77
  impact on cultural values, 44–46
  impact on stereotypes, 31
  informative strategies, 264–71
  miscellaneous types, 113–14
  out-of-home media, 109–13
  percentage of sponsors measuring, 293
  print media overview, 103–9
  regulation of, 34–39
  with self-satisfaction strategies, 281
  theme line support, 16–17
Advertising/display allowances, 174
Advertising Revenue Report, 347
Advocacy advertising, 93–94, 127
Aerial advertising, 97, 271
Affective brand attitude, 310, 312–14

Affective communications strategy
  basic features, 24, 77
  in call center case study, 411
  implementing, 80, 81*t*, 274–76
Agents, 165
Aggarwal, Raj, 116, 366
Agres, Stuart, 234*n*16, 241*n*19
Aguilar, Francis J., 207*n*6, 208*n*8
AIDA model, 167
Aided-recall measures, 304, 310
Aircraft industry, 163, 179
Air Jordans, 245
Airline industry, 174, 197–98
Ajzen, Icek, 256, 316*n*26, 323
Alba, Joseph W., 229*n*12
Albion, Mark S., 34*n*10
Aleve, 231–32
Alexander, Marcus, 218, 339
Allen, Chris T., 316*n*27, 316*n*28
Allowances, 174, 176
All-you-can-afford method, 350–51
Alsop, Ronald, 40*n*27, 40*n*28, 42*n*38, 314*n*23
American Express, 14
Analysis. *See also* Situation analysis
  for budgeting, 64–65, 84, 354–62
  defined, 54–55
  for marketing strategies, 247–53
  need to integrate, 67–68, 383–88
  in SMC, 63–65
  in systems context, 83–84
Analytic/planning model
  affective strategies, 274–76
  habit-formation strategies, 276–81
  informative strategies, 263–74
  overview, 260–63
  self-satisfaction strategies, 281–84
Ancestral totems, 44*t*
And 1, 385
Andrew, Wernick, 49
Andrews, J. C., 40*n*27
Anheiser-Busch, 102–3
Animal or thing, brand as, 306
Annual reports, 130–31
Anticipated sales, budgets as percentage of, 345
Anton, Jon, 256
Appalachian history books, 368
Apple Computer, 123
Application, positioning by, 242–43, 248, 252
The Apprentice, 293
Arabe, Katrina C., 167*n*11, 168*n*13
Arbitron, 102, 268
Area of dominant influence, 99
Armstrong, Gary M., 41*n*33

Armstrong, Larry, 197*n*2
Arndt, Johan, 356*n*14
Arndt, Michael, 327*n*1, 334*n*
Arthritis Foundation, 146
Associative strength, 307–8
AT&T, 37
Atari, 306
Athletic shoe industry, 384, 385
Atkin, Charles, 249*n*26
Atkinson, Claire, 261*n*
Attack ads, 93–94
Attention levels, 268
Attitudes
  measuring, 310–14, 316
  objectives based on, 296
Attitude toward brand purchase, 316
Attribute sensory modality, 264
Attributes, positioning by, 228–29, 248, 250, 251, 252, 399
Audience fragmentation, 15
Audiotext, 282
Auto-attendants, 406
Auto dealers, newspaper advertising by, 108–9
Auto makers
  brand identities, 56–57
  brand positioning, 234, *235*
  employee discounts, 188
  Internet advertising, 343
  MINI promotion, 89–90, 133
  use of price-off deals, 187
  use of rebates, 185–86
Auto racing, 122, 124–25
Availability of substitutes, 213
Availability of supplies and suppliers, 213
Average quarter-hour (AQH) audience, 102
Avery, Susan, 151*n*29
Avis, 231
Avlonitis, G., 232*n*14
Avon, 156, 282
Awareness. *See* Brand awareness
Axelrod, Joel N., 323

B

Baby Boomers, 379
Bagozzi, Richard P., 316*n*27, 323
Baier, Martin, 159
Bailor, Coreen, 145*n*13
Barban, Arnold, 8*n*6, 287, 335*n*14, 336*n*15, 336*n*16, 336*n*17, 337*n*18, 337*n*19, 339
Barbie dolls, 46
Barker, Robert, 180*n*41

435

Barnes, Beth, 88, 287, 335*n*14, 336*n*15, 336*n*16, 336*n*17, 337*n*18, 337*n*19, 340
Barnes, J. B., 225*n*6
Barnes, Jeremy Scott, 403*n*
Barnes & Noble, 187
Baron, Roger B., 116
Barriers to entry, 32–33, 212
Barry, Thomas E., 323
Bartos, Rena, 324
Barwise, Patrick, 147*n*22
Baselines for objective setting, 331
Basketball shoes, 385
Bass, Frank, 225*n*8
Battaglia, Andy, 184*n*57
Baugh, L. Sue, 28
Baumler, J., 70, 370*n*2, 392
Bawa, Kapil, 186*n*66, 187*n*68
BCG matrix, 205–7
Beach 'n Billboard, 97
Beach promotions, 97
Beatty, Sally Goll, 42*n*37
Beauty products, 179
Beer market, 32–33
BehaviorScan, 317
Belch, George E., 25*n*20, 87, 342*n*2, 356*n*13
Belch, Michael A., 25*n*2, 87, 342*n*2, 356*n*13
Belief strength, measuring, 302–3, 305, 311
Belk, Russell W., 45*n*
Ben & Jerry's Ice Cream, 123
Benefit segmentation, 21
Benefits, positioning by, 241–42
Benham, Lee, 33*n*9
Bennett, Christopher L., 147*n*24
Berg, Thomas L., 256
Berger, Arthur Asa, 49
Berger, Paul D., 159
Bergh, Bruce Vanden, 287, 335*n*14, 336*n*15, 336*n*16, 336*n*17, 337*n*18, 337*n*19, 339
Bergman, Thomas P., 159
Berman, Barry, 165*n*3, 180*n*, 187*n*
Berman, Dennis, 156*n*45
Berman, Ronald, 44*n*40, 49
Bertrand, Kate, 179*n*38
Better Business Bureau, 37, 38, 40
Betty Crocker, 246
Bianco, Anthony, 14*n*, 144*n*, 269*n*
Billboard advertising, 97, 109. *See also* Outdoor advertising
Blackwell, Roger D., 320*n*38
Blair, Tony, 130
Blasko, Vincent, 365, 366
Blattberg, Robert C., 191, 287
Block, M., 249*n*26
Block, Tamara Brezen, 287
Blogs, 133
Bloom, Paul N., 33*n*4
Bly, Robert W., 159
BMW
 campaign continuity, 9, *10*
 cooperative advertising, *177*
 MINI promotion, 89–90, 133
 product placement, 284
Body image stereotypes, 31
Body Shop, 8, 9
Bogart, Leo, 287, 335*n*14, 336*n*15, 336*n*16, 336*n*17, 337*n*18, 337*n*19
Bond, David, 193*n*

Bono, *130*
Bonus packs, 181, 182, 280
Bose headphones, 305
Boston Consulting Group (BCG) matrix, 205–7
Boston Properties, 38
Bounce-back coupons, 279
Boyer, G. Bruce, 235*n*17
Branch, Shelly, 38*n*24
Brand acceptance, 314
Brand-as-an-animal-or-thing test, 306
Brand-as-a-person test, 306
Brand associations
 defined, 77
 measuring, 305–7
 objectives based on, 298–99, 333–35
Brand attitude, measuring, 310–14
Brand awareness
 measuring, 307–10
 sample objectives for, 299
 strategic focus on, 77, 295–96, 396, 410–12
Brand-distributor tie-ins, 236–38, 252
Brand do objectives, 296
Branded Entertainment Reporting Service, 134
Brand equity, 4
Brand feel objectives, 296
Brand identity, 4
Branding, complexity of, 4–7
Brand knowledge, measuring, 302–5
Brand learn objectives, 296
Brand-listing procedure, 314
Brand loyalty, 249–50, 319–20
Brand preference
 measuring, 314–15
 objectives based on, 296, 299
 strategic focus on, 77
Brand profits, 296
Brand purchase, measuring, 317–18
Brand recall, 308
Brand recognition, 309–10
Brand repeat objectives, 296
Brands
 defined, 4
 institutional advertising, 123
 product categories and forms versus, 227
Brand sales, 296
Brand satisfaction, measuring, 318–19
Brand switchers, 249
Brand symbols, 251
Brand trial or purchase
 measuring, 315–18
 objectives based on, 299
 strategic focus on, 78
Brand unity, 6
Brand use, segmentation by, 21
Brand-user test, 306
Breakenridge, Deirdre, 256
Brenner, Robert, 167*n*8
Bressler, Martin S., 278*n*6
Brett, Daniel J., 47*n*47
Brier, Noah Rubin, 387*n*
Bristol, Terry, 41*n*33
British newspapers, 182
Britt, S. H., 324
Broadband, 294
Broadbent, Simon, 324, 365
Broadcast direct response marketing, 146–47

Broadcasting, 97, 274. *See also* Mass media; Radio advertising; Television advertising
Brochures, 397
Brokers, 165
Broniarczyk, Susan M., 45*n*44
Brooking, Pip, 185*n*59
Brooks Brothers, 239
Brown, Gordon, 324
Brown, Juanita J., 314*n*25, 324
Brown, Randall S., 356*n*14
Brown, Stephen W., 249*n*26
Browne, Beverly A., 47*n*47
Brucks, Merrie, 41*n*33, 253*n*36
Bruzzone, Donald E., 40*n*28
Budgeting
 all-you-can-afford method, 350–51
 in case studies, 397, 399, 401–2, 418
 changes based on feedback, 62–63, 82–83
 need to integrate, 66–67, 68, 380, 382–83, 386–88
 objective-task method, 350
 overview, 342–43
 previous-budget method, 351
 quantitative methods, 347–48, 358, 360
 ratio-to-sales methods, 345, 358
 in relation to competitors, 346–47, 358–59
 return-on-investment method, 348–50
 role of situation analysis in, 64–65, 84, 354–62
 Schultz et al. model shortcomings, 25
 SMC approach, 61–62, 351–54
 in systems context, 78
Bud Light radio campaign, 102–3
Buffet, Warren, 4
Buick cars, *230*
Buildup approach to budgeting
 elements of, 61–62, 78, 343
 in systems context, 84
Bulik, Beth Snyder, 175*n*23
Bulkeley, William M., 147*n*21
Bureau of Alcohol, Tobacco, Firearms and Explosives (ATF), 34, 35
Burke, Ken, 151*n*31
Burnett, John, 1*n*1, 116
Burrows, Peter, 197*n*2, 327*n*1
Burton, Scott, 249*n*24
Business magazines, marketing, 273, 275–76
Business-to-business marketing, 178, 179, 346. *See also* Trade promotions
Buy American campaigns, 233
Buy-back allowances, 174
Buyer-seller dyads, 166
Buying allowances, 174, 176, 280
Buy one, get one free offers, 182
Buzzell, Robert D., 33*n*6, 33*n*8, 348*n*6
Buzz marketing
 defined, 119
 in MINI promotion, 90, 133
 for movies, 119, 120
 viral marketing and guerilla marketing, 132–33

C

Cable & Wireless case study, 393–402
Cable television
 advertising reach, 99
 direct-response marketing growth from, 146, 147

growth of, 14
shopping channels, 283
Cagan, Jonathan, 256
Calderwood, James A., 34*n*11
California Milk Processor Board, 220
Call center case study, 403–12
Call centers, 145
Calvin Klein, 9
Camargo, Eduardo G., 46*n*
Campaign continuity, 8
Campbell, Andrew, 218, 339
Campbell's Soup, 242
Campus Connections, 74
Canada Dry, 244
Canned presentations, 166
Canning, Gordon, Jr., 211*n*11
Canon USA, 131
Cantor, Joanne, 47*n*47
Capital intensity, 212
Car dealers, newspaper advertising by, 108–9
Cardona, Mercedes M., 137
Card packs, 152
Careers as systems, 54
Carl's Jr., 41
Carlson, Les, 36*n*20
Carman, James M., 116, 365
CarMax, 274
Carnevale, Mary Lu, 36*n*19
Cartoon Network, 184
Case studies
  Cable & Wireless plc, 393–402
  Hancock Rack, 413–18
  UnitedHealth Group, 403–12
"Cash cows," 205–7
Cash flow, 203–4, 301
Catalogs. *See also* Direct marketing
  defined, 152
  electronic, 149, 151
  with self-satisfaction strategies, 281
  targeted communications with, 153–54, 155
Categories of products, 227
Cause marketing, 127
Cavaleri, Steven, 70, 392
Caywood, Clarke, 7*n*4, 7*n*5, 10*n*8, 12*n*10, 12*n*11, 28
Cease and desist orders, 35
Celebrities
  impact on brand attitudes, 312
  use in brand positioning, 245–46, 249
Cell phones, 148, 360
Cespedes, Frank V., 256
Channels of distribution
  defined, 163
  influence on brand/consumer relationships, 174
  power shifts in, 172, 175, 176–77
Chao, Paul, 232*n*15
Chewing gum distribution channels, 165
Chick-fil-A, 111, 238
Chiew Tung Moi, 182*n*45
Chiger, Sherry, 153*n*37, 154*n*39, 154*n*41
Children, advertising to, 34, 36, 37, 41–43
Children's Advertising Review Unit, 37, 40, 43
Children's Online Privacy Protection Act, 36
Children's Television Act, 42
Chrysler, 343
Chura, Hillary, 40*n*30

Churchman, C. W., 70, 370*n*2, 392
Cialis, 334
Cioletti, Jeff, 177*n*30
Circulation, 105, 108
Claiborne, C. B., 250*n*29
Claritas, 317
Clark, Shawn, 191
Classes of products, 227, *228*, 252
Claussen pickles, 241, 242
Cleland, Kim, 146*n*16
Clutter, 98
Coca-Cola
  brand image, 246
  C2 product, 221
  Montreux Jazz Festival participation, 125
  product class positioning, *228*
Cocheo, Steve, 142*n*9
Coe, John, 191
Coffee, 242, 306
Cognitive brand attitude, 310–12
Cognitive-structure indexes, 304–5
Colford, Steven, 36*n*22
Colgate-Palmolive, 342
College market, 73–74, 282
Colley, R. H., 324
Collis, David J., 218, 339
Colman, Stephen, 324
Color in advertising, 107
ColorStay makeup, 359
Commercial aircraft industry, 163, 179
Common look of communications, 16
Communications objectives, 23. *See also* Objectives
Communications strategy, 22, 23, 24. *See also* Strategies
Communications tactics, 23–25. *See also* Tactics
Community building, 9
Company position assessment, 207, *208*, 209–11
Company tours, 129–30
Compaq, 197
Competition, 32–33, 251
Competitive analysis, 205, 210, 211–12
Competitive-parity budgeting methods, 346–47, 359
Competitive structure of industries, 212
Competitive users, 20–21
Competitors
  budgeting in relation to, 347, 358–59
  positioning in relation to, 231–32, 249, 251
  setting corporate objectives in relation to, 330
  setting marketing communications objectives in relation to, 336
  setting marketing objectives in relation to, 333
CompUSA, 197
Computer-based training, 407
Computers, primary versus selective demand, 252
Computer technologies
  adoption by millennial generation, 282
  decreasing costs, 13
  IMC examples, 370–71
  impact on IMC, 15–16
  impact on markets, 214

reality versus, 379
shopping, 283
Computer-telephony integration technology, 406
Concentration of customers, 213
Concentration of suppliers, 213
Concerts, 125–27, 128, *130*
Condé Nast Traveler, 103
Condoms, sampling, 186
Conjoint analysis, 83
Conquesting, 188
Consent orders, 35
Consideration sets, 119
Consistency of message and media, 11, 23
Consultative selling, 166
Consumer-based approaches to IMC planning, 18–25
Consumer-based integration, 11
Consumer databases, 19. *See also* Database marketing
Consumer decision making, 247–48
Consumer experience, 249
Consumer information, 33*t*, 34
Consumer involvement
  defined, 249
  determining, 384
  impact on marketing budgets, 361
Consumer promotions
  defined, 163
  performance measurement, 187–88
  strategic elements, 180–87
Consumer-related factors in strategy selection, 247–50
Consumer societies, role of promotions in, 44–45
Consumer sovereignty, 32, 41–42
Contact management, 21–22
Contests
  consumer, 181, 184, 283
  sales, 173, 178, 284
Continuity, 8–9
Continuity plans, 182
Control
  in budgeting, 357–58
  corrective actions, 373–77
  defined, 54
  need to integrate, 67, 380–83
  sample scenario, 371–73
  Schultz et al. model shortcomings, 25
  in systems context, 82–83
  use of feedback in, 62–63, 370–71
Cooperative advertising
  with affective strategies, 274–75
  defined, 172, 173
  major forms, 174–76
Coordinated integration, 11
Coordination, monitoring and control of, 374, 375
Coppertone lotion, 242–43
Corkingdale, David, 324
Corporate advertising, 122–23, 275, 284
Corporate communications, 128–32
Corporate image, 209–10
Corporate mix, 76–77, 376
Corporate objectives
  alignment of marketing objectives with, 25–26
  budgeting from, 351–52, 356

in case studies, 395–96, 397–98, 408–9
examples, 298, 300*t*
implementing, 79–80
measuring, 300–302
monitoring and control based on, 371–72, 376–77
in system integration, 377–78
using situation analysis to set, 327–32
Corporate strategy. *See also* Strategies
in case studies, 395–96, 397–98, 408–9, 415
defined, 55
major approaches, 199–204, 297*t*
reassessing, 376
role of analysis in selecting, 204–15
setting objectives for, 79–80, 377–78
Corporate websites, 130–31
Corrective actions for monitoring and control, 373–77, 380–81
Corrective advertising, 35
Cortez, John P., 40*n*30
Cosmetic industry marketing budgets, 359
Cost leadership, 221
Cost per rating point, 100
Cost per thousand, 96, 268, 269
Costs, absolute, 264–66
Costs of sales calls, 167–68
Count and recount promotions, 174
Country-of-origin positioning, 232–33, 249, 250, 253
Coupon redemptions, 181
Coupons
defined, 181
evolution of, 182–83
with habit-formation strategies, 278–79
Courtney, Alice E., 47*n*47, 49
CoverGirl cosmetics, 243–44, 247, 359
Cramming, 36
Crate & Barrel catalog, *153*
Cravens, David W., 252*n*35
Creative decisions in advertising, 270–71
Creative selling, 167, 284
Credibility of marketing messages, 12–13
Credit card companies, 185
Crest toothpaste
brand knowledge about, 302–3
positioning strategy, 228, 251
product placement, 293
subbrands, 4–5, 53
Cron, William L., 191
Cross, Richard, 256
Cross-ruffs, 181, 279
Cross-selling, 144, 182
Cultural beliefs and values, advertising's influence on, 44–46
Cume or cumulative radio audience, 102
Curad bandages, *231*
Curry, Sheree R., 184*n*54
Customer analysis, 204, 212–13
Customer benefits, positioning by, 241–42
Customer factors in budgeting, 361–62
Customer groups, 226
Customer image, positioning by, 243–45
Customer loyalty, positioning by, 249–50
Customer surveys, 406–7
Cyclical demand, 212–13

D

Dacin, Peter A., 178*n*36
Daily effective circulation, 110
Dalrymple, Douglas J., 191
Danaher, Peter J., 116, 366
Danziger, Pamela, 379
Database development, 19
Database marketing
decreasing costs, 13
defined, 140
with direct mail and catalogs, 153–54
examples, 370–71
Databases
creating, 142–44
defined, 139
of mailing-list houses, 277–78
Data gathering
impact on trade promotion requirements, 175
in Schultz et al. IMC model, 19
sources, 142
on trade promotion results, 179–80
Data mining, 142
Dating, 172, 173
Davis, Frank W., 256
Day, George, 205*n*5, 207*n*7, 209*n*10, 211*n*12, 330*n*3, 330*n*4, 330*n*5, 330*n*6, 330*n*22, 331*n*7
Dayparts
defined, 98
radio advertising, 100, 101–2
TV advertising, 98–99
Dealer tie-ins, 173
Debevec, Kathleen, 313*n*22, 317*n*29
Debt relief concerts, 128, *130*
DeCarlo, Thomas E., 191
Deceptive promotions, 34–36
Decision-making concepts, 54
Decision-process test, 306
Decision trees, 55, 57–58
DeCloet, Derek, 184*n*55
Dedicated CSRs, 407–8
Deighton, John, 6*n*1
Dell Computers, 22, 327
Demand, impact on marketing budgets, 362
Demand cyclicity, 212–13
Demographics, 83
Demsey, John, 329
Designated market area, 99
Design engineers, 361, 362
Developing world, outdoor advertising in, 110, *111*
Diener, Ed, 45*n*42
Diet cola marketing, 221
Dieting infomercials, 282
Differentiation, 221, 252, 361
Direct-broadcast commercials, 146
Direct communications, 239–40
Direct mail, 152, 153, 277–78, 411–12
Direct marketing
broadcast direct response, 146–47
in call center case study, 411–12
catalog and direct mail options, 152–55
current status, 140–41
database creation, 142–44
defined, 140
direct selling, 155–56

electronic methods overview, 147–52
with habit-formation strategies, 277–78
with self-satisfaction strategies, 281–83
telemarketing overview, 145–46
total sales and contributions from, 139
Directory advertising, 113–14
Direct-response advertising
ACUVUE campaign, 6
defined, 152
with habit-formation strategies, 278
measurability, 349*t*
with self-satisfaction strategies, 281–82
Direct selling, 155–56, 283
Discounts, 174
Discover card, 185
Discovery Channel, 259
Discriminating criteria in media selection, 264, 267
Discriminatory pricing, 36
Disney, 261
Displays, 173
Distilled Spirits Council of the United States, 37
Distribution channels. *See* Channels of distribution
Distribution effectiveness, measuring, 210
Distributor-brand tie-ins, 236–38, 252
Distributor location, 238–39, 248
Distributor serviceability, 239, *240*, 252
Diversity, 4, 5
Divestment strategies
with BCG matrix, 207
budgeting for, 357
defined, 77
implementing, 203–4
objective setting for, 79–80
Doctors, email contact with, 150
Doer communications strategy
basic features, 24, 78
implementing, 80, 81*t*, 276–81
"Dogs," 205–7
Dolan, Robert, 89*n*1
Donato, Mary, 166*n*4, 168, 168*n*
Dongsub Han, 87
Douthitt, Robin A., 45*n*42
Doyle, Peter, 252*n*34
DreamWorks, 120
Duncan, T., 7*n*4, 7*n*5, 10*n*8, 12*n*10, 12*n*11, 28
DuPont
advertising budget study, 348
corporate advertising, 275
sponsorships, 284
Duracell, 36
Dutt, Jill, 225*n*5
DVD advertising, 113
Dyadic relationships, 166

E

Easterlin, Richard A., 45*n*42
Eastlack, Joseph O. Jr., 365
Eastman Kodak, 354–55
Economic conditions, 213
Economic issues in marketing communications, 32–34
Economies of scale, 33
The Economist, 154

Edwards, Cliff, 327*n*1
Effective net reach, 95
Effective reach, 95
Eisner, Michael, 4
Elasticity of communications tools, 348
Election campaign advertising, 93–94
Electronic catalogs, 149, 151
Electronic coupons, 183–84, 279
Electronic magazines, 104
Electronic mail, 148, 150
Electronic newsletters, 149, 151
Elgin, Ben, 327*n*1
Eli Lilly, 334
Eliminating criteria in media selection, 264–66
Elliot, Stuart, 38*n*24
Elliott, Richard, 88
Emmons, Robert A., 45*n*42
Emotional appeals, 274
Employee discounts, 188
Employee turnover, preventing, 202
End-aisle displays, 173
Enders, Albrecht, 159
Endicott, R. Craig, 342*n*1
Energizer Holdings, 36
Engel, James F., 320*n*38
Engineering functions, strategies emphasizing, 200–202
Enis, Ben M., 42*n*37
Enrico, Roger, 246*n*23, 256
Ensure, 240
Entrenched loyalty, measuring, 320
Environmental analysis, 205, 213–14
Epocrates software, 133
Erectile dysfunction drugs, 334
Ericksen, Gary M., 232*n*15, 251*n*32
ESPN 360, 261
Estée Lauder, 329
Esther, Thorson, 88
Ethics, 39–46, 267
Ettenson, Richard, 232*n*15, 250*n*31
Evan, W. M., 136, 137
Evans, Joel R., 165*n*3, 180*n*, 187*n*
Evansville-Vanderburgh School Corporation, 193–94
Event marketing
 with affective strategies, 275
 overview, 124–28
 with self-satisfaction strategies, 284
Everett, S. E., 7*n*4, 28
Everyday Adventures, 155
Everyday low price strategy, 183
Evoked sets, 251, 276–77
Experience curve effects, 210
Experience of consumers, positioning by, 249
Experiences, buying, 379
Experiential memoir symbols, 44*t*
Experimental method of budgeting, 347–48
External situation analysis, 204
Exxon brand identity, 4
Exxon Valdez accident, 4, 120, 121–22
Ezines, 104

F

Factor cosmetics, 359
Familiarity, impact on marketing budgets, 362
Farley, John U., 147*n*23
Farris, Paul W., 33*n*8, 34*n*10

Fast food advertising, 100
Fattah, Hassan, 148*n*
Favorability measure of attitude toward purchase, 316
Fazio, Russell H., 307*n*16
FCB model, 24–25, 261, *262*
Featherstone, Mike, 49
Federal Communications Commission (FCC), 34
Federal regulations, 34–36
Federal Trade Commission (FTC), 34–36, 42
Feedback, 62–63, 370–71. *See also* Monitoring and control
Feedback mechanisms, 62, 82–83
Feedforward, 63
Feeler communications strategy
 basic features, 24, 77
 implementing, 80, 81*t*, 274–76
Feit, Michelle, 159
Female stereotypes, 31
Ferguson Enterprises, 146
Ferrell, O. C., 218, 333*n*8, 333*n*9, 333*n*10, 333*n*11, 334*n*12, 334*n*13, 339
Fetto, John, 150*n*
Field, Catherine, 184*n*50
Finance functions, strategies emphasizing, 203–4
Financial factors in market position, 211
Firm changes, 331, 334–35, 337
Fishbein, Martin, 256, 316*n*26, 323
Fitzgerald, Kate, 38*n*24
Flamholtz, E., 70, 370*n*2, 392
Flint Joe, 38*n*24
Flip-flops, 97
Focus, in Porter's strategy model, 221
Focus group research, 334
Follett Corporation, 74
Food and Drug Administration (FDA), 34
Food Network, 146
Food product companies, 175
Foote, Cone, & Belding model, 24–25, 261, 262. *See also* Analytic/planning model
Ford, Neil M., 178*n*36
Ford Motor Company
 strategic product focus, 224, 229
 truck image, 251
 Volvo brand within, 57
Forecasts
 budgeting from, 345, 360
 setting objectives in relation to, 330, 333, 336
Forms of products, 227
Formula One racing, 122
Forward buying, 172
Fournier, Susan, 89*n*1
Franco, Mark Del, 155*n*42
Frazier, 414–15
Free-association test, 306
Freeman, R. W., 136, 137
Freeman, Sholnn, 186*n*64, 188*n*73
Free merchandise incentives, 173
Free premiums, 283
Free samples. *See* Sample products
Free speech rights, 42
Free-standing inserts, 104
Frequency, 95, 96
Frequent-flier programs, 143

Fuji Photo Film, 354–55
Functional integration, 11
Functionality versus value-expressiveness, 250
Fusaro, Roberta, 150*n*26

G

Gaeth, Gary, 232*n*15, 250*n*31
Gale, Bradley T., 33*n*6
Galvin, John, 290*n*1
Garby, F., 232*n*14
Gardial, Sarah F., 256
Gardisch, Walter, 143*n*11
Garfield, Bob, 40*n*30
Garrison, Stephen, 159
Gates, Bill, 4, *130*
Gatorade, 242
General Electric, 199, 207–8
General Motors
 college market promotions, 73
 corporate system, 65, *66*
 employee discounts, 188
 intangible factors positioning, *230*
 Saab brand within, 56–57
 use of patriotism, 233
GenZ Magazine, 74
Geographic selectivity, 266
Gerry, Johnson, 339
Ghemawat, Pankaj, 218, 339
Giant Eagle stores, 183
Gibson, 125
Gilligan, Colin, 365
Global call centers, 145
Global marketing agents, 165
Goals, 11, 58–59. *See also* Objectives
Goldberg, Marvin E., 41*n*33
Golden, Daniel, 36*n*17
Goldwasser, Joan, 185*n*63
Gonzalez, Gloria, 184*n*56
Goodwill Industries, 152
Goold, Michael, 218, 339
Gopalakrishna, Srinath, 178*n*32
"Got Milk?" campaign, 220
Government regulation. *See* Regulations
The Greats, 359
Greenberg, Karl, 90*i*1*n*2
Greyser, Stephen A., 40*n*28
Grimshaw, Colin, 174*n*21
Grocery industry weekly specials, 183
Gross rating points, 96, 110
Gross reach, 269
Group selling, 283
Grover, Ronald, 120*n*
Growth strategies
 budgeting for, 352, 357, 359–60
 in case studies, 408–9, 415–16
 defined, 77
 objective setting for, 79–80, 200–201
Guerilla marketing, 350*t*
Gunther, Robert E., 256
Gustafson, Robert, 31*n*1
Guth, Robert A., 150*n*28
Gutman, Jonathan, 324

H

Habit-formation communications strategy
 basic features, 24, 78
 implementing, 80, 81*t*, 276–81

Habits, media use, 267, 294
Ha, C. Min, 232*n*14, 232*n*15
Haefner, James E., 32*n*2, 32*n*3, 33*n*7, 39*n*26, 41*n*32, 44*n*39, 46*n*46, 49
Haidt, Jonathan, 45*n*44
Haire, Mason, 324
Hall, Floyd, 369
Halliday, Jean, 56*n*, 90*i*1*n*3, 343*n*
Halonen, Doug, 34*n*12
Hambrick, Donald C., 205*n*5, 207*n*7, 209*n*10, 211*n*12, 330*n*2, 330*n*3, 330*n*4, 330*n*5, 330*n*6, 331*n*7
Hamel, Prahald, 339
Hamermesh, Richard, 207*n*6, 208 *n*8
Hamm, Steve, 327*n*1
Hamper, Robert J., 28
Hancock Rack case study, 413–18
Harvest strategies
  with BCG matrix, 207
  budgeting for, 357
  defined, 77
  implementing, 202
  objective setting for, 79
Haspeslagh, Philippe, 205*n*5, 207*n*7, 209*n*10, 211*n*12, 330*n*2, 330*n*3, 330*n*4, 330*n*5, 330*n*6, 331*n*7
Hathcote, Jan M., 284*n*9
Hatton, Angela, 256
Hauser, Hohn R., 242*n*20
Haytko, Diana L., 193*n*1
Head & Shoulders shampoo, 241
Health care industry
  email use in, 150
  medical equipment training, 179
  referral systems, 273
  trade shows, 178
  UnitedHealth Group case study, 403–12
Health maintenance organizations, 273
Healthmax treadmills, 235–36
Hechinger, John, 178*n*37
Heckman, James, 36*n*21
Hedonistic values, 45
Hein, Kenneth, 185*n*58
Heineken beer, 133
Heinemann, Anna, 127*n*, 134*n*
Helsen K., 235*n*17
Henderson, Bruce D., 205*n*4, 206*n*
Herr, Paul M., 307*n*16
Herremans, Irene, 116, 366
Hershey's chocolate, 33
Heslop, L. A., 232*n*14, 232*n*15
Hewlett-Packard, 197, 228
Higher-order constructs, 57
High-involvement products, 262–63
Hill, Julie Skur, 46*n*
Hills, Gerald E., 252*n*35
Hilton, Paris, 41
Historical-statistical method of budgeting, 348, 358
Holiday Inn brand image, 306
Holloway, Bob, 185*n*62
Horizontal cooperative advertising, 172, 173, 174–75
Horwitz, Jeff, 45*n*42
Hostile takeovers, 197
Hotel/motel positioning, 234
House brands, 176
Households, 99–100
Households using television, 100
House lists, 154
How-brand-is-different test, 306–7
Hume, Scott, 36*n*20
Humphrey, Jack, 193
Hunt, Shelby, 53*n*1
Hutchinson, J. Wesley, 229*n*12

I

IBM, 197, 259
Idealization of celebrities, 245
Image
  brand positioning by, 243–45
  corporate, 209–10
  measuring, 304, 305
  of media, 268
Inbound calling, 145
Indiana Middle Grades Reading Program, 193–94
Indianapolis Grand Prix, 122
Indirect communications, 239–40
Industry averages
  budgeting in relation to, 346, 358
  setting objectives in relation to, 330, 333, 335–36
Industry factors in budgeting, 358–60
Industry group self-regulation, 37
Infomercials, 146–47, 278, 282
Information technology impact on IMC, 15–16. *See also* Computer technologies; Technology
Informative communications strategy
  advertising tactics, 264–71
  basic features, 24, 77
  in case studies, 400–402, 416
  implementing, 78, 80, 81*t*, 263–64, 385
  reseller support and public relations, 271–72
  word-of-mouth tactics, 273–74
Ingredient-sponsored cooperative advertising, 172, 173, 175
Innovation, 32
Innovation strategies
  with BCG matrix, 207
  budgeting for, 357
  defined, 77
  implementing, 203
  objective setting for, 79
In-Program Performance, 134
Inserts, 153
Instant coupons, 279
Instant messaging, 149, 151
Institutional advertising, 122–23
In-store advertising
  basic features, 111–13
  as reseller support function, 177–78
  with self-satisfaction strategies, 284
In-store coupons, 183
Intangible factors, positioning by, 229–30, 249, 251, 252
Integrated marketing communications. *See also* Case studies; Systems model
  ACUVUE example, 6
  company examples, 370–71
  conditions leading to, 12–16
  defining concept, 7
  implementing, 65–68, 377–88
  levels of development, 10–12
  major characteristics, 8–10
  planning approaches, 16–26
Integration
  defined, 75
  need for, 10–11
  within systems, 65–68, 85, 377–88
Intel, 175, 274–75
Interactive advertising, 277
Interactive Advertising Bureau, 347
Interactive marketing, 140
Interactive voice response systems, 406
Interlake, 414–15
Intermedia Advertising Group (IAG) Research, 134
Intermedia selection, 264–67
Internal situation analysis, 205
Internet
  advertising measurability, 349*t*
  American Express advertising, 14
  Cable & Wireless backbone, 394, 395
  direct marketing methods overview, 147, 149–51
  e-coupons, 183–84
  growing importance for business-to-business marketing, 178
  growth of advertising on, 343, 347
  impact on media habits, 294
  rebate redemption via, 185
  usage data, 38–39
Internet direct advertising, 149
Internet shopping, 379
Internet yellow pages, 79
Interpersonal medium symbols, 44*t*
Interplak, 356–57
Interviews, 129–30
Intramedia selection, 264, 268
Inventories, promotions to reduce, 185–86, 187
Involvement of consumers
  determining, 384
  impact on marketing budgets, 360, 361
  product positioning by, 249
iPods, 185
The Italian Job, 90, 133
Ivory soap, 306

J

Jackson, Rob, 28
Jacoby, Jacob, 251*n*32
Jaguar, 234, 235
Jain, Subash C., 207*n*6, 211*n*11
James Bond movies, 132
Janoff, Barry, 137*n*5, 385*n*
Japan, view of American culture, 46
J.D. Power and Associates, 272
Jensen, Elizabeth, 42*n*37
Jerry Lewis MDA Labor Day Telethon, 141, 142
Jhally, Sut, 49
Jiffy Lube, 225
Johansson, John K., 232*n*15, 251*n*32
Johar, J. S., 250*n*29, 250*n*30
Johnson, Bradley, 259*n*2
Johnson, Gerry, 218
Johnson, Michael D., 256
Johnson, Philip L., 242*n*20
Johnson, Steve, 154*n*38
Johnson & Johnson, 6

Johnson Controls, 303–4, 309–10
Jon, Lafayette, 292*n*1
Jones, John P., 116, 366
Jordan, Michael, 245
Jugenheimer, Donald W., 287

K

Kaatz, Ron, 287
Kahn, B. E., 235*n*17
Kahn, R., 70, 370*n*2, 392
Kapferer, Jean-Noel, 249*n*27
Kaplan, Robert S., 218, 339
Karr, Albert R., 42*n*37
Katz, D., 70, 370*n*2, 392
Katz, Helen E., 287, 335*n*14, 336*n*15, 336*n*16, 336*n*17, 337*n*18, 337*n*19, 339
Keene, Karyln H., 312*n*21
Keller, Kevin Lane, 16*n*15, 25*n*20, 28
Keller-Crescent Company, 193
Kenmore brand, 236–37
Kentucky Fried Chicken, 306
Key competitors. *See* Competitors
Kilburn, David, 46*n*
Kim, Ilchul, 87
King, C. W., 225*n*8
King, Karen W., 116
Kitchen, Phillip J., 87
Kleine, Susan Schultz, 316*n*27, 316*n*28
Kliatchko, Jerry, 87
Kline, Stephen, 49
Kmart, 183, 369
Knowledge-base software, 406
Kohnstamm, Abby, 259
Kolbe, Richard H., 47*n*47
Kotler, Philip, 25*n*20, 88, 199*n*3, 225*n*7, 250*n*28, 252*n*35, 300*n*6, 300*n*7, 348*n*8
Kruegel, Dave, 317*n*30, 324
Krugman, E. H., 304*n*8, 310*n*20, 324
Kuzma, John R., 284*n*10

L

Labatt's Brewery, 177–78
Labor market, 214
Laczniak, Russell N., 36*n*20, 305*n*9
Laddering technique, 307
Lancaster, Kent M., 287, 335*n*14, 336*n*15, 336*n*16, 336*n*17, 337*n*18, 337*n*19, 339, 356*n*14, 366
Lane, Ronald, 310*n*19
Lane, W. Ronald, 116
Lane Bryant, 370
Lang, Annie, 324
Lanham Act, 36
Larsen, Val, 46*n*45
LATimes.com, 107
La Tour, Michael, 47*n*47
Laurent, Gilles, 249*n*27
Lauterborn, Robert F., 18*n*17, 19*n*18, 28, 88, 287, 335*n*14, 336*n*15, 336*n*16, 336*n*17, 337*n*18, 337*n*19, 340
Lautman, Kay, 159
Lavidge, Robert J., 324
Lawton, Christopher, 105*n*7
Lazarde, Michelle M., 232*n*15
Learning, objectives based on, 296
Leasing companies, 163
Lee, Dong-Jin, 46*n*45

Legal restrictions on advertising, 266
Leiss, William, 49
Leno, Jay, 90
Leo, Bogart, 339
Lerner, A. Y., 70, 370*n*2, 392
Lester, Lisa Yorgey, 141*n*6
Levitra, 334
Lewis, Peter, 185*n*60
Liberty Mutual, *240*
Lichtenstein, Donald R., 249*n*24
Lieberman, David, 42*n*35
Liefeld, John, 232*n*15
Life satisfaction, 45–46
Lifestyle
 as mailing list criterion, 278
 positioning by, 246–47, 251
Lifetime values, 155
Lilien, Gary L., 178*n*32, 300*n*6, 346*n*3, 348*n*8, 359*n*17, 359*n*18
Linkages, 53
Linkner, Josh, 143*n*10
Lipman, Joanne, 40*n*28
Lippe, Dan, 42*n*34
Lipstein, Benjamin, 293*n*2, 324
Liquor advertising, 37–38
Little, John D. C., 116, 346*n*3, 348*n*5, 359*n*17, 359*n*18, 366
L.L. Bean, 155, 175, *176*
Location. *See* Place
Lodish, Leonard M., 287, 335*n*14, 336*n*15, 336*n*16, 336*n*17, 337*n*18, 337*n*19, 339
Logos, 410–11
Long-term objectives, 300
Lotus Development Corp., 197
Lower-order constructs, 57
Low-fare carriers, 197, 198
Low-involvement products, 262
Low price, positioning by, 234–36, 249, 250
Loyalty, product positioning by, 249–50
Loyalty/frequency programs, 143
Loyalty measurement, 319–20
Loyal users, 20
Lucas, D. B., 324
Lucas, George H., Jr., 218, 333*n*8, 333*n*9, 333*n*10, 333*n*11, 334*n*12, 334*n*13, 339
Luck, David, 218, 333*n*8, 333*n*9, 333*n*10, 333*n*11, 334*n*12, 334*n*13, 339
Lundegaard, Karen, 188*n*72
Lutz, Richard J., 305*n*9

M

MacArthur, Kate, 100*n*4, 221*n*
MacDonald, Maurice, 45*n*42
Machleit, Karen A., 316*n*27, 316*n*28
MacKenzie, Scott B., 305*n*9
MacMillan, Ian C., 205*n*5, 207*n*7, 209*n*10, 211*n*12, 330*n*2, 330*n*3, 330*n*4, 330*n*5, 330*n*6, 331*n*7
Madagascar, 120
MADD, 127
Maddox, Kate, 176*n*24
Magazine advertising
 basic features, 103–5
 costs, 266, 268, 269
 drawing attention in, 270–71
 sensory modalities, 264

Mahajan, Vijay, 205*n*5, 207*n*7, 209*n*10, 211*n*12, 256, 330*n*2, 330*n*3, 330*n*4, 330*n*5, 330*n*6, 331*n*7
Mahoney, Sarah, 137
Mail fraud, 34
Mailing-list companies, 277–78
Mail-in rebates, 185
Maintain position strategy, 79, 201–2
Majaro, S., 324
Major, Meg, 170*n*18
Management, relation to strategies, 58–59
Mandel, Ken, 151*n*30
Mandese, Joe, 259*n*1
Mangalindan, Mylene, 150*n*27
Mangleburg Tamara F., 41*n*33
Manning, Gerald L., 191
Manrodt, Karl B., 256
Manufacturer's agents, 165
Manufacturing functions, strategies emphasizing, 202
MapLinX, 298–99, 371–73
Marchetti, Karen J., 350*n*11
Marchetti, Michele, 166*n*5, 168*n*12
Market analysis, 204
Market changes
 impact on budgeting, 359–60, 362
 setting objectives in relation to, 330, 333–34, 336–37
Market diversity, 4–6
Market growth, impact on budgeting, 359–60, 362
Marketing communications. *See also* Advertising
 basic questions of, 1–2
 budgeting from strategies, 352–54
 complexity of, 4–7
 economic effects, 32–34
 level in decision tree, 55
 managing integration of, 65–68, 377–88
 social and ethical issues, 39–46
 superordinate processes, 76–77
Marketing communications mix, reassessing, 374
Marketing communications objectives
 brand awareness, 308–10
 in case studies, 400–401, 410–12, 416–17
 corrective actions to achieve, 373–74
 examples, 299, 300*t*
 impact on budgeting, 357
 setting, 80–81, 297*t*, 335–37, 353
Marketing functions, strategies emphasizing, 200–202, 203
Marketing mix
 adding prospects to, 221
 budgeting from, 353–54
 as communication tool, 23
 interactive effects within, 33
 reassessing, 375
 relation to strategic focus, 77
Marketing objectives
 alignment with corporate objectives, 25–26
 budgeting from, 352, 356–57
 in case studies, 409–10
 corrective actions to achieve, 374–75
 examples, 298–99, 300*t*
 measuring, 302–8
 monitoring and control based on, 372

442 Index

reassessing, 375
in Schultz et al. IMC model, 22–23
in system integration, 378–79
using situation analysis to set, 332–35
Marketing strategies
  analysis supporting, 247–53
  budgeting from, 352
  in case studies, 398–99, 409–10, 415–16
  overview and major models, 221–27, 297*t*
  for strategic place focus, 236–39
  for strategic price focus, 234–36
  for strategic product focus, 227–33
  for strategic prospects focus, 239–47
Marketing tools in Schultz et al. model, 23
Market position assessment, 208, *209*, 211–15
Market potential, impact on budgeting, 360
Market power, 33*t*, 34
Market-related factors in strategy selection, 251–53
Markets, defined, 225
Market selection, 225–26
Market share, measuring marketing effectiveness by, 301–2
Market size, impact on budgeting, 360
Market test method, 302
Marlboro campaign continuity, 9
Marra, James, 8*n*6, 287, 335*n*14, 336*n*15, 336*n*16, 336*n*17, 337*n*18, 337*n*19, 339
Mass media, 13–15, 265*t*. *See also* Advertising
"Matchbooks" approach, 16–17
Match-industry-norms method, 346
Match or outspend competitors method, 347
Materialism, 45–46
Maxwell House coffee, 306
Maybelline, 359
McCarthy, E. Jerome, 166*n*6, 166*n*7
McCarthy, Michael, 41*n*31
McCormick Place, 178
McDonald, Duff, 146*n*18
McDonald's restaurants
  decline in TV advertising, 14
  Monopoly game promotion, 283
  outdoor advertising by, 110
  use of premiums, 184–85
McGann, Anthony F., 287, 335*n*14, 336*n*15, 336*n*16, 336*n*17, 337*n*18, 337*n*19, 339
MCI, 37
McWilliams, Gary, 197*n*2, 327*n*1
Means-end chains, 75
Measurement. *See also* Objectives
  applying to objectives, 296–97
  basic advertising factors, 94–96
  company position, 209–11
  consumer promotions, 187–88
  corporate objectives, 300–302
  direct mail, 154–55
  direct-response broadcasting, 147
  direct selling, 156
  electronic direct marketing, 151–52
  event sponsorships, 128
  importance, 292
  magazine advertising, 105
  marketing objectives, 302–8
  market position, 211–15
  media habits, 294

newspaper advertising, 108
outdoor advertising, 110
personal selling, 170
point-of-purchase advertising, 112
product placement effects, 132, 133, 134
public relations approaches, 123, 128, 131–32
as purpose of objectives, 60, 294–95
radio advertising, 102
reliability and validity, 328–29
telemarketing, 145
television advertising, 99, 349*t*
trade promotions, 179–80
Media fragmentation, 14, 15
Media habits, 267, 294
Mediamark Research, 105, 110, 114
Media selectivity, 267
Medical equipment training, 179
Medical industry trade shows, 178
Meenaghan, John, 275*n*5
Mehegan, Sean, 146*n*17
Melillo, Wendy, 40*n*28
Memento symbols, 44*t*
Mercer, Dick, 35*n*14
Mergers, 15
Merskin, Debra, 47*n*47
Message/media consistency, 11
Message valence, 274
Messmer, Ellen, 152*n*32
"Me-too" products, 15
Mexico, view of American culture, 46
Michelin Tires, 122
Mick, David G., 45*n*44, 251*n*33
Microsoft, 360
Mid-calorie colas, 221
Milk Processing Board, 112–13, 220
Millennials, 282
Miller, Cyndee, 74*n*1, 346*n*4
Miller, James G., 70, 392
Miniard, Paul W., 320*n*38
Mini Cooper, 89
MINI promotion, 89–90, 133, 184
Miscellaneous advertising, 113–14
Missionary sales work, 167, 284
Mittal, Banwari, 40*n*27
M Media, 38, 39
Models, 18–26, 53
Moncrief, William C., 191
Monitoring and control
  in case studies, 396, 397, 400
  corrective actions, 373–77, 380–81
  defined, 54
  need to integrate, 67, 369, 380–83
  sample scenario, 371–73
  Schultz et al. model shortcomings, 25
  in systems context, 82–83
  use of feedback in, 62–63, 370–71
Monopolies, 212
Monopolistic industries, 212
Monopoly game promotion, 283
Monroe, Kent B., 253*n*36
Montgomery, Cynthia A., 218
Montgomery, David B., 348*n*7
Montreux Jazz Festival, 125
Moore, Jeri, 16*n*14, 18*n*16, 28, 88, 287, 335*n*14, 336*n*15, 336*n*16, 336*n*17, 337*n*18, 337*n*19, 340
Moore and Thorson IMC model, 18–19

Moorthy, K. Sridhar, 348*n*8
Morell, R. W., 71, 392
Morganosky, Michelle A., 232*n*15
Moriarity, M. M., 235*n*17
Moriarity, Sandra, 1*n*1, 116, 324
Moseley, Chris, 259
Mothers Against Drunk Driving (MADD), 127
Mouland, Wayne, 184*n*51, 185*n*61
Mountain Dew, 246–47
Movies
  advertising, 113, 349*t*
  buzz marketing for, 119, 120
  impact of technology on, 294
  product placement in, 132, 284
Mowen, John C., 249*n*26
Muehling, Darrel D., 305*n*9
Mulkerin, Jay, 393*n*
Mulkerin, Kristin, 393*n*
Mullis, Randolph, 45*n*42
Multiattribute attitude index, 311, 312*t*
Multiattribute attitude models, 83
Multifactor portfolio matrix
  in call center case study, 408
  company position assessment, 207, *208*, 209–11
  market position assessment, 208, *209*, 211–15
Multilevel marketing, 155–56
Multivariate measure of brand loyalty, 320
Murphy, William H., 178*n*36
Murray, Tom, 245*n*22
Mushiness index, 312, 313*t*
Music marketing, 294
Muslims' view of American culture, 46
Myers, John G., 365
Myron, David, 387*n*

N

Named sponsors, 124–25
Name recognition, 394–95
Narrowcasting, 99
NASCAR sponsorships, 125
National Advertising Division, 37
National Advertising Review Board, 37
National Association of Attorneys General, 37
National Association of College Bookstores, 74
National Do Not Call Registry, 141
National Enquirer, 268
National Football League, 4
National newspapers, 106
National Yellow Pages Monitor, 114
NBC, 38
Ndubisi, Nelson Oly, 182*n*45
Nedungadi, Prakash, 314*n*24, 324
Need for integration, 10–11
Needs, defined, 226
Need-satisfaction approach to personal selling, 166
Neelankavil, James P., 293*n*3, 324
Neff, Jack, 43*n*, 290*n*1
Nelson, Carol, 287, 335*n*14, 336*n*15, 336*n*16, 336*n*17, 337*n*18, 337*n*19, 339
Nelson, Emily, 179*n*40
Nelson, Scott A., 287
Nescafé instant coffee, 306
Nestlé, 175
Netemeyer, Richard G., 249*n*24
Net reach, 95, 269–70

Network Advertising Initiative, 39
Newman, Joseph W., 320n37
Newness of product, impact on budgeting, 361
Newsletters, 149, 151, 278
Newspapers
    basic features of advertising, 106–9
    consumer promotions, 182
    costs, 266
    declining readership, 13, 14, 269
    drawing attention in ads, 270
    sensory modalities, 264
The New York Times, 108
Nextel, 125
Nielsen Media Research, 99, 134, 268
Nike
    company tour policy, 130
    corporate image, 123
    positioning by celebrity, 245
    strategic prospects focus, 225, 243, 244–45
    symbolism in promotions, 44
900-Number Rule, 36
Nivea gel, 252
Nondedicated CSRs, 407–8
Nonstore retailers, 379
Nontraditional media, 89–90, 133
Nonusers versus users, 250
Nordstrom's, 169
Norms, 60, 297–98. *See also* Industry averages
Norton, David P., 218, 339
Norwegian Cruise Line, 220
Not-for-profit organizations, direct marketing by, 141, *142*, 146
NYTimes.com, 107

O

O'Connell, Vanessa, 137, 169n15
Objectives. *See also* Measurement
    advantages, 292–95
    aligning marketing with corporate, 25–26
    budgeting from, 351–54, 356–57
    changes based on feedback, 62, 83
    corporate-level measures, 300–302
    defined, 54
    examples, 298–99, 300t
    general factors in setting, 58–61, 295–98
    growth strategy, 200–201
    marketing communications–level measures, 308–20
    marketing-level measures, 302–8
    need to integrate, 65–66, 67, 377–79, 381–82, 384–86
    role of analysis in setting, 64, 84
    in Schultz et al. IMC model, 22–23
    setting at corporate level, 327–32
    setting at marketing communications level, 335–37
    setting at marketing level, 332–35
    in systems context, 75–79
Objective-task method of budgeting, 350
Obloj, Krzysztof, 70, 392
Ocean Spray Cranberries, 35
Offensive promotion, 40–41, 267
Off-invoice allowances, 174
Ogden, Joseph, 288, 335n14, 336n15, 336n16, 336n17, 337n18, 337n19, 340
Ogilvy, David, 116

Oil of Olay, 306
Oligopolies, 212
Olive Garden restaurants, 20–21
Olympic sponsors, 284
On-demand video, 261
One-look approach, 16
One-to-one selling, 283
Online lifestyle communities, 143
Online newspapers, 106, 107
Online shopping, 379
Online yellow pages, 79
OPEC oil embargo, 213
Opinion leaders, 273
Order taking, 167, 284
Organizational factors in budgeting, 356–58
Orlando/Orange County Convention and Visitors Bureau, 1
Oropesa, R. S., 45n43, 45n44
Osenton, Tom, 256
Oser, Kris, 78n, 107n, 343n, 347n
Outbound calling, 145
Outdoor advertising
    basic features, 109–11
    to beach market, 97
    drawing attention in, 271
    measurability, 350t
Out-of-home media, 109–13
Outside lists, 154
Ovations, 403
Owens, Bill, 178n33

P

Packaging, 182
Padgett, Tim, 46n
Paid circulation of newspapers, 108
Paired audiences, 269
Paired-comparison method, 315
Palda, Kristian S., 324, 348n9
Paltrow, Gwyneth, 329
Panels, 109
Papadopoulos, N. G., 232n14
Parente, Donald, 8n6, 287, 335n14, 336n15, 336n16, 336n17, 337n18, 337n19, 339
Parents Television Council, 41
Park, Andrew, 327n1
Park, C. W., 88
Parks, Liz, 183n47
Party plans, 283
Past sales, 330, 345
Pate, Cheryl, 412
Patrick, Aaron O., 182n44
Patriotism, 233
Patterson, Paul M., 177n29
Patti, Charles, 365, 366
Paul Frederick shirts, *236*
Pender, John, 393
Pepsi brand image, 246
Pepsi Edge, 220, 221
Percentage-of-anticipated-sales method, 345, 360
Percentage-of-past-sales method, 345
Percentage-of-purchase measure, 318
Percentage-of-unit-anticipated-sales method, 345
Percentage-of-unit-past-sales method, 345
Percy, Larry, 88
Permission marketing, 143, 144

Perreault, William, Jr., 166n6, 166n7
Personal computers, 252, 283
Personality, positioning by, 246–47, 251
Personal products, offensive promotion of, 40
Personal selling
    defined, 163
    direct selling versus, 155
    forms, 283, 284
    integration of, 11
    strategic elements, 165–71, 178
Personal-values test, 307
Personnel functions, strategies emphasizing, 201–2
Pessemier, E. A., 225n8
Peterson, Robert A., 319n34, 319n35, 324
Petouhoff, Natalie L., 256
Petrison, Lisa A., 88, 191
Pfizer, 14
Phillip Morris, 176
Phillips, David, 113n11
Photo industry, 354–55
Photosails, Inc., 97
Physical continuity, 8
Physicians, email contact with, 150
Picture-interpretation test, 306
Piercy, Nigel, 366
Pisano, Garry P., 218, 339
Place
    positioning approaches focused on, 236–39, 409
    strategic elements, 223t, 225
PlaceViews database, 134
Planned purchase measure, 317
Planning
    defined, 54–55
    need to integrate, 67–68, 383–88
    relation to strategies, 58
    in SMC, 63–65
    in systems context, 83–84
Pleasure-giving symbols, 44t
Pleasures fragrance, 329
Plugg Jeans advertising, 38–39
Point-of-purchase materials/displays
    basic features, 111–13
    as reseller support function, 173, 177–78
    with self-satisfaction strategies, 284
Political action committees, 94
Political campaign advertising, 93–94
Pollack, Judann, 152n34
Polo Clothing, 23
Popovich, Mark, 31n1
Popper, Karl, 71
Porter, Michael E., 21n19, 221n2, 256
Porter's model of competitive strategy, 21, 221
Portfolio models, 205
Positioning
    defined, 220, 223–24
    examples of success and failure, 220, 221
    impact of strategy on budgeting, 357
    objective setting for, 80, 332
    overview of major approaches, 224t
    relation to strategic focus, 22, 77
    for strategic price focus, 234–39
    for strategic product focus, 227–33
    for strategic prospects focus, 239–47
Post-it notes, 276
Potts, Leanne, 40n29
Powell, Martha C., 307n16

Powers, W. T., 71, 370*n*2, 392
Prahald, Hamel, 218
Preferred position, 106
Premiums, 181, 184–85, 283
Presentations, personal selling, 166–67
Press conferences, 128, 275
Press releases, 128, *129*, 272
Previous-budget method, 351
Price
    positioning based on, 234–36, 409
    strategic elements, 223*t*, 224–25
Price competitiveness, 210
Price consciousness, 248–49
Price discrimination, 36
Price elasticity of demand, 248, 249
Price-off deals, 181, 187, 280
Price-quality relationship, 250–51
Primary demand, 252
Primary research, 270
PRINT 05 & CONVERTING 05 trade show, 178
Print media
    advertising measurability, 349*t*
    information maximization in, 267, 274
Private-label brands, 33
"Problem children," 205–7, 408
Problems, positioning by, 241–42
Process hierarchies, 55, 57–58, 75–77
Procter & Gamble
    advertising expenditures, 342
    consumer products industry strengths, 180
    cosmetics marketing budget, 359
    sales growth, 289
    self-imposed ban on ads to children, 43
    toothpaste brands, 4–5
    TV advertising changes, 14
    use of sampling, 279
Product categories, 227
Product class, positioning by, 227, *228*, 252
Product differentiation, 224
Product effectiveness, measuring, 210
Product forms, 227
Product involvement, 360, 384
Production costs, 265–66
Production flexibility, 264
Product life cycle
    in BCG matrix, 205–7
    impact on budgeting, 359
    product positioning by, 251–52
Product-market matrixes, 226–27
Product/markets, 199
Product parity, 15
Product placement, 132–34, 284, 349*t*
Product-related factors
    in budgeting, 360
    in marketing strategy selection, 250–51, 415–16
Products
    high- versus low-involvement, 262–63
    positioning approaches focused on, 227–33, 409
    strategic elements, 223*t*, 224
Professional sports, 124–25, 132
Profits
    assessing company position by, 210, 211
    brand, 296
    measuring, 300–301
    strategies emphasizing, 202

Programming (TV), promotions in, 282
Projective tests, 305–7, 313–14
Promotional allowances, 174, 176, 280
Promotion effectiveness, measuring, 210
Promotion strategies, 222
Propaganda, advertising versus, 93
Proportion of sales method, 301
Prospects
    defined, 221
    positioning approaches focused on, 239–47
    strategic elements, 223*t*, 225
PSINet, 395
Psychographics, 83
Psychological continuity, 9
Publicity
    defined, 119, 272
    with habit-formation strategies, 280–81
Public opinion, influencing, 119. *See also* Public relations
Public relations
    with affective strategies, 275
    corporate advertising, 122–23
    corporate communications, 128–32
    defined, 118–19
    with habit-formation strategies, 280–81
    importance, 119–22
    with informative strategies, 272, 273*t*
    measurability, 349*t*
    with self-satisfaction strategies, 284
    sponsorships, 124–28
Puffery, 34
Pugh, Luke, 413*n*
Purchase cycle, 18
Purchase frequency, impact on budgets, 361
Purchase incentive measures, 317–18
Purchase intentions
    associating beliefs with, 303
    measuring, 316–18
    objectives based on, 296
    strategic focus on, 78
Putten, Marijke van, 182*n*43

Q

Qualitative measures (personal selling), 170
Quality of products
    countries associated with, 232, 250
    in Hancock Rack case study, 416
    relative price and, 234
    variations in perception, 252–53
Quality of services, in call center case study, 404–6, 407, 409–10
Quantitative measures (personal selling), 170, 171*t*
Quantitative methods of budgeting, 347–48, 358, 360

R

Rack Manufacturers Institute, 413
Radio advertising
    basic features, 100–103
    costs, 13, 266
    drawing attention in, 270
    of liquor, 37–38
    measurability, 349*t*
    seasonal effects, 267
    sensory modalities, 264
    theme line support in, 16, 17
Radio programming, 294

Rahmation, S., 71, 392
Ranking method, 315
Rao, Ambar G., 365
Rate base of magazines, 105
Rating points, 100
Rating services, 268, 270
Ratio-to-sales budgeting methods, 345
Raw materials, impact of availability on markets, 213
Ray, Michael L., 324, 360*n*19, 361*n*20, 361*n*21, 361*n*22, 362*n*23, 362*n*24, 366
Reach
    computing for media selection, 269–70
    defined, 94–95
    importance, 96
    radio advertising breadth, 100, 102
    TV advertising breadth, 98
Reactor communications strategy
    basic features, 24, 78
    implementing, 80, 81*t*, 281–84
Read, Brendan, 145*n*14
Readership of newspapers, 108
Reading program promotion, 193–94
"Real Men of Genius" campaign, 102–3
Rebates, 181, 185–86, 280
Rebello, Kathy, 197*n*2
Receipts, coupons on, 279
Recent reading, 105
Recognition measures, 303–4, 309–10
Redmond, Jack, 36*n*16
Reece, Barry L., 191
Referents for corporate objectives, 331–32
Referral awards, 181, 182
Referral systems, 273–74
Refunds
    defined, 181, 182
    when used, 185–86, 280
Regional editions of magazines, 105
Regression equations, 358
Regulations
    as constraints on media selection, 266
    impact on markets, 213–14
    overall influence on marketing communications, 34–39
Reichheld, Frederick F., 256
Reid, Mike, 292*n*2
Relationship-management integration, 12
Relationship marketing, 7
Relative price
    brand positioning by, 234, 249, 251
    product positioning by, 253
Reliable and valid measures, 328–29
RELPAX, 14
Repeat purchases
    advertising tools for, 277, 281
    direct marketing tools for, 278, 281
    loyalty programs promoting, 143
    measuring, 318–20
    as objectives, 276, 281, 296
    sales promotions for, 279–80, 283
Repurchase measure, 318
Reputation of distributors, 252
Research and development functions, 200–201, 203
Reseller support
    with affective strategies, 274–75
    in case studies, 401

with habit-formation strategies, 280
with informative strategies, 271–72
with self-satisfaction strategies, 284
strategic elements, 171–80
Resource allocation. *See* Budgeting
Retailing
    agents in, 165
    impact of consumer trends on, 379
    power shifts in, 172, 175, 176–77
    salesperson compensation, 169
    trade promotion issues, 172–78
Retired Persons Services, 404
Return-on-investment method, 348–50
Revlon, 359
Reyes, Sonia, 184*n*53
Reynolds, Christopher, 387*n*
Reynolds, Thomas J., 324
Rich, Greg A., 191
Richardson, G., 71, 370*n*2, 392
Richards, Timothy J., 177*n*29
Ries, Al, 224*n*3, 256
Rivkin, Jan W., 218
Roa, Akshay R., 253*n*36
Roach killer, 313–14
Roanoke Call Center case study, 403–12
Robb, F. F., 71, 370*n*2, 392
Roberts, Mary Lou, 159
Roberts, Steve, 159
Robertson, Thomas, 41*n*33
Robinson, William A., 191, 287
Robinson-Patman Act, 36
Rogers, John L., 147*n*24
Rolex watches, 250
Roll-form racks, 412–13
Rolling Stones, 125–26
Roman, Ernan, 28
Romano, Allison, 146*n*19, 147*n*20
Romeo, Jean B., 313*n*22, 317*n*29
Rossiter, John R., 41*n*33, 88, 116, 366
Rothschild, Michael L., 324
Rothschild, William E., 208*n*9
Rotzoll, Kim B., 32*n*2, 32*n*3, 33*n*7, 39*n*26, 41*n*32, 44*n*39, 46*n*46, 49
Roy, Mark, 141*n*5
Run of press, 106
Russell, J. Thomas, 116, 287, 310*n*19, 335*n*14, 336*n*15, 336*n*16, 336*n*17, 337*n*18, 337*n*19, 339
Russian Association of American Football, 46
Ruth, Julie, 176*n*25
Ryans, John K., Jr., 116, 366
Ryssel, Christian, 284*n*10

S

Saab brand identity, 56–57
Sackett, Victoria A., 312*n*21
Safer, Morley, 46*n*
Sager, Ira, 197*n*2
Saigon Cosmetics, 65
Sailboat sail ads, 97
Sales
    assessing company position by, 211
    brand, 296
    marketing budgets as percentage of, 345, 358
    measuring marketing effectiveness by, 301–2
    objective setting for, 330–32

Sales calls, 166–68
Sales contests, 173, 178
Salespersons
    defined, 165
    sales contests for, 173, 178
    variations between, 169–70
Sales promotions
    with habit-formation strategies, 278–80
    measurability, 349*t*
    regulation of, 36
    with self-satisfaction strategies, 283
Samli, A. Coskun, 250*n*29
Sample products
    for college market, 73
    as consumer promotions, 181, 182, 186–87
    with habit-formation strategies, 279–80
    in newspapers, 107
    stimulating word of mouth with, 273
Sara Lee, 156
Saranow, Jennifer, 187*n*69, 188*n*7
Satisfaction, measuring, 318–19
Sawyer, Alan G., 324
Schmidt, William E., 46*n*
Schmitt, Eric, 99*n*3
Schmittlein, D. C., 235*n*17
Schnaars, Steven P., 333*n*8, 333*n*9, 333*n*10, 333*n*11, 334*n*12, 334*n*13, 340
Scholes, Kevan, 218, 339
Schonfeld, Erick, 137
Schrage, Michael, 170*n*17
Schroer, James C., 116, 366
Schultz, Don E., 7*n*4, 11*n*9, 12*n*12, 16*n*13, 18*n*17, 19*n*18, 28, 87, 88, 191, 260*n*3, 287, 335*n*14, 336*n*15, 336*n*16, 336*n*17, 337*n*18, 337*n*19, 340
Schultz et al. IMC model, 19–25, 25–26
Schumann, David, 284*n*9
Schwartz, D. A., 324
Schwinn, Elizabeth, 141*n*8
Scott, Linda, 44*n*, 44*n*41
Screen Test USA, 35
Seagram's, 37
Search engines, 79, 147
Sears, 233, 236–37
Seasonal usage in media, 267
Season dating, 173
Secondary research, 270
Secret Sparkle Body Spray, 43
Segmentation
    in beach advertising, 97
    in Moore and Thorson model, 18
    of radio markets, 100–101
    in Schultz et al. IMC model, 19–21
    varied approaches to, 21, 226–27, 228*t*
Seibert, Larry, 182*n*46, 187*n*71
Seinfeld, Jerry, 14
Selective demand, 252
Selectivity of media, 267
Self-expression symbols, 44*t*
Self-liquidating premiums, 283
Self-regulation, 37–39, 43
Self-satisfaction communications strategy
    basic features, 24, 78
    implementing, 80, 81*t*, 281–84, 378
Seller, Patricia, 369*n*1
Selling agents, 165
Selling-formula approach, 166–67

Semantic differential measures
    attitude toward purchase, 316
    brand attitude, 312–13
    brand image, 304, *305*
Semiotics, 251
Sensory modalities, 264
Sequeria, Ian K., 178*n*32
Service, strategic focus on, 225
Serviceability, positioning by, 239, *240*, 252
Service quality, in call center case study, 404–6, 407
7Up, 227
Sex appeal, 38–39, 40–41
SFGate.com, 107
Shanklin, William L., 284*n*10
Shapiro, Benson P., 211*n*11
Share (TV audience), 100
Share of voice, 15
Share-of-voice/market method, 346–47
Sharon, Zukin, 49
Shaw, Jeff, 143*n*11
Sheehan, Kim, 49
Sheets, 109
Sherry, John F., Jr., 46*n*
Shipp, Shannon, 191
Shock advertising, 40–41
Shoemaker, Robert, 186*n*66, 187*n*68
Shop at Home Network, 146
Shopping networks, 146, 147
Shortbread cookies, 232
Short-term objectives, 300
Showing, 110–11
Shrek, 120
Shure, 125
Siemens, 229
Silk, Alvin J., 348*n*7
Silke Carty, Sharon, 186*n*65
Silver, Caleb, 41*n*
Similarity judgments, 307
Simmons Market Research Bureau, 105, 110, 114
Simon, Herbert A., 71, 392
Simon, Julian, 356*n*14
Simonin, Bernard L., 176*n*25
Simply Powder, 359
Simulating word of mouth, 275–76
Sin products, 40–41
Sirgy, M. Joseph, 46*n*45, 71, 250*n*29, 250*n*30, 370*n*2, 392, 402, 412, 418
Sissors, Jack Z., 116
Situation analysis
    applications of, 63–65
    with BCG matrix, 205–7
    for budgeting, 64–65, 84, 354–62
    in corporate objective setting, 327–32
    integration of, 67–68
    in marketing communications objective setting, 335–37
    in marketing objective setting, 332–35
    for marketing strategies, 247–53
    with multifactor portfolio matrix, 207–15
    need to integrate, 383–88
    process overview, 204–5
    in systems context, 83–84
Sloan, Pat, 359*n*16
Slotting allowances, 174, 177, 280
Small, William J., 121*n*
Smith, Janet, 256, 371*n*

Smith, Robert E., 305*n*10, 318*n*31, 324
Snapple, 127
Social issues, 39–46
Social observance symbols, 44*t*
Social status symbols, 44*t*
Social stereotypes, 31, 46
Sommers, M. S., 225*n*6
Southwest Airlines, 198, 225
Spam email, 150
Specialist firms, 225
Specialty advertising, 281
Spencer, Dale R., 42*n*37
Spiller, Lisa S., 159
Spiro, Rosann, 191
Spokespersons, 245–46
Sponsorships
  with affective strategies, 275
  measurability, 349*t*
  overview, 124–28
  with self-satisfaction strategies, 284
Sports
  product placement in, 132
  sponsorships, 124–25, 284
Sprint, *177*
Stability as corporate goal, 201–2
Stakeholder-based integration, 12
Stakeholders, 120–21
Stamminger, Eric, 284*n*10
Standard advertising units, 107
Standard Rate and Data Service
  magazine advertising measurement, 104, 105
  newspaper advertising measurement, 108
  outdoor advertising measurement, 110
  secondary ratings data, 268
Stanton, William J., 191, 225*n*6
Star Alliance, 174
"Stars," 205–7, 408
State Farm Insurance, 127
State regulations, 36–37
Steinberg, Brian, 293*n*4, 293*n*5
Steiner, Gary A., 324
Steiner, Robert L., 33*n*9
Stengel, Jim, 289
Stereotypes, 31, 46
Stern, Barbara, 9*n*7, 28
Stern, J. A., 366
Stevens, Ruth P., 191
Stockpiling, 235
Stoltman, Jeffery J., 305*n*9
Stone, Bob, 7*n*2, 159, 287
Straight rebuys, 167
Strategic business units, 199
Strategic marketing communications. *See also* Systems model
  analysis and planning, 63–65
  basic importance, 9–10
  budgeting, 61–62, 351–54
  consumer promotion tools, 181–82
  defined, 26
  direct marketing elements and methods, 146, 148–49, 152
  magazine advertising elements, 105
  newspaper advertising elements, 108
  objective setting, 58–61
  outdoor advertising elements, 110–11
  personal selling elements, 165
  radio advertising elements, 102
  role of theories and models, 53
  strategies versus tactics, 55–58
  system integration in, 65–68
  systems concepts, 54–55, 261
  trade promotion elements, 172–74
  TV advertising elements, 99–100
Strategic orientation, 9
Strategic partnering, 4, 124
Strategic place focus
  elements of, 223*t*, 225
  positioning approaches, 236–39
Strategic planners, 193
Strategic price focus
  elements of, 223*t*, 224–25
  positioning approaches, 234–36
Strategic product focus
  elements of, 223*t*, 224
  positioning approaches, 227–33
Strategic prospects focus
  elements of, 223*t*, 225
  positioning approaches, 239–47
Strategies. *See also* Corporate strategy; Marketing strategies
  changes based on feedback, 62, 82
  defined, 54
  as goals, 58
  linking to tactics and objectives, 60–61, 65–66, 377–79
  major corporate approaches, 199–204
  market pressures leading to changes, 197–98
  need to integrate, 65–66, 67, 377–80, 381–82, 384–85
  reassessing, 374, 375, 376
  role of analysis in selecting, 63–64, 83–84, 204–15
  in systems context, 75–79, 261
  tactics versus, 55–58
Strength of belief, measuring, 302–3, 305
Structural racks, 412–13
Subaru, 175, *176*
Subbrands, 4–5, 53
Subordinate elements, 55
Substantiation of marketing claims, 35–36
Substitutes, 213
Subway restaurants, 248
Suggestive advertising, 38–39
Sultan, Ralph G. M., 33*n*6
Sunday School Board, 370–71
Sung-Tai Hong, 232*n*15, 250*n*31
Supermarket weekly specials, 183
Superordinate elements, 55, 76–77
Superstations, 99
Supply factors in multifactor portfolio matrix, 213
Supply-side planning approach, 17
Surveys, 406–7, 412
Swatch, *124*, 125
Sweepstakes
  defined, 181, 182
  when used, 184, 283
Swickland, James E., 179*n*39
Swing users, 20, 21
Swinyard, William P., 305*n*10, 318*n*31, 324
Swire, Donald J., 205*n*5, 207*n*7, 209*n*10, 211*n*12, 330*n*2, 330*n*3, 330*n*4, 330*n*5, 330*n*6, 331*n*7
Switching behavior, 249

Symbology, 251
Symbols, 44, 251
System integration, 65–68
Systems, defined, 54
Systems model. *See also* Analytic/planning model
  analysis and planning in, 83–84
  approach to segmentation, 21
  budgeting in, 78
  communications strategy, 24
  contact management in, 21–22
  integration in, 85
  marketing tactics in, 23
  monitoring and control in, 82–83
  objective setting, 78–81
  overview, 74–75
  positioning in, 22
  strategies, tactics, and objectives in, 75–79
  use of well-established concepts, 25–26
Szybillo, George J., 251*n*32

T

Tabloid size, 106
Taco Bell, 100
Tactics
  in case studies, 399, 401, 417
  changes based on feedback, 62, 82
  defined, 54
  growth strategy, 201
  linking to objectives and strategies, 60–61, 65–66, 377–79
  need to integrate, 65–66, 67, 377–80, 381–82, 384–85
  relation to goals, 58, 59
  role of analysis in selecting, 63–64
  strategies versus, 55–58
  in systems context, 75–79
Talor, Thayer C., 167*n*8, 284*n*8
Tammaro, John, 370
Tannenbaum, Stanley I., 18*n*17, 19*n*18, 28, 88, 287, 335*n*14, 336*n*15, 336*n*16, 336*n*17, 337*n*18, 337*n*19, 340
Tao Li, 87
Targeted communications
  with catalogs, 153–54, 155
  decreasing costs, 13
  in magazine advertising, 103, 104
  for miscellaneous advertising, 113–14
  in newspaper advertising, 106
  in point-of-purchase advertising, 112
  for public relations, 123, 128, 131
  in radio advertising, 100–101, 102
Tawfik, Jelassi, 159
Taylor, Gail Ayala, 184*n*52
Technology. *See also* Computer technologies
  adoption by millennial generation, 282
  in call center case study, 406–7
  defined, 226
  impact on markets, 214
  impact on media habits, 294
Teinowitz, Ira, 40*n*30, 294*n*
Teleconferencing, 168
Telemarketing, 36, 145–46, 282
Telemedia, 282
Telephone Consumer Protection Act, 36
Teleshopping, 283
Television advertising
  basic features, 98–100

to children, 34, 42, 43
costs, 265–66, 269
drawing attention in, 270
growing costs and decreasing effectiveness, 13–15
infomercials, 146–47, 278, 282
of liquor, 37–38
measurability, 349*t*
percentage of sponsors measuring, 293
seasonal effects, 267
sensory modalities, 264
theme line support for, 16–17
Television households, 99, 100
Television networks
    acceptance of liquor advertising, 38
    declining viewership, 14, 261
Television programs, 97, 282
Television shopping networks, 146, 147
Telser, Lester G., 33*n*5
Terpstra, Vern, 232*n*14, 232*n*15
Terwilliger, Cate, 48*n*48
Texas Instruments, 370
Text messaging, 149, 151
Tharp, Marye, 44*n*, 44*n*41
Theater of the mind promotion, 193–94
Theme-lines approach, 16–17
Theoretical frameworks, 53
Theories, 53
Thinker communications strategy
    advertising tactics, 264–71
    basic features, 24, 77
    in case studies, 400–402, 416
    implementing, 78, 80, 81*t*, 263–64
    reseller support and public relations, 271–72
    word-of-mouth tactics, 273–74
Thin model image, 31
Thomas, Dave, 8
Thomas, Howard, 284*n*10
Thomaselli, Rich, 122*n*, 137
Thompson, Stephanie, 183*n*49, 329*n*
Thomsen, Steven, 31*n*1
Thomson, Stephanie, 175*n*
Thorson, Esther, 16*n*14, 18*n*16, 28, 287, 335*n*14, 336*n*15, 336*n*16, 336*n*17, 337*n*18, 337*n*19, 340
Thornton, James, 186*n*65
Thought-elicitation procedure, 312
Throckmorton, Joan, 141*n*4
Through the book, 105
Time consciousness, 379
Time frames
    for objectives, 60, 298
    radio advertising dayparts, 100, 101–2
    TV advertising dayparts, 98–99
Tippee, Bob, 137
Titleist, 237
TNS Media Intelligence, 134
Todd, Heather, 137
"Toon Tour of Mysteries," 184
Top-of-mind awareness, 308
Tours, 129–30
Tracking studies, 317, 318*t*
Trade allowances, 174, 176, 280
Trade journals, 417
Trade promotions
    with affective strategies, 274–75
    defined, 163
    with habit-formation strategies, 280
    with informative strategies, 271–72
    performance measurement, 179–80
    with self-satisfaction strategies, 284
    strategic elements, 171–79
Trade regulation rulings, 35
Trade shows, 173, 178, 417
Training
    computer-based, 407
    promotional value, 179, 272
    sales, 170–71
Transcendence symbols, 44*t*
Trojan condoms, 186
Trout, Jack, 224*n*3, 256
Tse, David K., 45*n*
Tupperware, 156
Turk, Peter B., 287

U

U2, 123
Ule, G. Maxwell, 350*n*10
Ultimate Shopping Network, 146
Unaided self-report questions, 314
Unilever, 342
Uniqueness, as goal of positioning, 223–24
Unit anticipated sales, 345
United 1K contest, 184
United Airlines, 197–98
United Colors of Benetton, 9
UnitedHealth Group case study, 403–12
United States Postal Service (USPS), 34, 35
United Way, 4
Unit sales objectives, 331–32
Unity, 5, 6, 16
Uprise shoes, 385
Upscale magazine, 14
Urban, Glen L., 242*n*20
US Airways, *129*, 197–98
USA Today, 107
USAToday.com, 107
Use-experience test, 306
User image, positioning by, 243–45, 249–50
Uses, positioning by, 242–43, 248, 252
Utilitarian values, 45
Utility symbols, 44*t*
UUNet, 395

V

Valence of advertising messages, 274
Valence property of beliefs, 303
Validity of measures, 328–29
Value added, 210
Value-expressive products, 250
Values, advertising's influence on, 44–46
Vanden Bergh, Bruce, 8*n*6
Variations in quality perceptions, 252–53
Vaughn, Richard, 261*n*4, 287, 288
Verrill, Glenn, 310*n*19
Vertical cooperative advertising
    defined, 172, 173
    elements of, 176, *177*
Viagra, 334
Video games, 349*t*
Video on demand, 261
Videotext, 283
Viral marketing, 132–33
Virginia Slims, 9
VisionTek, 371

Vogel, Craig M., 256
Voight, Joan, 40*n*28
Volvo, 57
Vranica, Suzanne, 36*n*17

W

Wachovia, 239
Wackman, Daniel B., 41*n*33
Wackman, Ward, 42*n*36
Wagner, Janet, 232*n*15, 250*n*31
Walkers cookies, 232
Wall, Marjorie, 232*n*15
Wall, Robert W., 288
The Wall Street Journal, 107
Wal-Mart
    gains over Kmart, 369
    impact of pricing strategy on markets, 183, 187
    product attribute positioning by, *229*
    strategic price focus, 224–25
Walsh, Ann, 36*n*20
Wang, Paul, 7*n*4, 28, 88
Ward, Scott, 41*n*33
Wartella, Ellen, 41*n*33, 42*n*36
WashingtonPost.com, 107
Wasson, Chester R., 252*n*34
Weather Channel, 292
Webb, Don R., 42*n*37
Web conferencing, 168
Weber, John A., 252*n*34
Websites. *See also* Internet
    in call center case study, 411
    defined, 149
    direct marketing methods overview, 147
    Goodwill Industries use of, 152
    importance, 151
    online lifestyle communities, 143
    public relations via, 130–31
Weekly grocery store specials, 183
Weighted average referents, 331–32
Weilbacher, William M., 88
Wellner, Alison Stein, 233*n*
Wells, William, 1*n*1, 116
Wendy's restaurants, 8, 245–46
West, Susan, 284*n*9
WGN, 184
Wheeler-Lea Amendment, 34–36
Whipple, Thomas W., 47*n*47, 49
White, Joseph B., 188*n*72
Whittington, Richard, 218, 339
Who concert, 126–27
Why People Buy Things They Don't Need, 379
Wildt, Albert R., 314*n*25, 324
Wilkie, Michael, 355*n*12
Williams, Jerome D., 178*n*32
Wilson, Laurie J., 288, 335*n*14, 336*n*15, 336*n*16, 336*n*17, 337*n*18, 337*n*19, 340
Wilson, William R., 319*n*34, 319*n*35, 324
Wind, Yoram, 205*n*5, 207*n*7, 209*n*10, 211*n*12,, 256, 330*n*2, 330*n*3, 330*n*4, 330*n*5, 330*n*6, 331*n*7
Wireless communication devices, 147, 148
Women
    sex appeal in promotions, 40–41
    stereotypes of, 31, 46
Wood, Michael, 250*n*30
Woodruff, Robert B., 252*n*35, 256

Worbel, Richard A., 320*n*37
Word of mouth
   with affective strategies, 275–76
   in call center case study, 411
   effectiveness, 118
   with informative strategies, 273–74
   viral marketing, 132–33
Workforce management software, 407
World Wide Web. *See* Internet; Websites
Wright, Newell, 46*n*45

Wrigley's gum, 165
Wybenga, Hans, 323
Wyer, Robert S., Jr., 232*n*15, 250*n*31

Y

Yale, David R., 288
Yankelovich Monitor, 317
Yan Yang, 156*n*47
Yeado, Brian, 168*n*14
Yellow pages directories, 79

Yoplait Yogurt, 127, 128
Young & Rubicam, 306

Z

Z3 roadster, 89
Zaltman, Gerald, 88
Zeelenberg, Marcel, 182*n*43
Zeithaml, Valerie, 252*n*35, 253*n*36
Zhou, Nan, 45*n*
Zoglin, Richard, 42*n*37